The Family

1920 – 2010

From Joan Y. Kelly

A History Told Through Memoirs
*and pictures courtesy of individual writers
and the Children's Home*

J. Andrews Smith

J. Andrews Smith, MSW

© 2010 The J. Andrews Smith Group, LLC

Without a witness, they just disappear.
- J. Andrews Smith -

In Memory of

Joseph L. Griffin, age 15
March 19, 1914
August 11, 1929
Killed by lightning
Final resting place J. H. Evans Cemetery
Greenville, North Carolina
Admitted - September 11, 1922

Wiley Robertson Watson, age 10
January 20, 1919
August 11, 1929
Killed by lightning
Final resting place not known
Admitted - October 12, 1923

Sandra Elaine Mercer, age 17
October 4, 1947
June 15, 1965
Died from kidney failure
Final resting place - Cabin Free Will Baptist Church Cemetery
Beulaville, North Carolina
Admitted – September 19, 1953

Contents

Foreword — 7
Author's Comments — 10
An Introduction — 12

1: The Griffin Brothers — 18
2: We Never Left Campus — 23
3: Molasses Ran Out On the Kitchen Floor — 36
4: I Will Always Be a Tar Heel — 39
5: I Cried the Day I Left — 43
6: The Hills of Home — 49
7: Recollections I Remember — 64
8: Scenes of Childhood — 80
9: The Best and Worst Day — 188
10: An Orphan's View — 197
11: A True Story — 209
12: Thanks for the Memories! — 212
13: We Were Twins Once — 222
14: The Shy, Barefooted Girl Who Became Valedictorian — 260
15: Tomorrow Would Be a New Life — 291
16: Reflection of a Fifteen-Year Orphan — 296
17: The Memory of Her — 305
18: The Loss was Compensated with a Strength — 313
19: Doris Ann, Willie and I — 354

20: My Memories of Childhood	359
21: A Peace Has Replaced the Wrinkles	365
22: I Will Be Eternally Grateful	371
23: The same Holy WOMB	380
24: Mama Knows Best	385
25: The Dirt Road	393
26: The Children's Home was a Fine Institution	398
27: The Lord Has Been Good	404
28: Benign Neglect	410
29: We Were a Band of Brothers	420
30: You're the Best of the Best!	432
31: Not Just a Home for Children	441
32: The Call	453
33: I Don't Feel Like I Sacrifice to Be Here	470
34: Omitted Stories, History and Tidbits	477
35: We Have Accepted the Challenge	492
Afterword	497
Acknowledgements	500
Appendix I	503
Appendix II	524
Index	525
About The Author	552

Foreword

With this book, J. Andrews Smith, MSW, makes a unique contribution to the fields of North Carolina historiography, sociology and social work. Almost 20 years ago, Clyde F. McSwain published a detailed account of his life at the Masonic Orphanage at Oxford, North Carolina (*Travels of a Printer*, 1988). Nearly 10 years later Richard McKenzie published a penetrating memoir of his life in the Presbyterian Orphanage at Barium Springs, North Carolina (*The Home: A Memoir of Growing Up in an Orphanage*, 1996). A few other full-length recollections of orphanage life may have been written and published, but there is no other book, I think, similar to this one by Mr. Smith. His is no less than a collection of firsthand accounts of life as lived by a succession of children in the Free Will Baptist Orphanage (or Children's Home) at Middlesex, North Carolina, over a period of nearly 90 years—from the second decade of the 20th century to the first decade of the 21st century.

Every society is, and during historical times always has been, faced with the problem of providing food, clothing, shelter and education/training for penniless orphans. For about 200 years North Carolina used a system of involuntary apprenticeship to cope with the problem. Under this system penniless orphans (who had no say in the matter) were brought before the county court where the justices of the court ordered each child to live with a master and serve him until reaching age 21. The master agreed to teach the orphan a craft or an occupation. All the orphan's labor while learning the craft or occupation belonged to the master. The master stood in "loco parentis" to the orphan, and agreed with the court to provide the child with the necessities of life and to teach him at least the rudiments of reading, writing and arithmetic. The master might teach the child a skilled craft, such as cabinet making, or house carpentry, or shoemaking, and so forth, or he might teach him farming. The object of this system was to train the child in a work he could use later to support himself as an adult. The rise of orphanages in North Carolina after 1885 helped bring to a close the old system of orphan and master.

The Freemasons led the way by establishing the Masonic Home for Children at Oxford, North Carolina, in the 1870's. They were followed by the various religious denominations in the state—the Baptists (1885), the Episcopalians (1886), the Presbyterians (1891), the Roman Catholics

(1899), the Methodists (1899), the Congregational-Christians (1904), the Reformed Church (1906), the Pentecostal Holiness Church (1909), the Free Will Baptists (1920), and so forth. Another fraternal organization, the Order of Odd Fellows, emulated the Freemasons and established a non-denominational orphanage at Goldsboro, North Carolina, in 1892. These institutions were scattered in the inner Coastal Plain and Piedmont regions of the state. Some of them were rural and some of them were urban. Some of them taught their children farming. Others taught skilled trades or occupations. Oxford Orphanage, for example, offered some skilled trades, including printing. The Roman Catholic Orphanage in Raleigh, Nazareth, offered clerical training—bookkeeping and accounting, stenography, typewriting, and so forth. As the reader will discover, the Free Will Baptist Orphanage, which admitted its first children in 1920, was originally altogether agricultural in its setting, in its philosophy, in its outlook and in its day-to-day life.

During the years following World War II the composition of the population of the state's orphanages underwent a basic change. More and more of the children for whom admission was sought came from dysfunctional homes or from homes broken by divorce rather than death. By the early 1950s, the various institutions altered their designation from "orphanage" to "children's home". Living accommodations changed from dormitory-style buildings to cottages. "Matrons" became "house mothers" and "house fathers". "Inmates" became "orphans" and later "orphans" became "children". Today, "children" are called "residents". Counseling by professional staff and individual tutorial programs were made available for the children. Family, parenting, marital counseling services, and family-centered outreach programs were offered to help dysfunctional families deal with stress. In short, the very nature of orphanages in North Carolina underwent a sea change during the latter half of the 20th century.

By the greatest good fortune, Mr. Smith has been able to gather direct testimony from the period when the institution at Middlesex was a full-fledged orphanage and undertook to rear a child to adulthood as if the child were a member of a large farm family. He has gathered testimony, too, from the period of transition to a "children's home". It is unlikely that any of the memoirs he has gathered will speak directly of this metamorphosis, but they will no doubt reflect it.

About half of my 37-year career as a professional archivist was spent working with the public records of the state and its hundred counties. The second half was spent working with the papers of private families of the state. For a reasonably clear notion of how people lived and worked and played, the historian needs to consult both the public records and private papers. I have a very healthy respect for both sources, but I also have a healthy wariness toward each category. In the case of that very special source of information, the memoir, it is doubtlessly unnecessary to sound a warning to the reader. It goes without saying that the memoirs presented here are meant to be as truthful and as candid as memoirs ever are. We all know, however, how treacherous our own memories may prove to be under the best of circumstances, and how reluctant we all generally are to expose all our foibles in print. Historians are trained as a matter of course to consider the shortcomings inherent in memoirs, and professionals who work in the field of social work may be just as well armed. Still, even with this caveat, it must be said that Mr. Smith has performed an important and unique task in perpetuating the testimony found in these pages.

George Stevenson, Jr.
Archivist (1970-2008)
North Carolina State Archives
Raleigh, North Carolina

Author's Comments

Sometimes, I've referred to my childhood family as my tribe. Fifty years ago I left the Orphanage of my childhood, but I have never left my tribe, the family born from my being there. My Orphan family will forever be non-blood family members. These brothers and sisters have been a greater part of molding my life than my AB negative blood lineage.

Everyone knows there are orphanages and/or children homes. Yet, there are no museums to record and display our history in North Carolina. At times, I feel we're a lost tribe. Sometimes, I feel many of us are like gypsies with bountiful wanderlust.

This book of an American family is based on recollections from those who have walked in the shoes of orphans and on the hallow soil of my childhood. It is not a scholarly work or comprehensive history of orphanages.

My first thought on writing this book was born years ago on a Sunday afternoon in my sons' childhood, nearly twenty-five years ago. We were visiting the Museum of History in Raleigh, North Carolina when the thought occurred - show Jerry, Jr. & Mark the history of orphanages. I wanted to find something in the museum about the Free Will Baptist Orphanage in Middlesex, North Carolina. I wanted my sons to know about my tribe, my family from the Orphanage. There was no such information about any orphanage on display in the museum. I thought to myself, we're a lost sub-culture. Without our history, our successes and failures will never be known to the general public and our sons and daughters will never know their non-blood family history. Like my first book, *I Have Hope*, published in 1978, I waxed and waned for some time before deciding to publish *The Family*.

This book spans ninety years, 1920 – 2010. To have a profound and reflective view of my orphan family's Middlesex experience, one should read these pages of cumulative memoirs from the Foreword to the Afterword. To skip over chapters while reading will not allow history to unfold as it happened. To bounce over chapters to read another may distort one's viewpoint and analysis of the historical event. There is a perspective gained from reading chronologically all memoirs of children's experiences within the imaginary wall of the Orphanage campus. You will gain most by reading stories built upon from one writer to the next. Some of the stories will be sad, others will bring humor, but all are part of our history. As the book's author, I have taken the liberty to date each alumnus' Middlesex years in parenthesis the first time the alumnus is written about within each chapter. This should give a dated perspective to those of you unfamiliar with names.

More than a few of us still exhibit detachment disorders. While many of our children and spouses have gain from our learned experiences, some of our families have felt the brunt of our unresolved childhood journey. Some alumni remain stuck in stages to resolution. Some are still in denial and some in anger. Even so, many alumni have found resolution.

While, for various reasons, some family members could not or would not write their story for public viewing, those who have written did so as a responsibility to the family and future children coming into substitute care. They felt it their task to get their story told for future generations and for history. As much as this book can convey, they yearn for the truth of their institutional upbringing to be told and by book's end for you to feel "The Family" experience. Some family writers felt my nudging for them to write. Others withstood my prodding for information. All alumni writers were recorded in the *REGISTER OF INMATES* book when they arrived on campus and years later, when they were discharged, their date leaving were verified in the register.

Family members (alumni) will find healing from this book. The common man will be educated. Professionals will have case studies to better their services. Churches will have an inside view of their child care ministry on the Middlesex campus since 1920. And, the birth of an accredited school of social work with a focus on institutional children, foster care and adoption may be realized on a college campus.

Today, there are over 2,000 family members and our numbers continue to climb. We're a blended family. We came to the family from different cultures, different races and different religions. You will read only a few of our stories. Every alumnus, staff member or their children, has an individual memory of the family and their life at the Orphanage/Children's Home. The content of this book has captured only a few of our memories but enough to tell the history as not told before. Alumni memories of the same event are meant to be truthful; even so, the same memory of a specific story may differ among alumnus; even the "nickname" spelling of the same individual will at times differ. Aging and time tends to grow stories as well as curb memories.

Enjoy your reading, and from the family, thanks for taking time to read our childhood experiences through our memoirs. You will feel what we felt. You are going to be there with us.

Meet the family.

Footnote: *J. Andrews Smith has allowed memoirs in this book to remain exactly as the writer intended, verbatim, without editorial input. He makes no representation about the accuracy for any memoir other than his own.*

An Introduction

The First 20 Years

The Reverend Dr. James A. Evans

The Free Will Baptist Orphanage of North Carolina had its inception several years prior to its opening. In the years of 1910-1915, some of our leading Free Will Baptists became interested in providing a home for orphan boys and girls of our denomination and state. We had men and women from the various Conferences and Associations, which embraced the entire state, that saw this great need, so they began to advocate the building of a home where we could provide care, training, and the necessary comforts of life for our children that would otherwise be supported by relatives or by County, State, or Federal Aid.

In the year of 1915, the interest became so great that the State Association voted unanimously to assume the responsibility of providing for those helpless boys and girls. At the annual session held at the Shady Grove Church, it was decided to elect a Board of Trustees to make the necessary arrangements to provide this home. There was not at this time any money provided or any land donated for a site. The trustees elected were: Elders J. F. Casey, W. R. Coats, M. C. Prescott, J. E. Davis and Brother W. J. Braxton. This Board of Trustees soon began their work and on January 1, 1916 they accepted a gift of fifty acres of land about two miles north from the Town of Middlesex, from Elder B. B. Deans, and a few years later, purchased the adjoining tract of 111 acres, making a total of 161 acres. Of this, about 68 acres are in cultivation and the remainder is in pasture and woods.

The first building was begun in the latter part of the year of 1916; this was a three story building with a basement. This building has 31 large rooms and is now used by the girls and is called the Girls' Dormitory. This building was opened for the admission of children on May 23, 1920.

The first application was passed on February 11, 1920. The first children admitted were Nellie, Helen, Dorothy and Carl Whitley on May 23, 1920. In just a few years it became necessary to erect another dormitory for the boys, which was built in 1925 consisting of a two story building containing 16 rooms, and is known as the Boys' Dormitory.

A modern building was erected in 1940 consisting of an adequate dining room, kitchen, storage rooms, office and reception room. The superintendent's home is an old building but has been remodeled and is now a very adequate nine-room building in which he and his family live.

Dining Hall, Kitchen and Office

Inside Dining Hall

There are several poultry houses, stock barn, dairy barn, shop, wash house, and several hog houses.

The following have served as Superintendent of the home during the 23 years of operation, viz.

Mr. L. B. Dunn, November 5, 1919 to March 23, 1920
Elder L. H. Wetherington, March 23, 1920 to July 1, 1921
Mr. C.G. Pope, July 1, 1921 to June 3, 1929
Elder J. R. Bennett, June 3, 1929 to December 20, 1934
Elder J. W. Alford, December 20, 1934 to January 17, 1935
Elder M. E. Tyson, January 17, 1935 to May 15, 1940
Elder J. A. Evans, May 15, 1940 -- now serving

The home was opened with only a very small number of children but soon began to increase in number, and in the year 1926, we cared for 84 children; in 1930 we reached 108, this being the greatest number in any one year. Last year we cared for 92.

During the 23 years we have operated, we have cared for 303 children on an average age of 8 to 15 years each. We take the children at an age of 3 to 12 years and keep them until they reach the age of 18 or the completion of high school and any other training that they might be able to receive.

It has been very encouraging to us to note the great improvement of the children after entering the home. The majority of these boys and girls have come from very poor homes that were destitute of the needed care and the proper environments of life, and some had never known anything about a place they call home. In a very short time after entering the home, we have noted great improvement in the life and disposition of the child. We have found in many of these boys and girls valuable talents that otherwise would never have been developed. The children of this home, after completing the course we have to offer, are filling important places in life. Some are preaching the Gospel, some are teachers and principals of various schools of the state, some are bookkeepers, stenographers, nurses, clerks, and some have married and established homes and have become leading citizens. We have sent many boys and girls out that are today rendering valuable service.

Our staff in the home consists of 12 persons who supervise and care for the children, operate the farm, dairy, etc. Our school work is all in the state school which is located nearby, and giving them a full high school course. The religious training is given in the home daily.

We have a concert class that we send to the various parts of the state (usually to the churches) that has been a great help in getting our people more interested in the Orphanage work as well as a financial asset.

Our operating expense has increased very rapidly. Last year, it cost $25,629.73 to maintain and operate the home. Our donations from the various churches, union meetings, conferences, and associations have been both liberal and regular.

We usually produce good feed and food crops on the farm. There is on the farm 75 to 100 head of hogs and pigs that produce a great portion of the meat and lard, 25 to 35 head of cattle, both dairy and beef, used in the home. We also keep 1,200 to 1,500 chickens which furnish all the eggs and chickens needed for the home for eating purposes, and also have quite a number to sell. We operate the farm with a tractor and four work stock. We have a feed mill which is a great asset.

We are at this time creating a fund to build a chapel as soon as war conditions will permit. We are investing the money in series "F" War Bonds and at this time, we have received for this purpose, $3,394 in actual cash.

In conclusion, we will set forth the operation of the home in terms of service rendered and cost per child per year. In 1942, we started out with 86 children -- 16 orphans, 70 half-orphans (5 with mother dead and 65 with father dead). There were 44 boys and 42 girls. We had 6 children under 6 years of age, 27 from 6-12 years of age, and 53 from 12-18 years of age, and 6 children 18 and over, giving us a total of 92 cared for during the year.

Physical Care of Children

Six children were given Tuberculin tests, 75 small-pox vaccinations, 75 typhoid vaccinations, 6 diphtheria, 6 Wasserman tests, 5 vision test, and 6 mental test.

We had 57 children who had been in the institution one year or longer who gained weight. There was one child who lost weight during that year. The boys' average gain was 10 pounds and the girls 9 pounds.

Thirty-five children spent one day or more in bed on account of illness or detention in cases of suspected illness. We had the services of Duke Hospital and Carolina General Hospital for examinations. We had two tonsil operations. Through the State Dental Department, we had 68 children given dental care -- 43 teeth were filled. Each child was provided with comb, brush, tooth brush, wash cloth, bath towel, face towel, sleeping garments and personal clothing.

The children consumed more than 7,000 gallons of fresh cows' milk which was produced in our dairy.

The physical education and recreational program of our institution is very limited because of work assignments and religious activities. We are hoping we may improve this phase of our work in the near future.

Library Facilities

We have the following volumes in library: Agriculture 36, Biography 45, Economics 9, Fiction 150, Geography and Travel 63, History 142, Home Economics 17, Literature 231, Religion 170, Science 101, Reference 67, other 210 -- totaling 1,041.

Religious Work

In regard to our religious activities, we have Sunday school each Sunday morning and church services each first Sunday afternoon. When a visiting minister comes in during the week, or any time, a service is held at that time. Prayer service is held in the boys' and girls' buildings daily, and on Wednesday nights they assemble together in the chapel for their regular service.

Discipline

Corporal punishment is permitted in extreme cases by staff members, which is safe-guarded in various ways. Reports are made to the superintendent on the cause and type of punishment given. Care is taken to see that no real injury is done to the child's body. We have a form of reward given to those who comply with the rules of the institution. They are known as "Children in Good Standing," and have extra privileges.

Social Service

A diagnosis of each applicant is made before admission by the superintendent. We study the needs of the child before it is admitted in order to determine how we can best help it. We work with the other social agencies of the community for placing the children who cannot be received through our institution. There is an extensive study made in placing children who are ready to leave. We seek jobs, schools and other opportunities for them. As has been stated, our educational work is carried on through the state school system two miles from our campus.

Many of our children are now in the armed forces of our country. The Alumni Association and the Free Will Baptist Press, through its weekly publication, help to keep alive the friendship and welfare of our children throughout our country.

The average operating expense per year for the past five years was $21,826.00 and in 1942 was $25,403.00. The cost per child per year, five-year basis, was $260.72 and in 1942 the cost per child was $332.73. There was an increase of $72.01 per child over the average for five years before.

The Orphanage is one of the outstanding achievements of the Free Will Baptists of North Carolina. It is the practical expression of the heart and soul of Christianity as it reaches out over the state and gathers the precious human fragments from among the broken ruins of North Carolina homes. One may point to the Orphanage and say, "There is Christianity at work!" It is an investment in North Carolina boys and girls; it is an abiding opportunity for voluntary, individual and personal expression of a feeling and desire to help others. It will remain as long as needy children of our state are bereft of homes.

*Footnote: *"The First 20 Years" was first published July 1943 by the Missouri Free Will Baptist Gem Magazine. It was originally published as "The Free Will Baptist Orphanage, Middlesex, North Carolina." Gem publisher, Gary Fry granted permission to use for this book. The Reverend Dr. James A. Evans was Superintendent of the Orphanage 1940-'49.*

1
Griffin Brothers
1922-31

Elmer 8, Joseph 10 and Russell 6

Cousins Lewis Henry Griffin, age 29, and Addie, age 14, married Friday, June 1, 1905. They had seven children born to their marriage.

On the weekend after Labor Day, 1922, Addie Griffin admitted her three youngest sons – Joseph, age 8, Elmer 6 and Russell 3 into the Free Will Baptist Orphanage in Middlesex, North Carolina. They arrived at the Orphanage on Monday, September 11th. Their father, age 44, had died on November 28, 1920 from a heart attack. Henry Griffin is remembered as a farmer, always neat and a good dresser. Their mother was pregnant at the time of their father's death and she gave birth to their younger sister Lillian on May 10, 1921, nearly six months after their father's death. The family owned a farm and after their father's death, their mom could not keep up mortgage payments and lost the farm after their neighbor foreclosed on the farm. It is believed mom might have felt overwhelmed with having to care for her seven children; and, with inadequate income, decided to place her younger sons in the Orphanage.

After the three brothers were placed in the Orphanage, their mother still had in the house their sisters, Lela, age 15, Sallie, age 14, and Lillian, age 1. An older brother Robert, age 10, was in the home, too.

> Middlesex, N.C.
> March 29, 1927
>
> Dear mother,
>
> I got your card Wednesday. We are getting a long all right. I hope you are getting a long all right. We are having a good time. Tell Bobby I said write me. I hope he is having a good time going to school. I am having a good time. I will close.
>
> your son,
> Joe

1927 letter from Joseph to his mother

In an August 2010 interview with Alton Griffin, age 61, son of Elmer Griffin, he shared the following information about Joseph's, Elmer's and Russell's stay in the Orphanage:

"Daddy went to the Orphanage at age 4 with his older brother Joseph and his younger brother Russell when their father died. There were two older sisters and one older brother and one baby sister who did not go to the Orphanage. Daddy spoke of work on the farm and in the dairy. He spoke fondly of traveling with a choir of boys and girls from the Orphanage to various churches to sing. He remembered the good meals provided to them. He spoke of occasions when members of the choir would spend the night in homes of church members when they traveled farther from the Orphanage.

"I remember Daddy talking of the day Joseph died. He said a storm was coming up and Joe, as Dad called his brother, sent Daddy away from the dairy barn to the residence or main campus. He said Joe was sitting on rails or dividers between stalls in the barn when the lightning struck and he understood the bolt exited Joe's body off his knees. I believe Daddy said Joe was killed and died on Daddy's birthday – his 13th. Dad's birthday was August 11. He was born in 1916 as his 13th birthday would have been in 1929.

"Dad used to like to reminisce about life at the Orphanage. Sounded like work was hard but there were happy times. Dad really enjoyed going back to the Children's Home for reunions to worship and fellowship with others who had been residents there. He also enjoyed receiving newsletters and correspondence about the Home.

"Daddy and Russell left the Orphanage May 8, 1931 when their mother remarried and the boys were needed to work on the farm. I remember dad talked about wishing he could have stayed at the orphanage to get his education. He loved animals and talked how he would have loved to become a vet. He helped everyone with their animals and he was very good at it"

Addie Griffin married the second time September 15, 1926. She married Robert Singleton, his second marriage, too. Yet, Addie waited nearly five years to remove Joe's brothers Elmer and Russell from the Orphanage. Shireyan Phelps, daughter of the Griffin Brother's sister Sallie, lived with her mother with Addie after her marriage to Robert Singleton.

In correspondence, August 2010, with Shirleyan Phelps, age 77, she wrote her thoughts how Addie Griffin cared for her family. She also gives insight into reasons Elmer and Russell might not have been taken out of the Orphanage until after she and her second husband Robert Singleton were married for nearly five years. Shirleyan's mother was a brother of the Griffin brothers:

"Mama (Addie) kept Uncle Bobby (Robert) the oldest boy at home; he probably tended what land was left; we have wondered often about how Mama took care of herself and the children at home. We think her brothers probably helped, as well as her father. The house sat right on the banks of Tranters Creek so they could get fish, some turtles and frogs. There was enough land to raise at least enough vegetables for them. The house is still in the family and through the earlier years could have provided almost everything. Mama was a good seamstress. It was a close-knit neighborhood with the railroad running right through it. They could also raise enough to keep at least a cow and chickens. When I lived in that house as a child, there was a large grapevine. Mother told me the first tea she ever heard of came about when Mama sent her to the store to trade eggs for something they needed and she was talked into taking it out in tea instead. As a child, I worked on those acres; almost everything was done by hand. I helped hand pick what we called stock peas. I doubt there was ever any tobacco. The area was rich with wild plums.

"As for why the children stayed at the Home until 1931, it was probably because of relations with stepparent; or, perhaps, too many children for Mama to care for? Mother told me during the years Mama was married to him, she (Sallie) lived out of a suitcase. Said she'd spend a couple of weeks with different folks. The children (and Mama) always called him Mr. Singleton.

"Mother (Sallie Verna Griffin Beacham) always told me Joe had been getting the cows into the barn ahead of a storm and that he crawled up to the eaves to wait out the storm and was sitting under the tin roof when lightening struck and killed him. Mother always said Joe was buried beside Papa."

Russell Griffin 74, died December 24, 1992. Elmer Griffin 90, died January 5, 2007. Joseph Griffin 15, was killed by lightning August 11, 1929 on Elmer's birthday. Joseph and his father are buried in J. H. Evans Cemetery outside Greenville, North Carolina.

Footnote: On July 11, 2010, a memorial was dedicated in memory of Joseph Griffin at the Free Will Baptist Children's Home. Along with Shirleyan Phelps and Alton Griffin, Dr. Bobby Taylor was helpful writing this chapter. Dr. Taylor was President/CEO of the Free Will Baptist Children's Home 1983-07.

2

We Never Left Campus

William Rich
1925-31

I was born March 17, 1921 in Asheville, North Carolina – but I have no recollection of my life until August 1, 1924. My family members have informed me of several things that happened prior to this significant day in my life, but none of them jogged my memory of those early days. It seems that, when I was just under three years old, my dad and grandfather were working on a T-Model Ford Truck and needed a wrench from the toolbox mounted onto a motorcycle. The motorcycle was parked under a barn shed approximately 100 yards from the garage where they were working on the T-Model. My dad sent me to get the wrench. I had to reach as high as I could to get it and, in my attempt to do so, I pulled the motorcycle, causing it to fall on top of me. According to the reports, my tongue was cut nearly off. My grandfather carried me to the family doctor who sewed it back with a needle and coarse thread. Later, in my teen years, I had an occasion to visit this physician, Dr. P. B. Orr. We talked about the incident and he informed me that my tongue had less than one-half inch of skin and flesh intact and the cut was from left to right. He examined the results and said I was lucky not to have a speech impediment.

During the depression years of the early twenties, jobs were scarce and most families in the South were living in poverty while enduring hunger and hardships. My dad was young and able to work, so with the advice and financial help from his dad, decided that the best he could do to support three young children and a wife expecting number four, would be to go to Detroit, Michigan to work in an automobile factory. He left for Detroit, had been there only a short while, and was exposed to Smallpox and died. His body could not even be returned to North Carolina for burial. I never even remembered seeing my dad. I was told he was buried in Greenhill Cemetery in Detroit. Later in life, I visited the cemetery but could not find his grave.

This resulted in many more drastic circumstances. My mother was pregnant with no income or means of support for herself and three young children. She, therefore, carried three very young boys, one about five years old, me (about three years old at the time), and one nearly one year old, to my paternal grandfather. Grandfather Rich was a minister and owned a home and about 45 acres, which he had inherited, there in the outskirts of Asheville. My mother went to her dad to help with his care, as he was in poor health, and the only place for her to stay at that time.

My paternal grandmother developed health problems soon after the three young boys became her responsibility. Her condition required surgery to remove reproductive organs and a long period of recuperation. Grandfather Rich, being a minister ordained by the Free Will Baptist Association and a pastor of a church that supported the Free Will Baptist Orphanage near Middlesex, North Carolina, was able to negotiate with the administration to accept my older brother, Alfred, and me. The orphanage was not equipped with a nursery and could not, therefore, accept my younger brother Lee.

Rich Family -Top L-R Alfred, William
Bottom L-R: Lee, Ray

On June 23, 1925, three months after my fourth birthday, my older brother Alfred, age 6 and I arrived at the orphanage just before dark. Our younger brother Lee, age 1 was too young to be accepted. We were the 89th and 90th children admitted to the orphanage. As we got out of that old T-Model Ford and began walking down the driveway to the orphanage, I began to cry. Alfred, as he grabbed hold of my hand, said to me, "Don't worry, little brother, I'll take care of you!" It seemed like that day was the beginning of my life! We arrived at the orphanage around 5:30 p.m. and walked to the kitchen, located in the basement of the girls' building. Frances Ledford ('22-'28) met us at the door, said, "Come on in and eat." Our grandfather left immediately after dropping us off. Alfred and I were sat at a table with six other boys. After eating, Mr. C. G. Pope, Superintendent ('21-'29), took us to the boys' building and assigned Alfred and me beds on the first floor with other boys. We slept in that room until we left the orphanage six years later. There were about 90 boys and girls at the orphanage at all times while we were there.

I was the youngest child there for more than two years...too young to attend school. We had two large brick buildings as dorms, one for the boys, one for girls. The superintendent's quarters, office, kitchen and dining area were all in the girls' building. There was also a chapel and study hall in the girls' building. Mr. Pope and his family lived on the first floor of the girls' building. Also, on the first floor was the co-ed study hall, which served as our chapel on Sundays and school on Monday through Friday. All grades, one through seven, were in the same room. Grades eight through eleven went to Middlesex High School. There was a piano in the room. Off from the basement, but connected to the dining room, was a kitchen with several stoves and a food pantry. Outside the entrance to the basement was the dinner bell and furnace for heating the building. The dinner bell was on a post, about 18 feet high.

The laundry room at the orphanage was in the basement of the old pump house. That building is still on campus and it is located across the road from a swimming pool dug on campus thirty years after we left there.

Behind the pump house was a hog pen and further back in the woods was a creek. We dammed up that creek in 1929 for a swimming pool. It was down behind the hog pens but up to the right of the hog pens because the water was running from the right down to the left, and the hog pens....we got into the fresh water before it got to the hog pens to make our dam and swimming pool. We, in all probability, made that thing, probably about, I would say, twenty-five or thirty feet wide and forty to fifty feet long. We dug it out with a team of horses pulling an old drag pan that you scoop up dirt with. We'd scoop it up out of the creek bottom deep enough to swim in and from the creek edges to build our dam across it. We took a bunch of old posts and drove them in the ground. There were two lines of wood posts driven close in line. We would take that scoop of dirt and drop it in between the two lines of posts. We lined each row of posts with big heavy boards. The dam was about six to eight feet thick, probably five, six feet high. Mr. J. R. Bennett, the new Superintendent ('29-'34), helped us arrange that. He also helped us so the water would never run over the dam with an overflow spillway that went around the end of the dam. The pool was every bit of seven feet deep; possibly eight feet deep at the upper end. We had a diving board off the bank. The boys and girls alternated every other day to go swimming. I remember when we finished, Clarence Mitchell ('23-'32) grabbed me and threw me in time after time. Just as soon as I could get up, he would duck me back in and I actually thought I was going to drown and Alfred did, too. Alfred jumped in and pulled me out. Clarence was one of the older boys and I was still the youngest kid on campus when this happened. Other older boys there were Haywood Howell ('21-'31), Larry Martin ('20-'32) and Horace Mixon ('23-'34).

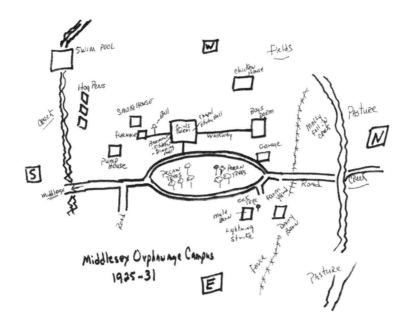

Drawn by William Rich 2010

    Clarence Mitchell was usually the one that did the barbeque for the Fourth of July and Thanksgiving. We'd kill hogs and build a big fire and barbeque it right there on campus. Clarence, too, was the one in charge of smoking meat in the Smoke House which was located just a little bit to the right of the Boiler Room (it furnished all the heat for the girls' building). I remember the smoke house was concrete flooring with a place to hang meat. They'd kill hogs, dress them and cut them up into parts to hang in the smoke house. I remember helping carry wood to the cement floor. We'd build two or three fires on that concrete floor and keep them going for maybe two or three days. You could see the smoke coming out up at the top right in the eave on each end. I remember helping Clarence build the fires. The smoke house was probably twenty-four to twenty-six feet long and maybe fourteen feet wide. We'd usually kill four or five hogs at a time. I remember the biggest one they had ever killed; estimated weight was over six hundred pounds. That was a big one.

Life was never dull at the orphanage and we learned a lot of lessons…some the hard way! I remember once just following a rain, there was a water puddle at the corner of the boys' building where the downspout had formed a small pond. To entertain myself and break the monotony of nothing to do, which rarely occurred, I found an old brush broom used to sweep the yard and tried to sweep the water away, resulting in wetting the corner of the building. Mr. Pope whipped me with a belt which, in my opinion, was unfair; however, this taught me to respect authority.

Clarence was rough with me at times. One time he was running after me and picked up a rock the size of a hen egg and hit me in the head. It just about knocked me out and I bled for quite a bit. Lucy, the lady that fixed Alfred's nose when he got it broke, patched up the left side of my head. Clarence was a little overbearing, about the oldest…closest to the oldest boy there and he seemed to be more in charge of things. I remember sometimes he would assign us to duty or tell us to do certain things and, if we didn't do it to suit him, he'd beat us up a little bit. He'd assign which ones would do cutting the woods and firing the furnaces and so forth. He probably slapped me around, I'd say, an average of once every week or two.

I recall on one occasion, while trying to get a calf into the barn, I stepped on a block which had a large nail, sharp end pointing up, sticking out of it. The nail went all the way through my foot. Ouch!

I can remember boys having fun riding a one-horse drawn wagon with no horse, shaft and bed removed from the wagon…just four wheels connected by a thick board. This took place on the dirt road (now called Children's Home Road) off of the circular drive. A short way down the road is a creek. The boys would push the wagon to the hill overlooking the creek at the bottom. One boy would sit up front and guide the two wheels with his feet, and one boy would sit in the back slowing the back two wheels with his feet. Other boys would push the wagon at the top of the hill to get it rolling down the hill. Several boys got limbs broken, one of the boys I remember with a broken arm was Randolph Wells ('25-'31).

To encourage churches to contribute more to support the orphanage, the office personnel decided to furnish envelopes to all Free Will Baptist churches. These envelopes displayed a picture of me, age 4 (the youngest boy), and Rachel Bissett ('25-'31), age 3, and youngest girl.

One of the most vivid instances I can recall is a summer electrical storm on Sunday, August 11, 1929. We didn't do any chores such as plowing and hoeing and things like that on Sunday. We went to Sunday school in the morning and then had our Sunday dinner. By the afternoon, it was hot and humid, fairly standard weather for the eastern part of the state in late summer. Thunder showers were forecast for the area. It was a lazy afternoon that Sunday. Some of the boys had a ball game going; other boys and girls were just enjoying the afternoon under the shade of trees; other children and matrons were sitting on their assigned building porches talking. Some were playing with the few dogs and cats on campus. Some of the boys were wandering around on the farm. We usually did whatever we wanted to until time to milk and feed the hogs and so forth. Many of us wandered down to the cow pasture near the dorm.

Wiley Watson, age 10, Alfred, age 10 and Joseph (Joe) Griffin, age 15 were playing together. One of the cows in the pasture, Joe Griffin really liked. He considered it his pet, although it was just one of the many cows in the pasture. Joe invited Alfred and Wiley to go with him to see "his pet." Before going into the pasture, they stopped at a nearby barn for Joe to pick up a chain. They opened the gate and went inside the pasture among cows and when Joe spotted "his pet", they went over to it. The cow appeared to know Joe. He smiled as he petted her on the head. Then, he put the chain around the cow's head and started leading her around the pasture. Joe noticed there was a lot of grass outside the fence and shortly, Alfred and Wiley followed Joe and the cow through the gate to greener grass outside the fenced-in pasture.

It was around three o'clock in the afternoon when a storm came up and it started raining. Most of us saw it coming and went to the boys' building. But, those three didn't run to the dormitory. Joe, in a short run, led his pet cow, followed by Rich and Wiley, under a big oak tree near the livestock barn. Shortly, they heard loud thundering, followed by lightning. With Joe leading his pet cow, they all moved inside the barn to escape the weather and wait out the storm. Joe put his cow in the second stall on the right and climbed up on the stall petition and sat holding the chain still around his pet's head. On the first stall on the left, Wiley and Rich climbed up on a stall gate and started swinging. Beyond Joe was another stall with eight calves in it. The rain was heavy, thunder loud and clashes of lighting seen over the nearby pasture. In low voices, the boys chatted back and forth with each other; Joe occasionally turning to the pet cow saying a few calming words. Alfred and Wiley were having fun swinging on the stall gate.

Then, there was a sudden loud bam, followed by a flash. Alfred found himself on the ground in a daze with his ears ringing. Lying nearby was Wiley, his white shirt on fire. Alfred, petrified and stunned, crawled, then jolted up and ran out of the barn into rain and thunder. With his ears ringing, Alfred sought shelter in a nearby shelter until the rain slowed. He then ran to the boy's building. His ears still ringing, sobbing, Alfred reported Wiley was on fire in the barn after being hit by lightning. He did not know the status of Joe at that time, as Joe was further in the barn with his pet cow. Word began to pass around campus of three boys in the barn during the lightning storm. By the time the information reached the superintendent, all three boys were believed killed. Alfred remembered what followed, "Well, shortly after the rain stopped, about thirty minutes after the lightning hit the barn and oak tree next to it, three black funeral hearses pulled up to the barn, but only two of them were used. I was the only one living. Joe and Wiley were killed. One of the eight calves was killed, but Joe's pet cow with a chain still around it head was still living. The oak tree later died."

I went with Alfred and several boys down to the barn to see Wiley and Joe. We stood nearby as their bodies were loaded in the funeral hearses. I was told later that Dr. E. C. Powell from Middlesex had been called to the barn to help Wiley and Joe.

There was no newspaper in Middlesex, but from nearby Raleigh – *The News and Observer,* August 13, 1929 edition reported the deaths under headlines:

"TWO ORPHAN YOUTH KILLED BY LIGHTNING – *Pupils of Free Will Baptist Orphanage at Middlesex Lose Lives."*

The paper went on to read – *"During the progress of an electrical storm which passed over this section Sunday afternoon, Wiley Watson, of Wilson County, and Joe Griffin, of Pitt County, were instantly killed by a stroke of lightning at the Free will Baptist Orphanage near Middlesex. Young Watson was sent to the institution from the Kenly section: Griffin from near Washington, N.C. The remains of Watson were interred in the Moore's Church Cemetery this morning at 9 o'clock. The remains of young Griffin were sent to Greenville and interment was made in the cemetery near that city this afternoon. Several inmates from the orphanage when the storm was coming up went out to drive a herd of cattle under shelter. Just as they got them housed lightning struck the shelter, killing Watson and Griffin, stunning another and killing a young calf."*

A day earlier, August 12th, *Wilson Daily Times* published a report with headlines – "Lightning Kills two Orphan Boys…Were Inmates of the Free will Baptist Orphanage Near Middlesex: Calf Which was Near Also Killed: One of them Wiley Watson from Wilson County."

The paper then wrote – *"Two orphan boys, Wiley Watson from Wilson County and Joe Griffin of Washington, N.C., were struck by lightning at the Free Will Baptist Orphanage near Middlesex yesterday afternoon and instantly killed. A calf which was near was also killed.*

"Word was sent by Dr. Powell to the Editor of the times by the driver of the Raleigh bus Mr. Lewis which arrived here yesterday afternoon asking us to notify the relatives of young Watson, but after phoning over the town and county to a number of the Watsons we were unable to secure any information as to the near relatives of the boy."

The memories of seeing these deaths still dwell in my mind! For several years after the incident, Alfred had ringing in his ears.

In that same barn, Alfred and I were involved in an incident of a mule attack! Some of the boys were assigned duty putting halters on the mules when they were not in use and leading them to a water trough to drink, then on to graze. The oldest mule of the three was named Molly. There was one white mule named Gladys and one other female mule named Rhoda. Molly was never accustomed to working with a team, so she was not used very much. I was attempting to take her to water and graze, and, as I approached her, she laid her ears back on her neck, rolled her eyes up, opened her mouth, brayed loudly and ran toward me trying to bite my head. I ran to the wide door which was on a rolling track at the end of the barn. The bottom of the wide door was high enough for me to crawl under and escape harm by old Molly. I was the first person that Molly attacked, but not the last! On one occasion, Alfred and a couple of the other boys attempted to harness her to cultivate some garden crops when she tried to pull her stunt again. One of the older boys had taken a long broken hoe handle in the barn for protection. When old Molly started for him, he threw the broken hoe handle at her, she dodged, and it missed the mule and hit Alfred, breaking his nose. Our farm boss, along with his wife and daughter, Lucy, who was a trained nurse, lived in the boy's building and served as supervisor of the boys. Lucy cut a finger from a lady's rubber glove, filled it tightly with cotton, and pushed it up Alfred's broken nose, holding it to its normal position for about one month. Later, the visiting doctor examined the broken nose and commended Lucy for a job well done. Old Molly later fell into a small stream, broke her neck and was buried near the barn. "Good riddance!"

Farm building, horses, mules and boys

We didn't really use old Molly near as much as we did the others because she was the oldest work animal that we had and we had two others...this was a white horse, and there was another mule that was a lot younger and we used them more. I think the horse's name was Dinah, because a little later, after old Molly, we replaced her with a young mule with the name Rhoda. I used to plow Gladys and Dinah. Dinah fell in the creek later and broke her neck, too. By age ten, I had started milking cows and feeding hogs.

Mr. Bennett helped me with my first fishing experience. I went to him for a fishing hook. He told me to go get a safety pin. When I returned with it, he bend it the shape of a fishing hook. He tied string on the head end of the pin. I found a few worms and headed to the woods. In the branch, I caught my first fish... a small brim.

Rev. J. R. Bennett replaced Mr. Pope as Superintendent in 1929. Rev. Bennett brought about some welcomed changes at the orphanage. As I said previously, he helped the boys design and construct a dam in a fresh water stream in order to have a swimming pool. Rules enforced a system whereas boys and girls took turns swimming every other day. There was no mixed swimming and no swimming on Sunday. The only co-habitation was in study hall, on the playground and in the dining room. Mr. Bennett tried to give each orphan a gift for his birthday. When I learned of my 10th birthday, he asked me to tell him my favorite candy. I told him peanut butter, because I thought I'd have more than if he gave me candy. My peanut butter came in a small metal pail with a lid and handle. That was my first birthday present!

Mr. Bennett encouraged boys to earn income by growing vegetables for the orphanage. He made available land, seeds, fertilizer and a mule with plow to boys to plant their own garden. My brother Alfred planted vegetables and Mr. Bennett purchased them from him to use in the orphanage kitchen. Mr. Bennett had us plant the pecan trees that are on campus inside the circular drive.

We didn't have a tractor until Mr. Bennett came to the orphanage. We grew mostly corn, but also all kind of vegetables for the dining room. I remember a lot of turnips. We had a lot of collards, lots of cabbage, watermelons, Irish potatoes, sweet potatoes, radish, cantaloupes, radishes, beans and, peas. The girls would use those old big three-legged pots that would probably hold twenty to twenty-five gallons. We had three of those and would build fires under them. They were outside the old kitchen. They would boil turnips and collards; we felt like it was a real treat. We especially enjoyed drinking the pot juices, called pot liquor, with cornbread.

We never raised tobacco while I was at the orphanage. We raised corn and oats to feed the livestock. Our main crops were stuff that we could eat in the dining room. We had peaches and picked blackberries and dewberries. A dewberry is black, similar to a blackberry but doesn't have long climbing briars way up high, it runs on the ground. It's a lot smaller vine. I remember picking some and I remember the girls would make jellies and jams. There was a wall in the kitchen, probably as high as the room's ceiling, probably seven feet, it'd be sixteen to eighteen feet long and maybe seven or eight shelves going up a foot high apart. Every shelf was full of jellies and jams, peaches and things that they'd preserved and canned. The girls made bread, cornbread and biscuits.

For meat, not only did we kill hogs, but chickens, too. We usually had sixty to one hundred laying hens. The chicken house was three to four hundred feet behind the girls' building. It was a big chicken house and had a big outside lot. I'd say, oh, probably the lot was one hundred to one hundred fifty foot square. We had the roosting area and nesting area in that house; chickens had a way they could go in and out freely from the house into this big lot. I remember gathering eggs. Sometimes, we would kill chickens to eat.

It was a great big occasion...usually in the spring. We'd separate the hens and roosters as soon as we could when they were young chicks. We always set the hens and they hatched their own eggs. The roosters, we killed for Sunday meals. Ninety kids could consume a lot of chicken each meal. We had all the milk we could use with twenty-five milk cows.

To encourage churches to contribute more to support the orphanage, the office personnel decided to furnish envelopes to all Free Will Baptist churches. These envelopes displayed a picture of the youngest boy and the youngest girl resident. My picture was on the envelopes.

On August 2, 1931, Alfred and I left the orphanage about 5:00 a.m. after an early breakfast was prepared for us, including my grandfather and my Uncle Hobert Ballard. Until that day, that morning, we had never been off the premise of the orphanage from the day we arrived.

The vehicle they drove to pick us up was a 1927 Chevy two-door with a four-cylinder engine. The distance to Asheville from the orphanage was 270 miles and top speed was about 35 MPH. So, after one stop to eat watermelon and two more stops for hotdogs and gasoline, we arrived home twenty-two hours later, at 3:00 a.m. the following morning. There were no interstate highways at that time. Climbing Point Lookout Mountain between Old Fort and Ridgecrest required low gear, causing the engine to overheat. We pulled over to put more water in the radiator at this place where there was a black bear chained inside a cage. We thought one of us would have to walk to the top of the mountain, but we were able to wait it out and continue on our way.

It was now Sunday morning, so even after the grueling trip, it was time for church. We went to Cedar Hill Baptist Church where I met, for the first time in my recollection, relatives and friends. Many are close friends until this day...others have passed away, but I have precious memories of them.

While at the orphanage, we were treated good, taught to work, behave, assume responsibility and respect others. All of us attended Sunday school, church and school and were offered a college education after graduation from high school. This period of my life is unforgettable and I am glad this care was available for me due to the circumstances. All the time while I was in the orphanage, I did not know I had a younger brother named Thomas Ray, born November 28, 1925. Neither did I remember ever seeing my mother and would not have recognized her if I had seen her face to face.

L-R; Alferd Rich, Jerry Smith ('49-'60) and William Rich (July11, 2010)

Footnote: At the Joseph Watson & Wiley Watson Memorial dedication on July 11, 2010, Alfred Rich, age 91, spoke to alumni attending homecoming at the Children's Home.

3

Molasses Ran Out On the Kitchen Floor

Fannie Holland
1925-35

L-R: Hazel and Fannie Holland

    Fannie Holland was born in Wayne County on June 23, 1917. She was the youngest of five children. At the age of eight, her father died and her mother killed herself. Her three older brothers and her older sister went to live with relatives but no one in the family was able to provide a home for Fannie. According to Fannie, one of her uncles took her to the orphanage and dropped her off on July 12, 1925. She was the 91st child to be admitted to the care of the home. Fannie lived at the orphanage for the next 10 years and left on June 22, 1935. She is now age 92 and the oldest living alumnus of the home.
    Fannie stated that her memories of the orphanage are very sketchy due to the length of time that has passed since she left. According to her daughter, her mother never talked much about her life at the orphanage until about fifteen years ago when she became interested in visiting the

orphanage again and attending the alumni homecoming in July of that year. Fannie stated that she was at the home when Alfred and William Rich were there and only learned a few years ago that one of them had a crush on her when they were at the orphanage.

Over the years, Fannie told her family stories of how she made biscuits for meals and how many pans of biscuits it would take to feed everyone. It was fun ringing the bell to let everyone on campus know that it was time to eat. She also relayed stories of other chores, such as working in the wash house, picking beans and canning vegetables.

When questioned about some of her fondest memories of the home, Fannie stated that it was having lots of children to play with and never feeling lonely. She also stated that she remembered one time when one of the boys, who was assigned kitchen duty, left the spigot on the molasses barrel open and molasses ran out all over the kitchen floor. What a sticky mess that was and it took several hours to clean it up.

Fannie stated that one of her saddest memories was the time a bad storm came up and some of the boys were sent out to the farm to get the cows in the barn and two of the boys were struck by lightning and died. She stated that it took a long time for the staff and children to get over this incident and the death of the two children.

Fannie acknowledged that in the summer for many years, she was chosen to go out on "concert class". She stated that the group would travel to the Free Will Baptist Churches in the state to raise money for the home. Fannie stated that this is how she met her future husband. She stated that her husband's family were members of Elm Grove FWB Church in Ayden and that when the concert class visited Elm Grove Church, she would stay with the Garris family. Evidently, Fannie made quite an impression on Mr. Garris because after she left the home, she married Wilbur Asa Garris and they were married for fifty-five years and had five children. Mr. Garris was a farmer and Fannie stated that she helped her husband work on the farm. They also raised a big garden and in the summer she would pick and can vegetables. She stated that the skills she learned at the orphanage helped her after she married. Velma McLawhorn stated that her mother was a great cook and she also made all of their clothes, some of them from feed sacks.

Fannie stated that, not only did she learn many useful skills that helped her as a wife and mother, but also her religious training stayed with her after she left the home. Her daughter stated that her mother was always very strict about what activities were allowed on Sunday. She stated that her mother did not permit them to sew or do laundry; only the very essential chores were permitted. Fannie has been a member of Elm Grove Free Will Baptist Church for more than 70 years.

In November of 2008 at the Friends of Children's Day Celebration at the orphanage, Fannie was honored by her son, Roger Garris and his family who established an endowment fund in her honor. They also donated a fifteen passenger van to the home.

Footnote: Due to medical reasons, Fannie's memories of her life at the home have faded and she was unable to write her memoirs or give the interviewer much information. The stories and information in this chapter of her early life was provided by daughter, Velma McLawhorn. Social Worker Cathy Hines Campbell ('57-'66) interviewed Fannie (age 91) and her daughter on January 9, 2009.

4

I Will Always Be a Tar Heel

Thelma Josephine Hatem
1933-43

Thelma Hatem

My father came to the United States from Syria as a teenager. He sold fruit in Wilmington, North Carolina where I was born. My birth was during the Great Depression years and my father died 12 days after my arrival. Mom had a rough time caring for me and my older brother. My uncle adopted my brother and I was admitted to the orphanage. Get out the violins...I never felt unlucky. I cannot remember arriving at the orphanage. I was told I arrived in June of 1933 at the age of 2 years and 10 months...left March 3,1943...and was always called Jo. I never saw my mother while I was at the orphanage and I do not remember her leaving me there.

My mother lived in New Bern, North Carolina until I went to the orphanage. She then moved to Hampton, Virginia and was in touch with me when, I believe, I was around 10 or 11.

Being that I was so young, I got to play outside most of the day...and, I believe, the older girls probably babied me. As I grew older, I had certain chores to do...after my bed was made, I swept the hall on the second floor in the girls' dorm and cleaned the bathroom. Later on, I helped with the laundry.   I used to love climbing the apple trees behind our building and eating the green apples, playing hopscotch, jumping board, playing ball, hide and seek and sitting in the circle looking for four leaf clovers.

On Sundays we would get dressed up in our Sunday best. After Sunday School and lunch, we would play tag, ball, etc. I was lucky; I received new clothes once a year from a Sunday School Class in New Bern. I believe a lady named Mrs. Leona Mercer sponsored me and she was responsible for getting me placed in the orphanage.

I remember looking forward to Santa arriving at the orphanage, coming over the hill to the circle with presents...bags of candy and fruit...and we would go from room to room checking each other's bag. I did not go anywhere for Christmas. I always spent it at the orphanage (and I enjoyed it because I received clothes and toys from the Sunday School Class in New Bern).

I did go on a couple of vacations to New Bern. When I was on vacation there, I stayed with my mother's cousin at their grocery store. I believe it was due to Mrs. Mercer in New Bern making the arrangements.

I remember the dinner bell ringing and knew it was time to get my face washed and hair combed and head for the dining hall. Originally, we ate in the girls' building in the basement. The kitchen and all the supplies were there. I do remember enjoying the delicious meals, especially the fried chicken.

When I disobeyed the rules, I was punished by having to sit on the steps in the girl's building for an hour, which seemed to me a lifetime.

I was given piano lessons at one time, which was a bonus, but I did not like practicing.

My schooling was at the orphanage in the early days, and then we were bused to Middlesex, which I really enjoyed. We were lined up and given our bag lunch... which consisted of a sandwich and a piece of fruit...then we boarded the school bus.

I remember some of the girls used to tell ghost stories...which would scare the heck out of me...(like seeing their grandmother at the foot of their bed in a rocking chair...rocking away). My nickname was "Possum," given to me by Earl Tippett. I had pneumonia when I was age six and I was carried up to bed while I pretended to be sleeping. They said I was playing possum. Afterwards, Earl called me "Possum." I must have been very mischievous.

We were drilled in our Bible Verses, the Lords Prayer and the 23rd Psalm. These have stuck with me throughout my life and I am very grateful. I was in the concert class for a couple of years visiting churches.

I remember a few of us girls gathering around the radio and listening to programs like Fiber Magee & Molly and The Shadow in the living room, and we listened to soaps in the ironing room.

I remember the pump house with the laundry around back...it was on the pump house steps I learned to whistle...and did not stop for days. I skated back and forth from the basement area to the pump house for hours.

During canning season, we peeled many apples, etc...and during the fall, I remember harvest time when they would use the hogs for making sausage, ham and other delicious items to be cured and placed in the smoke house.

I remember the quiet summer afternoon playing in the circle under the pecan trees...and running barefoot as soon as school was out.

I left the orphanage in March 1943 when I was 12 years old and in the fourth grade. My mother picked me up...we packed my stuff in some boxes and headed north by Greyhound. This was the first time I remember seeing my mother. No one visited me at the orphanage. My mother did start writing me when I was around 10 years old. She had remarried and had moved to Pittsburgh, Pennsylvania.

No one told me I was leaving the orphanage. Mother appeared one day to take me home to Pittsburgh and I became a Yankee (ha, ha), but deep down inside, I will always be a Tar Heel.

I did not have any relationship with my brother until I was 16 and already in Pittsburgh with my mother. We visited New Bern and that was the first time I met him. By this time, he was already married with a baby and in the Navy.

Too bad my buddy Earl Tippett ('28-'40) passed on; with him went so much of my childhood information. Thank goodness I did get to meet him before his death. The first time I attended the alumni homecoming, he gave his name and the light came on - I remembered his name and he remembered me. As a little girl, he was one of the people of whom I had a vague memory. He was a few years older than me, but I remembered seeing him work around the orphanage. He said he often wondered what happened to me when I left the orphanage.

Personally, I was very happy at the orphanage, because I had nothing to compare it to. When I left, I was very homesick for a few months, but finally adjusted to the Big City in Yankee country.

I do feel I was protected a little too much. I thought everyone was nice out in the world, but I found out that was not the case. I did learn how to cook, iron, sew and take care of myself physically at the orphanage. I was very self-sufficient and, in time, learned good coping skills. I believe someone there took special care of me and I am very grateful. So, all in all, my experience at the orphanage was good and much better than some other children who had a mother and father looking after them...struggling during the poor economic times.

5

I Cried the Day I Left

Mary Evelyn Pate
1933-43

Pate Family – Top L-R: Linwood, Ralph, Bessie (mother), Annie Lee Bottom: Mary Evelyn

I came to the Orphanage on August 12, 1933 with my two older brothers and my older sister. Ralph was 11 years old, Annie Lee was 9 years old, Linwood was 7 years old, and I was 4 years old. Our mother, Bessie Harper Pate, was 26 years old and a widow. Our father, Benjamin Franklin Pate, had committed suicide by drinking poison on December 24, 1932 at the age of 40. Because my mother was financially unable to take care of the four of us, we were taken from our home in Deep Run, N.C. to the Orphanage. The Reverend Clifton Rice from the Free Will Baptist Church in Deep Run and our mother and papa, who was our mother's father, were with us. We arrived in the afternoon after lunch. I would spend the next ten years of my life here.

There were several superintendents during my time there: J. R. Bennett ('29-'34); J. W. Alford ('34-'35); M. E. Tyson ('35-'40); and James Evans ('40-'49), who was there when I left the Orphanage. Mr. Evans' wife, Faye, was the dietician for a period of time. At the suggestion of the superintendent, we did not see our mother from the day we arrived until Thanksgiving on November 26, 1933. We had a picture taken of all of us with her at the Orphanage on that day. She brought us each a box of cookies.

Many names and faces have stuck with me through the years. Josephine Hatem ('33-'44) arrived in June and was the "baby" on campus when we arrived in August. She was age 3 and a beautiful child who looked like Elizabeth Taylor and we all loved her. Josephine, Hilda Harrell ('38-'53), and myself were the three girls who were not yet school age. Hilda and I shared a twin bed in the "Little Girls" Room on the third floor of the girls' dormitory. Two girls from the Orphanage were actually adopted, which was such big news to all of us. One was named Lily Sawyer ('40-'43) and the other girl's last name was Bryant. Jennings Lucas ('38-'43) and Jesse James Merritt ('41-'43) were my boyfriends. W. Burkette Raper ('36-'45) and Sterling Skinner ('37-'43) were living at the Orphanage during some of the years that I was there and I enjoy keeping in touch with them and seeing them at Homecoming.

I have heard that two boys were killed at the Orphanage. The story I was told was they were coming back from the cow barn carrying milk cans and they were struck by lightning. This would have happened before I came to the Orphanage. The matrons were always cautioning us during storms, probably as a result of the boys' deaths.

Each floor in the dormitories had a matron who lived on that floor. There was one girls' dormitory and one boys' dormitory and both had female matrons. The matrons were widows or old maids. Ms. Sybil Robinson, who had red hair, was one of my matrons. Ms. Daughtry was one of my favorite ones. There were matrons who were what would be considered today as abusive. They strongly believed in corporal punishment. Because I was somewhat mischievous, I certainly received my share of punishment.

The girls' dormitory had four floors. The basement was considered the first floor and it was where we had our meals until the dining hall was built later between the girls' and the boys' dormitory. We also did our homework in the basement. On the second floor was a parlor-like room which was used for church and for school when we had a teacher at the Orphanage. The ironing room was also on this floor. The third and fourth floors were the sleeping areas. The third floor was the "Little

Girls" Room with four twin beds with two girls to a bed. We had metal bed frames; and, if anyone was ever lucky to have chewing gum, she would stick it to the bed frame overnight. Often, someone else would decide to try it. My sister slept on the fourth floor with the older girls. We never shared the same room.

The dining hall was built while I was there. A time capsule was placed in the left corner of the building, if you are facing the hall. The bell was rung for every gathering, so it was rung for us to form a line so we could each sign our name on a piece of paper to be put in the time capsule, which was actually a quart jar. The girls and boys sat separately for meals in the dining hall and we were also separated by age. On occasion, on Sunday nights, we would have a bagged supper with a sandwich. Sandwiches were very rare in those days and we would line up on either side of the walkway to get our bagged meal. The chapel was built the year I left the Orphanage. The laundry house (called the pump house by some children) and the dining hall are the only two buildings that remain of the buildings that were used during my time there.

We all had assigned chores to complete. They would change usually in the spring and the fall. My chores were mostly laundry and housekeeping. We would collect sticks from a certain type of tree to make our brooms to sweep the yard as we did not have any grass. Everyone was expected to leave his or her room spotless. There was a working farm with chickens, cows, and hogs and a huge garden and a wonderful apple orchard. I did learn how to steam tomatoes in order to peel the skin. Mr. Evans' mother taught us how to clean out hogs' intestines.

We often had visitors to the Orphanage. People from the various Free Will Baptist Churches who supported the Orphanage would come. A county health nurse would come to give us our shots and a dentist would come and use an office that was set up in the front of the dining hall.

I had other contact with the world outside the Orphanage. I attended first through fourth grade at Middlesex School where I had my only friend who did not live at the Orphanage. Her name was Bonnie Williams. Sometimes, someone from the Orphanage would bring a basket of bagged lunches to the school for us instead of the school's lunch because this was a cheaper option. The "orphan young'uns" had to sit together in the lunchroom. It seemed like we were always referred to that way and we were always grouped together. Fifth and sixth grade for me was taught by a teacher who came to the Orphanage. The remainder of my school years was spent in Richmond where I went to live with my mother and stepfather.

Also, when I was 11 years old, I was chosen with about 10 other children to be in the concert class which was taught by Ms. Alma Broughton. For the summer, we traveled around to every Free Will Baptist Church in North Carolina to sing. This was a way to make money for the Orphanage because each church would take up a special offering for us after we performed. We would stay at the home of some of the church members. Mildred Johnson ('38-'49) and I always stayed together. Some host families would even take us to see a movie. I took my first trip to the beach with the concert class. We went to Cedar Island and I stuck my foot in the Atlantic Ocean for the first time!

The times when we left the Orphanage for a family visit, we would go to our grandparents' house in Deep Run, N.C. because our mother would be working. "Mama" was Annie Francis Harper and "Papa" was Blackledge Harper. My sister, Annie Lee, was allowed to go live with Mama in 1942. Our Papa had already passed away. Annie Lee was such a mother figure to me. I was used to seeing her on a daily basis and thought I couldn't bear it with her gone. So, when I was about 12 years old, I tried to run away. I was going to see my mother in Kinston. The other girls who were with me, as well as myself, were all spotted on the road and taken back to the Orphanage. I had to go to bed without eating.

My mother would visit us about every three months on a Sunday. I usually did not know in advance whether or not she was coming. Even now, Sundays can be a little difficult for me. Occasionally, she would send a letter to let us know she would be visiting. I loved to get mail but very seldom did. I would write her on occasion. I was told she was offered a job at the Orphanage when we first went to live there, but she declined because she thought she would show partiality to us over the other children. On one visit, she had saved up some sugar and she made fudge for us in the Orphanage kitchen. What a treat! Each child was "adopted" by a family to provide us with our clothing and special occasional gifts each year. The family would provide $40 two times a year per child. A matron would take us to Leder Brothers in Wilson to buy our clothes. I remember that a woman named Ada Smith from Tarboro would send a pair of socks for each child every Christmas.

I spent the holidays at the Orphanage except for one Christmas that I remember going home. Thanksgiving was my favorite holiday. We would all gather on the front porch of our dormitory and sing "We Gather Together". Birthdays were not acknowledged by the Orphanage staff. It was a time of economic devastation for so many and the Orphanage certainly was affected, too. There was always a huge Christmas tree. On Christmas night, we would gather and the gift with our name that was sent by our sponsor family would be passed out to us. We were also given a big bag of fruit and nuts. My mother would send us something as well. As for gifts, I had two dolls, one of which was a Shirley Temple doll. All of us girls loved Shirley Temple! I also had a green doll carriage. Somehow, I left the dolls and carriage at the Orphanage. My husband actually gave me a Shirley Temple doll one year as a surprise. For another occasion, I had received a burgundy corduroy jumper and a pink blouse from Mama. I had already put it on when I was told I had to stay home from school to help with the laundry, so I had to change. Another girl was allowed to wear my new outfit to school that day. I was so disappointed.

Easter was always celebrated at the Orphanage. We usually shopped for our spring clothes by Easter and I remember having a new dress to wear every Easter. I remember one particular Easter there was an Easter egg hunt in a field across from the superintendent's house. Candy eggs were hidden and once everyone finished the hunt, all the eggs were combined and divided evenly among the children. I'm unsure if there was a hunt every year I was there.

Because the girls and boys were separated, I didn't have a lot of interaction with my brothers. We would see each other in the dining hall and other gatherings. As I have said, I really cherished my sister and all she meant to me there. I also am so thankful for my relationships with my brothers as we became adults. Family is most important to me. My oldest brother, Ralph left the Orphanage after graduating in the summer of 1941 and moved to Wilson. He passed away April 26, 1993. As previously stated, Annie Lee left in 1942 and lived with our grandmother in Deep Run. She married and lived in Deep Run until her husband passed away, at which time she moved to Las Vegas to be closer to her children. Linwood left in the spring of 1943, as did I. We used to always say someone was lucky when he or she left the Orphanage but still, I cried the day I left. Our mother had remarried and we went to live with her in

Richmond, Virginia. Linwood joined the military and retired 28 years later to Fayetteville. He passed away on January 12, 2005. I moved to Wilson in 1955 where I met and married my husband, Jim. Our son, Reid, and his wife, Bobbi, have a son, Christopher, and a daughter, Elizabeth. Our daughter, Ginger, and her husband, Jay, have two sons—Trey and Vance.

    Of course, my experiences at the Orphanage have impacted my adult life. Ralph always said we ought to be glad that we were sent to live there. I don't remember my father at all, but Ralph did and he felt we were much better off living at the Orphanage than we would have been had we been with our father. The people at the Orphanage felt like a family to me. I do attend church, although not a Free Will Baptist church. When I went to live with my mother, because there was not a Free Will Baptist church nearby, she did not encourage us to attend a church. It was my dream to be a mother and to do all the things for my children that I might have missed out on. I chose to be a stay-at-home-mom which was very important to me.

    For awhile, I did not go back to the Orphanage. I returned for my first homecoming the year before I was married. I enjoy homecoming when we are able to attend and I always enjoy catching up and reminiscing with old friends from the Orphanage.

    After all, we are family.

6

The Hills of Home

Dr. W. Burkette Raper
1936 – 44

A Purview

My eight years at the Free Will Baptist Orphanage—now Children's Home—are epitomized by two days: the day I entered and the day I left. These two days characterize changes and new beginnings that formed the crucible which largely determined the kind of person I would become and the directions my life would take during the years that followed.

Recalling my years at the Orphanage has opened a floodgate of memories that lay buried deep in my innermost being—memories that are private, sensitive and at times painful, but lasting and meaningful.

There were two cultures at the Orphanage: one fostered by the management, and the other the self-made code by which the children lived. Bridging these two cultures was not easy; but in retrospect, I am indebted to both. It has been seventy-three years since I entered the Orphanage and sixty-five years since I left, and this span of time gives justifiable reason for those who might wish to question the accuracy of the story I tell.

Where I might be wrong about historical facts, I welcome correction. In terms of experience, however, each child reared at the Orphanage has his or her own story, and this story is the lasting impact—both positive and negative—that their stay at the Orphanage has had upon their life. This is <u>my</u> story and time has not erased the indelible imprint those years etched on my memory.

When I was at the Orphanage, it was an "orphanage," an institution where the children were frequently referred to as "inmates." The term was not meant to be derisive—"inmates" in that era was simply the accepted identification for those who were institutionalized. It would be another generation before the name would be changed to "Children's Home," to reflect the change in focus on the kind of care being given to those who lived there.

It is my belief that it was always the desire and intent of those who provided support for the Orphanage that it would be a Christian ministry of tender love and compassion for children. Indeed, it is significant to note that the Orphanage was the first ministry established by what was then the "State Convention of Free Will Baptists." And it has been my observation, through more than sixty years as an ordained minister, that one of the distinctive features of those rooted in the faith and heritage of Original Free Will Baptists has been and still is their loyal and generous support of the Home.

The institutional concept of child care, which prevailed during my days, was not restricted to the Orphanage at Middlesex. Some years ago, a distinguished alumnus of the Southern Baptist Orphanage at Thomasville, NC, wrote an account of his growing up in that orphanage, and entitled the book, <u>Tough Mercy</u>. It was an apt description of the kind of life I knew at the Free Will Baptist Orphanage. Now, to day one.

Day One – A Changing World

It was a hot July afternoon when I, my brother James Earl, and my sister Mary Lou arrived at the Orphanage. I was age eight, James Earl had turned five the day before, and Mary Lou had just reached age three. As the car carrying my mother and my uncle, who had brought us, disappeared down the hill and out of sight, I suddenly had the most lonely feeling I ever remember.

L-R: James Earl and Burkette Raper

It was not that I was alone—the large front porch of the old three-story building, which was the central focus of the campus at that time, was filled with dozens of children. Actually, there were one hundred children at the Orphanage at that time, but they were all strangers to me, my brother and sister. Mary Lou began to cry, and then we experienced our first act of kindness. Miss Velva Daughtry, a matron who was later to greatly influence my life, reached down her strong arms, lifted Mary Lou and said to James Earl and me, "Come with me." I see her yet as she carried us to the basement of the building where the dining hall was located and gave each of us a "Graham Cracker."

Back on the front porch, one of the "big boys," as I would later learn the boys of his age were called, named Ivy Linton, sat me on his knee and in a friendly voice said, "You are my buddy. If any of these boys bother you, you come to see me." Although I never had to go to him for rescue, I have never forgotten those bright blue eyes under that large straw hat.

Then a group of boys, slightly older than I—whom I would later come to know as the "middle size boys"—came over to where I was and said, "Come, let us show you around." They took me to the dairy barn where I saw the most cows I had ever seen. "You are in with these," the boys said. The tour continued to the barn where the mules were housed, to the chicken houses and to the hog fence. At each stop, I was told "You are in with these." Finally, I asked the meaning of being "in with," and the boys explained: "That means that these—the cows, mules, chickens, hogs and farm land—are as much yours as anybody's. They are ours—they belong to us." This feeling of ownership helped give me a sense of belonging and acceptance.

It wasn't long, however, before the words "in with" took on a fuller meaning. It was the policy of the Orphanage that every child have a work assignment. These assignments, however, would come later. In the meanwhile, life was like being shipwrecked upon a faraway island. A whole new way of life—far different from the intimacy of warm family relationships—had descended upon me.

The first test was emotional survival, but I was to soon learn that dealing with my emotional needs would be my own responsibility. In the environment of the Orphanage at that time, expressing emotion was considered a sign of weakness. Children who were overcome with a feeling of homesickness were taunted as "cry babies" by the other children who had already become hardened by the realities of institutional life. There were no shoulders on which to cry, not even the matrons.

Furthermore, the relationship between siblings was not fostered by the organizational structure of the Orphanage. The prevailing concept of management was fixed rules, discipline and established order. The boys were classified as "big boys," "middle size boys," and "little boys," with appropriate restrictions and privileges for each age division. In the minds of the boys, these classifications translated in something like a caste systems and younger boys did not intrude into the ranks of an older group. These ranks governed how the children lined up for going to meals, assembly and other events. We marched everywhere, and the line always formed according to size.

Seating in the dining hall was according to the arrangement of tables in descending order, according to the size of the children. The boys entered and left by one door and the girls by a different door. In the center of the dining hall, separating the boys from the girls, was what we children called the "Grown Folks Table" for the matrons and other staff members. The impact of this division of children according to size and gender resulted in the children identifying more with their age groups than with any siblings they might have at the Orphanage. During my eight years at the Orphanage, I do not recall ever sitting at the same table for a meal with my brother and sister, nor do I recall any occasion when I sat with them during a religious service or other gathering.

The occasions which most frequently brought us together as family members was when our mother came to see us—and she came as often as she could arrange transportation—or when we received a package of home-cooked goodies, which usually included layered chocolate cake and sea foam candy. Even when we went "home" for summer and Christmas vacations, for most of the time we were divided among various relatives. In retrospect, following the death of our father, I do not recall our mother and all four children celebrating a Christmas Eve or Christmas Day when we were all together. The truth is that for some years following the death of our father, our mother did not have a home of her own. It was out of this trauma of her situation that our mother explained to me why she placed us in the Orphanage.

Why the Orphanage?

It was the proposal of our maternal grandmother that we children be placed with various members of her family. According to her plan, my youngest sister Catherine, then fourteen months of age, would live with her; my sister Mary Lou would live with my mother's twin sister and her family; James Earl would live with one uncle and I would live with another uncle.

Our mother, however, was uncomfortable with this arrangement, but her options were limited. As she later explained to me: If I kept you with me—wherever that might be—I had no means to support you; if I found employment, I had no one to care for you while I was at work. During the Great Depression of the 1930's, child care as we know it today did not exist; nor were there state or federal programs for dependent children; and Social Security was just on the horizon. Our mother reflected on her own experience of having her education ended in the tenth grade in order to work on the farm; and she did not want that to happen to us.

Against the tide of family thinking, our mother turned to the Free Will Baptist Orphanage at Middlesex, but with a hundred children already under its care, the Orphanage was filled to capacity. Next, she considered the Methodist Orphanage in Raleigh, and I remember going with her on this visit. In the meanwhile, our father's older brother, Barney R. Raper, a member of Little Rock Free Will Baptist Church where our parents were also members, along with the pastor, Simon H. Styron, interceded on her behalf with the Board of Trustees of the Free Will Baptist Orphanage at

Middlesex. The minutes of the trustees record three different occasions when our admission was under consideration. According to our mother, a provision for our admission was negotiated: If she would buy the beds, the three oldest children would be admitted. From the sale of our father's farm equipment, she obtained the funds for this purpose.

As summer came on, our mother gathered the three oldest children to the home of her twin sister, Eulah, near Fremont, where she was also staying. I remember the days we were there—it was as if we three children and our aunt's two children were members of one family. My mother explained to me, however, that soon we would be leaving to go to the Orphanage. Then, one day after lunch, we were given wash basin baths on the back porch. Our Uncle Barney arrived and with him and our mother, we left for the Orphanage. Our journey to an unknown future had begun. The day was July 17, 1936.

Our sister Catherine was under age for the Orphanage and would live with our grandmother until she finished high school. By then, Rose and I were married and our home became her home until she graduated from East Carolina College (now University).

Of all the children at the Orphanage, our mother probably came to see us most often, and she would bring whatever special things—toys and clothes—she could. I think she never left without explaining to me why she placed us in the Orphanage: "It was not that I did not love you, but I had no means of caring for you. I brought you here because I wanted you to have the opportunity of an education and to be brought up right. I will never have anything to leave you. Whatever you have in life, you will have to earn it."

Although I have never forgotten her words or the compassion I felt in her voice, it would be years before I would come to understand the depth of insight and the wealth of wisdom in the legacy she wanted for us.

Education

When school began in September, I entered the fourth grade, and for the next four years—grades four through seven—I would have the same teacher, Alma Broughton, in the same room. In those days, grades 1-3 and grades 8-11 went to public school at Middlesex, two miles away. Grades 4-7 were schooled on campus. During these grades, we only went to school one-half day. In the morning, grades 4 and 7 attended classes: One grade sat in the front of the room and the other grade in the back, with the teacher alternating between the classes as she taught different subjects. In the afternoon, the same process would be used for grades 4 and 5.

The rationale for this system was to have some children always available for campus chores, like farm work and the washing and ironing of clothes. The laundry process was three wash tubs, each with a scrub board and with each garment passing through all three tubs. I remember when the Orphanage purchased its first washing machine—a Maytag—with the wringer at the top.

While the one-half day system for grades 4-7 had the advantage of providing campus work time by the children, it had serious educational disadvantages. The teacher could not adequately cover all subjects that students on a full-day schedule received. When I entered high school, I discovered that I did not have the background, especially in science and math, that other students had. It was a handicap that would follow me not only through high school but also into college.

Academically, my first two years in high school were marginal: I did what was necessary for passing grades, but with no strong motivation to excel. Upon entering my junior year, however, I had to make a major decision: Whether to take courses preparatory for college, including foreign language (French) and courses in mathematics beyond algebra, or the less demanding curriculum that would terminate my formal education with high school. My vision for the future had not yet come into focus, so at age 14 I took the easy route.

Two things happened, however, during my junior year in high school to change the course of my life. One was that through the helpful guidance of the superintendent, the Reverend James A. Evans, I came to terms with the unrest in my life regarding my relationship with God and made a commitment of my life to Jesus Christ.

Second, I told Mr. Fred U. Wolfe, my teacher in Vocational Agriculture, that I wanted to meet the requirements for an "A" in his courses, and he opened doors for learning and personal growth that I had never envisioned. He became a great encourager and under his tutelage I developed a sense of initiative and self-confidence that has remained a mainstay in my life.

One of the major features of the Future Farmers of America (FFA) is public speaking. During my senior year, I entered the speaking contest and felt well about my achievements when I won out in the Middlesex Chapter and also in the Nash County contest, and went to the State contest in Raleigh. There I was eliminated, and on the way back to Middlesex, I said to Mr. Wolfe: "I have made my last speech." We were chugging along in his old Ford at thirty-five miles an hour, the speed limit during World War II, and ahead of us was what appeared to be a steep hill. Without taking his eyes off the road, Mr. Wolfe said: "Watch that hill and see what happens as we approach it." As we moved toward the hill it seemed to flatten. "You see, Burkette, life is like that hill: The problems you see when you look ahead may seem big, but when you approach them with the determination to keep going, they are not as big as they look."

Suppose Mr. Wolfe had said to me, "Burkette, I think you are right—public speaking is not for you." Well, that might have indeed been my last speech! Instead, my educational journey would continue beyond my kin. But while there was the dream of going to college, there was little hope. The Orphanage did not have funds for students beyond high school, nor did my family.

During my senior year, a call to Christian ministry had crystallized in my innermost being, but no provisions for college were yet on the horizon. Graduation was barely two months away. One morning as I stood in line to board the school bus, Mr. Evans, Superintendent of the Orphanage, approached me with the question: "Would you be interested in going to Duke University?" Handing me a small slip of paper, he said: "Write this man and ask if you could come to see him."

The man was Dr. Charles Jordan, secretary to the University. With the help of Mrs. Dorothy Morgan, secretary at the Orphanage, I prepared a letter, giving some information about myself and my desire to attend college. Dr. Jordan graciously granted an appointment and Mr. Evans carried me. It was a memorable visit. I told Dr. Jordan I wished to enroll in a course of study preparatory for the ministry and gave him a copy of my high school transcript. The interview turned on two questions:

First, my academic eligibility. My grades during my junior and senior years were excellent, but I had not taken foreign language or geometry. Dr. Jordan said my deficiency in foreign language could be made up by my taking three years rather than two years of foreign language to meet the requirement for a Bachelor of Arts degree; but, I would have to have a course in geometry before I could be admitted. This issue could be resolved, however, if my high school math teacher would tutor me in a geometry course and certify it on my transcript. The Middlesex principal,

Mr. H. C. Bowers, was also the mathematics teacher, and he agreed to home tutor me in the geometry course during May and June.

<u>Second</u>, how would I finance the cost of attendance? Dr. Jordan said the University would provide a scholarship to cover tuition. He also agreed to contact the University food service for a work position that would cover the cost of meals. Then he asked from what source I would have funds for my room rent, laundry, books and miscellaneous expenses. Mr. Evans had prepared me for this question by telling me about the Anna Phillips Education Loan Fund sponsored by the Free Will Baptist Woman's Auxiliary Convention.

Religious Life at the Orphanage

A second vision of our mother in placing us in the Orphanage was that she wanted us "To be brought up right."

The Christian faith was the reason and the foundation for the Orphanage. Attendance of religious activities was never an option—attendance at every event by every child was a given. Included in these activities were dorm devotions before bedtime; mid-week services; campus vesper services during the summer; Sunday School and League each Sunday; Vacation Bible School in the summers; and preaching services when visiting ministers were available.

I have distinct memories of all these events. It was in the dorm devotional services lead by our matron, that we were encouraged to read the Bible daily and introduced to praying "in public" through the use of sentence prayers.

It was through the Sunday evening League service that I gained knowledge and acquired skills that I use to this day. In earlier years, Original Free Will Baptists had adopted the Sunday School as the "teaching ministry" of the Church; but it was only during my era at the Orphanage that the League was introduced as the "training ministry." I remember the late Reverend C. F. Bowen and his wife, Rose, coming to the Orphanage to organize the league on the campus. Both the Sunday School and the League had "quarterlies"—a printed publication which contained "lessons" for the Sunday School and "programs" for the League.

The Sunday School lessons were based on the study of the content of the Bible, while the league programs dealt with the practical dimensions of the Christian life. A major difference in presentation was that the Sunday School <u>teacher</u> would cover the entire lesson whereas in the League the program was divided into "parts," with each part assigned to a different person. It was through presenting the League program parts that I had my first experience of speaking to a group. This experience proved to be most helpful later when I participated in Future Farmers of America speaking contests.

Another feature of the League was learning how to locate verses of Scripture, which required knowing the order of the books of the Bible. I still remember the thrill I felt when I could stand up and quote this order from Genesis to Revelation. With this knowledge, I could compete in "Sword Drills," which tested how quickly we could locate a passage after the leader called out the book, chapter and verse.

Another dimension of the Sword Drill was who could first cite the location (book, chapter and verse) when a familiar verse was quoted by the leader. Obviously, this competition required memorizing key verses which were given to us in advance of the Sword Drill. Winners were chosen to go to the annual State League Convention, and my experience of going to the Convention in 1943 held at Sound Side Church in Tyrell County remains fresh and meaningful in my memory. Today, I cringe at the change that has taken place in our knowledge of the Bible when a minister announces a Biblical reference by book, chapter and verse and then feels the need to tell the congregation that the passage is found on page so and so of their pew Bible!

While Sunday School and League were fixed events every Sunday, it was not until my high school years that the Orphanage had a "pastor" and regular worship services on Sunday. The absence of a pastor, however, did not mean that we did not have "preaching." Whenever a visiting minister was available on Sunday afternoons or at night, the large dinner bell rang, and we knew to gather. This practice had its advantages in that it afforded us an opportunity to hear prominent ministers whom we otherwise might not have heard.

There was the Reverend J. H. Worley (1852-1946) of Selma, who at the age of 88, spent time on campus during 1940 supervising the construction of the dining hall, now known as Heritage Hall.

All the children who were at the Orphanage at that time will remember the morning, before boarding the school bus, when we were gathered in front of the dining hall while it was still under construction. Each of us was given a small slip of paper on which we were asked to write our name and place it in a glass jar that would be encased in the front corner of the building as a time capsule. In event this capsule should ever be located it would be a grand occasion for the gathering of all living alumni of 1940 to be present!

There were many others who impacted my spiritual development, including The Reverend Chester H. Pelt of Marianna, Florida. At the time of his visit in 1942, I was a junior in high school.

In addition to a Vacation Bible School with the assistance of his wife Mildred, Mr. Pelt conducted a community revival under a tent, which had been erected on the campus. At that time, I had not made a profession of Christian faith, but the question was resting heavily upon my conscience. At the age of fourteen, however, I was going through the typical adolescent stage of resisting—perhaps even rebelling against—any external authority or pressure upon my life. Although I did not respond during the revival to the invitation to commit my life to Jesus Christ, the sermons Mr. Pelt preached, along with the guidance of Mr. Evans, led me to make that decision on December 31, 1942.

My baptism by the Reverend Loy E. Ballard, took place on April 25, 1943 at Taylor's Mill, near Middlesex, and by the beginning of my senior year in high school that fall, my call to the Christian ministry had crystallized. Graduation from Middlesex High School was in early May, 1944.

Day Two: Leaving the Orphanage

The day was Saturday, July 1, 1944. World War II was reaching its climax. Three weeks before had been "D" day—the allies had opened a second front against the Germans by landing on the bloody beaches of Normandy in France. In the Pacific, U. S. Marines were paying a heavy price in casualties as they fought on a chain of islands, moving ever closer to Japan for the anticipated invasion of the mainland. Of the eight boys from the Orphanage who had entered Middlesex High School in the fall of 1940, I was the only one who had remained to graduate. The others had left for jobs in the war effort or were already enlisted in the armed forces.

I was sixteen years old. With everything I owned packed in one suitcase; with $50 in money I had earned from farm work or received from high school graduation presents; and a loan of $300 from the Anna Phillips Educational Loan Fund, I ate my last breakfast as a resident of the Orphanage and said good-bye to the children who had gathered in front of the three-story girl's dormitory—the site that had welcomed me eight years earlier when I arrived.

Mr. Evans walked with me the short distance to the Nash automobile, on which he would carry me to Duke University. The schedule called for me to be in an assembly of new students at 11:00 a.m. We stopped at Belks in Durham where I spent one-fourth of my $50 to purchase the bed sheets, towels and other items I would need for my dorm room.

During the hour I was in the assembly hearing the dean of freshmen welcome us and provide the information we would need for enrollment the next week, Mr. Evans waited. Then he went with me to the rooming office where I was issued a key to my room. Back to the car to get my suitcase, Mr. Evans accompanied me to my room. Very kindly, he wished me well and invited me to let him know if he could be of further help. Then he left. Seeing that one of the beds had been made up, it was evident that my roommate had already arrived, but he was not there and I was yet to meet him. I knew no one on campus, except Dr. Jordan, and only one person in Durham—a member of Edgemont Free Will Baptist Church who had done some plumbing work at the Orphanage.

Day two had ended—I had left the Orphanage.

Once again, I faced an unknown future, just as when I arrived at the Orphanage eight years earlier. Only this time, I was in a much larger world, and I alone was responsible for my finances and welfare. I had never written a check, I had never seen the ocean nor the mountains. I had never been out of North Carolina—in fact, I had never traveled farther west than Durham.

From a small rural high school with a graduating class of twenty-seven, I was now on a campus of several thousand students, most of whom were enrolled in the Naval Reserve Officers Training Corp (NROTC), preparing to become Commissioned Officers in the U. S. Navy. With World War II at a crucial point, the academic pace was accelerated and rigorous.

But for me, the course was set. The day I left the Orphanage, another boy was waiting to move into what had been my room. I did not have the choice of retreating—there was no place else to go. Not until I graduated in 1947 at the age of nineteen, would I remove my clothes and books from my dormitory. Duke University was now my home.

Life-Long Benefits from Living at the Orphanage

In what ways had my life at the Orphanage equipped me for the adventure that now lay ahead? The following thoughts are being written sixty-five years later, and I am sure they represent not so much my thinking when I left the Orphanage as my subsequent reflections over those years. In retrospect, I view those eight years as a providential journey—a journey that was not always pleasant but one that had a purpose.

- In the first place, the Orphanage provided the nurturing that guided me in making the fundamental decisions upon which my future would rest—specifically, my Christian conversion and call to Christian ministry.
- It was through the Orphanage that the door to higher education was opened, especially the opportunity to attend a major university which prepared me to continue my preparation for the ministry by enrolling in divinity school. Without the encouragement of the Reverend James A. Evans, Superintendent at the Orphanage, I might not have continued my education beyond high school and if so, it most assuredly would not have been at Duke University and Duke Divinity School. Notwithstanding that he had been admonished in writing by a well-known minister that if I attended Duke I would become so theologically "tarnished" that I could be of no meaningful service to Free Will Baptists, Mr. Evans held before me the vision of an education that would most effectively quip me for the ministry. Apart from his wise counsel, my future would have been drastically different—a future that certainly would not have included fifty years of work at Mount Olive College.
- At the Orphanage I learned a work ethic that has served me well. Each child was responsible for the order and cleanliness of his own room, including making his bed—a practice that my wife has not let me forget! In addition, we had specific work assignments. Some of this work required attention before breakfast, while other assignments were waiting for us when we stepped off the school bus. There were no refreshments between school and dinner. At one cycle of work assignments, my job was to rise at 5:00 a.m. and start the wood fire in the kitchen stove; at 5:30 ring the large bell as a wake-up call for the campus; set out the ten-gallon milk cans,

mix the feed for the cows, help milk the cows, assure that the dairy barn was cleaned after the milking; be in line at 7:00 a.m. for breakfast; and be ready to board the school bus at 8:00 a.m. Somewhere in between, I tried to find time to visit my rabbit boxes in the near-by woods. With this schedule, reporting for work at 6:30 a.m. in the Duke Cafeteria, where I worked for my meals, was like being on easy street.

- From my eight years at the Orphanage, I learned to be thankful. Life at the Orphanage was not easy: the discipline was stern; food was a precious commodity, often in short supply; clothing was very limited, and we were glad when good used clothes were sent in by the churches; the boys were expected to go barefooted during the summer—I remember being chastised for requesting a pair of work shoes during the summer before my senior year in high school; the Orphanage provided almost no supplies or equipment for recreation—for the most part, children had to improvise their own; there were no allowances—any "spending money" had to come from our families, and of course, that was very limited.

    I mention this Spartan lifestyle not to be critical—after all, my stay at the Orphanage was during the Great Depression of the 1930's and the war years of the 1940's. Frugal living was not restricted to the Orphanage—it was also the condition under which many people during this era lived, including those who gave of their limited means to support the Orphanage.

    Thanksgiving was the big day of the year. I still remember the trucks and trailers which came on that day—loaded with all kinds of produce from the farms—and the most sumptuous meal we would have all year—spread on a long wire table. That was the day when we children knew we would have all the food we could eat, and some left over, which we dared take to our rooms!

    In retrospect, it was through the austerity of life at the Orphanage that I learned to be thankful—thankful for plenteous food and the absence of hunger; thankful for good clothes; thankful for the comforts of a good home; and thankful for the opportunity to attain a good life. My experience at the Orphanage taught me that what some people consider entitlements are in reality gifts, and that much of what many people considered essentials are in fact luxuries. When my work as a student minister first carried me out to churches and into private homes, one of my major impressions was what I considered waste—things that people would cast aside that we at the Orphanage would have relished.

Beyond "things," however, I learned to be thankful for the kindred relationship I developed with the other children. To this day, many of those with whom I shared life at the Orphanage are like extended members of my family, and attending the annual Alumni Homecoming in July is in many ways like a family reunion.

- From the matrix of life at the Orphanage, I learned that I alone was responsible for the decisions I made. But I also learned that there were many good people—both known and unknown to me—who were responsible for the benefits and opportunities life has afforded me. These people gave of their time and resources without thought of benefit for themselves. In the spirit of our Lord, they gave to make life better for others. To them, I owe a life of gratitude.

Had it not been for the Orphanage, only God knows what would have been my future. Before Rose and I were married, I wrote to her that "Those red clay rocky hills will always be
THE HILLS OF HOME."

Footnote: Dr. W. Burkette Raper served as pastor of the church at the Children's Home October 1947-50.

7

Recollections I Remember

Fay Andreu Evans
1940-49

I must admit the idea for putting this on paper did not occur to me until June 10, 1977 while attending the high school graduation of our granddaughter, Olivia Fay Bass. We sat on the same row as Evelyn Pate Hill ('33-'43). She shared the following incident with me and a "great" idea was born.

Evelyn related a conversation she had with a friend just prior to the graduation mentioned above. Evelyn grew up on the campus of the Free Will Baptist Children's Home near Middlesex, North Carolina. She was one of four Pate children, Ralph ('33-'41), Annie Lee ('33-'42), Linwood ('33-'43) and Evelyn in age order. I, among other chores, was shopping for clothing for all the children. Evelyn said I met her on the campus one day and said, "Young lady, we're going special shopping for something you need". Evidently, that was not the first time I had noticed Evelyn's growth and development!

After this contact with Evelyn, I suddenly realized there was more of this in my mind and it was just churning around for several days. It seemed the only way for me to get relief was to put it down on paper.

To begin at the beginning, my husband, James A. Evans, and I, and our children, Anne 10, Lorraine 5, J. Arthur, 1 1/2 and Kay, 5 weeks old went to live at the Free Will Baptist Children's Home in May of 1940. Mr. Evans was Superintendent and I was to end up doing some of all the work in and around the buildings from "wash woman" (laundry matron) to Assistant Superintendent.

I was very reluctant to make the move and left our place in Kenly, North Carolina, weeping, and I soon realized I couldn't drive with tears running down my face. I managed to get control of my feelings, and we were on our way to those red clay hills and almost ten years of a tremendous experience. Every descriptive adjective in the English language could be applied to life at the Children's Home.

I told the wife of a friend that I was determined not to "absorb the Home nor allow it to absorb me". A few months later, this friend asked me what I had done about this issue. I had to confess that "I had done both".

When the children and I arrived at the Home, it was lunch time. Miss Velva Daughtry kindly took us in hand, after greeting Mr. Evans, found places for us to sit in the dining hall which was in the basement of the old girls' building. Miss Daughtry asked if I would like for the children to have milk for lunch. I answered yes, please. Later, I learned to my embarrassment that the Superintendent's children were the only children to have milk. At that time, there simply wasn't enough milk for all. From that time on, the Evans' children had strict instructions from their parents that they were under the same regulations as the other children when they were with them.

We also passed the same word to the various staff members. Can you imagine us sitting down among a sea of strange faces – not sure what was expected of us and how our children would respond? Needless to say, our children seemed much more at ease than their mother.

Evans Family – Back Row L-R: Ann, James, Faye, Lorraine
Front Row L-R: Kay, J. Arthur

Not long after going to the home, construction was begun on the present dining hall and kitchen, with two offices on the front. This was during the Second World War and a few of the men came from a distance and lived at the Home. There was no room for them to eat in the dining hall morning and evening so they took those meals at the Superintendent's home.

Since we had an infant, a toddler and two in school, I needed some help. After conferring with Miss Daughtry, it was decided that one of the older girls, Odell Jones ('33-'42), would live at our house and help me. We soon learned to love Odell and she was like one of the family. In the afternoons when there was ironing to be done and I could manage in the kitchen alone, Odell would set up the ironing board, turn the radio on and iron away until I needed her in the kitchen. Anne and Lorraine were too young at that time to help much.

Odell's sister, Estelle ('33-'42), would come over in the afternoons sometime to visit. Odell would ask Estelle to play the piano. So, with the radio going, the piano being played, plus whatever the other children were doing, we had an interesting time.

Estelle loved to push our baby Kay in the carriage. One afternoon, she had Kay in the carriage in the front yard and someway the carriage turned over, spilling a surprised baby who immediately protested loudly enough, so I went to see what was going on. Estelle was surprised also and somewhat frightened until we found no one was hurt and everyone went back to their tasks.

Rev. J. H. Worley was foreman for the construction and was one of the men who ate at our house. During this time, the older boys were catching rabbits in their boxes. Mr. Evans bought enough from them to serve to the men at our house for one evening meal. As you can well imagine, we had fried rabbit, baked rabbit and stewed rabbit. J. Arthur was eating at the same time as Mr. Worley and others. By the way, Mr. Worley called J. Arthur "Log Roller". After grace was said at this particular meal, J. Arthur raised his head and looked over the table and said, "Rabbit skip, rabbit hop". Mr. Worley laughed until the tears came. I did have some other meat on the table.

It was during this time that my husband and I began to enjoy coffee. One of the men, Robert P. Peele, liked coffee even better. Some foods were rationed during this period and coffee was one of them. Stamps were required to purchase coffee. Mr. Peele would share some coffee stamps with us and the coffee tasted better all the time.

While we were waiting on the chairs and tables for the dining hall, we used it to do some canning of corn. It fell my lot to take a group of the older boys and get the corn in the jars and down to the laundry to be processed in the wash pots. Another group, under the direction of a staff member, was shucking and cleaning the corn, another cutting. So, we set up an assembly line in the kitchen and went to work. All went well until one boy started grumbling and complaining. Much to my surprise Hicks Tripp ('35 - '43) took the grumbler by the collar and belt and marched him off to one side and told him not to rejoin the line until he stopped grumbling. It didn't take long before the grumbler took his place and the boys did a splendid job. There didn't seem to be any ill feeling over the incident, no anger. It was the easiest canning I have ever done! The other boys made no comment on the incident and neither did I.

And the laundry, oh the laundry! At that time, all of it was being done with wringer-type washing machines and wash pots bricked up in a furnace. This was housed in a building down the hill a ways from the girls' building. Miss Gladys Batten, the laundry matron, had her hands full with that operation. As I recall, there were some boys to help with the heavy lifting and firing the furnace. All the clothes were hung on outside lines to dry. Come rain, sleet, or snow, the laundry had to go on. I even helped take in the clothes when it was snowing. Thank the Lord for the means later to move this into the basement of the girls' building with a steam boiler, a commercial size washing machine (tumbler), an extractor to remove the water and a dryer. This was almost too good to be true, plus we had a steam press and ironer and a collar form for shirts. The weather didn't stop us then, nor did it effect the drying. The ironing was about the same.

We had some very interesting experiences in shopping for the children. Remember, this was during World War II and we learned to look for needed items wherever we were. In buying bobby pins, shoe laces, etc., we would get quite varied facial expressions and wild-eyed stares when we asked for them in large numbers. I recall being in Raleigh and stopping at a large grocery store for a few items and it seemed the store had some bananas, which we were not always able to find. Everyone on campus enjoyed banana pudding. I wanted enough for everyone. After talking to the produce man and explaining the situation, I was able to buy an entire stalk of bananas. I could hardly wait to get them to the kitchen crew.

Shoes were rationed also, as well as many food items, sugar, canned fruits and vegetables, gasoline, tires and many more items. It was necessary to arrange for the children to bring their stamps when being admitted to the Home.

I made frequent trips to town for shopping for the children, taking them to the doctors at Carolina General Hospital in Wilson, as well as some shopping In Raleigh. We were on good terms with the stores in Wilson and, when I would enter the store to find a long line of waiting customers, I would immediately fall in line. I would ask what the line was for and, if it was for something the children, staff or home could use, I'd remain in line. If not, I went on about my duties. I recall an incident with Mr. Hughes, manager of the Leder Brothers store at that time. Mr. Hughes replaced Mr. Leon Leder who went into military service. Mr. Hughes said he had something for me in the safe. He triumphantly led me to the store safe and presented me with a pair of nylon hose! This store was especially helpful in opening the store at night just for the children to shop after hours. The staff was so helpful. I recall how pleased we were when Mr. Leder, while on furlough, came to the Home to see us.

During this period, the National Association of Free Will Baptist, which we were part of at the time, was about to abandon the annual meeting. When we learned of it, we put our heads together and decided to invite delegates, ministers, and those necessary to carry on the business to meet at the Children's Home. The invitation was accepted. It fell my lot to do a house-to-house and almost store-to-store canvas to get food and lodging for the people. This was quite an experience for me. I always felt I could sell behind the counter, but house-to-house selling the idea and asking for the help was slightly different. The people were wonderful. Some could provide lodging and breakfast; some said they would serve breakfast if they could get some breakfast meat. We had hired a Home Economics teacher for the summer and she was asked to begin stocking the pantry. Two or three days before the convention, she informed us she had to go home. She was an only child of older parents and something had developed. She felt she had to leave. Here I went to the kitchen to try to help the kitchen crew plan, prepare and serve six meals each day for two days. The dietician, for some reason, did not have the pantry adequately stocked. With cooperation of everyone concerned, we did it! Miss Lillie Herring, who was in charge in the dining hall, had to explain to some of our guests what grits were and how to season them for eating. We learned also, one man and his wife and two young sons were asked by one of his sons to please go to the small café and get some breakfast. Many of the out-of-state guests did not know what grits were. The "squash" we served that morning were, in reality, perfectly good scrambled eggs. We found a number of families who were not delegates came and met other family members from different states. We moved all the boys to a vacant building to get sleeping places for everyone. I went to our home the first night after finishing up in the kitchen to find my husband had given our bed to some fellow minister. So, to the third floor of the girls' building I went to sleep on a mattress on the floor. I informed my husband if he wanted a cook to get these men out of my bed! He decided he wanted a cook! One couldn't walk on the third floor for bodies.

Everyone was caught up in getting ready for the National Association. It was warm weather and, of course, there were insects to contend with. Jesse Jump and his wife were in charge of the boy's building at this time and the boys had been moved out to a vacant building in Middlesex to make room for the guests. They slept in make-shift bedding for a few days, coming back on campus for chores and meals. We were serving six meals per day and washed dishes by hand. One of these days I felt like the kitchen and dining hall needed to be sprayed – we had accumulated some flies, with all the traffic in and out of the building. The boys usually did the spraying for us. Knowing everyone was tired, I mentioned to Mrs. Jump the need to spray and I was reluctant to ask the boys to do it. Mrs. Jump looked at me and in utmost simplicity and confidence said, "They will spray them". I was touched by her reaction. Needless to say, the boys sprayed the building. It was not unusual at all to visit the boys' building and see the boys sitting on Mrs. Jump's knees, the arm of her chair and some hanging over the back of her chair. It was surprising to me that so many wanted to stay at the Children's Home. The attendance was rather large and we practically had to step over one another. A good example of this was my husband filling the beds at our house with the guests. After one night on the floor in the girls' building, I informed Mr. Evans if he wanted me as a dietician, he would have to get our bed back. It worked.

Let me say again, the people in town and nearby were wonderful, as well as the merchants that were contacted. We could not have fed and slept the association without their help. We were a tired but happy group of people when the association adjourned. On the last day of the meeting, we were asked to have the noon day meal at a different time. Imagine our predicament on that day when our order for rolls and bread did not arrive until just minutes away from the meal. Trula Cronk, who worked at the home that summer, offered to help make and cook biscuits. The only substitute I could come up with at the time was saltines! You guessed it –

the adjournment was later and we could have had biscuits. I still regret having to resort to the crackers.

After this experience, I truly believe the Children's Home became "Our Children's Home" to the community. They were some of the finest people to be sure. I referred to the different "crews" earlier, let me explain. Each girl and boy was assigned a job in keeping with his or her age and ability. Some of the smaller children were too small to have anything to do. Some were only three years old. Those large enough were assigned either to housekeeping, laundry or kitchen. About every three months they were rotated to another area. We used all sizes of those old enough to help. In the kitchen, we had the smallest who were potato peelers and sometimes they would have to "peel the peelings". Those a little larger set the tables and the older group helped cook and wash dishes. Some swept floors. This way they were taught all phases of the work necessary to make a home.

The boys' building had a group of boys who were housekeepers there. Needless to say, they preferred outside jobs but they worked well. In each category there were some of the older children who could really help in getting the work done. Our children had their own work at home. Our Lorraine was about the same age, size and coloring as Hilda Harrell ('38-'53), the youngest of four Harrell children. Lorraine told Miss Mary Burton, girl's matron, that she would be glad when she could "hurry up and be a little orphan and live at the Children's Home!" I believe, on the whole, our children enjoyed the almost ten years there. As they grew up and the Superintendent's duties became greater, they did sometimes miss having more of their father's time and attention. I served as dietitian part of the time and found it quite a task to come up with appetizing, nutritious meals using what was grown on the farm plus what was donated. I was taught by my parents to waste not, want not, so I had considerable leftovers. Finally, when refrigerator space was filled, I would serve a different dinner on each table or mix some. On one occasion, I was mixing some leftovers and Margaret Taylor ('41-'46), one of the older girls in the kitchen, wanted to know what to call the mixture. I, not knowing myself, told her it was an "Evans" special. She instructed the girl who was serving the plates to be sure to serve some on her plate. We had a new name for leftovers!

Margaret was one of the two biscuit makers in the kitchen at that time. Two large dishpans were used for this purpose and I never tired of watching this operation and hearing the "slap" of each biscuit as it landed in the right space in the baking pan. Their speed was amazing and their aim quite accurate. It took about 24 pounds of flour to make biscuits for everyone, two to four gallons of vegetables for 75-85 children and staff. It was quite common for brothers, sisters and boyfriends to find a little something extra on their plates. I wondered then, as well as now, if the kitchen crew knew the dietician was aware of most of this!

Along this same line one summer, Burkette Raper ('36-'45) was helping someone in the neighborhood to harvest tobacco. Burkette's breakfast was served earlier. I went to check his plate to be sure there was ample food. Unknown to me, Irene Watson ('34-'44), one of the older girls, was watching me and I was prepared to have extra food put on the plate. You guessed it! Irene had neatly stacked extra slices of meat on the plate and, hurrying up to me, explained that Burkette needed some extra food because of the long hours and physical labor involved.

Burkette was in charge of the chickens for some time. Speaking of chickens, when we first went to the Home, some of the girls came over to the Superintendent's home one Saturday morning and asked me "how many chickens we wanted"? When I found out what was going on, the dietician was having chickens dressed for Sunday dinner and wanted to know how many the Evans' family wanted. Soon after this episode, the Evans' family dressed their own. The Evans' children had to be trained, as well as the children at the home. Getting the feathers off became less time consuming after Clarence Mitchell (Alumnus '23-'32) put together a motor driven "chicken picker". This was some something to behold. After all, this was in the 1940's and it worked very well.

Thanksgiving was the big day in the fall. Shopping for winter clothing was usually finished by this time and house cleaning began in earnest. We scrubbed, cleaned, polished each building from top to bottom and hoped and prayed it wouldn't rain on the big day because everybody and his brother, it seemed, came to visit and to bring money and food in various forms. It was truly a big day.

I have seen some of the older girls so tired they felt like crying and I wanted to join them. The theory then was to teach and train the students in all phases of everyday living and to be productive citizens when they left the Home. All of us survived and were very grateful for the food and money brought to us. I must tell you about our mountain friends. We sent jars to most of the churches in the state in early spring and they would fill them and return them to us in the fall. In addition to the filled jars from the mountains, the people brought truck loads of apples and cabbage. They would notify us when to expect them and no matter what time of night they came, everyone on campus got up to greet the people who came on the trucks and see the apples and all the other good things. It was almost Christmas in October. These good people canned their green beans after they were much more mature than ours and the children were a little slow in eating the beans. To be sure some food was left on the plates but not much. Everyone was encouraged to eat what we had and not to waste anything. It was very satisfying to prepare chicken, fish, hot dogs, etc. We knew they liked these items and watched them enjoy it. We, at the Children's Home, were people like everyone else who were privileged to live in their own home. We used the same day-to-day necessities as they did.

Harvest from the Mountains

At the time we went to the Home, bolts of material were purchased for dresses for the girls and brought to the home where Catherine West and later, Hope Allen, made the dresses. Later, we began taking the children to town in small groups to help choose their clothing and to be fitted at the stores. Underclothing for all, socks, shirts and pants for the boys were bought in quantity and fitted to the children. On the premier Thursday when I took the children to town, we could shop for their best clothing. We bought most of their clothing from these stores – Leder Brothers,

Belk-Tyler and J. C. Penney. All of the personnel in stores we worked with were very, very nice to us. Sometimes, treats were in stores for the groups. I recall once Mr. H. M. Jeffries, Sr., manager of the Belk-Tyler store, asked if he could buy them some ice cream. Permission was granted and the children enjoyed a cone of ice cream while sitting on the stair steps that led from the balcony to the second floor of the old store. During the war years, Montgomery Ward in Raleigh was most helpful in getting jeans for the boys. Along this same line, Mr. Evans was shopping in Raleigh for some items for the children when he was asked how many children he had. Without blinking an eye and with a straight face, Mr. Evans replied, "75". I will let you guess the salesgirl's response.

We also had various accidents to happen at the home. Some of the more serious ones are vivid in my memory. One Saturday afternoon, Mr. C. H. (Giddy) Pope had some of the boys in the woods for some reason. Anyway, Bobby Watson ('40-'48) wanted to swing from a pine sapling. He chose one which was too old and strong for him to bend down. After climbing the tree, he attempted to swing to earth, bending the tree as he came. The tree didn't bend and Bobby fell, breaking both arms. Mrs. Pope and I carried him to the Carolina General Hospital in Wilson. Dr. Kerr was summoned and single handedly, almost, set both arms. I recall seeing perspiration running down his face. There was no air conditioning at the time and it was mid-summer. He recovered quite nicely in time.

Charles Harrell's ('38-'51) accident was another I recall. He was walking ahead of the mowing machine driven by Julian McGee ('37-'43) and somehow the mowing machine got too close and almost severed Charles's leg. We were stunned – we felt like we would lose Charles. Again, a hurried trip to the hospital and to Dr. Kerr who saved the leg. The nurses told us afterward most any doctor would have amputated, but not our Dr. Kerr. All of the doctors and nurses were especially nice to all of us. These two boys came home slightly spoiled by all the attention they received! These were the more serious illnesses.

Of course, we had our share of measles. Many trays had to be carried to the sick in both buildings. It seemed at times, during single illnesses, the patient could not quite be satisfied unless Mr. Evans or I went to them. I recall very vividly getting up late at night to help Miss Mary Burton, girls matron, soothe the patient. It always tugged at my heart when these calls came. I could very easily visualize our children in the same situation.

It was always interesting to me to see the love and attention given to our smaller children by the older children. The small ones were never far from a staff member and the older children were just as attentive. When it was time for the noon day meal, one might see the little ones riding piggy-back on the back of the older boys and almost always returned to the boys' building that same way, half asleep. We didn't have girls that young at that time.

Speaking of little boys, at one time we had six or eight preschoolers with their matron, Mrs. Worthington, who took care of them during the day. She was quite fond and proud of her charges and the other staff members seemed well satisfied they were being cared for. I well remember walking near them and all of them would swarm around me. There just wasn't enough of me to go around! I feel sure others had similar experiences. The act of getting too emotionally involved with the children was brought home to me very forcibly in connection with Odell Jones living in our home and helping me. When it came time for her to leave the Children's Home, I was broken hearted. I wept as though I would never see her again. After that experience, I realized I couldn't' feel that way about each of the children and I wanted to be fair. I would soon be emotionally crippled and my own health and the welfare of my family would suffer.

One of the most interesting experiences I recall happened once when I was substituting in the boys' building for the regular matron. Clarence Mitchell was not married at the time and was living in the building. I went from the Superintendent's home to the boys' building for a final check before going to bed myself. As I walked across the campus, I realized something was missing from the campus. I did not determine what it was until a little later. All the boys were supposed to be in bed at that hour. I reached the building and, as I was quietly checking on the second floor, I heard quiet footsteps on the stairs. I stepped back out of sight and waited. Here came two of the older boys, Julian McGee ('37-'43) and Hicks Tripp ('35-'43) up the stairs with their shoes in their hands. They were as surprised as I was. Their eyes looked like small saucers and their mouths dropped open. They had "borrowed" the suburban and went for a ride. The car was what I had missed as I crossed the campus. The discipline involved I have completely forgotten – it must not have been too severe. Their faces, when they saw me, were something to behold. Clarence took charge of the situation and I returned to our house to look after our children.

I recall one occasion when Mr. Evans was away. I felt we needed some fresh meat. I asked Clarence if we had a hog that could be dressed. He decided we did and said he would dress it if I said so. Mr. Evans usually made decisions of this sort. Since he was away for a day or so, I made the decision and we had fresh pork. I told Clarence I would assume responsibility. Mr. Evans didn't mind when he got back on campus and all of us enjoyed the fresh meat. And Earl Tippett ('28-'40), I suspect our son J. Arthur had divided loyalties between his daddy and Earl. J. Arthur followed Earl like his shadow. J. Arthur was very young and had been heard to express a preference for Earl. I used to send Earl to town for anything from baby needs to groceries. He would always bring back what I needed. Part of Earl's duties was driving the truck for hauling necessities; Clarence's work was more confined to the campus.

One of my responsibilities was the store or canteen, which was opened once a week for the children to purchase candy, chewing gum, drinks, etc. We could buy one box of nickel candy bars a week. We saved these until we had enough for everyone on campus to have one. Wonder how many of the students remember this? Not as well as they remember the green apples that found their way to many of them, I'll venture to say.

CONCERT CLASSES

When we went to the Children's Home, one of the main sources of income was the Concert Class. A group of boys and girls was chosen and training began in earnest in the spring for the class to make the summer itinerary, giving concerts at the churches and receiving an offering. The class manager usually chose the program and rehearsed the children to be ready to start traveling when school was out. Sometimes, a group would go on weekends for special services. I soon developed mixed feelings about this practice. It did not seem to me to be a normal life for any of the group. Those who went with the class were often the recipients of special attention, treats, some gifts and other advantages. Those who couldn't go, obviously all could not, felt left out sometimes and less privileged. I do not, however, recall any serious consequences suffered by those who couldn't go. I do recall the anticipation when the class would come "home" for a short visit. Everyone was glad to see each other.

One summer a small group was trained on campus expecting Mrs. S. H. Styron of Pine Level to be manager. Something came up at the last minute and Mrs. Styron could not go. The itinerary was up and churches had been notified. My husband looked at me and said "you go". That was one place I had not worked nor expected to. He finally talked me in to going and prevailed on his mother, Mrs. Nettie Evans, known affectionately as "Granny," to stay with our children. It was not very easy for me to leave my family, but I went for about a month. Things went fairly well until I arrived at Rooty Branch Church and we had been assigned to the various homes. I waited until everyone was ready to leave and, when I started to drive away from the church, I saw Charles Kittrell ('41-'46), the oldest boy in our group under the steering wheel in one of the member's car. I froze and evidently Charles, seeing me observe him, must have had the same reaction because he ran into a sturdy tree. What makes this different was Charles was not a trained driver. I didn't know if he had ever sat behind the steering wheel and to make matters worse, the older gentleman who owned the car had a heart condition. We managed to get the situation under control and moved the gentleman, Mr. Summerlin, to his home where he didn't seem to be any worse from the incident. I called my husband who came to us and took charge. No one was injured physically, but all were rather shaken up. The incident was settled amicably to all concerned. Charles was very reluctant to take part in the concert that night, but I insisted the program had to go on. I felt that facing the church people, and singing a solo would have sufficient impact on him, that no other punishment was necessary other than a talking to. I felt Charles thought he could drive a car; he was not a destructive person by nature.

One of the most engaging classes of all was the "babies," as we called them under Miss Shearon. They were precious and my heart went out to her as she drove off with that group of little ones. Before long, she had to have help and an older girl, Irene Watson, was provided. Mr. Evans and I went to see them. After the program was finished, the children left the stage and, led by Haywood Stevenson ('42-'52), headed straight for Mr. Evans. No one seemed to mind, least of all the Evans. The offering was very good. At another time, we visited the class at Edgemont Church in Durham. During the course of the program, one small boy began to scratch on various parts of his body. The itching increased noticeably until the little fellow was going through quite a bit of gymnastics in attempting to relieve the situation. The audience controlled its mirth until the end of the program and then gave full vent to their emotions, physically as well as financially. The youngster had broken out with "mad itch" – a rash on his skin that soon disappeared when his excitement subsided.

Our daughter Anne took her class to the western part of the state. That class had some interesting experiences also. One was learning to adapt to different customs, preparation and serving of different foods and driving those mountain roads. Meeting and getting to know our friends and supporters from this area was a real treat.

Miss Fitzgerald, one of the class managers, found a husband on her tour. That class went into the churches in the eastern part of the state, where Miss Fitzgerald met and later married Garner of Newport. Miss Shearon served in this capacity longer than the others, as well as teaching music daily at the Home when not on tour. Several of the girls did very well at the piano. Marie Caulder ('39-'45) was one of these and played for the class I took out.

Miss Alma Broughton was class manager when we went to the Home and we had several others during the almost 10 years we were there: Miss Margaret Lewis, Miss Louise Edgerton, our daughter Anne, Miss Faustina Shearon and Miss Janie Bell Fitzgerald of Micro.

Afterword by daughter Kay Nell Evans

Our family had good relationships with the children on campus. Earl Tippett and my brother Jay were very good friends. Earl was an older boy but took a lot of time with Jay. Haywood Stephenson and I were named "orphanage sweethearts." There was a picture of us and it was used many times. Haywood's sister Joyce and I were buddies. In July 1943, Haywood's and my picture was published on the front page in the "Free Will Baptist Gem." Under the picture was written: The Orphanage Baby, Haywood Stevenson and the Superintendent's Baby, Kay Nell Evans.

One of my fond memories is sitting on the grass with other girls in front of the girls' building and dining hall looking for 4-leaf clovers. We made clover flower chains to see who could find the most or make the longest chain without breaking. I remember playing in the basement of the girls' building - close to the laundry room - as well as outside under a big "Chaney ball" tree on the dirt. Our play included making mud pies and jumping rope, as well as homemade jump boards, to see who could jump the highest and longest. It was fun spending nights in the girls' building just for fun and playing in the "big" sunroom on the front of the building - third floor, I believe. I was not allowed to go in the boys' building - obviously. There was a sick bay or infirmary for the girls on the back of the third floor of the girls' building. It was off limits for me, so I thought, but I would sneak in there occasionally. We sometimes fished in the pond over on the farm. The children were baptized in the same pond.

Thanksgiving was a "big event" with lots of people on the campus. There was plenty of good food on a long wire" (handmade) table under the trees between the unfinished chapel and the girl's dorm. It was a big celebration and a happy day! On Christmas holidays, the children would leave and spend time away with people and churches that sponsored them. It was lonely for me.

One of the Evans' Family stories from the orphanage has followed me through the years and is still told from time to time when there is a family gathering: My parents were away and my "granny" (daddy's mom) was staying with us. Anne, (oldest sister) was dating age (could actually leave in a car with her boyfriend at that time) but Granny would not let her leave the house and insisted on sitting in the living room "chaperoning" their date. No TV's back then. My bedroom was over that room and had a ventilator directly over the big space heater that provided heat for the house. The ventilator had a hard cover that was removable and a "basket like" thing held it in place by springs connected to the bottom grate. This allowed heat to go upstairs. Brother Jay loved to take the hard cover off so we could "peek" at whatever was going on in the living room – even when we were supposed to be in bed asleep.

That night, he was "observing the date" and I came upstairs after a bath - told him to "get out" so I could get my pj's on and go to bed. There were "ironed" clothes on my bed that needed to be hung up so I held them up high so they would not drag the floor - in front of my face. On my way to the closet, I fell, yes fell, in the "coverless" ventilator and was stopped by my arms with my legs waving wildly over that "hot" space heater. Anne's date shot out the front door (according to Ann) and Granny was yelling "Lord God, go get that youngin out of there before she falls through that thing!" I don't know how I was gotten out. It was said that Anne's comments were - "let her fall", I guess she was so angry and embarrassed. Jay (brother) had opened my door and was watching - laughing his head off. Yes, I was naked, yes really naked and old enough to be embarrassed myself. I was in elementary school at the time. I have never forgotten Anne's date's name either. This story (real) has been a funny memory for most of the family - not me!

My mother mentioned in her memoirs Odell Jones and how she was helpful in chores around the house and with us children. She frequently looked after me when mother was needed in the dining hall or other places. After Odell left the orphanage, she became part of our extended family and was always included in any and all important family happenings until her death.

Footnote: Fay Evans wrote her memoir in July 1977. Her story was stored with her papers given to daughter Kay upon her death. George Stevenson ('42-'52) made me aware that Mrs. Evans had written her memoir when he learned of my writing this book. I contacted Kay and Jay and they graciously agreed for their mother's memoir to be published. Kay's comments were made in 2010. Fay Evans, age 75, died January 28, 1984. Her husband, The Reverend Dr. James A. Evans, age 93, died October 25, 1999. Dr. W. Burkette Raper ('36-'45) delivered the eulogy at both funerals. Their final resting place is the Lucas Family Cemetery, Lucama, North Carolina.

8

Scenes of Childhood

George Stevenson, Jr.
1942-52

George Stevenson, Jr.

    I shall attempt in this to write some account of a decade, 1942-1952, from my childhood when I was living in the Free Will Baptist orphanage, located two miles in the country from Middlesex in Nash County, N.C. Even if I did not have to overcome the unwillingness of my memory to be commanded, I should still have difficulties. Chemotherapy has left me frequently unable to call up words and names at the time I want them. So, one may run into oddities of syntax, annoying slips from active voice to passive voice, omission of words, and so forth. This just has to be borne.

    Generally my memory is built up of eidetic images and not reminiscences, so a flowing narrative of connected events is improbable. My remarks are unlikely to be impersonal, impartial, and considered judgments. And last, the view is different from every level, so what I recall might be contradicted by a contemporary.

I do not know how many months elapsed between my mother's diagnosis of uterine cancer and her death on Feb. 2, 1942. At that time we, my family, were living in the neighborhood of Cash Corner, Pamlico County, N.C. My family consisted of my mother and father (who farmed and raised sheep), a half-brother and half-sister (13 and 10 years older than I respectively), my older sister Elizabeth (aged 7), my twin sister Joyce and me (aged 4 in July 1941), and my younger brother Haywood (aged 2 years in October 1941). Europe was at war, and it appeared to be only a question of time until the U.S. entered it – which it did in December 1941. This was a bleak outlook for a young mother facing certain death, and especially so as she regarded the fate of her four youngest children after her death. Her first concern was that her young children be kept together, and not farmed out to various kinsmen after her death. Another of her concerns was that we be able to care for ourselves to the fullest extent possible – to wash and dress ourselves, to tie our own shoes, and so forth. I can recall the hubbub of excitement in the house when I finally learned to lace my own shoes and tie the laces in the proper bow knot and not a hard knot. I remember, too, when my mother went to a neighbor's house nearby and had her long chestnut hair braided into a thick rich braid and cut so that it could, afterwards, be subdivided into six smaller braids for her children. It was a balmy day, like Indian summer, when she had her hair cut, returned to the house, hung the braid on a hook in the kitchen door, and began to get our supper ready. But of greatest importance was her choice of a home for us younger children when the time came. I cannot recall how many orphanages we visited – perhaps only a couple – but the home she chose for us was the Free Will Baptist Orphanage near Middlesex. True, it was an institution with lots of children from different backgrounds. At the same time, it came to being more nearly like the lives we had known than any other place. It had a rural setting. It offered a farm life, with plenty of work, depending upon one's size, strength, and ability. But most of all, even though my sisters would be housed in one building, and my brother and I in another, we would all be sheltered, clothed, fed, and kept together – and not scattered from Dan to Beersheba. Some few weeks lapsed between her death and our being collected by the orphanage superintendant, the Rev. James A. Evans ('40-'49), and taken to Middlesex. Both my half-brother and half-sister were beyond the age of admission. He soon joined the army, and she married young. We arrived well after nightfall. Everyone was already abed. We were taken to our respective buildings. Haywood and I were taken to a room reserved for little boys. As I recall, our entry caused some disturbance to their sleep. One little boy woke up completely, and rubbed his eyes as he studied my brother and me. I studied him right back and decided that I wanted that boy as a friend. That was not to be. He left the orphanage shortly thereafter, and Haywood and I inherited the bed that had belonged to Jamie, for such was his name. On the day following our night arrival, I was able to look about and get my bearings. Naturally I saw more than I could explore in a single day, or even in a single year. But bit by bit, and year by year, I familiarized myself with a great deal.

Campus

1942-L-R: Girls Building, Dining Hall, Boys Building

What I immediately saw when I first looked about me was that the public road leading to and from Middlesex terminated in a more or less elliptical drive that led around to the fronts of the principal buildings. These were a two-story brick dormitory for the boys, a sizeable one-story brick building called the "New Building" (that contained the administrative offices, the large dining hall, the kitchen and the pantries), and a three-story brick dormitory for the girls. To the rear of the new building, only a few steps from the kitchen stood a wooden single story storehouse filled with canned goods, dried fruits, peas and beans, potatoes, and so forth. To the right rear of the new building sat the smokehouse where hams, shoulders, bacon, and links of stuffed sausage were cured with smoke from a hickory fire that had been fed with the appropriate spices and herbs. It also contained salt boxes for the corning of some parts of the pork. To the left of the side entry to the girls' building stood another outbuilding a little distance away. This was the pump house, a small attractive brick building that was, to a small boy, both entrancing and fear-inspiring. When one entered the building, one immediately saw that the ground floor was almost altogether taken up by a great square concrete pit with rungs set in one of its walls. One supposed that the pump that furnished the water supply sat at the bottom. For me that was mere supposition; that pit looked so dark and forbidding to me that my fear of being drawn into it prevented my getting close enough to look down into it. If one pressed one's back against the wall and carefully inched one's way along the left side of the pit, one came to a small flight of wooden steps that led to a little half-story room. This was a shop room that was used in conjunction with maintenance of the pump. A high workbench held a large vise. Along the workbench, there was a series of cubby holes that contained an assortment of bolts, nuts, washers, screws, nails and a variety of small metallic junk. Below and to the rear of the building was a pair of large cylindrical cast iron vats suspended over a brick firebox. It was supposed by some of the children that these large vats had been used for washing clothes at a period before a proper laundry (with great rolling drums made of wooden slats into which dirty clothes were put with a detergent and then agitated in water) was installed at the entrance to the basement of the girls' building. I imagine, instead, that the laundry and ironing room had been part of the original design for the girls' dormitory and had been in operation there from the beginning. I seem to recall that the two iron vats were fired up once in connection with a hog killing (they were just the right size for that); perhaps there was an occasion when fat was reduced to lard in one of the vats. Before my mother's death, I recall our laundry days took place in the back yard where the clothes were washed in great cast iron pots under which a fire had been built to bring the water to a scalding temperature. I imagine that had been the practice in the homes of all the children before coming to the orphanage. It is understandable that an explanation for the pump house vats would have been extrapolated from a home scene of laundry pots in the back yard.

In addition to the large tumbling washing machines and their water supply on one side of the entryway to the basement of the girls' building, there was a long room on the opposite side of the entryway, where the ironing was done. There was machinery for pressing sheets and table cloths, forms for ironing shirt sleeves, and so forth, as well as the usual ironing boards and flat irons. Along the interior wall was a series of cubicles into which each child's clothes were put after they were ready for pick-up. Behind the laundry and ironing room, a hallway ran the length of the building. The left end of the hallway led to rooms on opposing sides. One room had large metal boxes with heavy lids. These boxes were partially filled with water that was kept cold by refrigerating coils that lined the interior walls. As the dairy cows were milked every morning and afternoon, the milk was gathered into five-gallon milk cans and transported to the refrigerating room and immersed in the cold water. Across the hall, in a long room, was machinery for processing the milk for use. One machine separated the cream from the milk. Another machine was used when milk was to be bottled, and it had a conveyor belt to move the bottles forward to receive the milk, to cap it with paper caps when filled, and to carry the filled bottles forward. Large metal sinks for washing and sterilizing the bottles and the milk cans stood against the wall of the room. Other interior rooms on the right end of the hall were disused while I was there. My impression is that meals had been prepared in these basement rooms before the "new building" was built. Since the girls' dormitory was built on a slight elevation that fell away to the left, a light-wall was constructed on the right side of the building so that light could be let into the basement rooms through windows that were very nearly below ground level.

    I have written more details than I set out to write, and have, thus, been led away from my purpose. What I set out to say is that the elliptical drive enclosed "the flower garden". What was left of the flower beds disappeared within a few years of my admission to the orphanage. Still, there were groupings of lobelia, quince, forsythia, and spirea with various persistent plantings of daffodils and grape hyacinths. Pecan trees stood at various places in the flower garden. It was here that wire fencing was pulled taut in a continuous horizontal surface every Thanksgiving and supports inserted at intervals to create a table. On that day women from many Free Will Baptist churches came with their families and with no end of truly delicious cooked foods. Of course, there was turkey, but there was also unbeatable southern fried chicken. Bowls of potato salad, and devilled eggs, and everything else, loaded the table, not to mention cakes and pies. Such a variety of pickles was never seen before. Thanksgiving was bigger than anything. Even Christmas was nothing to it. But, here I am getting distracted from my subject again.

I was speaking of the elliptical drive. When one entered it from the road to Middlesex, one passed the superintendent's house. It sat with the "new road" to its left, and the drive in front of it. It was a small, neat, two-story brick house, showing a degree of modest taste in its interior woodwork. To its left stood a gas pump with its buried tank--whether it was possible to keep up the supply of gasoline satisfactorily throughout the war years, or not, I do not know. I imagine it fell victim to gas rationing.

Continuing down the drive past the site where Memorial Chapel was subsequently built (but at that time a field of soybeans or oats or some other small grain), one came to three different spurs leading off the drive. The third, and last, of them led off to the left into the access road, or service road rather, that ran behind the principal buildings. This service road was used to deliver coal for the furnaces in the buildings, to deliver farm produce to the kitchen, to enable the man from the Sexton Foods Company to drive to the rear of the kitchen to receive and deliver orders for salt, pepper, seasonings, spices, and extracts, flavorings and cane syrup, and other similar wares. From the kitchen, the service road (screened by a tall hedge of ligustrum and privet) ran behind the girls' building, past the pump house, and under pecan trees, on toward the superintendent's house, to join the elliptical drive near its beginning.

Farmyard

The second spur at the bottom of the drive connected to a dirt road leading to "the other farm." I don't know the original extent of the orphanage property, but a Mr. Deans [Elder B.B. Deans Board Member ('20-'24)] added considerably to it by the gift of an adjoining farm—hence, "the other farm." Although the name of Mr. Deans ought to be perpetuated for his generosity, I do not know his forename. I was in school with his grandson, Gordon, but whether that had been the name, too, of the benefactor, I do not know. It was my understanding, though it might have been an erroneous one, that the land held by the orphanage, came to 200 acres. With its woods and branches, wild grapes and hickory nut trees, gardens, fields, pastures, and meadow, it was a wonderful place for a small boy. But, I begin to digress.

The first spur leading from the elliptical drive took one into the farmyard to the right, the heart of the original farm (which I shall henceforth call the home farm, though I never heard it so called.) The buildings in the farmyard were arranged on three sides of a square, the fourth side being nearly open. The first building was the farm shop, then came a feed house, and after that the dairy—these forming the first line of buildings in the square. A little distance, on a right angle from the dairy stood a large barn, and opposite it in the other corner of the square stood a stable. Behind these buildings the pastures swept back to the woods, on the edge of which was a wild crab apple tree. When in full blow in the spring of the year, this tree was a great glory with bees buzzing at its heart. There were occasions in the summer when a brief rain would fall leaving in its wake a rainbow that appeared to be attached to this very tree. Excited excursions to it always failed to reveal the end of the rainbow or the pot of gold that we little boys hoped to find there. The woods beyond were the preserve of the older boys (the "big boys" and "middle sized boys") who set their rabbit boxes there or hunted squirrels. One or two enterprising boys set traps for muskrats in order to take and sell their pelts. Rabbits and squirrels were killed, skinned, and cleaned. A fellow with such small game as this would have to persuade one of the "kitchen girls" to cook the meat for him. A meal of squirrel or rabbit bestowed a certain éclat on the fellow who had brought it to pass. They were a model for us little ones, as well they should have been, for when hunting in the woods, they used slingshots, not guns. It was a real feat to bring down a squirrel with a slingshot!

The pastures lay not only behind the buildings, but ran to the left side of the square, as well. A small stream ran through them, and the stream had been widened in places by the cows who, on hot days, ambled down to it and cooled themselves by standing or lying in it where a tree gave shade. This stream actually had its rise across the road leading to the other farm, in what was called the meadow strip. On occasion the meadow strip was sown in wheat which was harvested by a threshing machine, and the wheat straw mowed and baled for winter fodder. At other times it was a haven for wild flowers and butterflies. When the meadow strip was filled with ripening grain, it was home to families of rabbits. When the thresher, and later the mower, began to work its way from the outer perimeter to the center, the poor creatures withdrew for safety from the approaching machinery. Those of them who had not fled in time were finally driven into a small frantic group in the middle of the meadow strip. Some of these were caught by pouncing boys; others escaped in a daring dash. More got away than not.

The first building in the farmyard set on the edge of these pastures was the shop. It sat to the left as one entered from the drive. The small building had an anvil and a brazier with a foot-driven bellows that served as a forge. Here shoes were beaten into the right shape for each hoof when the mules and horses had to be re-shod. Like us boys, these animals required different size shoes, and blank shoes had to be fitted and shaped to each hoof after the hoof had been trimmed and neatened up to receive the new shoe. It was here, too, that farm machinery and equipment were kept in repair and in good working order by the man on the staff who was maintenance supervisor, and by any of the big boys capable of helping him. A once-of-a-kind effort was centered on the shop during the war (by which I mean W.W. II). All the buildings, outbuildings, and sheds on both the home farm and the other farm were searched for scrap metal and machinery past all hope of repair. This was in response to a call from the Office of Home Defense in Raleigh for the collection of scrap metal for the war effort. The gathering point was at the shop—but not in the pasture immediately beside it. This small enclosed area was the home of a small red bull with wicked looking horns. He was appropriately named "Tojo," after the Japanese prime minister who had led his country into war against the U.S. His stall, I believe, was at the rear of the shop.

Next in line was a small wooden building with a tin roof that was used to store salt blocks for the horses and cows, and sacks of cottonseed meal to be measured out so much for each cow at the time she was milked. The yellow salt blocks were mounted on stakes in the pastures where they were enjoyed by the animals and by the little boys, too, from time to time. This feed storehouse was more or less an adjunct to the dairy. It, the dairy, is where the cows gathered twice a day to be milked, and from which the fresh warm milk was taken to the refrigerated facility in the basement of the girls' building to be further processed and kept until needed by the kitchen. The dairy was a marvel in concrete and wood. The concrete floor supported a raised concrete walkway. Sets of head lockers were placed at convenient intervals on each side of the walkway, and at these places the concrete had been poured into a mold that created a basin-like depression. As the cows entered, each one walked, or was guided, to one of the head lockers which was snapped to. The cow had plenty of freedom for up and down movement. A generous portion of cottonseed meal was measured into the basin-like depression which lay at grazing level for the cow. She thus got the double comfort of being milked and of being fed some delectable meal at the same time. After each cow was milked she was released, and a new one took her place. I can't recall how many cows there were, or how many were milked at the time.

To the right of the dairy, forming a corner of the farmyard square stood a large barn. It had a large hayloft above and a series of horse stalls below. The large upper space through which bales of hay were hoisted into the hayloft generally stood open. There was a story connected to this barn, and it was told to a succession of little boys as a warning. It is probable that the story was true. It was told as truth. It was said that from the beginning of the orphanage up to the time I was there, only two children had died while residents of the home. These were two boys. They had gone, one Sunday afternoon, up into the hayloft in order to have a quiet smoke. A summer thunderstorm blew up while they were there. As the boys stood in the hayloft opening, smoking and admiring the storm, they were struck and killed by a thunderbolt. I was never entirely clear as to the warning that went with this tale. Was it to do with the dangers of smoking? Or with smoking on the Lord's Day? Or was it a warning not to smoke when God was "doing His work?"

Although there were stalls in the lower part of this barn, there was a separate building, opposite the barn, where the horses were usually stabled. It was here that "Silver" lived, a horse that was, like the Lone Ranger's mount, a silvery white. "Silver" had pride of place among all the animals, and though the farm manager, Mr. Massey, forbade anyone but himself to ride the horse, "Silver" was a great favorite with all the children. How well I remember the spread of the news when "Silver" stepped into a hole, broke a leg, and had to be shot. Some of us little boys were in the apple orchard stealing a few green apples to eat (a thing strictly forbidden) when the news came at dusk. I thought at first that the victim of this accident was one of the girls named Silvia Jean. While it was a relief to learn that it was "Silver" and not Silvia who had suffered a broken leg, it was a terrific shock. It was shortly afterwards, in cold weather, that a gentle mare named "Mary" came down with blind staggers. It was dreadful in the night to hear her frantic neighs, I nearly said screams, and wild thrashings as she attempted to destroy her stall. In the end, I think she had to be destroyed. Afterwards horses disappeared from the scene altogether. There were only mules, then. I should mention one capricious pair of mules who were willing to work with one another as a team. One was called Thunder and the other Lightning. When riding them to be unharnessed, one had to watch that the one being ridden did not turn back its head and attempt to bite ones kneecap. I don't mean to suggest that they, like all the mules, were not hardworking creatures when put to the plow or cultivator. It is just that they were not pet material.

Other denizens of the farmyard included a drake and his wife with their children, a mallard with his wives, some guinea fowls who eventually took to the woods and took up life there until they were, probably, eaten by foxes and a small gamecock and his wives. These latter were the private property of one of the boys who tended to them. He kept them in a small specially fenced area near the barn until they too, escaped and took up life in the woods for a short period. One other denizen of the farmyard was an old goat known simply as Billy. He was tolerant of the small children whom he'd allow to pet and play with him. He didn't appear to care for adults, and resented teasing by the older boys. All in all, he was a right good old goat who had the run of the place and was welcomed by all. By a most unfortunate happenstance, the principal meat dish served in the dining hall on the day of his death was a beef stew. I think it flew into the mind of nearly every child there that what we were being served was the remains of old Billy. I think, too, that a few of those boys who will take any dare, or do nearly anything to show they are not cowards, ate some of the stew. Otherwise the dish was left untouched on the table. I was prejudiced against beef stew for the next fifty years!

Apple Orchard

Probably I have given too much detail about the home farm and its buildings. If I have, it must be admitted all the same that not all has been described, nor has an overall sense of the place been given. Not a word has been said about the chicken houses and the gathering of eggs, or of the extensive vegetable gardens and the gathering of kitchen stuffs. For the moment it may suffice to say that the chicken houses were located beyond the apple orchard, at some distance from the kitchen, and fairly near the woods. Like the dairy, the chicken houses had a feed storehouse as a necessary adjunct. This had a tin roof, which was just the place to cut up apples stolen from the orchard and spread them to be dried by the sun.

That apple orchard was the source of never ending temptation as well as of apples. It commenced on the other side of the service road behind the girls' building and swept on to the rear of the kitchen, and back toward the chicken houses. Trees of "pear apples" grew behind the girls' buildings, and a golden apple that we called "the mellow apple tree" stood near the center of the orchard. No doubt the favorite was the "June apple," for it managed to produce small ripe apples as early as June. The mellow apple tree and the June apple tree both stood near a small building that had been built in the orchard as a brooder or a place for the hatching and raising of chicks to replenish the chicken houses as needed. As the apples in the orchard grew toward full size, they were surreptitiously preyed upon by the little boys, despite a strict injunction that they leave them to ripen on the trees. Mrs. Evans, the superintendent's wife, kept up as near a continuous vigilance as she could to prevent the boys' forays. The veil of dusk defeated her watchfulness from time to time. I hope that we never made such serious inroads on the apple crop that there was a shortage for canning. However, I do recall that there were times when the superintendent arranged for the delivery of bushel after bushel of apples from the North Carolina mountains. These mountain apples were supposed to be of supreme excellence. Perhaps they were. Memory tells me, on the other hand, that nothing equaled the June apple or the mellow apple from our own orchard.

Gardens

I have spoken already of the fact that the small field located between the superintendent's house and the farmyard, where Memorial Chapel now sits, was sown in small grain or in soybeans, and that the meadow strip sometimes lay fallow and was sometimes sown with wheat. The remainder of the land under cultivation at the home farm was given over to kitchen vegetables or to fodder for the horses and mules. The principal vegetable garden occupied a few acres, I suppose, and was located off the farm road leading to the other farm. It was bounded at the upper side and bottom by woods, and at the lower side by the pastures. There stood, too, at the bottom just inside the shade of the trees belonging to the woods, a pen in which young hogs were put up to be fattened for slaughter in the fall or early winter. On a line with it, but facing the farm road, stood a sizeable storage barn. Here were kept the various gardening implements that were needed throughout the year (rakes, hoes, funnel shaped hand planters, spraying pumps for insecticides, bean poles, twine, pegs (or dibbles) made from smooth lightwood knots used in pegging a planting hole for young plants, and whatever else might be needed for the planting and cultivation of a very large garden. Here, too, was kept a stock of corn to be shelled and carried to the fattening hog pen at the foot of the garden. A supplementary vegetable garden was planted one year across the new road opposite the superintendent's house. Earlier seed beds had been planted here, but in this year it was used, as I say, for a supplemental vegetable garden. It was given over to tomatoes, and perhaps some other vegetable, such as squash—it was not a very large space. Two other patches of ground were given over to sweet potatoes and corn. These lay at some distance to the rear and right of the kitchen, on a line with the chicken houses. A farm path that ran between the kitchen storehouse and the woodpile, along the outer edge of the apple orchard, led both to the chicken houses and, by turning right, to these two patches. The corn raised in this patch was for fodder, but the sweet potatoes were for our consumption. And good eating they were, too! They were so sweet that any juice that broke through the skin when they were baking, candied on the skin. They, sweet potatoes, were raised in the principal garden as well as in this patch, and a good thing they were, too, for we had a disaster with potatoes from the patch one year. It was decided to employ a new method whereby the sweet potatoes could be cured in the field. This would avoid the necessity of moving these great mounds of potatoes to a storehouse where they could be left to be cured out and be held safely through the winter for kitchen use. This new method required the digging of a shallow pit and lining it with pine straw. After the potatoes were put into the straw-lined pit, they were covered with more straw, and then a layer of dirt shoveled on top of the whole bed. Vents were provided at strategic points to prevent unwanted heat building up, and to supply air to the buried potatoes. It was based on the principles of a root cellar. Our design was a flop. Our whole cache of sweet potatoes rotted in the ground. The only good I got out of that potato patch, apart from the pleasure of helping grub and pile them up, was not even sweet potato-related. I had joined the Boy Scouts not long before, and was required to demonstrate my ability to tie certain basic knots before progressing in the Scouts. As anyone who has dug potatoes knows, the plant puts out fibrous runners from its root, and the new potatoes develop from them. It was with these long, fibrous, string-like roots that I demonstrated the tying of a Scout's basic knots to an older boy who was able to conduct my examination.

Woodland

Having spoken of the buildings, the farmyard, and the gardens of the home farm, it remains necessary to say a little something about the woods which enclosed the orphanage on all sides. How extensive were the woods owned by the orphanage, and what their depth, I do not know. One sometimes ran into a wire fence, however, and this fence might well have marked a boundary line, or it might have been only a fence to discourage pigs from straying out of their assigned territory. They, the pigs, had only one wooded territory on the home farm. I imagine the streak of woods that ran between the other farm and the home farm must have included an original boundary line. If my memory serves, the three principal buildings lay on a north-south axis: the girls' building to the south, the boys' building to the north; the "new building" about midway but to the west of the axis. Whether this is correct or not, I shall speak of directions as if this were a true statement of directional facts. By this scheme, the other farm and the streak of woods of which I speak lay to the north and ran east and west. It deepened and continued at its eastern end to run along the outer perimeter of the pastures. A small creek or branch ran through this piece of woods, and it, in turn, drained little branches from the other farm and from the meadow strip and pastures on the home farm before emptying ultimately into Turkey Creek or one of its feeders. Although I sometimes entered this part of the woods from the farm road leading to the other farm, I seldom walked on around to the woods at the eastern edge of the pastures. One would not like to interfere with a rabbit box or disturb a muskrat trap or startle such small game by going into these woods without a real purpose. These woods ran on across the new road and continued on, all along the road to Middlesex—though the orphanage property ran not so far. It probably did not extend much beyond a bridge in the Middlesex road that crossed a small branch that pooled and widened at this point. The woods on the east side of this bridge were generally held to be of little recreational interest. Still it was here, and only here, that one could find ground cedar and hepatica growing. They were not, however, sufficient enticements to a ramble.

It was generally acknowledged that the best section of woods lay to the south, below the girls' buildings and the pump house. A stretch of fallow ground lay between the woods and the plantings with ligustrum and privet that marked the end of the formal "campus," as we would now call it.

This fenced-in area technically belonged to hogs, I believe, but was generally occupied only by dog fennel, broom straw, "yellow top weeds" (a form of very bitter wild marigold, I think) and other such plants like thistle and, in season, Queen Anne's Lace. It was an example, to my mind, of what the prophet meant when he spoke of "an abomination of desolation." In later years somebody got the idea of building a brick outdoor fireplace for cooking hotdogs in this desolate patch. One was built, and hotdogs were actually cooked there a time or two. But it was not a success. It remained what it had always been—a fenced in stretch of uninviting terrain. A ditch that commenced behind the pump house led down to this patch. I suppose this ditch carried off the water from the laundry, the drain from which no doubt emptied into it. This ditch was overhung by willows, and in the spring its banks were covered by a profusion of well nourished violets. Practically nobody ever bothered to go behind the pump house, except for the occasional golden garden spider, so this spot of quiet beauty was a good place for those seeking serenity.

I appear to have strayed from my remarks about the woods but I really haven't. A path led from the basement of the girls' building to a gate in the fence that enclosed the stretch of fallow ground of which I speak. The path then led to a small storage building with a loft that was stocked with corn waiting to be shucked and shelled for the hogs penned up to be fattened for slaughter. A large sow with her litter had the run of this fenced area that included the fattening hog pen. This pen had replaced the one that sat in the edge of the woods at the foot of the principal vegetable garden. Like the other, this pen was raised and had a wooden floor, troughs for the shelled corn, and drinking troughs that had to be kept filled with water. It stood near a small attractive branch. This stream rose at a considerable distance to the west and flowed in a generally eastwardly direction onto the orphanage property, flowed under the bridge of which I have spoken, and continued on as a tributary of Turkey Creek. It was that part of the woods at the southern end of the orphanage property, that included this branch, that was the most desirable section of the woods, and I shall say more about these woods in due course.

The last quarter of woods lay to the left of the orphanage property and continued past the chicken houses, past the corn patch and sweet potato patch of which I have spoken, and terminated in the woods belonging to the other farm. It was here that large animal carcasses were dragged and left for the buzzards to devour. Here too was a footpath that led to the habitation of a black man known as "World's Troubles," and his large family of children and grandchildren. He occasionally helped with hog killings and might have been given work periodically. He could sometimes be seen cutting toward the field road leading to this quadrant, a sack on his shoulder, heading for the woods path that led him home. Although I once visited his house, I can tell nothing of his community or where the roads there took one. Some of the little girls at the orphanage would scare one another, as I recall, and perhaps the little boys, too, by threatening them with "the sack man." This was a libel on an old man who scratched out a hard living. The use of the nickname to terrorize another child was unjust to both the man and the child.

Farm

I have said nothing about the other farm except to indicate its existence. It was far too important to treat so shabbily. A dirt road ran to it, then passed through it to another farm, presumably belonging to Mr. Deans, through which it passed to connect with a county road. That part of the road that ran from the elliptical drive to the other farm ran between the meadow strip and the pastures. It made a slight decline before commencing a slight incline as one approached the woods and the farm. A small stream drained from the left side, as one went up the road to the other farm. In dry weather the little stream that crossed the road was hardly worth noticing, but in rainy weather, it swelled to a nuisance. The road went straight on for some distance, then turned sharply to the right and continued to the end of the farm. The odd thing about this farm is that I knew what I should see there before I ever went to see it with my own eyes. When I was carried there for the first time, I was filled with excited anticipation. I do not know how old I was, or why I was carried to it. Certainly there was nothing here for the littlest boys to do, and there was no occasion for preschoolers to go there. Yet I knew beforehand what I should see there, and when I went, I found what I expected. Perhaps I ought to do now what I should have done earlier. That is, make a sketch map of the principal buildings in relation to one another as I first knew them. One can then tell whether my indications of the compass points are roughly correct or wildly inaccurate, and adjust accordingly:

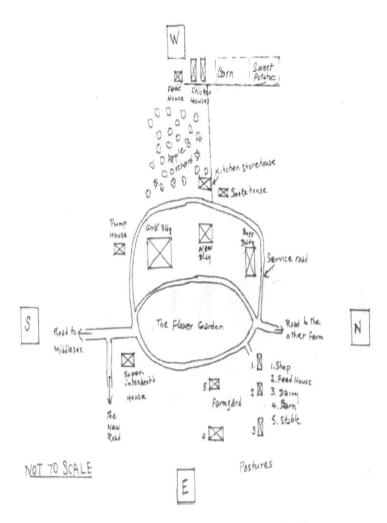

Drawing by George Stevenson-2008

    To return to what I was saying about the other farm, I found there what I expected to find. A nice, low, well-constructed farm dwelling house stood to the right of the road almost immediately upon arrival there. The house was, unfortunately, overhung by large evergreen trees that were both not the right sort of tree for this style house, and too close to the house as well. I expect they were a sort of spruce or (but less likely) deodar cedar. Whatever they were, the trees were too dark and gloomy for the low house. Beside the house sat its well with a chain pulley and metal bucket that could be lowered, filled with water, and then drawn up by turning a windlass. It was surrounded by neat stonework that rose a few feet above the ground and supported a roof and the framework for the chain windlass. The well itself had been dug straight down and perfectly circular in shape. One was lost in admiration for the skill of the workmen who dug it. I don't know how deep the well was, or the distance between the surface of the water and the surface of the ground. There was always an ample supply of very clear, very cold water in the well. It was probably far more dangerous for a child than the pump house well, but I felt no fear when gazing down into depths of this well and watching the splash and tilt of the bucket when it was lowered to draw up water.

Beyond the well stood the tobacco barns, tall log structures chinked with clay. The sheds that were necessary adjuncts stood with them, and cordwood for their firing stood stacked nearby. Farther back from the road, near the edge of the woods, stood a disused log cabin that was falling into ruin. It was said to have been a slave house, but childish imagination might have bestowed this history on it. It may have been no more than an old packhouse, and probably was such.

From here the road ran straight ahead for a small distance and turned sharply to the right at the corner of a small field where milo was grown one year as an experiment in finding a more satisfactory fodder for the live stock. It was just here, where the road turned, that one found several rambling canes of dusty, light red, flat, sweet smelling roses tumbling down into the ditch. Though they grew in so despised a condition and were frequently coated with dust from the dirt road, they persisted and perfumed the air. An attempt to remove them to a more choice location probably would have proved fatal to them. Farther along the road, on the right side, stood a small tenant house that was used for storage. It was here, on the opposite side of the road that a small pond was excavated by the generosity, I believe, of Dr. Hinnant of Micro. It was fed by a small stream at the far end. A diving board and platform was built at the end of the pond close to the road, opposite the house of which I speak. Fields opened from the road as one went down it. Beyond the pond, on the left side of the road, stood another farmhouse and its out-buildings. It had a small orchard attached to it, with trees of horse apples – big, ugly, and very sweet. Their distance saved them from sneak raids by the little boys. It was in these fields belonging to the other farm that crops of cotton and tobacco were raised. I may be mistaken, but I believe the orphanage itself did not raise tobacco, but leased land for that purpose (and the curing barns, and the nice farmhouse) to a farmer who sought the lease. I recall a pleasant family named Hedgepeth living there and, I believe, farming the tobacco. Cotton may have been raised the same way, or it might have been raised by the orphanage on its own account. Whether leased or not, the boys and girls helped tend these crops and harvest them.

Having said so much, perhaps too much, about the physical setting of the orphanage, I still ought to say one or two things more before speaking of life at the home. Remarkable changes in the physical setup followed close on the end of the war. The livestock, the farming machinery, the dairy operation, and the farmyard were all moved to the other farm. The old shop, feed house, dairy, barn, and stable were all demolished preparatory to building a new dormitory for the boys. The superintendent arranged to buy vacant U.S. Army barrack buildings that had stood at Camp Butner during the war and have them disassembled and shipped to Middlesex. They were reassembled and rebuilt on the site of the old farmyard, and given a brick veneer. In a space between the superintendant's house and the site of the old farmyard, where small grains used to be planted, a church, named "Memorial Chapel" was erected. The old boys' building was demolished. These changes were gradual, not instantaneous, and though it took four or five years to accomplish them, still they were unsettling. Life was not so compact as before, and as a result memories are more diffuse.

Financing

I wish I could speak with greater authority then I am able to do about the financing of the home. Since, however, an annual financial report was prepared for the N.C. State Convention of FWBs, and was published in an issue of The Free Will Baptist, the curious can consult the printed Convention minutes for an authoritative statement. In case, however, the annual financial statement will not be fully explanatory, my informal notions may be worth stating. From its earliest days, the orphanage was faithfully supported by Free Will Baptist churches all over the state. Even during the Great Depression, support was found for the orphanage. (It is possible that annual grants from the Duke Foundation were received by the orphanage as early as the Depression; they certainly were later.)

Besides funds sent throughout the year by the churches, special efforts were made to raise money by sending some small groups, called "concert classes," of children on tour to the churches in the early summer months. An adult who was able to play the piano; organize little skits and recitations; to train the children to sing solos, duets, trios, as a group, or what have you; to keep them together and in order; and to carry them from church to church and reconnoiter with local church leaders—these adults, usually one for the eastern churches and one for the western churches, took charge of their "classes" and made their tours of the churches. All this had to be orchestrated beforehand. Not only did one have to be certain that each church knew in advance the date of the evening when the touring class would visit, but arrangements had to be made among the women of the local "Ladies Aid Society" to take in one or more of the children to feed and lodge them overnight. This was tremendously hard work for all. No doubt the funds thus raised made it all worthwhile. But even if the fundraising was less than hoped, it was a valuable thing to take these children on tour to the churches so that the churches could see the fruit of their labor. The hearts of the church people were really in this work, and I am not at all sure that the churches have been given the praise they deserve. Many of the churches went beyond raising money for general operating expenses, and "adopted" a child to support during his lifetime in the orphanage. They made certain that the needs of "their child" were met with regard to shoes and clothing, school supplies, and so forth. Some might have sent some spending money from time to time (though I know of no such). They also made certain that "their child" received a present at Christmas. Some churches were more affluent than others, so some Christmas presents were nicer than others. But with regard to shoes, clothing, school supplies, and so forth, it is pretty clear that financial equalization took place in the superintendant's office. When the children were taken to Wilson, for example, to buy new clothing, they were taken in manageable groups based on age and size. Once in the store, they were fitted to the same brand and quality of shoes, coats, and clothing. The child, whose sponsoring church was a small struggling rural church in one of the poorer counties, fared no worse than the child whose sponsoring church was a large, flourishing one. If a sponsoring church requested to meet the child they sponsored, arrangements were made for such a visit. Otherwise, the churches and their Ladies' Aid Societies worked without recognition or reward, quietly and faithfully, year after year.

The clothes and shoes purchased for the children (and some clothes that were sent by Ladies' Aid Societies) were much the same as those worn by the ordinary child of the period whose parents farmed. Some clothes were purchased for church-wear only. Otherwise, overalls, made of durable jeans cloth, and brogans were standard attire.

From May until September, shoes weren't worn at all. It was a red letter day when shoes could be put aside, and a day of regret when they had to be resumed. Yes, there was always the danger of cutting ones foot on broken glass, or stepping on a rusty nail, or getting dew poisoning on unprotected feet. A little doctoring put that right, and one was left with a scar to be a memorial in later life of childhood's days of sunny freedom. Little, I think, could be done with dew poisoning except to keep the feet well washed and to stay out of dewy grass in the early mornings. Rusty nails, anyway <u>my</u> rusty nail, left punctures that required medicating with iodine, and, when a streak of fever like a red vein could be seen climbing upward from it, soaking the foot in a tub of very hot water to which a quantity of Epsom salt had been added. There was always the fear of blood poisoning and lockjaw resulting from a deep puncture, but in my case, the effect of the hot Epsom salt water was immediate and apparent. The streak of fever began to fall like the mercury in a thermometer. The badge of honor left by my most serious cut runs diagonally across the arch of my right foot in the form of a long silvery scar. This injury was so deep that we had to call on the services of Dr. Powell who was always available to come from the town of Middlesex, two miles away, to attend to any child needing his care. I have gotten entirely away from my subject, which was clothes. I meant to conclude by observing that one put on work clothes to perform ones morning chores, and changed into school clothes before breakfast. After school, one changed again – out of school clothes and into work clothes for the evening chores. Sunday clothes were donned for church.

Work Assignments

I see I have used the word "chores," but that was not a term that was in current use. Ones assigned work might be called a "job," but not a "chore." There was little or no work for pre-school children, but plenty of it for the others. No child was ever assigned work, or expected to perform work, beyond his capacity and ability. My first work was done in connection with the dairy. Once the cows came into the dairy building and took their places to be milked, a big boy took his seat on a stool and washed the cow's bag and teats. He then placed a milk bucket in place below and proceeded to milk his cow. They, the cows, were golden colored Guernseys and red Jerseys. The Jersey cows, I believe, gave more milk, but the Guernsey cows gave milk much richer in butter fat. Both gave very good, rich milk. One or two of the Jersey cows had the hateful trick of putting a hind foot in the milk pail and spoiling everything, if left to her own devices. Those cows had to have lockers fastened onto their hind legs to prevent them lifting a malicious foot and overturning the pail. Both the Guernseys and the Jerseys switched their tails in order to prevent biting flies from annoying them. My job was to stand between two of the cows being milked, beyond the milker on his stool at her side, and take the tail of each cow in either hand and hold on fast so that she could not switch her tail and hit the milker in the face.

I should say that this was not a regularly assigned job, requiring me to be present at the pre-dawn morning milking and the late afternoon milking every day. It is more probable that I was allowed by one of the big boys to follow him to the dairy and look on as the boys did their work of milking and cleaning out the dairy. No doubt one of the boys invented this little job of tail-holding just to give me a useful something to do.

Periodically, little tasks were found for us little boys. The most boring of all was the job of picking the heads of clover that had gone to seed and bagging them up for future use. The "lawns" in front of the three principal buildings were primarily of clover and were usually alive in the summer with little brown honey bees. Where the bees lived and made and stored their honey was anybody's guess, and it was impossible to form an opinion as to whether they all belonged to the same colony or not. There were certainly plenty of them when the clover was in blow and we barefooted boys had to be on the lookout for them when we walked there. When a sting occurred, a staff member who dipped snuff would remove a bit of the moistened snuff from her mouth and apply it to the sting. I was stung a time or two, but I never submitted to the snuff cure.

The clover seed might have been taken to the pastures and sown there. If so, they never sprang up in sufficient thickness to choke out two hateful weeds that grew on the northwestern edge of the cow pastures. These two weeds were the wild onion and the "yellow top weed." The "yellow tops," in blossom and foliage slightly resembled the marigold in a wild and weedy way and were twice as bitter. They thrived in poor soil and required little water. When they were flourishing, which seemed to be all summer long, the cows would stroll over and eat a bait of them. Everything else the cows ate was transformed into rich delicious milk. But even the four stomachs of a cow were not equal to the task of neutralizing the taste of wild onions or of the yellow top weed. Great groans went up from all the tables in the dining hall when the pitchers of cold milk that had been put out were found to contain the taste of these two weeds. As with the clover heads, we little boys would be sent day by day to the cow pasture to pull up these pestiferous plants. We pulled and pulled, and our hands stank and stank, but only a change of pastures ended the problem.

Another piece of work, a non-repetitive one, was the removal of stones from the northern section of the meadow strip. The orphanage property, woods and all, was scattered with naturally occurring rocks. Some of them were of white quartz and attractive to look at if they did not have to be picked up and moved. Some of them sported growths of moss and lichens and must have lain in the same spot for many years. Most of them did not. I was convinced that they were continually working their way up through the ground to the surface in order to lie in the sun – or just to get in the way of everybody. Our task was to collect the stones in the upper reaches of the meadow strip and make little piles of them. One or more of the big boys came by with a wheelbarrow, loaded the rocks onto it, and hauled them to a place where a small stream ran across the road to the other farm. The rocks were scattered about in that part of the stream bed that crossed the road. The idea behind this piece of work was to provide a solid footing for wagons, carts, and other farm equipment that had to cross the stream when using the road. I think this was not a very successful idea. The introduction of rocks into the stream's course caused the water to be diverted over a larger area. This required more rocks, and more rocks increased the area over which the water flowed. Eventually, a concrete pipe was laid to carry the water from one side of the road to the other.

Another job at which all of us boys worked together was the gathering of firewood. All our firewood was gathered in the early winter. It was taken from that part of the woods on the other farm that lay near the farm road. We all fell out for the wood cutting, taking our axes, wedges, and cross-cut saws to the woods where the trees were to be felled. The men and the big boys cut down the trees that had been selected in advance. Middle sized boys dressed them by lopping off branches after the trees had been felled. They cut the trunks of the trees to manageable lengths (say four feet), and did the same with the large branches. We little boys dragged the brush away to keep the workspace clear. After all was cut to lengths of no more than four feet, part of it was hauled to the tobacco barns and stacked as cordwood. Another part was hauled up the service road and unloaded at the woodpile back of the kitchen. Here the four foot pieces were laid on a sawhorse and sawn with a crosscut saw into shorter sections suitable for splitting into firewood for the kitchen range. I feel fortunate to have had the experience of gathering wood for fuel, for "helping" at the firing of the tobacco barns where this wood was used as fuel to heat the curing barns, and for working as a kitchen boy during the period that firewood fueled the great cooking range in the kitchen. Although I cannot tell the year in which the cook stove was modified to burn fuel oil instead of wood, it was after the war while I was the kitchen boy. Nor do I know how long it was before the method of heating the barns to cure tobacco was changed from cordwood to fuel oil, but with these changes winter wood gathering came to an end. Years later when I saw the painting in the Duc de Berry's <u>Book of Hours</u> that depicted peasants gathering wood in the winter, I not only identified with them, but felt that I had taken part in a way of life that had continued in unbroken succession for centuries.

As a boy became able to perform a task on a regular schedule, he would be assigned a job for which he had a daily responsibility. Chickens had to be fed and watered (and eggs gathered) as did the livestock. Or one might be a "house boy" or "kitchen boy." A periodic seasonal work such as plowing, planting, cultivating, tending, and harvesting was performed between the times set for feeding the livestock. Several boys would be assigned to help clean dung out of the chicken houses, stables, and barns so the burden would not fall only on the shoulders of the "chicken boys" or the "dairy boys" and so forth. Once loaded on the manure spreader (which we called the "s_ _ _ slinger," of course) several boys would attend it to the fields for distribution.

Chicken Houses

There was a period during which I, with another boy named William ('43-'54), but called "Pat," tended the fattening hogs. These hogs did not depend on kitchen scraps and forage for their food. They lived in pens with wooden floors raised above ground level. They were given shelled corn twice daily. Perhaps this compensated for their loss of freedom, loss of a nice mud wallow, loss of acorns and other forage that the unpenned hogs enjoyed, and such other pleasures as they may have enjoyed outside the pens. I am sure they were just as surprised when time came to slaughter them as they had been when the time had come to castrate them. They were slaughtered two by two throughout the morning—two of them being stabbed in the throat at one end of the pen while the remainder huddled in terror and looked on at the other end of the pen. Poor creatures! They made such delicious eating that it is easy to eradicate their terrified squealing almost completely from the mind.

I don't recall how long Pat and I tended to the fattening hogs. At the beginning of our work with the hogs, the fattening hog pen lay at the foot of the principal vegetable garden, just in the edge of the woods. We held this job still after the fattening hog pen had been moved into the woods that lay in a direct line from the basement door of the girls building. Our tasks were the same at either place—shell a quantity of corn at the small barn where the corn was stored in the ear, then carry buckets of shelled corn to the pen and pour it in the troughs. We were called from our sleep at 4:30 a.m. so that we could attend to the morning feeding, clean ourselves up, dress for school, have breakfast, and board the school bus in plenty of time. The afternoon feedings were done as soon as we returned from school and changed into our work clothes. Although the pigs were perfectly agreeable creatures, I cannot say that I took any real pleasure in feeding them. It was a cold business walking to their pen in the winter, especially when the pen lay at the foot of the field that had been the principal vegetable garden, but which was now denuded of all except cabbages and stiff collards. There was nothing here to break the wind which felt very bitter to my naked hands—especially if I had gotten them wet carrying pails of water to the drinking trough. My hands would get so badly chapped that the skin on the back of them cracked. The inside of the hand, especially the mound of the thumb, was sometimes blistered when using it to rub loose the kernels from the cob while shelling pails of corn for the fattening hogs. It was not easy work, but it was well within my ability to perform it.

I don't mean to harp on "ability." I do so because, while my constitution and general health were good, my body was not robust. I lagged behind my playmates in growth and physical strength. This may have been owing to the fact that my sister and I had been born prematurely. We weighed six pounds together and were not expected to survive the day. The few photographs of me as a child show a thin boy with arms like sticks. Not only was I below average weight, but I seemed to gain none. For a long time, the scales reported the same disappointing figures when I was weighed. Surely I wasn't stuck at 42 pounds, but I think I was. For a while I had to report to the kitchen porch late every afternoon and drink a daily supplementary half pint of cream—sort of like the fattening hogs. It was a fruitless effort. Unlike the hogs, I did not gain an ounce. I remark on this as an illustration of the care given the children in the orphanage.

I imagine it was the lack of strength in my upper body that led to my being given work as a hog boy. I had previously worked in the dairy rooms in the girls' building. I could lift a five-gallon can of milk from the refrigeration box with some effort and set it on the room's concrete floor. This was owing to the fact that the cans of milk were essentially weightless while they were nearly submerged in cold water. By giving a smart tug I could hoist one of the cans of milk up to the lip of the box, and then let its weight swing it to the floor. I could not, however, lift a can of milk from the floor and put it into the cooling box. Nor could I lift and carry a full can of milk. The milk rooms were the responsibility of one of the big boys, Charles H____('38-'51), who had had an Achilles tendon, and a foot, very badly cut in a mowing accident. Hay was being mown in the meadow strip, and Charles was walking in advance of the tractor and the mowing blade to remove any rocks that might be in the path of the oncoming blade. The mowing arm was so contrived that the driver of the tractor could raise or lower it at will. By some terrible accident, the mowing arm descended as Charles was walking, all unaware, in front of it. It caught and mangled his foot. I intend to say a little more about Charles in another place.

Have I spoken already of my work as kitchen boy? I had that duty on two separate occasions. I was kitchen boy first under Mrs. Evans, and the second time under Mrs. Mixon. There were some variations in my duties during these two periods. The first time I was primarily concerned with the great cast iron cook stove that stood in the northwest corner of the kitchen. It had at least two large ovens as well as warming ovens. Its top plates were made of cast iron and were rectangular in shape. Some of the rectangles had circular plates cut into them. All of them could be lifted by using a key (or even removed) and left tilted on one side or end to regulate the intensity of the heat coming to it from the firebox. My duties in connection with this huge cook stove, which burned wood as fuel, was to keep its ash drawer clean of ashes, and to keep a supply of firewood on hand. I have spoken already of the annual gathering of firewood and the dumping of a supply of it at the woodpile behind the kitchen.

A large wooden box that held firewood (or stove wood I suppose I should call it) sat conveniently near the stove. My primary duty was to bring stove wood in from the woodpile and put it into the wood box. It required several trips to bring in enough arms full of wood to fill the box heaping full. After the stove was lighted for the day, it required a fair amount of wood to be burnt in order to bring the cooking surface and the ovens to the proper heat. After the stove was good and hot, it took little wood to keep the cast iron plates and ovens at the proper temperature. Then I could fill the box and sit in a cozy place behind the stove and doze, or daydream, or read, or just rest. The kitchen with its busy-ness, voices, and clatter would die away, and I may as well have been in China for all the attention I gave my surroundings. A shake and a gesture toward a dwindling fuel supply would send me off to the woodpile to fetch in more wood. When the supply of cut stove wood began to get dangerously low at the woodpile, I would split more of the cut firewood, or I would saw up some of the lengths of small boughs that were in the pile. Then I'd begin carrying in armful after armful to replenish the wood box. I had learned early to be careful when loading my arms with wood so that it would not slip in my arms and pinch flesh or leave a splinter stuck in one of them.

In the summer when sitting behind the stove would have been unpleasant I frequently helped the kitchen girls prepare vegetables for the poor for canning. It was pleasant to sit and listen to the girls chat as we worked, or to join in their games. This work was done in the large enclosed porch. Here peas were shelled, beans were snapped, fresh corn was cut off the cob, potatoes were peeled, squash were washed and cut up, and so forth. The girls sat with baskets of vegetables at their feet and pails for peelings, pods, shucks, and what have you at their side. Pots and pans for the prepared vegetables sat to hand. The girls knew several games that could be played while sitting and the hands occupied with kitchen tasks. They helped overcome the drudgery of peeling one potato after another until enough had been got ready to feed 70 or 80 people.

One girl might announce, "I'm going to Jerusalem." "What will you take?" another might ask. "My blue nightgown," might be the reply. The second girl would then say, "I'm going to Jerusalem." "What will you take?" would be asked by a third girl. "My blue nightgown and my diamond ring," the second girl might say. Again the statement would be made by a third girl, "I'm going to Jerusalem." "What will you carry?" "My blue nightgown, my diamond ring, and a green piece of satin," might be the answer. And on and on the catalog of objects being carried to Jerusalem would grow longer and longer as the game was carried from girl to girl. The game ended when one of the girls stumbled in her exact repetition of the names of all the objects in order. A similar game of memory and repetition, but this time of bodily motions began, "Grandma Higgins died last night." "How'd she die?" "Just so, just so" (patting the left foot). The second girl would go through the formula and add a new motion, say nodding her head, while carrying on the original left foot patting. And on, and on until everyone was jerking, twitching, and laughing, and the game would break down under the physical impossibility of sustaining so many motions at once.

This game usually got us all in trouble. It was impossible to carry on the game and pay attention to work. It invariably led to wasted vegetables and ended in a rebuke.

A little perquisite went with the kitchen boy's job. He, like the kitchen girls, had to be up and doing long before sunrise, but he could listen to radio music in these early hours—usually gospel music played over radio station WPTF in Raleigh. Better yet, after school was over and everyone went about his work, the kitchen boy could help himself to a cold biscuit and molasses or to a fried meat skin (or "pork rind" as they are commercially called). Few things could be more welcome!

I have spoken of the fact that a few years after the war ended a new dormitory was built on the site of the old farmyard, now demolished and the stock moved to the other farm. Changes had already taken place in the livestock prior to the move. "Tojo" the bull was succeeded by a Brahma bull that became the cynosure of all eyes for a while. The Guernsey and Jersey cows were replaced by great lumbering black and white Holstein cows. They, the Holsteins, were said to give a higher yield of milk per cow than the others. I think, in truth, they did, but their milk had not the richness and taste of the milk given by their predecessors. Electric milkers were obtained, and a new dairy barn and silo to hold green fodder for them were built at the other farm prior to the move. I was never again involved in any way with the cows and their milking. The change affected me in other ways, too. After the removal of the boys into the new dormitory I was made one of the house boys. The house boys kept the toilets and the shower rooms clean, kept the floors clean, and from time to time cleaned the floors on hands and knees with old rags and a solvent solution to remove built up wax and to buff away scuff marks. Every child made his own bed and kept his sleeping area straight, so the houseboys hadn't that to worry about.

The most satisfying, and most tiring, work I was given to do (excepting cotton picking!) was in connection with the principal vegetable garden. This was especially true when the planting was under the direction of the superintendent's mother, an old fashioned country woman who knew what winds were beneficial and those that were injurious to planting. She was called "Granny Evans" by everyone, and she knew what seeds and slips ought to be planted during the dark of the moon, when the moon was full, or during the waxing or waning of the moon. She followed, too, the course of the moon through the heavenly mansions, and knew the beneficent or baleful influence of each zodiacal mansion while the moon was in it. Slips and roots and seedlings were planted by a team of three boys of different sizes. One went ahead and laid out at proper intervals the seedlings or the roots to be planted. Another followed with a lightwood knot peg, or dibble, with which he made a hole in the top of the furrow, inserted the cutting or seedling, and tamped it into place with another deft motion of the peg. It was very tempting to position the peg on top of the root tip of a seedling and push it down with the peg when making the hole. This saved the effort of placing the seedling in the hole by hand, but it might mean, also, destruction of the root tip and loss of the plant. It was a poor trick, and Granny Evans kept her eye peeled for it. The third boy in the team had to be big enough to carry along a specially made watering can. It was a long cylinder ending in a point, one side of the point being made to move at pleasure and release water by working a lever at the top. With the watering cylinder (as I shall call it for lack of its proper name) the point was put down at the newly planted seedling, the lever pulled, and a burst of water released to water the newly planted seedling. Cabbages, collards, tomatoes, Irish potato eyes, and sweet potato slips were planted this way. Seeds of plants that required planting rather than sowing, such as beans, peas, corn, squash, melons, and so forth were similarly planted by teams. One went ahead and pegged a small hole to the right depth, another followed and dropped in the seed, and a third came behind and covered the seed. Okra, which had to be soaked overnight before planting, might have been planted by a single person as were the vegetables that required sowing—radishes, carrots, lettuces, tender green, mustard, kale, and so forth. Once everything had sprouted and began growing, everyone pitched in and wielded hoes to cultivate, and to destroy weeds. Larger boys put up bean poles and strung twine to support the butterbeans and string beans that required support once they began to climb and form their beans. It was a very large garden—more like a field. Here all was quiet, the silence broken only by the cries of killdeers and the red winged black birds.

    Field crops were grown on the other farm, and I am unsure whether the "money crops," cotton and tobacco, were grown by tenants (the orphanage getting a rent) or whether they were raised directly on the orphanage's account. Of the two, cotton was more punishing than tobacco. It was picked by hand, the picker dragging a large bag behind him into which he thrust the cotton as he went up the row, pulling cotton from the open and dried out bolls. I was absolutely worthless at this work. Even with Granny Evans nearby to encourage the lackadaisical, I was no good. "Bow down to that cotton!" she would cry from time to time, directing our attention to the bolls that grew so low on the plant that one had to bend to get it. It was a backbreaking business, and if I ever picked as much as five pounds at a picking, I should be very surprised.

So far as tobacco is concerned, I worked with it only in the course of a single year. Beds were made for the sowing of the seeds in a wooded area near a corn patch that stood on the side of the new road opposite the superintendent's house. I had nothing to do with the making or the sowing of the beds. Tall, slender, straight trees (perhaps the tulip poplar) were felled and trimmed to frame the beds. After the seeds were sown, the bed was covered by a thin muslin cloth, called, for some reason, tobacco canvas. The muslin, or so-called canvas, was secured to the hewn trees that framed the beds, and in order to weed the beds, the muslin had to be rolled back from one side, and then put back into place after the weeding. When the plants were of a size that allowed them to be transplanted, they were taken up and carried to be planted in a field at the other farm. As the plants grew they had to be topped, work I could not do because I could not effectively reach the tops of the plants. Topping caused suckers to appear, and they had to be pinched out and thrown away so that the strength of the plant would go into the production of large handsome leaves of tobacco. It was underneath these leaves, unseeable from the top side, that some busy moth or another laid her eggs. The caterpillar that hatched from them gorged on the tobacco leaves and grew fat and sassy, was a vivid green, and had a horn sticking up from its tail. These creatures had to be picked off by hand and torn in two. There was no point in pulling them off and flinging them down onto the ground. They'd just crawl right back up the plant. There was nothing for it but to harden ones heart and tear the worms apart. Getting in the tobacco crop was a fairly complicated process and required the work of grown men and women, big boys and girls, and middle sized boys and girls. The men and big boys harnessed the mules to tobacco trucks (actually a sledge on wooden runners having uprights at the four corners from which burlap was hung to make sides) and went to crop the ripe leaves from the tobacco in the fields. When a truck was filled it was taken to the tobacco barns and sheds where the other workers waited. They had ready a large stack or bundle of tobacco sticks (cured pine sticks measuring about 3 ½ or 4 feet long and about 1 ½ inches on the four sides). Each woman had a kind of open stand like a towel rack that held a tobacco stick firmly in place on its two uprights, and held a large ball or cone of tobacco twine. The women who worked at these racks were called loopers, and they looped three or so leaves of tobacco at the time to the tobacco stick. When the full trucks of cropped leaves were brought to the workers at the barn, each truck was drawn up between the working stations of two of the loopers. The croppers had laid the leaves in the truck with all the stems pointing together. A hander, who might be a boy of 9 or 10, reached into the truck, took up three or four leave together (depending on the size) and handed them to the looper. The looper stood ready with the end of the twine tied to the tobacco stick and then running through one hand from the ball or cone of twine. The looper took the tobacco from the hander with one hand, whipped a loop around the stems with the other hand, and flopped the leaves alternately on each side of the stick as she filled it. When filled, she tied off the stick, broke the twine, tied it to another stick, and repeated the process. A rhythm was established between the hander and the looper so that the work went on with great precision and rapidity. As sticks were filled with the looped, green tobacco, they were placed on specially made racks in the tobacco shed. At the end of the day, the croppers came in from the field to the barns and hung the sticks of tobacco on tier poles that filled the barns from top to bottom. I think I have already said the barns were constructed of logs chinked with mud. Each barn had a firebox from which a flue extended all around the inside of the barn. Once a barn was filled with tobacco ready to be cured a fire was built in the firebox and kept fed around the clock with wood stacked by the cord and waiting nearby. A thermometer, hung just inside the door for easy consultation, enabled the fire tender to regulate and keep constant the heat in the barn. After the curing process was finished, the barns were opened and allowed to cool so that the tobacco could be removed and taken to a packhouse to be graded.

    My role in this process was that of a hander. It was a very satisfying thing to be part of a quick and smoothly operating looper's work. Certainly it was not skilled work; still to hand tobacco so as to win the approbation of the looper was a matter of pride. The firing of the barn was an enjoyable operation, especially to a small boy who was shown forbearance by the big boys and allowed to stay overnight with them as they fed the fire throughout the night. As night fell they talked and joked among themselves. They roasted sweet potatoes in the glowing coals and ate them as they lounged about the firebox. It was heaven to lie on the ground in the warmth of the fire, a silent spectator and, to some extent, participant. I felt secure and perfectly safe with them nearby, tending the fire in shifts throughout the night. At false dawn I was awakened and sent home. Once, and only once, I was allowed to do a little grading of the cured tobacco, getting it ready for market. Granny Evans showed me how to distinguish and sort out the various grades—from the first grade (the very best leaves) to the fourth (the very worst of tattered and torn leaves). She showed me how to make a bundle by putting together enough leaves that the stems filled the circle formed by touching the tips of the thumb and forefinger, tamping the stems down so that all the ends were even. She showed me how to take a leaf of the same grade and fold it flat over and over so that one was left with a wrapper as long as the leaf and about one inch wide. This was then wrapped around the stems of the bundle, the stem of the wrapper being inserted into the stems of the bundle. Apart from her instructions, there was no conversation. The two of us, alone, sat in the packhouse working silently, the door wide open to the serene morning light. Even now I can feel the coolness of the quiet, early morning and recall the supple texture of the cured leaf as it was handled.

Hog killings also required the cooperative work of men and women, boys and girls. The work had to be done in the cold weather to prevent spoilage of the meat as it was processed. I can't recall whether the full of the moon or the dark of the moon was preferred. A waning moon was avoided since it caused the meat to shrink away to nothing when cooked. The waxing of the moon had an undesirable effect, too, for the meat of animals killed under it would spatter hot grease all over the place when cooked. Eventually, the right day for killing hogs would come around. When it did, I saw why the fattening hog pen, to which Pat and I had carried many a bucket of shelled corn, had been placed where it was—close to a branch of running water. A great quantity of water was necessary to the job at hand, and the clear stream that ran over the rocks and sand furnished an abundant supply. To one side two thick upright posts had been sunk into the earth. They supported a stout beam from which the carcasses of the hogs could be strung. Between this and the pen stood rough work tables to be used for butchering the hogs when they were ready to be cut up. Large cans of scalding water were got ready and stood nearby. The pigs were, I think, curious about all the unwonted activity and the concourse of people who had come to their pen. They were used to seeing only Pat and me and the occasional person who might stop by. A group was a novelty. There is no point in dwelling on the terror of the pigs as they were, two by two, stuck with a knife and killed. They were quickly hung by the feet and bled, then soused with scalding water so that all the hair could be scraped off the body before it set. Old fashioned single-piece jar lids were used to scrape the hair away. The bodies were opened as they hung, and the viscera allowed to tumble out into waiting buckets. Very little of the hog was inedible (though I might not choose to eat it!). So much of the small intestines were saved as were needed to be cleaned and used for sausage casings, or to make chitterlings for those who fancied them. A portion of the large intestine was saved, too, for stuffing as a "Tom Thumb" of sausage. Unwanted offal was fed to the dogs so long as they could wolf it down. The remainder was put into the branch where I am sure the perch, robin, and crayfish had many a delicious meal. I imagine the dogs returned to the site to gulp down anything remaining on the following day, if anything remained for them. The carcasses, now hairless and empty, were moved to the improvised working tables. Here the men cut up the meat as butchers do—hams, shoulders, loins, sides of bacon to be cured as flitches, bellies to be salt-cured as "streak of lean, streak of fat", fat back, and so forth. Tails, snouts, ears, feet, and who knows what, were put aside for the making of souse. Heads were opened and the brains saved for serving in a delicacy of scrambled eggs and brains. Fat was cut away with the skin attached and stacked as slabs in a big tub. This was repeated over and over until the last pair of hogs had been slaughtered and butchered. All the meat to be cured, by smoke or by salt, was carried up to the smokehouse near the kitchen. Here Granny Evans had laid a fire of hickory to which any necessary herbs had been added. She had also made sure that the salt boxes that lined the walls were filled in readiness to receive their various parts of the hog. The hams, shoulders, and bacon were thoroughly rubbed in molasses, pepper, and other preservative spices and hung from hooks set in beams that ran across from one wall to another. Later, when the sausage had been made and stuffed into casings then twisted into link after link, it, too, was hung in the smokehouse. Granny, that wise woman, knew just how much wood, what kind of wood, and what arrangement of wood was required to burn slowly and keep the smokehouse filled with smoke for the period of time required to cure the meat. It was pleasure to be sent into the smokehouse later to help get a ham or a flitch of bacon, or whatever was required—or would have been a pleasure had not the pigs heads, now nearly denuded of meat, sat grinning at you from the salt box into which they had been put. My part in this major operation was in two areas. The first, which was not my favorite, was the cleaning of the small intestines. A smooth stick about two feet long was pushed through them to clear everything out. They went through washing after washing, continually working with the smooth stick. Something, I know not what now, perhaps borax, was added to the waters used for these washings. When the intestines were clean enough to satisfy Granny Evans, they were put aside in an enamel basin. Meanwhile the meats intended for sausage were cut and chopped into small pieces. This, too, was Granny's domain. It was she who measured out and mixed the peppers, herbs, spices, and salt to be used in making the sausage. They were thoroughly worked into the meat under her direction. While this was in progress, the sausage grinder was readied and put in place on the screened-in kitchen porch.

The sausage grinder was in the form of a cast iron cylinder standing perhaps 20 inches high and maybe a foot in diameter. It had an upright post that had been threaded like a male screw rising up the center. The lower part of this post was set with sharp blades. Below the blades there was a round opening leading to a cast iron spout that extended from the bottom of the grinder. An iron lid that fit precisely inside the body of the cylinder had a circular hole at its center that had been threaded like a female screw. One operated the grinder by turning a crank set into gears that caused the central post to turn. As it turned, its knife blades turned with it, mincing the spiced raw meat into a size suitable for sausage. At the same time, it drew the lid irresistibly down into the well of the cylinder, forcing the meat down onto the knives and extruding the minced sausage out of the grinder, through the spout, and into the casing that had been fitted over the spout. At intervals of about 8 inches, the stuffed sausage was given a twist to make a link of sausage. I had a well- developed spatial sense and took my turn at the spout, catching the stuffed casing and twisting it into links of sausage at proper intervals. When an entire length of casing had been stuffed, it was tied off then dropped in a wooden tub. This went on over and over until all the sausage meat had been stuffed into casings. It was then taken and hung in the smokehouse to be cured.

The other part of the work in which I was useful was the trimming of fat to be rendered into lard. The fat was cut into workable widths. It was a simple matter to draw a very sharp knife blade along the inner side of the skin and cut away the fat. The resulting blocks of fat were cut into smaller blocks to assist the rendering process. The clear grease cooked out of the fat was poured into cans to cool as pure white lard. The crumbs of meat at the bottom of the cooking pot were "cracklings" that some people thought tasty. The pared skins were cooked in large pans where they blistered and bubbled. We called these "meatskins," and I and everybody else thought them a great treat. I had done none of the big jobs during the hog killing, but the little jobs I did were valuable ones. I carried a feeling of achievement out of this work. I must have done a good job, too. Now that our hogs had been slaughtered, new jobs had to be found for Pat and me. I don't know what he did, but I started my first stint as a kitchen boy. I don't know to whom I owed this assignment, but I imagine it was Granny Evans. She had seen that I was worthless in the cotton field, but she had observed me grading tobacco, and she had observed me in the sausage and lard making. So I think she asked for me to be sent to the kitchen.

Our Relationships

I have suggested something of the tolerance shown to the little boys by the older boys in my account of the firing of the tobacco barns. Sometimes the relationship between the age groups went beyond mere tolerance, though naturally, the different age groups gravitated to one another. Left to their own devices the little boys played together, fought together, slept together, and ate together in the dining hall. The situation was not unlike that in a large family having brothers of very different ages. Older brothers usually ignore younger brothers though they are willing to take time to teach them things, and will protect them when necessary.

I remember a young boy coming to the orphanage. I don't know his age at the time of the incident I am about to relate, but I think he was in primary school. He had an undescended testicle. He seemed to have no sense of anything being out of the ordinary, but his situation was readily apparent in the shower room. How one of the big boys knew what to do, I cannot imagine. But he did know, and by exerting a downward pressure at the pubes he brought the thing down into the sac where it belonged. The various boys who had gathered in the little boys' bedroom to witness the procedure gave their silent approval of the proceedings. I think, though I may be wrong, that the little boy who was the recipient of these ministrations was not particularly grateful, and just took it for granted. This was an unusual case, but still one indicative of the relationship between big and little boys.

In the opposite direction, I recall that one of the big boys named Sterling S_____('37-'43) had a truly remarkable possession that was not intended to be shared with other boys. It was a collection of metal model cars and trucks in brightly painted colors. The paint was unchipped and looked fresh. He must have safeguarded them ever since he was a little boy. Certainly they predated the war, for until the war was over, it was impossible to find such metal toys. Everyone who knew of this treasure trove knew that these toys were not subject to unauthorized borrowing by any child there. Yet I had the inexpressible joy of playing with them once. Search my memory as I may, I cannot recall having permission directly from Sterling to play with these treasures, or whether his slightly younger brother (also a big boy ['37-'43]), Marvin, interceded on my behalf and arranged for me to have an afternoon's play with them. In any event, there were no repercussions; I didn't even get a cuff.

The introduction of the little boys to the pleasures of the woods was under the tutelage of the older boys. My first excursion into the woods was as one of a group of little boys being taken to the section of woods that lay in a straight line from the basement door of the girls' building. It was primarily to show us the branch of water that ran through it—especially a place in it where the branch pooled to make a little swimming hole. Here we stripped off our clothes and dove in. Thereafter we were free to return on our own if we wished. We were shown other areas, too. At one place there were vines that swung out over a marshy place. Those who knew Tarzan's yell gave it; those who did not imitated the others. There were other places in the woods where there were live wild grape vines that climbed the trees and bore a few sweet thick skinned grapes. I imagine they were wild scuppernongs. At the place where the road to Middlesex intersected this portion of woods, not far beyond the bridge, grew several trees that were eminently suitable for climbing. I must say to their credit that the big boys and the middle sized boys prevented us little ones from attempting to climb them. And a good thing, too. One of the larger boys climbed beyond the point where the branches were strong enough to support his weight. The branch gave way, and down he tumbled from the heights of the trees. He lay ashen faced and unconscious on the ground. The very worst was feared, but after he came to it was discovered he had broken a limb but nothing worse. If the big boys and middle sized boys continued their adventures here, the little boys did not, but were left at home. Like farm boys everywhere our rambles and play was free of adult supervision. But in this instance, the bigger boys learned a lesson and excluded us smaller ones from their more daring sports.

    Some group games, on the other hand, were played on the long stretch of grass and clover in front of the boys' building. They were games in which sides were chosen and one side tried to overcome the other. One game must have been called "Fox on the wall" for they were the opening words to the challenge called out at the beginning of the game when each team was strung out in a straight line opposite the other. The aim was for one of the teams to break through the others line and to get as many team members safely across the line without being tackled as possible. Surely, I do not recall the challenge, which was called out in alternating lines, in its correct words. I think it went thus: (1) "Fox on the wall;" (2) "geese in the gall;" (1) "How many chickens do you have?;" (2) "More than you can carry on your big toe;" (1) "Send them on then." With this, the two sides rushed at one another and scrambled to break through the others line. If only a few boys gathered to play, "Crack the whip" might be played as in Winslow Homer's painting. Sometimes a softball game might be organized near dusk. This was played in the ordinary way, players chosen alternately from the waiting boys. The weaker and unreliable were last chosen. I may as well admit that I was always the very last chosen. I didn't much care for the game on that account, but still I presented myself as one of the players until an open insult made me abandon it altogether. It had come up my time to bat. As I took my position, someone yelled out, "It's George! Everybody move up close to home plate." Of course everybody knew I could not hit the ball far, and it was this that made the insulting words so gratuitous. What made it so hateful, was not that one of the bigger boys called it out, but that it was called out by a grown man on the orphanage staff. The truth is, I can recall being jeered at only once by another boy, and that was a jeer from Pat one day when we were on our way to the fattening hog pen. We had recently been taken to see a movie, an unheard of thing. I think it was Walt Disney's "Song of the South" to which we were taken as probably being a harmless diversion unlikely to corrupt our minds. If it was not this movie, it was one in which a little boy was jeered at in these words: "Little Lord Fauntleroy, wearing a lacy collar." The words were called out in a sneering tone. What got into Pat, I don't know. It was possible that we were quarreling about something. I recall that we were not in the happiest of moods and that he was poking along behind me. Suddenly he began taunting me with the same words and in the same tone that had been used in the movie, "Little Lord Fauntleroy," etc. I turned and flung myself headlong on him. The suddenness and unexpectedness of my attack carried him to the ground, me on top and pinning him down. He was amazed. I was amazed. We were both amazed. He was a compact well-knit little boy who could have beaten the tar out of me in a fist fight. We both shook off our amazement, got up off the ground, and went on to feed the hogs. There were no more jeers, and our friendly relations continued as before. Pat was slightly older than I, had come to the orphanage with more age on him than I had had, and had an older brother in the Army who taught Pat things that the brother thought every little boy should know—some of them, like naughty limericks, Pat passed on to me.

I have got a little off my subject, which was the relationship between the older and younger boys. In speaking of Sterling S___ and his model automobiles I said that I had not been cuffed for having played with them. I did not mean to suggest that Sterling ever struck one of the little boys. I never knew of an instance in which an older boy struck a younger one. Fights, when there were any, were between boys of the same age group. An older boy might interfere in one of those only to be certain that the fighting was fair and that two children did not gang up on a third. I am not allowed to speak the caustic rebuke that was brought on by a ganging up situation (though I found myself hurling it forty years later at two schoolboys in London, a bully and his minion, who had ganged up on a third boy and forced him into an alleyway to beat him)—"two on one is coward's fun!" The rebuke was as effective in London as it had been at Middlesex.

The big boys and the middle sized boys might aggravate the little boys, but not hurt them. One year livestock (perhaps sheep) was turned into the meadow strip and an electrified wire was strung on insulated posts to keep the stock in. Some of us thought it would be a fun thing if we could use the electric fence to make a rooster dance. We caught us a rooster, hooked a wire around one of his legs, and threw the hooked other end of the wire onto the electric fence. I don't know whether the rooster was stupid, or whether he actually felt nothing. Anyway, he did not dance. We boys were left in something of a quandary. The question we were faced with was how to disconnect the rooster from the fence without getting shocked ourselves. A middle sized boy with peculiar ideas about the grounding of electric fences came by and made us disconnect the wire from the fence then release the rooster. He didn't care at all if we got a little shock or two ourselves for our heartless prank. He also obliged two or three of us in a row to seize hold the electric wire simultaneously with both hands. By his theory either only one or none of us would be shocked by the fence. We all were, of course, and the older boy laughed his head off. We were no smarter than the rooster—except we danced and he did not.

I have mentioned Charles H___ who had had his foot very badly injured by the mowing machine in that very same meadow strip. I worked for a while with him, you will recall, in the rooms in the basement of the girls' building where the milk was processed and refrigerated in large metal cases in which water was kept cold by refrigeration coils. My relationship with Charles alternated between patronizing me and tormenting me. I should say that Charles had various skills and that he was something of a youthful entrepreneur. He set up shop in one of the rooms of the ground floor of the girls' building where he cut hair. Or, at least he cut the hair of the little boys. I think the larger boys had acquired sufficient vanity to preclude them trusting their hair to Charles' skill. I don't know it for a fact, but I imagine Charles received some sort of financial remuneration for cutting the little boys' hair. Somehow he acquired a little capital, a few dollars, with which he stocked a small locker with candy and gum. This he sold whenever some gathering or other took place. Charles would open shop in the flower garden, under one of the pecan trees, and sell his wares as opportunities presented themselves. I was much flattered when he, having to leave briefly to answer a call of nature (or for some other sufficient reason), entrusted his wares to me. He might pay me a silver dime (which I quickly gave back to him to pay for a bag of hard lemon drops); once he paid me with a great big Baby Ruth candy bar. I thought I might open my own shop with it, if I could overcome the pride of ownership. For safekeeping I stacked a few bricks around it, like a little vault, in the sheltering roots of a large oak tree. It was discovered almost immediately by those busy, meddlesome fellows, the ants. It was tricky work cleaning them off the candy bar. I might even have eaten one or two along with the candy bar. That put an end to my attempt to emulate Charles.

About the time of the foot injury, or shortly thereafter, I moved from the downstairs of the boys' building where the smallest boys lived to the upstairs where the largest of the little boys, the middle sized boys, and the big boys lived. Lights were out at 9:00, I think, and all were supposed to be sound asleep immediately thereafter. Sometimes Charles, who lived at one end of the building, would send for me, who lived at the opposite end. As a result of the accident with the mower, Charles had lost a little toe, and perhaps the one next to it. He was much troubled by the ghosts of these two toes. Even though there were no toes there, they would continue to be painful or to itch. It was because of this that Charles would send for me. He would bid me to lie at the foot of his bed and rub the shattered part of his foot where the toes had been. If the truth is known, I was glad to be sent for. Not because I enjoyed rubbing his old foot. There was another reason. Charles owned a radio, and though it was past lights out, he kept the radio on at low volume. As I lay there in the dark massaging his foot, I got to hear programs I never should have heard otherwise. There were radio plays produced by the Hallmark Hall of Fame. There were serial shows like "The Squeaking Door" or "The Green Lantern" or "The Shadow". He could have got any of the boys of my age to massage his foot, but it pleased him to patronize me, and it pleased me to be patronized. Perhaps this all came about to make amends for his little bullying ways when I worked with him. The area where the milk was stored, like the containers, had to be kept scoured and clean. At scouring time, when the cement floor was good and wet, and my shoes damp, Charles would require me to go to the refrigerated metallic boxes where the milk was nearly submerged, in five gallon milk cans, in chilled water. Refrigerator coils inside the storage boxes kept the water cold enough to refrigerate the cans of milk. Charles knew very well that if you touched the top of the refrigerator boxes while standing on a wet floor you'd get a shock. As I say, he'd require me to go to the boxes at scouring time and to lay both hands on them palms down. Naturally I'd give a yelp and spring away. Charles would remonstrate with me and order me back to repeat my laying of my hands. He pretended to believe that I was play-acting, and that if I weren't, repetition would harden me against electrical shock. This is such a silly theory that I am left with the belief that he enjoyed compelling me to obey him, and never so much as when it caused me pain to obey. What a rat!

This was an unusual set of circumstances, however. The larger boys had their own interests, activities, and lives to prevent their taking up much free time with the little boys. Those only somewhat older, those in early adolescence, might spend some time with some of the younger boys. An older boy might show younger boys how to make and set rabbit boxes, how to place them in the woods where rabbits were likely to run, how to select places that could be found in the woods in early morning darkness, how to remove a captured rabbit and hold him aloft by his hind legs, how to kill him with a sharp blow to the neck just below the skull—these were things that had to be taught by show and tell from an older to a younger boy. They were good about taking the time to do it, too. Or, after the pond had been dug, boys of mixed ages would go gigging for bullfrogs. The smallest boys were not taken on such night ventures. The danger was too great of a small child falling into the pond on those dark nights. And water moccasins had to be looked out for, too, for the snakes enjoyed a tasty frog as much as boys did. Even so, the little boys were allowed to watch as the frogs were prepared for cooking. Since only the legs were eaten, this was a simple matter of cutting off the hind legs and skinning them, after which they were passed on to a friendly kitchen girl for cooking. The girls said the legs hopped out of the pan when they were being fried. I doubt that story. The cooked legs were brought on a plate to the boy who owned them while he sat at his place in the dining hall. He might or might not share them just as he pleased. I will say, in connection with the hopping claim, that I believe I have seen the cooked legs quiver on the plate. Imagination? Perhaps so, but that didn't stop my eating one of them when offered.

I can remember being afraid of only one or two of the big boys. Whether either would actually have hurt me or not is something of which I am uncertain to this day. There was a very brief period, perhaps only a year or so in the early 1940s when the orphanage had a small flock of sheep. I could have been no more than 6 or 7 at the time, and there was nothing relating to the sheep in which I could be useful. My father, however, had raised sheep in Pamlico County. Naturally I was glad to see these, to watch them as they were run through the creosote dip to kill any insects hiding in their thick wool, and to watch the shearing later. Both were done by the side of the service road that ran behind the boys' building. One of the boys of whom I speak, Billy P('38-'49), threatened to throw me into the dip. I needed no more encouragement to leave the area and find some other entertainment. Billy would also send me on impossible errands. Once he sent me to the shop to find a sky hook. When I asked what that might be he said it was what was used to anchor dirigibles, and he needed one. I ransacked the shop to find a thing that might be a sky hook. Another of the bigger boys found me rummaging there, and when I told him that I was trying to find a sky hook for Billy P., he picked out a cylindrical device with a pump and hose, used for spraying poison, for me to take to Billy. Another boy came by, however, and intervened when he found out what was going on. He made me return the object I had to the shop and forget the "errand" for Billy. So, here was a mixture. Billy was just mean. The other was a prankster, and the third had a kind heart.

One mysterious goodness will forever be a mystery to me. One warm afternoon in the autumn I lay down among the roots of a large oak tree where I was overcome with sleep. It was a deep sleep that I fell into. When I awakened it was near supper time. When I roused myself to go and get ready for supper, two large ripe pears lay where my head had been. The only pear trees were at the other farm, so this meant that they had been brought from there by a big boy. Who he was, and why he had made this anonymous gift to a sleeping child, I have never known. As I sit and write this sixty-five years later, I find my heart growing warm at the memory of this simple act of kindness by one of the big boys to a little boy who, wearied by the day, had lain down to sleep in the protecting roots of the oak tree.

Some memories are not as good. There are two terrible memories that linger. There was a most unfortunate incident caused by a miserable young dog named Rex. To begin with nobody liked the dog's name, and he was shamelessly tormented by the boys who would tie tin cans to his tail and watch him run in terror from the rattling noise that followed close behind him as he fled. He had been born to a young dog who found a litter of pups too early in her life. He subsequently mated with his own mother. Everybody, except Rex apparently, knew that this was an abomination. When that litter of pups was born, they were monsters. One of them had three eyes; all were deformed; all had to be killed. But the killings of the cats were even worse! One of the female cats gave birth to a litter just at the door in the boys' building that led to the dining hall. She had to be prevented from eating her own kittens. I don't think she ate them out of hunger. Anyway, they were saved, but to no purpose. It was declared that there were too many cats and it was ordered that they be killed. I had to help kill them. They were taken to the kitchen woodpile, and I had to hold those kittens to a chopping block while an older boy chopped off their heads with an axe and put their bloody remains in a box. The grown cats were not so easily killed, but they were all mauled to death with this axe before the day was over. The bloody box and its terrible contents were taken to that same section of woods where the carcasses of large animals were dragged and left for buzzards. In the case of the cats, however, a hole was dug and their bodies thrown into it and covered with dirt. On the following day one of the murdered cats appeared at the kitchen door, gashes clearly showing in its mauled head. The poor creature had dug its way out of the grave, had returned home, and now waited to be fed. It evoked terrible feelings of horror, not at all lessened by the fact that the only thing to do was to finish what had been started. I don't know why I was chosen to help the older boy kill the cats. Perhaps this was during the first period when I was a kitchen boy, and when the older boy discovered he needed someone to hold the kittens while he killed them, called on me merely because I was convenient to hand.

Outside Community

This has certainly taken me far afield in my remarks about the relationship between the big boys and the smaller boys. I'd better move to another subject. Perhaps it is worthwhile saying a few things about the relationship between the orphanage children and the general population. Until Memorial Chapel had been sufficiently completed that services could be held in it, the children were bused to a nearby church. One of them was a small rural church named Stony Hill Free Will Baptist Church, to which the children traveled by the orphanage bus. There was nothing pretentious about this church. It was just as plain as its window lights. One could look out onto the graves that lay in the churchyard, some of them with fresh flowers on them. Not a single piece of shrubbery was planted to grace the building. The piano had probably stood once upon a time in somebody's parlor. It was an old instrument with a tinkling sound. It was this sound, I believe, that western movies attempted to recreate in their pianos. The pianist was a red haired woman who played in a determined fashion, and at a tempo that prevented the hymns from being mournfully dragged out by the congregation. There was one hymn that must have been a favorite, for I think it was sung at every service I attended there. It opened with the words, "I have a Savior who's pleading in Glory". It spoke to the character of this church, I believe. My impression was that brotherly love prevailed here, and sincerity of worship. It was a case where public worship of the church sustained the life of the church. I did not know that then, but I came to surmise it later. At the time I am afraid that I went through the motions of worship without entering into the spirit of it. I remember, for instance, gazing at the neck of the farmer who sat upright on the wooden bench in front of me. I was fascinated by the color of the skin of his neck, a red that appeared even redder in contrast to the starched white shirt he wore. The sun had no doubt permanently reddened the skin which was crisscrossed all over with a pattern of lines that formed diamond shapes. I came to understand something of his devotion many years later when I called his image to mind and realized how he had faithfully donned his Sunday clothes week after week on the Lord's Day and had gone, whatever the weather, to worship God with his neighbors.

Sometimes we went to the Baptist Church in Middlesex, a different experience altogether. It was, to my eyes, a larger, prosperous, brick urban church. It had a baptistery at the east end of the church for the immersion of converts. It had tall stained glass windows with Romanesque arches at the top, and a small section at the bottom that could be tipped outward to create some ventilation when wanted. The stained glass images were sharp, clear, and richly colored. I don't remember whose figures were illustrated in the windows but I recall the ornamentation including crowns, crosses, lilies, and similar symbols. I think the last time I went to that church was an Easter Sunday. I must not have given my neck a good washing when I showered that day. A townswoman who set behind me must have studied my neck as intently as I had gazed at the farmer's neck at Stony Hill. For reasons known only to herself, she hopped up from her seat the moment the worship service was over and collared the superintendent, who had driven us to town, himself. I gather she accused him of not taking sufficient care of the children and of bringing them filthy to church. What her motive, what her purpose, what her satisfaction is anybody's guess. I know that when we returned home all the children but myself was cleared out of the bus. I and the superintendent remained.

I had had plenty of whippings before now, but never by a man in anger. This time, the superintendent used his belt with anger behind it. I think he regretted it later. In fact I am sure he did. He pulled me face down across his legs to whip me, and in the course of things I lost control of my bladder and peed all over him. I cannot imagine this happening at Stony Hill. It was only possible at the town church. The funny thing is, I did not blame the superintendent, but I did blame the woman who had so deliberately set him off. I still blame her. I never attended another service at that church.

The episode with the woman at the Middlesex Baptist Church was an unusual one. It was probably the occasion for a new scheme that was introduced by the superintendent. He called it the "buddy system" and spoke of the soldiers in the war as being his inspiration for it. My disgrace was not mentioned by him. If, however, I had given rise to the "buddy system", after all, I could not have been more annoyingly punished. There were two brothers at the orphanage, both of them red-headed. The younger, about my age, was called "Little Red", and his big brother was called "Big Red". When our buddies were announced, he and I paired; "Big Red" thought he had been made the boss of me. How well I remember how he'd come down the broad staircase in the boys' building, glowering around, looking for me to be on the first floor near the stairs, or waiting for him just below the landing on the stairs. "Have you done your chores?" he would ask in a loud, demanding voice. Within a few weeks we were avoiding one another, and our part of the buddy system collapsed in failure. No doubt the whole thing did. It was, after all, an artificial construct owing nothing to buddies as in the army in time of war.

Religious Life

I think I am going to make a digression at this point. My remarks about attending church at Stony Hill and at Middlesex want to make me divert my attention to the subject of the children's religious life at the orphanage. I'll return to my subject of relations in the public sector later.

I have mentioned nothing concerning the distribution of rooms in the girls' building, except for the basement rooms. The second and third floors were given over to the girls' bedrooms and bathrooms. At the end of the hallway that ran the length of the second floor was a large playroom that was built out over the front porch. The playroom was, in fact, a screened in play porch, screens being where spaces were for windows. A trapdoor in the floor to the right opened onto an iron fire escape that stretched upward from the concrete porch floor below. I describe this, though I never saw it. No boys, whatever their age, were permitted to go up the stairs to the girls' living quarters. The ground floor had rooms that were used for different purposes at different times. Some of the rooms had connecting doors so that they could be thrown together into a suite of rooms. These were the rooms that lined the left side of the wide hallway. Two staircases stood at either end of the hall, one landing at the front door and the other landing at the back door. Midway in the hall, under these staircases, stood a tall cabinet or closet, like a china closet or secretary, with wooden doors. It smelt strongly of the tall bottles of dark patent medicines with which it was stocked. I am sure the wood was so permeated that the smell could be eradicated only by fire. On the same side of the hall, through a door set in this same space between the staircases, was a room that served for a while as a bedroom for the little boys. I do not know why we were temporarily moved out of the boys' building and into the girls' building. Probably overcrowding in the boys' building had required finding space elsewhere for several months. Across the hall were rooms, or suites of rooms if necessary, used as living quarters by staff. If a child had a visit from relatives, a most seldom occurrence, a staff member would make their sitting room available for the visit. The room Charles H. used to cut the little boys' hair was a vacant one on that same side of the hall. Since I am about to speak of spiritual matters, I should probably suppress the fact that it was in this room one rainy day that a group of us little boys and little girls got together and player "doctor". This was a perfectly natural thing, of course. I think, though, that we played at it with a vengeance, as young as we were. This may or may not have been the reason that we were moved back to the boys' building to live, but we were. More than that, we were forbidden to return to our old haunts. The sidewalk leading to the new building marked the halfway point between the two dormitories. Mr. Pope who with his wife, was the principal resident staff member, issued an edict forbidding any of the boys from approaching the girls' building any closer than this sidewalk. They who should do so should be stripped and put into a frock. I fell a prey to this heartless ukase at least once, as did Rabbit B___('41-'54), and possibly one or two others. It could be that the sight of Rabbit and me, expelled to a section of the lawn, and unable to escape from it to the boys' building so long as we were dressed in those frocks and unable to resume our overalls, had the designed effect of warning off the other little boys.

The only room I have <u>not</u> mentioned, and the only one I really <u>need</u> to mention at this point, was the room just to the right as one entered the building. It was a good sized room—a double-cube as I recall it. It was used for a multitude of purposes, especially when the children were to be brought together in a setting outside the dining hall in the new building. (I shouldn't be surprised if this double cube room had not served as the dining hall before the new building was built.) This room had a piano in it, and those girls for whom the necessary fees were paid by their supporting Ladies Aid Societies, or relatives (if ever any relatives did pay), were given piano lessons and practiced on it. One of the girls for whom no one was available to pay for piano lessons had a natural ear for music. I shall have to break my rule about not telling a child's surname because my "chemo-brain" very wickedly is withholding this young girls' forename. I shall have to call her Miss Darden ('45-'50), for though the name "Christine" comes to mind, I cannot trust it. All Miss Darden had to do to play a piece on the piano was to hear it played once. What she lacked in correct fingering technique she more than made up for in gusto, enthusiasm, and enjoyment. How she loved throwing off a popular piece called "Down Yonder". This was not only a snappy, catchy melody, but it was flung from one end of the keyboard to the other. It was everybody's favorite (for "everybody" read, all of us small boys). She was prouder of having mastered a showy, formal composition called "Under the Double Eagle." This was probably a dance form of some sort, but I know not what—a Mazurka, a Polka, a gallop—who knows?

On Sundays this room served as a chapel for religious worship if the children were unable to go elsewhere for church, or if a visiting minister happened to be present to conduct services. (After Memorial Chapel was built, this room was wall-papered, painted, and decorated as a kind of drawing room where the big girls could receive boy friends who came calling.)

Occasionally some of the old superannuated ministers would visit for a day or two. I suppose, when they did, that they were accommodated in one of those rooms on the first floor of the girls' building and had their meals at the staff table in the dining hall. I remember visits by Elder Valentine who had many things to recommend him. First of all there was the general fragility of his appearance. He used a stick, but sat upright in his clean, starched clothes. His face had pretty much fallen in on itself, except for his prominent nose and large well-defined eyes—both probably made to appear larger by the ravages of time. He had a gentle speaking voice, and a perfect willingness either to answer a small boy's question or to sit quietly with him. I recall sitting once with Elder Valentine on the steps of the iron fire escape on the front porch of the girls' building in the midst of a thunderstorm, thunderbolts crashing overhead. It was a warm summer afternoon, much as it was said to have been when the two boys in the hayloft door were struck and killed by lightning some years earlier. Someone came, I think, to warn us of the danger of exposing ourselves as we were doing. Those two poor boys at the barn never entered my mind, and their warning was lost. I could not even begin to believe that God would let a bolt of lightning strike Elder Valentine or the fire escape, either, so long as he sat on it. With Elder Valentine confident in God, and I confident in Elder Valentine, we continued to sit and admire the power and wild beauty of the storm. Elder Worley was another of the superannuated ministers who came to visit. He, too, had been ordained in the 1870s or 1880s. Time had not been as kind to his looks as it had with Elder Valentine. Both had shocks of absolutely white hair, and both bore the marks of great age. Elder Worley, however, was afflicted with that ailment that leaves the eyes red rimmed to such an extent that it looked as if the lower lids had been turned inside out. That, and the apparent thinness of porcelain-like skin, made him look too fragile to be pestered by little boys. One felt the thing to do was to be kind and keep a distance.

It was during the war that another preacher and his wife appeared on the scene, The Rev. Mr. and Mrs. Ballard and their son Jerry. Mr. Ballard must have been doing evangelistic or revival work before he hove over the horizon. I imagine the gasoline shortage cramped him. In any event he brought with him a large canvas tent, like a small circus tent, that was pitched beyond the service road leading from the girls' building to the superintendent's house. Whether he meant to hold services in it, or only meant to air it out, I cannot recall. I do remember its sharp, pungent smell after the tent was pitched. I should be surprised if Mr. Ballard did not herd us in, make us sit on the grassy sloping ground, and preach to us. I know that he held worship services and preached to us in the large double-cube room. He seemed to like "go-gett'em" songs that were altogether unlike the songs sung at Stony Hill. Mr. Ballard had an older son, I believe, who was in the Navy, and was strongly influenced by the war. "Coming in on a Wing and a Prayer" and similar songs of recent creation that had snap and muscle and could be belted out with vim and vigor were more characteristic of his style than, "I Have a Savior Who's Pleading in Glory," or "Beneath the Cross of Jesus I Fain Would Take My Stand". Mr. Ballard also had a movie projector, screen, and a cache of filmed animated cartoons about the adventures of a character called "The Little King", the innocence and simplicity of which suggest that he might have been a forerunner of Babar the elephant king. Mr. Ballard's stock of these films was not limitless, so the showings were spaced out. He improved each occasion with a sermonette afterwards or a big brief uplifting story—frequently based on military heroism. During the summer months when there was plenty of light after supper and no school homework to prepare, Mr. Ballard held vespers on sloping ground to the left of the girls' building. We sat at the bottom of this little slope near some hedges while Mr. Ballard stood higher on the sloping ground and addressed us. It is hard to convey the extent of our delight when once we observed old Billy, the goat, appear and begin a slow advance on Mr. Ballard from the rear. He must have found Mr. Ballard an irresistible object, for that is where he exactly aimed. Mr. Ballard stood, as I said, at or near the top of the little slope in the yard. As he spoke to us he leaned slightly forward. We began laughing delightedly as the goat got nearer. Fortunately we did not ruin things by causing Mr. Ballard to turn around and look behind himself. Old Billy gave the softest of bumps to Mr. Ballard's bum; he lost his center of gravity and tumbled forward on his hands and knees, almost in slow motion. It broke up vespers for that evening. As the days grew shorter vespers were given up. We could have moved inside, but it was not the same. As a vesper hymn we sang, "Now the Day is Over, Night is Drawing Nigh". It was far more effective sung out of doors. Besides, the return of the school year and resumption of study hall to get up assigned homework would have made a continuation of vespers impracticable. I found vespers very agreeable, and I think a great number of the children, if not all, did so, too. I am confident that I and my siblings learned to say our prayers at our mother's knee, but disuse made me forget my evening prayer. It was during those months that we little boys were living on the first floor of the girls' building that some of the big girls came to put us to bed at night and taught us that ancient invocation taught to English speaking children everywhere—"Now I lay me down to sleep, I pray thee, Lord, my soul to keep." Vespers were just as comforting, but on a much larger and elaborate scale. My love in later years for Evensong can be traced directly back to vespers at the orphanage.

When, after the war, Memorial Chapel was built on the far side of the elliptical drive, across from the flower garden, in a space between the superintendent's house and the site of the old farmyard, the religious life of the children was put on a more regular footing. A Sunday school was organized, and there was a regular worship service every Sunday morning. Frequently, some of the girls would volunteer to sing a duet, often (perhaps too often) it was, "I Come to the Garden alone, while the Dew is still on the Roses". Occasionally there were flowers in a vase on the communion table—perhaps day lilies from the crossroads. Sometimes there were naughtinesses in the congregation, though I probably shouldn't say so. It was a slight wickedness in some of us boys that made us substitute words in standard hymns. For example, "On a hill far away stood an old rugged cross" became in our mouths, "On a hill far away stood an old Chevrolet" and so forth. The big girls had a more daring amusement during the sermon of leafing through the hymnal and looking for hymn titles they could make indecent by adding the words, "between the sheets". "Nothing between my soul and the Savior" was deemed daringly titillating when converted to "Nothing between, between the sheets". I am almost afraid to tell this for fear that anyone reading it will rush right out, grab a hymnal and start leafing through it. Fortunately the amusement soon palls.

Sometimes there were special services designed to awaken in a child a desire for a spiritual life--in other words, to convert him from his old life of sin into a better and blameless one. To put it another way, to help him to be "born again" as a Christian. It is funny that I have no recollection at all of having gone forward to the communion table to signify my conversion, but I must have done so. I do, on the other hand, remember my baptism. Arrangements were made to use Tippett's Millpond to baptize those who were candidates for this ordinance. (Free Will Baptists have no sacraments—only ordinances). I knew nothing about the arrangements and was at work putting soda to corn when someone came to fetch me. I was a little sorry to leave for I had just discovered some ripe fox grapes at the edge of the field. There was nothing for it, however, but to return with the messenger, get some spare clothes, and join the boys and girls who were to be conveyed to the millpond. As everybody knows,

Baptists are opposed to infant baptism, and hold as one of their principal doctrines a conviction that no one below the age of understanding could be effectively baptized. As I recall, 12 is the age of understanding, and 14 the age of discretion. Whatever our ages that day, I think we had no business being baptized. Since we were all to wade out into the millpond to the waiting preacher who would immerse us while repeating the sacred formula, we changed into old clothes that could not be injured by the mill water. That was the purpose of the extra clothes. We boys changed downstairs in the mill where, if someone entered from the outside at the wrong time and our nakedness was exposed, it would not much signify. The girls climbed up to the second floor to change. The floorboards in the mill were old pine boards an inch and a half thick and eight inches wide (or thereabout). They were straight sided boards, not tongue and groove, and no care had been taken to lay them tight to one another when put in. Consequently there were sizeable cracks running the length of the floor between the boards. The devil was present and flew into our heads. We tried to sneak about quietly in search of a vantage point where we could look upward through the cracks and see the girls' legs up their skirts. Our excitement caused our misdeeds to be discovered. An end was put to our carryings-on, and an adult put with us to make sure we behaved ourselves.

The girls were baptized first. They formed a line into the water, linking hands to make a chain, and waded out to water that was nearly chest high—certainly well above the waist. One by one the minister drew them to him. Then placing one hand in the center of the upper back, and the other cupped over the mouth and pinching the nostrils, he repeated the ancient, sacred formula as he lowered her into and under the water then raised her again. The rite was performed over and over, the baptized girl returning to the shallow water while the next girl moved out to the preacher. All the girls returned to the millhouse to dry themselves and change into dry clothes. They were perfectly safe from the prying eyes of the boys who were by now moving out to the preacher one after another. The day was marred by only one more gaffe. Rabbit B. was, astoundingly, one of the candidates for baptism. I am sure a mistake was made and that Rabbit had no more intention of being baptized than anything. I think he was under the misapprehension that we were taken to Tippett's Mill to go swimming. That is what he did. He was enjoying himself famously when an adult put an end to his sport. Still, "of such is the kingdom of

Heaven", as Jesus himself said. And further than that, who of us knows that Rabbit was not touched with a chrism other than water that day at Tippett's Mill? I should not care to deny the possibility.

I don't know whether the baptism did something for me or not. There was a period when I was drawn to religious things, perhaps too strongly drawn to them. The staff and the other boys very healthily ignored it, so it never got out of hand. It was only an aspect of my spiritual life, and eventually faded away. I must say one more thing before leaving this subject. I have heard accounts of people falling under a strong conviction of their sinful way of life and the likelihood of it taking them to perdition if the grace of God did not intervene. Old church histories and biographical sketches written by the Primitive Baptists are full of examples. I have never personally known of but a single example of it, however. This was a middle size boy, very nearly a big boy, named Charles P. I don't know why Charles told his troubles to me. I think it was because he was under such a burden of spiritual unhappiness that he looked for a sympathetic ear where he could find it. Or he sensed a kindred soul in me. There were deep wellsprings of goodness in Charles that even a child like I was could see. The love of God was on him like a mantle, yet he could not sense it. We lay in the grass near the new building and talked one time, and never again. It was an unusual thing for such a gap in ages as separated us to have a bridge thrown over it so that a confidential conversation could be had. I don't know for how long a period it was that Charles wrestled with his problem before realizing that he was, even then, held safely in the hand of God. As I say, we never had another conversation.

While on the subject of religion I must speak of one other figure, and that is the Rev. Moses L. Cummings. In doing so I may say more about myself than about him. I don't know the full story of Mr. Cummings, and what I do know may not be strictly true. When I knew him he must have been about 70 years old, or a little beyond that, and had a shock of thick gray hair. He was a compact, well-knit man, slightly below the average height, and tending to fleshiness. There was a serenity to his features often seen in elderly Sicilian men. His complexion and his luxuriant head of hair suggested why he had been called "Blackie" in his early life. He was always soberly dressed in a black suit rusty with age, a black hat, and a black bow tie. Mr. Cummings wrote an autobiographical pamphlet about "Blackie of the North Woods" that he entitled, "Avenues Leading to

Crime" and published it in Raleigh in 1922. He had it reprinted at Raleigh in 1947, shortly before I met him. It has been more than sixty years since I read his pamphlet, so naturally many details of what I read are now beyond recall. The sense of what I do remember is that Mr. Cummings was born in Canada, perhaps in British Columbia. His parents dying young, he was wild as a teenager and much given to drink. In fact, he became a common drunkard and a thief. As he said, he chose avenues that led to crime. He had been imprisoned at least once while in early manhood. Drink made him abandon his wife and little children. He continued the downward course of his life until he fell into the hands of the Salvation Army. It was a turning point in his life. The "Army" rescued him in every sense of the word. His life was so altered that he gave up drinking and took to preaching.

He made for himself a sizeable wooden case in which he carried objects that served as visual aids in his preaching. This case opened 180 degrees to form a small wooden platform on which he stood to preach. At the front of the platform, he inserted a "T" shaped contrivance. From one arm of the "T" he dangled a prisoner's chain and shackles, and on the other worn prison garb made of a rough cloth bearing alternating broad black and white stripes. Sometimes he donned the prison clothing while preaching or, alternately, put it up to view. His style of preaching was nearly that of a harangue. The few times I heard him preach, he said pretty much the same thing each time. He would begin by talking about his own life, punctuating his remarks with the prison garb and the shackles. He made his performance vivid by imitating a drunkard. It was a lifelike, if theatrical, imitation. The wonder is that he did not topple off his small platform in the midst of his simulated staggers. After appealing to his hearers to turn from sin and repent, he would invite them to give their life to Jesus.

I do not know how Mr. Cummings came to land at the orphanage, or under what terms he took up residence, or semi-residence, there. He was a considerable age, but nowhere near the age and decrepitude of Elder Valentine or Elder Worley. He must have been properly ordained, but I have doubts that he was ordained as a Free Will Baptist minister. I could not visualize him pastoring a church, but thought it probable, instead, that he was some sort of traveling preacher who went from town to town. He had a small coupe automobile. It looked as if he might sometimes live in it. I think Mr. Cummings was only a very nearly worn out preacher with little money and little hope of raising a regular income sufficient to support him in security. Whatever his life had been, it was blameless now. He presented no threat to the boys and girls he had come among. There were times when he would pack everything up, put it into his coupe and drive off to Middlesex. There he could turn left onto highway 264 and go to Wilson, or Greenville, or Washington. Or he could turn right and head off for Raleigh, a place one assumes he knew well. One supposes he might have set up his little platform in these or other towns where he might attract an audience, and put his little round basket at the front of his platform for the convenience of any who wished to make a small monetary offering. These, however, are nothing more than present day suppositions. Nothing of the kind entered my childish mind. I could see only that there were unexplained comings and goings of Mr. Cummings.

I was witness to a brief contretemps that shed no light on the status of the Rev. Mr. Cummings. He wrongly took advantage of an unusual crowd at the orphanage that appeared to offer him the opportunity of a large audience in the flower garden. It might have been on Thanksgiving Day when the temporary table had been put up, and visitors from many churches had come bringing boxes of delicious food to make a Thanksgiving feast for the children. The great crowd of adults was very unlike the handful of children who ordinarily might sidle up to Mr. Cummings to watch and hear him preach. He became like the old war horse who hears the trumpet from afar and flares his nostrils, pricks his ears, and paws the earth with a forefoot. Mr. Cummings got out his box and put up his preaching stand in its usual place under a pecan tree on the edge of the flower garden. There wasn't much of a stir when he flung out his opening words. A few people, I think, rudely laughed at his antics as he reeled about on his platform portraying the sad state of a drunkard. One or two of the women, who came over to investigate the goings-on, returned to their groups and reported that he was drunk. Word of these events was carried to the superintendent, busy in his office in the new building. He promptly sent words to Mr. Cummings that caused him, much mortified, to pack up his paraphernalia, put it into his coupe, and drive away with knit brows. He returned some days later. Some of the girls took Mr. Cummings' side, and thought he had been shabbily treated. My sympathy, I am afraid, lay with the women who had been alarmed, and with the superintendent. I don't know whether Mr. Cummings had placed a collection basket on the edge of his preaching platform, or not, but I thought he had presumed upon the day and the occasion. Was I heartless, I wonder? Or just a prig?

I lacked sufficient experience to realize that in Mr. Cummings I was witness to a genuine American genre. Years later, I encountered other examples (but of a different quality). Sometimes at Durham I would see an African-American woman who was a street preacher, dressed in white satin robes and a purple headdress. There was a man, too, frequently on the street, though he preached no sustained sermon. He walked up and down the streets full of lamentation, and crying in a loud voice, as he bowed up and down from the waist while he walked, "I tell you some of the women advertising these products, look like <u>heathen</u> women!" A man, more in Mr. Cummings' style, used to take his stand outside the Wake County courthouse in Raleigh when people were having their lunches in the open air and preach a short sermon that warned of coming evils and the need to repent. On Mr. Cummings account, it must be allowed that he thought he might, by the example of his life, be of genuine service to some of the children by warning them that our actions and our choices have effects capable of following us through life with evil consequences. No doubt he deserves to be presented in a more sympathetic light than I have presented him, but I am unable to pretend to a sympathy I did not feel.

In reflecting back on these days I wonder how many children gave up churchgoing altogether after they left the orphanage. Adolescence is a period in a child's life when resentments multiply and are thrown out in all directions and at any object-parents, teachers, school, church, government, or whatever stands as an authority figure with power to say "Thou shalt not." I should be amazed to hear that no child who was brought up at home with churchgoing parents ever made the same claim. These claims are, I think, put forward by young men and women who brought adolescent resentments forward into their adult life, rather than casting them off.

To be perfectly honest, however, it must be admitted that Memorial Chapel was an atypical church. It was almost an artificial life form. This becomes clear when Memorial Chapel is compared with Stony Hill—or nearly any other church. The other churches are living organisms that have an impact on the life of their community as well as on the lives of families that make up the congregation. In them their young people are married. In their churchyard their dead are buried. "The church visible and invisible." Their members band together to perform good works and to achieve common goals. They join their spirits to celebrate the sacred festivals of Easter and Christmas. From this viewpoint it would be surprising if any child carried with him from the orphanage an affection for Memorial Chapel. But the lack of affection for the orphanage church in no way supports a claim of having had religion forced upon a child.

Off Campus Activities

I had set out to write a few remarks about the relationship between the children at the orphanage and the large outside world before I ran off into a long digression on the subject of religion. It is possible that up to now I have given the impression that the orphanage was an enclosed world, separate unto itself, having nearly no contact with the outside. If I have, I ought to correct that impression. I will admit that during my very earliest years there, before beginning to go to school, my impression was almost exactly that. I had photographic images of my former home in my head, one of which included a scene of Vandermere, so I know that <u>those</u> places existed. I knew of no other places, however. When, eventually, I was taken on a trip away from the orphanage and passed through some communities and small towns, I found it difficult to believe in their objective reality. I supposed it more likely that "they" had arranged the scenes through which we passed by dismantling the town or community after we had passed through it, then reassembling it on the road up ahead to be passed through again and again. Many years later when I read about the villages in Russia that Prince Potemkin built in the wilderness then exhibited to the Empress Catherine in a tour of them that he had arranged for the imperial court, I was entirely sympathetic to the reaction of his enemies at court. They put out the story that the villages were unreal, being nothing more than false front buildings that the prince caused to be taken down after the court passed through, then erected again further up the road.

This state of mind was short-lived. I don't know whether attendance of the public school was primarily responsible for strengthening my notions of objective reality, or not. I am sure it helped. As I got older I enjoyed various occasions for participating in the world beyond our buildings and woods.

Very seldom there were excursions to the beach at the coast, or to the State Fair in Raleigh. Special arrangements had to be made for these, and money found for the children to spend. In the case of the State Fair, I imagine complimentary tickets were sent to the superintendent by the managers of the fair. I rather doubt that complimentary tickets for rides were sent, too—but they may have been. However it was managed, off we would go for an exciting afternoon, transported to the world of the fair with tickets of admission in our hands and some spending silver in our pockets. Some of my money went for a ride on the merry-go-round and on the Ferris wheel, a glimpse of a two-headed pig, and a magic show. To tell the truth, I'm not absolutely sure that I actually paid to see the magic show. I think it likely that the barker took one look at me standing at his feet and staring with all my eyes and just waved me into the tent. Here was excitement, indeed. Upon reflection I think the show was probably unfit for the eyes of children—or at least not all parts of the show. The tricks whereby the "magician" created the illusion of having sawn a woman in half, or stuck one full of daggers as one lay supine in a box, were not in the least impressive. When he caused a woman to float, and one could not figure out how he had done it, he raised my level of interest. I think that by this time I had achieved the status of a middle size boy, but that did not prepare me for the trick that was his great finale. The magician's equipment for this trick was an empty armchair, across the arms of which he had placed a sword, and to the side of the stage an upright guillotine. The woman who assisted him in his tricks put her head and her hands into a sort of stocks under the knife. She shook her hands as if she were full of fear—though she smiled at the audience, I think. He caused the knife to fall, and then appeared to remove her head, carry it to the armchair, and balance it on the sword. The eyes opened, the lips smiled. It was ghastly, and no scene for the eyes of a boy—even a middle size boy. Had I not slipped away and got into this show on my own, I should never have been allowed to see it. Except for "Song of the South" and "The Little King" we were not allowed to go to movies on the grounds of their probable bad influence. Looking at the "funnies" in the newspaper was frowned on, and comic books were out of the question altogether as corrupters of the mind. I recall once a magazine distributor made a gift of bundles of comic books that were unsold and were scheduled for destruction. The distributor meant well, but his stacks of funny books were brought up the service road and unloaded at the furnace room of the boys' building. The big boy in charge of the furnace had orders to destroy them bit by bit by feeding them into the furnace, and to prevent any of us boys from reading them. This order was more honored in the breach than in the performance. I certainly looked at as many as I could. Some of them were perfectly innocent—"Little Lulu", "Archie", and others of that ilk. Some were highly concentrated, illustrated versions of famous works of fiction—"The Cloister and the Hearth", "The Black Tulip", "The Three Musketeers", and so forth. Others opened worlds of fantasy and imagination—"Aqua Man", "Wonder Woman", "Superman", and all their fellow heroes. But one category was made up of lurid tales of murder, mayhem, and the walking dead. I don't know whether the superintendent condemned them all on account of this last category, or whether all were condemned on principle. I could not be kept away from them, no matter what, so long as even a shred of one remained. In retrospect I do not know whether the superintendent's comprehensive wholesale destruction of the comic books was warranted or not. Probably it was. It is very clear from my having been drawn into the magic show at the fair, and my compelling, irresistible urge to read any and all of the forbidden comic books, that I needed to be protected from myself and guarded against such unhealthy urges. These are my thoughts in retrospect and in no way reflect my thoughts at the time. Too, I should not leave the impression that all magazines were prohibited. There were never a great number of them lying about, but there were some.

Again I have wandered from my topic. Unfortunately the eidetic construction of my memory moves me, not chronologically or systematically, but from image to image. I hope this will not make nonsense of what I wish to say.

Occasional trips to the little town of Middlesex, two miles away, broadened ones experience. The drug store was a principal feature of the town, but my eye was caught by a small general merchandise store owned by, I believe, a Mr. Holland. When a larger grocery store came to town (no doubt one of a chain of stores), it must have cut deeply into his trade. He sold, however, some dry goods and notions and other wares that the big store did not offer. When one came to town, one encountered African-American families who had come to town to shop. My first experience of them was a revelation. I knew that there were black people in the world I inhabited, but for some reason, my mind had not taken in the fact that there was a sizeable number of families. An African-American midwife had delivered my brother. In the last clothes-washing in our backyard that I remember, my mother had to have assistance with this heavy work. She was assisted by a black woman who brought her little boy with her. As our mothers worked together, we played together. There was probably more than a single instance of this. So I knew very well from my earliest years that there were some black people. Years later when I started going to school, our school bus daily passed a school bus full of black children headed in the opposite direction. It was considered great fun for some of the bigger boys to yell out, "N_____, N_____, black as tar, stick your head in a molasses jar!" At the same time, the black bus erupted with cries of, "Soda crackers!" while some of the more daring little girls turned their rears toward the window, pulled up their frocks and mooned us. I don't know how it was determined which side won this daily yelling match. On a more positive side, the children of the orphanage were all familiar with the black man called "World's Troubles." But it was another thing altogether to encounter black families on the streets of Middlesex. Although I knew that "World's Troubles" lived in his small house with his wife, a passel of daughters, and grandchildren, I did not make the connection between him and his family with all those black pupils whose bus passed us daily. It did not occur to me that they, too, had mother and father and brothers and sisters and lived together as families in their respective houses. Consequently, the scenes on the streets of Middlesex opened my eyes to the fact that black children were like white children in that respect. This was an important discovery to me, and one I would not have made in the enclosed world of the orphanage. Another discovery I made on the streets of Middlesex, as I wandered around taking everything in, was negative in character. I have spoken already of the belittling taunts and rhymes the white school children and the black school children threw at one another from their respective passing busses. I think there was no real spirit of hatred behind these jeers and taunts on the part of either side. There was a belittling spirit, yes—but a spirit of hatred, no. I cannot recall what, if anything overt, that I saw on the streets of Middlesex that made plain the fact that a current of racial dislike eddied along the streets of the little town. It was there, however, and I felt it. I believe I am free of making a false claim when I say that within the confines of the orphanage, the children were not exposed to racial hatred or taught it by word or deed. This was at a time when there was still an organized Ku Klux Klan in the vicinity of Middlesex. I remember one of the boys in early grammar school revealing the secret, never to be repeated, that his father had a sheet outfit and was a Klan leader. The orphanage did nothing to interfere with the Klan and its teachings, but it at least insulated the children from it.

The chief point of contact between the world of the orphanage and the world outside it was the public school at Middlesex. In fact, in classroom and on playground, there was no distinction between the two worlds. Or perhaps, school and schoolyard constituted a third world that was called into existence for nine months of the year, having seasonal observances of its own.

The opening of the school year was marked by the disappointing necessity of donning shoes again after the barefoot freedom of summer, and the closing of the school year heralded the approach of the barefoot season. In between, lay holidays and the remnants of former holy days. The first of these was Halloween. In that rural community, this festival was not marked by children going from door to door with their demand of "trick or treat." Instead, it was a community event celebrated in the large auditorium-basketball court around which all the classrooms, both primary and grammar school, were arranged. (The high school had its own building, and it had no auditorium.) There were various booths, one of which was a fortune teller's booth, and the "haunted house" was called "the house of blue lights."

Nearly everyone came wearing homemade costumes, a very great many of them made of sheets to represent ghosts. Even though many of the details now evade me, I still remember the immense spirit of fun and excitement whipped up by the evening. Nothing else equaled it. The truly big holidays of Thanksgiving and Christmas were so much an individual family celebration, that little attention was paid to Thanksgiving at school, and Christmas was marked only by a special school program or concert. Thanksgiving was, I think, noticed only in the primary school where the students either tried to draw a gobbler or colored one already lithographed in outline onto a piece of paper measuring approximately 9x12 inches. It was clear that the children had no notion of the appearance of a real turkey. They were, all of them, either colored altogether in a drab brown or were given brown bodies with a spread tail colored like the rainbow – each feather in the tail being a different color. It was much the same at Christmas, except that drawings of Santas, Christmas trees, and fireplaces hung with stockings replaced those crude Thanksgiving turkeys. I say it was much the same, but I mean to say that it was much the same in the primary school. Because of its high sacred character, the school also mounted a special Christmas program or concert that involved both the primary and the grammar schools. This might be little more than traditional Christmas songs sung to a sort of pantomime. For example, "We Three Kings of Orient Are" might be sung while three pupils garbed as the magi slowly crossed the stage diagonally at a very slow pace while a large five-pointed star covered with silver paper and attached to a stout cord drawn through pulleys was made to traverse the upper region of the stage in advance of them. Or, "Silent Night" was sung to a manger scene near which stood, not stable animals, shepherds, and magi, but small students in their pajamas holding candles. Shortly after the new school auditorium was built, the school presented an ambitious Christmas concert. I think it must have been Christmas 1951. The highlight of the evening was the singing of the "Hallelujah Chorus" from Messiah. From someone, probably one of the big boys (by this time I was a middle-sized boy), I got a necktie to wear for the occasion. It was a very broad bottomed tie full of reds and blues and silvery grays. Perhaps it had a great trumpeting lily pictured on it. I have no doubt that this astounding tie was perfect for the bumpkin I was. Anyway, I thought it was perfect and kept casting my eyes down on it even while we were on stage singing. We had rehearsed the "chorus" in segments, never all together. Now, as we sang with all the voices in concert, I heard Handel's music for the first time. It took the top right off my head. My tie paled into nothingness. I stood rapt, my mouth agape. We could not possibly have sounded as well as I thought we sounded. Yet, I think perhaps we did. The genius and glorious beauty of the music lifted us all out of our ordinary selves and beyond our usual experiences.

In the primary school Easter was marked by the dying of eggs, and St. Valentine's Day was marked by the giving and receiving of Valentines. Had we not been introduced to this custom in school, I doubt that the children in the orphanage, left to their own devices, would have learned of it on their own. School also introduced us to some aspects of culture of much greater significance than the Valentine tradition. One of the educators, Mr. Fifer, on the staff of the State Superintendent of Public Instruction in Raleigh had a strong interest in the arts. Thanks to him the wall space between ceiling and blackboard was hung with colored reproductions of famous paintings: "The Blue Boy", "Pinkie", "Angelus", "The Man with a Hoe", "Feeding her Chicks", and so forth. It might have been the same man, or at least his office, who arranged for traveling cultural performances to come to Middlesex or a nearby city. The Grassroots Opera Company came and mounted a performance in English, of "La Traviata", and once we were bused to a baseball stadium in a nearby larger town to join pupils from other schools for a concert of music by the North Carolina Symphony. It was an overcast day with the threat of a slight sprinkle of rain, so the woodwinds did not make their appearance in the orchestra. I regret to admit that neither the opera nor the orchestra had the desired effect on me. Except for works by Mozart and Gluck, I never developed a taste for opera. Some years later, after I had left the orphanage, I would tune in to the "Texaco Opera Hour" on WPTF and dutifully listen in the hope that I might develop a taste for this art form. It was always a relief to me when my sister would demand that I "turn off those screaming mules!" The one traveling performance that came to the public school at Middlesex and made a great impression was of far less cultural standing than opera or symphony. It was a marionette show. The marionettes were made to enact "The King of the Golden River". I was bowled over. I built myself a little theatre from an old crate and made paper marionettes. I tried for a week to make them work so that I could put on my own performance of that thrilling story. After sadly admitting to myself that I could not bring it off I gave the project up.

It is likely that other group activities at school had greater developmental benefit of bringing children at the orphanage into non-academic contact with the other students. Although there were occasioned baseball games played on the weekend to which the children at the orphanage were transported, the ball game of choice was basketball. Some of the big boys were on the teams. Others of us were mere spectators. On one occasion I sat in the gallery above the end of the court farthermost from the auditorium stage and kept score on the scoreboard. Since I was worth nothing in sports, I got a lot of satisfaction from this.

I recall that when I was in the eighth grade I was the despair of the coach, who was also my homeroom teacher. He was unable to resist tossing a snide remark or two in my direction from time to time. Poor fellow! I am sure Coach A. had rather have had a mouse running around his basketball court than me. There was no point, none whatever, in his expecting me to throw a basketball up to the goal and make it go through the hoop. My life, and Mr. A's life, would have been easier if he could have just accepted that fact. It must have surpassed his powers of belief. Many more like me might have proved fatal to him. As it was, no permanent damage was done. Mr. A. lived to coach another year, and I left Middlesex. No other school coach was ever foolish enough to think I could do anything for him. So, we all lived happily ever afterward.

I cannot resist saying at this point that ten years later when I was in the U.S. Army and was undergoing basic training at Fort Jackson, the training officers held pragmatic views similar to those current at the orphanage: no task to be assigned that exceeded physical capacity. Although I could do the pre-dawn 40 foot crawl with the best of them, swing myself along on the overhead bars for long periods, and stand alone with the training officer at the end of a one-mile run with backpack and rifle (everyone else having fallen by the way), weakness of the arms interfered with some of my basic training. Accommodations were made. So that the chow line could move into the mess hall without hitting a snag while waiting for me to accomplish the mandatory pre-breakfast chin-ups, each of my chin-ups counted as three. I accomplished familiarization (or qualification) with all small arms but one: M-1 rifle, bayonet, pistol, carbine, bazooka, Browning automatic rifle, machine gun. I was made to stand aside during training with the hand grenade. There was some apprehension that I'd never remove the pin and throw the grenade over the stockade and to a safe distance before it exploded and injured the training officer and myself. No issue was made of it. We just went on to the next thing. I should like to add, too, that upon completion of my military service I was awarded the Army Commendation Medal. So there, Mr. A!

There were organizations where orphanage, school, and community came together. I think particularly of the Future Farmers of America, Future Homemakers of America, and the Boy Scouts of America. I was briefly connected with the latter only. Some of the boys were more faithful and more deeply involved than I. Some even attended the State Jamboree. I never did. In fact I attended but few of the meetings held in the evening in an empty store in Middlesex. I think I have told of my passing my knot tying qualification examination by tying the requisite knots in sweet potato roots when digging them in the field. While unorthodox, this accomplishment allowed me to camp out with the other scouts at Lake Charles. This small piece of water and campsite was situated at the end of a dirt road off the highway leading to Bailey and Wilson. One turned right at a small white church with large panes of colored glass in its windows. My treacherous memory will not let its name come forward.

A small number of us boys, some from the orphanage, some from town, and some from the environs of Middlesex piled into a truck with our bed roll, two eggs, and raw bacon and arrived at Lake Charles after dusk. After pitching our tents near the water we roasted hot dogs over an open fire. We were in our sleeping rolls and asleep soon after eating. We awakened with first light, built up our fires and cooked our breakfast of bacon and eggs. The scout master must have provided bread, water, and drinking cups. If I have ever had another breakfast as delicious and as satisfying as the one at Lake Charles, I do not know when or where it was. I had many a night and breakfast in the field while I was in Germany with the Army, but they were not a patch on my camping out with the scouts at Lake Charles. That was a high point in my young life.

School also allowed the boys and girls from the orphanage to enlarge the circle of their friends and to broaden the base for it. This was especially true with the boys who were on athletic teams. But children who were not athletes struck up friendships at school, too, and might be invited home for an after-school visit and supper with a friend's family. I recall once, while in primary school, there was a little boy in my class whom I greatly admired. He was my ideal of a schoolboy. He lived in town. I do not know what his parents did for a living, but I think they must have been fairly prosperous. This little boy, named Thomas Brooks, always looked as if he had had a dozen baths. Whatever the color of his pants, it complemented the colors used to print the fabric from which his shirt was made. It was all very subtle and understated—nothing flashy about him—and the colors of any stripes in his shirt were rich. They reminded me of the colors in some of the agates that the boys had for shooting marbles. His skin, his eyes, his hair, the roundness of his arms—I think I envied them all. I certainly admired them. You can imagine what a wonderful surprise it was to me to be invited to his birthday party. Not that I knew what such a thing was, never having heard of a birthday, let alone a party in honor of one. Somebody explained the nature of these occasions and told me that it was the custom to take along a little gift. The son of the superintendent, a buddy of mine, helped me scrape up a present—a little defective, admittedly, but, still a present. My only recollection of the party is of a room full of children dressed in their Sunday clothes, some games of which I was a little shy, the birthday cake, and the feeling that Thomas Brooks had honored me just by inviting me to come.

    A more boisterous good time was had at the home of another friend, a country boy named Johnnie S___. There was just a trace of academic rivalry between us. However, as arithmetic rolled along its inevitable course to long division, fractions, and decimal points, I could see that his quick mind "got" arithmetic. He actually enjoyed the business. It did not come easily to me. There was no further rivalry in that area. I conceded the field to him. One year after school took in, at the time grapes were ripening, Johnnie invited me to go home with him after school and eat supper with his family. While his mother got supper, Johnnie and I went out to play. If he had chores to do first, we got them out of the way. The paved country road ran near the house yard, and by it grew a tall tree that overhung the road. A scuppernong grape vine had grown up this tree, supporting itself on the branches as it grew upward to the light. If it is shameful to admit to greed, then I may as well expose my shame and get it over with. I have always been, and to this day am, greedy for grapes—fox grapes; black James grapes, golden scuppernong grapes. No praise of them is sufficient so I shan't pause to praise them. When Johnnie told me of their vine that had gone up into the tree and invited me to help myself to them, I accepted and shot up the tree like a squirrel, close behind him as he led the way. Up and up we climbed, eating as we went. We would pause briefly, lying on our backs on branches barely sufficient to bear our weight, as we reached above to pull grapes from an overhanging vine. The truth is we were vying with one another, our every climb to a higher, more dangerous branch, an unspoken dare conveyed in that silent manner so well understood by little boys. We both knew that if our agility failed us, if we lost our grasp, we would be dashed to our death on the paved road below. Some angel must have preserved us from our folly. If not, we certainly were by Mrs. S. coming to the back door and calling us in to supper. We clambered down and went to our supper. A very good one it was, too. It is one of the qualities of scuppernong grapes that a stomach full of them does not impair the appetite. In after years when grapes ripen my mind reverts to this adventure, and I am thankful all over again that Johnnie and I were preserved from our own folly.

    Shortly before leaving the orphanage I was invited to spend Sunday afternoon and evening in the home of a fellow student, Don Stone. I may as well say from the start what his surname was, for the minute I say anything about his family they will be recognized. His father, Jim Stone, had a very successful sawmill at Bailey, and he seems to have prospered as a farmer, too. He needed to. At the time I knew them there were, I think, nineteen children whose ages ran from early infancy to early adulthood. I think there were two or three sets of twins among them. They lived in a large, handsome, two story house with a great big kitchen. The then Mrs. Stone was the third, two previous wives having died. All pitched in and helped run the house and get the meals. They joked about their similarity to the orphanage and said that I ought to feel right at home—which I more or less did. The Stone children went to a school that had only primary and grammar school grades, transferring to Middlesex for high school. Consequently, I had just met Don at the time of my invitation to spend the day. I am unsure what, if anything, we had in common. He was all-alive-alive-oh and full of bounce and all those devices that enable a middle child to make and retain his place in so large a family. Perhaps it was out of pity, for I was nurturing a crush on his sister Katie. It was a hopeless business, of course. She was a year older and in a class ahead of me. She was also out of my class. She had great, soft brown eyes, skin like a magnolia blossom, dark hair that fell in ringlets to her shoulder, and a profile that would have bestowed beauty on a cameo. I was both innocent and ignorant when it came to girls. So far as I knew, their elbows and knees were glued to their bodies like dolls' appendages. That did not prevent my sighing and worshipping the beautiful Katie Stone. As I say, Don might have asked me to spend Sunday afternoon with him so as to give me a chance to see and speak with her in her home setting. The first part of the afternoon was spent with Don who took me with him to call on an older boy who was, I think, their preacher's son. I wonder if this can be correct. He was a wild boy of maybe 17 years who knew an awful lot about women and fast cars. When we got to his house, a two-story unpainted farm house with a car in the yard, it was somewhat after midday. The young man had not long roused himself and was cooking something to eat in the fireplace. I thought his conversation very racy and not the thing for a preacher's son. It was only later that I learned that his conduct and conversation were what was held proverbially to be characteristic of preachers' sons. After Don and I had returned to the Stone mansion, for so it must be termed, Mr. Stone took Katie and me for a ride in his small private plane. It was, in all aspects, a daring ride. Once before I had flown in a piper cub from Wilson to Red Springs, getting airsick along the way. I cannot imagine why I did not get airsick on this ride. Maybe excitement prevented sickness. The ride lasted only a few minutes, but what a ride it was. As we left ground the light from the setting sun was beginning to fail. Up we flew to where the air was brighter and more of the setting sun was visible than had been visible on the darkening ground below. A sudden nose dive sent us hurtling back toward the earth. Katie screamed, and I yelled pretty loudly myself. When Mr. Stone leveled the plane off just above the dead tassels of a field of corn below us, we both calmed down and discovered that we were clenching one another's hand. There was too much of the wrong sort of thrill to derive full satisfaction from having her hand in mine. Still, it was something. After supper in that great big kitchen we went to church. They attended a small country church of the evangelical and holiness kind. I imagine the Stone family was its chief support. I had never been to services of this kind before. Some of the congregation shouted in loud voices, some underwent jumping and jerking movements and others danced involuntarily. A few "spoke in tongues". I took it all in without knowing what to make of it. When the preacher's son was seized by the power that was at large and began a kind of dancing near the small stove that heated the church, I kept my eye on him to see if either Satan or God would not cause him to fall against the hot stove for his apparent hypocrisy. Several years later, after reading <u>Varieties of Religious Experiences</u>, I was better able to take in what I had seen. Moreover William James made me withdraw my resentment toward that young man. His life and his religion were none of my business.

Study Hall

This may not be the ideal place to do so, yet it may be well to say something about study hall at the orphanage before leaving the subject of school days behind. After we returned home from school, there were three more things to attend to before the day was ended. The first was to attend to our assigned work that remained to be done before nightfall-- milking, gathering the eggs and feeding the hens, attending to the brooder, currying and feeding the mules, filling the furnace stokers for the night, or what have you. By the time this had been done, the first bell would chime out to alert us to clean up and prepare for supper. A second pealing of the bell called us to the dining hall. By the time this bell was struck, all us boys were lined up by height, smallest to the fore and tallest to the rear. The matron stood by to see the line formed and to cast her eye over us. She might, upon inspection of our extended hands, send us back for more scrubbing. She always had us in apple pie order by the second bell, and on her word we moved in an orderly fashion up the sidewalk that connected the boys' building to the dining hall in the new building. On rainy days we naturally made a dash for it, but still preserving such order as could be preserved in a dash. At the dining hall we went to our respective tables to which we were assigned by size. It may or may not have been a factor in devising this seating scheme, but sitting by size at a table gave every boy "fighting chance" and prevented a small boy from being overawed by a bigger one. I don't mean to suggest the fights were subject to break out in the dining hall, but a squabble over one thing or another <u>might</u> erupt every now and then. The girls who waited in the dining hall had already laid the tables with crockery and silver and had placed bowls of food, platters of biscuits, and pitchers of cold milk on all the tables. The girls had all their tables on the southern side of the room and the boys on the north, the directions in which their buildings sat in relation to the new building. When a serving dish or a pitcher of milk needed replenishing, the boy at the head of the table raised his hand in the air to signal the girl who was assigned to wait on his table.

    Having said so much about the dining hall, I may as well say a couple more things before saying what I wanted to say about study hall. I have spoken of the girls having set the tables beforehand. There was a very brief period when this routine may not have been followed. The earliest crockery I recall was a heavy dining plate of earthenware that was divided into two small areas for vegetables and a larger one for meat. These plates were white with an impressionistic fat cabbage rose or two, with a couple of green splashes to indicate leaves, for decoration. These gave way to dishes of similar construction bearing the well-known willow pattern. No doubt there was a fair amount of breakage of dishes. Another "spoil of war" was secured so as to remedy the problem of breakage. A large stock of heavy, stainless steel, rectangular eating dishes (with the three familiar divisions wrought into them) was obtained from U.S. Army surplus after the war. Nobody liked these cold ugly things, and what is more they weighed too much to be handled easily by the kitchen girls. I imagine there was more than one instance of the weight of them toppling some little girl standing on a low stool right over into the large rinsing sink while they were being washed and scrubbed in the kitchen. My memory may be false, but I think when these were in use the boys got each his own and took it to his place at the table, and returned it to a kitchen counter after the meal. The next thing was a thin molded plate of a pale tan color made of some kind of plastic, or a forerunner of plastic. They were spiritless things, but still much to be preferred to those steel trays!

To return to study hall, it will suffice to say that after supper was over, the kitchen girls cleaned up the dining hall, washed and dried the dishes and the pots and pans, and readied the kitchen for the night. While this was underway the boys had a brief period of recreation or what have you. Afterwards everyone, boys and girls, returned to the dining hall, now a study hall, to complete their homework assignments for school the next day. The rules were few and simple: no cutting up; be quite; do your homework. Boys and girls could sit wherever they liked, and boys and girls in the same class (who had the same assignments, anyway), could sit and work together if they chose. Different members of the staff sat as a sort of invigilator. The one I most remember was Mrs. Wimborn, a widow well past fifty who managed to have a soft spot in her heart for little boys while retaining her ability to keep them in order. Her biggest challenge was probably Rabbit B., an active boy with a touch of mischief to him. She once remarked that he needed a daily whipping, just on principle. Yet the true state of affairs between them was revealed by the fact that she called him "Br'er Rabbit," and he called her "Br'er Wimborn."

Some of the older boys and girls who were sweet on one another managed to get a bit of courting done under cover of the study hall. It was a common ploy for a boy to have a buddy sit with him and his girl in order to escape immediate detection of their true activities. This never hampered the heart-struck boy nor prevented his flirting with his girl friend to his heart's content. The amount of whispered conversation had to be watched pretty carefully, but there was nearly no limit to the number of written messages that could be exchanged. And, let me tell you, some of them were pretty racy. I say no more.

I should like to speak of a memorable evening in the dining hall shortly after the end of the war. Two brothers named Parker, who had been in the orphanage together, served in the Army during the war. I don't know whether they learned to cook on a large scale during their stay in the Army, or not. They learned it somewhere. More than that, they had made themselves masters of rolling dough out, cutting out doughnuts, and cooking them to perfection. After their discharge they made a visit to the orphanage, bringing with them the makings for preparing doughnuts, the utensils for rolling out the dough and cutting the doughnuts out, and the equipment for cooking large batches of them. All of us children took our places at our accustomed tables and waited while the brothers cooked and cooked and cooked. I don't recall how many of us were there at the time—perhaps 70 or so. I doubt a single one of us had ever heard of doughnuts, let alone had eaten one. We ate our fill of those truly delicious creations that night. It is possible that I exaggerate when I say we ate our fill. I'm pretty sure, though, that we all had three or four of them apiece. It was a first-class treat that I think none of us who were party to it will forget. The two brothers opened what was for many years one of the favorite restaurants in Wilson—Parker Brothers Barbecue. Whether they included doughnuts on their menu or not, I do not know.

Let me speak of one other special use to which the dining hall was put and I shall then leave the place alone. I wish to say something about Christmas. As the great day began its approach packages addressed to individual children began to be mailed to the orphanage. Some were from a child's surviving parent and/or family member. Some were sent to the child by the church that had "adopted" him—that is, held themselves responsible for raising the money necessary to maintain him year by year. These were all collected and held in the administrative offices in the new building. A very large, shapely red cedar tree was located in the extensive woods, cut down, and brought to the new building where it was erected at the end of the dining hall opposite the kitchen. I do not know to whom the honor of trimming the tree belonged, but the job was invariably well done. The distribution of the colored lights was attractive and well balanced, and the many large colored glass ornaments could not have been better placed. All showed to greatest advantage. On the afternoon of an appointed day, all the presents were brought in and placed under and around the tree. The children reassembled and took seats. The superintendent then began taking up the packages and reading off the name of the child for whom each was destined. As a rule every child got at least one present—the one from "his" church. Some children with relatives or friends who remembered them got a second, and even, occasionally, a third. At the end the superintendent asked to know if any child failed to get a present, and, if there were such a case, he made provision for one so that nobody was in the end completely overlooked.

One year, perhaps the first Christmas I was there, it happened that I was the child to whom no present was sent. Perhaps I did not yet have a sponsoring church, or perhaps my tiny rural church that did so much for me over a decade, did not know to send a present. Whatever the reason, the whole business meant but little to me. It wasn't that I had never heard of Christmas, it is just that I wasn't sure it wasn't something best avoided. The first Santa Claus I ever saw terrified me greatly. It was a nasty little miniature creature in red and dirty white holding a Coca Cola to its mouth. It sat in the window of a grimy little country store. I yelled and jumped back in horror when I saw it. It helped not at all to be told that it was "Santa Claus". It looked to me like a small vicious animal, say a weasel or a badger, poised to spring in attack and do serious damage. To this day I care little for Christmas. On the occasion of the failed present, someone came up with a little gift for me by the time I had said my prayers and got into bed. It was a nice little framed picture of a small attractive house beside a body of water. It was a moonlit scene, but even so it was evident that roses clambered over the house door. I did not recognize the house, but since we lived at one point near the water in Pamlico County, I asked if it were my house. The big girl who had brought it to me said, "Yes," that it was. There was not only a hesitation in her voice that told me this was not true, but no photograph in my young mind actually included a house like the one in the picture. I decided, despite this, that it should be my house, and I demanded that it be hung then and there above the head of my bed where I could see it when I knelt to say my evening prayer. I never was much of a present getter. I don't know how my little brother fared in this department, but my twin sister was a champion present getter.

After the war when gasoline and tires were no longer rationed and people could travel more easily relatives of a child usually came to the orphanage, collected that child and took him with them to spend Christmas. Some children, myself included, had no place to go. That was perfectly agreeable with me. One Christmas a man and his wife did an unheard of thing. They were Herman and Betty Nobles of Greenville. They were childless. In a remarkable gesture of generosity Mr. and Mrs. Nobles sent enough single dollar bills to the superintendent that every child there was made a gift of one. But more remarkable than that, they invited me to go home with them for the holiday. I entered an entirely new world with them. I do not recall their house being an imposing one, but it was solid and substantial. There were Turkish carpets on the floor. The rich wood of their furniture was well burnished. Their silver gleamed. Their glassware sparkled. They had a housekeeper. Mrs. Nobles made me feel at home despite all this, and her kindness prevented my being overawed by all I saw. They took me with them wherever they went. I am not sure, but I think they probably bought me a little jacket to wear. The left pocket of my plaid flannel jacket had been filled with tar by some prankster—Pat L., I expect. The Nobles belonged to a fraternal organization called "The Order of the Red Men", and it was thought that at the Christmas meeting of the order, Mrs. Nobles would be chosen "Pocahontas", the highest distinction available to their women members. They took me with them to the meeting where I saw the ritual and saw Mrs. Nobles inducted into her new dignity. I had never seen anyone like Mr. and Mrs. Nobles. They were kind, gentle, considerate, generous, winning people. I am sure they gave me a present, but I have no idea what it was. I doubt that even then I could have told, if asked, what present they had given me. The fact of their having me in their home and making me feel briefly as if it were my home, too, beat completely hollow any Christmas present you choose to name. When I returned to the orphanage I came down with a malaise of some sort. I sat down to write a letter to Mr. and Mrs. Nobles, and while in the act of writing was discovered doing so by an older boy. He demanded to know what I was doing, and when I told him, demanded that I tell him about the Nobles. When I did, he jeered at me for writing and made fun of me for feeling homesick for a place that was not even my home. When he diagnosed my malaise as homesickness, I realized immediately that he was right. Knowing that I was homesick for the Nobles only made it worse, so I sat and boohooed for a bit. His jeering and making fun put an end to my letter, and made me pull myself together. The sequel to this affair is that the superintendent made a point of appearing in the dining hall one day shortly afterwards, when all the children were present and in their places, so that he could administer a rebuke personally. He informed us that not a single child, not even one, had written a thank you note to Mr. Nobles for his unprecedented gift of a dollar to each and every child. He told us baldly that we were all guilty of ingratitude and ought to feel shame for it. I did.

 A few years later, toward the end of my stay at the orphanage I went a couple of times to spend Christmas at my father's and once spent a week in the summer with him. I was glad of the opportunity to be with my older sister who had left the orphanage in 1944, but I felt no homesickness for them upon my return to the orphanage. These visits were not something that was looked forward to with anticipation or looked back upon with regret that the visit had come to an end. The truth is, I would have been content never to have made a visit anywhere at Christmastime. No doubt this sounds perverse, and I am sure this was not a view that would have been endorsed by the great majority of the children. The orphanage was, however, the home that my mother had selected for me. I belonged to it, and it belonged to me. Whether this attitude would have been preserved intact through the tumult of adolescence, or not, I do not know. I left the orphanage just as I entered those vexatious years.

I am sure that many of the children did not share my views, even though this was not a subject of discussion. I will say that among the children, the boys at least, a sort of rough delicacy prevented us prying into one another's private feelings and griefs. Nonetheless there were clear cases of great unhappiness in some of the boys that were apparent to all. I particularly recall one little boy, aged about 5 or 6, who came and stayed only briefly, Louis T. He was inconsolable. He could get through the day, but he invariably broke down at bed time. Louis did not lie in bed in the ordinary way, but hugging his grief to himself would compose himself like a Muslim at prayer, his rump in the air and his back sloping down to his head as it rested on the bed. And thus, gathered in to himself, Louis wept and wept until sleep finally came. There was not a thing any of us could do for him, so our relief was nearly as great as his when a kinsmen came and took Louis home with him.

The Woods

No doubt every child who suffers the loss of a parent at an early age also suffers a wound to his psyche. The grief felt by Louis was probably only different in degree and not in the nature of it. In looking back on that period of my life I am led to wonder whether I would have felt relief if another child had asked and I had told him of my mother. I doubt it. To this day her name is almost as sacred to me as the unspeakable name of God. As a result I am unable to get a credit card for I will not sully her memory for so crass a purpose, and the very first piece of personal information the credit card companies seek is to her maiden name.

It was seldom that a child's history was known by the other children. I know of only four exceptions during the period I was at the orphanage. One of these was a little boy whose only parent, his mother, had been murdered. I don't know how this information got out, but once it did it was common knowledge. These events coincided with a country and western song then being broadcast by the Raleigh radio station, WPTF. It was in the form of a folk song or ballad that related the murder of a young mother whose little boy, in the refrain, begged his mother not to go to town that night. We all thought this song told Charles Ray's story. In a way his grief was more terrible than the grief of Louis T. Grief, anger, resentment, betrayal had all been dumped on his young shoulders by his mother's murderer. He bore it grimly. I know now that I ought to have befriended Charles Ray ('44-'58), but I felt unable to overcome the dark barrier that surrounded him. The failing, however, was mine and not his. I could at least have gone with him to the woods and shown him the branch of water that ran through it, shown him where the hickory nut trees and walnut trees grew, and where to find wild grapes when they were in season. He, too, might have found as much pleasure in the woods as I. I speak as if he could have been introduced to the woods only by me. I don't mean to do so. It would have been mere vanity on my part to have supposed such a thing.

My way of speaking thus of the woods is grounded, not in vanity, but in an almost proprietary love for them. The woods on every side were all part of the same system. Despite this, there were subtle differences in the different portions of it. My favorite section lay to the south, beyond the girls' building. This was the section to which I was first introduced when very young by some of the older boys. They took some of the little boys with them one warm afternoon and made for the woods. After we entered, we went straight ahead until we got to a little branch of water. Here we turned to the right and followed upstream until we arrived at a place where there was a small natural swimming hole. We stripped off our clothes and jumped in. It was neither so deep nor so swift as to present a danger. All the same, it was borne in on us little boys that we were not to come by ourselves to swim here. For some time, three or four of us would go to the woods together. As we got older and my playmates had a purpose in going to the woods—to attend to their traps and to hunt squirrels with a slingshot—I found myself going for pleasure alone, or perhaps in company with only one other boy. It was best by myself. I could stay as long as I wished in one spot watching the water skimmers perform their trick of walking on water, or lying in wait to see a crawdad or a salamander come out of hiding, or just watching the water ripple over rocks, or looking for tadpoles and minnows. The land on the other side of the branch rolled down to the streambed. My favorite place was where the land did not roll gently down to the stream in the usual way, but dropped precipitously 12 or 14 feet, forming a rounded cliff of red clay. It was crowned by saplings and full grown trees. It was an invariable part of my routine to cross the branch and walk up this roll in the ground until I stood at the very top, surveying the branch below. It was a stiff climb, made easier by pulling oneself up it by the assistance of bushes and saplings. I called this spot the "Blue Ridge" though it had no more relation to the Blue Ridge than a kitten has to a tiger. Wild azalea bushes, which we called "honeysuckle bushes," grew here, but not below by the branch. Similarly, cattails grew near the branch where it flowed under the bridge on the road to Middlesex, but nowhere else. There were larger rolls to the land on the other side of the road, but no place where it had collapsed to form a cliff. Wild azaleas did not grow here, but trailing cedar and hepatica did. The woods on the other farm included a small swampy area where pitcher plants grew, the only place in the woods where I knew they might be found. Near them grew dog roses that produced large "hog apples" (as we called the rose hips). The dog roses were here and nowhere else.

My favorite section of the woods, the southern area, had a couple of swampy areas too, but no pitcher plants. The larger of these lay near the branch as it made its way to the bridge. It was filled with deep mire, covered with water at times—a regular slue. Though overhung with vines suitable for swinging, it was a place best avoided. It was probably an aquifer that fed the branch, but it was an uninviting one. A smaller place lay upstream in the sunlight at some distance from the branch. It was used as a wallow by an old brood sow that, when she had a litter with her feeding in the woods on acorns and roots, would squint with her ugly, red rimmed eyes and make a threatening sound or two to warn you off. She was not always at this place she used as a wallow, and its water stood shallow and clear. Once again, it is probable that one of the sources that fed the branch fed this wallow from a small spring below its surface.

Frogs were fond of this spot, as were the water moccasins that came here to sun themselves after gorging on the frogs. It was considered an act of derring-do to take along a hoe, spot a moccasin sluggishly digesting its meal, creep up on it, and kill it with the hoe. If it were a snake worth bragging about because of its size, or because of the number of large lumps along its body indicating the number of frogs it had swallowed, it would be taken by the tail and dragged all the way back to the furnace room of the girls' building. Here it was cut open with an axe to an audience of admiring, squealing girls, and the frogs removed. All had to be thrown into the furnace, of course.

When grapes had ripened, it was far more acceptable to climb a tree that had a vine growing up it and to fill a pocket with them. Another pocket might be filled with hickory nuts. These then might be brought back for a sister, or as shy offering for one of the girls. There was one little girl of extraordinary beauty, and I imagine she retained it in later life, name Rosalyn W____ ('43-'53). I don't think she carried her beauty with hauteur, but she was entitled by it to do so. In any event, it made me shy to be in her presence. Once, I brought back an offering of grapes and hickory nuts for Rosalyn, but I cannot remember whether I found the nerve to offer them to her or not. Some of the girls are lodged in my mind because of their beauty. The beautiful Lucy H. was a big girl when I was quite a little boy. The image of her softly waving light red hair, the nobility of her brow, the perfect composition of her face, are all fixed in my mind, perfect and unchanged after more than 60 years. Thelma B____ ('44-'54) was another whose remarkably good looks probably followed her through life. Her brother, Franklin ('44-'51), was a handsome, well set-up young man, to whom I imagine women later found it hard to say no. There was no brother and sister at the orphanage during my time to rival them in good looks unless it was Herb T. and his two sisters. These are purely objective observations. I was a little afraid of Franklin, and Thelma looked as if she might slap when vexed. So, favoritism does not cloud my judgment.

Before leaving the woods, I should like to say that during that idyllic period, a child might go alone into the woods and wander about in them in perfect security. They afforded countless hours of serene enjoyment. Having to leave them, and knowing that I could never return to wander in them, overshadows my recollection of them with a sense of loss that does not go away.

Orphanage Staff

I should like to say something about relationships with staff as I experienced them. But, before I do, I wonder if I need to clear up any doubt I might have unwittingly sown in what I have written. If I have conveyed the notion that I was a good little boy who obeyed his elders, did as he was told to do, and never got into trouble, let me correct that notion before I write another word. The truth is that I was always respectful, but not always obedient. I was what I should prefer calling strong-willed, but others might call stubborn. Sometimes I was quarrelsome and got into fights. I don't want to suggest that I was a bad child, but I think I was often an aggravating one. I got my share of whippings—a word or two on this subject may not be out of order.

Almost certainly, there was a stated policy governing the whipping of recalcitrant children, but I do not know what it was. Almost equally certain, there must have been a cut-off age beyond which corporal punishment was not employed as a form of correction for either boys or girls. Otherwise, it is probable that a fight would have taken place in which an adolescent boy or girl might have got the better of a staff member trying to administer it. I have a slight recollection of a whispered vague rumor that that is exactly what did happen once when one of the men on the staff set out to whip a big boy who turned on him. Good sense, if not stated policy, must have governed.

Very nearly all the whippings that I remember were given by women staff members. I do not recall ever being whipped by a male staff member, but I did get whipped at three various times by the superintendents. Once I was involved in a very novel whipping that may be worth recounting.

Soon after lunch one day, all, or most, of us boys were going on foot with a farm manager, Mr. Eagles, to perform a job that required us all. I do not recall what the work was, but we were going to it by walking down the service road that ran from the kitchen to the girls' building. For some reason that I can no longer recall, a scuffling and shoving match broke out between me and another boy. My treacherous memory will not supply me with the face and name of the boy, but I think it was either Jesse D____ or Jimmy H____. Anyway, Mr. Eagles stopped our procession right where we were. We had just come up to and were passing along a tall screen of ligustrum bushes. This shrubbery sends up tall slender shoots that are easily stripped and peeled, unlike privet with its crabbed stiff branches. Mr. Eagles announced that Jesse (or Jimmy) and I should settle our quarrel by fighting with switches. Thank goodness the hedge wasn't privet—we'd have torn one another's skin to pieces. He ordered us both to roll up the legs of our overalls to the knee, then step over to the hedge and select a switch for ourselves. I got me a good, serviceable switch of moderate thickness and length and stripped and peeled it. Jesse/Jimmy got himself one too, but it was the king of all switches. At its base, it was as thick as a man's thumb, and was six feet long, at least. Well, maybe only five. Anyway, it dwarfed mine.

The boys all drew back to give us room to go to work with our switches. I think everybody was astounded, I certainly was, when Mr. Eagles ordered Jesse/Jimmy and me to exchange switches. As I stood there holding the switch with which I was meant to be whipped, I was slightly stunned by the reversal. I was not going to hit Jesse/Jimmy with that monster switch, but he was unable to get by it to make a successful attack on me. The fight fizzled right out. I think Mr. Eagles made us shake hands, and then we proceeded on our way.

As I say, I was generally whipped by one of the women on the staff with either a slight belt or with a slender switch. During my first three or so years, I was whipped very frequently, too frequently I think. Afterward, they were on an "as deserved" basis. None of them were severe. There were three occasions, though, when I was caught up in allegations of wrong-doing so serious that the matter was referred to the superintendent for investigation and punishment. I have already spoken of the first of my whippings by the superintendent on the Easter when I was found to have gone to church with a dirty neck. It was the first and only time I was whipped in anger by him. I can only surmise that he had been made the object of an ugly confrontation in church and that his anger was still dangerously high when we got home. Had his anger cooled, he would not, I think, have whipped me as he did. He was, after all, an ordained minister of the gospel with children of his own. I remember my twin sister standing outside the bus as near as she could get to us, hopping up and down every now and then with all her feathers ruffled out like a little bantam hen, uttering threats against the superintendent through her tears of outrage. Poor thing, she took it worse than I–and still does.

I was never clear in my mind how I came to be implicated in the affair that led to my second whipping by the superintendent. It turned on the theft of a large clasp knife belonging to the superintendent. It was one that usually resided in the pocket of his hunting jacket which hung, I believe, on his back porch. One of the small boys came into possession of this knife by some means, and he sold it to another boy. I don't know how many times it changed hands before it came to the attention of the superintendent who, by this time, had discovered the theft of his clasp knife. I don't want to make Jesse D_____ or Jimmy H_____ my undeserved nemesis, but I think the first culprit in this affair was Jesse/Jimmy.

In the ensuing investigation into the affair, he said that he had got the knife from me—whether by gift, barter, or purchase, I do not now know. Not that it matters; it was altogether false. Unfortunately for me at this juncture, the special relationship I was thought to have to the superintendent's family, and the fact that I made daily deliveries of milk and cream to their house gave some color to the supposition that I had perfect opportunity to take the knife and walk away with it in my pocket. I had done nothing of the kind, but the accusation and appearances were against me. It was summarily decided that I must have had some role in the affair though the exact role could not be determined. There was nothing for it, but to bend over the desk in the superintendent's office while he laid on four or five strokes with a razor strop. They were methodical, but not angry strokes.

While the ins and outs of this affair were murky, they were nothing compared with my next visit to the superintendent's office for punishment. It was never clear to me just what the goings-on were or how I was connected to them, but somehow I was supposed to be implicated in some small outrage. This was under a new superintendent, Walter Croom (Alumnus '30-'39 & Superintendent '49-'51), a young man with a young wife and an infant child. I doubt that he knew what was going on, either. It happened that shortly before these events transpired I had been able to go to town—that is, to Middlesex. A bookstore had been opened there on a venture. I went to the bookstore and while there purchased a copy of <u>The Imitation of Christ</u> by the Blessed Thomas A Kempis. It was just the size to fit into the back pocket. Although this famous religious classic was beyond my intellectual level at the time, still I would pull it out and read in it from time to time. It was in my pocket when I went to the superintendent's office to be punished for this unknown offense. He spotted it, and told me to take the book out of my pocket. I did so and passed it to him. I heard him make a sound of surprise when he examined it. I got my strokes with the razor strop all the same, but they were not strong ones. I have never known whether he moderated his hand, or whether he naturally did not give blows to match the ripeness of those given by Mr. Evans (Superintendent '40-'49). When it was done, he handed my book back to me. I put it back in my pocket and left the room. This is very nearly my only memory of Mr. Croom. His tenure as superintendent was brief.

While I have next to nothing to say of Mr. Croom there are some members of the staff at the orphanage about whom I should like to write a little.

I have already made some mention of the Rev. James A. Evans who was superintendent until 1949. He was the one who collected my sister, my brother, and me and carried us to the orphanage early in 1942. I have said a few words, too, about his mother, known to us as "Granny Evans". I should say rather more about his family—especially his wife, his son James Arthur, and his youngest daughter, Kay Nell. His two older daughters Lorraine and Anne were considerably my seniors, so I saw little of them. Mrs. Evans was a truly remarkable woman. She was a lady in the old fashioned sense of that word when it conveyed a sense of good breeding, good taste, impeccable manners, and an underlying fortitude. Though she would think it indelicate of me to say so, she was like a piece of whalebone of the first quality—elegance combined with strength and resilience. Mr. Evans was a man of real ability and good administration. His sermons were difficult for me to follow, though they were carefully composed and clearly spoken. I was bewildered by them. Yet he seemed to be a good pastor when he had pastoral charge of a church. His mark was left in the lives of children in his care, and not in the ever changing physical plant of the orphanage. That may seem an odd thing to say since it was he who wrought so many of the changes. It was he who replaced the Guernsey and Jersey cows with Holsteins and got milking machines for the dairy. He restocked our fattening hog pens with Poland China pigs instead of the common pink and white pigs we had known. It was Mr. Evans who moved the farmyard to the other farm where a new dairy and stables and outbuildings were erected. He began the construction of a new boys' building, "Albemarle Cottage", on the site of the old farmyard, and up the road from it he began to build Memorial Chapel. Both progressed slowly. When money ran out work came to a standstill, and Mr. Evans would go out to raise funds to resume and continue the work. Some of the boys, anticipating the day we should move into "Albemarle Cottage," began to abuse the old building. I remember one room in which a hole had been knocked through the plaster and laths of the wall which connected to an adjoining room. It had to be lived with afterward until the new building was completed. It took years to complete Memorial Chapel and it, the chapel, was put to use long before all the finishing work had been completed inside.

No building, no change, bore the stamp of Mr. Evans. For many of us, Mr. Evans impacted our lives in different ways, but Mrs. Evans actually influenced our lives. That, in any event, was true in my case. Until the advent of the Mixons when Mrs. Mixon assumed the duties of dietician, Mrs. Evans acted as dietician. I don't know where she was educated, but she, Mrs. Evans, knew about food and how to prepare it in large quantities so that it was very tasty and wholesome. She had to rely on her mother-in-law, "Granny" Evans when it came to curing meat, making sausage, rendering lard, and so forth, but she was otherwise queen of the kitchen. Her neat figure moved among the girls as she oversaw the churning of butter, the baking, the peeling of vegetables, and cooking on the huge range. She was much opposed to waste, and even though potato peelings, the ends of snap beans, pea pods, and such other kitchen waste was hauled away to the hogs with the unwanted pot liquor, she kept a vigilant eye on the thickness of potato peelings, the size of the discarded broken ends of beans, and such. A word or correction would produce thoroughly washed pots and pans, and a clean and neat kitchen. It was hot and heavy work in the kitchen, and the girls assigned to work there did their work well. That they did so was owing to Mrs. Evans, and later her successor, Mrs. Mixon.

There was one area in which Mrs. Evans had no successor. This is not meant as a slap at Mrs. Mixon or anyone else. There were some things in which Mrs. Evans was unique. During meals she quietly moved about the dining hall, showing a child, when necessary, the proper way to hold and handle table silver, how to take a serving dish from a neighbor to the left by using the right hand, then after having served oneself to pass the dish to the fellow to the right by using the left hand. Food was made to be passed in counter clockwise motion. Food was to be chewed with the mouth closed. She did not insist on the left hand in the lap, but she did insist that elbows not be put on the table. Reminding us of the starving children of China she would persuade us to eat everything on our plate, even the hateful squash that appeared all summer long. I daydreamed of a row of large stainless steel cans at the top of the dining hall into which one could scrape unwanted squash, leftover collards or peas or what have you. In my daydream, these were capped and sent to China after every meal.

What was it, I wondered, about Mrs. Evans and squash? She was determined to serve them, and did serve them, at least once a day so long as the garden continued to produce them. To me they were watery, tasteless things with not even a hint of crunch about them. Mrs. Evans not only sent them from her kitchen with a dependable regularity, she also made it a point to glide about our quarter of the dining hall to make sure that we all took helpings of them onto our plates. I would be hard pressed to estimate the number of times that I left the dining hall with squash in my pocket instead of my stomach. Two cares had to be taken. The first was to pocket the squash without detection. The second was to get the watery mess emptied out of the pocket before engaging in rough and tumble games, or wrestling, after lunch. If my scheme of cans for China could be instituted, the whole problem could be solved—from stove to China was my idea. A beautiful, simple solution to the problem. It would have saved the girls the trouble of filling serving dishes with them and bringing them to our table, and would have saved us the trouble of pocketing them. Besides, those Chinese children might have been cunning enough to make them tasty. But it was not to be. The squash continued to make an appearance, and those of us who did not like them continued to fill our pockets. I regret that the squash remain to mar my image of Mrs. Evans. I had much rather remember her consulting her supplies on the shelves that reached to the top of the tall pantry as she placed her order with the man from Sexton Foods.

But there are plenty of other images of Mrs. Evans to call to mind. I think I have already said that when I worked with Charles H___ in the milk refrigeration room, one of my tasks was to make a daily delivery of milk and cream to the superintendent's house. Mrs. Evans never failed to say "thank you" though she might use words other than the usual formula to do so. Sincerity marked her voice every time.

I don't wish to make an invidious comparison, but at the risk of doing so I want to say another thing about my making a milk delivery. After the Evans had left and Mr. Croom was superintendent, I was on my second "tour of duty" as kitchen boy. One of my tasks was, once more, to deliver milk and cream daily to the superintendent's house. The family was made up of Mr. and Mrs. Croom and their infant child. For lack of experience, for failure to involve herself in the life of the orphanage, or for some other reason, Mrs. Croom's "thank you" was perfunctory, and delivery was at the open door. I don't recall once ever being asked to step in, as I was when the Evans were in residence. On a cold or blustery morning the warm kitchen was a good thing to step into for a minute or two.

The Evans not only involved themselves in the life of the orphanage, but they also brought up their children in such a way that no social distinction was made between the Evans children and the orphanage children. This was not always the case with staff families. The two youngest Evans children were playmates of mine and of other of the children. Jay, in fact, was a "buddy" to me and probably to several of the boys of his age. I recall that he was determined that I should share his joy and learn to ride a bike when he got his first bicycle. It was a disastrous experiment. I seemed to be drawn irresistibly to the ditch. In my last attempt I kept the bike in the road for some distance, rolling on with ever increasing speed as I descended the gentle decline leading to the bridge where the branch crossed the road. A fearful thrill froze my hands to the handle bars, and my arms stiffened as I began once more to be hypnotically drawn to the ditch. This time I crashed into the ditch bank, some distance below where the maypops grew, and crashed into the ditch bank with such force that I bent the front fender against the tire. I was skint up but unhurt. Jay kept his good humor even though he was unable to ride again until repairs were made.

He and Kay Nell often came over to the boys' building after supper to play with us boys of Jay's age. Perhaps it was only to catch lightning bugs as they bobbed up and down near the lobelia and quince bushes. Or we'd peer up through the dusk to see leather wing bats, or the occasional bull bat, and to try to charm them out of the sky. "Bat, bat! Come under my hat, and I will give you a slice of bacon. And when I bake I'll give you a cake, if (said very softly) I'm not mistaken." Jay was the only boy in the family, and Kay doted on him. Lorraine, I think, threatened him with dire punishments if he vexed her. Anne was away in school at Flora

MacDonald College at Red Springs. I recall once when Anne got a new frock called a "tea gown" she invited some of the big girls to come to see it and share in her pleasure. That's the sort of people the Evanses were.

I think I probably had a special relationship with the family. I felt that I had. They had a little dog that was totally unlike the mutts I was used to. It was a small, pure white little creature with pointed ears and sparkling eyes, named "Snowball". She was Eskimo Spitz, or something that sounded like that. Snowball was a canine version of Mrs. Evans—petite, self-possessed, and nice looking. Mrs. Evans would let me take Snowball on walks in the woods. I loved Snowball, and she showed every sign of liking and trusting me. She came to my call, and willingly returned home when I ended the walk—none of that going off and gadding about the woods on her own account like some dogs will do. We broke one another's heart on account of the careless dangerous action of a third party—a worthless third party to my way of thinking. One day Snowball and I went on a very long walk along the road that led to Middlesex. We were talking together and enjoying one another's company, and had got nearly as far as the Fulgham family's farm—perhaps a mile away—when a small car came upon us from the rear. It was hurtling along that narrow country road at far too great a speed. It was traveling from the direction of the orphanage going to Middlesex. We stepped off the tarred surface onto the narrow dirt shoulder. In spite of our precaution the driver managed to give Snowball a glancing blow. I am sure to this day that the driver was Miss M___, a young woman who drove in from town to work in the superintendent's office. She never stopped to see what damage she had done. Instead, she flew along her erratic way until she was out of sight. Snowball fled, yelping into the woods and disappeared. My anxious, plaintive calls did not bring her back. When I finally accepted the fact that she lay dead in the woods, I returned home to tell Mrs. Evans what had happened. She was all poise and calm as she quieted me. The loss of her beautiful little dog was a real blow, but she never uttered a harsh word or increased my grief with guilt. When I was told two or three days later that Snowball had returned home I was eager to see her. Alas! Our bond had been broken. She had no trust in me, and would not have crossed the yard with me, let alone gone for a walk. I think I am free of any grudge against Miss M___, who never admitted what she had done nor alluded to it, but I still hold it as a black mark against her that she could have done such a thing through carelessness, then driven carelessly away.

I cannot forbear saying one or two more things about Mrs. Evans. There was more authority about her than was warranted by her petite stature. True it is that she gave elegance to whatever she wore and that she always appeared at her best, no matter what. Even her galoshes, which she pulled on with the ease of gloves, were essentially her. They were marvels of engineering, having little high heels into which the heels of her shoes fit precisely. It was more than all this. She had presence, and never had to raise her voice. Her corrections and rebukes were gently, but firmly, spoken. She tried to instill some sense of good manners and politeness into us, and would have saved every one of us boys from becoming complete hooligans if she could. I hate to admit that my manners were never brought to the pitch of refinement she would have liked; still I never had to be ashamed in later life of my manners. I owe her a lot.

A considerable number of people joined and departed the ranks of the orphanage staff while I was there. I remember them all, I think, but I choose to write of only a handful of them. Some were good, some were bad, and some were mediocre. It is unnecessary, I think, for me to state the obvious fact that the staff, no matter how conscientious and caring, could not supply one of the most, if not the most, important necessity that every child requires. That is, affection. I mean the genuine article. Nowadays, the words "I love you" have been so abused, so misused, and so falsely spoken, that one shrinks back when one hears them or sees them written to oneself. The words are sometimes spoken by one person, whose face is corrugated in anger, to another, who hurls them right back. There are others who are unable to let friends depart from a casual encounter, or end a brief telephone conversation, without saying (or sometimes shouting), "I love you" when a simple "good bye" would sound more sincere. Children can be made to say "I love you" to a parent or a family member from whom they receive not a whit of affection. But children, like many animals, know when they are surrounded by love and affection and when they are not, for it is a power that flows back and forth involuntarily between two persons—it cannot be commanded. When it is not possible to muster affection, one can, unless completely heartless, at least exercise kindness. I make these remarks so that it will be understood that I in no way find fault in the orphanage because the staff was unable to do the impossible and shower the children with genuine love and affection. Exercise of kindness, however, should have been within the power of the staff. I do not mean that strictness and correction should not have been exercised, too, and there well may have been cases where displays of kindness were sometimes taken as displays of weakness. Yet, there were some of the staff whose management had an underlying kindness, and occasionally, there was one whose management did not.

Having got that out of the way, I should like to say a brief thing or two about the first of the staff whom I met. This was Mr. and Mrs. Pope. She was a well set-up woman who wore her glossy dark hair on a "rat" and dressed in serviceable frocks. Her husband was some years her senior, stout, out of shape and balding. They were up and waiting for us on the evening my brother and I arrived at the orphanage and were taken to the boys' building. Their apartment was on the ground floor on the right side of the foyer. It consisted of only two connecting rooms, a sitting room and a bedroom. Their bathroom was across the hall from their sitting room. Their bedroom backed up to the bedroom where the smallest boys slept, and to which my little brother and I were taken. I don't know where Mrs. Pope came from. She had a small magazine basket made of the shell of an armadillo that may or may not have hinted at her origins. Mr. Pope must have come from one of the nearby eastern counties. My guess would be Edgecombe, Halifax, or Wilson. My little brother's tender age (he was only about 2 ½ years old) elicited kindness on all fronts. It was considered best if we were not separated at night, so we shared a bed. Sometimes, he would be wakened by the blowing of the train's whistle which came clearly and loudly to us on the still night air from the depot at Middlesex, two miles away. We had never heard train whistles in the night in Pamlico County, and these frightened him. I would put my arms around him and hug him to me and tell him that he was safe—he was unconvinced. What he wanted was a mother to reassure him, which was the one thing he had not. Lying in her bed, Mrs. Pope could hear him on the other side of her wall. She would come in her nightdress, take him up in her arms, and bear him away to the safety of her bed. There were many such occasions when Mrs. Pope would comfort my brother in the night. I don't think Mr. Pope much cared for this, but her heart was two large to be inhibited by his grunts. Many years later when Haywood had sons of his own, he made a visit to North Carolina from his home in California. When he learned that Mrs. Pope, now remarried and bearing a different name, was living at Dudley, he made a special trip to visit and thank her for her kindness to him as a child.

Shortly after our arrival at the orphanage, I don't know how soon, there was a reassignment of the staff so that the Popes were transferred to the girls' building. The smallest of us little boys were transferred there, too, for a brief while. I think that I have told how Mr. Pope, after we little boys had moved back to the boys' building, laid an interdiction against our approaching the girls' building any nearer than the new building sidewalk. There was an occasion that Rabbit B. and I were punished for ignoring his prohibition.

There was another occasion, however, when we went over and escaped punishment. This was an occasion when one of the kitchen girls got a painful, but not serious, burn. Mr. Pope was said to be able to "talk the fire out"—that is, to stop the pain by an incantation. One would dare anything nearly to witness that. I pushed my way through until I stood immediately next to Mr. Pope and listened with all my ears as he muttered the charm. I was very disappointed. It opened with the words, "Mathew, Mark, Luke, and John, bless the spot that I blow on," (stopping here to blow on the burn). I cannot now recall the words that included the injunction for the pain to cease, but it doesn't matter. They were only words with no power in them. Or, if any, it was too weak to be felt in the open air.

When the Popes were reassigned to the girls' building, their place was taken at the boys' building by a woman named Mary Burton who hailed originally from Oxford in Granville County. I shall have nothing good to say of Miss Burton, so if this comes to the hands of family, friends, or admirers, they may wish to skip this section. I may as well say at the outset that upon my first meeting Miss Burton, I got off on the wrong foot, and never afterward managed to get on the right one. It is no more than just to say that she was a desiccated, angular, choleric old maid. There was something about her that put one in mind of a piece of cheap porcelain that had been crazed by long submersion in clear water. Not a single element of this description of Miss Burton is exaggerated.

The exchange of Miss Burton for the Popes took place not very long after we were admitted to the orphanage. I don't know whether she had been in charge of the boys' building earlier, or not. Some of the little boys knew of her and her methods, though, and this suggests she had been in charge earlier. I asked another little boy, who seemed to know things, to tell me about her. This little boy, a witty creature, knew that she was famous for her gleaming tablespoon and her two large bottles, one of which was filled with castor oil and the other with cod liver oil. This witty child, seeing a chance for a good practical joke, described those as being very delicious and much better than candy. He went on to say that she preferred to give out the cod liver oil in cold weather, but she was glad to let you have castor oil at any time. All one had to do was ask her for it. He said I should go right then and ask her for some castor oil. I did. She is bound to have been surprised by, and suspicious of, my request. I imagine I was the only boy in the history of the place to ask for castor oil. Miss Burton took me to the foyer of the building so as to get a better look at me in good light. She then drew out her great big spoon and carefully poured it full to the brim with the heavy, clear castor oil. I opened wide. She put in the spoon, and I closed my mouth and lips as she pulled the spoon carefully back out. The shock of surprise was very great, and I could not disguise it. Nor could I disguise my disgust. I can't recall whether I spat it out or not. Whatever I did, it wasn't the thing to have done. Forever afterward I was in Miss Burton's list of bad little boys.

For some reason, which I now think must have been emotional or psychological, I took to wetting the bed at night frequently. Each time was a fresh outrage to Miss Burton. She employed various tactics to break me of this practice, all of them humiliating. She would tell the other little boys what I had done, she washed my face in the wet sheets, and she compelled me to strip the sheets off the bed, take them with me to the shower room, and wash them as I showered while she stood by, switch or little belt in hand, to make certain I did a thorough job of it. None of these ploys had the desired effect. She eventually came up with a masterstroke. Miss Burton took a large sheet of paper, wrote on it the words, in capitals, "I WET THE BED LAST NIGHT," pinned the sign on my back and sent me off to school with a dare for me to take it off. I was one of the last of the children to board the bus that morning, and had hardly got aboard when the doors closed and the bus moved off on its way to school. I had hardly got aboard, too, when this piece of infamy was spotted by one of the big girls. She sprang up in outrage, pulled the sign off my back, and made for the school bus door, uttering imprecations and threats against Miss Burton. She was going to have it out with this matron, and would have, had the driver stopped the bus and opened the door. Knowing that this would give rise to a crisis that would keep us all out of school that day, he drove on. I don't know what this girl said later, or to whom she said it, but Miss Burton gave up trying to control my night bladder. The bed wettings ceased just as mysteriously and as suddenly as they had begun. I can't say that the trouble began with the appearance of Miss Burton at the boys' building and ended with her departure, so I shan't say so as if it were a fact. It might be exactly true; however, that such was the case.

Perhaps this is the place to say that my siblings knew nothing of my troubles with Miss Burton during those early years. Oddly, I have no recollections of my little brother ever falling into her hands. I think Mrs. Pope took him with her to bring him up herself at the girls' building. My older sister, who probably ought never to have been put in the orphanage, left it after a series of panic attacks late in 1944 (our father had remarried in the spring of 1943). My twin sister found out later, if she did not know it at the time, that Miss Burton was an enemy. I think that she knew nothing of the worst of my childish woes, however.

I once tried a ploy of my own on Miss Burton. It did not work. I have spoken of those momentous Thanksgiving days when a true feast was spread out in the flower garden. On one of these Thanksgivings, Miss Burton did not approve of the clothes I was wearing. Why she did not, I do not know. She looked about and found an ugly brown pair of knee pants (or plus fours) that had probably come to the orphanage in some castoffs that had charitably been sent in. I despised the ugly things. Nobody wore them in the 1940s, but Miss Burton was determined that I should. By dint of pulling and jerking and sewing and pinning, she got the things on me. As she was cinching the belt so they would not fall about my ankles during the course of the day, I took it into my head to smile at her. My, my! She gave me such a slap that I almost saw stars. "Quit grinning at me" she snapped. I never tried another smile on her.

She managed to get her hands on me once more, but only once, after she was reassigned to duty in the girls' building and left us boys in peace. It was an early Sunday evening, and I was on the first floor of the girls' building. It was strictly forbidden for one of the boys, whatever his age, to go up the broad staircase to the next floor—the girls had their bedrooms and baths on the second and third floors. Despite this prohibition, I was slowly making my way, a step at the time, up the staircase. My twin sister leaned on the banister above me and encouraged my actions. Suddenly, Miss Burton materialized out of thin air, her little belt in hand, and seized me nearly halfway up the stairs. She was flailing with all her might even before the suddenness and anger of her attack brought us both down on the wide, deep steps. I was determined to feel no pain, and in fact did feel no pain though she brought her belt down on my bare legs over and over. I turned my face up to her, and this time I did grin at her. She was as furious as she could be, and finally wore herself out and stopped, crying in frustrated anger. Just as on the Easter when I got a beating in the bus, my twin sister stood on the landing above, or rather hopped on it, all her feathers ruffled out as she cried in useless rage. I don't know whether I carried marks of the whipping on my legs, but if I did, they could not have been long lasting for the whipping never hurt at all.

I am going to leave the subject of Miss Burton in order to speak of Miss Annie P. Parker. I recall Miss Parker's coming as if it were yesterday. The superintendent came into the dining hall while we were at supper, as he did when he had a general announcement to make. (In an aside, I should say that when he announced peace and the end of the war, he did not wait until supper, but had the bell rung to assemble all of us together on the wide steps that swept up to the broad front porch of the girls' building and addressed us from the sweep below.) Anyway, on this spring evening, he told us that a new staff member would be joining us in a few days, named Miss Parker, and that she would work with the children who had not yet started school. In other words, she would be in charge of kindergarten, though he did not use that word. My ears almost grew pointed with excitement at his words. I knew in every fiber of my being that she was my savior and would save me from Miss Burton. After supper, I went onto the lawn to the left front of the new building in the lee of a ligustrum hedge that stood at a right angle to the girls' building. As I stood in the warm night air, a rising wind began to blow through the tops of the trees and to stir eddies on the ground. I was slightly drunk with excitement. As I stood with my arms extended straight out from the sides of my body in the hope that the wind would lift me up and help me fly, I chanted Miss Parker's name over and over. When she came, I felt I knew her already, for she looked just as I thought she should look – of a medium height and well formed, large eyes, hair pulled back from her face and carefully dressed, modest clothes, lisle stockings and sensible shoes. Above all, there was a pleasant interested air about her that foretold good days.

Miss Parker had a great fund of games suitable for small children: "Drop the Handkerchief," "London Bridge," "Rover Red Rover," "King William was King George's Son," "Bum, Bum, Bum, Here We Come,"

"Go In and Out the Window," "Simon Sez," and on and on. She taught us various ways of counting out in order to discover who was "it." My favorite of these was "William Trembletoes." She cut out and sewed up on three sides, rag dolls and small cloth animals that we stuffed then gave back to be sewn up on the side she had left open.

She recited poems to us: "Little Orphan Annie Came to Our House to Stay" (which was rather daring of her), "The Gingerbread Dog, and the Calico Cat," "Grandma Had a Little Grey Billy Goat" among them. I retain a vivid image in my head of the day we sat in a semi-circle around her in the flower garden as she read, "Who has seen the wind/ neither you nor I/ But when the trees bow down their heads/ The wind is passing by." As I looked up into the top of the pecan tree under which we sat in the hope of seeing either the wind or the tree bowing down its head, I discovered a great silver dirigible floating off to the south, moving from east to west. I didn't think that Miss Parker had made the dirigible appear just at that moment, but there was not another member of the staff for whom one would have appeared. For the brief period she was there, she stole my heart, put balm on my wounds, and was the very antidote I needed to Miss Burton's methods. This was the summer that I turned 6, so I started to school that fall. I had the very great pleasure of having Miss Parker as a teacher again when I entered the second grade. Here she encouraged my reading, and when she praised me, her praise surpassed gold. I never saw Miss Parker again after that school year, but I did not lose her. She has been with me ever since, and I praise her memory. Her simple kindnesses, coming when they did, strengthened my spirit and put my world on a better footing.

In this same vein, I should mention Mrs. Lena Wimborn, a widow, above middle age, with a benevolent face and air about her. I had no formal connection with Mrs. Wimborn, but I loved to be in her presence. She was attached to the girls' building, so my opportunities to be around her were infrequent. I have spoken of her in connection with study hall, and said something about her special relationship with Rabbit B. The truth is I think Mrs. Wimborn had a weakness for lively little boys, but she had an art for keeping them within bounds. It gave me much pleasure to pick long stemmed violets from behind the pump house and take them to her. On my last visit to the orphanage after I had left it, I walked the two miles to town to visit her, and walked back again after the visit. She was living on the edge of town with a younger woman. I found her looking very fragile and shrunken—a far cry from the stately white haired woman I had known only a few years earlier. Sometime after that visit, Mrs. Wimborn came to me by night in Chapel Hill to let me know that she had died. She was restored to her former vigor and glowed with well-being. She was still white haired, but had the appearance of a woman in her forties. I was so much struck by the appearance, or visualization, that I telephoned Middlesex the next day and made inquiries. I was told that she had died three days previously, by which I knew the visitation to be a true one.

   I have spoken of Mrs. Wimborn out of turn. I should have spoken first of the Mitchells. Perhaps it matters but little. Clarence Mitchell ('23-'32) had been reared in the orphanage and had gone into the U.S. Army during World War II. After he was demobilized at the war's end, he made a visit to the orphanage, riding on his fast motorcycle. My notion is that he not only wanted to show it to an audience of admiring big boys, but that he was also riding about the countryside looking for a girl to court. He found one, Mary Price, and married her. Not long after, they joined the orphanage staff. Mr. Mitchell was a largish fellow and not particularly tall. His small sleepy eyes saw more than one would have thought. Similarly, his girth concealed the fact that he had considerable strength and could move very quickly, indeed, when a situation required it. Mrs. Mitchell was probably no more than 18 or 19 when she came to the orphanage with her new husband. She was very handsome, rather than conventionally pretty. Her eyes sparkled, and she had a profusion of rich blonde hair that threw out glints of gold as it rippled to the top of her shoulders. Although I was no more than 8 or 9 at the time, I was keen to some of the elements of her good looks. I never tired of turning to look at her after she had formed us into an orderly line to move out to the dining hall. The arch in a woman's lower back and the line formed as it flares into the curve of the hip is not repeated elsewhere in nature, and Mrs. Mitchell had this to perfection. If I gazed in admiration, one may well guess her effect on the imagination of the big boys some of whom, after all, were no more than two or three years her junior. I recall sitting with my back to one of the rectangular columns that stood by the entryway to the boys' building, basking and daydreaming in the sun on a Sunday afternoon, while nearby one of the big boys attempted to flirt with her. Mrs. Mitchell knew instinctively how to turn him away while accepting his admiration, and how to do so without wounding his self-esteem.

How many times over the years, I wonder, have I paused to cast my mind back to Mrs. Mitchell? Whenever I do I am invariably filled with admiration of her pluck and self confidence in taking on the responsibility, at so young an age, of dealing with a horde of boys of all ages. She was little more than a young country girl with no great experience. She must have had a gang of brothers at home on whom she had honed her skills. From the beginning she had no trouble in imposing her will on her husband, on the big boys, on the middle size boys, and on the little boys. It helped to have, in addition to her innate ability, the authority to whip us when necessary. I suspect that it helped, too, to have Clarence Mitchell standing in the wings.

The term "house mother" conveys a clearer idea of Mrs. Mitchell's role in our lives than does the term actually used—"matron." Her relationship to our daily life and work was roughly analogous to that of the home room teacher in school. Except for those of us who had to rise very early at 4:30 to attend to our pre-breakfast and pre-school jobs, Mr. Mitchell went around and roused the boys from sleep. The very early risers were awakened individually by an especially appointed bigger boy who came to our bedside and touched our faces or softly called our names so as not to awaken our sleeping fellows.

Mrs. Mitchell neither assigned nor supervised our individual jobs of chicken boys, hog boys, dairy boys, kitchen boy, or what have you. These assignments were made by "them." "They" were adult staff members working in concert or individually. I hate to come right out and admit that during the duration of my stay at the orphanage there was always this division, separated by a gulf—"they" or "them" and "me" or "us." Except for the very brief period when Miss Parker, and later Mrs. Wimborn, flung a temporary bridge across the gulf, this division was permanent and enduring so far as I was concerned.

Albemarle Cottage built on right side of road

The work of the boys who were assigned jobs as "house boys" was supervised by Mrs. Mitchell. They were every day and all the day long under her immediate charge. My stint as house boy was not a long one. I think I was not very satisfactory. By this time we had moved into the new boys' building, "Albemarle Cottage." This building had had a former existence as three independent wooden army barracks at Camp Butner. I think I have already said that after the war Mr. Evans made big changes in livestock, having decided we should get considerably more milk from Holstein cows, and more lean meat from black and white Poland China hogs. He built a new dairy at the other farm, got electric milking machines to do justice to the new cows, put up a silo to store green fodder over winter, put up new stables for the mules, and so forth. In short, he moved the farmyard to the other farm and the livestock with it. He then used the site of the old farmyard to erect "Albemarle Cottage." The ground at this point began its slope down to the small branch that wound its way through the former pasture. He had the foundation laid, and built up at the rear, to receive the new building.

Albemarle Cottage built from old army barracks

The old barracks had been disassembled at Butner and shipped by rail to Middlesex, then transported by truck to the orphanage. There were three of them. When they were reassembled they were each made to form a wing extending back from a front passageway. The apartment for the Mitchells was at the center, and at this point a short wing ran back that was designed to serve as a "day room" for the boys. Otherwise the smaller boys lived in the right wing and the bigger boys in the left wing. Because of my size (I did not get my growth spurt until after I left the orphanage), I lived in the right wing. A brick veneer incased the former wooden buildings, and the inside featured gleaming wood floors, lots of pine paneling, and built in dressers and mirrors for each boy. This building, when completed, had two long wings at either end, and a truncated wing, or ell, in the middle. All joined to the long hall, or passageway, that formed the long front façade and resembled a giant capital letter "E" when viewed from above. It was suggested in jest that this was done purposely in honor of Mr. Evans. It was, I think, a groundless jest.

After the former barracks were reconstructed, the result was as unlike the old dormitory as anything could be. The barracks concept was retained in the new building, and all the bunks and their companion dressers were lined up in a uniform neat row one after another down the length of the wing. There might have been advantages to this living in the open, but it meant some loss of privacy and all loss of individuality. I did not like it. I preferred our old warren that had rooms of varying sizes up and down its hallways. True we slept sometimes six or eight to a room in the old dormitory, but at least the rooms there had doors, and rooms were shared by age groups.

One good thing about leaving the old building is that we left behind the earwigs that lived in its walls. Earwigs were handy for scaring new boys. They were warned about these harmless pale, watery centipedes, and told that they were dangerous things that loved to crawl into the ears of sleeping boys and eat their brains in the night. Karma has arranged it so that my house, built in 1939, has plaster walls on which the occasional earwig disports itself. I put cotton in my ears, now, just in case.

The old dormitory with its dark central hallway with bedrooms set on either side allowed us to get on with our cleaning jobs without a lot of "spit and polish." "Albemarle Cottage", on the other hand, was full of daylight that revealed to Mrs. Mitchell's vigilant eye all dust, dirt, and scuff marks wherever they lurked. There was nothing slovenly about her housekeeping, and she made sure there was none about ours. We scoured the bathrooms and their fixtures. We dusted and polished the furniture. We erased scuff marks with a solvent solution, and mopped the floors clean. We scraped old wax from the floors, rewaxed them with paste wax, and buffed them to a high sheen. The corners of the floor and the areas along the wall had to be buffed by hand and not by the buffing machine. The only thing remotely resembling fun in all this drudgery was in the buffing. Though Mrs. Mitchell discouraged such antics we sometimes buffed by dragging up and down the length of the dayroom floor a boy seated on an old wool blanket. As I said earlier I did not long hold the job of houseboy—if indeed I ever held it at all. Mrs. Mitchell was not above pressing any idle loafer into helping with the cleaning of the building if she chose to do so. And the new building, as I have said, afforded few hiding places for loafers. I might have been pressed into cleaning service just by being in the wrong place at the wrong time. She, Mrs. Mitchell, had a gift for binding us all to her will.

This gift meant she almost never had to resort to whipping a boy, and chose, mostly, to reason with one. At such times when I was involved, I was as polite as could be, full of "Yes, Mam", "No, Mam." Then I would go away and as likely as not repeat my offense. I think I must have been an aggravating boy from time to time. For her part Mrs. Mitchell loved fairness and it was characteristic of her that she always exercised it. She could not, with all those boys, rise to actual affection, but her honesty and sense of fair play was unfailing.

While I think I aggravated Mrs. Mitchell from time to time, I know that I aggravated Mrs. Mixon fairly frequently. Mr. and Mrs. Horace Mixon and their daughter and son joined the orphanage staff at the close of 1948. For a variety of reasons, I had less contact with them as a family than I had had with the family of the superintendent (Mr. Evans), who left in the year after the Mixons came. In the first place, their daughter was a year older than I, and it would have been unsuitable for her to seek playmates out of the boys' building. Her friendships were with girls, and her younger brother followed her example. Also, with the relocation of the farming operation to the other farm, I was less and less involved in it. As a result, my contacts with Mr. Mixon were sporadic. He and Mr. Mitchell shared responsibility for the farming. My impression is that Mr. Mixon was, or became, the principal supervisor for farming. He was a good farmer and skilled, as good farmers are, in a host of things. The first time I laid eyes on him, if I am not mistaken, he was shoeing a mule at the shop, heating the shoe in the forge and beating it on the anvil into shape for the mule's foot. He could help a cow deliver her calf, or a sow her litter. I believe he supervised some of the work when "Albemarle Cottage" was put up. His intention was to be upright and just, but I perceived him as stern and unbending.

In the case of Mrs. Mixon, the situation was different, for I found myself working for her for a considerable period of time. In some ways, she was a mirror image of her husband (though not physically so). She had a strong work ethic, a clear sense of duty, and an upright honesty in all things. She seldom laughed, but when she did, it was a joy to hear. If she had a weakness, it might have been the lack of a sense of humor, or one that was not easily tickled.

When the Evans left in the year following the arrival of the Mixons, Mrs. Mixon assumed the duties of dietitian. It was a true calling. I assume that Mrs. Evans and Mrs. Mixon worked together until the kitchen was turned over to the latter in 1949. She was a worthy successor, so far as food preparation was concerned. Mrs. Mixon had, or acquired, the knack of seasoning and cooking well in large quantities. She, like Mrs. Evans, hated waste, and tolerated no disorder in her kitchen.

I cannot for the life of me remember whether the great iron cooking range was modified when Mrs. Evans was still there, or whether it was altered under Mrs. Mixon. When it occurred, the stove was not the only thing that was altered. My duties altered, too. I have already spoken of the period in which the stove was fueled by split wood. It was converted to burn fuel oil.

Some clever artisan modified the stove so that it was fed a thin little stream of fuel oil just inside its door. From here, the oil ran down to the firebox and burned on a fire plate. The trick was to begin the stream as a trickle and let it run just long enough for the correct amount to pool, then set it alight without blowing the stove up—or drowning it out. When the trickle of fuel was lighted at the door, the door was quickly closed and the trickle took the fire down to the fuel that had pooled on the fire plate. When done properly, the great range gave a sudden "whoosh" that was most satisfactory to a boy. The flow of fuel could then be increased. The degree of heat in the stove was regulated by increasing or decreasing the flow of fuel from the fuel cock. If too much fuel pooled before lighting, the ignition could set off an explosion in the stove strong enough to knock askew the iron plates that formed its top. Or, too much fuel could flood the stove altogether. If that happened, the top plates would have to be lifted and all vents opened so that the excess fuel could evaporate. Or, if there were insufficient time to wait for evaporation to take place, the fuel would have to be mopped out before a fresh attempt to light it could be made.

I freely admit that I am one of those persons who hate change. Having admitted that, I still think I am justified in saying that no other fuel in the world has matched wood for heating an oven. Breads, cakes, sweet potatoes and roasts cooked in the oven of a wood-burning iron stove are unequalled. This judgment is based on experience with wood-burning stoves other than the orphanage stove. All the same, food continued to be sent from the kitchen by Mrs. Mixon as delicious as ever after our stove had been modified.

As one of those to be awakened early, I was roused at 4:30 and was at the kitchen by 5:00. If the cook stove had not already been lighted, I would light the stove. Then, I would go into the dining hall and prime and light the two large kerosene heaters that warmed the large room. These stood opposite one another on either side of the big room. One stood near the door by which the boys entered, and the other near the door used by the girls. By the time everyone was up, finished with their morning chores, and dressed for school, the dining hall was nice and warm for breakfast. As a rule I dressed for school before coming to the kitchen to work so as to be able to do everything and get to the school bus without a great rush. Sometimes this worked, and sometimes it did not. On one occasion, I missed getting on the bus before it pulled out and went on its way. I had to walk the two miles, and more, to school that day. One of my duties was to keep filled the fuel tanks on the two heaters. The kerosene supply was in a large drum lying on its side on an out-of-doors platform that stood head high. I would fill a fuel can from the drum, lug it into the dining hall, lift it up to the fuel tank on the heater and pour it in. I hated it when I spilt it, for I would get kerosene splashed onto my school clothes and shoes. If I hadn't time to go change my clothes, I'd wear them with the hope that the odor would disappear after the fuel evaporated. The heavy fuel cans were just about the fullest limit of my strength. Usually, there was no spillage.

After school, I'd return to the kitchen and fill the fuel tanks again for supper and study hall. But before tackling this, I'd find me a cold biscuit, poke my finger into one of the sides to make a hole, and fill it with molasses. Or, if I felt like living dangerously, I would surreptitiously lay my hands on a large can of golden cane syrup that had a lion's face on it [King's Syrup] and really make a treat of my biscuit with it. I knew that taking some of the molasses was okay, and that taking some of the syrup was not. But when the syrup was left out and ready to hand, what was a child to do? Was it a punishment, I wonder, that a meat skin, to which I could help myself, too, never tasted well with syrup? All that salt and all that sugar made no good combination.

Summer duties in the kitchen were unlike winter duties. I might be sent to the garden to get more tomatoes, or to cut some young tender okra for a meal. When sent for a few more vegetables from the garden, I never failed to take a salt shaker with me. While there I would pull a ripe tomato from the vine, wipe the dirt off onto my overalls, and then eat it, the tomato in one hand and the salt shaker in the other. I still remember the rich juicy tomatoes and their full bodied flavor. You could taste the sun in them. When necessary I might kill chickens, usually by chopping off their heads. I hated it when the chicken would hop to its feet and stagger about headless, splattering blood everywhere. I once thought I would try wringing the chickens' necks, and got through two or three of them without incident. I would hold them by the head and upper neck and fling their body around and around like a noise maker at a New Year's party. The last chicken was a layer, and what's more was ready to lay an egg for the day. I flung her around in my usual way and flung a perfectly formed hard shelled egg right out of her. I dropped her in great surprise. She made good her chance to escape and live another day. The egg splattered on the ground--a total loss.

   Summer months were canning months. String beans, beets, corn cut from the cob, fruits. All kinds of good things were put up in sealed jars and added to the shelves of the kitchen storehouse. Churches would send canned goods, too, particularly fruit preserves that had been put up by women of the church for our use. The large canner would be erected in the kitchen yard, and a fire built in its firebox to heat the water in the canner to sufficient temperature to seal the jars of food after they were immersed in it. Wire baskets would be filled with quart or half gallon glass jars of tomatoes, corn, string beans, or whatever was going. The filled baskets of jars, their lids screwed tightly down, were lowered into the hot water and left submerged there for a specific length of time, at the end of which the jars would be safely sealed against the entry of bacteria, molds, and other toxins. My job was to stay nearby and feed the fire and keep the water at the proper temperature. A cooking thermometer hung in the water so that the temperature could be checked. It was a tedious but not onerous job. I remember once having to tend the canner after the county book mobile had made its visit, and I had got a fresh supply of books to read. I don't recall what books I got on this occasion, but they included something that was powerfully good to read. (To be honest, I had developed such a passion, or vice, for reading that nearly everything was good to read.) When I took my seat by the canner that afternoon, book in hand, I may as well have been in China. Mrs. Mixon would spot me from the kitchen engrossed in my book, see that very little smoke was coming from the canner's chimney pipe, and send one of the girls to make enquiries. On one occasion the fire was all but out, and the mercury in the thermometer dropping below the correct range when I came to my senses and put things right. If Mrs. Mixon had discovered this state of affairs, she would have been justified in whaling the tar out of me. Apparently all the jars got properly sealed despite my lackadaisical performance. No one, in any event, came down later with food poisoning.

Looking back on these days I sometimes think what an aggravating boy I must have been to Mrs. Mixon. If sent to the garden to get a few more tomatoes, or what have you, I might dawdle beyond the point that whatever I was sent for was wanted. I might slip out the dining hall door on the girls' side and waste time by sitting on the stoop to see if a June bug might come by, or, failing that, if one of the girls might see me and come over to talk. Time to Mrs. Mixon was like a big potato in the sense that none of it was to be wasted. One day I discovered an actual hiding place into which I might disappear for 10 or 15 minutes without detection. I don't think this place was ever discovered by Mrs. Mixon. It was in the space formed by the rafters and joists under the roof of the smokehouse. A long opening had been left for venting purposes above the clapboards of the south wall, just below the roof that overhung to create a small shed. I found that I could stand on a chair, hop up, and catch hold to pull myself up and in. I was small for my age, and very agile. By looking around carefully beforehand, I could enter and leave this hiding place without being seen.

Mrs. Mixon was not fond of a switch, but she did not hesitate to use one when she thought it necessary. This was a part of doing ones duty. She had to do her duty on me from time to time. I should not be surprised to learn that she had said of me what Mrs. Wimborn had said of Rabbit B_____: that he needed a daily whipping on principle.

Smith Children

It was at about the time of this discovery that I met a young brother and sister who had come to the orphanage, Jerry and Nancy ('49-'60). I was much struck by Jerry, and when he took me with him to the girls' building and introduced me to Nancy, I was much struck by her, too. They closely resembled one another. They bore themselves similarly. Both had an open, candid look. The same clear light played about their faces. I felt by them as I had felt years earlier toward Jamie W_____., the little boy whose sleep my arrival disturbed and whom I wanted for a friend. I felt as though I had long known Jerry and Nancy—almost as if they had been a brother and a sister I had forgotten that I had had. I liked them immensely. But let me get on with my anecdote. Nancy had, and showed to me, some devotional cards having on one side a richly colored picture of a saint from the universal calendar, and on the other side a short printed account of his life. These were a gift to her from a grandmother, but whether she brought them with her to the orphanage or whether they were sent to her there, I do not know. I had never seen anything like them and was fascinated by them. I had never heard of the saints. (St. Nicholas and St. Valentine did not count.) These people reminded me of the Greek heroes, of whom I had heard, but these saints had lived in historical times and were Christian, not pagan. Nancy lent me three or four of them at my urging, and eventually brought me a few more of them. There was St. Martin of Tours, dividing his cloak with the poor beggar who turned out to be Christ. There was St. Lawrence with his gridiron, St. Christopher with the Christ child on his shoulder, St. Sebastian shot full of arrows, St. Elizabeth of Hungary with roses springing from her footprints in the snow as she went about feeding the poor, and others. They required close scrutiny and reflection. I took those she handed to me and leapt up with them to my hiding place. Here I put them aside for future study, and added others to them as Nancy let me have more. I may say in passing that these little cards not only broadened my sense of Christian awareness, but they also gave me a leg up when I came to study Western art. In the end Nancy had to insist that I return her cards to her, which I did, and a good thing, too. They exerted a strong pull on me, and I probably set a record in that brief period for sneaking off from the kitchen in order to study them.

  Not long after the arrival of Jerry and Nancy, I left the orphanage to take up life with my father. Consequently, I did not live with these two children long enough to cultivate a longer friendship based on day-to-day contact. The construction of my mind is such that time and distance matter but little. The friendly feelings I felt for those two have remained alive and enduring even though not developed further. In my departure I suppose it is fitting that the situation was reversed from my arrival. Then I wished to have as a friend Jamie W_____, who left; now I wished to have these two as friends, and I left.

  Nobody can tell about these things with certainty, but it might have been a very good thing that I did not remain to spend my adolescence at the orphanage. I have spoken of the removal of the farmyard as producing a sea change in my life there. The removal to "Albemarle Cottage" would have produced an even greater one. I bore barracks life okay during my weeks of basic training in the Army. It was bearable in the Army because it served a purpose and because it was for a period with a known ending. I was not a growing boy with nothing better to look forward to for the duration as would have been the case had I been at the orphanage and lived in the barracks-like "Albemarle Cottage."

I am aware of the fact that I have left a lot of things untold. I have said not a word about the health care given the children. I could at least have said something about the kindness of Dr. Powell who drove out from Middlesex to attend to us when we were sick. It seems particularly ungrateful not to have done so, for in our second or third winter there, my little brother came down with pneumonia, and Dr. Powell attended to him faithfully. The case was so severe that his life was despaired of at one point. Dr. Powell's care and Mrs. Pope's devoted nursing brought him through it safely. For surgery we went to the hospital at Wilson. My twin sister and I were there simultaneously by pure happenstance—me for a tonsillectomy and she for an appendectomy. Dental care was by a traveling dentist who was sent out by one of the departments or agencies of the state. He set up his chair and pedal driven drill and went to work. He solaced us with colored bird cards. I can't recall the name of the doctor who came to the orphanage to examine us as part of the program to eradicate diseases caused by the hookworm, called by the press, "The Vampire of the South." Perhaps he was Dr. Nash, who drove a Hudson; or he was Dr. Hudson who drove a Nash? The little boys, who liked bathroom humor, had fun with it, and the bigger boys blushed. The doctor had enlisted the help of some of the big girls, and it was an ordeal for the boys to have to crawl onto his table and lie face down while their naked bums stuck up in the air for all to see and titter at. The worst part was being swabbed and examined for signs of the worm. For those who knew what humiliation was, it was humiliating. So far as I know the examining physician found not a single case of hookworm at the orphanage. So far as humiliation was concerned, the orphanage was struck by three episodes far more humiliating. And, anyway, hookworm was endemic in the south. The three episodes of which I speak affected nearly every child there. One boy, whose name I shan't suggest, brought a contagious itch among us, and itch was caused by dirtiness. All of us had to be treated with a compound of stinking sulfur. Thank goodness this took place when school was not in session. The head lice, on the other hand, were probably brought in from school. I think it affected the girls only. It took days of medication and fine toothed combs to get rid of them. The girls went around looking like wet dogs and smelling far worse. Any of them who had tittered at the boys' bare rumps got their comeuppance in spades. I can't account for how we managed to get bedbugs in that enclosed world, but manage it we did. I think kerosene was used to kill them. The mattresses, every one of them, were carefully searched and treated. The bedsteads, bedsprings, bed splats were all dismantled room by room, taken out into the sunshine, and washed with kerosene (or whatever it was that we used to kill the bugs and their eggs). I have tried, without success, to figure out how bedbugs were brought to the orphanage. In my imagination I can see them, like army ants, marching through the woods until they came to our buildings where they made themselves at home. That's mere whimsy, of course. Do let me make it clear that these episodes of itch, lice, and bedbugs were onetime, and onetime only events. There was never a repetition of any one of the three.

The usual childhood diseases are hardly worth mentioning—measles, mumps, chicken pox. If one boy brought one of these diseases from school, he passed it on to his playmates. Consequently, there was a whole roomful of, say, mumps at the time. Overall this might have been a good thing. It simplified matters for Dr. Powell and enabled the staff to get the nursing for a particular ailment all done at once instead of in bits and dabs over an extended period.

There was something I wished to say about the school at Middlesex and failed to say. I shan't worry about that omission. It might have been something in connection with the principal, "Sneaky" O'Neal, so called because of his sometimes successful attempts to sneak up on the older boys at school who congregated behind the school water tank to enjoy a forbidden cigarette. Or it might not have been. I chose not to include some anecdotes because they were unnecessary to the point I was trying to make. One of these had to do with the terrible school bus crash of 1949. It did not involve the school at Middlesex, but all our students were assembled and told of it. A bus loaded with school children belonging to a sister school had a head-on collision with a Pine State Dairy truck in a blind curve near Turkey Creek. Perhaps as many as eight, or ten or twelve, children were killed outright. It was a dreadful piece of news that gave our students a shock. Each of the Middlesex students came to terms with the tragedy in his own way. The orphanage children had all encountered death before, and carried their personal grief privately buried within themselves. Our grief, those of us at the orphanage, was all one-sided. We knew firsthand what it was to lose a parent, but we lacked the experience necessary to imagine the grief of a parent over the loss of a child. I don't know whether we were better able to cope with news of the fatal accident than the other students, or not. All of us coped as best we could. That pseudo-profession of "grief counselors" had not yet been invented, so we were spared that. Perhaps I sneer wrongfully. Fifty or sixty years ago when people were born at home and died at home, death was integrated in day-to-day life. Both have been institutionalized and now seldom take place at home. As a result, I daresay most children in the U.S. form their notion of death from computer games, horror movies, television shows, and such. Perhaps the age we live in has called "grief counselors" into being.

    I have said nothing about runaways either, for it is a topic of which I have no firsthand knowledge. There were tales, kept alive among the boys, of runaways, but they may have been no more than tales. I remember only two occasions when a couple of the boys would pair together for support and run away together. In each case they were found and brought back before they got into real trouble in the world outside the orphanage. They were big boys who were only two or three years away from being discharged in due course. I have no idea what prompted them to run away. The reasons must have differed from boy to boy. There was no such thing as a "typical" boy, and no such thing as "typical" reasons for running away either, I imagine, unless adolescent rebellion played a strong part in it. I should have thought the boys would have been looking ahead at discharge in course with as much apprehension as anticipation. Or, perhaps not.

    I did not remain in the orphanage until discharge in course. Consequently, I do not know what provisions were made for a departing child. I'm sure he wasn't just shown the door and told to stay away. At the same time, whatever was done, and however it was done, I am pretty sure that it was made clear to the child that it was to be a clean break and that he could not return later and expect to be given bed and board. In one way we were like the typical farm family in which one of the boys might, after high school was finished, leave the farm, go to town, get a job, and strike out on his own. In another way we were unlike, for none of the boys could remain at home after high school and help with the farming. I never heard what responsibilities and obligations the orphanage assumed when discharging a child. There was no question of helping him obtain further education. Were they given assistance in finding a job to go to when they were discharged, I wonder? Were they given a small sum of money and transported to a nearby town? If they had family, were they taken in by a family member while trying to get on their feet? No doubt most of the boys went into the Army (and got two or three year's breathing space) as volunteers or draftees. If any ever returned to talk of their experiences, I never heard them. Their experiences must have been as varied as the boys themselves.

Little did I suppose when I met the brother and sister whom I wanted as friends, Jerry and Nancy, that this heralded the closing of the circle of my life that had begun in 1942 when I met Jamie W_____ and wished to have him as my friend. Now I look back and see that that is exactly what it was. The circle of my orphanage life closed in 1952 when I left. It has been characteristic of my life that when a period of it closed, I sealed it off like the chambered nautilus, and threw my heart, mind, and soul into the new period into which I entered.

It seems appropriate to me that now, 55 years later, as my life draws to its close, I should have been asked by that same boy, Jerry, now a grandfather several times over, to write a memoir of those years. I write at his behest, but for all who choose to read. I have little doubt that I have gone on for too great a length, that I have omitted many things, written too thinly of some things, and spoken in too much detail about others. Still, what I have written may serve to jolt the memories of others. What can it matter if our memories are sometimes at variance? They are sure to be. I can only say that in memories there is no single truth, but as many truths as there are rememberers.

Time has an art to change all things. It softens and blurs recollections of our experiences. It hangs a thin veil at the boundary of each period of our life, so that when we look backward, we gaze through veils that distort and partially conceal what we wish to scrutinize. More than that, it ought to be borne in mind that our perceptions are shaped to a large extent by our position at the time; at every level the view is different. While this need not invalidate a perception, it means that one must expect wide divergences in the interpretation of events.

Because of this, I imagine there are some who may feel I have written rhapsodic accounts of some aspects of my life at the orphanage, especially when they think back to their own experience. I am unwilling to say that I have put too fair a face on some things. I will admit freely, however, that I was fortunate in the years that I was there. There was some advantage even in my experience with Miss Burton. In later life when I encountered people of malice and petty minds, I merely reminded myself that everyone does not have to like us, and we don't have to like everyone. I had Miss Burton under my belt, and that helped me later to rise above the ill-disposed as I had risen above her. From my early childhood to the present day I have had my share of peculiarities and eccentricities. During the years that we boys were housed by age and size in small groups in our own rooms in the old boys' building, such things could be accommodated pretty easily. Not only that, but when there were only a few boys living together in a group it made possible a degree of camaraderie that would have been difficult to build and sustain in the barracks-like atmosphere of "Albemarle Cottage." And as for going off to your room to be sometimes alone, such a thing was out of the question in the new boys' building. There were no dividing walls and interior doors. There were only long open spaces with beds lined up side by side. One swift glance from the matron's eye could sweep the entire space in less than a second.

I don't know when it was that I first concluded that to go in "pursuit of happiness," as popularly understood, is to go on a fool's errand. Was I ever happy at the orphanage—or even afterward? I don't care to examine the question, and don't know what I should do with the answer should I find it. Was I content? Yes. Contentment is a very achievable and satisfactory state of being. So, while the orphanage was imperfect, the life I lived there, when taken as a whole, suited me. To my way of thinking our mother made a wise decision when she directed that my siblings and I be sent there after her death. I was, and still am, content with her decision.

Stevenson Family-L-R: Elizabeth, Haywood, George, and Joyce

Footnotes: George Stevenson completed his memoir November 1, 2008. He died September 23, 2009. Dr. W. Burkette Raper ('36-'44) officiated his graveside services. Jerry Smith ('49-'60) spoke at the services. George is buried in the Baptist Cemetery, Scotland Neck, North Carolina. He was 72. The dialect George used in writing his memoir is contributed to his love of the Elizabethan Era and Literature.

9

The Best and Worst Day

David John Lane
(1946-52)

The worst day of my life ended up being the best day of my life. The paths I have taken have been steered by the experiences and the lessons I learned which started one very warm day in August 1946.

David John Lane

I was a young 10-year-old boy living on a farm with my widowed mother, brothers and sisters. I had never been more than 15 miles from home until that day. I remember taking the longest ride I had ever taken. Someone came in a van and picked up me and three of my brothers, Durwood, age 8, Jacob, age 5, Robert Lee, age 4 and my sister Patricia, age 6, to take us the 60 miles from my home to the orphanage. It was called the Free Will Baptist Orphanage in Middlesex, North Carolina. When we arrived at the orphanage, we were greeted by the superintendent, Mr. James Evans ('41-'49) and house parents, Mary and Clarence Mitchell. I later learned that Clarence Mitchell was an alumnus ('23-'32) of the orphanage and a World War II veteran.

During this time, James Evans was the superintendent ('40-'49) of the orphanage, but later "Pa Smith" ('51-'55 & '56-'58) took that position. His real name was Stephen A. Smith. Carrold Little and I gave him the name of "Pa Smith." He was a good man who loved kids. He would put his arm around you when he talked to you and it felt good and it was comforting. That was the thing we were looking for. All kids need to know that someone cares and someone loves them. We found that in "Pa Smith."

One of the things I remember about being at the orphanage in the first few days was that I was put to work in the dairy barn. I was 10 years old and up until this point, I was just a farm boy who had worked odd jobs to help out my family. This job was new to me, as we couldn't afford cows and had never had them at home. The orphanage had about 30 cows to take care of. My job was to clean the barn every morning and every night. I would hose it down and make sure it was clean and ready for the day. This was quite a responsibility for a 10-year old. Later, I was given the job of helping milk five cows every morning and every night. I did this job for the next two years, until I was 12. I then was given the job of working in the laundry room and firing the boiler. This was an important job as the boiler provided the hot water for not only the laundry, but for all of the hot water used at the orphanage. I also helped with the laundry in the big commercial washer that was used to wash clothing. Both of these jobs, in the barn and in the laundry room, began each morning at 5:30 a.m. However, the job in the laundry room was a step up! In the barn, we cleaned seven days a week. In the laundry room, we only did laundry five days a week, but we did still fire the boilers each and every day. Clarence Mitchell was overseeing the laundry and the house jobs.

Part of our daily life in the orphanage was learning that hard work was expected and everyone had a job to do, but an education was just as important. I started the fourth grade at Middlesex Public School shortly after beginning my life at the orphanage. There were approximately 100 children in the orphanage when we arrived, about half girls and half boys. There were three of us Lane children who went to school with the other school age children that September in 1946. The two younger Lanes weren't old enough for school yet. Our days were full with getting up early and working our jobs and then getting to school and making sure we kept up with our studies. There were also jobs when we came home in the evening. The tone was set for our lives, to keep us busy. We worked hard, learned life lessons and we were exhausted by the end of the day. The lessons we learned during those years were the value of a job well done, respecting our elders and an education was expected. It was also during this time that I was given the very first Christmas gift I had ever received. It was a Roy Rogers sweatshirt and something I remember to this day.

During the time that my brothers, sisters and I were there, we did not have a family relationship. Because we were different ages, we were placed in buildings with other children the same age. We were not together. We were expected to work hard, go to school and behave. This did not include encouraging a relationship with other members of our family. It was very hard not knowing how your little brother or sister were doing. As a big brother, you felt responsible for them. However, I knew they were cared for. They had plenty of food to eat, a warm place to sleep and a good roof over their heads. Because of this, I was able to go on about my job of learning and working hard. In later years, my siblings and I have talked and as adults, we wondered why we didn't help each other out or why certain things happened the way they did. However, it was a different era and we knew no different. We only knew that our physical needs were being met and we were doing what we needed to do to grow and make something out of our lives. We were also only children.

In 1947, we began cutting bushes and removing trees from the low area where the creek flowed across the road, just past the farm buildings. The low area is where the present day pond is located. At that time, there was no pond, only a wet area with the creek running through it. Those working on this particular project were: Loyce Rogers ('46-'58), Carroll Little ('46-'53), John Rogers ('46-'52), Billy Powell ('38-'49), J. C. Butts ('37-'50), J. B. Outlaw ('43-'52), Franklin Bradshaw ('44-'51), Charles Page ('40-'54) and me. With bush axes and saws, we cleared the area, working into the spring of 1948. A bulldozer was brought in by someone from Wilson and the dam was built. One of the bulldozer operators invited me to spend the weekend with his family in Wilson. They took me to my first drive-in movie. That fall, during a church service held at the big girls' building by the Reverend W. Burkette Raper (Alumnus '36-'45), three of us were "saved"—Pearl Hill ('47-'55), Christabelle Tyson ('43-'52) and me. The first baptism at the new pond was held Sunday, September 26, 1948. Burkette baptized us three.

1948 Campus: 1. Girls Building 2. Administration and Dining Hall 3. Boys Building 4. Superintendent's Home 5. Memorial Chapel 6. Albemarle Cottage 7. Mule Barn 8. Dairy Barn 9. Road to Pond

2010: Pond

At the age of 13, I went to work on the farm with Farm Manager Horace Mixon (Alumnus '23-'34) and Loyce Rodgers. Loyce was my friend and a little bit older. Horace was my supervisor and also was an alumnus ('23-'34) of the orphanage. We farmed with mules most of the time, but I also learned to drive a tractor. I was very proud when I learned to operate the Farmall M Tractor. That became my job in the spring after school, and my full-time summer job. We were equally thrilled and proud that many days during spring planting and fall harvesting, Horace came to get us out of school early so we could work on the farm. That was a treat, as 13-year-old boys loved to be outside instead of in school! The big money crop that we farmed was tobacco. Horace and I rode a tobacco planter and Loyce drove the mules. Loyce was 15 years old at this time. Horace and I had the dirty jobs, because at the end of the day you couldn't tell what color we were. The red clay dirt of North Carolina stuck to us like glue! In the summer months and early fall, our mornings started at 6:30 a.m. and ended late in the evening, probably around 7:00 or 8:00 p.m. We didn't have lunch breaks to go eat back at the house; our lunch was brought to us in a bucket. We were growing, hungry boys and devoured our lunches. Our buckets were filled with "grubby" food, the kind that sticks to your bones and can stay with you while you are working. When we opened our bucket lunches, we were treated to meat and biscuits, sometimes country ham or pork chops and lima beans, corn, green beans, collards, stewed potatoes and corn bread.

It was also during this time that Loyce and I started experimenting with cigarettes. We felt that anyone who was old enough to drive a tractor or work the mules could sit down and have a smoke. Horace knew this and would sometimes leave cigarettes and matches at the end of the rows so that we could find them. We would get to the end of a corn row or a tobacco row and there, setting on a rock or bucket, would be a couple of cigarettes and matches. We were thrilled! Horace never gave us the cigarettes himself, but someone left them for us and we figured it was him.

One day when I was 14, I remember we were working in the tobacco fields and Horace needed a tool from his house. He told me to take his car and go get it. Remember…I was 14! There was a road across an earthen dam that I would need to cross to get to his house. I had never driven a car and was scared to death to drive across that dam. The car was a 1930's Chevy with a manual transmission. I got to his house, got the tool and drove back without driving the car in the lake. That was a real accomplishment and something I was very proud of.

We were young men and learning to drive that car, working hard and school were important to us. But equally important were the girls. On

Friday and Saturday nights, the boys and girls could see each other in the dayroom of the girls' building. We would sit around and talk. There wasn't much more you could do when you had people watching your every move. There was very little hanky-panky! But many lifelong relationships were formed during this time. Several of the people I knew ended up marrying each other and are still together today.

My first girlfriend was Lillie Faye Watson ('46-'54); now she is Lilly Faye Harrell. I also dated Doris Tyson ('43-'54) and Mrs. Sudie's daughter, Peggy Mixon ('48-'59). She ate dinner with us every night and we became good friends. Mrs. Sudie Mixon was our dietician, which was the reason we ate dinner together every night. In those days, we didn't have a lot of money, not a lot of freedom and we were too tired to do much, but we always had time for girls. On Sunday afternoons we would sit outside on the grass under the pecan trees and visit. Times were very simple, we were happy and we enjoyed those warm afternoons.

It was during this time that I joined the Boy Scouts. I was 14 years old and I remember being taught the Boy Scout motto and the laws by Franklin Bradshaw ('44-'51). We were fortunate to be exposed to those values.

In 1949, I had just learned to drive and I was driving a Willis jeep. My friend, Franklin Bradshaw was driving a 1949 Chevy Station Wagon and he crashed into me while I was in the jeep. If I remember correctly, the jeep wouldn't start, so he was pushing me with the Chevy to get it started. Then the jeep took off and I stopped it in front of the dormitory. Frank rammed me in the rear end. Frank got a whipping and I got a sore neck!

While working with Horace and his wife, Mrs. Sudie, Loyce and I were always playing jokes on her. That was one of our favorite pastimes. One afternoon when Loyce and I had been swimming in the lake after work, I took my underwear off and stuffed them in my pants to make a big bulge on my hip. I hobbled up to the house and told Mrs. Sudie that I thought I had broken my hip. Mrs. Sudie took one look, brought me in the house and said she had to take me to the hospital. As she put me in the car, she saw Loyce in the background cracking up. She knew we were pulling her leg and came unglued. (In 2008, I went to visit the orphanage and made a stop at the nursing home where Mrs. Sudie lived. My wife Norma and my sister Beulah came along for the visit and Mrs. Sudie shared the story of the broken hip with them. That prank we pulled and the story we told her was something she remembered about my childhood. I enjoyed that.)

Several times on Sunday mornings, Miss Bonnie Farmer would take several of the boys and girls to sing on WGBR radio. That was something I enjoyed. Loyce and I would fight over who would drive the Willis Jeep to get there! I remember that radio station's name as the call letters stood for "World's Greatest Baccer (Tobacco)".

In the fall of the year, Horace would take some of the older boys, which included Loyce and me, in the old blue school bus for a trip up in the mountains to visit a church where we would gather apples and homemade canned goods from the members. We would fill the bus with the food and that would help get the orphanage through the winter months. During the winter, we would also kill hogs. Horace would oversee the hog killing and we would kill 15-20 hogs at a time. I often wonder where that meat went. I never remember eating it. Sometimes, we would trap rabbits and Mrs. Sudie would cook them for breakfast when we had enough for the boys at our breakfast table. She would fix fried rabbit, biscuits and gravy! It was a wonderful treat! One time Mrs. Sudie asked me to kill a chicken for her family's dinner. I went out with a shotgun and shot the chicken, but killed two more behind the bush that were hiding! I also remember Miss Bonnie Farmer would take us twice a year to Wilson, and we would visit a store to buy our clothing. We would each receive $25.00 for clothes. We were never allowed to pick out our clothes, but we always had new clothes twice a year. My sponsor was the Free Will Baptist Church in Black Mountain, North Carolina. They made sure I had the material things I needed.

One time, I remember a beating I will never forget. I was supposed to help take care of the pigs on the farm. The pigs would root under the fence and many times would get out of the pen. One night the pigs got out and Clarence Mitchell blamed me for it. Clarence gave me a beating and I ran away from the orphanage that night. That night, I told him if he ever touched me again, I would kill him. I got as far as Middlesex and he brought me back and beat me again. Needless to say, my threat did no good.

When I was about 15 years old, it was the fall of the year and I had to travel with one of the Board of Directors of the orphanage. At this point in my life, this man molested me for two years. I will not name him, as I do not want to shame his family. This is the reason I left the orphanage at a young age. I left when I was 16 years old.

It was the worst and best day of my life, again. It was a cold day in January and I had to leave so that the molesting would stop. It was a hard decision to make, as the people and the orphanage were my home and my family. I had grown to love them. I felt as if I had been forced to leave my family again. My mother agreed to take me back home at this time. She took me out of school and I had to find a job to help at home. I worked for the Asphlund Tree Company and Carolina Power and Light Company for three years until I was 19 years old. During this time, I frequently went back to the orphanage several times a month on the weekends. I would hitchhike my way back and forth to see the girls. It was also during this time that I decided to enter the United States Air Force. I was at the orphanage one Sunday night and I had made up my mind I was going. I didn't have any money to get to Raleigh to see the recruiter. I borrowed $5.00 from "Pa Smith" so that I could get there. I paid him back later and it was the best $5.00 I ever spent.

Pa and Ma Smith

After joining the Air Force, I was stationed at Lackland Air Force Base in San Antonio, Texas for basic training. After completing basic training, I was transferred to Scott Air Force Base in Belleville, Illinois. It is close to St. Louis, so I would frequently head there with some of the other airmen to find things to do in our off time. It was in St. Louis in July, 1955 that I met the love of my life, Norma Jean Cunningham. We married at Scott Air Force Base and spent the next 21 years traveling with our three daughters, as I was stationed all over the world. Norma and I have now been married for 54 years and live near our three daughters, their families and seven grandchildren. We are very close to our children. Family is the most important thing to me, as this was something I missed in my childhood.

When I say in my story that the day I arrived and the day I left were the best and worst days, I need to clarify. The day I arrived was the worst day as I was taken from my home, my mother and the place I lived. However, I was placed in an environment that allowed me to grow to be a young man who knew what hard work was. I knew that hard work paid off and that integrity, honesty and family were important. On the day I left the orphanage, I felt that I had no choice and I again felt that I was leaving my home and family. In the end, all of these events led me to the place I am today. My life, my home and, most importantly, my family are the treasures I have gathered and are the way I measure my life. I would not change anything about the path that I took to get to this place and this time. Every single incident, good and bad, had an impact and an influence on the next decisions I made. And as I said....I am very satisfied and have what is most important to me. I have my wife, my family and there is always an arm around someone's shoulder reminding them that they are loved.

10

An Orphan's View

Alice Little
(1946-55)

On a fall day November 11, 1936 twins were born to Mr. and Mrs. James Little, Jr. from Farmville, North Carolina. My name is Alice and I arrived first, Doris was right behind on my heels. I am told many folk from near and far came to see the "Little" twins and their older brother, Carrold, age two.

The Christmas season of 1945 was only ten days away when sadness filled the lives of the "Little" family. My siblings, Sam, Joyce and Richard had completed the half-dozen under the age of twelve. Suddenly daddy became sick, Carrold assisted mother in trying to keep daddy in bed, while outside the beautiful snow was falling on the grounds. Later Carrold, Doris and I left the house after dark walking on the fresh fallen snow to get some assistance for mother to get daddy to a doctor. I remember losing my shoe in the snow and cried until one of us found it. To this day, when the ground is white with snow, I am reminded by Carrold and/or Doris to keep my shoes tied to keep from losing one of them.

It was daddy's (age 31) time to go home to the mansion built by Jesus for him. He died from spinal meningitis. It's hard even now to control my emotions as I write this. I'm so glad "God understands broken hearts and mends them as well." Life gets back as normal as it can, depending on what one calls normal. However; Christmas was very sad that year and reflected in our life in every way but normal. We missed our daddy and the comfort of our family being together. We missed the hugs and kisses only a daddy could give.

Arrangements had quickly been made for us to be admitted to live at the Free Will Baptist Orphanage at Middlesex, North Carolina. (Today, the home is known as the Free Will Baptist Children's Home, Inc.) On the first day of March 1946, drastic changes were brought to the lives of the "Little" children. Looking back, I can still have a vision of our mother and Richard, age 2, standing under that big oak tree as we were driven away.

Tears were running like a river from the five (5) of us: Doris & me age 9, Carrold age 11, Sam age 7, and Joyce age 2, as well as mother, as we departed from the comforts of her never-ending love with family members.

We sat as close as we could to each other all the way from Pitt County near Farmville to Middlesex in Nash County. As night was approaching and it began to get dark, we clung closer to each other. It was pitch dark by the time we arrived at the orphanage. The darkness did not allow us to be able to see the surroundings of where we were to live for the next few years. Strangers were everywhere we looked and everywhere we turned we could see someone eyeing us as if to say who are you? Food had been reserved for us since the staff knew we were arriving later than the scheduled mealtime. I can only remember one of the foods placed before me that night. It was the chocolate bread pudding, which I had never eaten before. To tell the truth, after all these years, "I still do not like bread pudding." I felt so alone in the big dining hall. It was a large area in the mind and eyes of a nine year old girl.

Little Family – L-R: Carold, Aunt Sudie Garris, Richard, Doris, Sam, Alice, Grandma Garris

Immediately, we became part of a larger family, our brothers were taken to the boys dormitory and we girls to the girls' dormitory. I thought I would never see my brothers again. But the next morning we saw them on the other side of the dining hall as we girls sat on our side at breakfast time. I was so happy to see them even from a distance. The boys and girls were never allowed to sit together to eat or at any other function this new place scheduled. We were told we could not go where our brothers were without permission of the house matron. That was a tough pill to swallow. (Let me insert – indeed rules have to be followed even when it hurts and we don't understand them.) Can you imagine having to just wave and not touch your brothers? The separation brought us closer together even in the years to come.

It was a MUST to be in all worship services whenever times were set, whether morning, noon or night. The only way you did not have to attend was if you had to pull kitchen duty or if you were sick. If you were sick, you had to stay in bed all day and have your meals delivered to you. So, we were taught lies as untruths have a consequence. Most of the children enjoyed and participated in the worship services. It gave us a feeling of belonging and someone to hold on to. We found it easy to always be able to pray to God.

In the third grade, with all new faces around me, I was scared the first few days. I felt so alone. By having been brought up by Christian parents, I knew that Jesus would take care of me. One thing for sure, we had been taught properly by them. Even to this day I can truly say I can stand on God's promises. I know He has never left me nor has He ever forsaken me. He is always near and lives in my heart. He helped me to stand even when it appeared I was standing along. Knowing the heavenly host is backing me up encourages the depth of my soul. It was true in those days and in the present day also. As a young child, I was always sickly. As I became a teenager, I grew out of the years of my sickness.

Each of the children was given chores to do at the home according to their age. My first chore was working in the laundry room. At other times, it was helping to keep the floors, bathrooms and etc. clean, as general house work goes. Most of the time, though, it was kitchen duties for me. I learned to cook then and to this day <u>I LOVE TO COOK.</u> First duty was setting the tables in the dining area by placing the silverware, plates and so forth on the table properly and keeping it clean before and after each meal. We also helped peel potatoes, apples and other foods as we were instructed. Sometimes, when the potatoes were peeled <u>too</u> thick, we found ourselves peeling the peeling so as to learn not to waste food. Many times when apples were on the trees behind the storage building, we dining hall girls would try to get ourselves freshly plucked apples so we picked them off the trees. Yes, many got caught and were punished, but I never got caught even though I spearheaded the venture. As I grew older, my duties carried me from the dining area waiting tables into the kitchen where the food was prepared. We learned how to actually cut up chickens!! It was hard to eat chicken the same day, but that was our meal for lunch or supper, so we learned to not remember what we had done only a few hours earlier in the preparation.

I can still recall how large of a pan we mixed the flour, lard and milk to make the biscuits. It was a large commercial round pan and most of the time the person mixing the ingredients had to stand on a stool just to be able to get into the pan enough to make the mix. The biscuit maker was covered in flour as she rolled the dough for the sheet pans. Biscuits were lined in these sheet pans eight (8) across and twelve (12) down. It was always fun when April 1st came and cotton balls were put in the middle of the dough and the biscuit were served as an April's fool joke. We made sure there was enough for each one who sat at each table. We would peek out the kitchen door and laugh as we awaited their reactions when the biscuit was bitten into. This joke was always received well and the next plates of biscuits were served "hot" with a smile. On Valentine's Day, we did the best we could to shape the biscuits like a "heart", but these biscuits were eatable and knowing if we particularly liked one of the guys, that you had made it just for him. Yes, the girls got the same cotton and heart shaped biscuits as the guys. It was an annual ritual and we looked forward to the coming year. We learned to make many chores fun and it helped us to move forward and never look back. We were aware that our future was ahead of us, knowing the best years would be brighter for us. From time to time, the boys would bring the girls in the kitchen frog legs that they caught in the farm pond to fry. It was amazing to see jumping frog legs frying in hot grease. Guess the muscle in the frog leg moved to work out the kinks. We were all just one big happy family and we enjoyed life as children. The special treat of the frog legs were just only for the guy who had caught them.

In winter 1948, we had a deep snow at the orphanage. School was closed and we had lots of fun playing in the snow. I remember Pat Lane (1946-58) got stuck in a drain line between the kitchen and girls dorm. Due to the depth of the snow, she did not see the hole in the line. We all laughed at her and with her. One of the girls got her out.

My family and I were very <u>blessed.</u> On July 21, 1951, our mother, Mrs. Lottie Little, came to work where we five children lived. Yes, she brought our baby brother, Richard, age 7, with her to live there also. I thought "heaven" had truly finally come for the "Little" children. Boy was I wrong! She wasn't put in charge of us, but she was the house matron for the smaller girls. Just think how hard it was to just wave at the brothers and now we had to do the same to our own birth mother. We could not just run to her when things did not go our way for comfort. <u>WE HAD TO HAVE PERMISSION.</u> It hurt to the depth of my heart for I loved my mother very much. Not only was it hard on us, it was hard on her as well. Today, as a mother of two (2) sons, I know that kind of hurt because on Labor Day weekend in 1975 my youngest son, James was hit by a car and died. I can truly say I know how hard it is not to see James daily or weekly or talk to him on the telephone. It had to be hard for mother to see us and not be able to hold us when we needed her or even when she needed us. The truth is, we needed each other and some way, somehow we found ways to see her. God only knows the way.

During the harvest of the fields and gardens, we had plenty of extra chores to do. After the evening meals, we would sit in the breezeway between the girls building to shuck corn, shell peas and butter beans or what we needed to do to get the harvest ready to can, freeze or just for the next day's meal. Being children, we found ways to making work fun. We threw the hulls at one another and blamed it on someone else. Of course, the area was cleaned up before bedtime. Watermelons were plentiful during the late summer months. Not only did we enjoy the meat of the melon, but the game played with rind was fun. Fun was always followed by a clean-up time shared by all.

Thanksgiving was a day we all planned to eat all our stomach could hold. Many people from near and far would come and bring any kind of food imaginable to us orphans. This particular holiday we could serve our own plates with whatever was on the table. Many times our eyes were bigger than our stomach and we could not eat all we had taken. Some of our plates had all of one or two kinds of food, just because it was a favorite. In addition to the meal prepared, these good people also brought canned food by the truck loads that they or someone else had canned or processed just for us. The storehouse reflected an overload of all kinds of food to be used during the next few months. Little did we know then just how much we appreciated these special people! By the grace of God it was a way for the Free Will Baptists of North Carolina to say they cared for children less fortunate than theirs.

Christmas time was a time when the many different Free Will Baptist Church groups and other organizations throughout the state came to make an "orphan" feel loved. Each group would have a program planned to help celebrate the full meaning of the Christmas story. Always after the program, we were given gifts and fruit bags. No one was left out. Had it not been for these groups, some of the children would not have had any Christmas at all. If a boy got a girl's gift or if a girl a boy's gift, sadness was shown on their faces. All in all it turned our great and we learned what thankful meant. Not only did these groups share their love, they also showed it in their giving and support.

There were some great young people at the home during my tenure. Even to this day we call ourselves "brothers and sisters." Yes, there have been great people there since the home became a place to live to those who were blessed to have the opportunity to live there. Our annual homecoming is on the second Sunday in July each year; come and join us in renewing our relationships to share this blessing. It is held at the Free Will Baptist Children's Home in Middlesex, North Carolina. Our connection was a bond of togetherness that has a common reason of belonging; we are no different than other children. We were and still are as normal as you who are raised in a home with your parents and loved ones.

In 1951 we orphans were asked to form a choir to sing on the radio station in Wilson, North Carolina. Miss Farmer always made sure she carried the best singers with her for this event. Both boys and girls were chosen to participate. We considered this extra outing fun and a way for us to get to leave the home and not be required to do our duties. Again, we referred to this as "singing for our supper."

On a special day in the year 1952, a BIG EVENT took place at the home. The girls' dorm received a TELEVISION. This was the first one on campus and we had it in our dorm, which brought excitement to us. As you know, the first televisions were not clear, but we could have cared less about the snow on the black and white set, we looked at it anyway. Before TV time, our school homework and assigned duties had to be completed. There was a lot of compromising since all of us did not want to see the same programs. TV brought disagreements, which caused the set to be turned off early and the troublemakers were sent to their room for punishment. We soon learned what time our special program time was and scheduled our TV time accordingly.

Outside pole lights were installed on campus in 1952. This was a giant step for those of us that were required to awaken early to prepare the breakfast meals. It meant no more flashlights to carry around and it also meant we could see the "bad one" who hid behind the bushes to jump out and scare us half-asleep girls. We promised the bad one that we would not prepare them any breakfast. Before each meal, the large Lincoln dinner bell was rung. In order to be the bell ringer, you had to be a kitchen worker. The bell was placed somewhere near the dining hall and remains almost in that location to this day. Each time we alumni return, we have a desire to want to "ring the bell" just one more time. The bell was used for any timing event of the home. It rang before meal time, before church time and before any time that required a gathering of us students.

In the summertime, some of us would work at the shelter during tobacco season. The monies earned would be divided among all the rest of the children. Others were chosen to go on concert class to different Free Will Baptist Churches in order to raise love offerings to assist with the expenses of the home. Speaking very lightly, we orphans called this venture as "singing for our supper." I was privileged to go out with the concert class two years. Due to the polio epidemic in 1948, the concert classes were forced to discontinue. It brought sadness to some because they seemed to be chosen each year for this activity. Miss Bonnie Farmer directed these classes and played the piano for them also. It was fun to visit the many different churches and to visit in the homes of good Christian people who still continue to support the home. They opened their homes to us and treated us as one of their own children, showing us Godly love.

A blessing came to me in 1954-1955 when Mrs. Lena Wimbourne chose me to assist her in the sewing room as my chore. The other girls called me her favorite or her "pet" due to Mrs. Wimborne's choice. She was a gentle and quiet lady who shared her love of Jesus as any Christian woman does in training young ladies. She was wonderful to me and I loved her dearly in return. It appears to be my calling because I have worked in sewing factories almost twenty-five (25) years of my adult life since I left the home. I feel that she took me under her wing to teach me the importance of being a Christian young lady. I was always a tomboy and liked playing tough and rough. I know some of her training later took hold of my life.

God blessed me with a love to play ball. At the home we played softball, basketball and baseball and even some football. It allowed me to release my energies and I drove headfirst into it. In the grade school, I played basketball and softball. I would play ball with the boys of our home. I thought it made me tough. The reality of it was it was Godly discipline for me. Entering high school, I set my sights on becoming a good basketball player. I am told that came to pass. I played basketball all four years in high school. I was one of the co-captains the years 1953-1955 for Middlesex High School (MHS). In 1954 MHS won the Nash County Girls' Basketball Tournament. I was chosen to be on the Nash County All-Star Team that year. Man was that great!! We were the best and we knew it to be so. As a thank you for a job well done, someone paid the team's expense to Raleigh to attend the ACC Basketball Tournament. I had the opportunity of seeing my favorite basketball player, Dick Hemric, play for

Wake Forest University. Even during basketball season, the kitchen duties seemed to always fall my lot.

Co-Captain and Nash County All-star

We attended Middlesex School in Nash County. I graduated in May of 1955 with honors. I was salutatorian of that class. I was also in the National Beta Club the last three years of high school. Children throughout Nash County, as well as the children from the orphanage, made up the school body. We rode an orange school bus to and from school. At lunch time a card was hole-punched to indicate we received our lunch meal. There were times we would trade our hot school lunch for a peanut butter and jelly sandwich with another student. We never carried our lunch from the home.

As teenagers, we learned that life without a high school education was not the road we were being taught to travel for the future. Education was becoming very important. With Mother's guidance after my high school graduation, Carrold, Doris and I returned Joyce and Richard to our Greenville home to live and continue their education. They both attended

J. H. Rose High School. Knowing our generation could be "world changers", we grabbed a hold the tiger of education by the tail in seeing that our younger siblings completed high school. They both did and we are proud of them for their accomplishments.

During our years of growing up, we were taught the need to accept Jesus as our Lord and Savior. This happened to most of us in our early years. If you received Christ and was <u>saved</u>, then water baptism was next. The only place we had to get baptized while I was there was the farm pond. Just think… snakes lived in that black water, as well as large fish we could not see. God surely took care of us since no one was bitten by a snake. I can still see that day, in memory of days of long ago, when Jesus became alive to me and it still is "so wonderful." There have been two baptisms in my life since the water baptism. I have been baptized in the Holy Spirit and also baptized in the Jordan River in Israel in March of 1984, while touring the Holy Land. There has been many infillings since and I look for many more as I grow closer to God in surrender and service through obedience.

As an adult, I can truly say that, with the assistance of the Free Will Baptist Church groups, I am a better person and Christian as I continue to work in my Father's vineyard. The Ladies Auxiliary of the Creswell Free Will Baptist Church took me as the child they sponsored and I truly thank them very much. During our stay, many excelled in high school academics and sports. You who are there now give it your best, "you are here for such a time as this," to fulfill that which God has ordained.

In the year 1958 I met the love of my life, Ned Holden Rouse. We married on December 2, 1960. We came to Greenville, N.C. to make our new home and have lived here even unto this day. Our home was blessed with two wonderful sons, Ned Holden Rouse, Jr. and James Earl Rouse. Holden and his wife, Cathy gave Ned and me one grandson, Christopher Holden and one granddaughter, Crystal Lynn. James, our second son went home to be with Jesus August 31, 1975 at the tender age of just nine years.

Beginning in 1961, we "Little" children have made the first Sunday of each month as a day we meet together in one of our homes, calling it the Little's First Sunday. It's like a holiday, all our immediate families are welcomed and most participate even to this day. None of us like to miss one of our First Sundays because we are so afraid of missing something, or it may be that we may miss the good food, or maybe we just want to keep up with what was going on with our families. All Little's know how to cook well, even the guys.

In 1969 I moved my church membership to the Black Jack Free Will Baptist Church, Greenville, N.C. I have been blessed to teach the Word of God to a wonderful group of ladies for more than thirty years. They are mighty women of God and we have learned and worked together for the right cause, the same right cause I learned at the Children's Home by striving to be one with Jesus as He is one with the Father.

During 1975, I met this wonderful Christian lady from Rocky Mount, N.C. She is The Rev. Ann Baines, Cross Country World Missions founder and pastor. Sister Ann has been a true friend, a prayer partner and a mentor for me as I continue my ministry. On April 2, 2001, I was ordained as a minister of the gospel of the Lord Jesus Christ under Revered Baines' ministry. Getting all things together in a nut-shell, the Lord had my path mapped out. "His word is a lamp unto my feet and a light unto my path." Ps. 119:105. The name of the ministry The Lord called me to minister is "<u>Beauty For Ashes</u>." The nucleus is to teach God's word with simplicity and understanding. By doing as Luke 4:18, 19 STATES, "The spirit of the Lord is upon me because He hath anointed me to preach the gospel to the poor, He hath sent me to heal the broken hearted, to reach deliverance to the captive and recovering of sight to the blind, to set at liberty them that are bruised and to preach the acceptance year of the Lord." My ministry is a one-on-one ministry. I have been commissioned to a ministry of reconciliation, teaching and helping others and encouraging them by the Spirit of the Lord to let go of the past. We cannot live yesterday, it is gone! Let go of the hurts, pains and unforgiveness so they can be healed. We have to be willing to follow Him when the days are bright and joyful just as we follow Him on the days we feel like crawling in a hole. Remember, Jesus wants to get in the same hole of darkness with us so He can brighten our life. Many are walking the lower road of disappointments, trials and injustices, etc. Isn't it time to take "the high road?" Jesus wants us to "come up" to where He is. Many times He comes down to where trouble is near. In James 4: 7,8a we read "Submit yourself therefore to God. Resist the devil, and he will flee from you. Draw nigh to God, and he will draw nigh to you." It is time we all learn to "walk on the water of His word."

No matter what has happened in my life, I can truly say God has been faithful to me. I am so glad He forgives! He has new trails and paths for each of us to walk so start your journey today. It can be the beginning of the "best day for the rest of your life." Why not allow God to use you and your life to get better every day. My stay at the Free Will Baptist Children's Home has an unforgettable impression on my life. I found the purpose-for-Godly-living example in the nine years of my stay. Jesus is the only way, so my challenge of this reader is to know and experience Him and you will truly love Him and follow Him the remainder of your life. In my life, as well as yours, there have been many highs and many lows. I can truly tell you God is with you in both situations. He has healed my body many times. In 1984 I was diagnosed with breast cancer. I can declare to you today that I am a survivor and cancer free. Twice in 1994 I almost hemorrhaged to death. In early 2009 I hemorrhaged again. Both times it seemed hopeless but God reached down and set me a path for healing. My life is still working and I will tell you very quickly that I walk in divine health. Jesus took all my "sickness and disease on the cross" and by "His stripes I am healed." This I know and truly believe. Faith in God and holding on to His promises has been my stay for many years. I am going to hold on to Him throughout this life and all eternity. God has chosen, designated and appropriated all we need. It is found in His son. It is time we accept with a grateful heart the wonderful things He has for us. Learn to love others as unconditional as He loves us. It will keep you on the right road to life eternal.

God has a purpose for all of us. Please allow him to complete His plan. That comes through obedience and full surrender on your part. Thank God for his provision for us. We prayed, played, cried, argued and laughed just as those in the outside world. We loved each other as well and fought one with the other because of a dispute, but if one, not of the home, came against one of our "orphan siblings" they had the entire crowd of children of the home to face. It was easier for them to back off than to fight us since we thought we were fighting for our survival. Somehow the orphan gang taught us how to stand for what we thought was right. We learned that the golden rule of DO UNTO OTHERS AS YOU WOULD HAVE THEM DO UNTO YOU certainly rested upon the shoulders of every child raised at the home. Loving others as Jesus loves us gave us a family we could rely upon. Knowing God was on our side made us winners and we strived for that. Just remember, God has no orphans since He is our father.

The raising, guidance and counseling received at the Children's Home prepared my adult life to witness to souls for Jesus. The basic learning we children received was free to all. How we chose to apply these skills was up to each individual. Since I did not have a standard type home to live in as a child, I am so thankful God's plan of life was for me to say, I was raised by the best people in the world at the Free Will Baptist Orphanage.

11

A True Story

Lillie Faye Watson
1946-54

    I would like to tell you a true story about a girl that I knew very well. She was born into a large family and her parents were very poor. When she was eight years old, she attended a little church near her home and she heard the pastor say, "If you accept Jesus as your savior, He will never leave you nor forsake you." She didn't know if this was true, but she knew she needed someone that she could always talk to who would be there for her. So she went to the altar and asked Jesus to come into her heart.

Lillie Faye

Only two years later her mother became very ill and died. She immediately went to live with distant relatives whom she had never met before. They were a young married couple and the wife was expecting a baby. The girl quickly realized that her role was to be housekeeper and cook. When the baby was born, they sent her back to her father and other brothers and sisters to live with them. There was hardly any food to eat and the living conditions were quite bad.

She began to pray that God would give her a home. She really had in mind a little white house with a picket fence and plenty of food to eat and clothes to wear to school. God answered her prayer, but instead of a little house He sent her and her sister and two brothers to an orphanage. It was far from her home and she did not see her father and other siblings for a long time. She was not sure that God had heard her prayer, but she later realized that God doesn't always answer prayer the way we have in mind.

At the orphanage she had food to eat, a bed of her own, clean clothes to wear and she attended school regularly. Things were not always pleasant at the orphanage. Some workers treated the children badly at times. She sometimes wanted to leave. But in her heart God kept saying, "I am with you always." So even through the hard times, she determined to do her best to take advantage of this opportunity to do something with her life. So she studied hard in school and did her chores at the orphanage. When she graduated from high school seven years later, she was Valedictorian of her class. This meant she had the highest grade average for four years of high school.

At that time, no girl who had graduated from the orphanage had ever gone to college. When students graduated from high school, they left the orphanage and were on their own. She had no money, but wanted to go to college and become a teacher. She was inspired by a young man who had graduated three years before and was working his way through college. She felt if he could do it, maybe she could too. After all, she wasn't concerned about the academics because she had always done well in school. The problem was money. Anyway, she and this young man had become sweethearts and they had talked about getting married one day.

With a small scholarship she earned by being Valedictorian and the money she made working the summer after high school, she entered college. She didn't have enough money for a whole year, but she got a job at the college Soda Shop and saved enough money to pay for the rest of the year. All this time she was going on faith that God would help her get through college, although she did not have any money. She believed He would pave the way and open doors for her to finish, and He did.

To make a long story short, this girl finished college, got married, later got her master's degree and taught school for thirty-five years. She has three beautiful children who all grew up and graduated from college and has four beautiful grandchildren for her.

I knew this girl well because I am that girl. One of my beautiful children is Kelly, a Bible Study teacher. She knows Jesus and so does her whole family. He continues to guide us with the Holy Spirit and His promises are true. I am now seventy-five years old. I have had many trials in my life, but Jesus has always been there for me to comfort me and to let me know that whatever happens, it will be all right.

Footnote: Lilly Faye Watson married Charles Harrell ('38-'51). Dr. W. Burkette Raper ('36-'46) participated in their wedding.

12

Thanks for the Memories!

Peggy Mixon
1948-59

The Mixon children ran and hid when Doctor Hinnant came to their home in the Core Point community of Beaufort County. Their father had died at age forty-six and their mother was no longer able to properly care for them. An aunt had arranged for them to live at the Free Will Baptist Orphanage and Doctor Hinnant had come for all except the oldest boy Edmund, who had become seventeen years old two months earlier. The other five were: Alice 15, Milan 12, Beulah 10, Horace 7, and Lula 4. They would begin living there on July 23, 1923, the sixty-sixth through seventieth children admitted.

My father, Horace Mixon ('23-'34) rarely spoke of his life in the Orphanage during the 1920's and early 1930's. He mentioned the boys killed by lightning but I never heard him really talk about it. When he did mention his life there, it was usually in a group setting or with his siblings. Times were not good in our nation at the time and the financial support of the home was meager, too.

The Orphanage school was on site and my father told of two teachers, one receiving very favorable comments. The other was very strict and if the students misbehaved, she would thump them on the head with her ring, similar to a class ring, and it would hurt badly. Someone reported it to the superintendent and that type of reprimand ceased.

When the Orphanage residents later attended school in Middlesex, Daddy would take a baked sweet potato in his pocket for lunch. At lunch time, after sitting on it, the potato would be flat. Sometimes the Orphanage students would trade their sweet potatoes for the peanut butter and crackers of the town students. This was quite a treat because the Orphanage students never had peanut butter and crackers.

There were summer races in Nashville, North Carolina in which Daddy participated. The other boys were attired in shorts but Daddy had none, so he had to wear his overalls. Ironically, the boy he raced was also named "Horace". The crowd yelled, "Run Little Horace, Big Horace is gonna catch you!" Daddy's long legs must have helped because he (Little Horace) won the race in spite of having to run in his overalls.

He told of the boys damming the creek to make a swimming hole. With a little ingenuity, they used a mule to pull a scoop to make the hole deep enough for swimming. I can imagine the happy times spent frolicking and swimming there. I understand that the area was still recognizable many, many years later.

Randall Bennett ('29-'34) from Bridgeton, North Carolina was Daddy's favorite superintendent and I was named for his daughter. When Mr. Bennett traveled to Raleigh for supplies, Daddy would go along to help. A great joy to a teenage boy was that Mr. Bennett would allow Daddy to drive!

On January 20, 1934, five days before his eighteenth birthday, Daddy left the Orphanage to live with a friend in Harnett County. It was there that he met and later married my mother on September 7, 1935. I was born in 1937, followed by my brother, Charles, in 1939.

Mixon Family – Back Row L-R: Horace, Sudie
Front Row L-R: Peggy, Charles

In the rural area of Harnett County where the Mixon family resided at Route 3, Dunn, North Carolina, but actually nearer to Buies Creek, my father, Horace Mixon, had the reputation of being an excellent farmer, the best in the area. After a meeting of the Orphanage Board of Trustees, a trustee representing the Cape Fear Conference of Free Will Baptists, informed him of their search for a Farm Manager. Daddy applied for the job, was hired, and our way of life changed when we moved miles away into the house on the farm in December of 1948.

Daddy, along with one brother and three sisters, had made the Orphanage their home after the death of their father. My assumption is that Daddy felt a connection to the Orphanage after having it as his home for over ten years. Or, perhaps he realized that it was an opportunity for a better life for himself and his family. I do not remember him giving a reason for removing us from the community, school, relatives, and church that were important to us.

Upon entering sixth grade at Middlesex Elementary School after Christmas of that year, the children of the Orphanage became my best friends and we continue to be friends today. These friendships strengthened as we matured and participated in elementary school activities, followed by high school activities such as Glee Club, school plays, basketball, and other school clubs. Our Middlesex High School graduation class had seven graduates from the Orphanage, including me (Pearl Hill '47-'55, Alice Little '46-'55, Doris Little '46-'55, Peggy Norris '48-'55, Eugene (Herb) Tyson '43-'55, and Lou Winstead '44-'55), the most of any class until that time. Five of us continued our education at Mount Olive Junior College, where Pearl Hill was my roommate.

Mama was not employed when we first moved to the Orphanage but was later asked by the superintendent to perform some substitute work to enable the full-time employees to occasionally have a personal day. Later, she assisted in the kitchen and after the retirement of Mrs. Winborne, my mother became the dietician. This brought more changes to our family as we would partake of our meals in the dining hall and not eat together as our family of four.

At every meal, the bell on campus was rung twice. The first bell signaled to stop what you were doing, clean up and get ready to eat. The second bell ringing was to enter the dining hall for breakfast, dinner or supper. The bell was usually rung by the kitchen boy, although girls did at times ring the bell. Mama told me that when Sam Little ('46-'56) was a kitchen boy, sometimes he would ring the bell longer than usual and the girls in the old girls' building would holler out the window for him to stop. He would come back in the kitchen laughing. My brother, Charles, said he could hear the bell when over at the farm. He recalled in the spring when he stayed in the afternoon for baseball practice, they could sometimes hear it at the high school several miles from the Orphanage.

Mama has mentioned that sometimes there were days that she would have to search the storeroom to find enough food of one kind for a meal, but conditions gradually improved. When the boys had success at hunting, she would fry their rabbits or make squirrel stew for them. There were positive comments about her barbeque sauce and also about the chili for our hot dogs. But many have said how much they appreciated the birthday cakes made for each child on their special day and letting them serve the ones at their table. Some had not experienced that excitement of a birthday cake and the recognition on their special day was memorable.

I always tried to be part of the big family and felt that I was accepted. I remember the long, tedious days of shelling peas, shucking corn, dressing chickens, and putting in tobacco. Once in a while on a Sunday I would volunteer to wash dishes so a kitchen girl would have more time off.

A day of helping in tobacco is very vivid! At the end of the work day, Lois Thigpen ('49-'53) requested to ride a mule back to the lot and asked me to ride with her. She held the reins and I held onto her. As we were leaving the area of the tobacco barns, John Rogers ('46-'52), one of the boys, hit the mule on its flank and that mule trotted all the way back, stumbling several times on the rocky dirt road by the pond. I have never been so frightened! Of course, the boys had a good laugh at our expense.

Another recollection also had to do with a tobacco day. We had been working in a mist or drizzle. Suddenly, a bolt of lightning hit in the nearby pasture. Those of us who were barefoot felt the electric shock but those with shoes, even though they were wet, did not. We quickly sought refuge in the tobacco barn but with all the metal inside, I'm not sure how much safer we were. That was the only lightning that day but it received our rapt attention.

Sandra Mercer ('53-'65), much younger than I, was very special to me. Her aunt was a beautician and that was exactly what she wanted to be when she grew up. She would ask if she could fix my hair and gladly I would sit as long as possible, enjoying every moment as she combed, parted, curled, and pretended to be a hairdresser.

I always liked to help during study time. A certain boy would seek my assistance with his algebra. He could tell me the answer but could not go through the steps on paper that the teacher required. It was fascinating that he could arrive at the answer in his head, and I always wondered if he was able to use his mathematical ability in his chosen vocation, but I lost track of him.

Some of the girls discovered a nearby creek with vines growing in a tree close to the bank. Somehow, we managed to use one of the larger vines to take turns swinging back and forth over the water. That came to an abrupt end one day when Teeny Butts ('46-'52) became so tickled and laughed so hard that she lost her grip and fell into the murky water. But, it had been fun!

Summer swims in the pond brought lots of enjoyment to all but on two occasions, there were unpleasant memories for me. I wore my mother's class ring but because I was afraid I would lose it, I hung it on a nail in the pier. While retrieving it, I dropped it into the water and it was gone forever when Daddy could not locate it. On another day, we were jumping from a rusty barrel in the water when I cut my big toe. A trip to the doctor in Middlesex required a tetanus shot that caused a severe allergic reaction, followed by the only time I have ever fainted. All the other times at the pond were good ones, including being one of many who were baptized in the same water.

Then, there were the leisurely times of hours of playing softball in the middle of the campus, walking miles around the circular drive, the occasional hot dog and marshmallow roasts on a Saturday night, and just talking about any and everything. As in a family, there were sometimes spats or disagreements but they were quickly resolved with no hard feelings.

Mama told me she and dad left to go on vacation to Blounts Creek, near Washington, North Carolina. When they were going across Hwy #301 toward Greenville in Wilson, they spotted Foy Watson ('51-'63) and Ray Worthington ('56-'63) thumbing. Foy and Ray thumbed them down without recognizing their car. They ran to the car with their suitcase and were surprised when they opened the door to see mom and dad. Dad asked them where they were going. They said to Kinston to see Ray's brother. Dad told Ray and Foy that Mrs. Everton (wife of J.W. Everton, Superintendent '58-'62) was in Wilson shopping with some of the children at Leder Brothers and they were going to take them there to get a ride back to the Orphanage. Mama said they told them that if something had happened to make them want to run away to tell Mr. Everton the truth about it. They put Foy and Ray off near the store and told them to see Mrs. Everton. They learned later Foy and Ray rode back to the Orphanage with Mrs. Everton.

Several special trips come to mind: being guests at a Harlem Globetrotters game and laughing so much that my sides were sore, and getting the autograph of the well-known clown Emmett Kelly at a football game at Riddick Stadium in Raleigh, when I recognized him as he sat in a car on the sideline awaiting his halftime performance in a game between the Oxford and Methodist Orphanages. There was my one and only train ride when residents of several childcare institutions were invited to Fort Bragg for a day, and being spellbound while viewing "The Greatest Show on Earth" at a theater in Wilson. And, how can anyone forget traveling to Parker's in Wilson for barbeque and fried chicken dinners? Or, the blue bus that afforded the transportation?

Who remembers the goat that roamed on campus? If you pulled his tail, he would chase you. Perhaps out of boredom or to rile a housemother, someone would tug on the tail, run up the steps of the girls' building, enticing him to at least reach the second floor, which he sometimes accomplished! I believe the goat enjoyed the attention and I do not think anyone was ever hurt. The goat disappeared and I heard that he would reappear in the dining room. For a long time, I would not eat anything that resembled beef.

Homecoming was always a special day when former children and employees returned to visit, renew friendships, and talk about old times. The lunch spread on tables in the middle of the campus was a treat! Sometimes, the men and boys participated in a baseball game in the area behind the Albemarle Cottage. Many were great players and we enjoyed watching them "play ball" so competitively.

Through the visits of people from throughout the state, a summer job, and visiting nearby churches, I met so many good people. If I did not get to know them personally, I remembered lots of names. I met a woman recently who is the daughter of a Whitley, the first family admitted to the Orphanage. My father came to the Orphanage a little later, but I immediately felt a connection with her.

Sometimes, I, along with a girl's trio (Faye Watson '47-'54, Thelma Bradshaw '44-'54, and Doris Tyson '43-'54), would travel with Rev.

Stephen Smith, Superintendent ('51-'55 & '56-'58), to churches on Sundays to raise awareness of the home and to improve finances. After he delivered his remarks, he would end by telling the true story, as only he could, of one little boy. The grandmother had brought her grandson, with his little box of belongings, to live at the home. She told Mr. Smith, "Take good care of him because he is all I have". Then, I would accompany the trio as they sang, 'Beyond the Sunset". You could hear the sniffles and the opening of pocketbooks. On one trip, Mr. Smith (Pa) asked us to tell our names and our hometowns. When it was my turn, I gave my name and my home as "Dunn". He teased me for years about my response. I had tried once to explain that I was a child of employees but the person had difficulty comprehending. I wanted to fit in and not draw attention to myself so it was easier to just do as the others.

The greatest effect on my future from my life at the Orphanage came in the summer of 1958 between my junior and senior years in college. "Pa" Smith asked me to be manager of a concert class of six children, two boys and four girls. The itinerary took us to churches across North Carolina, presenting seven programs a week, giving information about the home, and receiving an offering. I accepted the opportunity, not realizing until later what an awesome responsibility it was.

After church one night in Craven County, a woman approached me and asked if I would write to her son who was in a college forestry program that summer. I agreed, received a response from him soon after, and corresponded with him for three months. Then, we met for our first date and were married seven months later. For that summer job and meeting the woman who would become my mother-in-law, I will forever be grateful!

Life after the Orphanage included college (Mount Olive Junior College and Atlantic Christian College), with a degree in Elementary Education, and marriage a week after graduation, teaching in Craven and Washington counties, the births of my three wonderful daughters, the joy of teaching preschoolers back in Craven County, and the births of my three precious grandchildren. On a sad note, I lost my husband and best friend to colon cancer in June of 1997 after thirty-eight happy years of marriage.

As I reflect on the years lived in Nash County, the vast majority of the memories are positive ones. I am sure that, if I delved deeply enough, there would be some negatives. But, if they are that difficult to remember, they are not worth remembering. I am so thankful for what the Free Will

Baptist Orphanage meant to my father as a child and the warm friendship of so many to my father, mother, brother, and me during and after their sixteen years of employment.

Thanks for the memories!

Mother's Recipes

Over the years I've heard many of the alumni boys talking of mom's frying rabbit and cooking squirrels they had killed or caught in their rabbit boxes. I remember her cooking these for daddy and Charles at home. I would eat the front leg of a rabbit and the dumplings from the squirrel stew, but no more.

She may have fried the squirrels just like she did rabbits, but mostly she made the stew. For the rabbits: If she thought they were older ones, she would parboil them some first to tenderize them. Then, she would salt the meat, dip in flour and fry as you would for fried chicken. If she thought they were younger ones, she would just salt and fry. For squirrels: Mom would cut them into pieces, salt, and boil. When about tender, she would add corn meal dumplings. The dumplings were made from cornmeal with enough water added to form 2 to 3-inch patties. These were added to the stew, adding a little more salt if needed, and boiling until done.

Some of the desserts Alumni talk about are mom's birthday cake and apple dessert. The birthday cake was a "Pound Cake" and her recipe came from years ago when the cook used a pound of each ingredient. Mama was a good cook. I think the desserts came about after "Pa" Smith became the superintendent and got the Orphanage out of debt and there was more money coming in. Before that, the only sweets I remember were molasses and some fruit occasionally. If my memory is correct, the churches in the western part of the state would send canned goods. I think some of the applesauce came from that source and probably why it was so good. I think that daddy or other men would go and bring back a lot of homemade jar canned items.

These are her recipes:

Birthday Cake

1 pound of butter, softened
2 cups of sugar
8 large eggs
4 cups of flour
2 teaspoons of vanilla

Cream butter and sugar until light and fluffy. Add eggs and continue to beat. Gradually add flour and vanilla and mix thoroughly. Bake in tube pan at 325 degrees about 1 hour and 15 minutes.

Frosting for Birthday Cake

2 cups of sugar
¾ cup water
1 tablespoon light corn syrup
Dash of salt
2 stiff-beaten egg whites
1 teaspoon vanilla

Cook sugar, water, light corn syrup, and salt over low heat until sugar dissolves. Continue cooking until soft ball stage (let a drop fall into a cup of water to tell if it is this stage or you can let a little fall from a spoon and it will make a thread). Gradually add hot syrup to the stiff beaten egg whites, beating constantly. Add vanilla and continue to beat until the frosting is of spreading consistency.

Sunday Apple Dessert

Graham crackers
Butter (melted)
Applesauce
Added sugar and cinnamon (optional)

Crush graham crackers. Add some melted butter and press in a pan or dish. Spoon applesauce on top of the crumbs. Put remaining crumb mixture on top of the applesauce and chill.

Note—This was made before you could purchase boxes of Graham Cracker crumbs so the crumbs were not as fine. Also, much of the applesauce used was the homemade kind.

Note: Ms. Sudie Mixon is 92 years old and lives in Wilson, North Carolina. Her husband Horace died July 5, 1982 and is buried in Evergreen Cemetery, Wilson, North Carolina. One of the ministers speaking at his funeral was Dr. W. Burkette Raper ('36-'45). Two of the pallbearers were Billy Hines ('54-'62) and Jerry Smith ('49-'60)

13

We Were Twins Once

Jerry & Nancy Smith
1949-60

Ten sets of twins have been admitted to the Orphanage over the years. On August 27, 1949, we were the sixth twins to arrive on campus. Our Mother Martha passed away on July 25, 1945 from nephritis – a kidney disorder (failure) in which the kidneys become unable to filter waste materials and fluid properly. Mom was age 27 at her death. We were age three.

L-R: Nancy and Jerry Smith

After our Mother's death, we were passed back and forth from our grandparents in Dunn, North Carolina and grandparents in Lebanon, Pennsylvania. Often, we were separated, one staying with the Pennsylvania grandparent, while the other was with the North Carolina grandparent. Our Father never was a dad to us, he loved sport cars and had "wanderlust", traveling where he so desired.

The years before we started the first grade at Plain View Elementary School outside of Dunn, we were staying with our Grandmother Williford. We walked to school, about a mile and half from home. As we started first grade in 1948, Grandma wrote the Orphanage to admit us into care. She was age 66 and just could not care for us by herself. We only learned of grandma's letter to the Orphanage while writing our memoirs. We both called grandma, "mama". We lived with Grandma in a pre-Civil War farmhouse, wood shingle/tin roof. Part of the house was built from other homes that were dismantled. One part of the house was a log room. The chimney was made of homemade bricks. The bricks were made on site. On one side of the chimney brick were raccoon tracks from a raccoon walking on the bricks as they dried in the sun.

Our water was from an outside well where we would drop a bucket to the bottom and pull up a full bucket of water by a chain on a pulley. Our unpainted wood house was heated by a wood/coal burning heater in the kitchen and living room. The dining room and three bedrooms had no heat without opening the door to these rooms. To get to the living room and our bedrooms, we had to go through our grandmother's bedroom. Grandmother used oil lamps until we got rudimentary wired for lights. There were no light switches, only strings hanging from the light bulb in some rooms. Our bathrooms were outside at the "johnny." If we needed to use the bathroom during the night, there was bucket under our bed. Refrigeration was in an ice box on the wooden, back porch. Baths were taken by hand from warm water in a bucket or metal tub, with warm water being heated from a metal kettle sitting on top of one of the wood/coal heaters. During the summer, windows were kept opened during the day and we slept with the windows opened at night.

Grandma owned a small farm and we got our meat from hog killings and eggs from chickens on the farm. She had a small garden for fresh vegetables in the summer. Grandma canned a lot of vegetables for the winter months. If we were going to have fried chicken, grandma would send us after the axe. After catching one of the chickens roaming in the yard, she would attempt to wring its neck. Often after several tries, the chicken would just get up a little dazed each time Grandma threw it to the ground. Then, grandma would call us to bring the axe. With one hand, she held the chicken by the feet and in the other hand she held the axe. She would maneuver the chicken's head over a log and with one swift chop, the head would drop off and grandma would release the chicken to flip and flop over the yard. She fried chicken the best in the whole wide world.

When we needed soap, grandma would put all the ingredients into a big iron pot out in the back yard. After building a fire around the pot, she would slowly cook what smelled like grease for hours. After the fire went out and the pot cooled, she would take a big butcher knife and carve small blocks of soap from the pot. She used the soap for hands, baths and washing clothes. After washing the clothes in a tub by using a scrub board, they were hung out on the line to dry.

Grandma made her brooms from going to the backside of the fields and cutting tall broom straw, then binding it together with rubber from an old tire. These brooms were used for the house as well as sweeping the dirt yards. She made us clothes from flour and feed bags. During the depression years and into the early 50's, many country stores sold flour and feed in cotton sacks with different colors and designs. After flour and feed was emptied from the bags, grandmother made us clothes to wear, although we did have some store bought clothes provided by some of our relatives.

Our most lasting memory from grandma was she taught each of us the Lord's Prayer, having us to memorize and recite to her. The three of us attended Lee's Chapel Original Free Will Baptist Church religiously. We walked to church or rode on the back of a horse-drawn wagon when a neighbor stopped by to pick us up. We did not miss many revivals in the summer and, too, attended many funeral burials in the Williford Cemetery, named after grandma's father who donated the land for cemetery use. There never was a meal that our heads were not bowed and our thanking God for our meal before we ate. From this humble beginning, we have always had a feeling of looking after one another. We have always been each other's safety net.

Admittance to the Orphanage

Efforts to admit us to the orphanage begin September 7, 1948. Our Grandma Melia Williford wrote Superintendent James A. Evans ('40-'49) a letter:

Dear Mr. Evans:

I have two of my grandchildren with me. They are twins, a boy and girl. They are 6 years, 8 months old and ready to enter school. They are motherless children. I am not able to care for them as they should be. Their Mother wanted them to be placed in our Orphanage, so I am asking for the right steps to take to place them there. I will be glad to help with any information you request. So please let me hear soon.

On July 19, 1949, Ravin McLeod, a member of the Board of Trustees of the Orphanage ('49-'58), who lived in the Dunn area, wrote James A. Evans:

Dear Brother Evans:
Brother Coats has spoken to me about the two Smith children of the Lee's Chapel Community in Sampson County. He is of the opinion that applications are pending for their admittance to the Orphanage. Their Mother is dead and requested before her death that they be placed in the F.W.B. Orphanage. The father is a Catholic and lives up north somewhere.

If you desire to investigate this case come down sometimes and I will go with you. I know where they live.

James Evans reply July 22, 1949:

Dear Brother McLeod:
This will acknowledge your letter regarding Smith children from Lee's Chapel Community. We do have some information on this case, but due to the father being out of state, I have had difficulty getting the approval of the Welfare Department to transfer the case. I will endeavor to go by and see you regarding this case and two others during the week following first Sunday in August.

Letter to our Father, Andrew George Smith, from James A. Evans, August 18, 1949:

Dear Mr. Smith:
Yesterday I called on Mrs. J. H. Williford, your mother-in-law by first marriage and saw your children, Jerry and Nancy. As you probably know, Mrs. Williford is requesting us to admit the children to the institution. I left with her two application forms for which she is to use in getting your signature, consenting to the placement.

It is customary, when there is a living father of children and he is physically able to work, to require some help in the support of the children. I should like to have you consider what you can do toward the support and maintenance of the children if they are admitted to the institution.

Letter to our grandmother from Walter M. Croom (Superintendent '49-'51'), August 25, 1949:

Dear Mrs. Williford:
We are in the process of taking the final steps for the admission of your grandchildren, Jerry and Nancy Smith, into the Orphanage. Mr. Evans and I have discussed the matter and believe that if the necessary papers are completed by Saturday, August 27, that we will be a position to bring the children to the home at this time.
It is suggested that you get their clothing clean and packed in order that Mr. Evans may be able to get the children without any delay. He has indicated that he plans to be there by noon Saturday. Your cooperation in this matter will be greatly appreciated.

Thirteen days after James Evans wrote our Father on August 18 and four days after we were admitted to the Orphanage, our Father wrote Evans back on September 1, 1949:

Dear Mr. Evans:
I received your letter of August 18 and am answering to same. Mrs. Williford sent me the applications and I signed it. I, for myself, did not want to place the children in the home. But since they have been shoved around from one place to another, I think it will be a good place for them. I know they will get good treatment in your home, that is, if they are accepted. If they are not, I'll have to bring them back to Pennsylvania. Jerry and Nancy are fine children, that is good, only they lack discipline, and the reason for that is, they never had anyone to give it to them. Probably being with other children, and seeing how they behave, will straighten them out anyway. I hope it will.
Now Mr. Evans, I am not working full time at present, only three days a week, but I think I can manage to send at best twenty dollars a month. If you think that will help or not let me know.

Our Mother died July 25, 1945. Our Father remarried September 6, 1946 and his first child Stephen, from this marriage, was born June 2, 1947. We never lived with our Father in his second marriage. We never knew of his marriage or Stephen's birth until after we went to the Orphanage. Our Father had two more children before we left the Orphanage (Rhonda ['54] and Mike ['59]) and three children (Vonnie ['60], Mary Ann ['64] and Frankie ['67]) after we left the Orphanage. He never considered us living with him, and he only visited us a few times over the eleven years we were at Middlesex. Our Father was never a dad.

First Day, August 27, 1949

We woke up to a beautiful sunny morning, sheers over the windows in our bedrooms were moving from the early morning breeze. Grandma Williford woke us up around 7:00 a.m. and we could smell homemade biscuits, sausage and eggs cooking in the kitchen several rooms away. It was going to be a good day to go outside and play. We had our breakfast and exited the open kitchen door after pushing the screen door open. Grandma let us feed the chickens and a duck that we brought back from Pennsylvania several years earlier. The duck was given to us by our Grandmother Smith and rode in a basket tied to the front end of our father's car on our trip back to North Carolina. The duck loved tomatoes and during the summer we would pull cherry tomatoes off grandmother's plants to feed him (we later learned that he was a she). We both then spent the morning in the yard playing sometimes together, sometimes in our own little worlds. Little did we know that this was our last day staying with Grandma Williford? We have no memory of anyone talking to us about going to the Orphanage.

Around noon, we saw this car drive up the dirt path from the dirt road in front of the house. The path was near fifty yards from the road. After the brown station wagon stopped, a man got out and grandma invited him into the house; we continued playing outside. Shortly, grandma called and we headed to the house. She introduced us to James Evans and said that he was going to take us to a nice place to live where there were other boys and girls. We were confused, we did not understand. We refused to go. After negotiating with grandma and James Evans, we finally agreed to go to the nice place on condition our duck, named "Big Boy", could go with us. James Evans eventually gave in to the seven-year-old twins and agreed for us to take the duck with us. Grandma already had our bags packed, one for each of us. We had a quick lunch, afterwards went outside and found a basket, lashed it to the car's front bumper and put Big Boy in it. (This was not Big Boy's first basket experience. He was given to us by our Grandma Smith who lived in Lebanon, Pennsylvania. It was her pet duck and she give it to us when we left her house a year earlier to return to North Carolina. He was lashed to the front bumper of our father's car in a basket.) Our sixty-six year old Grandma hugged us bye and off we went, sitting in the back seat of the four-door brown station wagon heading to the nice place. We did not cry when we left grandma, we do not understand why, except maybe we had left our grandparents so many times to go to the other grandparents, we were just conditioned to load up and leave to stay somewhere else.

Late afternoon, James Evans stopped at a restaurant around dinner time. He asked if everyone wanted a hot dog or hamburger that he was going inside and purchase for us. We told James Evans, no, we did not want a hot dog or hamburger. We wanted a tomato sandwich and water to drink. He said we could not have a tomato sandwich, only what he offered. We refused and he finally agreed to our tomato sandwich. We got out of the car to eat when he returned with our dinner. We could hear noise from Big Boy's basket. We knew he was hungry and loved tomatoes. James Evans did not know we were ordering Big Boy's meal when we insisted on tomato sandwiches. Before he really noticed, we had slipped one of the sandwiches into the basket for the duck. Later, we sat one of the paper cups with water in the basket for the duck. In the dark of the night, we arrived at the Orphanage. We were age 7.

1949-50 First Year
Jerry

We arrived at the Orphanage during the night. Nancy was led to the girls' building, while I waited in the car. Shortly, Mr. Evans returned and helped me with my suitcase. As we walked up to the boys' building, sitting on the front porch was Clarence Mitchell (Alumnus '23-'32, now a matron) drinking a Pepsi Cola. Evans said, "Clarence, this is Jerry Smith." Clarence, looking at me, said "Let's go on in, the boys are all in bed, but we'll find a bed for you." The quack of a duck sounded in the distance and Evans turned to Clarence saying, "He has a duck. I'll go get it and bring it over." "That's Big Boy, he's my duck," I remember saying to Clarence. He smiled, looked at me and said, "Your duck will be okay and here for you in the morning."

Clarence then took me into the building, turning right down the hallway to the last room on the right. There were several double bunker beds in the room. He switched on a light; I could see several boys open their eyes, but quickly close them and went back to sleep. He told me where the bathroom was and where his and Mary Mitchell's room was located. Clarence helped me onto the top bunk, switched off the light and left the room. As I lay quietly in my bunk, wondering who the other boys were, I thought of grandma and Nancy. How was Nancy doing? How was Big Boy doing in the basket? I sure missed grandma. I remember saying a little prayer and after a while dozing off in sleep.

Early the next morning, I was awakened with the lights coming on and Clarence saying, "Get up." Shortly afterwards, I heard a bell ringing. As I sat up in the bed, one of the boys said to another, "He came in last night." Looking at them, I remember saying, "I'm Jerry Smith and I have a sister named Nancy." They told me to hurry up, that we had to get in line for breakfast and Mr. Mitchell did not like for us to be late. I tugged to put the clothes back on that I had worn to the Orphanage. My other clothes were still in an old suitcase grandma had packed. A second bell rung and as we lined up for breakfast, Big Boy started quacking. "That's my duck. His name is Big Boy," I said to the boys around me. The bell was sitting on the ground outside the kitchen. At that time, little did I realize that over my life at the Orphanage, that bell would be rung over two thousand more times, including for church and other special events.

As I entered the dining hall with 80-90 kids that morning, I could see girls on the opposite side of the room. I strained and found Nancy, waved at her, she saw me and smiled. I thought to myself – Nancy seems okay. I was happy. At tables of eight seats and ten seats, boys sat together and girls sat together. Nancy and I never sat together for a meal or slept in the same building the eleven years of our lives at the Orphanage. Many days we only saw each other at meals, often not being able to talk after a meal, especially if we had job responsibilities awaiting us. We were twins once; now we were among the mix of nearly 100 children.

As the weeks followed, my duck became part of the conversation on campus, as he would follow me everywhere I walked. Sometimes, Mary Mitchell would run him out of the house, as he would follow me in and get behind one of the chairs near the front cement porch. Everyone saw me calling Big Boy from time to time and him coming on my call. Sometimes on Sunday afternoons when visitors were on campus, Walter Croom would bring them over to the big boys' building and ask me to call my duck. Sure enough, my duck, usually sitting behind one of the bushes, would come to my calling. As Big Boy waddled to me, he would turn his head at an angle and his head would bobble up and down. He did not quack, but made a low pitch "duck purr" sound until he was in my arms. I did love that duck. The boys and girls and staff started calling me "Duck", thus the nickname that follows me until this day. Even in school, I would sign my papers with the signature – Duck. I soon realized that all the boys gained a nickname that stuck with them at the Orphanage – "Sack", "Rod", "Turkey", "Moose", "Toe", "Slugger", "Herb", "Rabbit", "Soapy", "Hog Eye" and more.

R-L *Jerry, Nancy, "Big boy", and other children*

The first boy to befriend me was George Stevenson ('42-'52), later Eugene "Herb" Tyson ('43-'55) took me under his wings. It seemed that every little boy had a big boy to look after him. Herb was the big boy that I thought looked after me. My earliest memory of competition among us boys was shooting marbles. There were no shooting for "fun" games in marbles. If you put marbles in a ring and did not shoot them out, the one that did got your marbles and, thereafter, owned the marbles. The game was usually played by drawing a fairly large circle in the sand. Participants would then put the same number of marbles in the circle and a straight line was drawn a distance away. Each boy would roll his "shooter" to the line, standing behind the circle of marbles. The order of shooting was determined by the order of marbles closest to the straight line. If you knocked a marble out of the circle on your shot from outside of the circle, it was your marble. If your "shooter" stayed in the circle, you could continue shooting as long as you knocked a marble out of the ring each time you shot and your "shooter" stayed in the ring. At times, you would see someone walking around with a pocket full of marbles he had won – looking for someone to challenge him in marbles. Horseshoes was fairly popular and once I caught one on my head. I was playing Roy Gasperson ('45-'57) and after pitching my shoes, I ran to the stake at the opposite end to wait for him to pitch his two shoes. After his two shoes had landed, I reached down to pick my shoes up as his shoes were closer to the iron stake. The next thing I knew, I was seeing stars. Roy had noticed another shoe near the pit and picked it up for a practice throw. He pitched it without seeing me bending over for my shoes. There was blood, but we never told anyone.

Another fun game was hitting rocks. John Thomas Rowe ('47-'54) and I would find small pebbles and an old tobacco stick. We would bat with the stick while the other threw pebbles to hit. When I struck out, I had to throw pebbles to John Thomas. Most likely this helped us both have an eye for hitting when we played baseball over the years. In later years, board games, checkers, monopoly, ping pong and more, were played with passion by us boys. The church did not approve the use of dice or playing cards with games, thus a "numbered thump board" was used to determine number of moves to make.

School started shortly after Nancy and I arrived at the Orphanage. The school bus made two trips from the Orphanage to Middlesex to transport all of us kids to school. Boys took the first bus and girls were on the second load. Never did boys and girls ride the bus together to school. Nancy and I were always in the same grade in elementary school and for that I have always been thankful. Our first year of school after we arrived at the Orphanage was in the second grade. Ms. Leitha Lewis was our teacher. I had a good school year and finished the year with an A- in reading, A+ in math, B- in conduct and B overall average. I remember vividly everyone going barefooted shortly after school was out and this continued until school started in the fall; shoes just were not worn a lot, even as we worked on the farm and did our assigned chores in the summer.

Before school turned out in the spring, the Orphanage was marketing us children for clothing. Headline for the April 15, 1950 edition of *The Young People's Friend*, a monthly publication of the Orphanage, was *"Children Not Adopted for Clothing,"* followed with a picture of five smiling children with captions below:

Back Row L-R: Arthur Jones, Joyce Thigpen, Jerry
Front Row L-R: Nancy, Bobby Thigpen

"The smiling boys and girls above would really have something to smile about if some auxiliary or other organization would adopt them for clothing. Arthur Jones is being considered and we believe he will be adopted very soon. However, the other children are without "parents" for clothing. We wonder if some of your friends would like to adopt one of them and have the privilege of supplying the money necessary to provide adequate clothing for one of them. Would you like to know something about them? We are setting forth a brief sketch of each of them. Select one and write to us regarding "adopting" a boy or girl for clothing!"

The advertisement of me:

"Jerry is Nancy's twin brother and came along with her to the Orphanage last August. Jerry is in the second grade and makes good grades. He enjoys getting mail and likes to eat. If you would like to adopt him, please write to us concerning the clothing adoption."

Only eight months after Nancy and I came to the Orphanage, no funds were available for our clothing. Apparently, our Father did not stay true to making his promise of $20.00 per month support for our "maintenance."

In June 1950, shortly after school was out, there was a revival in the unfinished Memorial Chapel on campus. Many children gave their lives to Christ, I was one of them. On Sunday afternoon in the pond over at the farm, Nancy and I, age 8, were baptized by the Pastor of our church at the Orphanage, the Reverend W. Burkette Raper ('36-'45). On that Sunday, he baptized 13 of us children. As I remember, the girls were dressed in white and the boys in white shirts and dark pants. As all the "orphans" and staff gathered on the banks of the pond, they sang the old spiritual "Shall We Gather At the River." Girls were baptized first. Other girls were Joyce Thigpen ('49-'52), age 10; Caroleen Jones, age 11 ('49-'57); Jo Ann Jackson, age 11 ('49-'56); Peggy Norris, age 13 ('48-'55); Katherine Jackson, age 8 ('49-'56); and Ruth (Velma) Gasperson, age 9 ('45-'58). Other boys were Justine Thigpen, age 9 ('49-'52); Arthur Jones, age 12 ('49-'55); Eddie Watson, age 8 ('47-'56); Robert Lee Lane, age 8 ('46-'59); and Charles Ray Hinson, age 11 ('44-'58). Later, we were presented a Baptismal Certificate, which I still have. It reads – This certifies that in obedience to the command and in imitation of the example of our Lord Jesus Christ, Jerry Smith, was "buried with Him in baptism" on the 11 day of June, 1950 at the Free Will Baptist Orphanage.

Later in the summer, July 31 – August 4, 1950, Reverend Raper directed Vacation Bible School on campus. It was good to attend with Nancy. We both were awarded certificates of attendance.

During that summer, on a Saturday afternoon, some of us boys walked over to the farm. Some of the older boys were riding the mules. As I recall, Haywood Stevenson ('42-'52) and I were playing with someone else near the barn. Suddenly, a rotten egg landed nearby. Gosh, it smelled terrible. We looked up and the older boys were laughing while throwing rotten eggs at us. They had found a nest of eggs and were having fun. We ran as eggs begin to score. There was a silo near, and we climbed up in it as the older boys kept throwing eggs up at us. I don't know how long we stayed in the silo. I do remember the first bell ringing and our coming down, running back to campus to clean up for dinner. We were three stinking little boys. The older boys smiled as we got in line for dinner.

Our Grandma Williford wrote James Evans on August 31, 1950 (one year after our admittance):

Dear Sir:

You are cordially invited to our family reunion to be here on September 3rd. We all would like for Jerry and Nancy to be here with us. It would not be complete without them. I don't know who might go after them at the present. We are looking for some of the family that doesn't come very often. If Jerry and Nancy cannot come, please do not let them know anything about the reunion.

I do not remember going to the 1950 family reunion held in Grandma's backyard. Looking back at that first year at the Orphanage, there were lonely times of missing my Grandma Williford. Helpful were relationships built with boys, and Clarence and Mary Mitchell, the boys' matrons, were as good as they could possibly be with over forty boys under their responsibility. I don't remember the term house parents used while I was at the Orphanage. Unlike living with grandma, I now had an indoor bathroom, shower and central heat. I still missed my grandma's cooking, hugs, smile, putting me to bed each night after my prayer(while on my knees) and doting over me. I, too, missed not having Nancy in my building, but seeing her at meals, church and school was helpful. Big Boy's affection was my hugs at times. For sure, by the end of the first year, I was institutionalized. When the first bell rang, it was time to stop what you were doing, get cleaned up and in line outside of the dining hall; when the second bell rang, it was time to eat. Thirty minutes after sitting down, it was time to leave and all food on my plate eaten. When the bell rang Wednesday night, Sunday morning and Sunday night, it was time to go to church. Showers were taken at 7:00 p.m. during the school year; 8'clock p.m. was bed time, no exceptions. No talking after you went to bed.

Nancy

After spending most of the day riding, we arrived at the Orphanage during the night. While Jerry waited in the car, James Evans led me into a large three-story building with many steps. Jerry and I were separated for the first time since birth. Climbing the stairs to the second floor with my baby doll held tightly in my hand, I was very scared and did not know what to expect. An older lady named Ms. Burton met me at the head of the stairs and directed me to a room where I was put to bed. I missed my grandmother and Jerry already and still did not understand why I was here. The next morning, I woke up in a room filled with giggly little girls my age. I made friends with Cora Lee Jones ('49-'61) right at the start. Maybe this wasn't going to be so bad after all, I thought.

It did not take me long to adjust to routines of institutional life, everything seemed to be scheduled, and the big bell near the dining hall rang at the same time each day for breakfast, lunch and supper. The first bell was to get ready for a meal and the second bell meant it was ready. I looked forward to those trips to the dining hall because I would get to catch a glimpse of Jerry, maybe a slight wave of his hand or a glance from him would bring me comfort. Then, I knew I would get through another day. From age 7 till I graduated from high school, I never had the chance to sit and eat a meal at the Orphanage with Jerry. As a child, I could not understand why at meal time we could not sit together. My memories of meals at Mama's were with the whole family sitting together and enjoying food and fellowship. I missed her wonderful meals, gentle smile, warm hugs and those wonderful walks through the field to pick blackberries and watching her get water from the well.

A different kind of loneliness swept over me those early days at the Orphanage; my nights were even lonelier. One night I woke up and there was this shadow of a woman sitting by my bed with a glow around her; in my mind, it was my Mother coming to my side to comfort me. It was scary and I hid under my covers because I knew also that Mother had died; yet it was still a comfort knowing that she was in heaven looking down on me. Sometimes at night I would think of Daddy and wonder where he was and would cry myself to sleep wanting him to come and get me. My thoughts were on mine and Jerry's last visit with our Dad before coming to the Orphanage. Jerry and I were in Pennsylvania staying with our Grandma and Grandpa Smith. One morning, Daddy and I went fishing, it was so cold, but it was a special time with him. Jerry decided not to go and slept in.

School started a few weeks after we arrived at the Orphanage and we entered the second grade at Middlesex Elementary School. As soon as we ate breakfast, we little girls had to hurry to our rooms, make sure our rooms were clean, bed straightened, hair combed and teeth brushed and be ready for the school bus. As little children, we had jobs to do at the Orphanage; my first job was emptying trash cans in the rooms and taking the trash out to a larger bin. The school bus was driven by one of the boys at the Orphanage; he would make two trips, boys first, and then he would come back for the girls. Boys and girls never rode together.

At the end of the school week, we had the week-end to play together and just be little children. The older girls would give us baths on Saturdays. I remember one Saturday Ms. Burton, the matron, came in and pulled me out of the bathtub, spanked me with a wooden paddle and told me I had better never wet the bed again. This matron sent me to my room for the rest of the day and I could not come out to use the bathroom. Of course, my being a little child, I wet in my pants and I was really spanked the second time for this. I would have episodes of wetting the bed; no one bothered to take me to the doctor to see if I had a problem until several months later, after I endured being spanked for this problem time and time again. There were times in elementary school when we would put our heads on our desk to take a nap and I would wake up wet. I was so embarrassed, but had to endure being laughed at and called "lemon water". Those were hard times for me.

Once, all of us little girls caught head lice. After our matron put medicine on our heads, I remember us going out to the sun porch and getting behind each other and using a fine tooth comb – we combed out the dead lice and the nits. Even in second grade, I could just move my head over the desk and those little critters would fall on my paper. Ugh!

The first year at the Home was getting to know the other children and learning the routines and finding where I fit in – staying out of trouble for fear of being spanked again with the wooden paddle. Most of that year was spent by myself as I sat back, watched, listened and tried to make something of this big change in my little life.

1951- 55 Middle Years
Nancy

I do not remember too much about the next four years of school, my third through eighth grade years. I did love my third grade teacher, Mrs. Wolf; she had a kind heart and always spoke softly. It was during this year that Linda Faye Owens befriended me and we spent this year through high school as best friends. I could tell her anything and knew that she had an understanding heart and would not tell any of my thoughts or heartbreaks. The fourth grade was one of the best school years, learning about foreign lands, science and etc. Mrs. Johnston was a very stern 4th grade teacher, but I learned a lot from her. Ms. Amspacher, was the seventh grade teacher, she was nice, encouraged me and Elsie Ward to do a food demonstration for 4H. We did and won, our reward was being on TV, making Welch Rabbit, a dish with a lot of cheese. Yum!

The eighth grade was the hardest of all; my teacher was Ms. Powell and she was nice, but strict. Math was my hardest subject and it was hard for me to get fractions in my thick head.

I always remember classmate Johnny Hales who (our class valedictorian) had it all together and math did not come hard to him – I wished I had his brains. During the eighth grade, I started liking music and would sing my heart out. I nearly failed the eighth grade. Ms. Powell called me in and said that she was thinking about keeping me back one year. I started crying and begged her to promote me to the ninth grade, that I would work hard to keep my grades up, and I wanted to be up with my twin brother, Jerry. She told me that it was going to be very hard for me through high school. At this point, I did not care.

There was a time during these years that the matron (Mrs. Lance) would walk with about eight of us girls to town and we would have about fifty cents to spend. Of course, back then you could get a drink for five cents, hot dog for ten cents and several pieces of candy for a penny. That was a fun and exciting time away from the home and we felt special.

Afternoons were spent playing hopscotch, Red Rover, Simon Says and hide and go seek; little children's games which we have all played. The swings were fun for me, swinging high to the sky. Also, a favorite game was jump the board. Where we would put several cinder blocks on top of each other, and then lay a long board across. One girl, Evelyn Jean

Darden (45-55), would get on one end of the board and I would jump on the opposite end, sending her high up in the air. When she landed on the board, it sent me flying high too. It's a wonder we didn't get hurt, but that never happened. Some afternoons, Evelyn Jean and I would slip to the dining hall and there she would play the piano. Boy, I thought those keys were going to fly off. Evelyn could play any song you ask her to. She really had a gift.

As these first years began to pass by, I felt that I was missing something in my life and it was at this time, around 8 years of age, I accepted Jesus as my personal Savior and my life changed. I had someone I could talk to anytime of the day or night and I knew He would listen. I decided to be the best I could be and make the best of my situation. This would be a very important turning point in my life, because it was His love and His grace that made me the person I am today. Baptism in those days was held in the pond on what we called the other farm. This was a refreshing event. From that day forth, I enjoyed going to church and being part of the activities. Church was twice on Sundays and some Wednesday night services. A lot of us girls didn't mind going to these gatherings because that meant that the boys and girls could mingle and talk.

I had the opportunity to be in a concert class that went out during the summer months to put on a play and sing at the different Free Will Baptist Churches. We did this to get support for the Home. We sung our hearts out. We would go to a church and people with friendly faces would meet us. Then, at least two of us would be taken to the homes of these gracious church people where they fed us and we spent the night. This was the time I met people of different walks of life, from the coast to the mountains, and I was touched by the way we were welcomed in their homes and made to feel as though we were a part of their family. I would like to give a big thank you to the Free Will Baptist families who were so generous and loving to have me in your homes. They were good memories.

The summer of 1955, I began to feel changes in my body, most likely the hormones getting ready to change me in to a young adult. These changes had never been related to me and I had to rely on the older girls at the Home to explain what was going on. This was the time I missed having a mother to relate to me what I was to expect, with the changes I was feeling. I do miss her so much. The older girls did a great job in this area, and now I sometimes sit back and smile at all those strange events.

Jerry

Many of the memories of these years run together. Thus, some events that follow may not be in the order of when they happened.

While we had hog killings at Grandma's, hog killings at the Orphanage took it to a higher level. We killed up to 35-40 hogs a year for our needs. A report in the February 15, 1951 "The Young People's Friend", gave details of our January 14th killing. "The fifteen hogs killed this day dressed an average of 250 pounds each and added to our meat supply another 3,750 pounds of pork. The 36 hogs killed during this winter season have provided us with a total of 8,320 pounds of pork, lard, ham, bacon, and sausage." This was my first experience of sometimes seeing unborn pig fetus when the cavity was opened for carving.

Several Christmas seasons at the Orphanage still come to my mind during holiday seasons. In 1951, we and 1,400 other children from orphanages across North Carolina were transported by train to Pope Air Force Base in Fayetteville. The Air Force had a huge Christmas party and dinner for everyone in one of the hangers on base. All children got gifts and ole Santa made an appearance. In 1952, the Air Force reached out to 4,500 orphans across the state and Christmas came by air. Over five days, Air Force pilots flew a helicopter loaded with gifts to orphanages across the state. I remember standing out near the church seeing Santa waving as the helicopter landed between the church and the superintendent's house. Every child got a gift. On leaving, Santa would throw candy from the helicopter all over campus.

We always had a huge Christmas tree in the dining room, but the tree I remember most was in 1950. Several of us small boys went to the woods and cut down a small cedar (3-4 ft.) and placed it in our bedroom in the old building. We decorated the tree by stringing popcorn Mary Mitchell popped for us. The tree was wrapped with tobacco twine that had been colored with crayons.

Thanksgivings were my favorite holidays. Grandma would find someone to pick me and Nancy up after our Thanksgiving program to the public, followed by food on the ground from visitors' baskets. It was always exciting to get her hugs and see her smile. One Thanksgiving I remember was when Charles Ray Hinson ('44-'58) taught me a few tricks on getting the best food before others emptied the serving plates. Charles Ray came to the Orphanage in 1944 and had been at many Thanksgivings. I remember following him as he explored the long outdoor table in the flower garden. As food was being removed from baskets and placed on the long wire-fenced table, Charles Ray introduced me to the art of food surveillance. He had learned not to get in line with everyone at one end of the table, but to work his way to the table center when it was time to eat. Charles Ray programmed my conscience that day – "Thanksgiving dinner isn't just a meal, it's an attitude." As the blessing was finished, I quickly followed Charles Ray to the center table, by-passing the turkey and the older boys and girls. Before anyone realized it, our plates were overly filled, excluding turkey. We went back for turkey after everyone passed; there was always plenty of turkey.

The Orphanage policy to keep girls and boys separated did not enhance mine and Nancy's relationship in those early years. I remember Mary Mitchell and Dr. Josephine Newell being aware of my being sad at times from longing to be with Nancy. They went to Superintendent Pa Smith ('51-'55 & '56-'58) with their concerns for Nancy and me not having enough time together. "It just was not right for twins not to be together," I overheard them say to one another. Apparently, Pa got the message and Nancy and I got to see each other more.

One summer Saturday afternoon, I picked a big jar of blackberries and asked Mrs. Sudie if Nancy could meet me in the dining hall to eat the berries when no one else was in there. She smiled, saying, "I can work that out for you two." I remember our sitting in the big dining hall all by ourselves, pouring carnation milk over the berries and eating them. Another thing Mrs. Sudie was so good about was cooking a birthday cake for everyone. Nancy and I usually were not at the Orphanage on our birthday – December 30. When we returned from the Christmas holidays with our grandma or with Aunt Annie and Uncle Dalton, Mrs. Sudie would make sure our birthday was not forgotten. The first week in January, two cakes were always cooked, one for Nancy and one for me. Her scratch cakes are still among the best I've eaten. Not many people knew Uncle Granville Byrd was first cousin to Mrs. Sudie.

To my amazement, my duck Big Boy started laying eggs. When I could find "his" eggs, I'd ask Mrs. Sudie if she would cook them for me. I felt real special to have duck eggs for breakfast while everyone else were having chicken eggs with their grits, bacon and biscuits.

Another good memory is that of listening to radio. I remember us small boys sitting around someone's radio listening to the Long Ranger, Gun Smoke, Black Shadow, Amos and Andy. As I got older, we would listen to boxing matches and baseball games. I remember one night (after we had moved from the old boys' building to Albemarle Cottage) listening to a fight with boxing champion Rocky Marciano defending his title. The lights were off, as it was bedtime. Several boys and I put a blanket over our heads and listen to the fight over the radio. It was not easy being quiet.

There were times I felt discipline was inappropriate. One time, someone had done something wrong and no one admitted to doing the wrong. All boys were put in a line and spanked until someone owned up to the wrong. Then, there was the time a boy missed getting on the truck after lunch to go over to the farm to work. When we came back that afternoon, two rows of boys were lined up in the back yard of the new boys' building. We were told to take our belts off. The boy was told to run through the line for missing work and we were told to hit him as he came through. The boy refused and a matron put the boy on his back and walked him through the line. Our belts were not hard, but he hollowed anyway to give the appearance of being hurt. Most boys were spanked for wetting the bed. Before I went to the Orphanage in 1949, I did not wet the bed. Sometimes after arriving, I would go through periods of bed wetting. It was always embarrassing.

One spanking, I really deserved. It was spring. Durwood Lane ('46-'52) and I were assigned feeding chickens and taking up eggs. Durwood was the older boy, I was just 10. As we passed the kitchen, we stopped and picked up an egg basket and continued pass the biddy house (half-moon metal building) to get to the chicken house. Durwood noticed Charles Hedgepeth (matron's son) following us. Durwood hollowed back and told him to leave. Charles got behind the biddy house. Durwood looked at me saying, "Duck, throw some rocks at the biddy house, maybe the sound of rocks hitting the tin will make Charles leave." I found rocks and started throwing. All the time, Durwood stood nearby smiling. We could hear my rocks thumping the building. Suddenly, we heard a scream. Charles came running out from behind the building, blood rushing down his face. Durwood looked at me and said, "Duck, I didn't tell you to hit him!"

The following morning, Durwood and I were called into the superintendent's office located in front room of the kitchen. Superintendent Pa. Smith ('51-'55 & '56-'58) asked Durwood who hit Charles with the rock. "Duck did it," he said. Pa looked at me. "He told me to throw the rocks," I responded. Durwood denied telling me to throw the rocks. I got a whipping, although Pa did not hit me hard. I've always regretted hitting Charles.

Still, there is another incident that sticks in my mind that happened when I was a teenager. I was slapped so hard by my matron I saw stars. I turned around and he said, "Look at me." To this day, I do not know what that was about. While I did deserve discipline for failing to feed the hogs one Sunday afternoon – the punishment did not match the wrong. I remember going to visit my grandma shortly afterwards. She questioned the black marks and bruises on my back. I told grandma I had fallen; not the truth – I had been beaten with a two-inch wide strip of wood.

One of my fondest memories at the Orphanage was catching rabbits. Herb Tyson and I were buddies. We set rabbit boxes together. I would go to the rabbit boxes before school each morning. When I caught a rabbit, I would put it into a covered bucket until I got home from school. We would kill and clean the rabbit. Mrs. Sudie would always cook it for us. While the other boys were eating the food of the day at dinner, we had rabbit. I caught 77 rabbits one year. Mrs. Sudie was loved by everyone for cooking a birthday cake for them on their birthday. Her apple sauce dessert is still my favorite. I suppose many women married to an "orphan" boy have found their cooking compared from time to time with Mrs. Sudie's recipes.

It was during this rabbit catching time of my life, I had my first girl friend. I call it "Rabbit Love." As I remember, it happened this way. My first girlfriend was Elsie Ward. She did not live at the Orphanage. We met in elementary school and would smile at each other during recess. She was a grade ahead of me. One day at the end of recess, she walked over and handed me a note folded into a one inch square. I stuck the note in my back pocket and headed to class. After school when I was alone, I pulled the note from my pocket and read it, my heart pounding.

It read, "Jerry, you have pretty blue eyes. Do you like me? I like you. Love, Elsie."

My first love note was pretty heavy on the ol' boy. It had three sentences and the "love" word. That night, as I tried to go to sleep, I kept thinking how to respond to Elsie's letter. The next morning after breakfast and before leaving for school, I put on my heavy coat and cap and ran to the woods to check on my rabbit boxes. Sure enough, I caught a rabbit that morning. Quickly removing the rabbit and resetting the box, I ran back to the dormitory and deposited the rabbit into a covered bucket. Gathering my books, I boarded the school bus after Mary Mitchell checked my ears for cleanliness. While riding to school, I realized that I had not written a reply to Elsie. As the bus bumped along the road at 35 mph, I took out a sheet of paper and wrote, "Elsie, I caught a rabbit last night. Do you like rabbit? Jerry." During recess, I passed my folded note to Elsie. She smiled at me. I smiled back. My heart fluttered and I was "deeply" in love. The next day at recess Elsie handed me a note. It read, "I like rabbit and your blue eyes. Love, Elsie." It's rather amazing how the male instinct kicks in during elementary school. It was about this time my "protect and provide" instinct became real. After writing many letters to Elsie on my rabbit catching skills, I decided one morning while riding the school bus to see if Elsie would like to have a rabbit. During recess, I quickly asked her if she would like to have a rabbit. She smiled and said yes, but she would have to ask her momma. The next day after recess Elsie smiled and handed me a note. It read, "Momma said I better not bring a rabbit home from school. Do you still like me? Love, Elsie." Now if Elsie had said yes, I don't know how I would have gotten that rabbit to her. For sure, Mary Mitchell, while checking my ears, would have suspected something from my bulging book sack.

I give credit for my love of reading to the bookmobile coming to the Orphanage during summer months. I would check out as many books as allowed and find a quiet corner to read all the books before the bookmobile returned. Reading books broadened my world and fed my dreams for future life. The more books I read, the more I hungered for more books. Even today, I read in excess of twenty books a year. The fire for reading kindled by the bookmobile years ago still burns.

Actually, my reading got me into a little trouble that most children never learned. In the back of comic books, there was an advertisement to sell flower seeds and win an air rifle. I filled the blank out and mailed to the seed company in Pennsylvania. When the seeds came, I was so excited and started trying to sell to other orphans. Well, as I should have suspected, no one had any money or really cared to have my flower seeds. The next spring, I started dropping seeds at different places on campus, telling nobody. As flowers started coming up and blooming, I got excited, but did not tell anyone I had anything to do with the flowers. I remember Ma Smith commenting one Sunday how pretty the flowers were on campus. I resolved my problem with no one purchasing my seeds, but then another problem started coming in the mail – a bill. At first, I ignored the bills, but as the bills begin to pile up, I got worried. I went to see Pa Smith and showed him the bills and told him the story of my purchasing the seeds and not being able to sell them. He asked me where the seeds were and I told him all over campus. Pa inquired where on campus I had stored the seeds. I told him to come over to the window with me and I'd show him the seeds. As we stood at the window, I pointed to flowers growing at different places. We went back and sat down. Pa looked at me, saying, "If I take care of these bills, will you promise me you will not order anything by mail again unless you have the money to pay for it?" I assured him I would. Leaving his office, I felt for the first time the feeling of being debt free and no longer getting bills from the seed company. I've never forgotten the teaching from those seeds. I learned then the peace that comes from being debt free. Today, I'm debt free.

For several summers I was in the concert class. One summer I was with Bonnie Farmer and the class that went to the mountains. The entire summer we traveled from one mountain church to the next doing our program and singing. Visiting in mountain homes, talking with families, waking up to the sound of a stream, view of a mountain ridge top and seeing waterfalls left a lasting impression of the mountains. I still remember walking on a swinging bridge and a family retrieving butter and milk from a spring one morning before breakfast – left there overnight to stay cold. My love for mountains and mountain people was kindled that year and, most likely, that experience played a role in my living in the mountains today. Nancy was with the concert class for many years, too. Often on returning from a trip, she would share with me some of the money families gave her. We still have today this insight into just knowing when the other may not be doing so good.

A bit of humor I remember happened after a holiday. To this day, I hate Milk of Magnesia. My memory is that both the boys and girls were given Milk of Magnesia (ex-lax) the same holiday. I cannot attest for the girls, but my memory is still vivid of the boys. We got back from the holidays and someone decided that the boys needed to be cleansed of all the bad stuff they ate while away. I still remember us lining up and drinking Milk of Magnesia. We had to swallow while standing in front of the matron. Of course, if all 40 boys take a laxative at the same time, everyone has to "go" the same time. I still can see the three commodes in the big boys' bathroom. No stalls, three boys sitting and talking while everyone in the three lines urging them to hurry!! During those years 20-25 boys used the same bathroom – forget about privacy (no locks on doors). *[Bathroom was institutional: Entrance was off hallway through standard door (no lock), room was 14' x 10', four individual sinks/mirrors, shower with three heads (no curtains), one window (no curtains) usually opened to release steam during showers, three commodes sitting side by side (no stalls/doors), drain in shower, drain in middle of bathroom floor and one overhead light. The floor was cement painted gray and walls were painted white. The small boys' bathroom was the same size but had a bathtub with showers.]* To this day, I abhor having to share a bathroom with anyone in the room when I'm there.

The summer of 1952 was an exciting time for us boys. Ralph Pate ('33-'41) financed and supervised the earthwork to build our baseball diamond located behind the Albemarle Cottage. The diamond was built in a cow pasture. (This was the same cow pasture where Joseph Griffin's ['22-'29] pet cow stayed prior to the 1929 storm that killed both Griffin and Wiley Watson ['23-'29]). As I recall, a dairy barn was on the property before the baseball diamond was built. Today, the dairy barn would cover 3rd base on the ball field.

We moved from the old boys' building into Albemarle Cottage in 1951. Before the diamond was built, I remember a homecoming when the alumni played boys still in the Orphanage. That game was played behind the church near the woods.

Friday, October 15, 1954 - Hurricane Hazel hit the coast of North Carolina as a Category 4 hurricane, packing 150 mph wind speeds and moving inland with a trajectory through the center of the state. Middlesex School opened in the morning, but turned out early. Shortly after noon, the eye of the hurricane crossed Middlesex. The first "eyewall" of destructive wind and rain came, then there was calm, little wind; followed by the back "eyewall" with a more intensified rain and wind. We went to school that morning, but were back home by lunch. As winds picked up speed, our matrons Mary and Clarence Mitchell called us to the halls of the Albemarle Cottage. They sat us down on each side of the hall facing each other. Electricity had gone out; and, as the winds howled and thunder roared, I'll never forget what Mary Mitchell said to us, "Shhh, we need to be quiet while God is at work." These words were calming to me. I was not afraid. Winds from the hurricane opened the cattle fence enough for our beef cattle to get out. For a week or more, we chased those cows all over the county. We boys were kept out of school. Pepsi Colas, nabs and canned sardines were often our lunch.

In 1954, many of us boys joined Middlesex Boy Scout Troop 64. I did not have a uniform, so my Grandma gave me one for Christmas that year. The next Thanksgiving, Eddie Watson ('47-'56), Robert Lane ('46-'59) and I were asked by Pa Smith to don our uniform and lead everyone into the church for our traditional services. There is a picture of that Thanksgiving floating among many alumni. Scouting was a great program for me. Mrs. Sudie always made sure we scouts from the Orphanage had plenty to eat and cook when we went camping at Camp Charles. A USDA can of beef was easy cooking, as I remember. The Boy Scout Motto, Oath, Law and Slogan are good guides for living and have always meant a lot to me. As a father, it was important that my sons were in scouting. Both earned Eagle Scout rank. Both sons' Eagle Scout projects were at the Orphanage. In '86, Jerry, Jr. built a campsite and shelter for kids on campus to camp. Leaving the Albemarle Cottage, going to the farm, the campsite is in the first woods on the left. In '88, Mark built a parking area for the campsite and an outdoor "johnny". I think it helped them have connection to their father's "orphan" family. I've always felt proud of their projects.

In 1986, I was voted Scoutmaster of the Year in the Wilson District and in 1989, I earned my Walking Wood Badge at Philmont Boy Scout Ranch, Cimarron, New Mexico. My sons and my success in scouting were kindled while I was in the Orphanage.

Another memory always brings smiles. On November 6, 1954, there was a celebration for the opening of Purina (feed mill), Highway 301, Wilson, North Carolina. The mill opening was on a Saturday. Ten or more of us boys from the Orphanage were transported to Parker's

Barbecue and told we were going to serve barbeque to the large crowd attending the opening of Purina. We were dressed in white and red checkered shirts for the noon serving of pig, slaw, cornbread, potatoes and sweet tea. I remember the queen of country, Grand Ole Opry Country Music Comedian Minnie Pearl, wearing her straw hat with the $1.98 price tag hanging off it and her knee length dress. Everyone wanted her attention and signed program. Country Music legend Eddie Arnold performed for those in attendance. Parker's barbequed 150 or more hogs. We served 15,000 plates with barbeque, slaw and cornbread at 75 cents per plate. No tea or drinks were served. Mellow Cup had a truck nearby for everyone to have ice cream. Free walking canes were giving out as long as they lasted. I have never forgotten the event. I remember wearing the Purina shirt given to us afterwards at the Orphanage. We were special orphans that day. Hanging on the wall in Parker's Barbecue today is a picture of that day.

By the time I reached my teenage years, baseball was a big part of my life. The Pittsburg Pirates was my favorite baseball team. I use to scrounge from old newspapers game results and knew the team's lineup by memory. I collected cards of as many players as I could. All the cards and news clippings were placed in a scrap book that I owned until a few years ago when I gave it to my son Jerry, Jr. who played baseball for the University of North Carolina at Chapel Hill.

Summer baseball at the Orphanage was so much fun. Of all the teams we played over the years, my favorite was the inmates at Nashville Prison Camp. We usually played them close until the last few innings, then, they started hitting the ball with homeruns going over into the cow pasture. When the game was over, you could walk in the outfield and find small bags of tobacco left for us boys to enjoy. One inmate, named Hula, took a liking to me. I remember a truck with him in it stopping at the Orphanage one day and him jumping out to find me. He handed me a leather billfold he had made for me. Inscribed in the leather was – DUCK. He said, "I wanted to make something for you, Duck." I thanked him and do not believe I ever saw him again. I do remember he was from the State of Hawaii and had killed a man.

I suppose the game I most love to talk about is the game some of us refer to as the "watermelon game". It was a game with a church team from Nahunta. Saturday, after working all morning and after eating lunch, the boys loaded up on our old blue bus with the words "Free Will

Baptist Orphans Home" painted on the side. Clarence Mitchell drove the bus. On arriving at the field, we took batting and infield practice. Clarence sat in the stands watching us and talking with fans from Nahunta. We fell behind several runs early in the game. Somehow, Clarence made a bet that we would eventually win the game. He was offered a load of watermelons, if we won. At the beginning of the sixth inning, with the score Nahunta 6, Orphanage 2 and us up at bat, Clarence came over to the dugout and talked with Rod Page ('40-'57) and a group of us standing near the bench. He told us of his watermelon bet he had with the farmer in the stands. He pointed to the man wearing the overalls. It was a challenge we accepted. Our team scored one run in the sixth inning and changed our defensive positions as we took the field. The first five innings of the game, I caught and Robert ("Toe") Lane pitched. We were younger players and the older boys wanted to give us a chance to play these positions. In the sixth inning, Rod Page took over pitching responsibilities and Herb Tyson caught. I was moved to second and Toe to the outfield. I remember some of other players on the team – Harold Rodgers ('46-'58), Charles Mixon ('48-'63), Alton ("Sack") Bryant ('46-'58), Jake Lane ('46-'59) and Roy Gasperson ('45-'57). There were other boys, but I do not remember their names. We scored two runs in the seventh, one in the eighth and one in the ninth; final score Orphanage 7, Nahunta 6. True to his word, the farmer led the bus to his watermelon field. Our equipment was moved to the front of the bus, watermelons filled the back of the bus. After dinner that night, the entire campus had a watermelon cutting.

    Nancy and I have always been able to communicate with each other in a different way than others. It might be telepathy, or just the sixth sense, but we know when the other is not okay. We have this sense when something is wrong with the other. Many times during these years Nancy came up to me after a meal and asked what was wrong or if I was okay. I would just say nothing was wrong, yet she was usually right about her insight. I had a need to look after Nancy and be strong for her, and telling her of my struggles did not seem to serve a good purpose. I never felt lonely at the Orphanage, just felt alone often. There were so many wonderful orphan brothers and sisters that were bright lights in my life while there. I will never forget them, but Nancy was my true safety net and I felt I was hers.

In retrospect, the day I accepted no one was coming back to get me and Nancy out of the Orphanage was the day I begin to deal with my situation. I stopped expecting others to care for my welfare, even love me. When I did stop expecting, I no longer felt disappointment from my Father or any other relative for my stay in the Orphanage. Today, I continue using this coping skill – good or bad. Like so many orphans today, I sometimes continue dealing with some issues with detachment. I'm more aware of the downside of detachment today than in past times. I've learned detachment does not kindle relationships.

1956-60 High School Years
Jerry

I'll never forget fall 1956. Dr. and Mrs. A. B. Edwards (he was a dentist) spent several weeks on campus. He placed a wooden dentist chair in the right front room of the kitchen. Over the chair was a one bulb lamp. Oh my, I can still remember standing in line with others waiting my turn. My negative image of dentist today comes from that experience. I'm sure Dr. Edwards meant well and most likely did a good job. But, that wooden chair is still an image in my mind.

Summer 1957, Foy Watson ('51-'63) and I were assigned to help Clarence Mitchell with grass cutting. In addition to grass cutting, we were required to care for and feed the 20 or more turkeys that Clarence ("Petey") had in a pen behind the baseball field. One afternoon after a heavy rain, we went to feed the turkeys. Foy was walking in front of me and entered the fenced area where all the turkeys were running around in the muddy yard. I picked up a stick and threw it in the mud and splattered mud all over Foy. In retaliation, he found a stick and intended to do the same to me. We were both laughing. However, just before Foy threw the stick, a turkey ran in front of him and the stick struck the turkey on the head. The turkey ran around in a circle with its head on the ground… then fell over dead. Foy was worried that Petey would find out he'd killed the turkey and a whipping would follow. After talking, we found our solution. We took the dead turkey into the woods behind the turkey pen and buried it. Afterwards, I started calling Foy – "Tarzan the Turkey Slayer" – as I thought it was so funny he'd killed the turkey. Several days later Petey was looking for his turkey. He asked me and Foy if we had seen his best laying hen and, of course, we both said no.

My years at the Orphanage during high school years were good years. While my basketball skills were not developed by my freshman year, I did make the Junior Varsity team and played varsity my junior and senior years. In baseball, I started every game during the years I was in high school. I was very proud of Nancy's cheerleading and chosen as the head cheerleader her junior year. Coach Enid Drake and Fred Wolf, our Agriculture teacher, showed a lot of interest in me. When I was a senior, I was president of FFA and Nancy was the chapter sweetheart. I represented the chapter in a public speaking contest. The speaking skills I learned from Mr. Wolf, I have used throughout my career.

In the winter of 1957, Asian flu spread throughout the country. It hit the Middlesex community fairly hard and I know of no one that didn't feel the symptoms at the Orphanage – fever, headache, tiredness, sore throat and dry coughs. In fact, Dr. Josephine Newell, who provided medical care for us, told me that everyone at the Orphanage was out of school with the flu.

Summer, between my sophomore and junior year in high school, Margie Herring ('52-'62) and I became boyfriend & girlfriend. I was smitten by her blue eyes, smile and tender heart. She was shy and very bright. Of course orphanage rules did not allow us to have a lot of close contact, but we did get a smile and occasional winks from one another across the dinning hall at mealtimes. It was one of those phenomena's that happens in orphanage life. One day, you're brother and sister, and the next day your boyfriend and girlfriend. If the relationship doesn't work out, then you go back to being sister and brother. We dated in the living room in the big girls' building on Saturday night, along with anyone else that was boyfriend and girlfriend. It was a good time for us both in our teenage years. She always sat behind me when I drove the school bus my senior year. I'd drive my first load of boys to Middlesex, unload, and return to pick up the girls. Our relationship lasted into my enrollment in Mount Olive Jr. College after my high school graduation. We've been friends through the years and she remains my "orphan" sister.

In my junior year, to earn my State Degree, I went to Farm Manager Horace Mixon (Alumnus '23-'34) and our Superintendent J. W. Everton ('58-'62) with my proposed project of planting pine trees. Coming from Middlesex to the campus, the pine trees for the project are planted on the left hand side of the road as you start up the hill to the campus, where the entrance sign can be seen. My FFA trees still stand today on the lot that is larger than an acre. In my sophomore year, Horace allowed me to purchase a pig on credit and raise it in the woods behind the chicken house. I thought I was going to lose the pig when wild dogs attacked it, but it survived and always had a limp for injuries incurred. After paying for feed and the cost of the pig, I made a little profit when the pig was sold at the stockyard in Rocky Mount.

On Sundays in the summer and fall of 1959, I played baseball for Union Hope, a semi-pro team in Samaria. Playing semi-pro baseball on Sunday was prohibited at the Orphanage, although we usually had a game between us boys on Sunday afternoon. Thus, for me to play with Union Hope on Sunday I could not be completely honest with staff. I would hide my uniform in the ditch between the Albemarle Building and the farm. Larry Whitley would pick me up after lunch to spend Sunday afternoon with his family, with the understanding I was to be back before church on Sunday night. We'd stop down the road and pick up my uniform I had hidden in a ditch on Saturday. Driving to the game, I'd change clothes in the car. Larry's father was the team manager. This went well until late summer. We played two games on Sundays. The second game went into extra innings and I was late getting back in time for church. Mr. Everton saw me sneak into the church. I could not tell him I was playing baseball and make it worse on the reason for being late. Thus, I was late for staying too late with the Whitley family. My punishment was I had to miss playing in a high school basketball game before the Christmas break. I was the starting guard/forward and had to miss the Red Oak game. Mr. Everton, who is one of my favorite superintendents, told me later basketball fans at Middlesex were upset with him. While I thought his punishment was a little hard, I broke the rules – but I did have fun playing baseball that Sunday afternoon. Wonder what Jesus would have thought of me playing baseball on Sunday?

My senior year I drove the school bus. I remember using some of my earnings from driving the bus to purchase a rifle, a 22 gauge, semi automatic Remington. Clarence Mitchell went with me to Henry Manning's store in Middlesex to set up credit for me to pay for the rifle. Each month I would go to Mr. Manning's country store to pay down on the rifle. It took most of my high school year to pay for the rifle from monthly earnings of $25.00. Prior to purchasing my rifle, I would borrow someone else's to squirrel hunt. In the winter of 1959, many a squirrel ended up on our dinner table from the crack of the rifle. Fried rabbit, which was caught with my rabbit box, also showed up from time to time. Mrs. Sudie was always good about getting one of the girls to cook our catch. Even in my earlier years when I caught bull frogs, Mrs. Sudie would ask the girls to fry fog legs for me. I guess one of the most amusing surprises was learning that my duck, "Big Boy", was not male after all. He started laying eggs and the girls would fry them at breakfast for me. Sometime, I would share my rabbit or squirrel with Nancy.

In the spring of 1960, at dinner on Wednesday night, Mr. Everton announced that anyone who did not want to go to church that night did not have to attend. I was the only one on campus that did not show for church. He came to me later saying, "Duck, there were others I thought would not attend, but I was surprised you didn't." I think it might have been my disappointment with punishment for the baseball issue, I don't know, but I just decided that night I was not going to church.

In 1960, I graduated from high school; the only boy from the Orphanage in the senior class. My classmates elected me Class President. At graduation ceremonies, my 78-year-old Grandma Williford, Aunt Ann, Uncle Dalton and my Father were in attendance. I was proud when my name was called for awards before diplomas were passed out. I was awarded the Public Speaking award, Most Outstanding Agriculture Student award and Most Athletic award. I stayed and worked at the Orphanage after graduation until I enrolled at Mount Olive Junior College in the fall with Nancy.

Nancy

Oh, the excitement of being in high school. We all have been through it. My morning started during the high school years by getting up at 5:30 a.m., going to the kitchen with the other kitchen girls and preparing breakfast for about 75 people, including boys, girls and staff members. We girls could whip up some fried eggs, toast, grits or oatmeal in no time. The frying pans were huge, so you could put about ten to twelve eggs in at a time. The pots for grits were large also. After breakfast, the kitchen girls would wash all the dishes and the dining hall girls would clean off the tables. We would then head to our building to bathe, dress and get on the school bus. At times, we would share each other's dresses and so forth, because we did not have a closet of plenty. I would check the town girls out once arriving at school and they were always dressed to the T, so to speak. Sometimes, I would think that I wasn't as good and that's when I would fall back into my shell. I always felt that us children from the Home was stared at and people thought we were low.

I remember at times that all the children at the Home would be invited to many of the Free Will Baptist Church homecomings. I did not like getting on the big blue bus with the writing "Free Will Baptist Orphans Home", it was like being singled out. But once we arrived and went through the Sunday service, it was time to eat all that wonderful food and it was then the big blue bus was forgotten.

There were days when several of us girls would be kept home from school to clean and dress chickens. Also, several of the boys were kept home from school to get the chickens ready for cleaning. We probably averaged cleaning around 150 or more a day getting them ready for the freezer. Of course, you could probably guess, chicken was for supper.

Birthdays were special at the home. Ms. Sudie Mixon, our dietician, would make the most wonderful cake for each birthday and her thoughtfulness will never be forgotten. Oh, how special we felt.

Other parts of the summer months were filled with shelling peas and butter beans under the breezeway at the Smith Cottages; once shelled, it was freezing time. Also, working in tobacco was an event. I couldn't quite figure out how to tie the tobacco on the stick once the boys brought it from the fields. It seemed that Doris Duncan ('46-'58) and Patricia Lane ('46-'58) accomplished this very well. I did enjoy tying tobacco to be sent off to the market. But the best part was break time when we would get an Orange Crush drink in the brown bottle and a Moon Pie. I would try to make it last as long as I could and savor each bite. The week-ends during the summer months were filled with games, such as jump rope, red rover, tag and swinging in the large swings. But, the most fun was watching "Billy" the goat chase the children; not sure what happen to old Billy…one day he was gone and a few days later we had stew beef for Sunday dinner.

There were times during the summer when all of the high school girls would be loaded up and taken to Rocky Mount to get perms. We came back with curls that were so tight to our heads we could hardly breathe. But, it was a nice jester on the part of the different shops there to give us free perms. It was an experience and a time to see a different part of the world.

I was a cheerleader for Middlesex High School and used to ride the big blue bus to the games. Of course, we girls would try to sit with one of the boys and not knowing that one of those young men I chose to sit with would become my mate for life. Jerry and I had parts in the Junior and Senior plays and that was lots of fun. Going to the Junior and Senior Banquet was a treat, I could get dressed up; and, of course, I borrowed a dress from a cousin of mine, but I did not care, because I felt special. My high school years weren't so bad, except Ms. Powell was correct; I had to struggle to get through my classes.

Thanksgiving was a time to make sure everything was spotless and clean. We children spent a lot of time practicing the Thanksgiving program for that special day. It was a day when folks from the different Free Will Baptist Churches would come with lunch and spend the day with us. Lunch was served on a long fenced-wired table. Boy, the food was delicious and we filled our stomach to the brim. I always looked for the banana pudding, one of my favorites.

Christmas time was spent with different Free Will Baptist Churches coming to the Home to give presents and goodies to us children. That was a fun time and we did appreciate the time spent with these people. We also looked forward to going home to family – Jerry and I could hardly wait to go visit Grandma Williford. I would just dream of the wonderful orange slices, chocolate drops and the stick candy that would be filling my stomach soon. Grandma made sure she had plenty for Jerry and me.

During these high school years was a time of gazing at the opposite sex; yep, I said the word sex – which was almost a sin to say. We girls always were checking out the boys, especially the ones at the Home. Dating time was hilarious, there would be about four or five couples in the same living room on about three big couches just staring at each other. No privacy at all. Only when we were seniors could we date off campus and then had to be back home by 10 or 10:30 p.m. Oh, and there was always that first love, when the butterflies would be in your stomach each time you would happen to see this love. My first little fellow was Eddie Watson who was at the home ('47-'56). It was at a Halloween carnival at Middlesex School, we went in to look at a cartoon; and, of course, the room was dark and Eddie made his move and gave me my first kiss ever from a boy. Not sure who had more butterflies, me or Eddie. I think the girls were more serious about the boys than the boys were about the girls. Boys were more interested in basketball and baseball.

I remember walking around the big driveway at the Home on afternoons and week-ends with other girls to have the chance to see someone special, maybe at the boys building, or even see Jerry. We were not allowed to talk with the boys except at functions such as church, on occasion in the dining hall during meal time or at school. The big driveway surrounded groves of pecan trees. During the harvest of the pecans, some of the boys would climb the trees and shake the limbs. Not sure what happen to all the pecans, maybe they were sold for support for the Home.

Twice a year it would be shopping for clothes time. Usually different Free Will Baptist Churches would adopt a boy or girl and provide money for clothes. Jerry and I had been at the Home over a year before anyone or a church adopted us for clothing. Also, it was usually twice a year when we could visit family and Jerry and I were always excited to go see our Grandma Williford in Dunn. Those hugs and kisses were worth millions. I remember my Dad coming only four times during the eleven years Jerry and I were at the Home – once to take us to Pennsylvania for Christmas vacation, once to just spend the day with us, Dad happen to be in the area; one summer when I was out on the concert class in the mountains and for Jerry's and my graduation.

Afterword
Nancy

My life has not always been peaches and cream since I left the Home. There have been a lot of hurdles that I had to get over; one of them has been insecurity. I did not think I was good enough for my kinfolk or my classmates and if applying for a job, I was afraid that I would be told no. I could have used my situation to make things harder for me, to be a problem, not getting along with my peers, making others miserable because of not feeling included, or adults not understanding me. My choice was to better myself. I had to be patient rather than losing my temper. I had to forgive and not hold a grudge. If I had had the encouragement when growing up from kinfolk as well as from staff at the home, my life could be different. But the love of my Grandma

Williford during the eleven years spent at the Home will never be forgotten. Even though Dad did not get it, "being a Dad ", I still loved him and stayed in touch with him after leaving the Home. Dad did write to me while in college. My visits to see Dad, my step-mother, three half brothers and three half sisters were during the summertime. I visited many summers with my immediate family. I felt that it was important for my children to know their granddad. Most of all, I needed that contact with Dad to feel a part of him. Dad died December 1986. A week or so before he passed, I visited him in the hospital, he was in a coma. I prayed with him, told him that I loved him and wished our lives had been different. I knew it was too late and I would never hear the words "I love you" or "good job Nancy". But, in all of this, there has been one important factor – I had my brother Jerry who was a crutch to hang on to during the changes in my life; and, most of all, I had my Heavenly Father who never gave up on me.

After I graduated and left the Home, life was tough. I had to be on my own and I did not how I would manage this. I enrolled in Mount Olive Junior College and went for one year. It was hard for me, or maybe I just did not know the skills of applying myself. The year after college I began to work in the drug store in Bailey, N.C. and worked there until I was hired as a Health Care Technician at Dorothea Dix Hospital in Raleigh – working with the mentally ill was a new experience. I later worked in Medical Records and finally the Reimbursement Office. I then transferred to the Controller's Office for the Department of Human Resources in Raleigh. Working with the mentally ill was an experience of helping others, which I loved and I always wanted to be able to help others. One day while walking from one Unit to the other, I saw someone that looked very familiar to me; so, on my way back through, I stopped and spoke to the young man and it happen to be Alton Bryant ('46-'58) who grew up at the Home also, it was like seeing a brother. We sat and chatted for a few minutes. I was still very insecure in everything I did and not feeling worthy or as good as my co-workers. But I kept my head held high and did the best I could to cope. It was important for me to work hard at any task set before me in my job, which was instilled in me at the Home. I was not one that played around and waited to the last minute to get my task done. It was important to hear from my peers, job well done.

I retired with 32 years of work for the State of N. C. During those first years, I married Jacob Lane, who was raised at the Home ('46-'59) on August 3, 1965. I was determined whatever obstacles came about, I could get through them. It was also important for me to make my marriage work, because of my belief and what my Bible states about marriage. I wanted for my children what I did not get from the Home, praise, "good job", I love you and those wonderful hugs. There is not a time when I speak to my children that I do not tell them I love them. I did not have adults that I could mold my marriage after. It was a learning experience, I did want to instill in my children honesty, respect for others and do the best they could at whatever came their way. Looking back today, I say a job well done on both mine and my husband's part.

I still have a problem feeling close to others, a little insecurity is still lurking around and that is probably why I do not have many real close friends. It's hard for me to trust and feel worthy. I am afraid to get too close because I may be rejected. But one thing I did learn about at the Home, and it remains with me still, is my relationship with my Heavenly Father. If I keep my eyes on Him and keep Him in my heart, things will be okay.

Jerry

Now, in my later years in life, I am better prepared to look back at the Orphanage years and see the impact in my life. Too, I can now understand my Mother Martha's decision and her desire for Nancy and me to go to the Orphanage. She knew our Father would never be a dad for us. It was his failure to be my Dad that propelled me to be a good dad to my sons and I'm thankful I use my disappointment of my Father in modeling what I felt dads should be to their children.

After leaving the Orphanage, I met with my Father and offered to forget the past and start a new relationship. He agreed, but it only took a few years to see he gave nothing to the relationship. I stopped expecting him to give back in 1965. I divorced my Father and told him that, if I ever was his son, I no longer was. I removed the heavy sack of expectations from my shoulder. The day after Thanksgiving 1986, I called and ask my Father if I could see him. (He had never visited in my home with me or my sons.) I drove from North Carolina to see him in Lebanon, Pennsylvania. We did not have any serious conversation. I just hung out with him for a couple of days. That December, he had an aneurism while bowling. I got there late at night and found him in his hospital room alone. After talking with the nurse and realizing there was no hope of him living, I sat near his bed alone in the room just looking at him. My Father was not conscious. After a time, I got up and leaned close to his ear. "I forgive you for not being my Dad," I said. I then left the room. He died the next morning, December 27, 1986, at age 73. I was sad we never had a relationship. At his funeral, there were no tears.

My work ethic was taught at the Orphanage and it has proved good for me throughout life. So many times I've listen to people whining about work when I thought how little they had to do. The system of changing chores every three months provided an opportunity of learning skills I would not have gained otherwise. I suppose most boys admit the job most disliked was cleaning the dormitory. I always enjoyed the kitchen job and working around the girls.

While my religious experience at the Orphanage influenced my attending church today, the fundamental religion left me with many questions about God's influence in my everyday life. Till this day, I am still trying to work this out. My minor in college was religion and philosophy, a direct influence of my formative religious experience at the Orphanage.

One of the influences of my college education may be directly related to my educational experience in the Orphanage and really nowhere to go after leaving the Orphanage. Leaving there, I knew there was not room for failure. Where would I go? I don't recall anyone influencing me to go to college. I think, from all my book and newspaper readings, I concluded attending college would be mental stimulation and would help prepare me for a better future. My career in Social Work was influenced by my childhood. My business management style was influenced by awareness of each adult's child management system in the orphanage while I was there. I actually started studying systems from observing matrons and other adults' ways, and I learned how to get into their system, around their systems and find a way for their system to work for me while in the Orphanage. This learned skill was huge when I was placed in positions of managing people in my professional career.

Finally, forming and maintaining relationships was part of living with 80-100 children and that experience prepared me for forming and maintaining relationships throughout life. Too, at the Orphanage, I learned some relationships were not healthy and could be a barrier for my well-being. This carried over to my adult life and I have avoided relationships that were not healthy for me, my family or my career. My relationship with Nancy remains as strong today as in our childhood. As in the Orphanage, we continue to be a safety net for one another.

Mother's Decision

Our Mother died a painful death. We've both at times wondered why she wanted us placed in an orphanage rather than with our Father. In hindsight, we now see what she knew. She was such a strong woman to make the decision at a time she struggled with her life. Our Mother Martha saw our future with our Father, and she was correct. We love her so much for her decision. We're eternally appreciative for her being our Mom until her grave. If our Father had only been our Dad?

When we left the orphanage our duck "Big Boy" was living near the chicken houses, running free. He had only one eye as someone shot him will an air rifle. From time to time "Big Boy" comes up in family conversation. We still remember "his" low pitch "duck purr" sound as he approached to get in our arms. I still carry the nickname "Duck" to many.

Our Grandma Williford (Mama) died June 9, 1963, age 79. In later years, we've been told of her sadness and tears the day we left her for the orphanage. She was our safety net until her death.

Stepmother Mildred, 85, has loved us and always remembered our birthday and holidays with cards. She should know our gratefulness.

We'll always love our "orphan" brothers and sisters. We're most grateful to Lee's Chapel Original Free Will Baptist Church near Dunn, N.C. for providing aid to us while we were in the Orphanage. We, too, are thankful Original Free Will Baptist people were there when Mom needed help. We will always be grateful to staff at the Orphanage who cared for us in our childhood.

THANK YOU!

Footnote: Paternal grandparents are Austrian-Hungry immigrants to America in the early 1900's. Elias Peter Kovacs and Mary Besci were married in Lebanon, Pennsylvania November 3, 1908. Andrew George Kovacs, father of Jerry and Nancy, was the second of three siblings born to the Kovacs. On January 23, 1922 the grandparents became American citizens. In 1926, Elias Peter Kovacs legally changed the family last name from Kovacs to Smith. He felt the change would help prevent discrimination against him (Hungarian – American) in his efforts for employment.

14

The Shy, Barefooted Girl Who Became Valedictorian

Margie Elizabeth Herring
(1952-62)

My Early Childhood

The year was 1944, a leap year: World War II was still raging—19,000 U.S. soldiers were killed in the Battle of the Bulge, one of the deadliest battles of the war; Franklin D. Roosevelt was elected to a four-year term as President of the United States; the GI Bill of Rights was passed; the CIA was formed; meat rationing ended in the U.S.; the cost of a gallon of gas was fifteen cents, a loaf of bread ten cents and a stamp three cents; Chiquita bananas were introduced; the average cost of a new house was $3,450; and, the average wages were $2,400 per year.

Margie Herring

I am what some people call a "war baby"—I was born during World War II in Duplin County, North Carolina on September 19, 1944 at 4:00 a.m. I was the second of seven children born to Willie R. and Norma S. Herring. Mother had an illegitimate child prior to her marriage to Daddy and his name was Ray Stanley. Daddy also had three other children by a former marriage—I only knew one of them, William Herring, who lived in Goldsboro. We lived on Route 2, Mount Olive, somewhere in the vicinity of B. F. Grady School. We did not have a motor vehicle so we walked just about everywhere we went. We were as poor as church mice—I do not remember ever having a piece of money until I became an orphan.

My early childhood—prior to seven years old—is vague; in fact, I do not remember what my Daddy looked like except he was a balding, dark-haired, big man. The only way I know what he looked like was because of a picture I saw of him in his casket. That's a sad thing to remember, but it's the truth. I have pictures of my Mother and she was beautiful and thin.

Daddy was a tenant farmer who worked from sun up to sun down, barely getting home in time to eat and get a few hours of sleep. We children never had a chance to jump up on his lap or have him read to us or do what fathers do. All work and no play seemed to be his lifestyle. He enjoyed alcohol and stayed drunk most of the time when he was not working. Mother kept house and took care of the children. Mother was no angel, something my sister Evelyn and I discussed frequently. There were times when salesmen would come to the house and the children were made to go outside; however, curtains or shades were not closed, so we peeped through the windows and saw what went on. These scenes caused Evelyn and me to have many mixed emotions throughout life. Life was difficult. I do not remember ever hearing "I love you" from either parent.

Nine people lived in a one-bedroom house (I assume it was a tenant house since Daddy farmed the land); there was a big den area where my parents slept and a kitchen in the back of the house. All of the children slept in the bedroom with two double beds—four boys in one and three girls in the other (the youngest girl was not born until after our father's death). We took baths outside in large wash tubs and had "outhouses" instead of toilets—no indoor plumbing. We played on dirt (no grass or trees); our favorite game was "doodle bug". Our house was on cinder blocks, so we were able to crawl underneath the house and hide. I enjoyed sitting in the swing with my Mother and listening to her sing and pop chewing gum. I picked up one of her habits—I like to pop my gum, too, which annoys many people. If Mother needed to discipline us, she would send us across the road to a forest to get a switch—we always got a big one because the little ones hurt the most.

One favorite memory I recall is coming home from school and eating cold biscuits and cold boiled potatoes. That is all Mother had on the table. I cannot remember eating sweets. According to health records, my siblings and I were very malnourished; yet, I do not remember ever being sick. I am sure I was exposed to childhood diseases because there were so many children in one small house.

On December 9, 1951, at the age of 53, my father died due to a cerebral hemorrhage and cirrhosis of the liver caused by alcoholism. Mother, age 33 and pregnant with my youngest sister, was left to take care of seven children, four boys and three girls. She could not financially provide for us so our family was torn apart by the Duplin County Welfare Department. Apparently, there were no family members who were able to take us into their home, so other arrangements were made by the state authorities.

I lost contact with my other siblings because they were adopted—James, Tommy, Janice and Alice, ages 4, 3, 1 and 4 months, respectively. I did not actually lose contact with Alice because she was adopted by my Aunt Virginia Hamler, Mother's sister. Later in life, Aunt Virginia told me the story of Alice's adoption. When Alice was just a couple of weeks old, Mother took her to Aunt Virginia and asked her to take care of her because she could not feed her and she was very malnourished. Apparently, a few weeks later, Mother picked her up and it upset Aunt Virginia. Not long after that, Mother took Alice to Aunt Virginia again—for the same reason—and Aunt Virginia told her she would take Alice but Mother would not be able to get her back. Mother left without her little daughter and Alice became Aunt Virginia's daughter. Alice was very blessed to have been adopted by two wonderful Christian parents. Our oldest brother Ray, age 10, became a resident of the Caswell Training School in Kinston because of medical problems. I did not see him again until 1988.

Can you imagine a pregnant mother losing her husband and having eight children taken from her within six months? What did she go through? What happened to her? At one time, we were told she had remarried but we never met the man. Some said she could have lost her mind and was institutionalized—no one knows, not even her own brothers and sisters. Every road we traveled to find her led to a dead end. I believe I could rest better if I could find out whether she is dead or alive. I do not hold a grudge against her. I would love to tell her how much I love her, no matter what the circumstances were then and now.

This was when my world began to crumble—my Daddy had died six months earlier; I was taken from my Mother due to circumstances beyond her control; I was separated from the youngest members of my family because they were adopted; and I was placed in an environment like none I had ever experienced. I had no idea what was happening and to be honest, I do not remember my last day prior to becoming an orphan. In the years to follow, none of my uncles and aunts discussed my Daddy or my Mother. I wonder what they had to hide.

Prior to being admitted to the Orphanage, I was given a battery of tests and a psychological examination in Raleigh, N.C. They stated that I was "a neatly dressed, barefooted little girl who bit her fingernails during a good deal of the interview and appeared to be normal", though I appeared "sad and emotionally disturbed". It was also noted that my score on the Revised Stanford Binet Scale placed me in the "dull normal group." I was above normal in reading but I had a comprehension problem. My IQ was considered average. "Being placed in a more normal environment where I was loved and accepted and where some effort could be made to understand me and to satisfy my needs would help me make a good adjustment", they said.

ORPHANAGE LIFE

On June 13, 1952, Bobby, Evelyn and I, ages 8, 6 and 7, respectively, were admitted to the Free Will Baptist Orphanage ("Orphanage/Children's Home") near Middlesex, North Carolina. We had no say whatsoever in the decisions made for us. Application was made for our brother James to be admitted but he was denied for reasons unknown. I am not sure who picked us up at our home in Duplin County and how we got to the Orphanage; I think Field Director James Evans (Superintendent '40-'49) picked us up in one of the Orphanage's fancy cars and put us out on the large campus—Evelyn and I walked very slowly up the large walkway to the old girls' building and Bobby went to the Albemarle Building, the new boys' building. We had no idea what was happening and never before had I felt so lonely. We had nothing but the clothes we were wearing and they were later thrown away. What a difference from the small house we had left behind in Duplin County! I soon forgot Bobby and Evelyn were my blood brother and sister—they became just like all of the other boys and girls at the Orphanage, just another face in a group of ninety or more boys and girls.

After Bobby, Evelyn and I became "orphans" in 1952, Mother visited us at the Orphanage only two times. The last time she visited us, I mashed by thumb in her friend's car door. Due to the pain and blood, I got sick on my stomach and had to lie down. When I went back outside, she had left and she never returned. I felt guilty for a long time after that, wondering if I had upset her when I was injured and could not visit. What was it about that visit that prevented her from coming back remains a mystery; it also caused me a lot of pain due to having to grow up without her. I wanted my Mother and she deserted me. She could have at least continued visiting us. She was not forbidden to see us. To be sure she had friends who could have driven her to the Orphanage. The last time I saw her was at the Marlboro Free Will Baptist Church when I went out on a concert class, but she did not talk to me. She sat on the back row and left as soon as the program was over. That might have been the last time I saw her, but that certainly was not the last time I thought of her. I still feel her loss today—there have been many times I've needed a mom to share my thoughts with; I've needed a "best friend"—you know, most of the time a girl's best friend is her mom—but I did not have that privilege.

I do not have very vivid memories of my first years of my life at the Orphanage, but I am told I was a skinny, toe-haired little girl who was very bashful and scared. Alice Little ('46-'55), one of the older girls, became my "hero" and took care of me. NOTE: Alice and I are still each other's "hero"; in fact, she has adopted my husband as her "hero", too. Alice would say and do just the right things to make me smile—she was good at throwing pea hulls. Evelyn and I first stayed in the old girls' building (three stories high, with a basement that housed the laundry) and later moved to the Smith Cottages; as stated before, Bobby stayed in the Albemarle Building with the boys. Brothers and sisters were not allowed to live together or have any contact with each other as we did at home. In fact, I did not even think of them any different than the other boys and girls that I lived with. We were all one big family.

I do not remember doing any work in my home prior to becoming a resident at the Orphanage. However, after I got settled in, things changed and I soon learned what hard work was all about. We had to learn what it took to survive in the "outside" world. Mind you, I was only seven years old, but we were taught to make our own beds when we very young and to pick up our clothes. We also had to empty waste baskets. We shared a closet with another girl. I honestly do not know when I was assigned my first three-month assignment. When we were youngsters, I would say younger than 10, we had opportunities to play and be mischievous. While living in the old girls' building, we used to beg to sleep on quilts on the hall floors; and when the younger girls got to sleep, the older ones would go down the hall and stick our hands in water to make us talk and tell our deepest secrets. I guess my biggest secret was that I wet the bed at night! By seven years old, one should not be wetting the bed. I was told I did due to emotional problems. I do not think I was the only one! Our noses were rubbed in the wet sheets and we were spanked. I understand the boys had different punishments, some more severe.

One of our favorite pastimes in the old girls' building was sliding down the banisters and, quite often, we would get caught doing it and received punishment. I don't think we ever got any splinters in our various body parts from sliding down those rustic banisters. The little girls enjoyed spying on the older girls when they were in the parlor dating. We enjoyed playing many games on the steps of this old building. New buildings were built and we had to see the "old girls' building torn down. My favorite game in front of the big dorm was hopscotch—we drew our diagrams right on the walkway and played until the matron called us inside.

We had an old bell that was rung when it was time to gather for special occasions, such as eating, worshiping, having parties, etc. The bell was rung two times for each meal, thirty minutes apart, and when it was time to eat, we were ready. We would all meet at the side door of the girls' cottage, line up and walk together to the dining hall. The girls were seated on the left side of the dining hall as you entered from the front; the boys were on the right. The staff members, other than the house parents, were seated in the middle of the room nearest the kitchen. When the old girls' building was demolished, the bell was relocated next to the dining hall. The sound of the bell could be heard around the community, not just at the Orphanage. I was disappointed recently to learn that the bell has been relocated to the front of the dining hall underneath the front stoop.

My sister Evelyn ('52-'63) was a very quiet, pretty little white-haired child who did not cause trouble. However, she once took the blame for Doris Duncan's ('46-'52) gold fish being killed. All of us had to walk around the driveway until someone confessed to killing the fish. Even though she was innocent, Evelyn confessed to the incident just so we could stop walking. I learned many years later that someone else also confessed to destroying the fish; apparently, they were innocent too. The person responsible for this incident still remains a mystery to some; I, however, learned in 2007 who actually killed the fish and I was amazed. To the young lady who committed this tragedy, Evelyn never held a grudge against you for doing the evil deed and not confessing to it! She confessed to make it easier on all of us who had to walk for something we did not do. That's the kind of person Evelyn was. She loved everybody, no matter how she was treated. I do not remember Evelyn dating anyone at the Home. Evelyn was smart in school and college. She also worked hard throughout her entire life to provide for her daughter. Many times she and I had discussions about how little we had growing up and we were going to make sure our children did not do without.

I was in the second grade when I became an orphan. My orphan classmates during my school years at Middlesex ('52-'62) were Billy Hines ('54-'62), Bobby Thigpen ('49-'52 & '57-'60), Nancy Pope ('52-'61), Louise Morris ('52-'59), Flora Hines ('57-'62), Richard Little ('51-'56) and Jo Etta Worthington ('54-'62). Louise and Richard left the Home and did not graduate with us.

I found school to be boring and difficult at times, especially during my elementary and middle school days. Nancy Pope and I stayed in trouble when we were in the fifth grade. Mrs. Annie V. Hilliard used to give us "U's" (which stood for unsatisfactory) on conduct because we would throw rocks at each other during break. Our grades were good—our conduct was rotten! My fingers got sore many times because I used to have to write "I will not throw rocks" or "I will not talk in class" a thousand times each time I was punished (believe me, it was more than once). I felt like the teachers hated me and that they "singled" me out too much. Mrs. Naomi Powell, my eighth grade teacher, was my favorite teacher and it was during her classroom that I finally caught on to what school was all about and I began to enjoy learning. I still found school to be boring because I was so fast in doing my work that I finished before others and I had to sit still while others completed their assignments. Here again, I probably got marked down on conduct because I was bored and felt I had to talk out loud. I must have been hyperactive and no one recognized it. No one had heard of Ritalin!

I remember many things from my school days at Middlesex High School (grades 2 through 12). I especially enjoyed my high school courses, such as typing and shorthand, because they were classes in which I was constantly active. I did not have to sit still—I was busy. Because I finished my assignments ahead of everyone else, I assisted the teachers in grading papers. I was a member of the Beta Club, 4-H Club and played basketball (as a forward) for four years; I was co-captain in my senior year. Mr. Enid Drake was one of my teachers and coach and he saw the best in me. He pushed me to excel, both in class and in basketball. In one of his United States History classes, we had to give an oral report from a current newspaper. I stood up, hurriedly gave my speech and sat down. Mr. Drake said, "Now Margie, I know your report was probably good but I do not know a word you said because you spoke so fast. Please stand up and give your report again." Well, I felt like I was going to die, I felt tears build up in my eyes, my head started hurting and I felt my chest would explode. Why in the world would he embarrass me like that, knowing I was shy? I slowly stood up and managed to present the report again, but not without my blood pressure hitting the roof. Mr. Drake knew I could do better and he proved it. That's the way he was as a coach—he pushed us beyond what we felt we could do.

    I was an honor student and a marshal during my junior year (based on scholastic average) and valedictorian of my senior class at Middlesex High School. I had no idea I was even close to being at the top of my class until the day before the graduation ceremonies. At graduation, I was scheduled to give the valedictorian speech to my class. I wrote the speech and intended on giving it, but when the time arrived, I just could not bring myself to do it. With my shyness and lack of self-confidence, I refused to speak to the class. I carried the weight of this for years. I also received two other awards that night—one for service and one for academics. Looking back at what the tests and psychological examination revealed in 1952, I can say without a doubt that I "proved them wrong" and I am so thankful I was able to accomplish my goals. I was smarter than they thought! The Children's Home enabled me to attend school and excel.

    Acne is a young teenager's worst nightmare and I was not exempt. I used to get these very large, under-the-skin bumps which embarrassed me. Every month, just like clockwork, they would pop up. I always felt inferior when it came to good looks. Frequently, I would cry because I never felt pretty enough to get the boys to look at me—it was always someone else who stole their attention. Not only did I have an acne problem, I had a big gap between my two front teeth that I always tried to hide. Some people say the gap represents intelligence, but I let it bother me, so smiles were few and far between. Having pictures taken at school was useless because I would always tear up mine because the ugly bumps would always pop up at the wrong time—picture time—and I never wanted to show my teeth; so, my pictures would always show me as being sad or mad when I wasn't. Being shy did not get me too far in life without my working hard to overcome it. Believe it or not, I am still shy today and find it difficult to carry on conversations. I wish I had taken public speaking in high school or college.

In order for us to have clothes to wear and other necessities of life, Free Will Baptist Churches throughout North Carolina would send money to the Home for the children. My sponsor was the Greenville First Free Will Baptist Church and I visited with several families there during holidays and vacations. I have no idea what the cost was to provide for me. I am forever grateful to this church, as well as all of the other Free Will Baptist Churches, that supported the Home.

Twice a year we were taken to Wilson to shop for clothes. We were allowed two dresses, two pair of shoes, socks and underclothes. We were also given tooth paste, tooth brushes, deodorant and things like that. We exchanged clothes throughout the school year—one would wear a dress one day and another one would wear it within a day or two. How embarrassing! I remember Ms. Sanderson, our laundry matron, put so much starch in our crinolines that, when we sat down, our skirts would fly up over our heads and anyone looking could see our underclothes. Sometimes, when we didn't ask someone if we could wear a blouse, skirt or dress of theirs, the owner would fuss at us. Jean Thigpen ('49-'52 & '57-'60) never liked to share her clothes. She always wore nice things because her sister Lois provided them. Pat Hester always wore nice clothes and shared hers to some extent. Shoes were never exchanged.

To this day, I have dreams of never having enough clothes to wear. I dream about getting ready for school or work and being late because nothing fit, or there wasn't anything to wear except what someone else wore the day before. The dreams have gotten farther and farther apart, so I must have enough clothes now! When I was first admitted to the Orphanage, wearing shorts and slacks was out of the picture. Rules were later relaxed and we were allowed to wear slacks. I do not remember blue jeans being in our wardrobe, especially the ones with "holes". Dresses (or skirts and blouses) had to be worn to all church services. Also, the skirts and dresses had to be below our knees.

The Orphanage girls used to go to Rocky Mount twice a year to get permanents in our hair. We didn't volunteer; we were made to get them. Some of us would cry for several days because the perms "fried" our hair and it was frizzy, but we handled it the best way we could. We dreaded going to school the next day because our hair told the story. When we were in the younger girls' dorm, we had to have our hair washed in alcohol and some other stinking substance monthly to prevent lice. We were made to take castor oil or Milk of Magnesium to keep our innards clean!

We had good medical and dental care. A dentist would come during each summer and perform the necessary dental work on each child. I do not, however, remember having yearly physicals. If we had a medical problem, such as the mumps or measles, infections, etc., we were taken to see Dr. Josephine Newell in Bailey and she became our friend, as well as our doctor. My only surgery during my childhood years was a tonsillectomy performed at Woodard Herring Hospital. I had the chicken pox, German measles and Red measles at the same time, chicken pox, infected knees and many colds. I also had fainting spells very early in the morning. I remember once when I was in the dining hall, standing behind my chair at the table and waiting for someone to bless the food. I fainted and slipped down to the floor. I was not injured, only embarrassed. I was never taken to the doctor for my fainting spells, so I never found out why I had them.

There was an occasion during the mid 50's when everyone at the Orphanage suffered with the Asian flu. Dr. Josephine Newell and a few others came to the Orphanage to take care of us. Also, one Saturday night we were served fried shrimp for supper and approximately 40 of us got food poisoning and threw up for a day or two.

When we were about 15 or 16 years of age, Flora Hines caused a lot of concern when she swallowed a sewing pin. That girl was a trip. I think she did it for attention, but who knows! She was taken to the hospital in Wilson for an x-ray. I can't remember whether or not she had to have surgery, but it eventually disappeared.

I owe a great deal of gratitude to several staff members, whether they were employees or contract workers, who helped me adjust to life at the Orphanage and taught me the valuable lessons I needed to learn in order to succeed in the "outside" world:

Superintendent Stephen A. Smith and his wife, Bertha ('51-'55 & '56-'58) – known as "Pa Smith" and "Ma Smith";

Mr. Grover C. Hill (farm/maintenance work) and wife, Helen (girls' matron) ('51-'53);
Superintendent J. W. Everton and wife, Hattie Mae ('58-'62);
Superintendent R. H. Jackson and wife ('55-'56);
Mr. Horace Mixon (farm manager) and wife, Sudie (dietician) ("Ma Sudie") ('23-'34);
Mrs. Lottie Little (matron)
Mr. and Mrs. Clifton Hedgepeth (farm work/relief work);
Mr. Carl W. Powell (farm work) and wife, Iris (relief work);
Miss Bonnie Farmer (concert class director);
Mr. Cornell Lucas (farm work) and wife, Daisy (big girls' matron);
Mrs. Daisy Owens (relief work);
Mrs. Emma Maiden (laundry);
Granny Sanderson (laundry);
Mr. and Mrs. Herman Stocks (farm work/relief work); and
Mrs. Thelma M. Rulli (girls' matron). (More on Mrs. Rulli later.)

As I reflect on the days when we used to all eat together in the dining hall, I think about Mrs. Sudie Mixon and cannot understand how she knew the amount of food to cook. "Ma Sudie", as we called her, was one of the best cooks in the world. She made sure the larger boys got enough to eat because of their hard work—extra food went their way! We had good food except for Thursday night—this was "left over" night and most of us did not like that. Some of us did not like Sunday morning breakfast because we did not like cereal or milk. If we worked in the kitchen, we were fortunate enough to eat leftovers—hot dogs and chili buns were our favorite. Ma Sudie could make the best chili. Once in a while, there would be a few left over drinks and we were allowed to drink them. On Saturday, while cooking fat back for lunch, one of my favorite foods was a peanut butter and fat back sandwich! Yum! I have not had this combination of foods since I left the Home. I should have been fat then because of what I ate, but I weighed less than 90 pounds.

Ma Sudie taught the girls how to cook. She used to fuss at us when we cooked eggs too long, especially scrambled ones. "Get those eggs up now, they are done enough. Don't you know they are going to cook some more when you take them out of the frying pan?" Sometimes, they were cooked so hard you could play ball and jacks with them! If we did not listen to her, we were chastised. Just imagine having to cook enough fried eggs (yes, some over easy—we frequently broke the yolk!) for 100 people to have two a piece? We peeled potatoes with a knife until a potato peeler was purchased. Once in a while when we peeled potatoes, we would peel them so thick that we had to go over the peeling—no surprise to what we found—enough potatoes for two or three people. When the potato peeler was used, we fussed about having to get the "eyes" out of the potatoes. We could never be happy. When I married and had to cook for two, it was tough; I always cooked too much.

We also liked to pick up pecans and have Mrs. Mixon make us fudge or pecan brittle. Sometimes, she would let us make the candy and we enjoyed that. Wild berries and apples made good pies, too. Mrs. Mixon always made birthday cakes for everyone. I used to love to lick the bowl and spoon each time she made a cake. Happy birthday was sung to each person having a birthday. You had to share your cake with the children at your table and also give those at the "head" table a slice. You really did not have too much left to carry back to your dorm. It was nice being able to send a piece over to a boyfriend.

Most of our fun consisted of childhood games such as "Mother May I", "Red Rover", croquet, jump rope, jump board (Evelyn Jean Darden ['45-'55] used to jump so hard on the board that she would send us higher than we wanted to go), picking four-leaf clovers and making chains, softball, hopscotch, swinging (I remember being thrown over the top of the swing because the person pushing me wanted excitement), building houses out of rocks and china balls (those stinking balls that grew on a tree down by the old pump house—you didn't want to squash them in your hands because of the smell), and picking violets that grew down by the stream which flowed from the pump house. That stream was later filled in and a swimming pool was installed. During my stay at the Home, the farm pond was the only swimming hole we had—I hated it because I was afraid of snakes and did not like filthy water. Once in a while, the girls were permitted to watch the boys play ball behind their building. We sat on the hill behind the catcher and yelled for our favorite team. That was one of the few times we were permitted near the boys' building.

The pump house holds a lot of memories for many; nothing comes to my mind except the violets down by the stream! In other words, the pump house holds no "love" memories for me. I went by the pump house several times on my way to swing, pick flowers and play with rocks under the trees. I have heard many comments about what went on there. I just thought it was an old building where they kept the lawnmowers, shovels, maintenance equipment, etc. I personally feel the building should never be destroyed. Now, according to rumors, there were other "secret meeting places" that I knew nothing about. There was a boiler room behind the kitchen used as a secret rendezvous. When the coast was clear, the boy would take a shovel and bang on the boiler to make a noise indicating to the girl that he was waiting. One time a couple met, kissed and got caught by Mrs. Rulli. Oh well, you probably guessed the ending to that story!

Sunday afternoons were fun. We walked the driveway and occasionally were allowed to "walk up the hill" toward Middlesex. I wonder if they ever thought we would run away when we walked up that hill? Some children did run away but they were picked up before they walked too far. Sundays were filled with visiting with family and friends and we were allowed to leave the campus for a ride. Occasionally, Stanley Brantley, one of our high school friends, would pick some of us up and ride us around Middlesex and Zebulon. He would drive extremely fast, especially over railroad tracks, and we were thrown up out of the seat and our heads would hit the top of the car—we would scream to the top of our lungs. Luckily, we never had an accident. It was great to "let loose" and have fun.

Television was monitored and dancing was not allowed. We would come home from school, change clothes and head straight for the study hall to turn on the television for just a few minutes to watch Dick Clark and Kenny and Arlene on American Bandstand. Believe it or not, we did not have many quarrels as to who was going to watch what on television. We heard some wonderful music on the radio; and, occasionally, some of us girls would get in one of our bedrooms and bop to rock and roll music, such as "Rocking Robin". If we had no one to dance with, we would hold the bed post and dance with it. This was taboo, but fun! I learned to dance from watching American Bandstand. I still like to dance, especially the bop and the shag. I played the piano every chance I got, which wasn't very often because there were so many others who could play and they deserved their time to play. I was afforded the opportunity to play the piano for church services and that was an honor. I got my first radio from Aunt Bebe, Aunt Ginny and Papa Dildy.

We were punished for misbehaving, whether guilty or not; of course, that depends on what one calls misbehaving. J. W. Everton ('58-'62) was my favorite superintendent while I was at the Home, but he was very strict and believed in punishment. I remember one time Jo Etta and I were punished for missing our curfew. Our excuse was not accepted even though we told the truth about making a wrong turn and getting lost.

Evelyn Jean Darden and I were mischievous during our days of waiting on tables. She was older than a lot of the girls and dared us to do things. One Saturday morning during breakfast, we were both assigned to wait on tables—I had the girls section and she had the middle-age boys section. As we were standing and watching for uplifted hands, she dared me to tie her apron strings around the two of us. She did not think the strings were long enough and I told her they were. Well, just about the time I completed the tying, a hand went up in the boy's section where she was assigned duty and she didn't give me time to untie the apron. Out I went with her, embarrassed to death. Ma Sudie didn't like it either. She punished us for the whole morning—we had to stay tied together until lunch time. Evelyn Jean was twice my size and I had trouble staying up with her. Ma Sudie felt we had learned a lesson.

Another instance of punishment was when some of the high school students from the Orphanage went to a party at Larry Whitley's home just outside of Middlesex and we were told not to leave the house for any reason. After we played a few games, such as "Spin the Bottle", "Post Office", and "Fruit Basket Turnover", we became bored. We disobeyed the orders given to us by the superintendent and a bunch of us took a ride in Larry Whitley's car. Upon our return, Mrs. Mitchell, the boys' matron, was waiting for us. On the drive back to the Orphanage, her eyes and her voice told us what we already knew; we could feel the belt on our behinds! The superintendent did not whip us, but we were restricted from going off campus for several weekends. I managed to keep my nose clean and didn't have any problems after that.

Have you noticed the pine trees on your left as you drive up the last hill from Middlesex to the Home? They were small seedlings at the time they were planted. That is a beautiful sight to me because Jerry Smith ('49-'60) was responsible for getting those trees planted in 1958 as a special agricultural project for him. I don't know who added the azaleas, but they enhanced the area. The house on the corner was not built at the time the trees were planted.

I was entering the ninth grade when I fell in love for the first time--he was an orphan and junior in high school. Jerry was my first boyfriend and the only one I had who was an orphan. I think our blue eyes were the big attraction! Jerry and I used to meet behind the kitchen after mealtime just to grab a kiss or hold hands for a few seconds. You had to stay alert because you would often get caught and sometimes you would get punished. The front seat of the school bus was mine because Jerry was the bus driver! While the other girls were exiting the bus, he and I chatted and held hands. We grabbed every moment we could just to smile and say hello to each other. Riding "big blue", the Orphanage bus, to attend special church functions, ballgames, etc. didn't bother us because we had a chance to sit together for a short while.

Dating rules were terrible at the Orphanage. We could start dating at 15, but we had to sit in the living room where the matrons would peep out their bathroom windows (remember, the blinds in the living room had to be open) to see if you were hugging or kissing. When we became a little older, we were allowed to double date and leave the campus on a car—yeah! Jerry and I used to double date with Cora Lee Jones and Phillip Anderson. No date is complete without a good night kiss, so standing on the breezeway to say good night was tough because you knew the matron was peeping out the window at you and you were suppose to say good night and that was it—hugging and kissing were out of the picture! I was a very naïve person and did not know anything about sex—hugging and kissing—that's all I knew and that came naturally. We never had any group discussions on the subject of sex, only in physical education at school. If any hanky-panky was going on around campus, I did not know about it. Even though I am personally unaware of pregnancies among the girl residents, I am told by other alumni that there were some.

After Jerry graduated, he left for Mount Olive Junior College (MOJC) and as time passed, his letter writing became less frequent. Unfortunately, as the case is most of the time, he met a young lady at MOJC and we drifted apart.

I began dating other boys from school and the surrounding area. I was jealous of several of the girls at the Home because the guys I really wanted to date did not even know I existed when they were around. I was not an outgoing person, and as I stated earlier, my acne and teeth took away my self-confidence. There was no other special one in my heart until I entered college. Yes, in college I fell in love again with a young man from Kinston and he used me just to get good grades—I got my heart broken for the second time. I ended up dating a guy from Pink Hill and I broke his heart. I was afraid to get close to anyone else. I hated rejection and I was determined I was not going to get hurt anymore.

My job assignments during my 10-year tenure at the Orphanage included housekeeping, cooking, waiting on tables, washing dishes (because of a fungus on my hands, I was exempt from this chore during my last two years) and ironing. It was tough washing dishes because we had to lean over the large sinks filled with the hottest water imaginable. We would be soaking wet when we finished cleaning the kitchen. When I became a senior, I wanted to work in the superintendent's office but Jo Etta, who I felt was a "pet", was chosen. I was upset, but I soon got over it. Summer was full of work: we shelled peas and butter beans, shucked corn and cut it off the cob, picked and canned tomatoes, harvested, looped and tied tobacco, etc. Barning tobacco was hard work, but it was fun. It beat having to iron, clean house and cook. Around 9:00 in the morning, Ma Sudie would send us drinks and peanut butter crackers, or moon pies, for a snack. The boys who harvested the tobacco would make sure there were tobacco worms in the tobacco truck. Occasionally, if they found a snake, it was put in the truck to scare the daylights out of the barn crew. Hanging the tobacco in the barn wasn't fun. It was tiresome and the tobacco juice would get in our eyes. When fall came, we would all go to the pack house and work in the dry tobacco until supper time.

During the summer, a truck load of beans or peas was dumped on the cement breezeway between the Smith Cottages; and, as we sat shelling them, we would frequently throw "unshelled" ones into the pile of hulls so we would get through faster. Yes, that was wasteful, but we did not think that at the time we were doing it. We were tired and didn't care. We threw hulls and occasionally spit peas at each other. Thank God we never got caught. Some of us shelled faster than others and we would get upset when we saw others goofing off and not shelling their load.

Freezing corn was the hardest job of all. The dump truck would drive up behind the kitchen and the corn was dumped on the rocky ground. I do not recall the number of ears of corn we prepared at one time—too many to count. We all had a responsibility, whether it was picking, shucking, cleaning off the silks, washing, blanching, cutting it off the cob or whatever, it had to be done in order for us to have food throughout the year. Once in a while, we had ears of corn containing more than corn—yes, worms—and we had a good time throwing them at each other.

The worst assignment I ever had was "chicken detail". About four times a year, several girls and boys stayed home from school for a whole day just to prepare chickens for future meals. I do not recall how many chickens lost their lives at a given time, but it seemed like 500 or more. The boys killed the chickens and plucked off the feathers; the girls removed the guts and made sure they were cleaned prior to freezing. What a stinking mess! To top it all off, Ma Sudie wouldn't wait until a later date to serve fried chicken, she would have it for supper the same night we cleaned them! That was hard to swallow.

Those assigned to kitchen duty also had a lot of fun. Making biscuits took the longest time; I bet we had to cook ten or more large pans full each time they were served (biscuits with molasses and butter became a favorite for all of us). Jo Etta told me that, one time when she was rolling out biscuits, she threw a ball of dough up to the ceiling and when it fell down, it went right into the frying pan of hot chicken grease, splattering the grease all over Miss Bonnie Farmer who was filling in for Ma Sudie. She was not happy. The girls enjoyed having one of the older boys working as the kitchen boy. We liked playing tricks on them. On one occasion, Barry Rogers was carrying in a crate of drinks and slipped on banana peelings that Jo Etta had thrown on the floor. Barry fell and never once let go of the crate of drinks. Believe it or not, Barry did not get hurt nor were any drink bottles broken. Jo Etta did not get into trouble either.

Occasionally, tempers would get the best of some of the girls while working in the kitchen. The Pope girls, Nancy, Mary Belle ('52-'61), Daisy ('52-'63) and Johnnie Faye ('53-'66), were known as "tough girls". You didn't pick on one without the others joining in to help. Well, one time Ma Sudie and Nancy got into a scuffle (I do not know why) and the other sisters felt they needed to rescue Nancy. Each one of them began to wrestle their way into the fight. They were all squirming on the floor and the fight became serious enough that Mr. Everton had to step in and resolve the matter. That was scary to me. I didn't know what was going to happen; I did not want anyone to get hurt. I do not like friction of any kind.

I recall Mrs. Dovie Barbour (mother of Stacy Barbour ['57-'64]), matron of the small girls, used to make one of the youngest girls (I do not recall her name) sit at the table long after everyone else had left to make her eat her food. The child cried every time; the more she cried, the more the food was forced into her. The child just did not like the food but Mrs. Barbour forced her to eat it more times than one. I hated that; I really felt sorry for that little girl and I wonder what impact that might have had on her eating habits once she became older.

Holidays were favorite times of the year. I looked forward to leaving the campus with family and friends each Thanksgiving, Christmas and summer vacations. There were three special families that would take me home for the holidays: Leslie K. Dildy and his two daughters, Ginny and Bebe of Wilson, Othal and Rose Minshew of Kenly and Mr. and Mrs. E. L. Jones of Walstonburg. I hated returning every time. Aunt Bebe told me that when they took me back, I got out of the car and held my head down and looked very sad as I walked to the dormitory. I would cry every time Rose and Othal or Mr. and Mrs. E. L. Jones took me back up that lonely hill. Prior to her death a few years ago, Mrs. Jones sent me a Christmas picture I had drawn and given to her and Mr. Jones during one of my Christmas visits. They were wonderful people and I loved them a lot. I could not believe she had kept the picture for so many years and thought enough of me to send it back many years later.

Thanksgiving was a special time because all of the children, boys and girls, were required to sing for a special Thanksgiving service for people who visited from the various churches throughout the state. The children sounded good as a group. Having lunch spread out on the tables in the pecan orchard (some call it "the flower garden") was a fun time and we got to eat food that was brought by guests—yum! Then, the children would leave the Home with friends and relatives for the Thanksgiving Holiday.

At Christmas, we would gather in the dining hall for a big celebration. Each child received gifts from their church sponsor and special friends. As usual, some children received more presents than others. Bags of fruit were also distributed to everyone. I do not remember ever getting a baby doll for Christmas. One Christmas Santa Claus came to the campus in a helicopter and gave us all toys. We all enjoyed these special moments.

Easter was a lot of fun because we had Easter egg hunts in many different locations around campus. My favorite place was out in the grassy field area behind the store room. The grass was just tall enough so the eggs could be hidden but could be seen by the smaller children. What a blast—when the sound was given for us to begin the hunt, we ran in all directions, some of us tripping and falling and messing up our pretty Easter clothes. Prizes were given to the children with the most eggs. Louise Morris' mother always brought her lots of Easter candy. No, she did not share with us. Like a lot of other children, she was stingy because she wanted her candy to last longer.

Speaking of candy, I took care of the candy store for a while. Anyone wanting to buy candy could see me. I always had to make sure I had enough money to pay for the next load of candy coming in. I really enjoyed the Baby Ruth candy bars and the Oatmeal cookies. Sodas were kept in each dorm and we were occasionally given one without having to buy it. Sometimes, popcorn was served while we watched television on Saturday night.

Aunt Bebe and I feel the same way as to why we were brought together 54 years ago. I was no one special, just an orphan who felt nobody loved her. I was an eleven and a half year old girl who needed someone to care for me, to love me, and to make me part of a loving family. So, when she called Mrs. R. H. Jackson ('55-'56) and asked if there was a young girl who needed a special family, I became that little girl. Little did we know that God had a plan in 1956—I needed someone to care for me then; Aunt Bebe needed me 50 years later. So, in 2006, Michael and I invited her to move in with us so we could care for her. A nursing home was out of the question. Here is what Aunt Bebe said to me at that time: "I feel that God's putting you in my life 50 years ago is one of the greatest gifts He ever gave me. He knew I would need you later on."

Aunt Bebe and I have had many conversations about my upbringing at the Orphanage. When I visited her family in Wilson, she said I always behaved and never broke a curfew. The rules of the Orphanage applied in her home and I respected that. If I dated, I had to obey the dating rule; in fact, I was always home earlier than the curfew. Recently, Aunt Bebe made the following statement: "I have never known anyone with higher integrity than Marge has." That says a lot about me because that was instilled in me while I was in the Children's Home.

Othal and Rose Minshew "adopted" me late in my teenage years. I was in high school when they first took me home with them to Kenly. When I graduated from high school, I stayed with them in Clayton upstairs over a funeral home where Othal worked. Rose used to take me shopping and we would have more fun than a barrel of monkeys. She loved to spend money and I loved every minute of it. They helped me get my first car after I got out of college. We are very close today—"Mama Rose" and "Daddy Othal"—two very special people. Rose's mother and daddy, "Ma Flossie" and "Pa Jesse" and her sister Patsy and her brother John became my family as well. Evelyn also spent a lot of time with this family.

At this point, I want to bring up the issue of adoption. I never could understand why no one wanted to adopt me, especially my Mother's family. Uncle Walter Stanley, my Mother's brother, wanted to adopt Evelyn (he tried to bribe her with ice cream) and Bobby, but not me. Aunt Bebe wanted to adopt me but was unable to due to financial reasons. Othal and Rose had only been married a short time when they came into my life and I was in my teens—too old for adoption. Aunt Bebe once told me that she tried to get Ralph Pate (Alumnus '33-'41) to adopt me, but he felt he couldn't because he already had two or three children. Do I think my life would have been different had I been adopted? All of the people I have named herein would have been wonderful, loving parents, but I am glad they did not adopt me. I love them and will always be appreciative of their contributions to put meaning in my life; however, growing up in the Children's Home was a blessing, not a curse. Just look at the large family I grew up with.

Sometime during 1987, I was having some health problems and I needed closure from being separated from my other siblings for over 35 years, so I decided to search for them. I knew where Alice was and we had stayed in touch, but I needed help to locate the other four. With a couple of names and addresses given to me from a gentleman who lived in Mount Olive, I located James, Tommy, Ray and Janice in Duplin County. Seven of us, along with our families, had a reunion in the summer of 1988 and we had fun talking about our lives since 1952. It was as though we had never been apart. We've been a family ever since. I did not physically locate Janice—I found out who she was and that she had gone to school with my youngest brother Tommy. I saw a picture of her in Tommy's school annual and I thought I was looking at myself—she looked a lot like Alice and me.

I have always wanted to sing, but I cannot carry a tune. I do not know what Concert Manager Bonnie Farmer saw in me, but she wanted me in the concert class every year and she made me sing alto (I sounded like a male). I was always so embarrassed to get up in front of a church and sing because I knew the concert class sounded terrible. We would put on our white blouse and blue skirt (or pants for the boys) and look so pretty! We did our best and I am sure God was pleased with our performances. After the program, we would run outside the church and play until it was time to leave. We had a lot of fun on the concert classes and yes, we were spoiled. One lesson I learned early in life was that I would never be a singer or an actress.

I was involved in my first car accident during one of the concert class tours in the mountains. Miss Farmer was driving and it was raining at the time. All I remember is that the vehicle we were in had to be replaced because of severe damage. Thank goodness, none of us were hurt. On another occasion while in the class, I was standing on the running board of our suburban and fell off of it, breaking the window and cutting my arm—I had to have several stitches.

I am not a swimmer and I hate murky waters. One summer while on tour, I was swimming in a pond on one of the church member's farm; and, as I slid down the "slimy, green cement dam, I fell backwards and hit my head very hard. I was sick for two or three days, unable to perform due to a severe head injury.

While in the concert class and visiting in the various homes of church families, I was molested twice. I did not understand what was happening at the time; I was young and naïve. I never told Miss Farmer or anyone while I was at the Orphanage. I was embarrassed and afraid no one would believe me if I reported it. It was while writing my memoirs that I decided I must release the guilt, so I told my husband and the writer of *The Family* of the molestation. It hurt me to tell it because I felt dirty, and I was embarrassed to reveal such personal emotions, but I think letting it out was a healing process. I've learned others were also molested and never told about it. I have no idea how or why things happen to children, how they grow to be adults when there is so much evil in the world.

Miss Farmer also tried to teach me piano lessons but I was too impatient. I wanted to do it my way, so I quit taking lessons and played "by ear". I could read music just a little; but if I heard the song, I could play it. I took lessons for a very short time at school, but that didn't last long either—I did not like the teacher, she was too slow for me. My first and only piano recital was a disaster because of my shyness and I kept hitting the wrong notes due to my trembling hands. I enjoyed playing the piano for church services and for the quartet that went to various churches with Mr. Everton.

My relationship with God began during my stay at the Home. I accepted Christ as my Savior and was baptized when I was 13 years old. I especially liked the Wednesday night services because, quite frequently, we had to stand and quote a favorite Bible scripture. If the superintendent did not think your verse was what it should be, you had to quote another one. For instance, if someone stood up and said, "Jesus wept" and that was it, he would make that person give another verse. After a while, the children learned to do it right the first time. We had League on Sunday night and the Bible drills were and Vacation Bible School gave us another opportunity to learn more about God. Boys and girls could sit together in church. I couldn't wait for Sunday night services to be over because we could spend a little time dating or have someone ride to Rock Side and get us a hot dog, candy, dill pickle, or anything we could afford.

Money was scarce during my tenure in the Children's Home. I remember the superintendents used to give us money on Friday night (most of the time it was a roll of nickels) so we could attend basketball games or we could use the money for snacks, etc. We were rich! If you were fortunate to go out on the concert class, you were given spending money by some of the church members.

Pa Smith was my kind of disciplinarian. He never used his hands to whip the children. Even though I was good and never had to go before him for punishment, I heard from others as to his way of disciplining. He used to beat his belt on the desk in his office and made everyone think he was spanking us. If he used a belt, it was so soft that it would not have harmed a fly. I always got hugs from him. He was a wonderful man and he loved all of us. We were very saddened by his departure from the Home, but we carry fond memories of him in our hearts.

Around 1958 or 1959 when they were approximately 14 or 15 years old, Bobby Thigpen ('49-'52 & '57-'62) and my brother Bobby ('52-'59) ran away from the Home because they did not want to go to school. They were gone for two days and Pa Smith went out looking for them and found them and brought them back. He decided that their punishment would be to stay out of school for a week and to work on the grounds around the Home. He also decided they should plant bushes and shrubs around the driveway, which they did, and the landscaping is still there today. I do not think my brother ever became acclimated to life at the Orphanage. He was smart but he did not apply himself. He left the Home without getting a high school diploma.

I am aware of various forms of discipline that were used at the Orphanage: leather straps, belts, 2 x 4 boards, paddle ball bats, shoe horns, hands and feet. There were probably other things used I know nothing about. I do know there were severe punishments that should have been prohibited. Sometimes, the punishment was more severe than it should have been for the wrongdoing.

My brother Bobby and I were not close for many years because of an incident that occurred when he was working as the "kitchen boy." One day as I was walking out the back door of the kitchen, he propositioned me to go to the storeroom with him for something other than getting food and I was shocked. I got mad and scared of him. I immediately told him he was crazy and I held that against him for over 45 years. I never told anyone at the Children's Home. I later learned from my sister Evelyn that he had done the same thing to her. Prior to his death, he told me he was sorry and I was able to forgive him—I am glad I did. Prior to his death, I witnessed his acceptance of Jesus as his Savior.

One of the saddest times during my stay at the Orphanage was the sickness and subsequent death of Sandra Mercer ('53-'65). The onset of her leukemia was prior to my high school graduation and after I left for college, I heard little about the suffering she endured. She was such a pretty girl and her death due to kidney failure created confusion for everyone, especially the children. Death was something we knew little about. I had left the Home when she died in 1965 and I was unable to attend her memorial services. I remember her gentleness and her smile, and she will always have a special place in my heart.

I was always classified as Mrs. Mixon's "pet". Louise Morris and I had a mother-daughter function to attend at school and she needed someone to go with her. She went to Mrs. Mixon and said, "I know you are probably going with Margie, but if you are not, would you go with me to my mother-daughter function?" She told her yes, but when it was time to go, something prevented both Louise and Miss Farmer from going, so Mrs. Mixon and I went together anyway. I never considered myself being anyone's "pet." I just behaved myself. I still visit Ma Sudie in assisted living quarters in Wilson and she always asks me if I remember this incident.

Talking about pets—humans, not animals, Cora Lee Jones and Jo Etta Worthington were, in my opinion, pets of many of the matrons. One time Cora Lee had a pair of glasses she disliked and tried to get a new pair. There was nothing wrong with the glasses, Cora just hated them. Well, she told Jo Etta about wanting to break the glasses and asked her for help. They took the glasses and did everything they could to break them—threw them on the floor, threw them up against the wall, twisted them—they tried everything and couldn't break them. So, they left the situation alone. A few days later, Cora accidentally knocked the glasses off the dresser and they fell to the floor and broke. Yeah! A new pair of glasses was bought for her.

Cora also had an allergy to poison ivy/poison oak—every year she had a severe case to break out on her entire body and her eyes swelled to the point she had trouble seeing. I really felt sorry for her, especially when she had to stay out of school.

The only staff member who I felt disliked me was Mrs. Thelma Rulli (Alumnus '23-'30), girls' matron, and I'll never be able to figure that out. Mrs. Rulli was an "inmate" at the Orphanage for seven years so she should have known what life was like for an orphan. I never argued with her; I did not look at her when she was talking to the girls as a group and that annoyed her. Maybe that's what she disliked about me. I do not have to look someone in the eye to grasp what they are saying, but I could not get that across to her. She was always saying, "Look at me when I'm talking to you." The thing that made it so bad was she would say it in front of the other girls. That degraded me and I hated every minute of it. I think back and realize that is probably one thing that made me sad a lot of times—being degraded in front of my peers. No matter the differences between us, I felt she helped me through some tough times. I do not remember ever seeing her smile or act like she was having a good time. Isn't that sad?

Let me tell you about an instance when I felt Mrs. Rulli "had a heart"—after Jerry and I broke off our relationship, she saw the hurt I was experiencing. She called me into her bedroom one day and told me that she had spoken to Jerry and he wanted to meet me in the living room at a certain time on a certain day, which was out of the norm. Well, little did I know, she had called him and told him that I wanted to see him at the same time. When we met in the living room, we questioned each other as to why we were meeting and we discovered Mrs. Rulli had "set us up". She wanted us to rekindle our relationship. Now, wasn't that sweet of her! Her plan worked for a while; Jerry then entered the Army and that was the end of our romance.

Life after the Orphanage

After I left the Children's Home in the summer of 1962, I moved to Mount Olive to attend MOJC and Dr. W. Burkette Raper, President (Alumnus '36-'45), employed me to work in his office prior to my starting college. He believed in me and I was given a chance to further my education. Even though I received a scholarship to attend Atlantic Christian College, I chose MOJC because it was where Dr. Raper was and I knew that he would take care of me. After all, I was one of his "orphanage sisters" and I needed "a big brother" to look after me. I am deeply indebted to him for all he has done for me and I love him as a brother and a great mentor. He is one alumnus I look forward to seeing every year. He and Rose never seem to age!

The "orphan" issue came to light early the first year I was at MOJC (1962). First of all, I had no money so I had to earn my way through my two years of college the best way I knew how. I accepted a janitorial job at the College in the girls' dorm upstairs above the offices and classrooms. I felt I had been taught at the Orphanage how to dust, sweep and scrub floors and clean toilets. I hated what I had to do and I was embarrassed every time I was seen sweeping and scrubbing the staircases, especially when the guy I was dating saw me. I kept telling myself it would be okay, but I would go upstairs to my room and cry and have a "pity party" all by myself. By the time my first year came to a close, I didn't care who saw me working like a cleaning lady.

During the summer after my first year and during my second year at MOJC, I worked for Dean Roy O'Donnell—no more janitorial duties! I was able to earn enough money so that I only had to borrow a little more than $700 from the Children's Home for both school years. I was so proud when I sent in my last check to pay off the loan in 1974—ten years later. I paid $50 per month; yes, I got behind at times, but Superintendent M. L. Johnson was very understanding. Again, I graduated from college with honors and I was proud and very thankful for the opportunities afforded me. I earned my way and I appreciated what I had accomplished. I was presented with the M. L. Johnson Business Award for outstanding achievement and a Certificate in Business which helped me throughout my working career. Here again, the testing and psychological evaluations given me in 1952 were proven wrong!

I wanted to further my education at East Carolina College and actually moved into a boarding house in Greenville just prior to the school year. However, due to financial difficulty—not wanting to increase my debt obligations—I decided my school career would end. Yes, I regret making that decision…hindsight is beautiful! I moved to Wilson and began a working career, utilizing the work ethics and knowledge I had received while at the Children's Home and MOJC.

On August 7, 1966, I married Gerald W. Matthews from Wilson. Our marriage ceremony was performed in the Children's Home Chapel by the Reverend J. W. Everton, former superintendent of the Children's Home. In

1972, we moved to Raleigh where Gerald worked for the Internal Revenue Service, Criminal Investigation Division (CID). In September 1979, we adopted our son Christopher. We then began a journey to various places in Florida where Gerald was to end up as Division Manager for the CID in Orlando. I was blessed with an 11-year career at the Walt Disney Company ("Mickey Mouse") in Lake Buena Vista, Florida. In 1993, Gerald had a nervous breakdown on the job and we returned to Wilson in June 1996; he committed suicide on July 21, 1997.

I attended only one or two alumni homecomings after graduating in 1962 and that was because I could not let go of feeling inferior to everyone else and the resentment I felt toward Mrs. Rulli. I had nightmare after nightmare due to this lady and I could not let go of my hatred for her. I cried many tears because of the way she treated me while I was at the Home, but I cried even more after I left due to bad dreams involving her. Also, I did not think my attendance would make a difference. I was robbing myself of some precious moments and some wonderful hugs by staying away. I regret letting one homecoming go by without attending.

After being away for over 30 years, I decided I needed to go back to the Home; I had been gone long enough. I was the one to blame for not going back, not anyone else. During the time I was attending my 30th high school reunion in Middlesex, I went to see the one matron I had hated all those years because she made my life so miserable at the Home—Mrs. Thelma Rulli was a thorn in my side. I was tired of having nightmares and waking up crying because of pain inflicted on me by Mrs. Rulli. I did not think Mrs. Rulli would recognize me but once I started talking and told her who I was, she smiled and we had a wonderful conversation. I held her hands and told her what had bothered me for so many years. We both started crying as I asked her forgiveness for blaming her for the hate and pain I had carried in my heart for so long. She immediately told me she was sorry and forgave me. She had no idea I had such feelings. Mrs. Rulli asked me to forgive her for the way she treated me and I honored her request. After our wonderful visit, the nightmares and crying stopped. I began returning for the homecomings and have found a lot of love and joy. Forgiveness is important in letting go of the hurtful past.

After Gerald's death, my son and I decided to return to Orlando, so I sold my house in Wilson and headed south in April 1998. I was asked to direct a wedding for a dear friend in Wilson in June 1998 so I returned for a short visit. It was during that time I attended First Free Will Baptist Church in Wilson and met the wonderful man God had chosen for me to spend the rest of my life with. I went back to Orlando, sold my house and returned to Wilson in August—all of this was done in a four-month time span.

Michael and I were married on November 24, 2000; Dr. W. Burkette Raper performed the ceremony. I will tell you up front that Michael is 18 years younger than me, but as the old saying goes, age is just a number. We have a wonderful marriage and God is foremost in our lives.

Michael and I were attending a Southern Gospel singing in the fall of 2007 when I released much of my childhood "baggage"—rejection, unresolved and often misdirected anger, having no roots, and feeling inferior. My eyes glowed over in red and became watery; tears crawled down my face as I listened to the Talley Trio from Morristown, Tennessee sing the lyrics of the song "Orphans of God:"

"Who here among us has not been broken
Who here among us is without guilt or pain
So oft abandoned by our transgressions
If such a thing as grace exists
Then grace was made for lives like this

"Come ye unwanted and find affection
Come all ye weary come and lay down your head
Come ye unworthy you are my brother
If such a thing as grace exists
Then grace was made for lives like this

Chorus
"There are no strangers
There are no outcasts
There are no orphans of God
So many fallen but hallelujah
There are no orphans of God"

Sitting, holding hands with Michael, listening to the music, I sobbed while quietly thinking—"Thank you God, I cannot escape being an orphan here on earth, but I'll not be an orphan in heaven." Tears continued to roll down my cheeks as I listened to the words of the song. "There are no orphans of God" struck me like a bolt of lightning. "Amen," I cried out, and when the song ended, I finally realized my "orphan" days on earth were over; a burden had been lifted. Indeed, I had a Father and one day I will meet Him face to face. I came to accept that, throughout my entire life, I really had never been alone because God had always been my constant companion.

After the 2007 gospel sing, I was at peace with myself, but not without pain I was having from a liver disease caused by hepatitis and hemachromatosis (too much iron in the blood). My condition became terminal without a transplant. I was very weak and stayed in bed during most of 2008 and the first part of 2009 due to liver failure. I couldn't drive, cook, attend Gospel singings (one of my favorite pastimes), talk on the telephone or work—I couldn't do anything except sleep and depend on someone else, something I was not accustomed to doing.

The long-awaited day arrived. On May 25, 2009, at 11:30 p.m., the telephone rang advising Michael that the day had come—they had a liver for me. It took us less than two hours to drive from Wilson to Chapel Hill. On May 26, 2009, after eight hours of surgery, God blessed me with a new liver. A young man had been accidentally killed and his liver was donated by his family. When the doctor told me I had received a "male" liver, I was shocked because I didn't know they would put a male liver in a female or vice versa. I do not feel any different because of my 27-year old male liver. I was in the hospital six out of eight weeks between May 26 and August 1 because of complications, including a light stroke. It was a "touch and go" situation but God, in his infinite wisdom, healed me. In September, I showed signs of rejection and was hospitalized for a week. My anti-rejection medication had to be changed. I am thankful I am alive today and thank God for the donor who made it possible for me to have a second chance at life. My only regret was that someone had to die so I could live. I cried more about this situation than I did about the possibility of dying. My greatest concern during this time was for Michael and Chris, wondering what life would be like for them if God chose to take me home. Today, as I awake every morning, the first thing I do is to thank God for another day of life. Throughout the difficulties we faced, Michael and I never were bitter; we never asked "Why us, Lord"; we had faith that God would supply our every need. Believe!

POSTSCRIPT

As I reflect back over my years at the Home, I realize and appreciate what God did for me when he removed me from a very poor life style and placed me in a safe environment. Where would I have gone—would I have received the training, education and religious upbringing that I received by being an orphan? I tremble, and yes, I sometimes cry, when I think about what kind of life I might have had. I believe I would have suffered tremendously and would have died at a young age. I am thankful I was placed in the Orphanage at the age of seven because it gave me a better opportunity to mature above everyone's expectations. The psychologist in 1952 was right: "In a more normal environment where she is loved and accepted and where some effort is made to understand her and to satisfy her needs she should be able to make a good adjustment, whether this is in an orphanage or a foster home." The Orphanage/Children's Home provided that environment for me.

I must admit, when Jerry told me he was writing a book containing alumni memoirs, that there was no way under the sun that I could put on paper some of the memories I had from growing up at the Orphanage. I did not want to write something that would hurt another human being. There are things that happen when we are young that stay with us throughout our life, good and bad. I harbored some hateful feelings that I had not been able to shake since 1951 when my family was torn apart—I lost a daddy, mother, four brothers and three sisters. Yet, the more I wrote my heartfelt feelings on paper, the more I began to realize that the hate and anger I felt was from within. It was time I quit blaming others and understand God's purpose in my life. The more I wrote, the more I cried; and suddenly, I could feel the burdens being lifted. I kept telling Jerry that I did not feel what I had written was meaningful, but I wanted those who read my story who had not been able to put the past behind them to be able to do so now.

Life is what we make of it and we are given choices. Life is too short to let unhappiness and unforgiveness get in your way. Choose to move on and replace the hurt with happiness. Think about it—being an orphan was not all bad; if we had not become residents of the Orphanage, we probably would not be as successful as we are today and our morals would have been less desirable. Forgive those who hurt you in the past—they cannot hurt you anymore, but they will if you constantly dwell on the hurt and pain they caused you. We all had lots of baggage and different personalities when we were admitted to the Orphanage, but I believe we all had similar circumstances that brought us together as a family.

The Orphanage/Children's Home provided us with a warm building and nice beds to sleep in; we had good food; we wore nice clothes; the girls were taught how to cook, iron, clean house and preserve food for future use; the boys were taught housekeeping, yard maintenance, and farm work; we were given a chance to attend school; we were given money to spend, maybe not as much as we wanted; and, most importantly, we were taught about God and the importance of doing what is right. I can tell you, without any hesitation, that I would never have had life as rich as I had at the Orphanage had I stayed in the poor environment from which I came. Yes, I grew up without a mother, a father and most of my siblings and the love of my blood family, but look at the family members I came to love, respect and appreciate by being an orphan. I will cherish my Children's Home memories forever, the good and bad.

I presently live in Wilson with my husband Michael, Aunt Bebe Dildy, and my two dogs, Abby and Mimi. I have one son, Christopher Matthews (adopted at seven months old by my first husband Gerald and me), age 31, and one precious seven-year old granddaughter, Lillian Elizabeth (named after me). I believe I am the happiest I have ever been and I am content with what I have. I am truly blessed by God. Ray, Bobby and Evelyn are deceased (1996, 2003 and 2010, respectively) and I miss them terribly. I stay in touch with my other brothers and sister I located in 1988, James, Tommy and Alice—they all have children and grandchildren—having them in my life means everything to me. I recently told them that I'm the oldest of the four remaining and they will have to take care of me! They were blessed because they were adopted; Bobby, Evelyn and I were even more blessed—we grew up as "orphans"—but remember, in heaven there are no "orphans". There will not be a sign on our back with the word "orphan" on it; instead, it will read "Child of God."

One prayer I have is that all of my family and friends will come to know Jesus and accept Him as their personal Savior before it is too late. I have tried my best to live as Christ-like as possible so I can be an example to them.

I want to thank Jerry A. Smith, author of this book, for extending me the opportunity to openly express myself. It was one of the hardest tasks ever put before me, because I have included some things that caused me a lot of pain and embarrassment, but it has enabled me to unload all the baggage I kept inside for many years. I hope I have not offended anyone in any way. As adults, we realize there were things in our childhood that we aren't proud of but there are also memories we do not want to forget. As the old saying goes, "It is what it is." I would also like to say to all of my "orphan" brothers and sisters—you are so precious to me and I love all of you.

I am proud and thankful to be a part of "the family".

15

Tomorrow Would Be a New Life

Mary Belle Pope
1952-61

A rainy October 26, 1947 my father passed away. He was 70 years old and very religious. He named me Mary - after the mother of Jesus. After his death, life was hard for my mama. My father left her with a tobacco farm and four small girls - Nancy, Daisy, Johnnie and me. I was six years old and the oldest sister. My mama sold the farm and moved us near Blackjack Church, Greenville, North Carolina.

L-R: Daisy, Mary Belle and Nancy Pope

Nearly two weeks after Christmas, on a snowy Monday morning, January 7, 1952, mama woke us early for breakfast. After packing a few clothes, each of us girls carried a box of clothes as we walked down a gravel road to Mrs. Marslander's house. We climbed into a 1945 Studebaker, as mama explained to Nancy, Daisy and me that we were going to live in an orphanage. I was ten, Nancy age seven and Daisy was six. Our youngest sister Johnnie, age four would come later. The black Studebaker pulled away and as I watched in the rear view window, Mama, with Johnnie in her arms, waved until she just faded away.

After an hour of riding in the Studebaker, Mrs. Marslander parked the car facing the dining hall on campus. A man came over to the car. He introduced himself as "Pa Smith "(Superintendent '51-'55 & '56-'58). We got out of Mrs. Marslander's car and got into a car with "Pa" and he drove us to Middlesex School. Daisy was in the first grade; Nancy in the second and me a third grader. I was seven years old before I started to school, so school made me happy. I liked my teacher; her name was Mrs. Johnson. She had a kind nature and cheerful way of teaching. At 3:15 p.m. school was dismissed. Jean Thigpen ('49-'52 & '57-'60), another orphan girl, walked me to the school bus. The bus returned to the orphanage and stopped in front of a huge building with concrete steps and hedges to one side of the steps. Later, we referred to it as the old girls' building. A Ms. Carroll met us at the front door and took Nancy, Daisy and me up a wide staircase. At the top was a long hallway. The end room on the left held three beds. That night we lay in our beds and cried ourselves to sleep. I thought to myself that night – "tomorrow would be a new life for us."

Our new life was fairly regimented. Our school day schedule went something like this from that day until I left nine years later:

5:30 a.m. - First bell rings and we are awaken.

6:00 a.m. - Second bell rings and we go to breakfast. After breakfast we returned to our building, did our chores and got ready for school.

8:00 a.m. – Loaded on the bus for school.

3:30 p.m. – Returned home from school.

4:00 p.m. – Did our chores until dinner.

5:30 p.m. – First bell rings and we get clean for dinner.

6:00 p.m. – Second bell rings and we go to dinner. After dinner we did chores, study hall, bathe and brush our teeth.

9:00 p.m. – Lights out, no talking.

Each day would start all over again with the same schedule. The bell kept up moving from one job or place to another. Sometimes the bell annoyed me. Our free time was Saturday and Sunday evening. Sunday morning we were in church. There were three bells on Sunday morning – two for breakfast and one for church.

In church we learned the Bible and were taught how to live a religious life. Sitting in church was a remembered time. Everyone attended church every Wednesday night, Sunday morning and Sunday night. We had communion, including the washing of feet. There were baptisms. We had Bible drills that went like this. We would stand in line in front of everyone in the audience with our Bible down to our side. The leader would say:
Attention – Signal for us to stand up straight with Bible at side.
Salute – Bring our right hand to forehead and salute.
Draw Swords – Bring Bible up in front of you with one hand on bottom and the other hand on top ready to search verse.
Go – Leader would give group a Bible verse. Everyone would wait for this signal to start. The first person to find the verse was the winner of the contest. This was a game to teach us familiarity of the Bible.

*Washing of the Saints Feet during Communion
Mary Belle's feet washed by Louise Morris ('52-'59)*

On Sunday, August 23, 1953, my sister Johnnie was admitted to the orphanage. She had a difficult time adjusting to the orphanage, even staying in the same room with me, Daisy ('52-'63) and Nancy ('52-'61). Johnnie ('53-'66), for the longest time after being admitted, called me mama. We were fortunate to stay in the same room together most of our years at the orphanage. My sister Annie, born after me, died at age two from a childhood disease. I felt a need to protect my sisters in the orphanage; I even feel that way today.

In 1953 the new girls' building opened and nineteen little girls were moved into the dorm. Later, the big girls followed into the second wing of the building. Mrs. Thelma Rulli (Alumnus '23-'30), our housemother was a nice lady, but had little time for nineteen girls. I do not believe she ever noticed me. There was some jealousy among us girls. Some had negative attitudes, but we always worked out our differences. As we grew older, the girls were boy crazy, dreaming about Elvis and the day they would grow-up. In the summer, we picked peas and worked in tobacco. We all had jobs. Sometimes, we had to cut up chickens, shell beans, and freeze and can vegetables. On many nights, bedtime was a welcome time. There, too, were times that punishment was reflected of punitive institutional discipline. I remember one unpleasant incident that a bath tub was left with dirty water - no one let the water out. No one owned up to using the tub last or leaving the tub full of water. Every girl that took a bath that night had to stand outside the building until someone owned up to the wrong. After nearly two hours. I decided - let's just get this over with. I did not do it, but I owned up to doing it so all the girls would not have to keep standing outside. My punishment: For one week, I could not look at TV and had to go to bed early every night.

Another incident was when someone killed another girl's goldfish. No one owned up to killing the fish, thus the matron made us all walk around the driveway until someone admitted killing the goldfish. It was a very hot day and each time we came around the drive way in front of the girls' building, the matron would stop us to see if anyone would admit to killing the fish. Nobody ever admitted to killing the fish. I, however, decided to own up to killing the fish so the girls would not have to keep walking in the sun. I did not kill the gold fish.

The girls I knew in the orphanage shaped my life and I felt special from them. Today, they are my friends. At the home, I learned to function in society in a way that would later in life be beneficial to me. The home freed me from many dangers in the real world. It provided an education, shelter, clothing and plenty of food. I saw my mother once a year while in the orphanage.

In 1961, I graduated from high school and enrolled at Mount Olive Junior College. The world was waiting for me and all was well.

Today, looking back on my years in the orphanage, I know the experience impacted my life and in these ways:

- The foundation for my religion was learned at the orphanage and led to my worship of God. Today, I have a loving relationship with Christ. I feel I can do anything if I work hard and keep Him in the center of my life.

- From the orphanage experience of growing up without parents, I came to realize just how important I was to my children and the importance of parenting skills in raising children. I am a good mother.

- From the orphanage experience of learning how to live with different children and different people, I have been able, even today, to build relationships with others I meet.

- From the orphanage experience, I learned work ethics and the importance of doing a good job, whatever I do. I've had many jobs, but done all well.

- From the orphanage experience, I learned that education was important and have encouraged my children and grandchildren to gain their education as a means to their future.

16

Reflection of a Fifteen-Year Orphan

Philip Mercer
1953-68

As I sit writing this, the Holiday Season has just past, which to me begins on Thanksgiving Day and extends through Christmas and to New Years Day. This time of year always brings to me recollections of my years at the Free Will Baptist Children's Home at Middlesex, North Carolina. Thoughts come flooding into my mind of thanks to the many people who have touched my life; some I know and so many I will never know. We may never know all the people who touch our lives or all the people we touch throughout our lives. Let me say thank you to God and to all the people of the Original Free Will Baptists of North Carolina who provided a place like the Children's Home for me and many children. I should start at the beginning for me.

L-R: Ona, Phil, Woodrow (father) and Sandra Mercer

I was born on May 14, 1950; my family lived at Beulaville, Duplin County, North Carolina. The family consisted of me with two sisters (Sandra and Ona) and both parents Woodrow and Lillian Sandlin Mercer.

In the fall of that year my mother died and, I suspect, threw the family into turmoil. Of course, I knew little of the circumstances of my early life. I am told that my grandmother and father tried to keep the family together but were unable to do so. Stephen Smith (affectionately known as "Pa Smith") was Superintendant ('51-'55 & '56-'58) of the Children's Home and I assume arranged for the Mercer Children to go to the Home. I remember little of this early time at the Home so most of my remembrances come from stories that were related to me. But in 1953 we became residents of the Home. I reluctantly use the word resident of the Home as this place became my Home and that is why I express my thanks to the foresightedness of the organizers and sustainers of the Children's Home.

I often hear some of my acquaintances talk about their large family; they say they had a large family with four, five or more brothers and sister. I say I had a family with as many as seventy to ninety brothers and sisters at the Children's Home. When I tell them that I grew up at the Children's Home, they begin to feel sorry for my having to grow up in an orphanage. But I say do not feel sorry for me, because I had a large family and we grew up as a family at the Children's Home. I hope to relate in this message how this Children's Home affected me and now affects my immediate family.

My recollections of Thanksgiving Day are a wonderful time for me at the Children's Home. I remember that on that day many Free Will Baptist from North Carolina would visit the Children's Home and attend Thanksgiving service at Memorial Chapel with all the children standing before the congregation and singing a song for those in attendance. I seem to remember that one song we would sing was "Faith of Our Fathers"; this song still brings me many recollections of the Children's Home. Also, I remember spreading the long picnic table in the flower garden with the abundance of food which the visitors would bring to the home. You know there are many, many very good cooks in North Carolina. To me, the abundance of food was a marvelous sight and we were able to eat until we were about to pop. This was a great time for me and I know that the people who came that day should know they made many good and lasting impressions on me. Another important time of the Holiday Season was Christmas. I feel that we should combine Thanksgiving Day and Christmas into one holiday and call the season "Thanksgiving for Christ". What more should we give thanks for than the birth of our Lord and Savior Jesus Christ. However, Easter should also be included in this holiday, for even more we should give thanks for the death and resurrection of Jesus to ensure our salvation. But let me get off of my soap box and get back to this story.

Christmas at the Children's Home was a most wondrous time. I remember the many groups that came to the Children's Home and sponsored a Christmas party. I will not attempt to name these groups because I simply do not remember the names of all the groups, but they know who they are and I express my thanks to them. They would bring a toy for each child at the Home and they probably thought that these gifts were small, but the gifts were not small to me. The gifts made me feel special to someone that did not even know me and this made me feel special that someone would be so kind to me.

I should interject here and express many thanks to a special congregation of Christian believers; the good people of Free Union Free Will Baptist Church located near Snow Hill, North Carolina. As I understand the situation, the Ladies Auxiliary of many FWB Churches selected a child at the Home to sponsor. I am not aware of the extent of this sponsorship but I felt that I was special to this group of Christians and to feel special to anyone was very important to me as an "orphan". I am unable to express the extent of my gratitude to the members of Free Union Church.

As I attempt to relate my recollections of my life at the Children's Home, it is most difficult to know where to start for there are so many recollections of people and stories. But I will try to tell some of these stories and the people that influenced me, but I can only tell some of the stories. Where do I start?

Because I was only three years of age when admitted to the Home, I do not recall much of the early years. Mary Mitchell, house mother for the boys, has told me that the first few nights I would stand at the back door and cry for grandmother and say that I would fall off the bed if I was not there sleeping with her. I wish I could remember more of my grandmother and mother.

My earliest recollection at the home was an incident that occurred with Marshall Heath ('53-'68), Steve Mitchell (Mary Mitchell's son) and me. As best I recall, we decided that we wanted to go fishing at the pond. We gathered fishing poles, from somewhere, dug worms and walked to the pond. Mind you we were less than five years in age but we went fishing. I do not recall if we caught fish, but I do recall Pa Smith coming to get us and I do remember the punishment that followed; we needed the punishment. I cannot imagine the distress and agony that we caused the adults at the home when they discovered we were missing and frantically searched for us.

Let me say at the start, anyone that attempts to relate their family life cannot say that their family life was perfect. There were good times and there were bad times. This is not only at the Children's Home but in all "normal" family lives. To me, we children and adults at the Home operated as a family, although a big family. We all had chores to do and were assigned various chores at different times. Some boys were assigned chores on the farm, some were assigned chores with maintenance, some were assigned chores with upkeep of their respective cottage and even one was assigned chores as "kitchen boy". I loved the job of "kitchen boy" because that boy had the pleasure to interact with the girls; the majority of the time the boys and girls were segregated except at meals or church.

The girls were also assigned various tasks with housekeeping of their respective cottage, as wells as chores such as cooking and doing laundry for the entire family. Of course, the children were under the supervision of an adult whether it was the farm manager, the maintenance manager, the kitchen manager or the laundry manager.

Tractor Story

Had to be in the summer of 1966 or '67; we had put in a barn of tobacco and were leaving the field. Terry Edwards ('65-'73) was told to take the Farmall Super "A" tractor to the barn. I jumped on the rear plow lifts to ride to the barn with him. Off we went, WIDE-OPENED. As we approached the barn shelter, Terry said "Watch me spin this tractor around and back it under the shelter". (He said something to that effect). I just stepped off the rear of the tractor to watch. As Terry turned the tractor hard to the right, I saw the right wheels slowly begin to rise; I remember the entire incident was in slow motion. As Terry continued to turn the wheels, the tractor continued to rise until it fell on the side and then rolled with the wheels standing up in the air. The tractor looked like a dead animal. My immediate thought was…where is Terry? You cannot imagine my relief when his head popped up on the other side of the tractor. I know the situation could have been very tragic, but I would love to have a picture of the expression on Terry's face across the under belly of that tractor. Terry's immediate response was … (How should I put this?)… "Mr. Henry [Henry Mitchell, Farm Manager] is going to kill me … Mr. Henry is going to kill me!" That was his greatest concern. Looking back, the entire situation seems to be very comical. I do not recall but I am sure he was punished. Mr. Henry had a temper, once he got an (electric) hog shocker after us in the back of the pickup truck. I do not remember the circumstances but we were probably just being boys. It could have been Terry had not forgotten the truck incident. It may have been everyone was so relieved that there were no injuries and there was no punishment. Terry's anxiety may have been enough. We must have been 15-16. I do not think Mr. Henry would have let younger children drive the tractors. Sometimes, I wonder how any of us "escape the numerous evils of childhood and youth".

One person who still has a great impact on my life and I think of, if not every day or at least several times each week, is Clarence Mitchell (Alumnus '23-'32); known to many of the boys as "Oscar" or "Petey" but we did not call him that to his face. To his face he was called him Mr. Mitchell and he was Mr. Mitchell. Petey had the task of maintaining the yards and what we now call the infrastructure of the Home. I do not know what his job description stated (we probably did not have job descriptions back then, most employees did what needed to be done), but his job was to take a group of boys and maintain the physical plant that made up the Home. The most important characteristic I remember about Mr. Mitchell was his ability to figure stuff out; I say stuff to include a multitude of problems and challenges. Looking back, he was probably the most resourceful man I have ever known. He could face the most difficult challenge and find a way to resolve the problem. The solution may not have been perfect but the problem would have been solved.

What I gleaned from Mr. Mitchell is the ability to confront any challenge with the expectation that there is a solution to a problem if I will diligently look for the solution. I now feel that Petey believed in a principle that I have come to strive to live by; that "time, patience and perseverance will accomplish all things". One example is the concrete benches still located in the flower garden. One day Mr. Mitchell acquired a concrete bench from somewhere. I helped him build a mold from this one bench and then make several other benches. When I return to the Home and see those benches, I think of Mr. Mitchell and the times we interacted.

'60's Baseball Team with Petey

With some hesitation, I will share another incident with Petey that made a lasting impression on me. As I view all authority figures, I viewed Petey as being infallible and larger than life. At times I think I am infallible and can do all things myself, that I am greater than life. When we begin to feel that way, we may think we are gods and are thus infallible. But let me explain. One day a group of boys was playing baseball; must have been at least four or five on each team. Petey came by on his way to the "turkey pen" and I think he asked us if he could play. I thought that was kind of neat having Petey to play ball with us boys. I do not recall another time that Petey had that type of interaction with us. Back to the story…..Petey came to bat with me pitching; he hit the ball and made it to first base. I do not recall who was on first base, but we picked Petey off, however' Petey began to run toward second base. But Petey stumbled and fell and was tagged out. Petey got up, dusted himself off and headed to the "turkey pen". Now what lasting impression did this make on me? Well, Petey was still Mr. Mitchell, but I began to realize that he was human and had the same feelings and challenges as everyone else; he was not infallible. None of us are infallible and we have shortcomings; we cannot do all things without some help. Even if we appear to do all things ourselves, we have God-given Talent to assist us.

Another important person to me was Milton Johnson ('62-'69); he was superintendant of the Home in the mid 1960's. Several important things occurred in my life that still affects me. During this time, my sister Sandra became sick and ended up in Memorial Hospital at Chapel Hill, North Carolina. I do not recall all the events surrounding her sickness nor at the time had a clue about the extent of her illness. Sandra died due to kidney failure at an early age; I think about sixteen. I have a picture that Cathy Hines ('57-'66) gave me of her at the Junior-Senior Prom; I look at it often and think of her.

What I remember of Mr. Johnson is his driving to Chapel Hill to see Sandra in the hospital; he would take me along and I can remember our trips and vaguely remember our conversations. Although, I think he did most of the talking and had to drag conversation out of me. I think his wife, Mrs. Pearl Johnson, would stay at the hospital with Sandra. This must have been a trying time on their lives. I appreciate all that Mr. and Mrs. Johnson did for me at that time, as well as through my life.

Mr. Johnson was also responsible for the construction of two new buildings at the Home, one which was to be a boy's dormitory that would put two boys to one room and these two would share a bathroom with two other boys. This building segregated the older boys from the younger boys and spread the task of one house parent being responsible for so many boys. Looking back, this was probably a revolutionary idea as the older boys were allowed to have a more normal home life than the dormitory style of the old building.

I recall the boys assisted with the construction of this building; not with the major phases of construction but helped nonetheless. I remember the construction of the basement area of the building. There was a trench beside the concrete block exterior wall. We installed "tar paper" to the exterior of the wall as a vapor barrier and gravel along the bottom of the trench for drainage and of course filled the hole. I recall standing around with the adults discussing how to waterproof the basement walls and adding drainage. I do not recall who was involved in this discussion, but I am sure the group included Mr. Mitchell, Mr. Johnson and whoever was the main builder in charge of construction. Why is this important? This incident revealed that two or three heads are much better than one; working together as a group can accomplish many things.

Another important thing Mr. Johnson did for me was regarding my college life. I do not know how things happened, but one day in early 1968 Mr. Johnson called me to the office; I wondered why I was in trouble now. But, he handed me a college application and told me to fill it out; I am sure he helped me with it. This was an application to The Citadel and I had never even heard of The Citadel. For those who may not know, The Citadel is the Military College of South Carolina located at Charleston, South

Carolina. My plans had always been to attend college (Where did I get that idea?) but had planned to attend Mount Olive Junior College and transfer to NC State. But, with the help of Mr. Johnson and I am sure God was involved, I was able to attend The Citadel and graduated in 1972. I thank The Citadel and all those responsible for my attending The Citadel, which has greatly influenced my life. I cannot get started on my experiences at The Citadel because that is another story. My experience at the Children's Home and the regimental life style at the Home greatly assisted me with life at The Citadel. I must say that I owe a huge debt to The Citadel.

We children at the Children's Home attended Middlesex School; this was a first through twelve grade school located at Middlesex, North Carolina. I also have many fond memories while attending this school for I was enrolled at Middlesex for twelve years. There are so many memories that it is most difficult to start. Let me start with my eighth grade teacher (Mrs. Naomi Powell); by the way, this was the last school teacher to punish me (anyone my age knows what punishment means). It seems that Mrs. Powell had left the room and I decided that it would be a good idea to play catch with someone by throwing the erasers across the room. However, when Mrs. Powell returned, one of the erasers passed just in front of her nose. You could say I was caught red handed and punishment ensued.

But this is not the main reason I remember Mrs. Powell. In the summer of 1967, several children from the Home were privileged to go to the World's Fair at Montreal, Canada with Mrs. Powell to accompany the group. The best I can remember, the Duke Endowment paid the expenses for the children to go on this trip; I thank the endowment for providing such a great experience for the children. It is still hard to believe that we orphans were allowed to travel to Canada by bus with stops at such places as Harrisburg, Pennsylvania, Niagara Falls, New York, Montreal, Canada, New York City, and Washington, DC. The Expo 67 at Montreal was a sight to see, especially for a country boy from Nash County. All the different places we visited had many marvelous sights. This was a great experience in my life and I still have many fond memories of this trip.

There are so many recollections and stories that could be related here but space does not allow. However, I must reflect on my immediate family, my sisters Ona and Sandra. I have always been proud of Ona. She was very smart in High School. I remember her as being a cheerleader for the school and graduating at the top of her class (I think she was second in her class academically). After High School, she went to nursing school and graduated from Baptist Hospital as a Registered Nurse. She now resides near Chapel Hill with her husband of many years and has two grown sons.

My recollections of Sandra are of a pretty, happy girl. I do not have many detailed recollections of her at the Home due to the segregation of the boys and girls. This is the reason I do not recall much of the events surrounding her illness. One of the shortcomings of the Children's Home is the separation of the immediate families. Most of my recollections of interaction with my sisters occurred when the children spent time at holidays with their respective blood-related family. For me, this time was spent with my mother's sister Sarah Bolin. During Thanksgiving, Christmas and about two weeks in the summer, she and her husband, Dr. Paul Bolin, would travel to the Home and collect us and return to Beulaville. This allowed interaction with my sisters that was not available at the Home. I have many fond memories of these times with my sisters and these memories will always be precious to me. There are not sufficient words to express my gratitude to Aunt Sarah for all the time and love she gave to us.

At present, I reside at Richlands, North Carolina with my wife Karen, who has put up with me for many years. We have two children, Michael who is attending college and working; and Amanda who has graduated from Campbell University and is now married to Zach. Amanda has recently delivered us our first grandchild, Milly. I am so proud of both of my children and the love for them is hard to express.

My marriage and acceptance into Karen's family has allowed me to be a part of a more traditional family that I missed while growing up at the Children's Home. When I reflect on my life at the Children's Home and my life after leaving the Home, I cannot but wonder how my life might have been different had it not been for the Free Will Baptist Children's Home.

17

The Memory of Her

Sue Heath
1953-67

Sue Heath

    My family came to the Free Will Baptist Children's Home in Middlesex, North Carolina in August of 1953. There were six of us, ranging in age from 14 months to 10 years old. My mother had been diagnosed with cancer following the birth of my youngest brother, Clarence Ray. She really suffered for a long time and had to make the hardest decision of her life; to make sure that her children were taken care of. Since my father was an abusive alcoholic, my mother went through Social Services to make sure that we would be together instead of being placed in different homes. The day after my mother's funeral, five of us: Wilbert Earl 10, John William 8, Michael Faye 6, Marshall Glenn 2, and myself Sue Heath 4, came to live at the Children's Home. Because a child had to be at least 2 years old to be accepted at the home, my youngest brother was left behind with my father who eventually allowed him to be adopted by a childless couple, but we always stayed in contact with him.

My first day at the home is a mixture of both jumbled and vivid memories. I don't remember who took us to the home or how but I do remember sitting on the swings with my Daddy. One by one, someone would come to get us until we were all separated. First, the boys were taken to the boy's dorm, then my sister Faye was taken to the girl's dorm and finally me. I was taken to a room where my waist-length hair was cut off, then trimmed up to my ears with short bangs across the front. Next, my new dress which had been bought for me to wear to my mother's funeral was stripped off of me. Then, I was placed into a bath tub and given a bath. My hair was washed with kerosene and rinsed in vinegar which was for lice control. I didn't even have lice, but this was the standard routine. All my clothes, which were not many, were taken and burned. This included my new dress and new red shoes. I was so proud of that dress and those shoes. It was the only time that I ever remembered having new clothes and shoes. To this day, I can still describe that dress! It was white with red, blue, yellow and green sail boats on it. My shoes were bright red leather with two straps that buckled across the front. On one of these straps was a tiny bell that jingled when I walked. I absolutely adored those shoes! I never saw that dress or those shoes again. I was really upset about all that was happening to me and I couldn't understand all that was going on. I didn't even know when my Daddy left! I never got to say "good-bye" to him. It was quite a while before I saw him again, although he did visit two or three times a year.

I was given a stack of clothes; dresses, slips, underwear, socks and shoes. Then, I was taken to a big room that had six single beds, two dressers, two chest of drawers and three closets. I was assigned a bed, two drawers in each of the dressers and one side of one of the closets. I was shown how to fold and hang my clothes. Everything had to be done a certain way, very neatly and precise. My initials were marked in all my clothes and shoes. This routine continued for all of the fourteen years I lived at the home. I was given one towel and one wash cloth which was hung on the head of the bed, exactly in the center. It was folded in a certain way, always the same. I was given a toothbrush and a cup which hung from a hook in the bathroom. It, too, had my initials on it. Each morning the matron (which is what the women were called) would line all of us up and go down the line placing toothpaste on each toothbrush. I quickly found myself to be the last one in the line because I played around making faces in the mirror. After many, many spankings, I finally moved up the line!

I was taught how to make my bed, which meant no wrinkles whatsoever! If your bed did not pass inspection, the covers were thrown back and you had to remake it. Every time anything had to be redone, you got a spanking. I learned quickly to do everything correctly the first time! Baths were taken each night, two girls at a time in the tub for 15 minutes. When you got out of the tub, you were expected to dry off, put on your pajamas, wash out the tub, then hang up your towel and wash cloth. Fresh towels and wash cloths were handed out once a week.

Following baths each night, we would get together for devotions and prayers. This was something else that I knew nothing about since I was only four years old and could not read yet.

All this stuff was pretty confusing to me, coming all in one day. Later in the afternoon, the matron gave me an ice cream cone which I began to slurp loudly. She said, "Say thank you." I said, "What for?" She replied, "Because it is good manners to say thank you when you're given something." I quickly replied, "Well, I don't want to say it." She informed me that if I refused to say thank you, then I had to give the ice cream back. By this time I was really getting upset, so my cussing habit kicked in and I threw the ice cream right in her face and said, "You can take the blankety, blank thing, I don't want it anyway." Well, that was the first, but certainly not the last, time that I got my mouth washed out with soap and my fanny spanked! Boy! That wood paddle sure did hurt! On top of all this, I was told to sit down in one of the big chairs on the front porch. The matron said, "Don't get out of that chair until I come back out here and tell you that you can!" Well, while I was sitting there crying, feeling all lonesome and abandoned, my little two-year-old brother Marshall came walking up the sidewalk pulling a red wagon. He looked up at me and said, "Wanna ride?" I said, "Yep!" and quickly jumped down out of the chair and ran down the steps to get into the wagon. Then, just as Marshall started pulling me down the sidewalk, out stepped the matron who had originally placed me in the chair! Needless to say, I got my second spanking of the day and Marshall was told that he was not supposed to be on that side of the driveway because the boys and girls were separated. Then, I had to sit in that hard chair for another whole hour. I never knew an hour could seem so long, but by the time I was allowed to get up, it was supper time.

There was a huge silver bell mounted on a stand with a long rope hanging from it, which was rung every morning at 6:00 a.m. This was our wake up call. Everybody got up at this time, washed our face and hands, dressed, combed our hair, made beds, dusted our beds, dressers, blinds and window sills, and then swept our rooms. All this was completed in thirty minutes, at which time the bell was rung again. This was the signal to all of us that it was time to line up and go to the dining hall. As we went into the dining hall, the girls went in the front door to the tables on the left side. The boys came in a side door and went to the tables on the right side. You stood behind your chair at your assigned place, six children at each table. There was absolutely no talking allowed! You stood until all the announcements were made and the blessing was said. When you were finished eating, you were not allowed to leave the table until every person at your table was through. Then, one person would ask the matron if we could be excused.

The bell was rung for breakfast, dinner and supper. Following each meal, there were chores to be done and the work assignments were changed every three months. The superintendent made out the list which was then posted on the bulletin board in the dining hall and the dorms. You had no input about your assigned job, you just did it! For the girls, the jobs were: kitchen, dining hall, big girls' dorm, little girls' dorm and laundry. Following breakfast each day, we went to our assigned area to work on chores until time to leave for school. For instance, if your work assignment was dining hall, you ate your meal thirty minutes prior to mealtime so that you would be available to serve food and beverages. When meals were finished, you cleared the tables, scraped the dishes and took them to the kitchen. Next, you cleaned the tables and refilled the salt, pepper, sugar, vinegar and napkin containers. We would then reset the table with clean dishes and silverware for the next meal and the floors were swept. When you completed all four of your assigned tables, and if you had any time left, you could use it any way you needed to. For example, if you had not completed your homework, you could use this time to do it. This was risky though, because we did not always have extra time.

Then, we all headed off to school, which we attended five days a week. Each morning the school bus would transport the boys to school first and then return to take the girls, which is also the way we were transported home. Although the girls had Home Economics Classes in school, the matrons taught us hand sewing and basic mending. This was how I learned to cook, clean, wash clothes, freeze and prepare food, sew and live an organized life. I didn't really value or appreciate any of this until I was grown, married and had my own family.

I quickly fell into the routine of things. We became one big family and loved each other as sisters, although some we became closer to than others. Johnnie Faye Pope ('53-'66), Sandra Mercer ('53-'65) and I became close friends. Other friendships were formed as new children joined the group. As small girls, Johnnie Faye, Sandra and I seemed to stay busy doing most of the things that were against the rules. One example of this was sliding down the banisters. We would take turns, always looking out for each other. Breaking the rules was great fun for all of us.

One of the most challenging escapades we came up with was jumping the drainage ditch. This was a long, deep ditch behind the pump house. It was about three feet deep and varied in width in different places, but best of all, it was definitely off limits! The challenge was to see who could jump across the widest part of the ditch without falling in. Well, one Sunday afternoon, Johnnie Faye, Sandra and I, along with some other girls, decided to jump the ditch. I still had on my Sunday black patent leather shoes when we headed out for our afternoon of fun. Well, we were keeping up with the older girls pretty good until we got to a really wide place where we knew we might not make it. Sandra immediately backed out, but Johnnie Faye and I rose up to the challenge! Johnnie Faye backed way up so she could get a good running start and sailed across that ditch like it was nothing, so I proceeded to copy her. Just about the time I thought I had made it across, my foot slipped and down I went, into the grey water. Johnnie Faye was cheering me on when she saw me slip and tried to pull me out before my shoes got messed up, but it was too late! I mired down into that nasty, stinky, grey muck up to the calves of my legs. After Johnnie Faye pulled me up to the other side, I still had to retrieve my shoes out of that mess. I laid down on my stomach while she held onto my ankles and lowered me down into the ditch. When I got my shoes out, I wiped them off on the grass, the best I could. Then Johnnie Faye and Sandra hid me between them as we snuck back to the dorm. Johnnie Faye and Sandra helped me get cleaned up and into a change of clothes. I washed my shoes out in the sink, praying the whole time that they weren't ruined. I made sure I shined them up more than usual that following Saturday night.

Every Saturday night, two of the oldest girls in the little girls' dorm shined all the shoes for school and Sunday. They always used cold biscuits to shine the patent leather shoes. I definitely used more than one biscuit on my shoes that Saturday night! Those biscuits must have had extra lard in them or the good Lord had mercy on me, because my shoes turned out just fine.

We had good times and bad times. One Christmas, Santa Claus landed in a helicopter and that was the first time I got a baby doll for Christmas. That doll had real hair that was glued on but Sandra talked me into pulling all the hair off of it so it would look more like a real baby. That was one ugly doll after that!

I remember getting new clothes and shoes for Easter. The Ladies Auxiliary at the First Free Will Baptist Church in Kinston, North Carolina was my sponsor for the entire fourteen years that I was at the home. These little ladies poured out to me from their hearts. There was only ten or twelve of them, but they were so precious to me. They went above and beyond all that they were required to do. Every Easter they bought me a hat, gloves and a purse to go with the dress and shoes that the home provided. Everybody did not receive these extra items. As long as I was small, these special ladies completed my Easter outfit.

At Christmas we all made a list of three things we wanted. This list was mailed out to each child's sponsor and you could expect to receive at least one of the three things you listed. For all fourteen years, my sponsors sent me all three things on my list.

My sponsors paid for me to take piano lessons for ten years and voice lessons for four years. They also sent me an allowance of $4.00 a month the entire time I was at the home, which was a lot of money at the time! Even after I left the home, the Ladies Auxiliary gave me a wedding shower and a baby shower. I am sure they are all deceased by now, but their special place in my heart lives on! I know the Lord has rewarded them greatly for all the blessings they bestowed on me!

One of the bad times I remember was being given four tablespoons of Milk of Magnesia every six months, whether we needed it or not! We had to line up and take our medicine. Afterwards, you had a choice of two Tootsie Rolls or a half of a Dr. Pepper. I always chose the Dr. Pepper so I could wash the yucky taste out of my mouth! To this day, I cannot stand to even look at a Dr. Pepper, much less drink one. We also had to line up to get shots at regular intervals. It was a big thing to see who screamed or cried!

One of the most devastating times of my life at the home was when Sandra Mercer got sick with a kidney disease and eventually passed away. Sandra and I came to the home about the same time. We were close friends, sisters and roommates. When she went home on vacation to her Aunt Sarah's in Beulaville, North Carolina, I went with her many times. Her Aunt Sarah became my Aunt Sarah. Sandra and I double dated to the Junior-Senior Prom. Aunt Sarah paid for our prom dresses and for us to get our hair done at a beauty salon. I went with Don Brantley and Sandra went with Bennie Morgan. She was so beautiful that night; her dress was like a bridal gown, all white and lacy. In my heart, I think she knew that she was going to die. She and Bennie were 16, madly in love, and right before the prom was over, they disappeared. Since Bennie was our driver, Don and I had to find another ride home that evening. By the time we got back to the home, there was a big commotion going on in the living room. Sandra and Bennie were planning on eloping that night, but Sandra got really sick and was admitted to the hospital. So I stayed in her hospital room for several days and nights. Since we were roommates at the home, I knew where to find all her things. She asked me to bring her big box that was filled with all the letters that Bennie had written to her.

For days, I read those letters to her, every single one, over and over. Before she went back to the hospital, she asked the superintendent's wife to drive her around the circular driveway very slowly so that she could see everything one last time. I told her she would be coming back, but she was right; that was the last time she ever saw the Children's Home. We were called back from summer vacation for her funeral. The memory of her in that casket is forever engraved in my heart and mind. She was buried in her white prom dress and a red rose was placed in her hand. I remember leaning down and touching her face as I kissed her good-bye. My heart still aches when I think about her. When I moved to Richlands, North Carolina, I went to her grave site at Cabin Free Will Baptist Church in Beulaville, North Carolina. I stood talking to her for a while, telling her all that was going on in my life. I left feeling as if she heard everything. Her death at such a young age made me more eager to live my life to the fullest.

I've made many mistakes and bad choices, but God has covered me and I have known His blessings. He has blessed me with a sweet, gentle, loving husband who loves the Lord. He is ever faithful to read, study the Word and walk in what the Lord speaks to him. I have three sons and ten grandchildren. My first great grandson was born in March, 2009. My family is very dear to me and we have a close bond between us. We always hug, kiss and say, "I love you" as many times as possible. I don't remember ever being hugged or hearing the words, "I love you" in the fourteen years that I lived at the home. That's why it is so important for me to show my love, not just to my family, but also to my friends.

God laid my spiritual foundation at the home. I learned to pray, read the Bible and sing. To this day, I love to sing and play the piano. God has given me many songs that have blessed me and encouraged me in my walk with Him. I am so glad that I was raised at the Children's Home. God surely answered my mother's prayer as well as all of mine.

18

The Loss was Compensated with a Strength

Stephen Worthington
1954-63

I am writing my memoirs of my life at the Children's Home at the request of another Free Will Baptist Children's Home resident – Jerry "Duck" Smith ('49-'60). Jerry and I re-connected in 2008 when he came to Washington, DC for a meeting with his son and we met for dinner (I live in Arlington, VA – five miles from Washington, DC). Shortly thereafter, "Duck" e-mailed me and asked if I would write my memoirs of my years at the Children's Home, from 1954-1963, for a book that he was going to write. I readily agreed – both out of friendship and out of the very fond memories I have cherished all my life of the nine years of my childhood at the Free Will Baptist 0rphanage/Free Will Baptist Children's Home, hereinafter referred to as the "Orphanage" or the "Children's Home". You will note I also use "Orphanage" and "Children's Home" interchangeably because the name change occurred while I was there and in my memories, I think of each name separately, depending on what time frame I am recalling.

Standing with their father, L-R: Steve, Ronald, Raymond,

JoEtta and Stuart Worthington

My family was all from the Ayden-Grifton-Winterville area in Pitt County in Eastern North Carolina, near Greenville (East Carolina University). My family members were mostly all farmers. My Father was a "sharecropper" tobacco farmer. A "sharecropper" means that you own nothing but your labor. You live on the land in usually a wooden or cinder block house provided by the landowner. The landowner puts up the land and the equipment and the sharecropper puts up his labor. The sharecropper had to split all the costs with the farmer and then split the profits. The sharecropper was usually in debt to the farmer until the tobacco sold in the fall. That system of farming dates back to when the U.S. was a colony of Great Britain. It phased out as a way of life mostly during the 1960's era as equipment technology was introduced and back and sweat labor moved on to factory jobs. Factories started moving into Eastern North Carolina in the late 50's, all through the 60's and 70's and changed a whole way of life – for the best.

I was admitted to the Orphanage in June, 1954 when I was 8 (my birthday came a month later on July 7 and I turned 9), along with four siblings: older brother Stuart, age 11; older sister JoEtta, age 10; two younger brothers Ronald, age 7 and Glenn, age 5. We had a younger sister who did not go to the Children's Home – Muriel. Muriel was two years old when our Mother died. She was adopted right away by my Father's older sister (Aunt Helen) and her husband – they had no children of their own. Muriel was given a very nice home and good childhood with luxuries that we other five did not know growing up. But there was never any jealousy or resentment from the rest of us. We were happy for her.

My first year at the Home (1954), especially that first summer, remains sweetly vivid in my memories. It was a time of strangeness, a time of adjusting to a group environment and group rules. It was also a time that I began to experience stability and freedom from "scarcity". Prior to coming to the Orphanage, my brothers and sister and I often moved from one family member's home to another. After our Mother died (Christmas Day, December 25, 1951- I was six and a half at the time), we six kids were split up. Two stayed with an Aunt and Uncle. The other four of us stayed with our Grandmother (our Father's Mother). I was in the first grade at Grifton, North Carolina when our Mother died. I finished the first grade at Winterville – living with an aunt and uncle with five kids of their own. Then, I went to my Grandmother's where I attended second and third grades at Ayden.

Several times during the two years that four of us kids (Stuart, JoEtta, Glenn and I) stayed with our Grandmother, she was severely ill – twice suffering heart attacks. During those times of her hospitalization and recovery, we were sent to other relatives' homes to stay. In my second and third grades, I had lots of difficulties with my school work and was considered low IQ and learning-disabled. Also, I was constantly in trouble for fighting. Then, as now, there were always bullies who made their reputations by "beating-up" on the "underdogs". It seems that I had to fight back constantly – on the bus and on the schoolyard – to keep from being "picked on". Many a mornings, I started the day in the principal's office – often getting a lecture followed by a paddling. Seems I never could get it understood that I was not the one starting the fights – I was protecting myself.

My first experience at the Orphanage was not having to daily and constantly deal with bullies. Not that we didn't have a few; but there was a system at the Orphanage where the older boys largely took responsibility for the smaller boys and protected them from the bullies. That summer of 1954 – arriving at the Orphanage - was the first time since my Mother had died (1951) when I did not have to deal with fear as a constant factor in my life.

Although I arrived a little scared and a little overwhelmed with being in the midst of so many other children, ages from about three years old to 18 years old, I soon began to feel that I had landed in heaven. Let me explain.

First of all, there were three full meals each day. I had not known the luxury and experience of having eggs, toast, sausage (or bacon), oatmeal, grits and milk for breakfast on a daily basis. In our dorm, there was running water – bathrooms with showers and sinks with hot and cold running water and flush toilets instead of the outhouse that I had known the first nine years of my life. The buildings were heated in the winter time – all rooms – not just a living room with a coal stove and a kitchen with a wood-burning stove, which was the case at home before coming to the Orphanage.

Over the nine years I lived at the Children's Home, a number of staff workers affected my life there – almost all in a positive way.

First, at the boys' dormitory there was "Ma Mitchell" (Mary Mitchell) and "Petey" (Clarence Mitchell) – the house parents for the boys. Petey's job doubled as both the house father for the boys and as the campus maintenance manager.

The superintendent when I came to the Orphanage was Stephen A. Smith ('51-'55 & '56-'58) ("Pa Smith" and his wife "Ma Smith"). If I remember correctly, they were from Beulaville, North Carolina. Pa Smith wore grey or brown pin-striped suits and a fedora hat and smoked a stick cigarette smoker – all in the style of Franklin Delano Roosevelt (America's President during the Depression and during World War II [WWII]). This was not uncommon in those days for men to "affect" the style of the most popular president of American presidents – this was only nine years after the end of WWII. The superintendent's office, at that time, was two large rooms in the front of the dining hall, one on each side as you walked through the front entrance.

All who have lived at the Children's Home remember the system of the three-month job assignment. Every quarter, we all were assigned jobs for three months at a time. For the boys, the jobs were either farm boy, yard boy, house boy, kitchen boy or laundry boy. A larger boy (usually ninth grade or older) was assigned to the kitchen or laundry duties to do the heavy lifting and moving. (I held each of these jobs twice and quite enjoyed them – will speak about them later when I reach that time period.)

The very first job I was assigned – at nine years old – was farm boy, but with a specific assignment – I was the chicken boy. I fed the chickens twice a day and collected the eggs twice a day and took them in wire baskets from the chicken house to the big cooler in the big storeroom right behind the kitchen. My boss was Horace Mixon, the farm manager. The assistant farm manager was James Lucas (known to all as "Luke"). Luke and his wife Daisy were also the house parents for the older girls. Grover Hill and his wife, Helen, worked at the Orphanage 1951-1953; he worked on the farm, performed maintenance work around the campus and did whatever needed to be done. Mrs. Hill worked as a house parent in the old girls' building. They had one son, Grover Jr. ("Peanuts") who was my age.

The house mother for the girls was Thelma Rulli. Mrs. Rulli was a widow; she was also Clarence Mitchell's sister.

Clarence Mitchell ('23-'32), Thelma Rulli ('23-'30) and Horace Mixon ('23-'34) had all grown up at the Orphanage in the 30's and early 40's. I wish I knew more about their lives and times at the Orphanage; but, I do not recall them ever talking much about it but I am sure that they did. I do, however, remember both Horace and Clarence speaking about the hard times during the Great Depression and the eating of "parched corn", which is how the corn was continued to be food after it had ripened and hardened.

Mrs. Sudie Mixon (wife of Horace Mixon), affectionately known as "Ma Sudie", was the campus dietitian and kitchen manager.

The laundry manager was an elderly lady known affectionately by all as Granny Anderson. Granny Anderson stayed only a year or two after I came and then she retired. She was replaced by a lady named Emma Maiden from Zebulon.

I think that these eight people were the entirety of the staff running the Orphanage when I first arrived. As a business owner with 35 employees, I think back with amazement and awe to consider what these eight staff workers were able to accomplish by themselves – running what was a very sophisticated "child-care" institution.

The staff had children of their own: Clarence and Mary Mitchell had two children, Steve and Brenda Lee; Horace and Sudie Mixon had two children, Charles and Peggy; and "Luke" and Daisy had two children, Patsy and Carlton.

Other people who worked at the Orphanage while I was there – they were not there when I came to the Orphanage in 1954 but joined the staff later and did not have long tenures at the Home – were:

Mrs. Dovie Barbour (mother of Stacy Barbour ['57-'64]) was the house mother for the younger girls. Mr. and Mrs. Cornell Lucas left the Home, Mrs. Rulli became the house mother for the older girls and Mrs. Barbour replaced her as the younger girls' house mother.

Mr. and Mrs. Carl Powell had their residence in two rooms in the boys' dorm. Carl worked on the farm with Mr. Mixon and Mrs. Powell, as I recall, was a "relief worker" – working in the boys' dorms and the girls' cottages when the house mothers had their day off. On other days, she worked in the kitchen, the laundry or wherever she was needed. They had two children – a boy named Lanny (who we nicknamed "Lambert") and a daughter whose name I don't recall. The Powells only stayed about two years and they moved on. Life at the Orphanage as a staff worker was hard on a family and some contributed but moved on.

Herman and Mrs. Stocks: Mr. Stocks worked on the farm with Horace Mixon. Mrs. Stocks worked as a "relief worker" for house mothers on their day off and assisted in other duties on the campus. Mr. Stocks was there during my freshman and sophomore years in school (I was 14, 15, and 16 then). My particular memory of Mr. Stocks was that of being the "hog boy". Another resident, Bobby Thigpen ('49-'52 & '57-'62), and I were responsible for feeding and caring for the hogs and pigs – we had lots of them in those days – a big part of our diet and food during the winter.

I recall a time during the winter of January-March 1960 (I was in the ninth grade) when we had a hog cholera epidemic and many of our hogs were dying. It seemed that almost every day, Bobby and I had to bury a hog. Mr. Stocks would drive the Massey-Ferguson diesel tractor with its bucket to the hog parlor, then Bobby and I would have to load the dead hog into the bucket. We would hop onto the back of the tractor and Mr. Stocks would drive out into one of the fields. Bobby and I would have to break the frozen ground with our shovels and dig a deep hole into which to dump and bury the dead hog. The hole had to be deep enough so that the hog was far underground so that the cholera disease could not spread to the surface. We had to do this every morning after breakfast and before going to school. Often, this would take so much time that we were not able to catch the school bus so we were driven to school on one of the campus cars. I dreaded every morning going to the hog barn – it was freezing cold – being in January-February, and the work was very distasteful. Our hands would be frozen by the time we finished burying the hog. And, I always wanted a hot shower before dressing and leaving the campus to go to school at Middlesex. But this was a job that had to be done and Bobby and I were ones with the assigned job. Over life, that experience has given me the capability to do unpleasant tasks; but I did them because it was "my job".

Mr. and Mrs. Francis Garner ('67-'70): Francis Garner was not at the Children's Home when I lived there ('54-'63). He was there when I worked at the Home ('67-'68) after I graduated from the University of North Carolina. Francis worked on the campus supporting Clarence Mitchell, assisted on the farm and did various other tasks that came up. I developed a special friendship with Francis and his family. He had three children – two daughters and one son. They were very young then. I playfully nicknamed them – I called his older daughter "Twinkle Toes", his son I nicknamed "Archie" and his youngest daughter – Pamela – I never did give a nickname. This family was special to me during my 16 months working at the Home after graduating from UNC-Chapel Hill and before enlisting in the Marine Corps. This period of my memoirs will be near the end of my recounting.

One of my first big pleasures and happiness at the Orphanage was when I had my ninth birthday – July 7, 1954. All children's birthdays were always singled out and on their birthday they had a cake (at lunch, if in the summer; at supper, if in the school months). The superintendent announced the child's birthday and everyone in the dining hall sang "Happy Birthday" to the special person. I felt special, important and "cared about". That was a great tradition - many thanks to the superintendent or staff worker who started it.

One of the great advantages of growing up in an orphanage or a large group environment is that you always have lots of playmates. In our free times, which were at nights after supper and Saturday and Sunday afternoons, we played lots of games. The boys had a big playground – all the grounds around our dorm and the big baseball field. I enjoyed and looked forward to the evenings after supper when we played games such as "Steal the Baker", "Red Rover", etc. I was not yet into softball, baseball or football until a few years later. It was such a pleasure to smell and feel the lush green grass on our playgrounds. Grass gives off such a nice aroma in the evenings.

On Saturday nights, we would often be treated to an outdoor movie. There was a fellow named Clyde Coppedge who lived in Wake Forest. Clyde, if I remember correctly, was either an engineer or a salesman for IBM. He would bring a screen, a projector and a sound system and set up an outdoor movie. He would bring reel-reel films such as "Ma & Pa Kettle", Gene Autry, The Bowery Boys, Red Ryder, Bud Abbott & Lou Costello and we would have a night outdoor movie. At that time, there was an old two-story (with basement) brick dorm that had previously been the girls' dorm. In front of this building was where Clyde would set up his equipment. This building was across from the "flower garden" between the dining hall and the pump house. Two new dorms had just been built for the girls – one for the small girls and one for the older girls. This building was now unused except for the basement where Granny

Anderson had the laundry. The building had a large colonial-style porch and we sat there and out on the grass. Seats, of course, were first-come, first-served. I do not know much about how Clyde Coppedge came to know about the Orphanage or what prompted him to give up his Saturdays and bring equipment and movies to the Orphanage; but he certainly made a lot of kids very happy and he helped expose us to the world beyond those orange clays hills. Later, Clyde adopted as his son one of the residents from the Orphanage – Eddie Watson ('47-'56). Eddie had two sisters at the Orphanage – Lilly Faye ('47-'53) and Betty Jean ('47-'58). He also had a younger brother – Foy ('51-'63) – who became my best friend when we both got into high school.

Living at an orphanage gives a kid a very large family. Arriving there in the summer between my third and fourth grade years, I was in awe of the older kids – those that were juniors and seniors in high school. They were soon to graduate and leave the Orphanage to go out into life. But, they were part of our family. They stood out in our childhood eyes as heroes, older brothers and sisters, someone to be like someday. They graduated from high school and left the Orphanage but remain an image in our eyes as someone of heroic proportions. The ones I remember, in the faintness of my memories, are: Eugene "Rod" Page ('40-'57) ; Alton "Sack" Bryant '46-'58); Harold Rogers ('46-'57); Sam Mace ('46-'55); Arthur Mace ('46-'57); Herb Tyson ('43-'55); Charles "Wiley" Hinson ('44-'58); Roy "Gap" Gasperson ('45-'57); Benedict "Jackie" (also "Abel") Morris ('52-'57); and Martin "Cain" Morris ('52-'59). Girls are: Shelby Jean Price ('48-'57); Ruth Gasperson ('45-'58); Carolyn "Gabby" Jones ('49-'57); and Lou Metta Winstead ('44-'55). There are others, but I was only nine at the time and my memory fails me to remember all of the oldest kids there at that time.

The Orphanage was started in 1920. Being a resident of the Orphanage gives one a very large family where we all shared a common experience. All of the residents of the Children's Home shared the same grounds and similar experiences with hundreds of other "orphans" who lived there at some point in their lives. I hope that Jerry "Duck" Smith's book will find residents of those 90 years so we all can know more about that large family that we were all a part of and shared some very common experiences – at different times in the Orphanage/Children's Home experience.

Moving on – I am writing these Orphanage/Children's Home memories in chronological sequence, so while I might digress, I will try to work myself back to the sequence of those nine years as they come into my recall.

Going back to my first summer at the Orphanage (1954), I want to speak about the concert classes. The concert classes were both a promotion and fund-raising activity of the Orphanage. The concert classes would visit virtually all of the Free Will Baptist Churches (F.W.B. Churches) in North Carolina each summer. There were two concert class groups and they would split the state and churches between them. Their purpose was to raise funds for the Orphanage and to make the F.W.B. Churches aware and updated on what their monies were doing to support the care of orphans in their orphanage to which they gave money to support. Each concert class consisted of two boys, four girls and a chaperone. The boys and girls in the concert classes were usually between the ages of six to twelve. Our job was to appeal to the hearts and pocketbooks of the church members in all of the F.W.B. Churches across North Carolina and get them to continue to support the Orphanage with their monetary contributions.

We would be at each church for just one day. We would give a night program which consisted of songs, poems, a Biblical play and then a slide show by the chaperone about the current events (and needs) of the Orphanage. The minister of the church would introduce us and make his remarks; we would give our performance; the chaperone would give her presentation on the Orphanage and its needs and projects; the minister would then take back over the event and make an appeal for monetary donations. The collection plate would be passed, the money given to the chaperone and she would deposit it the next day at a local bank; it would then transfer to the Orphanage's bank. The next day, we would move on to another church. We six kids would stay with various families in the churches that we were visiting. Someone might take one boy or both boys, or any such combination of kids.

Staying at the various homes was quite a treat. We were often treated as very special guests and the families would go out of their way to show us a good time. We were taken to swimming pools (a big deal in those days), to picnics, sightseeing, etc. Many of the families had children of their own and their kids would treat us as special playmates and go out of their way to be especially nice to us.

To those of you who lived at the Orphanage/Children's Home and never went on a concert class, this will be news to you. We few fortunate and lucky kids got a chance to experience a life outside of the daily summer life of the Orphanage. We were treated to parties, ice cream, sightseeing, games, fun and spending money given to us by the families we stayed with. We went from the coast to the mountains of North Carolina. We did a good service to the Orphanage because we brought in a lot of money to run the Orphanage; but at the same time, we enjoyed a life each summer so different from what the children were doing back on campus, working in the summer fields or tending the yards and grass mowing. I was in the concert class for three and a half years – from my first summer there at nine years old through my summer of twelve years old.

One chaperone lady was a fixture and a God-send for years – Miss Bonnie Farmer. Miss Bonnie ran the concert classes for years. She did so much good for the Orphanage. She was totally professional in her work. Every F.W.B. Church that we went to, Miss Bonnie was acknowledged, respected and loved. This was in 1954-1958; people in North Carolina (and the rest of the U.S.) did not travel. She made it real to them as to what and who their donations were going to when they gave money to support the Orphanage. (She – and us kids – made it possible for the Orphanage to keep its high standards of support for the kids there.)

I had mentioned earlier that there were two concert classes: The other class was chaperoned by a beautiful young woman named Mattie Quinn. Mattie did the concerts for several years and then when she left, Peggy Mixon, daughter of Horace and Sudie Mixon, did one of the concert classes for several years.

Kids that I remember being on the concert classes with me were: JoEtta Worthington ('54-'62); Margie Herring ('52-'62); Ann Worthington ('55-'65); Eugene Waller ('53-'64); Johnny High ('57-'69); Ona Mercer ('53-'64); Leroy "Lace" Miller ('52-'60); and Sue Heath ('53-'67).

I went out for four summers on the concert class – '54, '55, '56, and '57 (9-12 years old). I did not stay at the Orphanage for the summer and work on the farm until the summer of 1958 when I was 13 years old. Usually by the time one was 12 or 13 years old, they were "retired" from the concert class – mostly I think on the theory that the various F.W.B. Church members across the state would best respond to the plight of "orphans" and give more generously if the "orphans" were young and therefore more "in need" of help and support. (As a current business owner, I recognize and commend the creators of the fund-raising concert classes as being very smart and savvy marketing and business people.)

As mentioned earlier, part of our concert program was to present a Bible Story play. The first summer, I played the part of the little boy who had the basket of fish and bread that Christ blessed and multiplied and "fed the multitudes". The second summer, I played the part of Daniel in "Daniel and the Lions' Den". The third summer, I played the part of King Asherius, who was married to Queen Esther in the Biblical story of Esther, who saved her Jewish people from annihilation at the hands of the evil court advisor Haman.

My sister, JoEtta, played the part of Queen Esther. Eugene Waller played the part of Haman. Eugene also played the part of Eli the Priest in the previous summer play of "Daniel in the Lions' Den".

We all came back at the end of the summer with money in our pockets that various people we stayed with at each church over the summer had given us. That money made us very popular and we had friends – at least until the money ran out. I would use my money to buy ice cream for me and my friends at the morning break at Middlesex School. We kids all called the pocket money that the people gave us as our "earnings" and each morning, when we would leave one church on our way to the next, we would ask each other "how much money did you earn?"

I am spending a lot of my writing space on the concert classes and should move on because I have nine years of life at the Orphanage to cover. I am doing so because this part of my life at the Orphanage made such an initial impact on me and my impressions of life. It was such a new and novel experience for me – one that was new, exciting and adventurous and so different from the world I came from prior to coming to the Orphanage.

I feel that I could write a separate book about those four summers of my life between the ages of nine and twelve (before my fourth grade year to before my seventh grade year). I remember many of the churches and many of the families I stayed with those four summers and the fun and adventures I had and the things I got to see from the coast of North Carolina to the mountains of North Carolina.

Two last things and I'll move on:

We gave seven programs a week – one each on Monday through Friday nights and two on Sunday (morning Sunday service and evening Sunday service – we were the program in substitution of the preacher's sermon).

Saturday nights was our "night off" and we all looked forward to it. We got to "play" that full day and most of the families we stayed with treated us special and showed us kids a very good time.

One little amusing story – I stayed with a family one summer whose last name was Rice. The father was a mortician and owned a funeral home. A few weeks later at another church, I stayed with another family whose name just happened to also be Rice. That father was in the tombstone business. In my youthful mind, I thought that there was a connection, so I asked him if the other Rice was his brother. Once I explained why I asked that, he was very amused and had quite a laugh. There was no connection except both had the last name of Rice; and, coincidentally, both were in related businesses.

In October of 1954, Hurricane Hazel struck. It was on October 15th – a Friday – that the Hurricane struck our part of North Carolina. We were supposed to go to a barbecue dinner that night at Corinth-Holder High School – about 10 miles or so from Middlesex but in a different county. We did not go, of course. Everyone was "buttoned down" – not only at the Children's Home, but all over the state. Petey and Mrs. Mitchell assembled us all in the study hall as the storm started building up that evening and night. Everything was solemn and there was an atmosphere of fear in the air although Ma Mitchell and Petey tried to assure us all that we were safe. The wind howled with such ferocity and intensity – loud and fearsome! Sometime early that night, the electricity went out. We all were sent to bed, but I remember Ma Mitchell and Petey coming to our areas many times to assure us that things would be okay and that we were not in danger.

The next morning – a Saturday, if my memory serves me right – the scene across the campus at the Orphanage was one of downed trees and limbs everywhere. One of the columns on the front porch of the boys' dorm was blown away and the front porch roof was sagging. Petey and the larger boys went outside to assess and start fixing the damages. I was only nine years old then – all we smaller kids stayed inside most of the day while the older kids worked to restore working power to the dorms and to handle the damages of the hurricane. I seem to remember that Ma Mitchell led us in a prayer to thank God that we all had passed the Hurricane in safety. "Google" says that in North Carolina, 90 people lost their lives in Hurricane Hazel.

This was my first five months at the Orphanage and what an impression those five months made on me – from the concert classes, my birthday cake and Hurricane Hazel.

A very important positive change occurred in my life that first year that followed me the full nine years of my life at the Orphanage and the four years of my life in college and the university. I started my fourth grade year at Middlesex Elementary School. Almost at the very beginning, I found myself – for the first time in my life – being able to understand things in the classroom at school and being able to easily comprehend the subjects that we were studying. At the time, in elementary school, grades were S's, N's, and U's (for Satisfactory, Needs to Improve and Unsatisfactory. I made all S's the whole year. This was such a change from my first through third grade experiences because before coming to the Orphanage, I was a failing student and was considered a "marginal" student at best. In the fourth grade at Middlesex, I was the top student in my class.

This academic success stayed with me throughout my nine years of public school and my four years of college and university. Looking back on that change, my understanding and explanation for it was that at the Orphanage, I felt secure, safe and cared for and in that environment, I was able to thrive and grow and use my God-given abilities. In my three years after my Mother's death, my brothers, sisters and I were loved (not neglected nor abused) but our lives were so unstable – moving from one family member's house to another family member's house and no stability in our lives. The Orphanage gave me stability and predictability and in that environment, I was able to grow and use what was inside me natively and grow accordingly.

While we lived our lives on the campus of the Orphanage, we went to the Nash County public schools and our lives were interacted with the other kids of the Middlesex community who were not residents of the Orphanage. My fourth grade teacher was a lady named Mrs. Johnston. My fourth grade year was the year my life changed. That year I discovered that I could read and learn and that I was not "mentally limited". Mrs. Johnston was very influential in that she praised my accomplishments and let me know that I had abilities.

In the fifth grade, my teacher was Mrs. Annie V. Hillard. She had been married to Gus Hillard who owned the drug store in Middlesex. Later, she changed her name back to Annie V. Powell. I remember that year as being fun and exciting, as I continued my growth and education and understanding of the world.

My sixth grade teacher was a Mrs. Amspacher. It was during my sixth grade year that Russia launched "Sputnik" and put the USSR (Union of Soviet Socialist Republics, as Russia was known in those years of the "Cold War") in the forefront of the space race and America feared for its dominance as a world power. Later, Russia put Yuri Gagarin in orbit around earth – the first man into space and America was doubly concerned about its role as a world power being subjugated to second place behind Russia. Also, it was about this time that Francis Gary Powers, a high-altitude jet pilot, was shot out of the skies over Russia and put on trial in Russia as an American spy. Those were momentous chapters in American history.

My seventh grade teacher was a Mrs. Bissette. That was the year that I "fell in love" for the first time – with a girl who was from the community – not from the Orphanage. Unfortunately, she was not in love with me.

My eighth grade teacher was Mrs. Naomi Powell – a person whom I have always respected and credited with having a major impact on my life. Mrs. Naomi challenged me to reach into myself and develop my mind. She encouraged me to reach beyond the average and to reach out beyond my horizons to explore new worlds. She also recommended books for me to read that took me beyond the world of Middlesex and the Orphanage – mostly historical novels. In particular, I remember reading "Mary, Queen of Scots" that opened me up to the history of the English royalty and the English throne and crown and the decisions and actions one has to take to hold on to power and face up to insurmountable opposition and difficulties; and to hold on to honor and duty even in the face of death as a consequence. It made a powerful impression on my young mind at the time.

I was fortunate to have had such gifted and dedicated pre-high school teachers who took an interest in me and exposed me to a vast world beyond my horizons.

Impressions I have of my first five years at the orphanage:

Pets: We had a Collie dog named "Sam". Sam slept on the front porch at night. He was a loving and playful pet. Sam was there when I came to the Orphanage. We also had a bulldog (forget his name), some terrier hunting dogs that belonged to Petey (sometimes they were let out of their pen for us to play with) and a raccoon named "Ring-eye" that was the pet of

Wilbert Earl "Scram" Heath ('53-'60). He had been found as a baby and raised by Scram. We had various other dogs scattered throughout the houses and buildings of the farm which were there to greet us when we showed up.

Flowers: Ma Mitchell loved flowers and we had flower beds and roses – one of which, a red rose – was grown on a trellis at the left-end of the front yard and just seemed to bloom profusely year after year. The campus had lots of trees and shrubbery, was very well-maintained by Petey Mitchell, and was a very pretty and stately environment in which to live and grow up.

Insects: There always seemed to be butterflies, bumblebees and fireflies everywhere in the summer. Often, dragonflies and grasshoppers would show up near the dorms. And, the crickets always chirped at night.

The Night Sky: Being on a farm with thousands of acres, the night sky was always very visible. One could always look up at night and see thousands of stars and the night moon. Also, the day sky is an integral part of my life and my memories of the Home. The clouds, the sun, sunrise, sunset, rains – all stand out in my memories. Most of my adult life has been in the city (Washington, DC and Arlington, VA). With tall buildings, street lights, power lines, etc – all canopying overhead, the sky – day and night – is more or less screened out. In the city, one's vision becomes very horizontal. I miss the experience of the night sky – in order to have that experience again, I often go to the mountains and to the Shenandoah National Park to see and experience the sky.

Grass: The grass always seemed to be green from early spring to late fall. The smell of the grass was so sweet in the spring, rich in the summer and nostalgic in the fall. In spring through fall, there seemed to always be dew in the mornings and the evenings; and frost on the grass in late fall through winter into early spring. I loved the sensation and smell of the grass when playing in it or when walking in it. At that time, it was a natural part of country existence; today in a world of concrete, asphalt and pollution, it is a rare-to-be-experienced sensation.

The Farm: I did not start working on the farm until the summer of 1958 – just before my starting the eighth grade. The previous summers, I had been on the concert class during the summer. The summer, of course, is when the hardest work is done on the farm. I hated the hot, hard days out in the sun working in the tobacco fields, the bean patches, the vegetable gardens. It was hard, back-breaking and sweating work. But, I did especially love working on the farm in the spring and the fall. I enjoyed being in the corn fields in the fall pulling the dried corn; or, being in the wheat fields in the late spring loading the bales of wheat straw. I loved the feeling of being young and muscular; of using my body to do manual labor; of smelling the rich fragrance of both plants and the soil.

In the winter, we usually did clean-up and repair of the farm buildings and grounds and getting things readied for the spring planting. One pleasurable memory I have is in the fall, Horace Mixon, the farm manager would take a lard stand and pop popcorn over the open fire that was built as we cleaned up and burned tree limbs and old timber on the farm. We would make a big fire to burn off the wood. The smell of the fire and its warmth still lingers with me today. Even today, my palate tingles when I think of the lard stand popped corn. The summer memories are of the tobacco fields and barns, harvesting the green tobacco and "looping" it at the barns. And, the summer days spent picking butterbeans, corn, field peas, etc. and then all afternoon shelling them under the trees back on the campus so they could be blanched, frozen and stored for our winter food.

Those years on the farm and the hands-on skills learned have stayed with me for a lifetime. Although my career has basically put me in an office environment, I am very capable of picking up hand tools and handling any everyday task that comes along.

On summer nights and Saturday/Sunday afternoons, we enjoyed playing softball, baseball, and football or choose-up-sides games. These were our "free" times and we lived them to the extreme. Several hours of recreation before the dark set in and we had to go inside. The camaraderie of teenage boys playing in fun and competition has probably been the experience of boys down through the centuries. At the Orphanage, with so many boys, we had the ideal scene for playing and enjoying so many games. Sometimes, Petey would load us up on the farm truck or bus and take us over to the lake for a swim. I loved those late afternoon – after supper – swims in the lake.

Meals: The meals at the Orphanage were always something that I looked forward to. We had great meals with a variety of meats: chicken, pork, beef, turkey, fish; and always a variety of vegetables. Sunday dinners were always special – fried chicken or turkey. Breakfasts always consisted of eggs, bacon, sausage, ham, grits, oatmeal, toast, jelly. Sunday morning breakfasts – the one day we got to sleep late – we were served cereals –

Cheerios, Corn Flakes, orange juice, etc. For Saturday night supper, we almost always had hot dogs. The Orphanage hot dogs were the best! Even today, I compare every hot dog I eat to those we were served at the Orphanage. Especially great was fixing one or two (usually two) hot dogs with chili – after finishing supper - and taking them back to the boys' dorm and hiding them in our chest of drawers to retrieve later that night to enjoy with our Saturday ration of a Pepsi while we watched "Gunsmoke" on T.V. That cold hot dog, with its congealed chili, was absolutely divine to savor and enjoy later that night as we watched our favorite Saturday night shows. Even today, it is very difficult to get meals that had so many great vegetables mixed in with the meats. I think all Eastern North Carolinians still love their butterbeans, field peas, squash, farm-grown corn and okra. Living around the U.S. and the world over the last 40 years and sampling and enjoying foods from all over, I still miss my North Carolina Orphanage/Children's Home meals. Ma Sudie and the kitchen girls did an incredibly great job of preparing meals for several hundred people that were appetizing and delicious and very enjoyable.

Television: Those were the days of black and white T.V. We would watch "The Honeymooners" starring Jackie Gleason, June Allyson and Art Carney; and, the unforgettable "I Love Lucy" show. On Sundays nights, there was "The Wonderful World of Disney". Walt Disney was alive in those days and he always hosted his show. There were all the great Disney movies and the unforgettable "Davy Crockett" six-part series. In the late weekday afternoons, there was "The Mickey Mouse Club". I was in love with Annette Funicello. Every year, there would be the "Wizard of Oz" movie brought back. Every Saturday night – to end the night – there would be "Gunsmoke" with "Marshall Matt Dillon, Deputy Chester, Ms. Kitty and Doc - coming on at 10:00 - after which there was always bedtime and lights out for everyone. Other shows I remember was the suspense and supernatural shows of "The Squeaking Doors" and the "Inner Sanctum"; the Saturday morning cartoon shows (when I was very young) of "Howdy Doody" and "Tom Terrific and his Wonder Dog – Mighty Manfred". There was "Death Valley Days" with Ronald Reagan long before he became a politician. Other western shows that were big in those days were "Maverick", "Paladin", "Bonanza" and "Rawhide", the T.V. show that starred Clint Eastwood in his magnificent career playing the part of the impulsive, hot-tempered cowpuncher named "Rowdy Yates". The theme song for "Rawhide" was sung by Frankie Lane. Also on Sunday afternoon in the winters when we could not go outside, there would be the "Evangelical" programs, especially those with the Reverend Billy Graham or the healer, the Reverend Oral Roberts. With the Billy Graham Crusades, there was George Beverly Shea with his incredible bass voice singing the unforgettable and soul-stirring "How Great Thou Art". There were the afternoon "soap operas", which I never watched, but the women and the girls in particular did and they often discussed them, such as "The Guiding Light".

In the days of black and white T.V., they would often show re-runs of the classic movies of the 30's, 40's and 50's. One of the great re-runs of that time was "High Noon" which starred Gary Cooper and Grace Kelly. This was a classic western and was the last movie that American-born Grace Kelly played in before she married Prince Rainier of Monaco and left Hollywood and became a princess, in fact.

Also, there was the great "Ed Sullivan Show", a talent show that came on Saturday nights, which featured the best talent of the time. I will never forget when Jacob "Jake" Lane ('46-'59) came running down the hall heading for the T.V. room yelling, "He's on", announcing that Elvis Presley was making an appearance on the Ed Sullivan Show. This was 1956 and I was 11 years old at the time. Here is a "Google" reporting of that momentous occurrence:

"Elvis Gyrates on Ed Sullivan's Show (1956): Elvis Presley had already appeared on other national television shows (such as the Stage Show, the Milton Berle Show, and on the popular Steve Allen Show) when Ed Sullivan booked Elvis for three shows. Elvis' pelvic gyrations during his appearances on these other shows had caused much discussion and concern about the suitability of airing such provocative and sensual movements on television.

"Although at first Ed Sullivan said he would never want Elvis on his show, Sullivan changed his mind when the Steve Allen Show with Elvis as a guest had about twice as many viewers as Sullivan's show that night (they were competing for the same audience since they were in the same time slot). After negotiating with Elvis' manager, Ed Sullivan paid Elvis the huge sum of $50,000 for appearing on three of his shows: September 9, 1956, October 28, 1956, and then on January 6, 1957.

"For Elvis' first appearance on the Ed Sullivan Show on Sunday night at 8 p.m. on September 9, 1956, Ed Sullivan himself was not able to host since he had recently been in a very serious car accident that left him in the hospital. In his place, Oscar-winning actor Charles Laughton hosted the show. Elvis was also not on location in New York for the show since he was in Los Angeles for the filming of "Love Me Tender". Laughton hosted from New York and then when it came time for Elvis' appearance, Laughton introduced him and then cut to the stage in Hollywood with Elvis.

"Elvis appeared on a stage with large, artistic guitars as decoration. Wearing a plaid jacket and holding his guitar, Elvis thanked Mr. Laughton and then said, "This is probably the greatest honor that I've ever had in my life." Elvis then sang "Don't Be Cruel" with his four back-up singers (the Jordanaires), followed by "Love Me Tender," which was the not-yet-released title track from his new movie.

"Although the cameras stayed mostly from the waist up on Elvis' first appearance on the show, the second time he appeared that night, the camera widened out and the T.V. audience was able to see Elvis' gyrations. During this second set, Elvis sang "Ready Teddy" and then ended with a portion of "Hound Dog."

"Elvis' appearance on The Ed Sullivan Show was a major success. Over 60 million people, both young and old, watched the show and many people believe it helped bridge the generation gap for Elvis' acceptance into the mainstream."

I was only 11 years old at the time. I was not into "Rock and Roll". I did not even know who Elvis Presley was. My big interests in those times was in exploring the woods with my "Blood Brother" (Wilbert Earl Heath - "Scram"), so I did not even go into the T.V. room to see what the commotion was all about.

Jake Lane ('46-'59), by the way, was the first to wear "calypso pants" which was a new fad which only lasted a couple of years. Calypso pants were Caribbean-style pants which came up to the calves and tapered off and ended. Even then, we "orphans" tried to emulate the clothes styles of the times.

What a time to be growing up – T.V. in its infancy; America moving from being a rural (country) nation to an urban (city) nation; the U.S. (and the world) going from pop and country music to rock and roll; the "Cold War"; the U.S. moving out of a "one-car" nation to a "two-car" nation. We kids at the Orphanage – and in the little rural and isolated village of Middlesex, North Carolina, were somewhat isolated; but we were not cut off from what was going on in mainstream America. I, along with my fellow residents at the Orphanage, was being pulled into the direction that American culture was going in.

In the midst of all these cultural changes, there was a presence at the Orphanage that was from an era and a time long before the '50s and the 60's. This presence was the Reverend M. L. Cummings. "Preacher Cummings", as we called him, was an old evangelist who somehow had found his way to the Orphanage where he lived in one of the two bedrooms that were behind the study hall in the boys' dorm. Preacher Cummings always wore a black suit, white shirt, string bowtie and a big round-brim black hat. He came and went – sometimes he was gone for the weekend and returned on Monday; other times he was gone for several weeks. It was rumored that when he went off, he went to various cities where he conducted street evangelist services and preached. Preacher Cummings had a past. In his youth in the Black Woods of Canada, he was frequently involved in fights (mostly knife fights) and was often in trouble with the law.

Here is the only information that I can find on him on "Google". The first article is from the "Ocracoke News" around 1930 and the second is from one of his two books.

"M. L. Cummings, Evangelist, visited Ocracoke in the 1920's. He held meetings in a large grassy area near what is now called Creek Road, close to Suzie's hair studio. He sold a 32-page booklet, <u>Avenues Leading to Crime</u>, and <u>Blackie of the North Woods</u>, His Life and Conversion, for 25 cents. The chapbook, which told of a life of vagrancy, crime, alcohol, drugs, sex, and conversion, relates details of southern jails and chain gangs, and was probably autobiographical."

Preacher Cummings had an old black Model A Ford (about a 1930's as I recall) which he didn't seem to know much about operating. Every Saturday when he would leave the campus to head off to his street-corner evangelistic work, we boys would have to push his old Model A to get it going. Usually, we pushed it out on the baseball diamond and finally would get his car going and him on his way.

When he was on the campus, he often would sit on the front porch of the boys' dorm in his black suit with his wide-brim black hat and his cane (always carried a highly-polished curved handle cane). Our old collie dog, "Sam", would be curled up at Preacher Cummings' feet. There was a "simpatico" between those two old guys.

I liked Preacher Cummings and would often sit with him (I was 9-10 at the time) and he would tell me stories of his youth in the Black Woods of Canada (not sure where that area is).

One of the amusing anecdotes about Preacher Cummings was his "deafness". He could not hear very well. Often at lunch or dinner in the central dining hall where all the people on the campus – boys, girls, staff, staff's children, etc. – had our meals, when the superintendent would either offer the blessing himself or call on someone to give the blessing for the meal, Preacher Cummings would think that he was being asked to pray and he would start out. In kindness to the old man, whoever was the intended one to give the blessing would stop and remain quiet and let Preacher Cummings do the blessing.

Ma Mitchell was very kind to Preacher Cummings and treated him as if he were her old grandfather. She would do his laundry, hang his clothes, press his suit and white shirts, and pack his suitcase when he went off for his weekend evangelist missions. I have always remembered the kindness and love that Ma Mitchell showed to the old man – a love and service that came from her heart. She had her hands full looking after the full boys dorm; but she made time in her over-busy schedule to be kind to an old man who – like us orphans – had no other home to go to.

When Preacher Cummings passed away, Ma Mitchell cleaned out his room and handled the disposal of his very few life possessions and his clothes. In his room was a box of his paperback books. Ma Mitchell gave me a copy of his autobiography book – "Blackie of the North Woods" which I read through several times. It was probably around 1956 when Preacher Cummings passed away.

Another illustrious character at that time was a fellow who showed up once or twice a year – the "Goat Man". When the word was out that the Goat Man was in the area, we would all be loaded up on the farm truck and bus and head out to Zebulon – to the intersection of N.C. 97 and U.S. 264. This was where the Goat Man usually stopped off. Here is what "Google" has to say about the Goat Man and I'll leave it at that – for those of you that this was a chapter in your lives as well:

"Charles "Ches" McCartney, the legendary "Goat Man", was a wanderer, who spent decades traveling across the country while guiding a massive iron-wheeled wagon loaded with pots and pans, pails, bales of hay and car tags, lead by a team of goats. The "Goat Man" entwined himself in the folklore of rural America for more than six decades.

"The Goat Man led a very colorful life. At age 14, having a reputation as an eccentric, he left his hometown in Iowa for New York. There he married a Spanish maiden and became a target for her knife-tossing act for two years. In the 1930's, McCartney hit the road with his wife and son. His wife later tired of the travels and returned home to Iowa while McCartney traveled on with his son.

"He was somewhat like a prophet with his long, grey beard and travel-worn clothes, spreading the word of God to any man, woman or child who would listen. From 1930 to 1987, legend has it that he walked 100,000 miles preaching the gospel in 49 of the nation's 50 states."

In those years around 1956 or so, it was rumored that Elvis Presley had passed through the area in his famous "pink Cadillac" and had stopped off in Zebulon where a number of people had seen and talked to him. I don't know if that was true or not; but at that time, I would not have paid much attention. I was into the "outdoors and the woods" and paid little attention to rock and roll music.

My Best Friends at the Orphanage/Children's Home: I had many friends at the Orphanage/Children's Home over the nine years I lived there; but two stand out as my "special" friends – Wilbert Earl "Scram" Heath and Foy Watson.

Scram and I became friends about the second year that I was at the Orphanage. Wilbert Earl was about two years older than me. He was skinny and wiry and could run forever, which gave him his nickname of "Scram", from running or scramming quickly from any place you did not want to be in or from any danger or intimidating person; or just to be able to quickly go from one place to the next. Scram and I shared a special friendship and love of the outdoors and the woods. We spent a lot of our free time exploring the hundreds of acres of woodland on the Orphanage property and the surrounding properties. We liked to build tree houses in the woods, find and establish "Tarzan vines" over the creeks and water branches in the woods. We built and placed rabbit boxes to traps rabbits and squirrels – which if we caught, we would skin and clean and take to the kitchen to be cooked for us. Mrs. Sudie Mixon, the director of the kitchen and the campus dietician, was so understanding and so accommodating. When we caught wild game or fish, or picked wild blackberries, she would have those prepared for us. Even though it must have been quite an inconvenience to her and the girls working for her in the kitchen to take time from their preparations to feed several hundred people at each meal, they would fix the rabbits or squirrels we brought in or make pies from the wild blackberries that we had picked and brought to her.

Scram and I would be up at 4:30 in the morning to go out into the woods to check our rabbit boxes. We would have our flashlights and our heavy winter coats because the nights were often very cold. The woods are so different and sometimes a little intimidating at 4:30 in the morning. It was quite an adventure at 12 years old.

To express and confirm our deep and devoted friendship, Scram and I once took a pocket knife and cut our wrists and let our blood run together. We became "blood brothers" in the tradition that we had heard came from the Native Americans – the Indians who walked the woods long before white Europeans came to the North American shores. In that act, we vowed to each other our mutual friendship and protection. When I became Scram's blood brother, my life at the Orphanage literally changed. Scram was a known "fighter". No one messed with him. As his blood brother now, "no one messed with me". (Reminds me of the Korean Karate fighter and trainer – Jhoon Rhee – who advertised on the T.V. in the Washington, DC area when I moved there in 1977. He owned and ran a chain of karate schools to train youths in karate and self-defense. The line used in his T.V. ads was a little Korean boy saying "no one bother me".)

Scram was several years older than me so I was able to go about the campus without being harassed by any "bullies". It was a very good life having a friend so respected (and feared) by the others that no one would mess with me since I was Scram's "blood brother".

Unfortunately, as I neared my high school years and started getting interested in baseball and basketball and "the woods" became less of interest to me, Scram and I started drifting apart. Our worlds changed and we spent less time together; but, we remained "blood brothers" and we were always there for each other. Scram left the Children's Home, as I recall, when he finished his sophomore year in high school and I lost contact with him after that.

Foy and I became good friends, I think, in our tenth grade year. I was then into high school sports – I was on both the basketball team and the baseball team (catcher) at Middlesex High School – the public school where we all attended. Foy and I shared our friendship with a common interest of music – particularly Elvis Presley. He was a very excellent, natural artist; and, I – along with others at the Children's Home – appreciated and enjoyed his great artistic talent. Foy was the one friend to whom I opened up and we shared between us our feelings, our dreams, our teenage concerns and hopes for the future.

When we graduated from high school and left the Children's Home in early June 1963, we connected again in September 1963 at Mt. Olive College where we were both freshmen. Foy and I worked together in the dining hall at Mt. Olive College where we had jobs to earn our meals. In the late fall, we both gave up our jobs in the college dining hall and took jobs as waiters at a steakhouse near Warsaw, North Carolina – about an hour and fifteen minutes drive from Mt. Olive. At the steakhouse, called "The Country Squire", we were able to earn excellent money in tips which gave us both some spending money which we sorely needed.

The Country Squire was then famously known as the "Home of the 64 Ounce Steak". If a customer wanted to take up the challenge and eat the 64 ounce steak, their meal was free. I worked at The Country Squire for about a year. I don't remember anyone successfully taking up the challenge and winning. When we first started working there, I had a '49 "Flat head 6 Ford" which got us back and forth to work. Later the car played out on me and Foy bought a car. I don't remember what it was; but, I do remember that for every fill-up, we had to put in a pint of oil. The car smoked a lot; but it got us back and forth.

After our freshman year, Foy dropped out of school and joined the Army. We saw little of each other after that. I finished up at Mt. Olive and went on to UNC-Chapel Hill for my junior and senior year and during my senior year, Foy called me – he was in the Army then and stationed at Fort Jackson, South Carolina. He came to Chapel Hill to visit me. It was in the winter and during a light snow storm. We drove to somewhere up near the Virginia border to drop one of his army buddies off at his home. Foy and I spent the weekend together; we double-dated and we went to see an "Elvis" movie.

I saw Foy several years later when I had finished my enlistment in the Marine Corps ('68-'72). It was 1973 and I was working for the State of North Carolina and I was on a business trip to the Charlotte area. I spent the night with Foy and his wife, Shirley, and his family and we caught up on the years in between. That was basically the last time I saw Foy except at a class reunion many years later – I think it was in 2003, which was our

Middlesex High School's 40th year reunion. Unfortunately, we did not get much of a chance to talk in the short several hours that we were there.

In my memories, when I think back on the Children's Home, Foy always comes up in my memories as a very special friend that I shared some years of my young life with. Wherever he is today and however he is doing, I give him my sincere thanks for a special friendship. (Further on in these memoirs, I will speak of Foy again.)

Superintendents:

There were four superintendents of the Orphanage/Children's Home during the nine years that I live there:

1. Stephen "Pa" Smith and "Ma" Smith ('51-'55 & '56-'58)
2. R. H. and Mrs. Jackson ('55-'56)
3. J. W. "Wilbur" Everton and Mrs. Hattie Mae Everton ('58-'62)
4. M .L. Johnson and Mrs. Pearl Johnson ('62-'69)

My memory may not serve me quite well, but these are the years I think that they were there at the Orphanage/Children's Home as superintendent:

Pa and Ma Smith: I seem to recall that they were there during my first two years – from '54-'56. They were like an institution, highly respected and deeply loved by all. Earlier in my memoirs, I have described "Pa" with his "Roosevelt" demeanor – grey pin-striped suit, hat, long-stemmed cigarette holder.

Here are two of several memories I have of Pa and Ma Smith:

We were invited by a local farmer to go to his fields and pick field peas (or butter beans) to can for winter food. This particular farmer had an apple orchard. Somehow, most of the boys ended up in the farmer's apple trees picking his apples. Apparently, he complained to Pa Smith and we were all to be punished. We had to line up outside the office and Pa had his paddle and was to spank us (whack each of us on our "buttocks" – as "Forest Gump" would have said). When I came up in the line, I was only nine years old then and had just been at the Orphanage only four to five months, I remember Pa asked me if I had climbed the trees and knocked down the farmer's apples. I told him that I had. He looked me in the eye and then "lightly" tapped my butt with his paddle and told me not to do again. I felt that Pa and I shared something special between us since we both had the first name of "Stephen".

I remember Ma Smith wearing her kerchief and working with us in the fields picking butterbeans; back on campus she helped us shell, blanch and prepare them for freezing and storage for the winter. She was so much one of us orphans. Even though she was the superintendent's wife, she worked right alongside all of us and made us feel that we were all one family sharing our common hardships, labors and enjoyments together. I was only nine then, but Pa and Ma Smith's devoted work made such an impression on my youthful mind. The current world that we live in has a short supply of such superior persons.

R. H. Jackson and Mrs. Jackson: Mr. and Mrs. Jackson had two daughters, Connie and Wilhelmina. If my memory serves me correctly, Mr. Jackson was a craftsman and a man who loved to use his hands and to be outside working more so than being cooped up in a superintendent's office.

My one big memory of Mr. Jackson was his love of carpentry and his being on the roof of a new chicken house that we were constructing – in his coveralls and swinging a hammer. His two daughters, Connie and Wilhelmina, were very attractive and I remember how the "older" boys would talk about them and try to make an impression on them.

Also, I remember that one Sunday Mr. Jackson was to go to a F.W.B. Church somewhere to deliver the Sunday sermon and he took Foy and me (and, I believe, Jimmy Cantrell ['53-'64]) to accompany him. That afternoon, after the sermon and a dinner in one of the parishioner's home, he took Foy and me to an area that had been a pre-historic sea and we were able to dig for sharks' teeth.

J. W. "Wilbur" Everton and Mrs. Hattie Mae Everton: Mr. Everton was the superintendent who served the most years while I was at the Children's Home. I was 13 to 16 years old when he was there. These would have been the years of my older memories. I especially admired and appreciated Mr. Everton. He always gave me such an acknowledgement and recognition. He always called me "Mr. Steve". I always felt so important when he was around. He treated me as a responsible adult and made me feel important and respected. I felt that I had to live up to his expectations and did so even when he was not around.

Mr. Everton was an excellent manager. From my later training as a Marine Corps Officer during the Vietnam War, I remembered and recognized his excellent management abilities. He always inspected his areas of responsibility. He always made his junior people in charge of those areas important and let you know that he both depended on you to do your job and he respected and appreciated you if you lived up to your responsibilities.

Mr. and Mrs. Everton had three children of their own. They had two sons who came to the Children's Home with them: Jeff and Randy; a daughter, Rebecca, was born while he was as superintendent.

Mr. Everton, as I remember, had been a military man. He had served time in the U.S. Navy; afterwards, he had attended the Free Will Baptist Seminary in Nashville, TN where he was ordained as a Free Will Baptist minister.

On campus Mr. Everton was in my mind like a young John F. Kennedy – full of life, youth, vigor, dreams and aspirations which he sought to impart to us orphans. After leaving the Children's Home as superintendent, Mr. Everton, I think, took over as pastor of Johnston Union Free Will Baptist Church. Sometime after that, while he was serving as pastor of Daniels' Chapel Church in Wilson County, he developed a brain tumor – as I recall – and succumbed to it. His death was the passing of an extraordinary and beautiful human being. I was too young in those days – and too involved in my own life's struggles – to understand and appreciate the passing of a truly wonderful human being. Youth – and rightfully so – is excused from not understanding the comings and goings of "great beings" and people who have personally given so much to them. Only, it seems, in later age – if ever - do we recall those wonderful beings of our childhood who gave so much of themselves to make it possible for us to survive and to grow to our maximum potential (or at the very least, to live lives that are more protected and easier in comparison to those who preceded us and sacrificed for our better well-being).

M. L. Johnson and Mrs. Pearl Johnson: Mr. Johnson came to the Children's Home the summer before my senior year in high school ('62-'63). Mr. Johnson was a different kind of superintendent than the Orphanage/Children's Home had seen before. He was a dreamer, a builder and a business manager. Mr. Johnson's dream, as I understood it, was to convert the campus life from that of a dormitory-style life to one of a cottage-style life. He dreamed of giving each orphan/resident at the Children's Home a life that was as close to a family life as possible – even in an orphanage environment. He dreamed of building "cottages" that would more represent homes than dormitories or military barracks-style living. Mr. Johnson carried out his building plans over the next several years – adding a boys' cottage which housed the 16 oldest boys – with two boys to a room and a bath shared with one other room. This was quite an improvement over the old boys' dorm which had beds in row after row with no room and no privacy and two big open common bathrooms and showers – one for the younger boys and one for the older boys. A staff workers' cottage was built for those who were not house parents and did not live in the resident dorms. Houses were also built for the farm manager and assistant farm manager. More about Mr. Johnson later in this narrative.

My Favorite Jobs

As mentioned earlier in this narrative, all the residents except for the pre-schoolers were assigned jobs on a rotating three-month basis – first through fourth quarters of the year. Over the nine years I lived at the Home, I held all of the jobs at least once – farm boy, yard boy or house boy. I enjoyed and/or benefited in developed skills and know-how from each one. But the three that were my favorites were:

Kitchen Boy: The kitchen was run by all girls under the supervision of Mrs. Sudie Mixon, with the exception that there was one boy assigned to the kitchen. The boy was needed to: (1) do the lifting and emptying of the heavy garbage cans; (2) do the lifting and moving of the large heavy food containers in the storeroom; (3) tend the coal boiler every day and do the full maintenance service every Saturday morning; (4) keep the yards around the kitchen swept and pick up all trash; (5) keep the sidewalks and porches at all four entrances swept daily; and (6) wash and disinfect all the garbage and trash cans on Saturday morning. I thoroughly enjoyed working for Ma Sudie – she was an excellent manager, an excellent teacher and would let you know how your work was coming along. She would not hesitate to praise if she felt you were doing a good job. The kitchen boy job had some extra perks that came with the job – chance to get snacks and leftovers from supper to take back to the dorm with you; chance to sneak a Pepsi on Saturday and Sunday afternoons when you left playing to go to the storeroom and put the required number of crates of drinks in the cooler for Saturday and Sunday night suppers; also, it gave us a chance to drink some orange juice from the cooler on a hot Saturday or Sunday afternoon when putting the drinks in the cooler. The kitchen boy had keys to the kitchen and the storeroom. There was always the privileged position that the kitchen boy had of being the only boy working in a crowd of girls. (At that time on the campus, there was very little permitting of the boys and the girls to co-mingle and socialize. Both were kept primarily on their own campuses except for the meals in the dining hall). The only other job that put boys working around the girls was that of the laundry boy job – more about that later.

One special event I have often remembered with pleasure is when my best high school friend and Children's Home resident, Foy Watson, was the kitchen boy during one of the winter quarters. Often, the kitchen boy would have to get up in the middle of the night and go up to the kitchen to "stoke the boiler" since the kitchen boiler was old and had the tendency to go out on cold, wet or snowy winter nights. Foy would wake me up and we would go up to the kitchen together and I would give him company (and help) as he worked. One night that I especially remember was on a very snowy night, Foy had to make sure the boiler was burning well and would not go out. We got up in the middle of the night, left the dorm and walked up to the kitchen. After we tended the boiler, we then went into the kitchen and made ourselves several sandwiches from left over country-style steak that we had for dinner the night before and took a quart of milk with us. We went back into the boiler room, sat with the door open and watched the snow come down while feasting on those delicious cold steak sandwiches. With the heat from the boiler, the cold from the snowy night and the delicious sandwiches and milk, we stared at the coal fire from the open boiler door and talked until late in the night. We finally returned to the boys' dorm and got a few more hours of sleep in what remained of the night.

Laundry Boy: A second favorite job was that of "laundry boy", which I had twice. I worked for Ms. Emma Maiden who was the manager of the laundry. I particularly liked this job, as I worked independently; as long as I did my job well, I worked with very little oversight and direction. When I first started the job, Ms. Maiden trained me on operating the giant washing machines, extractors and drying machines. Since we did huge laundry runs with so many clothes and bed sheets, etc. to wash, the laundry equipment was large heavy industrial machines and it took a lot of effort and strength to pull the heavy wet clothes and sheets from the washers and then the extractors to transfer to the dryers. The laundry girls always had a radio going with the latest pop and rock music and they ironed and folded clothes. Along with the independence of the job, there were two other fringe benefits: (1) working in a room full of girls (just like the kitchen boy job); and, (2) there was always small change in the machines from residents who left coins in their pockets. So, the job also provided me with a small amount of pocket-change spending money.

Yard Boy: I worked as a yard boy my last two summers at the Home ('61 and '62). I worked for Petey Mitchell, the campus maintenance manager. This was my most favorite job of all the jobs I held while at the Home. We maintained the grounds and the buildings at the Home. I learned to service and operate lawn mowers, fix broken windows, make small plumbing repairs, etc. The second half of my first summer and the entirety of my second summer as yard boy, I operated the tractor mower. I loved the solidarity and the independence of this job. I worked by myself and on my own all week. Monday morning, I would show up at the pump house along with the rest of the yard crew. Petey would give us our assignments for the day. Usually, I would start out the week mowing grass the furtherest from the campus – around the farm barns and houses. Over the week, I would work on the campus. By Friday, I was mowing the flower garden, the grass around the superintendent's house, the office, the church, the kitchen, and the girls' and boys' dorms so these areas would look good for the weekend and weekend guests of parents and F.W.B. Church members and groups who might be visiting the Home over the weekend – especially on Sunday. On Saturday morning, I always mowed the baseball field so it would be in the best shape for our Saturday afternoon baseball game. I developed a special relationship with Petey. Often during the week, I would bring the tractor mower (which was a small Farmall Cub) to the pump house so Petey could sharpen the blades. He and I would sometimes talk for several hours while he sharpened the blades or did other repairs to the tractor. I enjoyed his stories of his life as a resident of the Home ('23-'32) and I enjoyed hearing his stories of his war experiences in the Army during WWII. He became a very special person to me during my last two years at the Home as a result of my working directly for him and getting to know him and to learn from him.

One occurrence that has remained in my memory was early on that first summer, when I first started driving the tractor, I did not understand much about tractor maintenance and I let the oil level go down too far and it damaged the pistons on the tractor. When I brought the tractor into the shop after hearing the strange noises and knew something was wrong, Petey immediately knew that it was burnt pistons from the oil level being too low. First, he told me what was wrong and what I should be doing in checking the oil and filling it to top levels each day; then, he said something to this effect: "Okay, what's done is done; now I am going to show you how to fix it." I spent that whole day with him and he showed me how to break down the engine and to pull the pistons, sleeves, etc. and re-grind the valves and repair the engine damage.

I never forgot the kindness Petey showed me that day. He could have severely reprimanded me for neglect in what I should have known (and he had shown me), but I forgot that day to check the oil. Also, he could have pulled me off the tractor mower job and downgraded me to a lawn mower pusher. Instead, he used the occasion to teach me a lot about the maintenance and repair of equipment and he let me keep my job as the tractor mower driver. In appreciation to him for that gesture, I always did my job far beyond the expectations. Just before I graduated and left the Home (June, 1963), he told me that I was the best boy he had ever had doing the tractor mower job. If I were, it was because of the way he handled things that particular day when I damaged the tractor and he chose to instruct me, to give me a second chance and to keep me on the job that I enjoyed so much.

SPORTS AT THE HOME

At the Home, we had lots of playground room: a big campus with lots of grassy places; a great baseball field that also served as a football field in the fall; an outdoor basketball court and pole-mounted basketball backboard and metal hoop; a fishing lake on the farm which also served as a "swimming hole"; plenty of road on which to ride bicycles; and lots of woods to explore and play in.

Games that I remember playing after supper in the warm weather were "Steal the Baker", "Red Rover" and "pile-up", which was a sort of "choose up sides and fight". Sometimes in telling friends and associates stories about growing up in an orphanage, I would relate the "choose up sides and fight" game and their eyes would widen.

When I first went to the Orphanage, I don't recall us having our own baseball team. Some of the older boys at that time – Gene "Rod" Page;

Alton "Sack" Bryant; Harold Rogers, to name a few – would dress in their baseball uniforms and leave campus to play for a team called Union Hope (if I recall correctly). I remember the awe I had seeing them in their baseball uniforms – in my young eyes, they were like major league players.

Later on, we formed our own Orphanage/Children's Home summer baseball team. I may not be remembering this correctly, but I seem to recall that Petey had a hand in forming up the team. One game, in particular, that I remember was the Home's baseball team playing a baseball team from the local prison which was, I think, in Bunn, NC – about 20 miles away. The prison bus would arrive with the prison baseball players who were all "trustees". There would be three to four prison guards with shotguns – one near the benches and one in each outfield. The prison team had one player who stood out. He was from Hawaii and was nicknamed "Hula". Hula joked and chattered a lot (like Mohammed Ali) and he was a long-ball hitter. All we young kids liked it when Hula came up to bat. We also played the baseball team at the Kennedy Home – an orphanage that was located in Kinston, NC. There was also another orphanage that I think was in Wake Forest that the Home played. I was small then and was not on the baseball team at the time. I started playing on the Home team the summer of 1959.

Jerry "Duck" Smith ('49-'60) was our catcher at the Home (he was also the catcher for the Middlesex High School team). When I was 14 – summer before my ninth grade year, I started playing on the Children's Home team – I played the outfield. The spring of my freshman year (ninth grade) in high school, I went out for and made the high school team where I was mostly a bench warmer. I became the catcher for the Children's Home team – Jerry trained me to replace him as he would be graduating and leaving the Home after the twelfth grade – his last year at the Home. Jerry was three years older than me, so I was the catcher for the Home team my last three summers at the Home.

We joined a summer baseball league that was comprised of teams from Middlesex, Mt. Pleasant, Zebulon, Spring Hope and Bailey. Six teams – the Children's Home team was the best team in the league and the one that all the others particularly wanted to beat. The other teams came with baseball uniforms, baseball shoes and top notch gloves and bats. The Children's Home team wore blue jeans, tennis shirts, white tee shirts, had – for the most part – rag-tag, hand-me-down baseball gloves; and, we had homemade bats made at the pump house by Petey. Most of the players on the other teams also played on their high school teams during the school year. Only a handful of the Children's Home players also played on Middlesex High's baseball team. I have often reflected on that team and why we so consistently beat teams that had superior players. I think the reason was that we were "a team". We were all at the Home – we lived together, worked together, played together, fought each other and later made up and remained friends. We had a team spirit and a camaraderie that outmatched our opponents.

It was while playing on the Home baseball team that I was given my nickname of "Reno". When I was the catcher for the Home team, as I squatted behind the home plate, I would run my mouth and harass the batters – trying to distract them. One of the players on one of the opposing teams gave me the nickname.

By the way, most every kid at the Home had a nickname – especially the boys. The nickname could come because of some physical feature, it could come because of some personality characteristic or it could come as a result of some action one did – especially if one "screwed up". Here are some of the nicknames – to any former Home resident reading this, you'll recognize if it was your nickname: Soapy, Preacher, Elvis, Ears, Stony, Tip Toes, Duck, Toe, Sack, Rod, Bad-Eye, Scram, Sarge, Garcia, Chi-Chi, Dobie, Higgy, Presley, Hi-Tie, Red, Turkey, Hanged, Me-Too, Lace, Cain, and Abel.

Over my lifetime, I have used that experience to form teams that defeated superior teams – when I was an officer in the Marine Corps and led a platoon of Marines; when I was a sales manager and developed a team of sales people; and when I was a business director and managed a business group. Often, I did not have the superior talent in my group, but I molded my group into a cohesive team and we more often than not out did other groups made up of more talented members but lacking in true team spirit. If you think back to the American Revolution, that is how George Washington led an army primarily made up of farmers, merchants and laborers and defeated the mightiest professional army in the world at that time – the Redcoat Army of Great Britain – the world's super power in the 18th and 19th centuries.

In high school at Middlesex, I played on both the baseball and basketball teams – all four years. Enjoying various sports both at the

Home and at school are among my treasured memories of my nine years at the Home.

Other memories I have, not in any chronological order and not necessarily related, include:
- Picking and shelling butter beans and field peas.
- The apple orchard behind the kitchen with its apples in the fall and covered with ice and icicles after several heavy snow or sleet storms. Once one winter, the water tank overflowed and the apple trees beneath it looked like ice castles where the overflowing water froze on them and formed such a delightful sight.
- The second apple orchard which was on the farm; also, the several pear trees that were on the grounds of the old stone houses on the farm.
- Going to the Wilson County Fair every fall and having dinner that night at Parker's Barbecue. When I was a senior, I won the gate ticket drawing for a bicycle which I had always wanted growing up – by the time I won it, I now wanted a car. All the small kids who did not have a bicycle wanted to ride mine. There was a little kid named Johnny Ray Whitley ('61-'69). I made Johnny Ray the manager of the bicycle. He could ride it any time that he wanted to. In exchange, he took care of the bicycle and would set aside time for the other kids to ride it also. As a result of this action, I became Johnny Ray's special "big brother". When I graduated from high school and left the Home, I gave Johnny Ray the bike.
- Going to the circus every year when it came to Wilson; and, again having dinner at Parker's Barbecue that night. (I think that one of the owners of Parkers, Henry Brewer, spent time at the Home.)
- When on the house boy three-month job, we spent Saturday morning house cleaning, mopping, and waxing. I remember the smell of soapy mopping water and the smell of wax, the humming of the buffer machine and the shine of the wooden hall floors and linoleum floors in the study hall.
- Again when a house boy, on Wednesday and Saturday mornings – before breakfast, laying out sheets in the hallway and pulling all the dirty clothes from the clothes hamper and bundling them in the sheets, tying the sheet into a big bundle and balancing it on my head; and going across the campus in the dark to take the bundles to the laundry. Wednesday was for dirty clothes; Saturday was for

both dirty clothes, sheets and pillow cases. All bed linens were changed on Saturday morning, with the dirty sheets being laundered that morning.
- Each boy had to go to the laundry on Wednesday night after supper and Saturday afternoon after lunch to get his own clean laundered clothes and take them back to the boys' dorm and put them into their closets and drawers.
- Dating in the living room at the older girls' dorm.
- F.W.B. Church Homecomings: The Home was invited every year to maybe a half-dozen church homecomings. After the morning service and sermon, there would be a big picnic served outdoors on long tables made of stretched fence wire. I was a big lover of coconut pie and I would scout out the entire table just before the dinner blessing and would position myself by the best-looking coconut pie I could find. As soon as the blessing was said, and we were free to "dig-in", I would immediately help myself to two slices of the coconut pie, then go look for fried chicken and barbecue, in that order. There was always the afternoon singing after the noon meal. I usually enjoyed the singing; but, sometimes I had a difficult time staying awake.
- Jerry "Duck" Smith giving his "I Believe in the Future of Farming" speech. This was in the fall of 1959. Jerry was a senior at Middlesex High School. I was a freshman at that time. Jerry had Agriculture as one of his courses at school. He had entered a public speaking contest and had chosen as the subject of his speech to be on the future of farming. He titled his speech "The Future of Farming". At that same time, the Children's Home was doing a promotion of the Home and a fund-raiser for a series of Sundays at various F.W.B. Churches in Eastern North Carolina. A group was formed, of which I was one of the members, and early on Sunday mornings, we would board the campus bus and head out for the F.W. B. Church where we would be the featured event in lieu of the Sunday morning sermon. We did singing and other presentations and then Jerry would be introduced by Mr. Everton who would be explain that Jerry was participating in a speech contest and Jerry would then give his speech to the church congregation. I heard that speech so many times – perhaps six to eight – that his opening words still remain in my mind: "I Believe

in the Future of Farming – with a faith born not of words, but of deeds".
- Several special high school teachers: Margaret Williford (affectionately known as "Ma Willy"). Ma Willy taught the science, biology, chemistry, physics and French classes. This was not uncommon in small rural and small town schools at that time; but, even so, very few teachers commanded such a range of subjects as Ma Willy did.
- Jasper Enid Drake, the baseball and basketball coach and the history and civics teacher. "Coach Drake" was both respected and loved by all who encountered him in his classes and/or on his baseball and/or basketball team. He was an exceptionally fine human being. My four years of high school sports were a great experience which I cherish in my memories – largely in part to Coach Drake. I was not particularly skilled in sports when I started high school; but under Coach Drake's tutelage, push and encouragement, I developed into a good athlete and learned how to push myself to physical levels I did not think I could do. In particular, this experience came to play and helped me more easily develop into a Marine Corps officer (of course, Marine Corps boot camp also played a big hand). There are many memories of my four years in sports under Coach Drake, but one in particular comes to mind. It was in my freshman year during basketball practice. At that time, Middlesex High School still had an old gym – about 1940's vintage. Coach Drake had us running laps around the gym and around the bleachers. While we were running, Coach Drake began whistling – he had a marvelous whistling voice. The song he was whistling was "Danny Boy", a great and lovely Irish folksong that had recently been popularized by country singer Conway Twitty. That beautiful whistled song seemed to resonant all over the gym and throughout the empty bleachers; and, to me, it was such a great experience to be running laps and gasping for breath and trying to make the next lap and hearing this beautiful melody being so harmoniously whistled while we ran.
- My Father – Raymond Worthington: He came to visit the five of us very often. He would come visit us consistently almost every other Sunday. Some of the kids at the Home were not so fortunate – their remaining parent (most of the kids at the Home

were half-orphans and had one or the other of their parents still living) did not visit often. Many times it was because they were not able. The U.S. was not as affluent in those days as it is today. Today, everyone has a car and most have cell phones and computers – easy to travel and communicate; but that was not the case in the '50s and the 60s (and before). The Children's Home was for many a long journey from where they lived in North Carolina and with limited transportation and/or money, they could not visit often. We also spent all of our Easters, Christmases, Thanksgivings, and week in the summer with him. He arranged ahead to prepare to have us with him and with various family members.

Here's a little anecdote about my Father. He was handsome and had lots of girlfriends. Also, he had this thing about new cars – he never owned one. He believed in buying an old used car and driving it into the ground, ditching it and buying another used car. Over the 10 years that we five Worthington kids were at the home, he owned maybe a dozen cars. Among them were a Buick, a Nash Rambler, a Ford, a Studebaker, and a Kaiser which the kids at the Home nicknamed the "Batmobile". Whenever my Father came to visit, the kids would speculate whether or not he would come with a different girlfriend, a different car, or both.

There is a little more to the story of my life at the Home which I will relate near the end of this memory recollection.

I graduated from Middlesex High School in early June, 1963 and left the Home. In the fall, I enrolled at Mount Olive College (Mount Olive Junior College at that time). I spent two good and memorable years at Mount Olive College and I have warm, cherished memories of those two years (September, 1963 – May, 1965). There were many kind and helpful staff at Mount Olive College who contributed to my life and my experiences there; but I am especially grateful to Dr. W. Burkette Raper (Alumnus '36-'45), the founder and President of Mount Olive College, for his support and encouragement. Dr. Raper – as most of you know – was also a resident of the F.W.B. Orphanage.

After finishing my sophomore year at Mount Olive College, I transferred to the University of North Carolina where I graduated with a Bachelor's degree in August, 1967.

At that point, I connected personally with the Children's Home again. I was visiting the Home for Homecoming in July. The superintendent at that time was M. L. Johnson who had been the superintendent my senior year at the Home (he came there in July, 1962). Mr. Johnson had stayed in touch with me throughout my four years of college/university and had encouraged and supported me to stick with it and get my degree. He asked me what I planned to do when I graduated. I had no definite plans – the Vietnam War was on and most likely, I would be drafted; but at the time, I had orthodontic appliances (braces) on my teeth and until they came off, I could not be drafted. Mr. Johnson asked me if I would consider coming back to the Home and being the house father for the 16 teenage boys living in the new older boys' cottage which had just been finished about a year earlier. You might recall that I mentioned earlier in my memories - in the section on the superintendents who served at the Home while I was there – that Mr. Johnson had a dream of turning the "dorm life" of the boys' into a "cottage life". He had built a "cottage" which housed the 16 oldest boys. It seemed, however, that his dream had encountered a problem that he had not anticipated – the older boys, now with more privacy and more privileges, had become a little bit unruly and unmanageable. Mr. Johnson thought (and hoped, I'm sure) that I – having just left the Home four years before and having been invited by him to share in his dream when I visited him over the four years in college – would be able to relate to the older boys and they to me and that I might be able to be an understanding, yet effective, house father to the 16 teenage boys and bring some discipline into the dorm.

    I accepted his request but with some concerns. I was 22 years old and did not especially want the life of a staff worker – especially that of a house parent with all its restrictions on my personal life. I was young and wanted the life of a 22-year old male. Working as a house father meant 6 days a week and 24 hours a day. I had Tuesdays as my day off and one weekend per month. Not much of a life for a 22-year old male who had just graduated from the University of North Carolina. I wanted to make some money to pay off college/university loans and have some spending money to get a new car, buy clothes, have dates, etc.

    The pay of a staff member was never what they could have made out in the commercial world. The staff and workers at the Home were talented and capable individuals and could have done other things with their lives. For many workers at the Home, their tenure there was a calling of God and the Church and their Christian faith and it was a "Labor of Love". Most did not have to be there – they could have done other things with their lives – made more money, had more time for themselves and their own kids and families; but had they not made the sacrifice, who would have? And, what would we kids there have had for better and more loving and caring house parents, farm, campus, kitchen, laundry managers? I personally am grateful for every staff member and worker that was there during my nine years at the Home. They gave so much to all of us so that we could have a much better life than that we would have had – had we not been fortunate to live at the Home.

Considering Mr. Johnson's request, I also felt that I wanted to contribute back to the Children's Home – it had provided for me and gave me a good life for nine years and a good upbringing. I needed and wanted to give something back. Also, Mr. Johnson had supported me during the four years I was in college/university and now he was asking my help and support and I needed and wanted to repay the kindness and support he had given me.

I accepted his request and became a staff member of the Children's Home in August, 1967 as the house father for the older boys. I worked at the Home from August, 1967 until December, 1968 – when all the kids went off for Christmas vacation.

I felt that my 16 months working at the Home made a difference. Within about three months, I felt that I had created a relationship with the teenage boys and that they respected me as their house father. I brought order and discipline into the cottage while at the same time – allowed as much self-determinism and freedom to the boys as I could without sacrificing discipline, order and good conduct.

There were 16 boys under my charge those 16 months. I have tried to recall all 16 of them but have only been able to come up with 14. If anyone of you reading my memoirs know who the missing ones are, I would be pleased if you would contact me with the missing names. Also, if any of you in my listing were at the Home at the time but not actually in the older boys' cottage, you can also let me know. In my mind, I can still see the cottage and the layout of the rooms and where each boy was and who roommates were.

Here are the boys who – to the best of my recall - were under my charge at that time: Marshall Glenn Heath ('53-'68); Jeff Thomas ('60-'70); Terry Thomas ('60-'71); Andrew Hartsfield ('59-'69); Phil Mercer ('53-'68); Claudius Elmore ('60-'73); Sidney Suggs ('58-'70); Jimmy Merritt ('65-'72); Ted Worthington ('56-'69); Ray Harris ('57-'69); Johnny High ('57-'69);

Edward Connor ('73-'71); Mickey Newton ('59'71); Terry Edwards ('65-'73).

They were all special to me and I hope that life has been good for all of them. I know that two members of that group are no longer with us: Andrew Hartsfield died in a crash of his private cub airplane many years ago at a very young age. Terry Edwards passed away – also at a young age - with incurable cancer.

I joined the Marine Corps in the fall of 1968. Our country was at war. I felt that we were obligated to defend South Vietnam. The United States had made a treaty with South Vietnam and other countries in Asia – the treaty was called SEATO. As a nation, we pledged and obligated ourselves to come to the defense of our treaty partners if they were attacked or aggressed upon. I did not wait to be drafted – I voluntarily enlisted. I served in the U.S. Marine Corps as an officer and a platoon commander – as a Lieutenant and later a Captain from January, 1969 – December, 1971.

One of the dreams I had while at the orphanage was to visit Disneyland in California. I visited Disneyland three times while a Marine at Camp Pendleton, CA in 1971. I have also visited Disney World in Florida four times. Disney World did not exist when I was at the Children's Home. My last trip to Disney World was over New Year's week – 2009. I find that at 64 years old, I am still a kid who likes to play.

I married in 1983 and have two daughters. The oldest daughter, Stephanie 22, just graduated from Virginia Tech; the youngest daughter, Virginia 20, is in her sophomore year in college.

You all know how it is with us orphans – particularly those of us who lived and grew up at the F.W.B. Children's Home in Middlesex, North Carolina - we can manage and do anything. The years we lived there, what we were taught, what we experienced and what we learned gave us the ability to do things and make things happen. We grew out of being victims of the circumstances that put us in an orphanage to being masters of our fates. We took the help, the support, the sustenance and the strengths that the Orphanage/Children's Home life and experience gave us and went on to survive and build our lives and the lives of our own families. The experience of being an orphan and of growing up in an orphanage has its own special advantages. We learned things that kids growing up in a more or less "normal" home never learn or experience. Those years of sometimes loneliness, sometimes sadness, sometimes wishing we had a normal family with both parents – the loss was compensated with a strength that other kids in normal families do not often get.

Overall, while life may have dealt us a bad hand at making us orphans, it also blessed us with the experience of the F.W.B. Orphanage/Children's Home.

My love and my best regards to all of the children who have lived at the F.W.B. Orphanage/Children's Home in Middlesex, North Carolina from its establishment 90 years ago to the present. I would also like to acknowledge the staff that worked there and thank them for dedicating a portion of their lives to the service of helping "orphans".

19

Doris Ann, Willie and I

Tommy Lancaster
1955-65

Here I am, fifty-five years later, on the deck of the Carnival Fascination ship, somewhere between Jacksonville, Florida and the Bahamas. I am still pondering over our lives; where we were, where we have been and the life we lead because of the hand that was dealt us in life.

The years prior to 1955 hold very vague memories of the life we were living; however, I do remember my brother Willie and I and some of what we experienced. We came from the small town of Vanceboro in Eastern North Carolina. My sister, Doris Ann, Willie and I were three of six children, three of which were much older and did not experience what we did.

I never realized until later years how poor the circumstances were in which we were born. We lived in a four room house consisting of a kitchen, living room and two bedrooms. We had no inside plumbing (pitcher pump on back porch), we stayed warm by a wood stove and heater and there was one light bulb in the center of each room. Plain as it was, it was home; as far as we knew, we were comfortable.

As poor as we were, I can still remember things we did as a family to help us survive from season to season. We would net herring (a fish) when they were spawning or migrating inland, pack them in salt and brine water in barrels to eat during winter months. We would salt and smoke pork (hams, sausage, fat back and side meat) to have throughout the year, along with as much canned vegetables as time and expense would allow. We grew tobacco and corn for the money needed to clear our debts of charged goods from stores in the small town of Vanceboro. My daddy had a "stick mill" for cutting tobacco sticks and sell to other farmers to help support our needs.

The year my mother died, Doris Ann, age 8, stayed with my older sister Mary Alice until she was placed in the Free Will Baptist Orphanage (as it was known at that time) on Tuesday, August 30, 1955. Willie and I stayed at home.

As young as we were, I really did not experience the feelings of separation from Doris Ann that normally would accompany such trauma. I knew there were changes being made, but the realization of all those changes would come to Willie and me at a later date. Being poor and mischievous (as children are), the things I remember about us for the next few months seem to have been normal for the time and circumstances.

I can remember us having a pet goat that crashed through the screen door of our house while chasing us. While the goat was in the house, he decided to relieve himself at a time our dad was coming home. Without too much thought, we grabbed his hat, cleaned up the mess and dumped it in the yard.

L-R: Tommy and Willie Lancaster

Willie and I made do and played with things that could only have been fun in the 50's. Willie pushed a set of transplanter wheels, while I scooted around on a tricycle (too small to ride) with a car antenna fastened to it. I know if anyone came by they would have heard us making the motor noise with our mouths. We were always busy, grown up passed the four to six years we actually were and very happy as far as we knew.

Life as we had known was about to make some drastic changes. One Saturday night, the Swift Creek was flooding and out of its banks, the creek waters were rushing at a dangerous pace. The local police picked us up, as a precaution for our safety, took us to a county facility and housed us for a couple of days.

Unbeknownst to us, our mother had made our sister promise she would try and have us placed in a home somewhere together. We were picked up by Superintendent R. H. Jackson of the Free Will Baptist Orphanage on Tuesday, November 22, 1955 and carried away from our home. The feelings I thought I was too young to experience hit me and stayed with me until this day.

When processing us in was complete, Willie, age 6 and I, age 7, were separated because of age differences and for the first time in my life I was totally alone. Not knowing where we were, I knew we were a long way from the life and places (as poor as were) that I had known all my life. I can remember sitting on the porch of the Albemarle Cottage and staring up the road, past what I later called the flower garden. The lump in my throat was so large I could not speak, tears at a point of flowing. I sat and waited for someone to come get me and carry me back to the life I had always known.

I heard this loud ringing noise and could see all the boys start to converge and gather where I was. This was frightening to me, but then I saw Willie being lead out to where I was. I started to cry but tried hard not to show it. We were together again and for a brief moment everything seemed to be all right again. The second bell rang out and we all began to walk toward the building located in the center of campus. We all lined up and were directed to go in to what was to be the dining hall. We all took our places and I began to look around. I saw my sister Doris Ann, our eyes met and I was elated. I still could not get to her because of the darn rules that were related to group living (institutional, as it may have been called then). Although we were not physically together, we were all in one place and I did start to feel a little relief.

In the months to follow, the hurt seemed to vanish and we began to enjoy the company of the many boys and girls that had come to the orphanage. A lot of the children there had experienced some of the same things we had. As time passed, we began to make friends and enjoy the company of local people, going to school and playing competition sports. Little did I know at the time, a lot of us boys and girls would become brothers and sisters and share a bond that could not be broken.

All through the years that Doris, Willie and I lived at the home, we never stayed in the same close quarters as a family. However, I could always count on the presence of all when that bell rang. We could look across the room at one another, smile and know that we were safely together.

Doris Ann graduated and went to school in Raleigh; worked her profession for a while and then was married. She worked as a mom and housewife as long as she needed to and then went into business for herself. Over the years, if she needed anything, she would call and I would respond as soon as I could. If I needed anything, the same came my way. What you would expect from family.

Willie graduated and went (as it was known at that time) to work in utility construction and did well for himself, wife Paula and two sons. A few years passed, Willie experienced some health problems and was forced into an early retirement. He and Paula had made some good decisions and have done all right. Paula has since gone back to school and earned her Master's Degree in Education and with the Lord's help, they are doing quite well.

When I left the Children's Home, I enlisted in the army for four years. I pulled my time and I returned home in 1970. I began to look for work and found it in electrical construction. Willie bought me my first set of tools (I've tried to repay him ever since when I can). I worked in construction and maintenance for the next 24 years. I went in business for myself in 1994 and have been blessed. I have been married two times; have four children and five grand children.

In 1996, Doris Ann was taken from us all too soon. She was always proud of having been at the Children's Home and worked diligently for the Home and Alumni Association. The shock of losing Doris from a car wreck took me back to the porch of the Albemarle Cottage in 1955, the same feelings rushed in and I knew I would never see her smile again here on earth. The thoughts of her gone, visiting her grave in Smithfield, make me so sad. Even at that, my visits make me feel a bit closer to her. Knowing that one day that Bell will ring again, I'll look up and see her again. Everything will be okay.

She often spoke of "Duck Smith ('49-'60) and Ray Worthington ('56-'63)" to me. These two were special to her.

The Children's Home furnished us a stable place to grow up in; we all have some stories to tell, some good, some not so good. For the most part, we all can be grateful to the Children's Home for the opportunities offered us and for being able to grow up in a Christian-based atmosphere. High morals were instilled in us and we received a good education through example and hard work.

My thoughts and memories of the home have diminished over the years, but I can always rest assured that each year I will get a refresher at the homecoming. Every year I learn more about my orphan brothers and sisters that I never knew. I learn things that happened at the home that I hear for the first time.

I look forward every July to the Homecoming. I still like to walk by and pull that old rope on the bell and hear it ring one more time. I pause to remember all of my inherited family that are still here and those that have gone on ahead of us, knowing they are keeping things in order until we will all get back together.

This is life, no matter where you grow up. I look at everyone as they return and know that there had to be good coming from the home. Nothing says it better than looking and knowing that most have lived a good and prosperous life, none of which would have been possible without the opportunities afforded us through the Children's Home.

20

My Memories of Childhood

Yvonne Rouse
1955-69

I was born in a house at Wooten Crossroads, which is located near Walstonburg, N. C. It was called this because five roads met in the middle. My Pa ran a country store there. I remember living in a house attached to the store. My brothers tell me I was born in a different house and later the family moved to the house I remember. At the store I remember having lots of men living nearby gather around the pot-bellied stove and talk for hours.

    On weekends we would have a community cookout at the store. I remember a lot of fish stews. My oldest brother Daniel said they would alternate weekends between barbecuing a hog and cooking a fish stew. My parents were older parents; Pa was 70 when I was born and Mama was 43. As a very young child, I remember always being around my Pa at the store and that his health wasn't the best. My Mama, brothers and I would attend a church down from the store on Sundays. It was Free Union Free Will Baptist Church, which would later get involved with us going to the Home.

When I was four, I remember Hurricane Hazel (October, 1954) coming through Wooten Crossroads and knocking down part of our store roof. My Pa was asleep in the store at the time. I was watching him sleep while sitting in a window that passed from the house into the store. My brothers and I always used this window as a passageway.

My Pa passed away (January 15, 1955), three months after the hurricane. He was 74. After Pa's death, somehow the FWB Church near the store and relatives got involved with the Welfare Department (called Social Services today) who made us wards of the state, saying my Mama wasn't able to take care of three small children and my teenager sister alone.

I remember being taken out of my Mama's arms, when I was four, kicking and screaming, and put into Mrs. Thelma Rulli's (Alumnus '23-'30) arms. I watched them drive my Mama away, and then I remember being surrounded by a circle of little girls, as I sat crying in Mrs. Rulli's lap. I was the third youngest girl at the Home. Margaret Ann (Last name?) and Bobbie Jean Langston ('55-'69) were younger than me. I think all three of us were four years old. My brothers Daniel, age nine, and Steve, age seven, were in a separate dorm from me and I got to see them mostly at meals in the dining hall. Everyone ate in the dining hall for all three meals. We ate at very long tables. When I got older we changed from the long tables to tables that seated six. We came to the meals at the ringing of a bell.

L-R: Steve, Yvonne and Daniel Rouse

"That Infinite Bell" was our signal for everything: eating (once to make us ready and another 30 minutes later for us to come to the dining hall to eat); for Church on Sundays; or for anything when we needed to meet together, like on Wednesday nights (prayer meeting). I wonder how many of us (orphans) have a bell in our homes now. I know I have a small one on my porch, and I know Billy Hines ('54-'62) has one in his front yard. How many others? I don't use mine, but that "bell" will live in my memory forever.

A lot of the boys at the Home were given nicknames, like Ears, Yogie, Doc, Scram, Duck, Owl, Higgie, and Turkey. I'm sure there were others but my brothers couldn't remember any more. Must be a boy thing, huh? My brothers Steve and Daniel were given nicknames as well. Steve was given the nickname "Soapy". According to Steve, Barry Rogers ('48-'61) gave him that name. I tell everyone it was because my brothers and I had a vocabulary that was "very colorful" (something we no doubt picked up hanging around the pot-bellied stove at Pa's store). Ha! During that time, we were often threatened to get our mouths washed out with soap for using such language (hence, the name "Soapy"). This explanation sounds good to me and anyone who knows Steve. Ha!

My brother Daniel said he thought Barry Rogers also gave him the nickname "Moose". It started out as Mussolini after the boys saw a movie about the Italian Dictator and said Daniel looked like him. I never knew this until recently, so I went on the internet and looked at pictures of Mussolini and I didn't see the resemblance. The name was later shortened to "Moose".

I like my version better. I thought my brother was called "Moose" because he was so quiet and shy, slow to anger; but when riled, watch out (like the animal). "Moose" has been shortened again by Steve's grandchildren as "Uncle Boo". Makes you wonder (girls) if those boys gave us nicknames we don't know about. Ha!

Mrs. Sudie Mixon was our kitchen matron. She planned our meals and assigned us our kitchen duties and dining hall tables. She would make each child a cake on their birthday just for them.

We were assigned jobs by the Superintendent for three months. The girls' jobs were: kitchen (cooking and washing pots and dishes), dining hall (waiting tables and cleaning tables, sweeping and mopping), laundry (ironing and folding lots and lots of clothes, sheets and towels), and cleaning the little girls' and big girls' dorms. I enjoyed the dining hall and hated the laundry. I don't iron very much today. Thank God for permanent press fabric! Ha!

The boys' jobs were the farm, grounds, and animals. One boy was assigned kitchen duty to do the heavy lifting and the laundry to run the huge washers and dryers. I remember my first job at six was taking out trash and washing out the trash cans in my dorm. Mrs. Barbour (in 1957) replaced Mrs. Rulli as my matron when I was around seven or eight. Mrs. Rulli went to the big girls' dorm. I didn't like Mrs. Barbour as well as I did Mrs. Rulli. The bright side of this was I would eventually move over to the big girls' dorm at around 13, and be back with Mrs. Rulli.

All the children went to the public school in Middlesex (for grades 1-12). I went there until my 11th grade, and then all the small surrounding schools in the area consolidated into one Senior High school. I left the home just before my 12th grade year. The home had its own school bus and one of the older kids drove it. My last school bus driver was Phil Mercer ('53-'68). The bus would make two trips to the school - the boys first, then the girls.

I remember during the summer some of the kids would go out on a concert program. We would go to other FWB Churches around N.C. and do plays and sing. I started in this program around six. Miss Bonnie Farmer was in charge of this program.

I remember my Mama coming to visit my brothers and me on Sundays. Sometimes, she would come on Saturday and spend the night in the boys' dorm. We were able to go home with her at Christmas, Easter, summer vacation, and Thanksgiving.

Our summer vacations were three weeks long. It started in July at homecoming. I remember the long tables (made of chicken wire) being set up in the middle of campus and people from other FWB churches and parents would come and bring food. Then, we could go home with Mama.

When we returned, the tobacco and garden would be ready to harvest. It seemed like long periods of shelling peas and beans, shucking corn, killing chickens and tying tobacco, along with our other duties.

'50's Pea Shelling at girl's dormitory.

I remember the boys would bring watermelons from the garden and leave them under the tree in the middle of the campus. Mrs. Barbour or Mrs. Rulli would have us go get some and put them in the cooler to eat later.

However, we always had Sunday off (except for cooking and dining hall duties). Sometimes on Sundays, we visited other FWB Churches (for their homecomings), loading up the Home's activity bus and a few cars for the trip. My Mama and relatives would occasionally show up at these churches at the same time we attended. These trips started in the summer and went through fall.

In December, during our Christmas vacation, we would go home with Mama. A few weekends before leaving, we would have parties. Churches and Woodmen of the World would come and we would meet at the dining hall, sing carols, and receive gifts. I'll always remember the net stocking filled with candy and fruits and a paddle ball from the Woodmen Club. I would also receive one present from my Woman's Auxiliary (the FWB Church club who sponsored me).

We always had an Easter egg hunt down where the old pool used to be, behind the old pump house/maintenance building. I don't remember who came to put on the hunt. Maybe it was the Woodmen of the World or a Free Will Baptist Church. We children would be told to stay inside our buildings while they hid the eggs. The eggs were not the hard plastic kind that is hid today; they were the real Easter eggs (the hard candy outside with soft centers) wrapped in cellophane. One year (can't remember how old I was) some men (three or four) parachuted down to the area where the egg hunt was. They were a surprise from the people who gave the egg hunt. We were in awe and keep running to where we thought each person would land. We always went away for Easter vacation and the egg hunt usually occurred the week-end before Easter.

As a little girl, I enjoyed watching the big girls dress up for their proms. They would come out of their dorm in their evening dress and we would do our "ohs" and "ahs." When I got older, I dressed up too. We were allowed to go to the high school basketball games and the sock-hop after the games when we were in high school.

I remember playing hide and seek in the corn field behind our dorm and swinging on the big swing set in the middle of campus. Sue Heath ('53-'67) was my hero, she could bob and go completely over the top (complete circle). I later did it myself. We would test ourselves to see how high we could jump out of the swing while still in motion. "We had no fear". Ha! We girls played softball in the middle of campus. Two of the trees (still there) were our first and third bases. Third base was a pecan tree.

In 1967 I remember going to the World's Fair in Montreal, Canada. An anonymous donor left the Home a lot of money and said it was to be spent on something the children would enjoy (not material things). Superintendent M. L. Johnson ('62-'69) chose this event. We (boys and girls) and two or three matrons loaded onto a Trailway Bus and toured the upward states on our way to Canada. We went to a Mint, Niagara Falls, Ontario, Montreal, and New York City. We were in "AWE" of everything.

These are some of my memories and I'm sure I could think up a lot more. Anyone (especially the "Orphans") who reads Jerry's ('49-'60) book, come back to the Home at homecoming and share your memories. Even if you weren't there, but lived around us or attended school with us "orphans" (children), come share.

I was at the Home from June 14, 1955 until June 5, 1969. I was the 446 child; my brothers must have been 447, and 448.

In closing, I hope you enjoy reading about my memories and I think it's great that someone is finally writing our memories down. A book like this, with lots of the "children" remembering something different or alike, shows others how we lived as children, what we learned and who it makes us today. It also shows how the Home has affected our lives now and maybe in our future. I pray and hope that these memories in this book will become a sequel for other people's memories to be written.

21

A Peace Has Replaced the Wrinkles

Ray Worthington
1956-63

My father was a farmer and my mother stayed at home to care for my older brother John, my sister Ann, younger brother Ted and me. We were content and I thought we had it all. Our grandmother Lillie ("Nannie") lived with us after our grandfather's death. She was the greatest person who ever lived. She was a saint on earth. Mother was beautiful, calm and enjoyed being at home with us. When daddy was not farming, he played in a band and sung. He played baseball and could write some very good poetry. He named my youngest brother after baseball great Ted Williams. Dad would use his belt to discipline us.

In 1951, my father was infected with tuberculosis and shortly afterwards our mother was diagnosed with breast cancer. My father and mother realized the seriousness of our family situation and they decided if both died, we children would be placed in the orphanage. Mom died in December 1952 and dad passed in November 1953. Nannie took care of us children and our parents during their sickness until their deaths.

We attended Friendship Free Will Baptist Church near Walstonburg, North Carolina, located a few miles from our home. Prior to his death, our father contacted Reverend Robert Lee Norville about helping to get us into the orphanage. Until our placement in the orphanage, Nannie looked after us. Ann, age 10, was admitted to the orphanage Saturday, December 31, 1955. Ted and I were admitted in 1956. Our brother John was too old to be admitted and stayed with Nannie until he graduated from high school.

On Monday, June 18, 1956, Ted, age 4, and I, age 12 were admitted to the orphanage. Pastor Norville and Nannie were in the car that day. When we arrived our matron, Mary Mitchell, told Jesse Hines ('54-'65) to take us to swing in the flower garden across from the chapel. After we were there for a while, Nannie and Reverend Norville had to go. I remember seeing their car leaving as it went past us in the flower garden. I felt uneasy and anxious seeing them leave. Ted was all right until we got back to the cottage and Nannie was gone. He had to sleep with me for a while. My first night was full of apprehension and confusion and Ted peeing on my leg. He peed on my leg many nights. He would not let go of my leg during the days (that meant I didn't have to get on the farm truck for work).

Prior to my going to the orphanage, our family history had been about God and we were a church family. All my relatives were Bible-first people. When I went to the orphanage, I thought they laid a good foundation, not without errors, for a child to grow to form a good perception of God and man.

Our holidays at the orphanage were always a little exciting. At Thanksgiving everyone always seemed happier. At Christmas we got small gifts from churches before going home for the holidays. I really never expected much for Christmas and always enjoyed songs around the season, especially listening to Brenda Lee sing "Rocking Around the Christmas Tree." I was just contented with just a basketball and a dollar.

The dinner bell on campus was always a part of our life. I always felt it meant order and dependability. It reminded me to be thankful for food to eat. When I rung the bell, I always felt a little power surge. The best individual dinner bell ringing was on my birthday, May 30, of every year. That's when Mrs. Sudie Mixon made me a birthday cake and I shared it with everyone at my table. There was a work ethic taught at the orphanage; it instilled in us to do our part. We were responsible for our work area and living area. Our matron used to say, "It's hard, but it's fair." This ethic has carried me through life. Just like at the orphanage, work has been hard, but doing it has been easy for me. The orphanage prepared me.

The orphanage taught respect for other people. The steps were put in place for you to learn to give a little and stand up at the same time. You were given your space and expected to respect another's space. I learned a lot about teamwork and working for the same goal. I believe each of us has an instilled personality (laid back, quickly to anger, quiet, loud, etc.), and the orphanage helped where help was needed to teach us to act appropriately to the situation.

In the summer of '61, Foy Watson ('51-'63) and I were filling sacks with corn that had been stored in the old rock house just past the pond. We both had been in some sort of trouble and just like teenagers felt that we had been wrongly punished. We began to talk about how great it would be to be able to leave the Orphanage. Somewhere during the conversation, we began to talk about running away, but where would we go? I told Foy my brother John lived in Kinston and we could stay with him. So, our plan was to pack our suitcases sometime during the next day and to leave after everyone was asleep that night.

About eleven o'clock we slipped out the back door and ran across the baseball field into the woods so no one would see us. We were lucky that a full moon gave us enough light to see. We exited the woods just past the pond and were on our way down the dirt road that came out to the highway on the back side of the Orphanage. After walking on the highway about 15 minutes, a car with three teenage boys stopped and picked us up. I don't remember what reason we gave them for being on that highway late at night with two suitcases. They took us to Bailey and dropped us off at a school in town. We found an activity bus that was open so we spent the rest of the night sleeping on the seats. The next morning we walked a few blocks to a service station that was on the road to Wilson. We had several dollars between us so we each bought a drink and a candy bar. At this point, our plan was to hitch-hike to Wilson and then to Kinston. After a short time, we were picked up and dropped off in Wilson near Leroy Miller's ('52-'60) home. He had left the Orphanage the previous year.

After a short time visiting with Leroy and telling him we had run away, we caught a ride on Hwy #301 to the Kinston highway. We were excited that we were making good time. We were let out by a four lane highway with lots of traffic so we knew we had a good chance to get a ride. Sure enough, we had been thumbing about five minutes and a car pulls over just ahead of us. We started running toward the car and, lo and behold, it was Horace and Sudie Mixon, farm manager and dietician at the Orphanage. They were taking a weekend off and just happened to come by at the wrong time for us. To our surprise, both Horace and Sudie were so nice to us. They told us that Mrs. Everton (wife of Superintendent J. W. Everton ['58-'62]) was in town shopping with some of the children and we could catch a ride with her back to the Orphanage. We agreed that was the right thing to do. They dropped us off near Leder Brothers Department Store and we caught a ride with her and the other children back to the Orphanage. We did get into trouble; I think we were grounded for a month.

My early experience could have made me bitter, but I chose to make the best of the situation. Playing sports, especially basketball, helped me forget the past and find fulfillment. Some of the early influences of my interest in sports were from Jake Lane ('46-'59), Duck Smith ('49-'60) and Charles Mixon, son of Mrs. Sudie. Watching them play sports motivated my interest in playing. Of these three, probably Duck Smith had the most influence with his playing basketball and baseball at Middlesex.

Ray Worthington

In high school, Coach Drake gave me the opportunity to achieve in basketball. In the 1962/63 basketball season at Middlesex High School, I set the highest single-year school scoring record with 529 points. My scoring average was 20.2 points per game and shooting accuracy was 42 percent of field goals attempted. On Friday, January 4, 1963, I scored 43 points against Wendell High School and didn't play the last four minutes. That record still stands at Middlesex High School.

In 1965, Bruce Creedmoore, a local DJ, was looking contestants for the Jaycees' sponsored Miss Zebulon Beauty Pageant. A Children's Home employee's daughter showed Bruce a picture of my sister Ann, then a senior in high school. Bruce contacted the Zebulon Jaycees and Ann received an invitational letter to be a contestant and attend a meet-the-contestant party sponsored by Pepsi Cola Bottling Company. Ann was excited and interested in participating in the pageant.

While home in Farmville to visit with Nannie, Ann told our grandmother about the invitation and Nannie was happy for her. Ann and Nannie contacted Pat Hester ('54-'63), an alumnus Ann befriended when Pat was in the home. Pat was so kind and excited for Ann and later drove her to Zebulon for the Jaycees' sponsored meet- the-contestant party. They met the other six girls participating in the pageant. The Jaycees talked to the girls, learned each girl's talent and helped all the girls to get to know one another.

A week later at Zebulon High School auditorium all the girls met to learn the basics of how to walk and self presentation. Ann was very nervous, wanting to do well. Her talent was to sing "Moon River". She had an opportunity to sing with a small band and they were able to give her tips on how to relax. She learned how to answer the judges' questions and proper walk in a gown and bathing suit. Ann did not relish wearing a bathing suit for the pageant.

Back at the Children's Home, Ann received support from other girls, boys and staff. Her strongest support and inspiration came from Sandra Mercer ('53-'65), a seventeen-year old high school junior on campus. Sandra was very sick, but despite her illness, she was eager and so happy for Ann having the opportunity to compete in the pageant. Sandra seemed inspired to fight her own illness from Ann participating as a child from the Children's Home.

Sandra's support and illness was motivational for Ann. She knew Sandra was seriously sick and was competing with her sickness to live. It put the pageant in perspective for Ann, knowing that it was minute compared with Sandra's battle with her diseased kidneys. Ann became more relaxed and strong.

On Saturday, April 27, 1965, the Zebulon Pageant was held. Our brother John and his wife Gracie and Nannie attended. Nannie questioned Ann on how she was going to feel if she did not win. Ann told her grandmother winning was the last thought she had. She just enjoyed the whole experience and that was what mattered.

Back stage before the pageant the girls were busy preparing and were assisted by their mothers. Ann had her matron Mrs. Rulli (alumnus '23-'30) with her. Mrs. Rulli told Ann she felt like she should be doing more. Ann thanked her and told Mrs. Rulli her presence was enough. Ann told Mrs. Rulli she had dressed herself all her life and could do it then.

Ann sang "Moon River" and felt very good about her performance. It was a happy experience and she was better for it. Her night was capped off winning the "Miss Congeniality" trophy. Brother John almost squeezed her into celebrating and Nannie…well; all she had to do was look at Ann to show her how proud she was. Everyone on the Children's Home campus was pleased with Ann winning the trophy. Sandra Mercer glowed with pride when she learned of Ann's performance and winning "Miss Congeniality".

Ann graduated from high school in May. In June, Sandra passed away on Tuesday, June 15, 1965. Ann, along with many alumni, returned to attend Sandra's funeral at Memorial Chapel.

At our homecoming held each year in July, I see the faces that I've known since 1955. They've aged but a peace has replaced the wrinkles. I'm so impressed and happy with them all. We've become even closer in later years and it's been good for all of us. We have so much of our "orphan" family for which to be thankful.

22

I Will Be Eternally Grateful

Cathy Hines
1957-66

Cathy Hines

I guess you could say that my journey to the Children's Home began in June of 1948 when I was born. I was the youngest of nine children born to Bertha and Frank Hines, who were tenant farmers in Edgecombe County. In June of 1952 when I was four, my mother was diagnosed with tuberculosis and was admitted to the TB Sanatorium in Wilson, and then in December of 1952 my father was also diagnosed with TB and admitted to the sanatorium. By this time, my oldest brother Marion was married and living close by, my next to the oldest brother Keith was in the army and serving in Korea and my oldest sister Lois had left home and was married. My older sister Flora and I went to live with my Aunt Betty and Uncle Herbert in Beaufort County. They were childless and were happy to take us in and provide a loving home for us. My four other siblings went to stay with my oldest brother Marion and his wife, but it was obvious to them that their sister-in-law did not want them there. My brother Billy left and went to live with a former neighbor and friend, Willis Phillips. On August 24, 1954, my two youngest brothers, Billy age 12 and Jesse age 8, went to live at the Children's Home. They were the 441st and 442nd child admitted to the care of the home.

My parents were discharged from the sanatorium in 1955, but were disabled and unable to care for their children, although my sister Flora returned home to live with them at that time. My mother was pleased with the care that Billy and Jesse were receiving at the Children's Home and wanted Flora and me to grow up with our brothers, so she requested that we also be admitted. I did not want to leave my aunt and uncle because I was happy there and it was quite a traumatic and emotional experience for me to have to leave them when I did not understand why. My aunt and uncle were also very distraught about losing me. My older sister Flora, age 12 and I were admitted to the home on January 9, 1957, when I was 8, as the 456th and 457th child. I adjusted quickly to life at the home even though I went from being an only child with my own room to sharing a room with five other little girls. At the time of my admission, Mrs. Thelma Rulli (alumnus '23-'30) was the housemother for the little girls and there were twenty-four girls living in the dorm. The Reverend Stephen Smith was the Superintendent ('51-'55 & '56-'58) of the home and I remember him as being very kind and fatherly. He and Mrs. Smith were better known to the children as "Pa and Ma Smith". I was in the third grade at the time of my admission and we attended public school at Middlesex. Mrs. Wolfe was my third grade teacher and there were five other children from the home in my class. The school bus from the home had to make two trips to take the children to school. The boys went on the first trip and then the bus returned for the girls. I enjoyed school and learning and have very vivid memories of all of my teachers and the impact they had on my life.

My first summer at the home, I was chosen to go out on concert class. The concert classes traveled all over the state to the Free Will Baptist Churches presenting a program of music and a short play or skit to help raise money for the home. It was very exciting, traveling and seeing new places and becoming familiar with the churches and people of the Free Will Baptist Denomination who supported the home. These summer adventures included my first trips to the beach and to the mountains. The children in the concert classes who I traveled with changed from year to year as well as the as the staff person who traveled with us. I traveled with the group until I was fourteen. Some of the staff I remember traveling with were Miss Bonnie Farmer, Miss Peggy Mixon and Mrs. J. R. Bennett. Not only did the churches give monetary support throughout the year to help pay for the on-going expense of running the home, but also each child had a church or women's auxiliary that supported them.

My sponsor was the Ladies Auxiliary of Kenly Free Will Baptist Church. During the nine and half years that I was at the home, I came to know and felt very close to many members of this church. I would often spend weekends and holidays with Mr. and Mrs. Richard Oliver and their children. The Olivers were a very loving family and always made me feel welcomed and loved. I have some very fond memories of the time I spent in their home and have remained in contact with them. I also remember how supportive the Olivers were in that they attended many of the important events in my life, such as piano recitals, high school and college graduations. I also spent time with Mr. & Mrs. J. T. Raines and their family. The women of the Kenly church not only provided money for my clothes when we had our annual spring and fall shopping trips, but also remembered me on my birthday and at Christmas with gifts. The summer I turned fifteen they paid for me to attend a week at Cragmont with the youth from their church.

Life at the home was very regimented by the necessity to keep everything running smoothly. Every child who was old enough was assigned chores to do. I remember when I was in the little girls' building, I had to make up my bed and help keep the bathrooms clean. When I was older, around age 12, I was assigned to work in the dining hall waiting on tables and cleaning up after meals. Then, when I moved to the big girls' building when I was 14, I was given more responsibility. Jobs were assigned on a three month basis and they were kitchen, laundry or cleaning the two girls' dorms. The kitchen and dining room were located in a separate building which also housed the offices for the superintendent until a separate office building was built in the 1960's. When I was assigned kitchen duty, I had to get up at 5:30 am, prepare breakfast, wash dishes for approximately 80 children and staff and scrub the kitchen floors. Having kitchen duty was where we learned to cook and make biscuits under the patient guidance of Mrs. Sudie Mixon. Only as a wife and mother could I appreciate the enormous responsibility that Mrs. Mixon had in planning meals, buying food etc. for 80 children and staff. Years later, at one of the alumni homecomings, Mrs. Mixon asked me what I thought about the meals we had at the home. I responded that we may not have always liked and appreciated the food we had but it was always good. Over all, kitchen duty was not so bad in the summer but rather tough duty during the school year.

The job I disliked the most was having laundry duty during the summer time because it required standing on a hard cement floor and ironing all day. The laundry building we used was built around 1957. One of the boys was assigned laundry duty and his job was to run the commercial size washers and dryers while the girls did all of the ironing. We tried to make laundry duty fun by listening and singing along with the radio tuned to WKIX in Raleigh. Also, another girl and I came up with the idea of sharing our ironing duties. We decided that if I ironed the collar and sleeves and she ironed the body of the shirt, we could finish our wash tub of shirts quicker. I must admit I hate ironing to this day. During the summer, not only did we have our assigned chores to do, but we also had a huge garden that had to be picked which the boys did. Then, they would bring us truck loads of corn, peas and beans. After we finished shucking the corn and shelling the peas and beans, then we would have to blanch and freeze the vegetables, so it was an all day process. The most difficult job that I had to do while I was at the home was clean chickens. As I recall, this happened about twice a year and we usually had to miss a day of school. I only remember having had to do this twice; however, this job would make me so sick that I could not eat chicken for several months afterwards. Not only did the Children's Home raise a big garden and chickens, we also had turkeys, pigs and cows which the boys took care of. We also had a tobacco crop. I never worked in green tobacco while I was at the home but did help with tying dry tobacco in the fall after school.

The boys were also assigned jobs for a three month period. My older brother Billy ('54-'62) told me a story about his job assignment of looking after the turkeys. He stated that the boys who were assigned yard duties also had to water and feed the turkeys. The turkey pens were located behind the boys' dorm and they had to carry water from the basement of the boys' dorm to the turkey pen because they did not have a water pump at the pen, although later on they installed one. Billy stated that sometimes the turkeys would get out of the pen and roam around the campus. It was his job to follow the turkeys and find out where they were laying their eggs and nesting because eventually the eggs would be removed from the nests and placed in an incubator for hatching. He said the turkeys were very smart and, if they sensed that they were being followed, they would not go directly to their nests but instead lead him on a "wild turkey chase". So, he would have to be very discreet and hide behind trees, shrubs, buildings etc. so the turkeys would not know they were being followed. One of their favorite nesting places was behind the old superintendent's home where there was lots of kudzu. Billy earned the nickname of "Turkey" due to his persistent pursuit of the turkeys.

Life at the Children's Home was not all work and no play. There was time for fun and with so many children together in one place we certainly had some advantages that others didn't. For example, if we wanted to play softball or basketball we had enough for two teams. Some of my fondest memories of growing up at the home were having friends to play with. As a little girl we played house and with our dolls, we learned to hula hoop, ride a bike (although I never had my own bike) and roller skate. We had the perfect place to skate; we had a cemented breezeway between the two girls' dorms that made a nice smooth skating rink. I also remember making mud pies one time, and then getting into a mud pie fight. Needless to say, our housemother was not too happy with us and that was the same day the Pepsi man brought us some paddle balls. I am sure the housemother wanted to use the paddles on us for tracking all that red clay into the dorm but she didn't. Instead, she told us that if we did it again, we would be punished and asked if we knew what our punishment would be; one little girl spoke up and said that we would probably go to hell. I think the housemother smiled at this and assured us that our punishment would not be that harsh. Also, I remember learning to love to read. Some of the first books I remember reading were the Nancy Drew mystery series. I looked forward to the local bookmobile bringing us books in the summer and later when I was senior in high school and working in the superintendent's office being able to choose the books. Reading is still a passion of mine.

When I was in high school, the Children's Home had a pool installed. I don't recall if any of us knew how to swim but we learned. It was wonderful being able to play in the pool in the summer after working all morning or all day. In high school we were able to participate in activities at school. Many of the children played sports, I didn't, but was a cheerleader so I was able to go to all of the basketball games. We all rode on the bus from the home or the activity bus from school so it gave us an opportunity to socialize. Because Middlesex was a small high school, the only sports that it offered were basketball and baseball. Also in the fall, the local chapter of the American

Legion would treat all of us to an afternoon at the Wilson County Fair and a meal at Parker's Barbecue afterwards.

I also remember dating. I dated boys from the home and from school. The home's policy regarding dating was that boys and girls could not date until they were fifteen and at that age they were not allowed to leave campus and had to date in the living room. So, I guess we had what would be called group dating since most of the time there were at least four couples in the living room at the same time. We didn't have a television in the living room to entertain us and I don't recall us playing any board or card games, so we must have done a lot of talking. When we reached our sixteenth birthday, we were allowed to double date. We could not leave campus until 7 pm and our curfew was 11 pm. Some of our favorite places to go were the Starlight drive in theater in Wilson and the Creamery for ice cream and milk shakes. When we became seniors in high school, we were allowed to go on single dates. One of my most memorable dates was when I got permission to go with my boyfriend to see the "Sound Of Music" movie in Raleigh. I thought that was the most wonderful movie I had ever seen and it is still one of my favorites. I also remember going to the junior and senior proms. This was a very special time since we got to choose and wear a long dress, and if we were lucky, to have our hair styled.

Religious training played a major role in our life at the home. Every morning before breakfast we would have a bible reading by one of the staff. We attended Sunday school and Sunday morning church services. On Sunday nights, we would have "Bible sword drills" which was a competition to see who would be first in finding selected Bible verses and reading the verses. There were also Wednesday night prayer meetings. During the summer, we would have vacation Bible school which I loved. We would have lessons and crafts and also I remember memorizing the books of the Bible and scripture. Sometimes the superintendents, who were ordained ministers, would preach and sometimes we had a minister from outside the home. When I was in elementary and high school, I remember the Reverend C. H. Overman from Ayden being the minister for the home. I also remember the superintendents, Reverend Wilbur Everton ('58-'62) and Reverend M. L. Johnson ('62-'69) preaching as well. One sermon that I have never forgotten was one that Reverend Everton preached on the "Sins of Omission". Over the years when I failed to do things that I should for others that sermon would come to mind. We also would have revivals and that is when I and many of the children at the home accepted Jesus as our personal savior and were baptized. In the fall, some of the churches close to the home would invite us to their annual fall homecoming. It was a nice break from our usual Sunday routine, plus we all loved having all that wonderful food to eat as well as riding on the bus with the boys.

    I have many memories, both happy and sad, of growing up at the home. Some of my favorite memories are of Mrs. Mixon cooking a birthday cake for me and all of the children on our birthday and getting to choose the flavor of the cake and having everyone sing "Happy Birthday"; it really made each birthday very special. I loved hearing Miss Farmer play the organ in the church and thinking that one day I would take organ lessons. Although I took piano lessons for many years, I never did achieve the goal of learning to play the organ. I also loved hearing the church chimes on Sunday morning as we made our way to church. Every time I hear church chimes now, it evokes special memories of the church chimes on campus. Also, I remember "the bell" at the home that we rang at meal times or when there was a special gathering in the dining hall. I remember trips to Rocky Mount to get free hair perms that were donated by various hair salons there and also having some free time to shop. I remember how exciting it was to go shopping in the fall and spring in Wilson for new shoes and clothes and being even more excited when I got to wear my new outfits. I remember special friendships that I made both at the home and at school and how wonderful it is each year at alumni homecoming to see these special friends and renew their acquaintance.

    One of the most difficult and saddest times I can remember was the summer I was seventeen and I lost my roommate, Sandra Mercer ('53-'65) to kidney disease. Sandra had been very ill for some time and was in and out of UNC Memorial Hospital in Chapel Hill. I can remember visiting her at the hospital with Reverend Johnson, but I don't think I truly realized how ill she was since she had such an amazing spirit and personality. When Sandra's condition would stabilize, her doctors would send her home and she would return to school. Sandra's passing was my first experience with death and the realization that someone as young and vibrant as she could die.

    While all of our basic needs were met on a daily basis at the home, there were gaps in our care that only could be met by a loving parent or parents. Also, the home was very strict about the separation of the boys and girls. Not only were we housed in separate dorms, but we were also separated at meals and in church. There was very little time for talking and socializing with our siblings and because of this, I do not feel that the family bond that holds and keeps siblings close was as strong as it would have been. Although my housemothers, Mrs. Rulli and Mrs. Barbour probably did the best they could, I certainly did not always agree with their methods. However, as the mother of two girls, I can only begin to imagine the daily challenges of caring and being responsible for twenty or more girls. I remember Mrs. Rulli as being a very reserved person. I had her for a brief period of time as my housemother in the little girls' dorm and then again when I moved to the big girls' building. Mrs. Barbour came to the home to work as the house parent in the little girls' building shortly after her son Stacy ('57-'64) was admitted to the home in August of 1957. I remember Mrs. Barbour as being very stern with strict rules about schedules, cleaning, clothes etc. I remember how she would make us wear our clothes two days in a row and how embarrassed I would be to go to school in the same clothes that I had worn the day before. Of course, I now realize no one probably noticed. I also remember when I was in the sixth grade and a shoe store donated shoes to the home, I ended up with some orange shoes with plaid ties that looked like brogans. I remember some of the boys at the home, as well as school, laughing and teasing me about my ugly shoes. Instead of being thankful that I had shoes to wear, I was totally humiliated and begged my Aunt Betty to buy me a pair of stylish shoes.

One of the most bizarre things that Mrs. Barbour had us do was line up about twice a year for our semi-annual purging. I don't know what the medicinal purpose of this was except maybe at that time it was thought that if we had our systems cleaned out we would stay healthy. So, we all had to line up and take our dose of Milk of Magnesia. Of course, her thinking may have been a little flawed since having twenty some girls all take a laxative at the same time with only four toilets available was utter chaos. Now that I look back on this, I find it very humorous.

I will be eternally grateful for the care that I received at the Children's Home and the opportunities that it afforded me. Also, I will always treasure the friendships that I made while living at the home. I know that without the encouragement of the Reverend M. L. Johnson and Miss Bonnie Farmer, I would not have gone to college. I remember my senior year in high school not knowing what I wanted to do after graduation. I knew that there were jobs and careers that I was not interested in pursuing but I really did not know what I wanted to do. Also, I remember being scared to graduate because I knew I would be on my own. After applying and being accepted to Mt. Olive College for the fall semester of 1966, Faye ('46-'54) and Charles

Harrell ('38-'51) (who grew up at the home) invited me to come live with them for the summer and work in the library at the college. I will always be thankful to them for helping me make that transition from the home to college life. Once I was on campus and became a student, I still didn't know what I wanted to major in. I thought that maybe I would be a piano teacher since I had taken piano for many years; however, I learned very quickly that even though I could read music and play, I really didn't have an ear for music or any talent in that area. Then I thought about becoming a librarian, I loved working in the library and being surrounding by all the wonderful books I had yet to read, but I still felt that this was not what I was meant to do. After graduating from Mt. Olive College, I continued my education at East Carolina University and it was there I decided to go into the field of social work. I felt having grown up in a child care facility gave me a special insight into some of the problems that children face when their parents are unable to provide a home for them.

I remember when I was at the home, how I envied my friends at Middlesex School who lived with their parents in what I considered to be a normal home. I would often wonder if they knew how fortunate they were and did they appreciate what they had. I have often thought of this as my husband and I have reared and tried to provide a loving stable home for our two daughters. I hoped that they would realize how blessed they were to have two healthy parents to love and care for them. On the other hand, unlike most of the children at the home, I had two living parents so I was not a "true orphan". However, my parents were disabled and could not provide a home for me and my siblings so I felt very blessed compared to the other children and the circumstances that had brought many of them to the home. I certainly feel that choosing a career in social work was part of God's plan for my life and gave me the opportunity to give back and minister to others in need.

23

The Same Holy WOMB

The Reverend Dr. Tom Everton
1958-62

I have no memory of my first day at The Children's Home, because I was only two (2) years old when that day took place. I arrived, not as an "orphan," but as the youngest of three sons of The Rev. James Wilbert Everton, the new Superintendent ('58-62); and his wife, Hattie Mae Everton. Jeff and Randy were my two older brothers. My memory box does open around the age of three (3).

Everton Family – Back Row L-R: Jeff, Randy
Front Row L-R: Wilbert, Becky, Haddie Mae
and Tom

At the age of three I started going to the local bank in Middlesex with Dad as he made daily deposits for the Home. Then we'd cross the street to get an orange-aid at Gus' Drug Store. Gus had light brown hair and a smile that would make the biggest bully blush. My main "buddy" at the Home was another two (2) year old, Claudius Elmore ('60-'81), who was one of the residents. He lived down at the Boy's Dormitory under the care of his house parents, Mr. and Mrs. Mitchell. Claudius and I would play together on the swings and sliding board. We'd play "war" with little plastic army figures and all the other usual "boy" stuff.

When we became four (4), we were allowed to attend the county fair in Wilson with the rest of the children, as well as eat at Parker's Barbeque for supper. I recall the two of us literally dancing to the tune of "ring around the roses" on the afternoon of the fair. The excursion (for us) seemed larger than life.

I recall another time when one of my legs got stuck in the "Flower Garden" in what must have been a hole dug out with "hole-diggers" that someone forgot to fill. I was just a cryin' when Claudius went to Mrs. Mitchell for help. In just a little while, I was free.

It seemed like everyone had a nick-name. Mine was Tinker and later was shortened to Tink. Don't know who gave it to me or why, but often wondered if it was because I was always "tinkering" with something. Probably something I wasn't suppose to be messin' with. I remember the baseball games the older boys played in at the Home. It felt like the Big Leagues to me, the way things often do through the eyes of a four (4) or five (5) year old boy.

Once I was sittin' on the Big boy's bench watchin' the game when two of the big boys were "warmin' up." They were throwin' horizontally behind us, and I thought nothing of it. They were lined up and throwin' the way I had seen other boys do dozens of times. Well, one of the fellows threw such a wild pitch that it headed straight for our bench. I just happened to turn around as the ground ball approached. I remember thinking, "shaw, that thing's goin' so slow, even if it DOES hit me, it ain't goin' hurt." Well. . . . You guessed it. That ball took a weird bounce and hit me in the kidney area. It plum knocked the breath out of me. John William Heath ('53-'62) picked me up, threw me over his shoulders, and took me up to Mrs. Mitchell.

I ended up in the hospital for eleven (11) days and wasn't allowed to have anything to eat for the first eight (8). Dad told me my "garbage can" had been hurt and two of the doctors wanted to take it out; but, the Big Honcho Doctor said, "No." No carried the day and I'm forever grateful it did.

The last major event that took place during my stay at the Children's Home was the birth of my sister. Rebekah Jane Everton was born with a head full of dark hair. You would have thought she was a queen, the way everyone swooned over her; especially the girls. I think they would have "eatin' her up," but just a few weeks after "Becky's" birth, we moved to Johnston County, where Dad became Pastor of Johnston Union Free Will Baptist Church.

My mother often talks of our time at the Children's Home. She enjoyed going with the children to some of the local Free Will Baptist churches for their homecoming services. She said they always had church at the home, but it was a special treat to go to these services. Mom also enjoyed taking children shopping for clothes at Belks and Leder Brothers in Wilson every year. She would also take children to their doctor and dentist appointments.

On one of the shopping trips to Belk's in Wilson, she looked across the street at a small sandwich shop and saw one of the boys who had been staying at the Children's Home, but had "run away" and somehow made it to Wilson. She went over to the shop and talked with Foy Watson ('51-'63). She finally told him that it was up to him, but, if he wanted to go back with her, to be at her car when they finished shopping. He was there waiting to go home.

One special time each year that mother remembers is going to the County Fair with the children and afterwards stopping to have dinner at Parker's Barbecue restaurant in Wilson. She also recalls the "mounds" of peas and butterbeans that would be unloaded under a shelter at The Children's Home, and how everyone would shell and shell and shell.

My mother's memory of her "own" children when living at the children's home are probably close to anyone else's childhood events although a couple of things did stand out to her. When the new swimming pool had been installed she looked out the front window and saw my brother Randy diving off the high diving board. She did not think he could swim and she nearly had a heart attack!

As far as my Dad and sibling stories when I was at the Home: I have very, very few memories of them. Dad was absent, overworked and on the road frequently (raising money). I'm proud of him, loved him, (and), will always be grateful for the two long talks we had towards the end of his life. Dad died on Thursday, March 4, 1971 from a brain tumor. He was 45 years old when he died, and Pastor of Daniel's Chapel Original Free Will Baptist Church. Dr. W. Burkette Raper (Alumnus '36-'45) participated in the funeral. My brother Randy played for our dad's funeral. Dad is buried in East Duplin Memorial Gardens, Beulaville, North

Carolina. Near his grave are the graves of Uncle Stephen and Aunt Bertha Smith, known to most of the children as Pa and Ma Smith. My father's mother (Gertie) was Ma Smith's sister.

There must have been something going on in the deepest part of my soul during those four (4) years of living at the Home, because, even though I was only six (6) years old when I left, I kept going back. When I got old enough, my parents would take me back during the summer and let me stay for a week or two. When I turned 16 I began driving my '63 Dodge Dart up to the Home with my eight-track tape player playin' "Grand Funk Railroad." I'd pull right up to the boy's Dorm driveway and would often stay over on week-ends.

Mickey Newton ('59-'71), Charlie Warren ('67-'73), Randy Faircloth ('67-'75), Kenny Warren ('67-'72), Ted Worthington ('56-'69), Sydney Suggs ('58-'70), Dwight Elmore ('59-'72)and others, became my buddies. Later I developed close friendships with two of the older boys who had already left the Home when I became old enough to drive up - - - Ray Worthington ('56-'63) and Jerry "Duck" Smith ('49-'60).

In a deep and special way, I identified with the "orphans," and still do. Even though I had parents, the boys at the Home "adopted me" as one of their own. To this day, at age 54, I feel as close to them as my own "biological family." As the ole' sayin' goes, "God works in mysterious ways." All I can say is, "I feel enormously graced and blessed to have the Children's Home and the children who were reared there, as part of my family history."

I received at least two (2) gifts from my days spent at the Children's Home:

Number 1.) The gift of never taking myself "too" seriously. If anything, the experience at the Home was real. You had too many fellow pilgrims who could see through your B.S. to let you get too big for your britches.

Number 2.) : The gift of knowing I'm part of Something bigger than my own little separate self. Both the Buddhists and the Christian mystics know this is true. There is no real "self" that is not part of everything and everybody else. Our Buddhist brothers sometime call it the face you had before your parents were born. We Christians call it the True Self, the Divine Spark in each of us; what Jewish scripture calls " the image of God within us." Whatever we call it - - - it brings me such joy to know I'm MORE than my own little self-centered "self." There's something true within each of us that goes beyond our own little group, denomination, religion, party, opinions, feelings, or country.

We in the English speaking world call it "God." Jesus called it, "Abba" (Daddy). This "Something" was nurtured at the Home, and still is by my friends who were reared there. This Something is real and alive, and yet, I can't fully know it with my mind. I can't figure it out. I can't put my finger on it. I can only experience it. I know it, and yet I don't "know" it. But somehow, in the "not knowing," I am Known. And there's grace and humility inside it.

So, as I reflect on my days at the Home, I still don't fully understand what it was that kept drawing me back. I STILL can't put my finger on it. I can't explain it. But, if I had to TRY to explain it in one word, it would be "family." I guess it shouldn't surprise me, since all of us there, and everywhere, ultimately came from the same Holy WOMB.

Footnote: *The Reverend James Wilbert Everton was superintendent December 1, 1958 – July 31, 1962. Reverend Everton, 45, died March 4, 1971. Dr. W. Burkette Raper participated in his funeral. Tom's mom, Hattie Mae Everton, 84, resides near Wilson, North Carolina.*

24

Mama Knows Best

John Elmore
1958-65

Elmore Family – Back Row L-R: John, Ottis and Buddy
Middle Row L-R: Dwight and Loucindy
Front Row L-R: Ronald, William and Donald

I am John Bailey Elmore and I was born September 24, 1947. Marvin and Emma Elmore were my parents and neither had an education above the third grade. I have five brothers and two sisters; seven of us were raised at the Free Will Baptist Children's Home in Middlesex, North Carolina. We were a hard working, poor family but I don't think any of us children thought we were poor. Days were full of work and fun, we were happy. Our father passed away in November of 1956 with pancreatic cancer which made things hard for the family. Mama, Dorothy (oldest sister), and Ottis (my older brother) went to work in the fields while I stayed home with four brothers and one sister. Three of the boys were in cloth diapers and all four were on the bottle--I had a busy job. Helen Strickland, a neighbor, picked us up and took us to Lee's Chapel Free Will Baptist Church, located on Highway 421 about five miles out of Dunn,

North Carolina. Mrs. Edna Baggett went to our church and she was instrumental in helping Mama place us in the Children's Home.

Ottis (age 13), Loucindy (age 8), and I (age10) went to the Home on September 5, 1958. It was a nice warm, sunny day. Mama, Mrs. Edna Baggett and our Aunt Alyne Elmore went with us that day. My other brothers and sister stayed home. Mrs. Clarence (Mary) Mitchell, house parent, met us and showed Ottis and me where we would bed and keep our clothes. Rod Page ('40-'57) was on the porch leaning back in an old wooden chair, smoking a cigarette. He was friendly and gave us encouragement about being in the home. It must have been around three o'clock that Mama and company left the Children's Home. As they were leaving, I stood in one of the chairs on the front porch so I could see the car until it was out of sight. I was now in a strange place and my family was broken up. I felt sad, upset, scared, crying and lost as I watched the car disappear out of sight.

Not too long after Mama left, a school bus pulled up in front of the building and about forty boys of all ages got off. Some spoke as they entered the door in an orderly fashion. They put their books in a bookcase located in the Study Hall, went to their bed area, changed into work clothes, and lined up to get a Pepsi and a piece of cold toast with peanut butter on it. When snack time was over, it was off to do chores: farm boy, house boy, kitchen boy, yard boy, laundry boy, etc.

The first night was a new learning experience. A bell rang and we had to stop what we were doing and get washed up and ready for supper. When the bell rang the second time, we all gathered on the front porch and when Clarence Mitchell (alumnus '23-'32), house parent, said "Lets go," we walked as a group to the dining hall facility. When we got there, we had to line up with the shortest person in front and the tallest to the rear. After the line was established, we walked into the dining hall and went to our assigned table seat. Older children were heads of the table and kept things in order. Everyone had to finish eating before the table could be dismissed. After supper, you completed your special chore or were required to get your bath and then prepare for study hall. When study hall was over, it was bedtime. Each child had a single bed, two drawers of a four-drawer chest and shared a closet with one other boy.

Time was structured, as it had to be in order to manage a large number of boys. But it was totally strange for me. I was used to washing in the washtub that had been filled with water in the morning and heated by the sun during the day. No study hall was required to do my homework, and when I went to bed, I slept with two or three brothers. I ate supper with my family and helped wash dishes when it was over. The only indoor plumbing we had was cold running water. You could equate my living conditions to that of the Jefferson's on T.V. Going to the Home put me in the "moving on up" status; all the living quarters were heated, indoor bathrooms, hot and cold running water and showers. None of this mattered to me that first night; I was in a traumatic state of mind. I didn't like it; I wanted to be with my family and I did not sleep very well that night. My Mama and others told me things would be better for me at the Home, no one could convince me that was the truth that night.

Dwight, my brother (age 8) came to the Home on August 23, 1959; William, also known as Claudius (age 5) arrived on July 4, 1960; and the twins Donald and Ronald (age 6) arrived on August 7, 1962. Their arrival made it feel more like my family was with me, but I still wondered about Mama and how she was doing. One day in September 1959 we returned from school to find out the house Mama rented had burned down and she had lost everything. That was frightening and I wanted to help but I couldn't because I resided in Middlesex.

As time passed, things became more routine and I adjusted well to the structured environment of the Home. I began to learn what to do, how to do it, and became more at ease with the children that I had to live with from day to day. Many remain life-long friends.

We had a bell at the Home that started and ended our daily routine. It was a big bell and when it pinged you could probably hear it at least two miles away. The ringing of the bell was to call us in to eat a meal. Ivan Pavlov was a Russian physiologist who did a study with dogs; he rang a bell and fed the dogs. After he did this for a while, he decided to change and ring the bell but not feed the dogs. He found that the dogs salivated when the bell rang even if he did not feed them. When I heard the bell, I knew it would soon be time to eat. I must say the food was good and on our birthday, Mrs. Mixon, the dietician would make you the kind of cake you requested.

Mama did not want to place us in the Home, but she knew she was not able to physically care for us the way we would be cared for there. After Mama left the first three children at the Home, she did not return for thirty to forty-five days. I am sure that is was a rule to allow the children to get into an acceptable routine. When this time elapsed, she came about once a month; she would come shortly after lunch and leave just before supper. Once in a while she would spend Sunday night and leave the next morning. We never knew of her planned visits. I'm sure that work and money were the driving factors that dictated her schedule. One thing for sure, we were all glad to see her arrive and hated to see her go.

One day during my early stay at the Home I had to sing for Ms. Bonnie Farmer, a worker at the home. She must have thought I had a pretty good voice because the next summer I was going out on class concert. Class consisted of six children, four girls and two boys, and Ms. Farmer. For the next eight weeks this group traveled to many Free Will Baptist Churches. At each church we would perform a play and sing songs. Ms. Farmer would give a presentation on the Children's Home. A "love offering" would follow Ms. Farmer's presentation. This was one of the mechanisms used to raise money to support the Home. Our travels took us from the mountains to the coast. We performed each day and after the service ended, we packed our bags in the car and moved on to the next church. The pastor and some church members would greet us at our next church. People that met us were the ones that would feed us, wash our clothes, and provide us with a place to sleep for the night. Doing this was much easier than doing the work the children were doing back at the Home. We met many good people on our class trips. They were the people that helped provide money desperately needed to raise the seventy-five children at the Home. Concert class was work, it was fun and it was like traveling on a vacation. Each day was a new adventure. We visited historical and tourist sites around the State, and singing for your supper was a good learning experience.

One of my fondest memories at the Home revolves around my participation in sports. With forty boys around, you could usually get up a baseball, tag football or basketball game. A baseball game usually required the older guys and a few of the younger ones. I was one of the younger fellows on a day I will never forget. We played the game for real, no matter the age; we hit, tried to steal bases, turn double plays, just like an organized game. On this particular day I was playing second base and Jerry Smith ('49-'60) was catching. Jerry was the catcher on the Middlesex High School team. Whoever was on first for the opposing team decided that he was going to steal second and I was covering second base. Jerry threw the ball and I tried to tag the guy out before I caught the ball; the ball hit me in my left eye, so off to Wilson Hospital I went. When I arrived, they transferred me to Rocky Mount Hospital. I needed an eye specialist to evaluate my condition. I was admitted to the hospital and had to lay in bed with little movement. I recall a scary moment when two doctors were checking out this thirteen year old boy. The doctors' conversation included "If this double vision does not go away by tomorrow, we will have to operate." I had about seven stitches, a large area of numbness and double vision. Thankfully, the double vision went away and I was released from the hospital after about a week. My baseball playing did not include second base after that, but I did end up wearing glasses.

I attended Middlesex High School in Middlesex, North Carolina. Mr. Enid Drake was our history teacher, driver education instructor, and basketball/baseball coach. Basketball was my favorite sport. I played junior varsity and when it was over that year, Mr. Drake put me on the varsity team. Being put on the varsity as a ninth grader was a special treat because I was the only ninth grade player on the bench. I was about 5 feet 11 inches tall, weighed about 180 pounds, and could lay my hand at the wrist over the rim. If I had bigger hands to grip the ball, I could have dunked it. I could shoot the ball pretty good, but I shot foul shots poorly. In my senior year, Ottis and I were both on the team. He jumped center for us. He was about 5 feet 10 inches and had a very quick vertical leap. That year we played a Coopers' team three times. We lost to them by a total of four points. In one game we came from twenty-one points down, went twenty-one points ahead, and lost by one point. Mr. Drake was a good coach and we highly respected him. I would venture to say that he played an instrumental role in the lives of the children from the Home that he coached.

Clarence "Petey" Mitchell; maintenance worker, house parent and husband of Mary, was not a very cordial guy. I was assigned to yard maintenance off and on over the years. Petey was the man to whom we had to report. I was scared to let him know that I had a varsity game so I returned to the Home after school. The superintendent came to check why I was not at the game. Petey didn't know I had a game and told me to let him know the next time I had one. Somewhere in that gruff man was a heart that was not often seen. There were a large number of old broken bicycles in the basement of the boys' dorm and within the storage space beneath the dorm. One Christmas Petey got parts for all the broken bicycles and repaired them. All the boys who did not have a bike received his personal bike that year, courtesy of this man's effort.

Thanksgiving and Christmas were times that you couldn't wait to arrive; you were going home with your family for a while. Christmas was a joyous time of the year. Before we went on vacation, all of us would gather in the dining hall. The Christmas tree and presents sent by the church that sponsored us were to be found there. My church was Union Grove Free Will Baptist Church in Fremont, North Carolina. We would sing carols and the presents would be passed out. It was just like Christmas morning at our house. Upon permission, the paper was flying, all the children were excited, each looking to see what the other got. Finally, we went back to the dorm for final packing of our suitcase for vacation with your family.

When one graduated from high school, it was required of you to leave the Home. This created a crisis for some of the children. We were not counseled on our next step in life. A family member or someone you knew had to meet you on graduation night and take you home with them. Making a transition from an environment made safe for you into an environment that YOU had to make safe for you could be more than a little daunting. Life skills you learned at the Home; hygiene, housecleaning, farm work, teamwork and attending church were all you were armed with to meet life. The graduating child was thus cast into a new environment with little or no real preparation. A few were able to attend college, but a large number went into the Armed Services.

Jessie Hines ('54-'65) and I graduated in 1965, and we both joined the Air Force. I stayed in the Air Force for over 27 years. I chose the Air Force to learn a trade and it provided security for the insecure. I would eat three times a day and could make a little money. This environment was similar to the one at the Home. My life in the Air Force went well. I married Ann Worthington ('55-'65), the love of my life from the Home. We were blessed with three children; John David, Catherine Ann and Angela Gail. Additionally, we saw a lot of the world in our travels; Viet Nam, Thailand, Saudi Arabia and Germany were unaccompanied assignments, while England, California, Oklahoma, Virginia, North and South Carolina were accompanied. I was stationed at Cam Rhan Bay in Viet Nam. One day while in the hutch, I was pleasantly surprised with a visit by Tommy Lancaster ('55-'65) who I shared a closet with and bunked next to at the Home.

Family life for newlyweds was hectic and stressful. I was a lowly enlisted guy and my pay was marginal. We managed to make it through the hard times; electricity shut off, door-to-door salesmen, no money for Christmas, etc. Some of my assignments were unaccompanied. Ann's role went from being a mom to being mom and dad. Also, family stress was elevated due to overseas assignments. Ann was a stay-at-home mom and she provided home care, love, education and training for the children. I was the wage earner and enforcer. I helped with the children, but my primary duty was wage earner. At the Home, one did not receive hugs or enjoy the intimacy normally developed between parent and child or brother and sister in a normal home. I'm sure that Ann and the children did not receive the normal expressions of love and affection from me. They did receive material blessings as I was able to provide. From my observation of my brothers and some other alumni, I would say the boys from the Home were excellent providers, but not very good at expressing their love, affection and care to others.

At the Home, we all received religious instruction. I had to learn a Bible verse and say it from memory at the Wednesday night service. I went to church every Sunday morning and we had League for our Sunday night service. A preacher from one of the churches would come and hold revival. It was at one of the revivals I accepted Jesus as my Lord and Savior. Over the years, my faith declined, I could only be described as a nominal Christian. I cussed, did not attend church, and my priorities were not where they should have been. Work, golf and tennis were high on my priority list. I did not drink nor did I do any wild things. When the children came along, we attended church more frequently. There was no Bible study, blessing of the food, or praying as a family. As the children grew older, church attendance increased. When the children left home, I backslid into the old routine of golf, tennis, sleeping in, and watching television. God must have wanted to get my attention. I had stage III cancer; Ann and I divorced following over 30 years of marriage. My life was in turmoil. God put His plan into action. He sent Pastor Elvin Butts, who I did not know, my way. I received numerous cards and phone calls from people I did not know. I started praying and reading my Bible. Dr. Rao took care of my medical needs. When I was released from the hospital and strong enough to attend church, I went to Pastor Butts' church. I have been cancer free for over seven years, Church now has a high priority and I continue to read my Bible, pray and help others as I am able.

I would say that Mama's decision to put us in the Home was the best for us. The training, care and living environment were much better than they would have been with Mama. After leaving the Home, we Elmores did well. We worked hard and provided for our families without welfare assistance. William ('60-'73) became an optometrist; Dwight ('59-'72), Donald ('59-'72) and I retired from the military; Ottis ('58-'65) became a brick mason; Loucindy ('58-'69) married and her husband retired from the military and Ronald ('62-'75) became a preacher. I would surmise these accomplishments would not have occurred if we had not been placed in the Home. All of us had rather been home with Mama, but Mama knew best!

25
The Dirt Road

Mickey Newton
1959-71

My story begins on a dirt road, in a little house in Greene County, North Carolina. My mom was sick when I was born and would die before I turned two. My dad did his best to earn a living, but my sister Debbie and I spent a lot of time with other family and friends as Dad also had a drinking problem. Mother had died in 1955.

Dad remarried and we had a stepmom (Eva Dail) for a while. She was very strict and once she became very angry that we had gotten dirty while playing in the yard. When we entered the house, she began to beat my sister with a stick from a bush until her legs began to bleed. When she reached for me, I ran out the back door to an old house in the back yard calling for Dad. He had been drinking but came to see what was going on. As we approached him with Eva Dail chasing me, I saw him make a fist. With his bottle in his left hand, he hit her in the stomach. I will never forget the moment or the scream. Even the violence of the act surprised me. I saw my dad as a hero for protecting us. Eva Dail left us and was no longer a part of our lives.

I do have other memories of her before she left. One of the most vivid memories was being awaken in the morning and finding her in the kitchen pouring whiskey down the sink. Dad had hidden it in the house. I do think she tried. I only saw her once after she left.

There were many fun times on the dirt road before Dad died. I remember going fishing a lot and cleaning fish on the back porch. I remember Dad and I turning on the dirt road once and a quail flying into the windshield. Dad took time to stop and pick up the bird. I knew we were poor when we had the bird for supper.

Another nice memory was of Dad pitching me baseball as a kid. He would pitch to me and my cousin in front of the tobacco barn. I can still remember the look of pride on his face when I hit one over the barn. Dad liked baseball and would take me to games being played on the fields back home. I still remember he and I being the only white people there as we watched all black teams play. He would always tell the players I was going to be a player one day. (Years later when I was out of college and had returned from the Peace Corp, I had just finished a softball game one night and was not ready to leave so I was watching the next game when three older guys [in the 60's] stood by me watching for a while when one of them finally spoke. He said, "You know something? Your dad could play also." The fact that they could tell who I was, and who my dad was by watching me play, is one of the best moments of my life.)

Dad continued to drink and was having other problems so we moved around quite a bit staying with our cousins. Uncle Hubert and Aunt Mildred had two children so we had someone with whom to play. On the last Thursday in August of 1959, my cousin Nelson and I were playing baseball while the girls were inside watching Aunt Mildred cook. I had just hit the baseball into the garden and as Nelson chased it down I was running back and forward to score as many runs as possible before he found the ball.

Even though I have been an orphan most of my life, my life is a collection of many wonderful childhood memories. The day I went to the Children's Home is one of them. It was a warm sunny Thursday, the last of August 1959, and my sister and I were with Aunt Mildred and Uncle Hubert on one of the many dirt roads in Greene County.

L-R: Mickey and Debbie Newton

I must have been on the 10th run when a car came down the dirt road and pulled into the yard. Nelson and I did what we had been taught to do and ran into the house telling everyone that a car had arrived. Little did I know that this car would be the beginning of my new life. Aunt Mildred and Uncle Hubert put a few things in a bag and put my sister and me in the car for the trip to the Children's Home. The man, Superintendent J.W. Everton (('58-'62), was nice and very soon we arrived. We were taken to our dorms and our new beds.

I remember I wet the bed the first night there, but never again. It was the wake-up call the next morning at 5:30 a.m. that let me know that my care-free childhood had changed for good. After breakfast, a bus came and took all of us to the farm to work. We picked up rocks from a field all day. Most of the rocks were huge to my six year old eyes but I enjoyed working with everyone. The day went quickly and soon days had turned into weeks.

My Dad died when I was in the second grade. My sister and I got out of school to attend his funeral. Shortly afterwards, Debbie and I were at Aunt Joyce's house and saw our stepmother Eva Dail for the first time since she left home. She gave Debbie a dress and me my first baseball glove. I never saw her again.

The first time I heard the bell I had no idea what to do. It soon became the clock on which my days would all begin. The 5:30 a.m. bell started my day and at 6:00 it rang again as we marched to the kitchen. The bell rang again at 5:30 p.m. and 6:00 p.m. when supper was served. The 5:30 p.m. bell on Saturday evening was my favorite as we gathered for 30 minutes to watch TV as our favorite wrestlers went at each other before we would eat. Saturdays also meant hamburgers or hot dogs, with the leftovers going to the boys' building for a snack late at night.

My most vivid memory of the bell came on a cold snowy winter night when I was a kitchen boy. It was time to ring the bell as I went out 6:00 a.m. The wind was blowing the snow everywhere. I was pulling the rope down when I heard a crack. I moved back as I pulled the rope one more time as the bell fell to the earth. I was scared for a moment, but my imagination was soon off and running. The smallest kid at the home had brought down the bell. In my mind I was David and I had slain Goliath.

Of all the work we did at the home it was a winter I spent making cement post that I remember most and from which I have been given the most joy. I really enjoyed working in large groups but I was left mostly alone on this job. Each day after school, I had to mix up cement and make two more post. Before I could start, I had to take out the two posts from the previous day, mix the cement and pour two new posts. Petey (my house parent Clarence Mitchell [Alumnus '23-'32])) had me place metal rods in each one so they would not break easily if hit by a car. I also had to paint the post. It was a long cold winter, but I liked the work and solitude very much. The week when we finally dug the holes and put the poles in the ground was a proud time for me. The poles are still there today and I love seeing them when I visit.

Of all the things I remember about growing up at the orphanage, the one that flashes through my mind most often is how we were able to enjoy even the most unpleasant tasks. Even cleaning out the hog, chicken, or turkey pens would turn into a fun time. I can remember always laughing as we worked and making a game out of everything. We would end up in trouble sometimes but it made the job easier and not stink as much.

One of the favorite games we would play while we worked would be hitting rocks with sticks as we waited at the end of the rows (tobacco, beans, or corn). I look back at this now and I am amazed that no one lost an eye.

Yes, life at the home was fun even when working. Cleaning bathrooms with the "pink stuff," cleaning and playing ball and climbing from the first and second floor in the church, kitchen duty and working in the fields all provided home for playing. We learned to make all our chores fun.

If not working, I enjoyed playing sports with the other kids. After a week of work and chores, time off was passed playing football, basketball, or baseball. I always enjoyed playing and still do so today. I think being at the home and working so much helped me appreciate and value my free time.

I do believe this part of my life has helped me enjoy my adult life so much. I feel so lucky to be so happy and able to enjoy even the simplest aspects of my life. I still enjoy working in groups and I still enjoy physical manual labor even though I do not work as hard as I once did. By making the hard work we did fun, I think we learned not to complain about our fate in life.

Looking back at my early days at the home now, I only have good feelings about my early days there. I was always looked after and cared for by someone. At times this may not have been by an actual worker at the home but an older child playing a support role. We always seemed to know each other's needs and helped each other when possible.

The best things about the home are the things I take with me now. Having a place where I can say I grew up, great memories and wonderful friends and best of all, some of the best stories a child could ask for. It hurts me in some way when kids today grow up without stories to tell when our childhood was one story after another.

The longest lasting aspect of life at the orphanage to me has been the friendships that I formed while there. There is a core group of friends that I still see on a regular basis and it is a wonder to me how comfortable I feel around these people. To be able to slide back into a conversation, a story, or even a joke that was told years ago is the best feeling I know. My friends from the home have always been a big part of my life. I love the way they accept my other friends into the group. They are a kind and gentle group of friends. At certain times of the year, I find myself longing to be in their presence again. This is usually around the holidays when we all want to be with our families. That's exactly what my friends are to me. They are my family.

I am sure my personality was formed before I went to the home, but I do know I also changed in many ways. I was very shy except with other kids at the home. I really began to talk and joke when I was at Mount Olive College. It was at the home that I first started to think about college. Phil Mercer ('53-'68) won a scholarship to the Citadel and he would return to talk to us. Later, more and more kids went to college after leaving the home. I was lucky that my dad was a veteran of WWII and his benefits had been saved for me. It was an opportunity that many of my cousins on the dirt road did not have at that time. After college, I joined the Peace Corps and my life changed as I never imagined. I still feel that the two and half years I spent in Colombia helped me become a more complete person.

When I look at my life now, I feel very lucky. I never had set many goals for myself, but my life has progressed and evolved into a wonderful life. I have great friends and know many people who care dearly about my being. It's hard to think back to a time in my life when I have not had everything I need.

26

The Children's Home was a Fine Institution

Josephine Newell, M.D.
1951-69

Dr. Josephine E. Newell, daughter of Dr. Hodge A. and Mary Hayes Newell, was born in Henderson, North Carolina in 1925. She is the youngest of four siblings. Other siblings are Hodge A. Jr., Sue and Jane. All the siblings are now deceased. Jane spoke six languages and was an interpreter for the 1945-49 Nuremberg Trails.

Josephine Newell

Dr. Newell entered the University of South Carolina at age 14 and completed the undergraduate program in two and one-half years. She chose her father's alma mater, the University of Maryland School of Medicine for her own medical training and at age 16 1/2 became a full-time student. She graduated from the School of Medicine at age 21, but could have graduated at age 20. School policy required physicians to be age 21
to graduate. To meet the requirement, Dr. Newell dropped out of the School of Medicine between age 20-21 and taught math and science at

Henderson High School, her alma mater for one year. Afterwards, she continued her studies at the School of Medicine. Dr. Newell is a seventh generation physician in the Newell family.

In 1951, Dr. Newell opened her medical practice in Bailey, North Carolina, where she practiced family medicine for 24 years. As a country doctor in a direct family line of seven doctors, Dr. Newell was inspired to honor the memory of the 19th century country doctor. In 1968, along with Dr. Gloria Flippin Graham, Dr. Newell inspired the effort that culminated in the dedication of the Country Doctor Museum in Bailey to honor the memory of country doctors. She was President of the Board of Directors from 1967-87 and is now President Emeritus…continuing. The museum was accredited by the American Association of Museums in 1972.

In 2010, Dr. Newell, age 85, was interviewed for this book. She had lost most of her vision from Macular Degeneration and no longer could read or write. This is her story.

"Shortly after Stephen ("Pa") Smith became Superintendent in 1951, he visited my office in Bailey and asked if I would be the primary physician for the Orphanage. I asked him if I could have some time to think about his request. Several days later, I called him and agreed to provide medical care to the children. For the next 18 years, I was a constant visitor to the campus and always available in my Bailey office for children as needed. During the 18 years of services, I never charged for my services. Until I became the primary physician, medical care for the children was provided by Dr. E. C. Powell in Middlesex and doctors in Wilson. Dr. Powell had provided medical care for the children since the '20's and continued for a short while after I accepted Pa's offer.

50's - Pa Smith with youngest on Campus

"In 1957, Asian Flu spread across the state and the home was not passed. There were 115 children in bed at the same time. Ma Smith was the only person on campus not sick. My nurse, Juanita Haskins, R.N., and I stayed three days and nights on campus to help out. Juanita had a husband and four children at home during her stay at the Children's Home. The house parents were sick but did their best to help the kids. I particularly remember Clarence and Mary Mitchell; they were very sick, yet up and helping the boys. The Home could not afford to send children to the hospital. Up to that year, it wasn't the norm for everyone to get a flu shot. After that year, everyone got a flu shot yearly. We, too, gave measles and other needed vaccinations. I really enjoyed working with the children and staff.

"I often visited the Home at Pa. Smith's invitation for dinner. I enjoyed eating with the children and fellowship with Pa and staff. I'd come into the dining hall and sit with the Smiths and/or others that sat at the center table. One night during dinner, I told Pa Smith that the boys needed to be in the Boy Scouts. Shortly afterwards, a troop was formed in Middlesex and boys from the Home were invited to join. With no money for uniforms, I got busy soliciting funds to purchase uniforms. Pa would bargain stores for the best price and all the scouts had uniforms. Ma and Pa personally measured each boy for the right size.

Thanksgiving Services

"I was always invited to Thanksgiving services at the chapel. Pa Smith would ask me to walk in with him and the trustees to the front seat after everyone had been seated. Pa would say to me as we walked down the aisle, "Now don't you tell anyone you're an Episcopalian. These Free Will Baptists will not understand." Then he'd quietly laugh as we settled into our seats. The church would be full with visitors and family who were there to take children home after the Thanksgiving services. The children marched in and took the stage for their program after we were seated.

"Once I was asked if the children I saw from the Home experienced depression. My comment was most children were better off than where they came from. There might have been some depression the first four to six weeks after admittance, during the adjusting period, but none afterwards. Another question asked was if there was bedwetting by the children. I was not made aware of any bedwetting by children.

"I recall an experience with the Smith Twins (Jerry and Nancy '49-'60). Jerry had this duck. He said to me one time his only friend was his duck. I thought it was the saddest thing I'd ever heard a child say…my friend is my duck.

"Boys and girls were separated and they could not meet. Girls lived in one building and boys in another. Jerry and Nancy were not allowed to be together. Matron Mary Mitchell and I fought a war on getting them together. We went to see Pa Smith together and Pa allowed them to be together occasionally.

"I am only aware of one child abuse incident during the years I provided medical care for the children. It was in the late '60's. I was called to the Home during the day. A young boy was trimming grass on his knees along the walkway in front of the chapel. Something happened and an adult hit him with a hoe handle damaging his kidney. I rode with him to Wilson and his kidney was removed. It was sad. For years after the child left the Children's Home, he'd call and talk with me.

"While I was there, Sandra Mercer ('53-'65) had kidney failure. We don't know what caused it. She is the first person I ever knew to be on dialysis. She was in the hospital for several weeks at the University of North Carolina Hospital. She received dialysis treatments once a week; now days treatments are given more often. On my day off on Thursdays, I would take her to Chapel Hill for her treatment. Sandra realized she was going to die. She would tell me, "I'm not going to live". Sandra died June 15, 1965.

"The Children's Home was a fine institution and did good work with the children."

Thoughts from Children

Jerry Smith ('49-'60) - "One Sunday afternoon during a baseball game I hurt my arm throwing to second base during an attempted steal. My arm hurt so bad I was taken to see Dr. Newell in her Bailey Office. She gave me a shot to relieve the pain. I never had any more problems with the arm. I've always viewed Dr. Newell as the strongest female in my life during childhood."

Margie Herring ('52-'62) - "I remember Dr. Newell, especially her dedication to helping children at the Home. She was always stern in her approach but made me feel that I would receive the best medical help she could provide. When I was in my teens, I had infection in both of my knees and she was responsible for providing my medical care. I found her to be a warm and loving person."

Alma Pope ('53-'66) - "I've thought about Dr. Newell so many times in my life. She was a life saver to me. One morning about 3:00 I awoke and Dr. Newell, Mrs. Rulli and Ma Smith were standing over my bed. The room had been cleared of all the other girls. (They actually thought I was going to die.) I was about 10 years of age. Dr. Newell sent me to Duke Hospital. I stayed there for two weeks. They performed all types of test. I was placed in a room with midgets (little people). I didn't know what they were at that time. They wore diapers but talked like old people. They were just a few feet tall. (They were running around me and talking.) Some of that period was a really bad experience for me. They drew fluid out of my spine, put needles in my head, glue on my hair and gave me shock treatments. I walked like a zombie when I left Duke and went back to the Home. Ms. Farmer and Ma Smith knew what I went through. I never told anyone."

Jo Etta Worthington ('54-'62) - "I remember at Christmas one year Pa Smith presented her with a diamond watch from the children and staff. She was so elated and proud of the gift. She gave a little speech thanking us. I remember her giving me flu shots."

Steve Worthington ('54-'63) - "Dr. Newell scheduled me for a tonsillectomy and adenoids removal operation when I was 10 years old. Jimmy Cantrell ('53-'64) and I were scheduled together and we both had our operations at the Wilson County Hospital. At that time, there was the false belief in medicine that the tonsils and the adenoids were appendages that were useful on the evolutionary development of the human body; but were now defunct and were no longer useful; but were often harmful causing colds, nose and throat infections, etc. Many of the kids at the Orphanage were scheduled to get their tonsils and adenoids removed. This was maybe 1955-1956. Dr. Newell also treated me when I was in high school - I had a growth on my arm - near the bicep - had cut it on the farm and a growth formed - probably because I did not treat it with the usual Merthiolate or Iodine. She burned it off."

Cathy Hines ('57-'66) - "I remember a couple of visits to Dr. Newell for severe ear infections and I remembered that she had to refer me to an ENT specialist in Wilson. I do remember her as being very straightforward and efficient. If I had to describe her, it would be as a 'ball of energy'."

Dr. Newell not only served the Home for medical care, but she also knew the children's struggles and cared about their future; using her day off to sit with a child in a hospital, listening to a child after he/she left the Home and encouraging others to reach their potential in life. She modeled to the girls and boys a strong woman. She took personal interest in every child.

Footnote: Dr. Newell was honored by the Raleigh News & Observer as Tar Heel of the week in 1971. She was elected the first female president of the North Carolina Medical Society ('81-'82). After retiring from practice, she went on the faculty at Duke University Medical School. Today, Dr. Newell lives in Magnolia Glen, a retirement community in Raleigh, North Carolina.

27

The Lord Has Been Good

Pearl Johnson
1962-69

My husband Milton and I went to the same church, Hopewell Original Free Will Baptist, when we were young. Milton and I both lived on farms near Smithfield. Milton and I had several boy and girl friends before we started going together. When I was fourteen, I stopped school in the 9th grade to care for my mother who had TB and she later died. I continued caring for my younger brother and sister. The 9th grade is all my former education.

Pearl and Milton Johnson

Milton and I got married when we were 18. Milton was already licensed to preach by then. He continued working on the farm and preaching when he could. We stayed in the Smithfield area until after our first daughter Glenda was born. Then we moved to Duplin County where he was Pastor of Snow Hill Original Free Will Baptist Church.

Milton continued to farm while pastoring the church. Eventually, he was pastoring four churches while we were there. Rotha, my 19 year old brother, came to live with us and helped Milton with the farming. In the middle of getting our tobacco out of the field, my brother got pneumonia and Milton got pleurisy. He was in a lot of pain. I'll never forget those church members. Without them, we'd never got the crop in that year.

In the early 50's, Milton pastored Marsh Swamp Original Free Will Baptist Church in Rock Ridge. In the summer of '57, we moved to Mount Olive to help get the college started. Milton was the Treasurer and Business Manager and I managed the cafeteria. We worked for the college for years before going to Newport for two years for Milton to pastor Holly Springs Original Free Will Baptist Church.

Then, we moved to the Children's Home in 1962 where he was superintendent. Those were fun years and I enjoyed the children and staff. I helped out with taking children to the doctor and their clothes shopping in Wilson. Most of the shopping was at Leder Brothers.

One little girl, Sandra Mercer ('53-'65), will always be special and part of my memory at the Children's Home. As I remember, Sandra was a happy, go lucky girl, into mischief and always seemed to have a good time. She went home one Christmas and came back with a sore throat. We learned from taking her to the doctor, she had a kidney disease. Sandra stayed in the hospital for a long time and I often stayed with her. Her sickness led to her death June 15, 1965. We were all saddened. Milton preached her funeral held at the Children's Home. Later, Milton had her picture framed and it hangs in the Children's Home Chapel today.   My favorite houseparent at the Children's Home was Thelma Rulli. She was a child at the Children's Home 1923-30. She was very good. Another houseparent I enjoyed was Mrs. Dovie Barbour. Her first husband was my first cousin. After his death, their son Stacy ('57-'64) was admitted to the Children's Home. She later became a houseparent.

I thought Dr. Josephine Newell was a nice lady and really cared for the children. She was interested in the children and went out of her way to help them. I love that lady.

L-R: Dovie Barbour, Thelma Rulli

Milton was a fair and honest person. He worked hard at everything he did. When he died, I did not know what I was going to do. One day I received a call from Louisburg College offering me employment as a houseparent for one of the dorms. The president of Mount Olive College, learning of the vacant position, recommended me for the job. No longer was I Mrs. Milton Johnson. Now I was Pearl Johnson. Later, I moved to Raleigh to be a houseparent at St. Mary's College. In February 1991, I married James B. Hunt, Sr., father of Governor James B. Hunt, Jr. James passed May 7, 2003 and is buried at Marsh Swamp Original Free Will Baptist Church. He was 91. Dr. Burkette Raper (Alumnus '36-'45) officiated his funeral.

I've enjoyed my whole life. It's been hard at times. I've always dwelled on the good, not the bad. I've have a good time and I love the Lord. Today I'm 95 years old and live in an assistant living facility in Smithfield. My daughter Wanda calls me every day. The room I live in is my home until I die. I'm so happy and satisfied.

The Lord has been good to me.

Afterword by daughter Wanda Johnson

My memories of the Free Will Baptist Children's Home (or Orphanage as I first knew it) cover almost my entire life. I remember going to the Home on several occasions as a pre-schooler. Church meetings, playing with the children, hearing them sing as a group, picnics on the grounds, and watching the pet goat are among my memories. My childhood memories of the Home are tied very closely to my relationship with Rev. and Mrs. Stephen A. Smith.

Rev. Smith and my father Rev. M. L. Johnson were both young Free Will Baptist ministers and the best of friends. As the Smith's had no biological children of their own, I enjoyed the attention I got when our families were together. We visited when we could while we were living in Wilson County and they were living in Beulaville. Happily for me, when Rev. Smith became superintendent of the Home, our times together were more frequent. They were always "Uncle" Stephen and "Aunt" Bertha to me even after they became "Ma" and "Pa" Smith to the children and friends of the Home. My father spent much time working on the completion of Memorial Chapel. I got to know many of the children during this time. When Aunt Bertha's niece Donna Jan went to live with them at the Orphanage, I had another reason to enjoy my visits. I remember playing on the swings and slides, eating in the dining hall, going swimming in the old pond, riding on the old blue bus to ball games and other activities, all the children going to our church (Marsh Swamp Free Will Baptist) for Bible School at least one summer, and many church services, especially the annual Thanksgiving service and picnic.

In 1962 my father became superintendent at the home. I was a college student at that time. I stayed with my parents while attending Atlantic Christian College (now Barton College) for a year and a half. After I began teaching in Havelock, North Carolina in 1964, I still spent many weekends and part of several summers at the Home. I did some relief work in the girls' cottages and filled in other places as needed.

Living at the Home as a young adult was very different from visiting as a child. Although I was only a few years older than many of the children, I quickly learned to love the children and ministry of the Home. Having lived a relatively sheltered life, I was touched and somewhat shocked by the reasons some of the children were at the Home. I was aware that adults were often indifferent and even cruel to each other. However, realizing that some parents (especially mothers) made choices that practically removed their children from their lives was hard for me to understand or accept. At the same time, I was very favorably impressed with parents and other relatives who, although unable to care for their children fulltime, were very supportive of the Home and their children's life there.

Some of my special memories of living at the Home included supervising very happy children in the pool, preparing vegetables (peas, butter beans, corn, etc.) to be frozen, visiting in the breezeway between the two girls' building, Christmas parties, meeting new children, watching pick-up ball games behind the boys' building, Sunday worship services in Memorial Chapel (where Rev. C. H. Overman often shared the "Gospel According to Peanuts" with us), taking children to doctor's appointments as well as ball practice and other school activities, and Homecoming activities.

Our years at the Home were very special to my father (and our entire family). He loved the children and was loved by them. This was a very different ministry from the others he had served in the Original Free Will Baptist denomination. He became ill in 1968 and died February 11, 1969, at age 53. Dad was buried at Marsh Swamp Original Free Will Baptist Church in Wilson County. This was a sad time for our family, but the love and concern expressed by the entire Children's Home family provided many sweet, happy memories as well.

My mother remained at the Home as acting superintendent until the fall of 1969, when she went to work at Louisburg College. I continue to visit the Home often. Participating in alumni activities at the Home continues to be a very special time for me. The majority of the most active alumni were raised at the Home when either daddy or Uncle Stephen was superintendent. I am proud of them all. Homecoming weekend is truly like a big family reunion.

Because of my association with some of the children at the Home, I met Patricia Anderson, five months old in 1969. When she was eighteen months old, she was living with her aging grandparents and father. Her father agreed for her to live with me. In spring 1972, I was given legal custody of Patricia who was age three. Her brother Andrew, age 2, was later admitted to the Children's Home April 4, 1972. We visited the Home to see Andrew until he left in 1978. Patricia lived with me until her marriage in 1987. Although there have been challenges for both of us through the years, Patricia has certainly enriched my life. Thanks to her I now have two granddaughters, a great-granddaughter and a great-great grandson who are an extremely important part of my present life. Patricia and her brother Andrew have an excellent relationship.

Mom lives at Carolina House Assistant Living in Smithfield, North Carolina.

Footnote: The Children's Home Board of Directors appointed Pearl Johnson Acting Superintendent at the death of her husband M. L. Johnson. Reverend Johnson served as Superintendent '61-'69. Mrs. Johnson was Acting Superintendent for three months until the board appointed Reverend Edward W. Miles ('69-'71). Milton Johnson is buried at Marsh Swamp Original Free Will Baptist Church. Reverend R. H. Jackson participated in his funeral. R. H. Jackson was Superintendent of the Children's Home 1955-56. Wanda Johnson lives in Smithfield, North Carolina.

28

Benign Neglect

**Charles Warren
1967-73**

*Warren Family - Back row L-R: Lacy Mack (Dad), Jean Carolyn
Mary Catherine (Mother)
Middle row: L-R: Kenny Ray ,Thelma Lou
Lacy Mack, Jr.
Front row: L-R Charles, Mary Ann, Judy Lynn*

There were seven children born to Mary Catherine and Lacy Mack Warren. Following his army service in Europe during the Second World War, Lacy Mack and Mary Catherine married and lived their lives together as share croppers in Hertford County North Carolina. Having a large family ensured that there were enough hands to attend to the many chores of life on a farm. Life was, at best, a meager existence; food, clothing, bus rides to school, and church on Sundays, an existence not unlike the daily lives of millions in Rural America.

Daddy Dies

Awakened by the sound of someone falling to the floor, my brother and I jumped out of bed to discover our father lying with his head up against a dresser, with white foam dripping from his mouth. My mother was frantic as she called out to Lacy Mack, with no response. The oldest amongst us, Lacy Jr., was sent down the road to the next house to use the phone and call for help. When the ambulance came, I was waiting by the road to flag it down, but it did not stop. After a time, the ambulance returned to our house and stopped. They brought Lacy Mack down the stairs sitting upright in a chair because the stretcher couldn't be maneuvered into the bedroom. As they placed him in the ambulance, none of the children watching the scene understood that their father had died. Sometime later, Mary Catherine returned in a car with the words "Hertford County Coroner" on the door. Without saying anything to anyone, she ran crying into the house. At this point, we all now understood that our daddy was gone.

Mary Catherine Doesn't Cope

Jean Carolyn, only 17 at the time, had married and moved away. Lacy Jr., at 14, was the oldest still at home. Mary Catherine would leave for days at the time, leaving us kids to wonder where she was and what she was involved in. When Mama wasn't at home, all six kids would gather in the same room. Lacy Jr. had a shot gun by his side and Kenny Ray had a 22 rifle. Through the night, we would huddle in fear, convinced every sound we heard was some evil out to get us. When the school bus came in the morning, we would wave it on and try to figure out how we would eat and from where the food would come.

On one occasion, Mary Catherine returned home after several days' absence, dropped off by a North Carolina State Highway Patrolman, walked quickly by us kids and disappeared into the house. Collectively, we confronted her. Where had she been? Why hadn't she come home? Why wasn't she at home with us as she was supposed to be, attending to our needs, making meals, doing the stuff of everyday life? When I became particularly vocal and aggressive in my questioning of her, she turned towards me, threatening to get the belt. When my father was alive, the threat was different—"wait until your father gets home." As I ignored her scolding, it felt strange, as though she no longer had the right. Now it was different. As she approached me to grab and hit me, I turned and ran. Never would I have run from my father, never. It seemed to me that now she had no right to spank me. She, after all, was the one misbehaving. She was no longer a mother, but rather just someone waiting for the next best opportunity to get away from her kids and escape with the next man who presented himself as a convenient means of transport to some other place, with less responsibility and burden. She could not be trusted as a mother.

As she continued to disappear for long periods of time, we became more vocal with our dissatisfaction when she returned. Disrespect for your mother was not easy when you were raised in the rural south, in the Bible belt. Hungry and disillusioned, we would scream at Mary Catherine with our questions about where she had been, what had she been up to, what man had she been with this time? We broke the liquor bottles whenever we discovered them.

My brothers, sisters and I became quite good at finding and destroying the liquor bottles. When she realized that we had taken them out into the woods and broken them, she became angry and threatened us with punishment. Each time we knew it was just a matter of time before she would be gone again and days before she would return.

Neglect Conviction

Mary Catherine went to prison. Sentenced to prison for neglecting her children, she served 12 months. What she was guilty of was not coping well with a difficult situation. Lacy Mack had died suddenly of a heart attack. He was the provider for the family and had always made sure there was food on the table. Mary Catherine was left to face raising six children all alone. Given her eighth grade education and limited means, she possessed few skills and lacked any understanding of how to improve her situation.

A Year with Relatives

At ages ten and eleven, my brother Ken and I were hitchhiking from the town of Ahoskie, NC to the place we lived in rural Hertford County. The car that stopped to pick us up was familiar. It was our cousin, daughter of our mother's sister. When she pulled over to pick us up, we got into the car and began to answer her questions.

Later that evening at the police station, our Aunt Ora Bell, sister of our father Lacy Mack, came to take us to her house. When the police officers asked where we wanted to go and which relative they should contact, we gave the name of our favorite aunt, Ora Bell Rogers. As a single mother, she had a family of her own, with three kids still living at home. She drove the ninety minutes from her home to the police department in Ahoskie, NC and took all six children home with her.

Aunt Ora Bell and Aunt Gladys were both sisters of Lacy Mack and split the responsibility of taking us children. Working with the Hertford County Department of Social Services, we were all enrolled in school and attempting to get on with our lives. For the next year, we lived with aunts and uncles and attempted to fit into situations that were uncomfortable and strange.

Going to Live at the F.W.B. Children's Home

The air was cold and damp, the sky overcast and gray. Kenny Ray and I were left outside the administrative offices of the Free Will Baptist Children's Home, while the adults attended to the legal and administrative requirements of intake for children admitted into care. The F.W.B. Children's Home, located just east of Raleigh in Middlesex, North Carolina, seemed a long way from Ahoskie.

As he was leaving, Uncle Johnny Frank made small talk with me and discovered I had used the money I had earned in the tobacco fields to buy a pocket knife. He questioned why I needed it and whether or not it was a good idea for me to have it. When I could not offer an explanation that suited his purposes, he gave me the two dollar price I had paid and took the knife with him.

The knife, of course, was my response to the fear and concern that I had about life in an orphanage. Would the other kids be mean? How could I protect myself without a weapon? All that I knew about orphanages I had learned from my limited exposure to books and television. Oscar Wilde, I suppose, had given me the notion that, for a kid living at an orphanage, you had better be prepared to defend yourself.

Life in Albemarle Cottage (The Little Boys' Building)

My brother and I went to live at the Children's Home in February. Kenny Ray was 12 and I was 11. With a population of 103 kids, there was no room for our sisters, Thelma, age 13, Judy age 10 and Mary Ann age 9. They would come later in June when it was expected that room would be available.

Mrs. Mary Mitchell, the Albemarle Cottage matron, led us to our beds. They were the last two beds in a row of beds separated by a couple of feet of space. She showed us where to place our clothes and indicated that we should join her in the study hall when we finished putting our things away. In the study hall, there were several smaller preschool kids preoccupied with their play.

Later when the school bus arrived, the building came to life with boys of all ages from six to eighteen. Most kids seemed to know where to go and what to do as the building filled with boys. Mrs. Mitchell and her husband Petey barked out specific instruction to those in need of prodding and cajoling in order to meet their after school obligations. There were chores to be done before the first bell rang for dinner at 5:30 PM. Later in the evening, there was study hall and an early bedtime.

Chores at the orphanage were assigned on the basis of a three month schedule. For the boys, it was pretty straight forward. You were a yard boy, a farm boy, or a house boy. Each designation meant that you reported to a staff member who had that area of responsibility. Petey Mitchell was responsible for maintenance and directed the activities of the yard boys. Henry Mitchell was the farm manager and the farm boys reported to him.

The house boys worked at the behest of Mrs. Mary Mitchell. For a house boy, you were assigned cleaning activities on a daily basis, with additional activities on the weekends. Each older house boy had responsibility for several smaller kids. You had to ensure that they got dressed on time, took baths and attended to their homework.

Life as a yard boy was doing whatever Petey Mitchell decided needing doing outside. Mowing grass, raking leaves and assisting in making repairs to the buildings and facilities was generally the kind of work designated for the yard boy. Over the course of the summer, there were other tasks. We made cement benches using molds that Petey built. The job was one of mixing the cement in wheel barrels and shoveling it into the forms. It took several days to dry and the forms were removed.

During the spring and fall, we could make two benches after school and before supper each day. These benches were placed around grounds on campus and still remain there in use today.

When the dinner bell rang, everyone gathered in the front part of the building to hear from Petey and Mrs. Mitchell of any new rules or instructions required to keep order and maintain the discipline required to have it all work. When the second bell rang at 5:55 p.m., Mrs. Mitchell would take the lead with the smaller kids and Petey would bring up the rear. We would all make the 100 yard walk to the central cafeteria single file and without excessive conversation. Once inside, we each had an assigned seat in the designated area for each cottage where we stood behind our chair and waited for Mr. Johnson, the superintendent of the Children's Home, to make his entrance through the kitchen and into the dining room. After Mr. Johnson made any announcements, someone would say grace and we sat down to eat. If there was a birthday, we all sang while a cake was brought out to the table of the lucky birthday kid.

Feeding the population of the Children's Home was no small matter. There was a kitchen staff of two who directed and supervised activities for meal preparation and cleanup. There were designated "dining hall girls" whose responsibility it was to fetch additional food or to fill tea glasses during the meals. When you needed something, you raised your hand and one of the girls would come over to your table and take your request, breakfast, lunch and dinner every day. When you were finished eating, it was generally a good time to spend a few minutes visiting with your sisters. Because the campus was strictly segregated, there were only select times to mingle with the girls.

The Death of Our Patriarch

After almost two years living at the home, life had become somewhat routine. Summers were filled with chores. In addition to attending school, everyone contributed to the effort of keeping the Children's Home operational. Farm crops, such as tobacco and corn, a large garden, along with hogs, cattle and turkeys, provided ample opportunity for everyone to pitch in.

During the summer, a few lucky kids were chosen to go out on concert class. This was a tour around the state of North Carolina, visiting Free Will Baptist Churches, with a small group of four to five kids and the concert class leader. The kids would sing religious and patriotic songs and usually perform a short play. At the end of the evening, a donation was taken and the kids moved on to the next church. The concert class did not perform chores at the Children's Home, as they were on the road living in the homes of members of the Free Will Baptist Church denomination throughout the summer months.

During the 60's, life at the home was based on routine, rules, and repetition. But there was one constant in everyday life that created a kind of calm, comfort and assurance that no matter what was going on in your life, it would all be OK.   At the end of each day, as we gathered for supper, the entire population came together for supper. As we each stood behind our chairs, we waited for the arrival of our superintendent, Mr. M.L. Johnson. There was a certain level of comfort that we all derived from waiting, and then watching as he made his entrance. With a smile that filled his entire face, Mr. Johnson would come in through the kitchen, stopping to say "hello" to the kitchen girls as he made his way to his seat. We all stood and faced him and waited for him to speak. Mr. Johnson would usually make some announcements, share things of interest going on with kids, birthdays and anything else worthy of celebration.

He always had dinner at the dining hall. His wife and family could have chosen to have their meals at their residence. It is as if he knew that his presence there at meal time sent a message that we all needed to hear. We all found comfort in it.

My recollection is that it was in the morning on that Tuesday in February, 1969 when, while in class at Middlesex School, an announcement came over the public address system. It was the school principle asking that all kids from the Children's Home come to the auditorium as soon as possible. This struck us all as odd, because the kids from the home were integrated into the public school in Middlesex as much as possible and were not typically called together as a group.

When we arrived at the auditorium and took our seats, the principal, Mr. Williams, made the solemn announcement that Mr. Johnson had died suddenly. At first, there was quiet throughout the gathering of Children's Home kids across all grade levels. And then, slowly at first, the sobbing began as everyone processed the news in their own way. After a few minutes, some kids were crying uncontrollably while others just seemed shocked.

I suspect that every kid who passed through the Free Will Baptist Children's Home remembers their first superintendent, executive director or CEO. This role today is more administrator than active participant. But during this time in the history of the home, the superintendent was a central figure in the life of the children who lived there. The passing of Mr. Johnson was a sad day for all the children who lived there.

Moving On To Rogers Cottage (The Big Boys' Building)

At the age of twelve, I got to move to the big boys' building! Ken had moved over several months prior and it was good to join back up with him. Rogers Cottage had individual rooms with two boys in each room, sharing a bathroom with the boys in the adjacent room. Set up much like a college dorm, the arrangement allowed for more privacy than the little boys' building.

As a teenager, sports became much more a part of everyday life. The baseball diamond seemed to always have at least a few kids playing catch. There were at various times a Children's Home baseball team. We played other loosely organized teams at local churches. At one time, we even had uniforms. On Sundays, pickup games got a lot of attention. Mr. Henry Mitchell, the farm manager, would call balls and strikes and the girls were allowed to come down to the baseball field and watch the games. Teams were determined through some arbitrary and loosely formed process, in part selection by a designated captain, and in part volunteering to play for a team. Games would go on all afternoon until Mrs. Mitchell would call everyone in to get ready for dinner.

High School

During the formative years of life, the exposure you have to positive influences can have a life-long impact on your life. For me, this came in the form of my relationship with my high school football coach. Having little more than a love of the game, at 155 pounds, football was not a likely outlet for personal expression. I was fortunate to be able to play all four years, earned my letter as a junior and was named all-conference my senior year when the first winning team ever in the short history of Southern Nash Senior High was in fact undefeated during the regular season. As a linebacker, tight end, and special teams player, my biggest asset was my intensity. Coach Jerry Ball took a special interest in me. He and his wife Judy were very supportive. During a Thanksgiving holiday, when I had no place to go, Coach Ball invited me to spend the holiday with him and his family. During my high school career, he provided much guidance and council, providing a very positive role model and influence.

Retrospective

After spending much of my time at the Children's Home filled with resentment towards my mother, I made peace with Mary Catherine when only a few short years ago my brothers, sisters and I purchased a tombstone and placed it on her otherwise unmarked grave. Mary Catherine died alone, a tortured soul. When she was released from prison, she visited us only once at the Children's Home. During her visit, she spoke of how she was going to regain custody and we would all be together again. Even at my young age, I knew that was not an option. She soon fell back into her old lifestyle of excessive drinking and bad company and sealed her fate of an early grave. She died of a heart attack at 48.

Looking back on my time at the Free Will Baptist Children's Home, I can only surmise that it was for me and my brothers and sisters, a life saving experience. As kids without supervision and largely neglected, we were headed for certain trouble. Living with relatives was uncomfortable and we did not feel welcomed. At the Children's Home, we were allowed to take part in a life style that provided discipline and the basic needs of life.

I left the Free Will Baptist Children's Home in 1973 at the age of eighteen. Now, at the age of 54, each year I look forward to visits from my "orphan" pals. We follow each other's personal lives, are in regular contact and behave more like family than friends. We are bound by common experience.

The friendships and relationships formed during life at the Children's Home are marked by the intensity of shared experience. Neither the passing of time nor the distance of vast geography can diminish the feelings of closeness and kinship between those who have lived through this experience together. Even now, much later in life when the brilliance of memory has faded somewhat, whenever I meet someone who lived through the experience of spending a portion of their childhood at a children's home, I feel an immediate emotional connection. While I sometimes vacillate in my assessment of the emotional impacts of my time at the Free Will Baptist Children's Home, I always arrive at the same ultimate conclusion—it was for me a positive, overall experience coming at a time in my life when the kind of care provided was desperately needed. Without the opportunity to be a part of life there, I don't know what may have become of my brothers, sisters and me.

29

We Were a Band of Brothers

Randy Faircloth
1967-78

Randy Faircloth

It's the summer of 1966 on a bright sunny day as the car crests the last hill before descending down into the land of a thousand kids. Mrs. M. L. Johnson (never did find out what M. L. stood for) had told me and my three brothers so much about the Children's Home that I could hardly wait to see it for myself. I don't know how my brothers felt about the change in our lives, but I guess I was amazed about the whole story. As we come to the bottom of the hill and I look to my right, all I can see are kids, kids and more kids. At first glance they appeared to be playing in the woods. My first memory would be something similar to the scene in "The Sound of Music" where kids are hanging from the trees. Only later would I know better to think such a thing could happen with Clarence "Petey" Mitchell in charge. I would later find out that they were not playing but instead raking leaves and pine straw that had fallen from the trees. I would all too soon experience the pleasures of the fine art of raking leaves.

As the car stops and we tumble out, my eyes are amazed to see even more kids in all directions. With the administration office almost in the center of the orphanage, you could see buildings all around. Mrs. Johnson had not lied when she said there were lots of kids and horses with which to play. For a nine year old kid, this looked like heaven. Maybe living here would help soothe the pain of having to leave our dad and uncle behind. So went the first day at the Children's Home.

I guess I should go back a little bit and explain what the circumstances were that brought me and my brothers to the home. I have three brothers, from oldest to youngest they are Rick, age 10, myself, age 9, Terry, age 8 and Johnny, age 6. We are basically a year apart in age except for Johnny who is two years younger than Terry. My mom and dad divorced when we were very young. I'm not exactly sure, but I would guess when I was about 5 or 6 years old. We wound up living with my dad. He was a kind man who had his own issues. He was a disabled veteran and an alcoholic. Most all of his money went to buying alcohol. If there was any left over, he would buy some food for the family. I can remember times when the only meal we would have in a day would be a cake of cornbread cooked in an iron skillet. My brothers and I had free reign during the short time we lived with my dad since most of the time he was not able to care for us. As a result, we pretty much came and went as we pleased. We roamed the streets of Chadbourn at a young age because we didn't really have any direct supervision. I don't know for sure but I firmly believe someone in the community saw what the future held for us if things didn't change and must have gotten the Department of Social Services involved. Thank God for their foresight.

When social services finally did get involved, we were on our way to the first of five different foster homes. We were first placed with a lady who was recently widowed. We were not mean kids but four young boys was a lot to ask of one person. That didn't last very long (from what I remember it was about two weeks) before we were divided among two families. Rick and I went to one family and Terry and Johnny to another. Later, we were divided yet again, Rick stayed with the family he and I were with, I went to another, Terry and Johnnie were split up as well. At one time all four of us were with four different families. Eventually, someone had the wisdom to recognize that we were growing up not knowing each other and decided to do something about it. With all the moving and changing going on, it was enough to make a young little boy very confused about the whole situation.

And then Mrs. M. L. Johnson came into the picture. Mrs. Johnson was the wife of the Superintendent Milton L. Johnson ('62-'69) of the Children's Home. I will never forget her soft voice, gentle touch and that wonderful smile.

If memory serves me correctly, there were around one hundred children at one point during the time I was there. It was pretty even with about half boys and half girls. Many of the children were just as my brothers and I, more than one child from the same family living at the home. No matter, we all eventually became one big family. We may have fought one another at the Children's Home but when we were at school and some other kid got in a fight with one of us, they had to deal with all of us. We were truly a band of brothers.

Although several people helped me learn the game of baseball, I would have to say Mickey Newton ('59-'71) and Ted Worthington ('56-'69) were the two who took me under their wings and taught me the game. I guess you could say I was blessed with a strong left arm. They either recognized that I had a little talent and wanted to help develop it or they were suckers for a confused little kid looking for something to give himself a sense of belonging. With their help and my determination, I was able to prove to others that I could make it at something.

When times were tight and money was tighter, we learned how to make do with what was available. I remember making a "baseball" ball one time when we didn't have one to play with. It was an old sock tied in several knots, wound with some old tobacco twine and then covered tightly in black plastic electrical tape. It was hard to throw a curve ball with it because it had such a slick surface, but it sure played well in the rain.

As you can imagine, keeping that many kids in line could be a chore. There were all ages and backgrounds to deal with. Clarence "Petey" Mitchell was the man for the job, at least for the boys. He was ex-military and would not be caught dead with anything on except the khaki colored looking clothes you see in the military. Add in a hawksbill knife and he could put the fear of God in anyone. But when he came out with the oak paddle, it was your worst nightmare. He had what seemed to be an endless supply of those suckers. He also seemed to take great pleasure in demonstrating the laws of physics as it pertained to the force of an oak paddle applied directly to the rear-end of a disobedient kid.

Petey had the belief that he was an expert barber. He specialized in one style, the buzz cut. Many times he would ask a kid how they would like to get their hair cut, only to see the look on their face when he went to his specialty.

During the time I was at the home, kids were assigned chores to do. With several hundred acres of land to farm and numerous buildings to maintain, there was plenty to do. There were several "details". There was farm detail, kitchen detail, maintenance detail, turkey detail, etc. You rotated around at different times of the year. Although Petey was gruff at times, he did have a soft side if you could ever find it. The guys always wanted to get on Petey's maintenance detail because they knew one of the perks was that he would go into town often. Going into town was like you had won the lottery. You got to see other people, shop for things like lawnmower parts, get a drink and/or a candy bar. You were in high cotton! I think what really made this so enjoyable was the fact that you were doing things that ordinary families were doing so you felt almost normal, or at least I did for a short while.

Farm detail was another assignment I enjoyed. Mr. Mixon and his family were pretty much left in charge of the farm when I first got there. They were a very loving, caring and humble family. They were in it with all the children for reasons other than the meager salary he earned for his family. Their children were not children that had been admitted to the home but rather were part of the home as the result of being children of parents who worked there. They easily could have had resentment for being associated with "orphans". However, they have and will always be considered a part of the big family of the Children's Home. A relationship closer than a brother or sister is a bond that defies description.

One of the many fond memories of my experience at the Children's Home was working on the farm that they operated. After the combine had gone through the fields and picked the ears of corn, we would come along and gather the remaining corn that had fallen to the ground. As the tractor was pulling the trailer along through the field, we would find an ear of corn laying on the ground and immediately drop back to pass in the land of make believe, fire a wobbly spiral (corn was never designed for tight spirals) toward our imaginary receiver (the trailer) only to see it over shoot the mark and put a nice goose egg on the forehead of the unfortunate soul near the trailer.

One of the things that sticks out in my mind while at the Home was the ownership of a vehicle (or in some cases a motorcycle). I guess the earliest I can remember anyone having a vehicle would have been Marshall Heath. I could be wrong on this, but I definitely remember him being around cars a lot so I may have thought some of them were in fact his.

Some of the more outstanding memories about cars and motorcycles would be Denny Edward's ('65-'73) Chevy and Claudius Elmore's ('60-'73) Honda motorcycle. Denny had what I thought was the most beautiful car in the world at the time. Remember, at the time I was a younger man and was infatuated by the thought of owning something so desirable by so many other guys. His car was jacked up in the back with raised white letter tires on Cragar chrome rims. I'll never forget it. It had the sweetest metallic moan when it was started up.

And then there was Claudius' Honda motorcycle that I worshipped all most as much as he did. He kept that thing so clean it's amazing any paint stayed on it as much as he washed it. If he parked it outside on a sunny day, it had so much chrome on it that planes flying in the area had to detour around the Children's Home because of the glare. It was sweet! And I wanted to ride it. So, one night he made the mistake of leaving it unguarded. I also knew where he would hide the keys. I had an obsession with that bike. It was love at first sight. I can't be blamed for my actions. It was a full moon and I could see well enough to maybe ride it around the ball field a few times. I quietly pushed it out of the basement and down the hill by the ball field so as not to be heard by anyone. Fired it up and started cruising around the field. It was a great feeling to be able to scratch that itch I'd had for so long. No harm, no foul, right? Wrong! Who was I fooling, once I fired it up everyone at the entire Home must have heard me doing doughnuts on the ball field. At that moment, I didn't really care; I was fulfilling a need.

In the mist of doing my doughnuts, I laid it over on the side a few times, just enough to cover some of that shiny chrome with ball field red clay mud. After my "Paul Revere" night ride, I took great care in making sure I placed the bike back in exactly the same place it was in. But in my haste, I failed to remove the incriminating evidence. I tiptoed back up stairs and crawled into bed as if I were fast asleep.

Next thing I hear is Claudius stomping down the hallway saying something about killing somebody. I had a gut feeling he may be talking about me. I knew the best chance I had for survival was to play "possum" or I might be dead. When he came storming into my room yelling for me to wake up, I did the best acting job Hollywood had ever seen. My eyes were closed tight and I held my breath, hoping he wouldn't notice I was shaking like a leaf under the covers. He yelled and yelled some more but I wasn't about to move an inch so that he might think I was waking up.

Now, I knew Claudius was a smart guy and he had to know that I wasn't really asleep just scared sh--less. I think somewhere during the venting he realized he didn't want to kill me after all because if he did he knew he would have to answer to Petey. That would have been even worse than my fate. So he tortured me by just leaving me there to lay awake all night long wondering if he would come back in the middle of the night and finish me off when there would be no witnesses.

Seriously though, I would say that allowing the kids at the Home to own a car or motorcycle was a great learning experience. We learned to appreciate what we had worked so hard to buy. I know why Denny and Claudius were so proud and protective of what they had. They had worked hard for what they had and no one was going to take it away from them without a brawl. The same thought process carried over into many other things. Hard work translated into reward and when you were thrust into an environment as we were, you needed as much reward as you could to temper the pain.

I don't want anyone to misunderstand me, when I say pain I do not mean physical or mental abuse. I have never felt that way about the Home. When I was punished, it was because I deserved it. I'm talking about the pain of confusion, the pain that came with not completely understanding why I was there in the first place. Claiming ownership to something of value, although it was material in nature, gave me a sense of belonging. I always struggled trying to describe my feelings but I guess I would say it made me feel like I was worth something to somebody, just like the objects we treasured.

Children of unfortunate circumstances will never know any better unless they are offered an alternative. The Children's Home became that alternative. It has produced a great number of executives, government officials, doctors, lawyers and many other respectable professions. I firmly believe that giving us, the children of the home, a chance to experience a different way of life than what we were accustomed to made the difference in many of our lives. I thank God someone cared enough to get me and my three brothers placed at the home. There is no doubt it saved my life.

You have heard it said many times; "I would not trade my experiences for anything in the world." Without any doubt, that is true for me. I would not be the person I am today without going through the things I have in my life. I have a better understanding of the value of money because I had so little. When I did have some, I was very careful in how I spent it. But more importantly, I know how it is not to have certain things and I would like to believe I am more sensitive to the needs of others as the result of my experiences while at the home. I think you will find that most of the children from the home have a willingness to share with others because of such an experience.

The Shirt

One incident that occurred while I was at the home will always stand out in my mind. At the time I did not know it would make such a lasting impression on me. Now, looking back on it, I see it played a big part in molding me to be who I am today.

The Children's Home used to accept used clothing for the children to wear. One morning, while I was in high school, I remember frantically searching for a shirt to wear to school. It was getting late and I knew the school bus was about to arrive. Missing the school bus was a definite no-no. We really didn't want to have to answer to Petey. That didn't happen very many times before you had an automatic appointment with the infamous oak paddle. Since the clothes were used, occasionally you would find a small tear or maybe a stain on them. After a long search for the right shirt to match my pants I found what I thought to be just the right one. A deep rose color that was perfect. I scanned it carefully for any holes or stains that might lead to later embarrassment. It looked good so I quickly put it on, buttoned it up and readied myself for the school bus to arrive. Not long after getting on the bus and finding a seat, someone promptly asked what was wrong with my shirt. I had no idea what they were talking about since I had just recently spent a good bit of time looking over the shirt before putting it on. They pointed out the collar as their reason for the question. I quickly started tugging at the collar and twisting my head back and forth in an effort to get a peak at what they were talking about. As I grabbed the collar to look, small pieces of the material crumbled in my hand. It appeared the collar had been burned while being ironed, making the material very brittle. The more I touched the collar, the more the material came crumbling off, exposing the white part underneath that was used to stiffen the collar and make it stand up properly.

As you might imagine, a deep rose-colored shirt with a crumbling collar against a white background stood out like an orphan at a country club social. I couldn't hide, so the next best thing was to somehow play it off. A lot of the kids on the bus were from the home so I could deal with that, knowing they probably felt for me. Getting to school was a whole different situation. I had the entire day to worry about who would notice my ratty old shirt and what they would think. I had no way to change so I had to live with it.

Looking back on it, I don't recall my friends ever making as big a deal of it as I did. Knowing my situation, I have to believe they had no desire to pile on. At the time it really bothered me. I already felt like I was different than the others kids and this just made me stand out in a more visible way. I could hardly wait to get back home so I could get that shirt off. I would guess, as much as anything else, that may have lead to me being so particular about my clothes in the future.

More than anything, I learned that it's okay to be different. In fact, sometimes it's better. You can set your own path in life and don't have to just follow the masses. I suppose that shirt would be considered cool, based on the fashion of the youth today. Most of the guys had jeans with holes in them. We didn't know we were so cool at the time.

I also learned that what matters is who you really are and not what others perceive you to be. So many people want to be like someone else. Not satisfied with who they are. The poor want fancy clothes and fancy cars. The rich want wrinkled shirts and tattered jeans. Most of my close friends know who I am. I am certainly not ashamed of it. A true friend, to me, is just like family and family would give you the shirt off their back if you needed one and that is what really counts.

During my time at the Children's Home, the children went from a small community school called Middlesex High School to the newly built and much larger school called Southern Nash High School, which pulled kids from several communities in the county. This meant a much bigger school campus and a lot more kids. For an insecure kid like me, this was overwhelming. In so many ways it was like starting over again. I had to try to establish new friends all over again only to be asked "where are you from?" and then having to explain that I live in an orphanage. More often than not that would be followed by "why are you there?" At that time in my life it was quite embarrassing to have to explain my family situation. It was not until I got in college that I was able to talk about my past and be proud of it rather than be embarrassed by it. Now, as I look back on my experience at the home, I'm more ashamed that I ever felt embarrassment at all. I am very proud of who I've become despite the obstacles I had to face at an earlier age. I believe it had a lot to do with preparing me for the future.

After I graduated high school in the summer of 1975, I left the home and from then on was basically on my own. I stayed in the college dorm during the school year. When the school year ended, I had to move out of the dorm and find a place to stay for the summer. This meant finding a job to afford rent, food, utilities and car expenses. You grow up quick when facing those type decisions as a teenager. Looking back, I wouldn't trade them for anything. They prepared me for life and it made it much easier to accept certain situations later on in my life rather than complain about them. Like the saying goes, I was able to roll with the punches, and there were plenty of punches.

Among the many faults I possess, the one that has pushed me the most in my life I would say is pride. Although pride can destroy people, it can also be a strong motivator. I believe it has been the driving force behind any success I may have attained. Hearing and knowing the stories of how and why the children came to be at the Children's Home had an enormous impact on my outlook on life. I was determined to show the world that although I did not have a mom and dad like the traditional family, I could still accomplish anything I set my mind to do. Knowing there were a hundred others kids with similar situations as mine, I wanted to succeed at whatever I tried, not only to prove to myself that I could do it but also to encourage the others. I felt like I was carrying the banner for the entire home, although I know that I was not. It is very hard to explain but I felt as if I was justifying the existence of the Children's Home and myself. I am very proud to say that I am from the home. In order to survive mentally from the traumatic experience of separation from the only parental figures I knew, I had to seize any positive feedback as my motivation and continually suppress any doubts that would arise about whether any one cared about me at all. When I was able to do that, I felt a strong sense of accomplishment.

I will always remember telling myself that, as long as I am able to work, I will never be poor again. I knew what it was like and I didn't like it. I also remember telling myself that one day I would be a millionaire. I have since come to realize how misguided my thinking was at the time. Success in my life is not measured by whether I become a millionaire or not. Success is when you can take what you have and be happy with it.

Specifics about certain people and things that happened while I was at the home have become blurred. Maybe it's partly due to the length of time that has passed and partly due to the desire to suppress deep emotional events. To me the most important thing to reflect on is how they had an impact on who I am today.

As you can imagine, with as many people as we had at the Children's Home over the course of its existence, there have been plenty of characters to go around. There certainly was during the time I lived there. For whatever reason, we were prone to giving people nicknames that stuck. Higgy, Bo and Turkey were just a few that come to mind. I guess it was our way of identifying someone without getting to close to them. You never knew when a kid might be "redeemed" by a family member. I was never in the military but I feel certain it was something similar. You bring several people together from all walks of life, expect them to get along together and then suddenly you lose one that you had become great friends with. It can create great voids in a person's life. It can also create very strong bonds. A bond that is so strong that, when your friends hurt you, you hurt even more. These are friendships that you can't adequately describe to others that have not had the same experience.

One of the characters that I will always remember was a kid named Tim Pittman ('64-'76), "Birdman". While many of us were into others things like sports and girls, more often than not in that same order, Tim was completely consumed with the outdoors. He loved being outdoors and learning about wildlife. During school days the rest of us were thinking about sleeping to the last second before the school bus came to pick us up for school. Tim, on the other hand, was probably out breaking ice in one of the creeks around the home to check his traps at 4:30 in the morning on a freezing cold day before going to school. When he wasn't actually doing these things he would be reading about wildlife and the outdoors. Most of us kids could care less about sitting down and reading on our own. We did if we were forced to for school work, but on our own, forget it! Tim could be seen many times carrying a book around as if it were magnetized to his hand. He amazed me at how he was so focused on what he loved. I guess I was the same way about sports but just didn't recognize it at the time. As I have told my kids, you must have a passion to have a life. Passion can be demonstrated in many ways. Tim's was the love for the outdoors. Mine was sports. My way of self-identity and belief in myself was developed through my passion for sports. I think you will find that many of the children who have gone on to lead productive lives developed that passion for something early on in their lives. I also think it was a way of identifying who we were and not just accepting ourselves as castoffs from society.

My experience at the Children's Home gave me my view on family. Although I cannot fully convey to my children what it meant to be raised at the home, I have tried to share with them what it was like. Hopefully, they will have a better understanding about who I am and what I stand for as the result of our talks.

As I have told my children, family is everything. Money comes and goes. When others may have abandoned you or the money has run out and you don't know which way to turn, family will always be there for you. Even if you have burned enough bridges along the way to make the Union Army blush, true family will always be there to help you cross any chasm you may face. You may not be able to build a fortune, but you certainly can build a name. I am living proof of that very fact. We all as Faircloths have an obligation to each other to build the family name not tear it down.

One thing I have found about myself is that I am not the most organized person you will meet. Ideas pop into my head and many times they pop out just as quickly before I even have time to act on them. So many times I do not complete a project I have undertaken until much later or until my wife pushes me enough before I finally get it done.

I would consider myself to be a dreamer. I am sure the experiences at the home had a lot to do with that. When I didn't have money or I felt that I wasn't being recognized, which was a common theme for all the children, I could at least dream of such times. Those dreams are what kept me going.

The Children's Home or the children would not have survived had it not been for all the support from the many, many people over the years. So many of these people will never be mentioned by name for their help, but I know I speak for all the children when I say they will never know how much we truly appreciate all their help.

I could not possibly write about my experiences at the home without mentioning the Nunnally family. I am who I am because of this family and the matriarch, Bertha Mae Silverthorne Nunnally. Growing up in the very rural area of Whortonsville, in eastern North Carolina, Bertha Mae Silverthorne lived every day of her life with family in mind.

I first met the Nunnally family when they came, one of the many times, to the home to pick up another kid to come and visit with them. I hit it off early on with their two sons, Wave and Paul. They also had a daughter named Anne. I found someone who had the same passion for sports as I did and it was on from there. We would play some sport, whatever one was in season at the time, take a break and talk about sports and then go right back to playing again. We were eaten up with it. We have had many a battle over the years competing against one another and shared many a laugh along the way as well. These were the kind of things that ordinary families with siblings might do. That's how I was drawn to this family, through the common thread of sports.

Eventually, I was accepted into the family as if I were a Nunnally by birth. You don't really know what love is until you have someone bring you into their family unconditionally. When I would visit at Christmas time, I would get just as much and sometimes more than any of their own three children. I still get overwhelmed with emotion every time I think about how someone could do so much for me without expecting anything in return. I have come to understand what true love is all about.

If I had to characterize who I have become as the result of my experience at the home, I would have to say I am a person who is deeply loyal to friends and family. As I reflect back on it, I am humbled knowing so many people showed interest in a confused little boy.

30

You're the Best of the Best!

Brenda Mitchell
1946-65

"Bootie Baby" is a name my Dad gave me when I was an infant at the Orphanage. My little feet would kick and dance in the air when he came up to the crib and spoke to me - so he called me his little "Bootie Baby". I would be so happy to see him and I loved him so much and could recognize him and my little feet in booties would just kick up a plenty!

L-R: Clarence, Brenda and Mary Mitchell

Every once in a while when I'm in the vicinity of Nash County and Middlesex, North Carolina I get this familiar urge to drive the back roads leading to the campus of the Free Will Baptist Children's Home . The memories ebb and flow with emotion just bittersweet, as I ride through the countryside past the farm and pond. I remember the animal barns and shelters that are no longer standing, along with the two homes that once stood in the vicinity. I recall climbing the apple orchard trees for sweet green apples to munch on, the beef cows grazing, pigs, and chickens…all needed to help feed the children throughout the year.

Slowly, I reach "the hill," as it was called back then, separating the campus from the farm. I see the campus today and remember the years past with the sounds of activity and laughter. The kitchen bell calling us to meals flooded back to my memory. I could almost smell the fresh cut grass and the dusty road running in front of the boys' cottage. Many days and evenings we sat on that old front porch when we were tired, hot and needing to be cooled from the heat, to keep the rain off, or just the smell of a summer rain on a dusty, dirt road after an afternoon or evening shower, brings the flooding of memories. Looking back and realizing those years could be defined as the best of times and the worst of times for my psyche.

I don't go back often to the yearly "homecomings." Somehow, it is just so hard for me to endure. I dab at my eyes constantly and feel embarrassed, seeing people looking my way in the chapel as the designated speaker recalls the memories from the time they spent at the Home.

That brings me to the real reason for writing about the Mitchell family. I am the daughter of Clarence Lee and Mary Harriet Price Mitchell. My name is Brenda Lee Mitchell Overton and my brother, Clarence Steven and I lived in the boys' cottage over the years as Dad and Mom were employed there. I might also add my Aunt Kay, Thelma Kay Mitchell Rulli, my Dad's sister, also was employed in the girls' dormitory. They were both reared at the Home, but two other siblings, older sister Effie and baby sister Arleetha, never joined them in Middlesex. Arleetha died from complications due to burns at three years old, and Effie, the oldest sister, died after giving birth to a daughter later on in adult life. The siblings were orphaned in the great flu epidemic of 1918-1919. They lost their Daddy one day and their Mother the next; they are buried in pauper graves in Wilson County. They lived with family relatives for a period of time and then my Dad (Clarence Mitchell ['23-'32]) and Aunt Thelma Kay Mitchell ['23-'30]) eventually coming to the Home. My Dad said the hardest thing he and Aunt Kay endured was the absence of relatives who would or could have made an effort to visit and never did for seven years.

Dad said he entered the Home around seven and Aunt Kay was two years older, as best I recall. Their parents' grave markers were only letters and records were destroyed in a fire at the cemetery. I've seen the graves but a long time ago…pauper graves. There were no names, just a white cross with a letter engraved. "Info" in the office matched the letters. There were no death dates for either parent, but they were probably between September, 1918 and January, 1919.

I remember Aunt Kay speaking of her shyness, sadness, loneliness, and crying in the night for her Mother and Daddy while living in the old dormitory that once housed the school, laundry, living and sleeping area for the children. Even though the old dormitory has been long torn down, she recalled how austere life was for them both at the old dormitory and their life at the home. Yet, both were thankful for a place to live, plenty of good food, other children, but they missed the most important unit needed to be a family--their parents and sisters. It hurt them, but they endured by living one day at a time for years...dreaming of their family again.

Recalling events of their years spent at the Home was interesting and sad. Dad spoke of the 1929 storm and the lightening strike that took the lives of two of the boys working at the dairy located where the boys' cottage is today. Another story relates to a haircut he was giving one of the boys outside. As a plane flew over, they both looked up...Daddy took his eyes off the haircut and the young boy just long enough to nick the top of the ear off! For the remainder of his life that mishap stayed in my Daddy's mind... he truly was sorry it occurred. Loneliness and a fear of harsh punishment from Superintendent C. G. Pope ('21-'29) due to his behavior patterns was a constant reminder during his 1923 to 1932 years spent at the home.

Dad left the Orphanage on Saturday, December 31, 1932. He stayed with the Reverend and Mrs. Bennett from Beaufort, North Carolina. Shortly after leaving, while he was crossing a road or street, he was hit by a car, had surgery and had steel pins put in that leg afterwards. He received a settlement from the injury. He worked for a while at a sawmill and then worked at cargo docks and on Merchant Marines boats. Dad moved out of the Bennett house in the late 30's or early 40's and went to work as a single man at the Orphanage in Middlesex.

Aunt Kay left the Orphanage December 5, 1930. She worked in Maysville, North Carolina, the Odd Fellow's Building in Goldsboro, and, I believe, Cherry Hospital. She met the handsome John (Johnnie Rulli) from New York State. He was first generation Italian living in the USA. He was in the Air Force...met her during the war... had been overseas in England and Africa. They married in either 1942 or 1943, not sure of the month, but before Mom and Dad, I believe. Aunt Kay worked at Bloomingdale's in Manhattan in the lingerie department and sometimes filled in at the candy department (they had chocolate covered grasshoppers and crickets to sell, she told me-ugh!) John sold Electrolux vacuum cleaners. They had a convertible sports car and lived in an apartment in Astoria, New York. He had bone cancer and died in 1953 and is buried at Calvary Cemetery in New York. She had two miscarriages during their marriage. The Rulli's were a big family that was close. Oh, the Italian food was delicious. She felt alone after his death, so decided to move back to N.C. to live and work and be close to My Daddy.

Aunt Kay was my second Mom, or so it seemed. We were close and I was the daughter she never had in life. She made me clothes and cut my hair. We had many talks and discussed anything I felt, thought, or believed in. I loved her dearly.

Dad and Mom were married March 2, 1943, while he was in military service. Aunt Kay traveled to Texas on a train with Mom where Dad and Mom were married. It was some little place near Belton and Killeen, Texas. Dad was 29 and mom 17. They lived off base and Mom had a picture of the two of them on steps of their house. Dad talked about serving in Guam, Mariana Islands, Camp Polk in Louisiana, and Fort Hood, Texas. I'm not sure of all of his overseas duty, though. He was a sergeant in the Army and worked on repairing engines. He was so good at the craft… he was like a "go to guy" for questions on how to evaluate a repair or what needed to be done to repair or rebuild an engine at the repair unit shop when others had a problem or couldn't get the vehicles back on the road again…so he said.

I was born October 12, 1946 at Carolina General Hospital in Wilson and my mother brought me home to the Orphanage. We lived in the small, still standing house across the road from the pond. Then, we lived in a white colored two-storied brick building for boys located where the young girls have dorms still standing today. I lived at the Home around 16 years. In my early teen years, I ironed and pressed clothes for the older boys in the dorm when they found wrinkles in their shirt prior to a date. People always said to me, "I just can't believe you live in a building with all those boys." The boys were like brothers to me.

Dad was hired by Superintendent James Evans ('40-'49) to work at the Orphanage prior to his entering the Army during WWII. Shortly after he was released from the Army in 1945, he and Mom returned to the Orphanage as matrons for the boys. My Mother chose to work with Dad at the Home and they worked there until 1950. I believe Superintendent

Walter Croom ('49-'51) terminated my Dad's employment. Walter Croom ('30-'39) was a child in the Orphanage with my Dad. They may have had differences in childhood that carried over into adulthood.

My parents moved to Keener, North Carolina in Sampson County. Dad ran a dairy as the production manager for a wealthy doctor who owned milk cows. They processed white and chocolate milk in huge stainless vats from this little plant. J. C. Butts ('37-'50) left the Orphanage May 30, 1950 and went to work with my Father. He bought a motorcycle and he and Dad would ride at times. The doctor gave us a collie dog named Sam that was used to round up cows. We, along with Sam, returned to the Orphanage in 1953 and I entered the first grade. I lived 15 years of my childhood at the Orphanage with my parents. They both worked in the boys' dormitory as house parents. Dad worked on the farm, maintained the grounds and, at one time, was the barber at the Home (remember those short cropped do's, guys?). During later years, after we had a swimming pool installed for all the kids to enjoy, he worked there and at the laundry on certain days. Turkeys were raised and an incubator was used for turning and hatching the eggs located in the boiler room at the back of the boys' building.

Bootie with Jerry's duck - "Big Boy"

My parents were disciplinarians--some delegated from the superintendents and some of their own doing. They were human and we all err in life, but they both loved the Free Will Baptist Children's Home and the children there. They tried to teach the children how to stand up on your own two feet and have a good understanding of what was right and wrong and to have a backbone. Hardships were a part of it already…they cared about the outcome for each child, as it wasn't going to be as easy for some of them as for others. Dad used to say he never could forget the people in his life who reached out to help and support him. He stopped to pick up strangers and hitchhikers along the roads and Mom and I would fuss at him. He would say, "Look, if someone had not stopped along the way and reached out to help me from time to time along this journey from an orphaned child to a grown man, I don't know where I might be today."

Jerry Smith ('49-'60) was one of the boys that stands out in my mind from years past. He was popular, enjoyed sports and excelled. Girls thought he was really attractive. His sister, Nancy ('49-'60) was a beautiful, sweet girl and kind to all. Jerry had a duck he brought with him to the Orphanage that he called "Big Boy," and this little duck followed him everywhere. Jerry was serious about his life and what he was going to achieve. He used to help me with math problems, when I would ask. Jerry and Nancy's father would come to visit in a convertible sports car…just the envy of us all. Mr. Smith was very personable and friendly during his frequent visits to see his children.

Some other boys that also excelled in sports and were handsome brothers that the girls wished to date were Jacob ('46-'59) and Robert Lee Lane ('46-'59)! Rod Page ('40-'57) and Alton Bryant ('46-'58). Not very far behind in memory is the Elmore brothers, with Otis Elmore ('58-'65) probably my closest friend who operated the candy store, or so we called it. Phil Mercer ('53-'68) lost his sister, Sandra ('53-'65) while at the Home. She was so brave. Daniel Rouse ('55-'64) and his brother Steve ('55-'66) were good guys. Bobby Herring ('52-'59) could always make me laugh to tears. Billy Hines ('54-'62) and his brother, Jesse ('54-'65) were good people. Glenn ('54-'62) and Ronald Worthington ('54-'63) were always funny. Steve ('54-'63), their brother, would help me when I asked for help with math problems. The Cantrell brothers, Jimmy ('54-'64) and David ('53-'65) were such funny guys. Tommy ('55-'65) and Willie Lancaster ('55-'66) and Jerry Langston ('55-'67) were good guys.

I remember Ray Worthington ('56-'69) telling me, "Bootie I remember the first time I ever saw you. You had on a cowgirl hat, your blond hair in pigtails, a gun and holster set strapped around your waist, and a tobacco stick between your legs, galloping around the corner of the building pretending you were riding your horse!"

Barry Rogers ('48-'61) was always saying to me, "Bootie, if you keep eating the way you do now, we are going to have to start calling you two-ton-Harris!" He was a funny boy and never meant to hurt me, but used to love to tease me...I did my share of teasing him, too. I'll tell you, at 12 years old it made me start thinking and I would run a lap or two around the circle at night to keep my figure in check in later years.

Sweet Andrew Hartsfield's ('59-'69) was such a joy to know and be around; so was John William Heath ('53-'62), Wilbert Earl Heath ('53-'60), Foy Watson ('51-'63) and Eddie Watson ('47-'56). I just adored J. C. Stallings ('52-'62), nicknamed "Higgins," and his brother Jerry ('53-'60) was a sweet person. Eugene Waller ('53-'64) was cute, well handsome. Arthur Mace ('46-'57) was so kind, sends cards and always asks about the Home and everyone.

At Christmas one year, former Governor Jim Hunt came by on a black limousine late in the day. He left a huge ham-- or was it a turkey, or maybe both-- for the Home. No kids were there because they were on vacation. Dad accepted the food gift. He put the food in a freezer at the storage room behind the kitchen and later reported the gift.

One of the boys who lived at the Orphanage, Billy Powell ('38-'49), was accused of murdering someone. Years later, after released from prison, he came back one afternoon and took us to ride to the hill and back in his convertible--yes, this really happened!

Dad told my husband, Wayne, that he helped the state people map the creeks/branches on the Children's Home property. Since there was no name for the branch behind the baseball field/turkey pen, the man from the state named that branch after my dad and now it's called Mitchell Branch.

The old pump house still stands today where my Dad and the boys worked so diligently over the years. I can still smell the sawdust, grease and clover from freshly cut grass. Keeping the Home going day to day for all of us seemed our duty...we did it too! Just one big family, until we lost sweet Sandra Mercer ('53-'65). Her death hurt all of us...she was so very young and lovely. Her portrait hangs in Memorial Chapel as a remembrance to her.

After we found out Daddy had terminal cancer, he and Mom came by to visit and eat dinner with me one afternoon after visiting the mausoleum where he would be entombed. He wanted a baked ham with brown sugar and raisin sauce and potato salad. Later, he and my oldest son, David (just five at the time) sat on the back porch in the sun. Dave told him about the bumble bees and wasps in the yard. Dad asked where were they and little Dave showed him the holes in the wooden fence post. Dad collected small sticks and pushed them in the holes at each post and broke them off, looked at Dave and said, "Now the bees won't sting or chase you and Brian (my youngest son) when you play in the yard." Many days we sat under a huge oak tree in a swing in our back yard and some evenings watched fire flies (lightening bugs) before he or Aunt Kay or Mom went back home. He loved us and our family has never really been the same unit we once were before he passed on. He was tough and could also be gentle as a lamb.

Dad died in 1975. Rabion Bryant ('41-'54) sat with him the week before he died and was at his bedside the night before his death. Daddy was a Mason and Mom secured a Masonic ring for him to wear. He was a member of Roger Lodge #525 in Middlesex. He talked often of how you could tell a true mason by the way they shook your hand--by the way they held the fingers--suppose to be secretive and he would never tell us how due to some oath.

Mom is 84 years old and in a skilled nursing facility due to medical problems. She still loves to talk of the 40 years she spent at the Home. I used to say, "Mom, these folks don't care about your 40 years at the home." She would turn my way and say, "But I care and you should too…because I love those boys and girls who were raised there, they were my life."

The Gay Brothers---Delma Gay ('66-'77) has helped by sitting with Mom and feeding her when we weren't sure whether or not she was going to make it due to congestive heart trouble. Johnny Gay (('66-'76) traveled from Ohio recently to visit and boo-hooed like a baby. I paid Ronnie Gay ('66-'76) to paint her little home once. They are the nephews of Rabion and Alton Bryant ('46-58). Bobby Thigpen ('49-'52 & '57-'62), Daniel Rouse ('55-'64) and Jerry Smith have visited with Mom during her sickness.

L-R: Steve Mitchell, Phil Mercer and Marshal Heath

    Steve and I will never forget the Home, as we felt like outsiders because we had our parents and they could be with us each day. It was hard for us, too…I choose not to recall names or quotes or conversations. If my Dad and Aunt Kay (Ms. Rulli) could open their eyes from eternal rest, they would smile at the mention of the Home, I am sure. Each one of you is special and loved, regardless of your situation. They, too, would often say "why me" just as each of you have at some time in life. Just remember: if any of you feel any less of a human being for having been at the Home, don't. If you have problems or situations that aren't resolved, just remember--"You can't find peace until you find all the pieces."

    All of you were special and I love you…you were my Children Home brothers! I'm glad I knew you, for you're "the best of the best"!

Footnote: Clarence Mitchell worked at the Orphanage '45-'50 & '53-'75. He died September 1, 1975, age 60, and is entombed at Oakwood Cemetery in a mausoleum, Raleigh, North Carolina. Dr. James Evans (Superintendent '40-'49) officiated his funeral. Jimmy Cantrell ('53-'64) and other Alumnus were his pallbearers. Thelma Kay Mitchell Rulli worked at the Orphanage '54-'79 and died June 13, 1994, age 81. Dr. W. Burkette Raper (Alumnus '36-'45) officiated her funeral. She is buried near the curb at the meditation garden, Evergreen Cemetery, Wilson, North Carolina. Mary Mitchell, 84, is in Guardian Care facility in Zebulon, North Carolina.

31

Not Just a Home for Children

Stewart Humphrey
1970-72 & 1977-81

Humphrey Family - L-R: Back Row Todd, Stewart, Linda
Front Row – Mark

When orphanages or children's homes are mentioned, our minds usually immediately recall an individual we know or have known that spent a portion of their life in one of these "homes". For many, these thoughts are positive. Like so many experiences in our society, being raised in a children's home or orphanage was the very best thing that could have happened to the individual in mind from our perspective as well as theirs. On the other hand, the story more often told in the media, is the other one, the one about abuse, loneliness and disappointment. The writers in this book, and there are countless other positive stories out there, tell of a life filled with opportunity and hope a "home", though not necessarily perfect, where they were loved and cared for and, yes, disciplined as well; a "home" where staff became surrogate parents who laughed and loved and cried along with them. It is they/we, the "staff" I write about in this chapter.

As staff, our lives were forever changed by having lived at the "Home" as well. We came from all walks of life. There were pastors' widows who had lived in the shadow of their husband's ministry through the years who now felt the call to carry on in ministry. The "Home "became their ministry and their "home" as well. Seminary students from the local seminary found a home, a ministry and a new perspective on life. <u>But of all those who deserve a larger measure of credit are the individuals who grew up at the "Home" went off to war or to find their fortune and made the circle back, to become lifelong house parents, maintenance men and had families of their own, who like they themselves, grew up at the "Home"</u>.

My own journey was not unlike many of the superintendents/executive directors. Many of us were pastors who were called on by the Board of the" Home" or, in my case, a friend who was the superintendent at the time, to serve. I had been pastoring for half dozen or so years and had spent several summers working at our church youth retreat in the mountains of North Carolina as a camp counselor with that same friend. As a pastor, I encouraged the churches I served to form Boy Scout Troops. I enjoyed camping with the Scouts and spent several weeks in the summers as the camp chaplain for the Scouts. My training was centered in Christian education and Social Work. So, I guess in some sense I had been preparing for the role for a long time without knowing it.

In 1970, I became the Director of Campus Life, sort of like the Assistant Superintendent I suppose, of the Children's Home. All the time I had spent with young people was no preparation for the immensity of the task before me. In those days, there were few men on campus and they had limited responsibility for the care of the children other than working them in their particular area of expertise, usually maintenance or the farm. With the exception of one cottage, all were "manned" or "womaned" by single females who worked a month at the time with a two-day weekend off. The kids ate in the cottages so she had to prepare all the meals with the help of the children and an occasional aide. That left my friend as the "HEAD MALE" and me as "NUMBER TWO MALE" in 60 children's lives. At least that's how we perceived it. Today, when you ask about the people in their lives, the answer is more likely to be the farm manager, the maintenance man or a teacher at school. But when it came to permissions for outside activities not related to daily life, we did have a role to play. As you can imagine, it went this way. When the kids couldn't get their way with the house parent, they came to me. When they couldn't get there way with me, they went to my friend the superintendent. On occasion, we all agreed; but, more often than not one of us knuckled under and let them have some semblance of their way. What a way to run a railroad or a children's home, but it was life. It was family. It was surprisingly like most other families, only there were more members and the grocery bill was humongous.

The children presented many challenges, of course, but as most administrators will tell you, often the staff was the greatest challenge. I had not been in town long before through my open bedroom window one early morning I could hear a house parent verbally abusing one of the children outside the cottage before school. Later that morning, I confronted her about her behavior and she denied every allegation. This individual had been reported by the children before, but because of a perceived lack of confirming evidence which led to many atrocities in these kinds of facilities, both then and now, no action had been taken other than a reprimand. "But I heard you this time with my own ears", I told her, and she still denied the incident. I asked her to pack and be gone before the children came home from school. I had just fired a fellow human being. She was very upset. She felt I had wronged her. And, I was having feelings unlike any I had ever had before. I think it was probably then that I realized what it meant to have real power over another human being. I had not felt that power before in hiring people to work, in making decisions for or against a person's will. For the first time, I felt the curse of power over another. Justified as I was in the decision to let the individual go, I would feel that curse again. There is a sermon to be preached here about the use and abuse of power but we will save that for another book.

The Bill and Marty (their names have been changed to protect the innocent) event is remembered well, not only by myself, but for at least one of those youngsters involved as well. We had the opportunity to visit together some years later and he asked if I remembered the event and I told him I did. That was the most embarrassing evening I have ever spent. Two of the boys had gotten into a fight. Both were about the same size, both bigger than I and they were going at it pretty well when I arrived. Rather than stepping in immediately, I hesitated for a few moments and they quickly grew tired. One had a pretty nasty cut on his face. Both were great kids and, no sooner had the fight ended, whatever it was that sparked the fray was forgotten. The less injured was genuinely concerned over the welfare of the other. The cut looked pretty deep, so I suggested that the "winner" might want to take his cottage mate to the emergency room. Believe it not, we actually let kids drive agency cars and school buses back then. It was the wait at the emergency room that did the trick. "Having to explain that it was me who inflicted the wounds was the most humbling experience of my life", he told me 25 years later.

There were many times during those years when I had to decide to let nature take its course rather than step in and try to enforce my will on a child or an adult. One night I was working in my little shop area I had set up in the storage room off the garage of the superintendent's home. One of the boys wondered in the door. I suspected something was up, but I continued to work on my project and we talked about this and that. After a while he said, "I guess I had better get back to the cottage." "What are you doing out", I asked? "Well, I was running away," he said. "I got mad and decided to leave, but I guess I will go back." I don't know if it was something I said or didn't say. One thing I had learned was that everyone needs a moment once in awhile and if we don't try to rush in to save the day, it is surprising how a fight or flight might turn into a great learning experience for everyone involved, including those of us who think we have the power to protect others from their mistakes.

Of course, there were times when I second-guessed some of the decisions I made. I have had poor vision all my life. One night one of the girls fell and hit her head pretty hard. It fell my lot to take her to the emergency room. I asked a couple of the other girls to go along to assist their cottage mate. She was bleeding pretty badly and I felt the need to make the trip to the emergency room, about 30 minutes, away as quickly as possible. I headed to Middlesex (there was no by-pass then) and as I neared town, I thought that a police escort would be of assistance since it was growing dark and I couldn't see that well anyway. The town police car was an old Chevy, probably worn out by some other town, and the policemen on duty were great fellows but a little like Barney Fife and Gomer, the deputies on the Andy Griffith show. They convinced me we could get to Wilson faster if we all got into the police car. So there we were, three kids in the back and Barney driving, me in the middle and Gomer riding shotgun. "Oh what a night"! I quickly learned the old car could run much faster than I ever dreamed. With tires crying and the car skidding around the curves, I came to believe that the girls would have been safer riding with me in the van even with my poor eyesight. Funny how the dynamics change when you find yourself totally in the hands of someone else. Remember, Barney is at the wheel. I wondered how many times children looked at us as their caretakers and wondered if we had their best interest at heart, or if we had the car under control from all the slip-sliding we seemed to do when they pressed us for answers, or when life was scary.

As I will allude to later, we had the opportunity to work at the "Home" twice. We learned things change over time. During our first term there, we would hear someone was going to run away that evening so we would sit in the Pine trees to catch them and save them from their wandering ways. Of course, they never came. I suspect they knew exactly what we were doing and were in their rooms laughing hysterically, knowing we were out there in the cold. When we were there the second time, we heard that some kids had run. Our Director of Campus Life asked me to take a ride with him. Not far out of town, he turned on a side road and in a few moments we came to the train tracks. He stopped the car and turned it off. "What now", I asked. "Just wait a few minutes", he said. A few minutes later here they came down the tracks. He simply opened the car door and stood smiling. They got in the car and giggled as we drove back home.

The impact that living on a children's home campus has on one's own children can be as traumatic as life at the "Home" is for the children who came there because of abuse and neglect. It is not uncommon for those of us who feel "called" to ministry to fling ourselves into our work without thought of our own health and welfare, as well as that of our own families. The afternoon my three-year old son stood at the screen door with tears in his eyes, shouting to the "Home" kids coming up the driveway, "Go away, he's my daddy", jolted me into reality. It had never occurred to me that I might be neglecting my own child (or at least he perceived I was neglecting him). No matter what I thought or felt, my young son was feeling he was losing his dad to all those other children that came calling. I soon learned that fact even more forcefully when he began calling me Mr. Humphrey rather than Dad. He had learned that I answered more quickly to what the other children called me. No, it was not just a home for "the children", it was also home for my child and I had failed to notice.

"Growing up on the hood of a Dodge Van", is a phrase that strikes fear and terror in my mind today. There was a time when we didn't know or were unwilling to admit that safety belts save lives. During the early days as Director of Campus Life, the Home had an old green Dodge Van. We drove it to school, the doctor's office, shopping, it went everywhere. It was about all we had at the time other than an old bus. There were no social workers, no extra staff to ferry kids around, it all fell on the shoulders of the Director of Campus Life. As I look back, it seems my greatest memories were made in that old van. On those trips with small groups of kids, you had the opportunity to interact with them individually. The banter between them as we traveled about provided more information than we could ever gleam from a more formal conversation. You can imagine how much you could learn when the kids thought you weren't listening. On most all those trips, perched on the engine cover inside that old van was my young son. His mom was attending classes at the local college and he rode with me when she was at school. We had some good times. He began to feel like "one of the kids". He had my attention, too. These strange kids who came to rob him of his dad had become his "brothers and sisters". His memories of the years we spent at the "Home" are pleasant ones. We often reminisce about the kids and where they might be and what they are doing. What a family!

Food from the store house or "manna from heaven"? Security or becoming institutionalized? We had been in the pastorate prior to coming to the" Home". Our first child was just a couple of years old. We were paying college loans and the wife was going to school part time. Pastors' salaries were meager. Many pastors had second jobs to meet the needs of their families. We had a full-time church so we did not have the opportunity to have a second job, so times were tough. You can imagine our surprise to find the" Home" had the "storehouse". The storehouse was the on-campus grocery store. It had everything the downtown grocery store had and it was FREE. Food and housing were provided for those who lived on the campus. In the pastorate, we had struggled many times to have the basic things in life. We ate a lot of cheese and macaroni. The storehouse was like going to "food heaven". Reflecting back now after more than 30 years, these wonderful blessings we enjoyed so freely and were needed so desperately at the time would also alter our lives in ways we could not imagine. <u>The lovely homes we enjoyed and the benefits of food, in addition to all the many other benefits that communal living affords, develop a false sense of security. There was no worry about where we would live or the rent going up, or whether there would be enough in this month's pay check for food, or if the utility bill had been paid.</u> We talked all the time about how to prevent the children from becoming "institutionalized" and had lost sight that we were as institutionalized as they.

After nearly 30 years living in a home provided for you and the benefits of food and the security of a huge extended family, we realized what that had come to mean as we bought our first house and had to pay for all the food, utilities and taxes! The one advantage we had, of course is that we had not grown up as a child in the "Home" and lacked the self-reliance one learns at an early age as a child in a traditional family setting. We had innate coping skills related to the outside world that the "Home" children never had. Struggle as we might to prevent it, there was and always would be a blank spot in their development that most of us had filled by loving parents from birth through our childhood.

One of the things that bothered me was the lack of involvement in the Alumni Association by the former children of the "Home". They came to events and the annual reunion but didn't participate in the leadership of the Association. I encouraged them to nominate each other for offices in the Association and a slow transition began to take place. Over time, the former children dominated the leadership. I will never forget one particular reunion. It began on Friday evening and concluded on Sunday afternoon. The kids living at the" Home" made pallets on the floor and let their senior brothers and sisters have the beds. Those beds went unused for the most part. The entire crowd stayed up all night…both nights…talking and sharing the "good old days" and some of the pain as well. For me personally, it was one of the highlights on my years at the "Home"--generations coming together, acknowledging their common past and present and creating memories of family for the future.

We had two opportunities to serve at the Children's Home. Our first term was as Director of Campus Life. We were there for about a year and a half. Leadership changed during that time and the new leadership had different goals. I felt that it was best to let the new leadership accomplish those goals in their own way, so we went back into the pastorate for four years. They were wonderful people, but something was missing. We had become infected with the wonder and joy of seeing children whose lives were disrupted by family problems bloom and grow to their potential within the safety and security of the "Home". We, too, as we said before, had come to appreciate that safety and security. While life moved on, another son was born, educations completed, and there was a deep longing that at the time we could not put our finger on. Then the word came that the Superintendent, Executive Director as they were now called" at the Children's Home was leaving. It didn't take long before I let the Children's Home Board know I was interested. Just the thought of being able to return was enough to energize me as never before. For four years I had been dead and when they asked me to come back, I was alive again. Little did I know the challenges that lay before me nor how my life would once again be altered by being a part of the Children's Home family.

In 1964 the Civil Rights Compliance Act had been passed. The Children's Home was not integrated and signing the Compliance Act required integration. Many private agencies signed right away but others chose to put it off. In 1976, when I returned to the Children's Home, that task had yet to be done. Over the next four years, it became clear to me that this step needed to be taken for many reasons. First, I believed it to be the right thing to do. All children are God's children. Second, many of the financial resources that were available to private agencies were beginning to require the signature of the Compliance Act.

Thus began one of the most defining phases of my life. It was the Children's Home Compliance dilemma that bought me to the "line in the sand" regarding my beliefs about racism. I had made hollow statements about what I would or would not do if I were ever in the position to stand up for people of color, but the test had never come. To that extent, the Children's Home became more than a ministry which I loved as much as life itself; but, it also became the greatest battle ground in my life theologically. So, the journey began.

Over the next years, I presented the case for Compliance. I went about it with the same passion as I did everything else in life. I traveled to and fro across the state telling all I encountered and the reasons why this was the right thing to do. I believed I had fully convinced leadership that this was the right thing to do. But when it came to making the decision to proceed, the support wasn't there. Right or wrong, the rank and file of the supporting body was not ready to take this monumental step, even though

I believed they should and many of them believed they should as well. I was stunned.

A few months passed and it became clear to me that something inside of me had changed and life was never going to be the same. It wasn't my passion for the children or the sheer joy I had for having this wonderful opportunity to minister in this way. I came to believe that my primary mission was to make a personal statement for myself and what I believed about the future of the Children's Home. I came to believe that the best way to make that statement was to leave this mission field for another that more closely mirrored my beliefs about this issue. So, I asked for direction and, as usual, God was faithful. He sent me to a place where Compliance had been signed but with other challenges that needed immediate attention.

My four years at the Children's Home and the struggle for Compliance was not wasted. A couple of years later the leadership again tackled the issue and this time reason prevailed. Lesson learned? We are where we are for a reason. We are in that place at a particular time for God's purpose even though we may not realize it. Our perception of what is happening at a particular place and at a particular time is limited to the present moment. We cannot see the future we might be helping create.

Contrary to what many believe, children's homes were among the innovators in children's services. During the 70's Original Free Will Baptist became a licensed child placing agency. A number of foster families were recruited and trained to be foster parents. These families served the children under 6 that were referred to the Children's Home. Often sibling sets had to be broken up when they came into DSS custody, but with the addition of foster care, now these families could be served together and receive the same supports they would have received if they had lived on campus. In addition, older teenagers who were aging out, could be placed in a foster family and begin to experience what life was like living in the community in a smaller family group.

Another innovative service offered during this time was an independent living program. The Albemarle cottages were renovated into apartments. Young people who wished to continue to live at the Children's Home after graduation, to work, prepare for college or just mature a bit more could live in one of the apartments under the supervision of the staff at the Home.

The Original Free Will Baptist Church also experimented with programming that has become popular across the country. A retirement community was developed on the same property. Senior citizens lived in housing next door to child care cottages. One of my favorite stories is of the retired bus driver from Durham who used to sit on a bench under the trees with children gathered round, telling bus driver stories. What a positive image that conjures up in one's mind. What a grand way for children who were separated from their grandparents to learn who grandparents were and the role they play in children's lives.

Leadership changes and so do the programs and services that ministries like children's homes provide. Change is inevitable. Good or bad, only history will tell.

A good bit has been written and TV news has often had a hay day with the alleged abusiveness that went on in orphanages and group homes through the years. Having lived a good portion of my life at an orphanage and having become acquainted with generations of individuals who lived out most of their lives in one of these facilities, there were times when the discipline did not seem to fit the gravity of the incident. Often in anger staff said and did things that they were later sorry for. There were the incidents of what seemed to be outright cruelty at the hands of care givers. And yes, there were those persons who should have never been allowed to work with children. Individuals who took advantage of their power and physically and sexually abused the children in their care.

Many of us grew up in what might be called a normal family with a mom and dad present in the home. We went to church every Sunday. Our parents were poor yet we were fortunate to have what we needed. However, within these "normal families" there were unspeakable moments of anger and abuse. Child abuse, by all standards today, but for the time, the education level of parents, the cultural norms around "not sparing the rod" led to what would be considered by many today as a dysfunctional family. What I saw during my years working at the orphanage (Free will Baptist Children's Home '70-'71,'78-'81 and Eliada Home for Children '81- 2001) were incidents that reminded me of my own childhood. Most staff were competent caring people who committed themselves to loving and caring for homeless children. They tried hard to make this world a safe place for children to grow up and become good citizens. But they, too, sometimes broke under the stress and said and did unkind things to children. They, too, were guided by the way their own parents had raised them and being the "good Christians they were saw corporal punishment (albeit got out of hand sometimes) as an accepted method of disciplining children."

Adults' preying on children was not limited to orphanages and instructional facilities, then or now. Our society has always had those who took advantage of the weaker members of society. Our prisons are full of them and they didn't all choose their victims from among children in orphanages. My point is simply that life at an orphanage, the good and the bad, was not all that unlike the experiences of children who were raised in "normal families" in the community. What we all know is that family is important. Children will choose to remain with a dysfunctional family rather than going into foster care or an orphanage or group home. For many that was not an option. Their families were simply not there for them. Due to death, separation because of war, or numerous other reasons the orphanage was "home". The staff was their surrogate parents. And, they experienced life, the good and the not so good, much like all other children in society. Some of those raised in an orphanage saw their glass as half empty and hopeless. Others saw their glass half filled with opportunity, hope and promise. Not so different from any other child out there in the world.

This is by no means a defense of any of the times a child suffered in group care. Group living in itself presented a power struggle between care givers and those being cared for. More often than not I suspect the care giver was as much the victim as the victimizer. I would compare it to a theme we often hear today. Parents often fail to discipline their children because they are afraid their children will come back at them with the words, "I hate you or you don't love me". In a group setting, I suspect the care givers often saw the maintaining of the balance power as much a protection for the whole group rather than intentional abusiveness of any one child. Maybe flawed, but nevertheless, with the exception of a few of those who should have never been caring for children in the first place, their best effort to provide a safe place for children to grow up.

Another lesson learned from the children? When it's over, it is over. Some might think I moved on from the Children's Home with some bitterness in my heart. No, not at all. Some disappointment maybe, but not bitterness. You see, I had seen too many children whose families had failed them miserably, turn the page and go on living. Chapters could be written on children who overcome great adversity and grow up to be fulfilled adults. Pity we "normal" adults can't manage that as well in our own lives. We too often become hardened and cynical. We harbor grudges and hatreds. Not children, more often than not they pick up the pieces and move on. Many children who wind up in places like the Children's Home find caring adults who have often themselves been hurt by life, who help them on their journey to wholeness. And so it goes--generation after generation--the human race moves on to a better understanding of itself and its reason to be.

If children ruled the world, there would be many things that would not exist. There would be no fractured families, no spousal abuse, no child abuse and no need for children's homes. If children ruled the world, there would be no recognition of race or class. Everyone would be chosen to play on the team and get a turn at bat. If children ruled the world, everyone would have a house to live in and food a plenty. There would be no time for war, only the curious exploration of the world and learning about those who are in it. If children ruled the world, the kingdom of God would be real right here on earth because Jesus said, "The children get it".

32

The Call

Dr. Bobby Taylor
1982-07

Taylor Family - L-R: Stephen, Bobby and Wes

I have been blessed with many wonderful privileges during my lifetime, but there is one, which stands out among the rest, living and working at the Free Will Baptist Children's Home. I am sure there are many who have lived in a children's home who do not consider it a privilege, for all children, well at least most, want to live with their families. But living at the Home was a privilege for me, and it was my choice as well as the choice of my family. I remember vividly the night I received a telephone call from Mrs. Rebecca Davenport, who was serving on the Board of Directors('69-'90). At the time of her call, I had just accepted a position at the Home. Mrs. Davenport wanted to know why (off the record) I wanted to come to the Home. She asked me, if I understood the current financial situation the Home was facing. I considered these fair questions, ones asked out of her concern and love for both the Home and for me.

When I began working at the Home, I had been in the ministry for about ten years, all the time continuing my education seeking a minor in religion, and majoring in psychology. God had placed upon my heart a desire, a passion for youth and for working with them; and my ministry had revolved around that calling, whether I was serving in the church as pastor, leading in summer camping programs at Cragmont Assembly, located near Black Mountain, North Carolina, or serving in community volunteer programs for youth. During this time, I would always be drawn to what was happening at the Children's Home in Middlesex. The number of children being served had been on a steady decline for several years. The Home had lost State funding due to legislative changes. During this time (1978 – 1985), the national trend in caring for children was moving from residential care to family foster care.

After several years of praying and talking with others about the needs of our children in the Home, I discussed it with my family and friends, and shared with them that I felt led to seek the possibility of serving at the Children's Home. When the position of Director of Child Care came open (1980), I met with the Rev. Stewart Humphrey, executive director of the Home ('77-'81), and later applied for that position. Sometime afterwards, the Rev. Humphrey called me and informed me the Board had made the decision not to fill the position due to the status of the Home and its financial situation. In about a year, the Board announced it was seeking a person to serve as Executive Director. So I applied, but did not get the job. The Board hired Howard Cayton to serve (1981). Within a few months, Mr. Cayton called me and said he was looking to hire a Director of Child Care. He wanted to know if I would be interested in applying. I submitted my application and got the job. I resigned the pastorate; and three months later, on December 1, 1982, my family and I moved to the Children's Home to begin our lives as part of the "Children's Home family." I had no idea as to the role the Home would play in my life and the lives of my children. Stephen and Wesley, still to this day, see the Home as their home of origin, the place where they grew up.

LIFE IN THE HOME

With the blessings of the church I was serving as pastor (Pleasant Grove Free Will Baptist) and the help of several of her members, we moved into a small home provided for the Director of Child Care on the edge of campus. We were looking forward to the opportunity to meet the children and staff; and we were presented this opportunity during the morning worship service on campus the next Sunday.

After the service, everyone gave the impression they were okay with the new folks who had moved in, but there was no celebration. They had learned over the years a lot of people think they want to work and serve in a children's home, only to discover it was not really their calling, so the Home's family were used to seeing people come and go. Everyone was hospitable, willing to see how long the new folks would stay. The term "new kid on the block" took on a new meaning for us.

Living in a children's home is like living in a small, private, but closely-knit community, where everybody is "kin," so to speak. There is the outside world and the inside world of the Home. The inside world is like this, you know all your neighbors. You know when they leave and when they return. You know what they are having for breakfast, lunch, and dinner. You know where everyone works, goes to school and his or her respective grade level; you know where they shop, get their hair done, as well as what schedule everyone has. You know who's sick and who's getting better, what doctor they saw and what medications they're on. You know what time those who live in the outside world (off campus) come to work and when they leave. You live together, work together, go to school together, eat together, study together, worship together, play together, and host events together. Yes, there is a lot of "togetherness" in a children's home. You even learn not to mess with the children's home kids on the school bus – they are together, much like with blood siblings: they can smack each other around but no one else better try!

When we moved on campus, our son Stephen was three and a half years old, and Wesley was just six months. They were the youngest children on campus and became the center of attention. All the children on campus treated them like little brothers. All the girls wanted and carried Wesley around all the time, and Stephen was the sidekick of the older boys; they were received by the children and staff as official members of the Children's Home family.

I remember walking to the office on that first day of work. I saw the children getting on the school bus and thought what an awesome responsibility to have entrusted to any individual. I had been coming to the Home regularly for over three months now. I had traveled to different parts of our State taking training offered by The Group Child Care Consultant Services of The School of Social Work at the University of North Carolina, Chapel Hill, North Carolina, to help in preparing for what would be a much longer journey than I could imagine.

FIRST CHRISTMAS

Christmas is a wonderful time of the year. It is the time in which we celebrate the birth of the Christ child and our thoughts are on sharing, appreciation, singing Christmas carols, decorating, cooking, and sharing a spirit of love. I had no idea what Christmas would be like at the Home, but I was about to learn.

One of the first things passed to me upon entering my office was our December schedule of activities. I looked at it, stared at it, and still could not believe it. You see there are a lot of wonderfully unselfish people who care about the less fortunate, especially children. There were twenty groups scheduled to visit within twenty-two days to share their Christmas spirit. That did not include the scheduled "private" events of the Children's Home family, which included our Christmas dinner, church services, Christmas program, cottage Christmas, and visitations, etc. Needless to say, it was an "eye-opening" experience which came with the challenge to get all this done in some organized manner.

LEARNING THE REAL MEANING OF A SUGAR HIGH

Almost every evening, visitors arrived on campus with every conceivable dessert to share with our family – cookies large, medium, and small. Candy overflowed containers, red, green, white, and every color of the rainbow. There were sweet breads, cupcakes, big cakes, sliced cake, with icing dripping – rich and sweet. We had hot chocolates, cold chocolates, drinks of all flavors offered with love and concern. We were led in singing Christmas carols, some we knew and ones we did not; and, of course, there was the Christmas story, loved and shared by all.

Each evening, the children would leave their cottages and we all assembled in the Recreation Center for the evening's celebration. As we entered the second week of celebrating, I was tired, the "family" was tired, and staff was tired. But guess what: more sugar and we were good to go. I guess you could say all of us were a little unstable: a sugar high is a real thing – we know.

We enjoyed this first Christmas and all the celebrations, but I decided next year would be different, for we would limit the number of parties held on campus by asking groups to come at different times of the year. We called it "spreading the joy" – and they embraced the idea as much as we did. Do I need to add there were sighs of relief? This shift allowed the children to have a more normal schedule, but also amble time to keep up their schoolwork and get the rest they needed. And, of course, the staff found this arrangement to offer much more stability and peace.

LEARNING THE REAL MEANING OF CHRISTMAS

As I recollect my experiences, I feel compelled to share this with you; it is one of those life-changing experiences. In December of 1984, three children entered our care, Joanne 5, Dorothy 8, and Eugene 10. These sweet children had a very tattered look, and entered care with very little. They came out of a difficult living situation, being removed from their home by personnel of their respective Department of Social Services because their parents could not provide the care they needed.

This sibling group entered care during that busy time when we were celebrating the Christmas season. The children had been in care about two weeks and individuals from the Woodmen of the World fraternity were on campus for their annual Christmas visit. There must have been sixty adults and children; they had come to share the spirit of Christmas. Also, Mr. and Mrs. Claus were in toe to visit with us. The building was warm, the glow of logs burning in the fireplace added an ambiance, and the laughter and warm greetings of Christmas joy filled the air. The tables were covered with sandwiches, chips, nuts, cakes, candy, and all the other wonderful treats, which these good men and women had prepared. There was a pastor in the group (whose cheerfulness was likened to Saint Nick himself) who led this gathering of young and old alike in Christmas carols as all shared about the birth of our Lord.

After making merry, singing, eating, fellowshipping, and of course Santa and Mrs. Claus visiting each one there, it was time for our generous visitors to take their pilgrimage to their own homes. All were ready to call it a "good night." The Woodmen and their families were preparing to leave, so I took the opportunity to say thank you. As I was doing so, I felt a tug on my jacket. I looked down and there was one of the newest members of our Children's Home family, little Dorothy. She asked if she could sing a song. Seeing the sincerity on this child's face, I said, "Sure." I got everyone's attention, and helped Dorothy stand in a chair beside me so everyone could see her. I noticed as I looked up, that all eyes were fixed upon this little girl. I announced, "Dorothy has something she wants to say and she wants to sing 'Away in a Manger' for you." Everyone in the building grew quiet; and a sweet still spirit settled. Dorothy, this tattered looking child who had only been in care about two weeks, began in this sweet childish voice, one you would almost imagine an angel to have: "I…I…I want to thank…you…for everything. It's the best Christmas we (speaking of herself, Joanne, and Eugene) have ever had."

Everyone's eyes began to glisten, and tears began to move slowly down Dorothy's cheeks. She was so thankful for the refreshments and gifts. This was the second party they had attended, and there were several more to come, not to mention our "campus family" Christmas. I have no idea where she learned the song and actions of "Away in a Manger," but somewhere in her short life of experiences, someone had taught her the meaning of Christmas in its very essence. The building became even quieter as this little girl's expression of thankfulness poured out from her heart (the heart of this little girl who had so little and looked so tattered). She acted out the words to the song as she sang. I looked around and saw I was not alone; tears were running down everyone's cheeks, as she sang,

Be near me, Lord Jesus, I ask Thee to stay
Close by me forever, and love me, I pray;
Bless all the dear children in Thy tender care,
And fit us for heaven to live with Thee there.

The real meaning of Christmas had fallen upon us, never to be forgotten. I guess you are wondering what happened to these children. Well, Joanne and Dorothy lived at the Home for three and one-half years and were adopted. Eugene remained in the Home for eleven years before leaving.

MEETING THE BOARD OF DIRECTORS

A board of directors governs the Free Will Baptist Children's Home. Those who serve do so by appointment of the Convention of Original Free Will Baptists. They give their time freely; they pray, give resources, serve on committees, and travel from all over the State because they care about the Home and its ministry. When I began to serve at the Home, I knew many of the Board members because they were active in the denomination, and I had seen most of them at various denominational meetings. Over time, I would get to know them much better while sitting with them, praying with them, laboring with them, and fellowshipping with them.

At least once a year, a dinner would be served prior to a Board meeting. This gave those who served in leadership a time to be around both the children and staff. They always enjoyed this time. They cared about the children we served, and always wanted the best for each child there; they also found time spent with staff to be special, too.

The Board was meeting in regular session in February (1983). During the meeting, Mr. E. Howard Cayton ('81-'83) resigned; he left on May 2, 1983. The Board appointed me to serve as Acting Director, while the search committee began its search for a replacement. As the Board was accepting applications for the position, I prayerfully considered the post and submitted an application. I was interviewed during the May meeting and hired as the new Executive Director, to begin my new position, July 1, 1983. Having served as Acting Director during the Home's time of transition, I was better prepared to make the move into my new role as the official Director. We cannot see the future, so I had no thought of the road before me, nor did I know I would travel that path for the next twenty-four and one-half years.

As I previously mentioned, the Board members are dedicated individuals and our relationship grew as we journeyed together through the years. These men and women were always serious about the business of our ministry to children and families. They continually offered their prayers, support, and assistance whenever called upon. Many times the meetings were long, the discussions deep, and decisions were prayed over as we sought God's direction. I could not have asked for a more dedicated team of Christian men and women that provided the leadership and guidance for our calling to God's mission in serving children and families.

THE FIRST MAJOR QUESTION

Every meeting included many questions and a lot of discussion; but the first major question asked was, "Where are we?" "Where are we heading?" This question would come up each time we prepared the long-term strategic plan. As I stated earlier, the number of children being served had steadily declined for several years. The Home had lost State funding due to legislative changes. The national trend in caring for children was moving from residential care to family foster care.

The Children's Home ministry began as the Free Will Baptist Orphanage, opening its doors on May 23, 1920, and receiving the first four children into care that day (Nellie ('20-'27), Helen ('20-'30), Dorothy ('20-'32) and Carl ('20-'31) Whitley). Over the decades, the Home experienced many changes, and in 1956 the name was changed from the Free Will Baptist Orphanage to the Free Will Baptist Children's Home, which reflected its progression in services to children and families.

In the 1960's, the Home began to build cottages to replace the existing dormitory-style living situation. No longer would children have to go to a central dining hall for meals; meals would be prepared and served in each cottage. Also, laundry would be done in the cottage. The concept was to make the cottage as close to a "regular home" as possible. Other services would be provided through the Department of Family Services established in the 1970's. The goal of this department was to help families deal with their crisis to the point of reuniting children back with their family.

MINISTRY CHALLENGE:

The Civil Rights Act of 1964

When I became the Director, the main issue facing the Home was the Civil Rights Act of 1964. My predecessors had been working with this challenge since its inception. In 1970, the Board of Directors signed the Home into compliance with the Act. Even though the Board had moved forward, the Convention voted to rescind the action of the Board during its Annual Convention. This action caused the Home to withdraw from compliance. For a number of years, not being "in compliance" did not affect the Home and its services, or its financial status; State funding continued. This was due to the fact that legal custody of many children was given to the Home prior to their placement into care; and legal custody was the criteria for receiving funding for children being served by children's homes. Although these criteria had been in place for some time, legislative changes made by the General Assembly mandated allocated funding (State Grant in Aid) to childcare facilities be tied to compliance to the Civil Rights Act. Only children placed into care by local county Departments of Social Services were eligible to receive funding. The Departments of Social Services were mandated to place children only with agencies/ministries in compliance with the Act. Before this time, all children placed at the Home came through private placement.

Once again, this became a strong point of discussion within the denomination for several years (1977-83). For years, the Board kept returning to the point of discussion and evaluating the need for the Home to be in compliance. In 1983, the Board, once again, signed the Home into compliance and asked the Convention to support its action. During the 1983 Annual State Convention of Original Free Will Baptists, the delegates at the Convention voted to support the actions taken earlier by the Board.

After the Convention in September, the Home received its first African American child in care, Francis "Travis" M. King('83-'85); he entered care on November 7, 1983. Over the years, the Home had served children of different races and nationalities, but Travis was the first African American child. Of course, as one could imagine, there had been much discussion at all levels of our denomination, from the local churches, conferences, to the Convention. Questions akin to, "What would this do to our ministry?" "How would compliance affect the children who were already in care?" "How would it affect our funding and support?" "How would the staff care for these children? "Would the government take control of our Home or dictate how we serve children?"

The Home's ministry is representative of its slogan, "A Christian Home for Boys and Girls." While it is true children from different cultures draw from their own respective cultural experiences, the basic needs of children are the same. Children need a safe and secure environment, food, clothing, shelter, medical care, proper education, religious training, and most of all love. Most children have the resilience to adapt to new environments if their basic needs are met, and this was found to be true.

The children and the staff of the Home spent nearly a year discussing and preparing for the transition of the Home to serve all children, no matter the race, color, creed, or national origin. In-service training was provided; all staff attended workshops. All staff and children were involved in the planning for the transition and they also visited other ministries that had been providing care to minority children for decades.

THE TRANSITION

The family remained the same, "family." Children and staff came together to ensure the values and principles on which the Home was founded remained; the same is true today. The Home exists to provide "A Christian Home for Boys and Girls."

DINNER IS AT 5 O'CLOCK

I always lived by the philosophy - being Executive Director includes executing whatever needs to be done. When I think of this belief, an event quickly comes to mind: I remember one of the houseparent couples was called away one afternoon at 3 o'clock due to a family emergency. There was no other staff on campus available to fill-in, so I called the house and told the family to pack bags; we were going to spend the night in Smith Cottage. Stephen and Wesley got excited about the opportunity to stay in one of the cottages. We arrived at the cottage where there were 12 children ranging in age from 9 to 13 years old. So our immediate family had grown in number to 16.

The first thing I did upon entering the cottage was to greet the children, all who had gathered around to check out these relief workers. Next, I had to find the "cottage schedule," which was posted on the bulletin board to determine the remaining activities for the day. There it was: 5 o'clock dinner. I looked at the clock and it was 4 o'clock, one hour before dinner. Needless to say, panic set in; we were already behind where we needed to be - we needed "a miracle."

Well, I had often cooked for the 4 of us at home, but for 16 – WOW! Where does one start? A couple of the older girls took us to the kitchen and showed us where things were. The staff had things laid out: meat was thawing in the refrigerator and staples were on the kitchen counter. The girls had made a cake the day before, and half was left. So we put our bags in the relief room, and set in with the children's help to prepare the evening meal.

These children were great, pitching in and knowing what to do to aid these inexperienced "green horns." I guess it goes without saying we did not have dinner at 5 o'clock, but we did manage to get it on the table by 5:30 p.m. As we gave thanks that evening for the food, we also thanked God for "a small miracle." I can still tell you 27 years later, what we dined on that night: spaghetti with meat sauce, tossed salad, green beans, Italian bread, milk, tea, and cake.

After dinner, the children did their chores, which included some of the residents assisting with helping to clean the kitchen and dining room; and they did a great job! We were running behind schedule, but all was going well. To assure things went smoothly, I needed to get back to check the schedule (schedules are important to keeping everything running right). Looking at the schedule I found listed: study time, free time, snacks, devotions, baths, and bedtime 9 o'clock. Everything was set out and structured for the children.

We had been in a whirlwind since entering the front door. Now the cottage was quiet, well, I should say, quieter; I could still hear some of the children talking. They didn't seem to be as tired as I was, and I had paperwork to do. At the end of each day, houseparents completed daily logs on each child's day. I remember thinking, "the family," all 15 of them, were in bed and things had gone well. I finished doing paperwork about midnight and walked the cottage to make sure all was well. One more thing to do before retiring for the day was to check tomorrow's schedule. The first thing I saw was: get the older girls up at 5 a.m., and the younger children at 5:30 a.m., breakfast at 6:15 a.m., morning chores 6:45 a.m., school bus arrives at 7:15.

I have always remembered how well this family worked together, and how this family had come together to get things done. And I learned just how important a "cottage schedule" was in keeping the "togetherness" together! Now I was off to the office (8:00 a.m.) to learn the houseparents would return about lunchtime. I bowed my head and thanked God for such dedicated people.

THE FIRST ALUMNI HOMECOMING

THE PREAMBLE
We, the former children and employees of the Free Will Baptist Children's Home, in order to promote the general welfare of the children at the home, to build closer relationships among ourselves, and to maintain a harmonious and working relationship with the Board of Directors of the Home, do establish this Constitution for the Alumni Association of the Free Will Baptist Children's Home.
The Constitution of the Alumni Association of the
Free Will Baptist Children's Home

As I mentioned earlier, I became Director, on July 1, 1983, and the Alumni Association's annual homecoming always met at the Home on the second Sunday in July, only a few days away. This would be my first Homecoming.

As with all "firsts," there are a lot of questions that run through one's mind: "How would this Association accept a new administration, and what would be their expectations?" "What had to be done to welcome these former residents and their families?" Many of these former residents had spent a large portion of their childhood in this place they called "Home." Even though they had been gone many years they still felt the draw to return each year. It is an inimitable circumstance, it was their home and still is the home of their childhood, yet it is the personal home of the current children and staff. "Home" is the term we use to describe the protected place in one's heart that is private; and yet in this case, it must be shared. I wanted the alumni to feel their ownership of their childhood home, and I wanted the current children to be assured their home was not being invaded.

The staff and I had been planning and discussing the expected visit for weeks, but I must confess I was nervous. Today, Homecoming is a one-day event for the campus; but in the early eighties, it was a weekend event for some of the alumni. Some would arrive on Friday afternoon and stay until Sunday afternoon, if we had space on campus for them to stay. But most would just attend the events and stay off-campus. The events included a meal on Saturday (usually a cookout) and breakfast Sunday morning. The main event was Sunday morning worship, followed by an Association meeting and lunch (catered by Parker's or Bill's Barbecue).

After lunch, many of the alumni would gather under the trees in the park. This was a special time, as they would share stories of growing up in the Home and the relationships they established. Each and every alumnus had stories of his or her own. It was a real delight, as well as quite informative, to hear these adults talk about their childhood at the Home. Many who were in the Home in the 1920's, 30's, 40's, and 50's shared how hard life was in the Home.

As I looked at the records related to those periods, it was difficult times for the Home financially. Being a new ministry and operating during the "Great Depression," it is only by God's grace, and caring Christian people the Home was able to maintain. People brought baskets of potatoes, chickens, canned vegetables, apples, and all sorts of food provision to sustain this ministry. During those times, the children worked on the Home's farm, caring for livestock, farming corn, tobacco, soy beans, and large vegetable gardens, and whatever else could be raised for food and to improve the Home's income.

It was a simpler time, but the Home provided for the basic needs of the children: food, clothing, shelter, education, and spiritual training. In the early part of the 20th century and through the late 50's, the attitudes of adults toward children was much different than today. Children were to be obedient and in most cases seen and not heard (they were only to speak when spoken to). Parents worked hard and long hours to provide the basic necessities for life. Many individuals who work at the Home during this period reflected this mindset. Some were very demanding and showed the children little affection; and then there were those who were very loving and caring. Both made an impression upon the children's lives. When the alumni told their stories, you could easily tell into which category a staff person fell.

GETTING TO KNOW THE ALUMNI

After years of seeing these alumni each year, one learns about their families. Many alumni would bring their children, grandchildren, and even great-grandchildren with them for Homecoming. This would allow for their families to see where Mom or Dad had grown up and the stories of the past could and would come alive.

One must remember every family has its own respective story, but each narrative is different because of its unique set of circumstances: details related to the size of the family, the relationships, the sharing of a common bond based on different situations beyond the natural family's control. As one listens to these life sagas, it moves you to tears, moments of joy, and in most cases appreciation for how God has blessed you.

I met and got to know so many of the alumni and their stories of being at the Home. It would be difficult to list them all, for that would be a book within itself, but I will share one with you: I met a gracious couple, Shirley and Sterling Skinner ('37-'43) whom I got to know very well. They started attending Homecoming shortly after I went to the Home. I don't think, the best I can recall, Sterling had not been back to the Home since he left on February 28, 1943. Sterling, his brother Marvin ('37-'43), and his sister Elva ('37-'42) came to live at the Home on January 4, 1937. Sterling, in his comments, put it this way, "I was a very mischievous young man." According to his own admissions, he got into everything and seemed to stay in trouble. He could tell story after story of his deeds and misdeeds during his residence at the Home. You look at this generous man, with his huge smile and kind manner, and wonder if all those misdeeds really could have happened. But, I know Sterling to be an honest and reliable man, so there was no need to doubt his tales.

After knowing Sterling and Shirley for a few years, while in the process of planning for the next Homecoming I came up with a way to recognize Sterling and add a touch of humor. The plan resulted in the following, which would be given during the Association meeting:

Presidential Pardon
Be it known to all people on this fifteenth day,
Of July, in the year of Our Lord, Two Thousand One,

That
Sterling Skinner

Has been granted a full and complete pardon
For all miss deeds while an inmate
Living at the orphanage.
Be it further known to all people,
That
Sterling Skinner
Is granted all the rights, privileges, and honors as
An alumnus of the
Free Will Baptist Children's Home.
Sign: *Bobby R. Taylor, D.Min.*
President

Awarding this pardon made for an additionally fun-filled day for all the alumni who had gathered once again to share, reminisce, and catch up on all that had happen since they met the year before.

As mentioned earlier, the first children to enter the Home were the Whitley children (May 23, 1920). Nellie lived at the Home for 7 years; Helen, 10 years; Dorothy, 12 years; and Carl, for 11 years. When I became Director, Nellie had deceased, but I was privileged with the honor of visiting in the homes of Helen, Dorothy, and Carl. Meeting Helen, Dorothy, and Carl were experiences I will never forget.

THINGS HAPPEN

What was a "normal" Sunday morning worship service in Memorial Chapel, located on the Children's Home property, became a very unusual one (the year was around 2000). A local pilot had taken his Piper Cub out for some flying time. Shortly after taking off from a Triangle-area airport, the single-engine craft began to sputter. Unable to return to the airstrip from which he had left, the pilot looked for a place to land. He spotted the dirt road, which ran in front of Albemarle Cottage and determined to sit the craft down. The pilot landed the plane on what is now Buck Deans Road, between the campus and farm ponds. Those in church heard the noises of the event, and said the "Amen" of the benediction to walk out and see the plane and pilot within an easy walking distance of the Chapel. It appears the pilot did not check his fuel before leaving that morning. His wife was glad to hear he was fine but offered an ultimatum relative to him never flying again.

THROUGH THE YEARS

Since the beginning of this ministry much progress has been made in attitudes relative to the physical care, programs, and quality of services to the children, as well as to the physical campus. The Historical Summary published by the Home is an outstanding resource for anyone who would be interested in a chronological list. Many of these visions and challenges did not come easily.

This ministry was brought into existence by The Free Will Baptist denomination. It was the result of a visionary call. The members of this body, worshiping in multiple churches across the State saw many children and families in need. Sometime it's hard for us to realize the advances in health care, financial stability, and an overall improvement in the quality of life that have occurred since the beginning of the Home. Life expectancy around the turn of the twenty-century was much lower than it is today, and technology has advanced beyond our ability to comprehend. This was recorded in 1915, during the Annual Convention of Original Free Will Baptists: those present "adopted a resolution of conviction to build a home for orphans." During the next five years, a caring people labored together and the ministry came into existence.

Since its meager beginning of 50 acres and the first main building in which all services were provided, the Home has provided direct care on its campus for over 2,000 children. Today the campus consists of approximately 50 acres, with the addition of farmland measuring approximately 400 acres, of which 200 acres are farmed; and there are 20 buildings on campus. This is a testament to God's many blessings through a kind and caring people.

I will not list all the improvements accomplished to services and the physical plant, but I do want to speak of several from 1983 to 2007. First, in November 1983, was the establishment of a program for teenage residents called "Preparation for Independent Living." The title implies the mission of the program, to assist teenagers in their preparation for independence.

The second was the building and completion of Whitley Center (gymnasium), November 1988, named in honor of the first four children who entered care May 23, 1920. This multi-purpose building offers opportunities for the children, staff, community, and campus events. Third, on July 1, 1992, the Home developed services through its emergency care program (Genesis House Emergency Shelter, Wilson, NC). The program continued to grow and now is operated on the main campus

The fourth thing I will mention is a goal talked about back in 1983 during a meeting of the Board of Directors, but did not come to fruition until 16 years later. During the meeting, I shared with the Board a vision - one day our ministry would be nationally accredited. Fourteen years later, in 1997, we began the process of seeking accreditation. It was a major undertaking and involved the participation of all the staff, children and Board of Directors working together many long hours, days, weekends, and months to follow.

As I think back, it was only by God's grace and Spirit we were able to bring this 16-year dream into reality. During the month of November 1999, the Home celebrated receiving national accreditation from the Council on Accreditation of Services for Families and Children, Inc. The Home, since that first accreditation, has gone through the process two more times and remains an accredited agency today. It was a high benchmark, but one which has raised the quality of services to children and families.

TIME CAPSULES

Time capsules are a way of looking back at a point in time. Such a reminiscent look offers a momentary glimpse at a particular point in history for the one who finds the capsule and considers its contents, as much can be gleaned there from. Information about what was happening, as well as considered to be significant is often contained within the buried item. There are two time capsules buried on the campus of the Children's Home. One was buried during the construction (1940) of what is now Heritage Hall (the old central dining hall). Witnesses have stated it was placed in the right hand-corner of the foundation facing the main entrance. The other was placed beneath the Church near the furnace room in the basement (2000) by children and staff. It is scheduled to be open on the hundred anniversary of the Home (May 23, 2020). Both hold significant items related to residents and activities of the Home at the time of placement.

MEMORIES TO TREASURE

...DREAMS TO FULFILL!

Today as I think about the Children's Home and its mission, its future is best stated on the back page of its Historical Summary:

The Free Will Baptist Children's Home is one of the outstanding achievements of Original Free Will Baptists, and one of its greatest mission fields. This ministry is an investment in the future, founded in the heart and soul of Christianity. It exemplifies Christianity by providing "a Christian Home for Boys and Girls"; a place to live free from abuse and neglect; a place to restore faith in themselves and others, a place to build memories they can treasure, a place where they can fulfill their dreams, a new chance at life.

33

I Don't Feel Like I Sacrifice to Be Here

Donald Batchelor
1975 – Present

Donald and Joyce Batchelor

Two days before my 64th birthday, it was my honor to assist in moving the campus bell to its final location in the Bell Tower, Heritage Hall. Through the years, this bell has been rung to give notice to children and staff of meals, church services, parties and other events in their campus lives. While only one original building (Pump House) remains on campus since the Home was founded in 1920, the bell is remembered more in stories by alumni. It is the one image of campus life to those who have left the home remember more often. Alumni still like for it to be rung when they attend homecoming each year. Some alumni have a small bell in their yard, symbolic of this bell from their childhood.

Thursday, January 21, 2010, 2:00 p.m. was a cold, rainy day. The day's low was 40 degrees, high 43 degrees. It was very, very cold. Dillion Construction Company was hired to move the bell. They drove on campus a Boom Truck to lift the bell off the two-pole silver stand. Before the bell was removed, I spray painted it the same color it has been since I've been on campus, silver. We put a new hanging bolt on the bell. It appeared the bell had been repaired from a fall in the past. It had two big welded places on it. Somebody did a good job putting it back together.

The truck lifted the bell and set it up in Heritage Hall Bell Tower. We immediately noticed the bell was too high for the bell to be seen from the street. Using a fork lift, the bell was lowered and positioned in its present location. Five of us helped transport and mounted the bell on a steel frame made in Raleigh. Before 5:00 p.m., the bell was firmly secured under a covered roof for the first time and will be preserved for generations of the past, present and future. It was my honor and I'll always remember the day. Now, at night, when the light is shinning on the bell, it's so beautiful.

Bell Locations 1920-10: 1. Girls Building, on one 12 foot wood pole, ten feet from side entrance. 2. On ground next to dining hall. 3. Mounted on two metal poles next to road. 4. Current location.

Never could I realize in 1974, when my family first started visiting the Children's Home, I'd be part of the bell history to so many. In the latter part of '74, my favorite Christmas story from the Children's Home took place. We had started coming to the Children's Home to pick up a little four-year old girl, Dorothy Johnson ('74-'81), that our church, St. Mary's

Free Will Baptist Church, Kenly, North Carolina was sponsoring. We would take a weekend to bring her into our home. We had three girls of our own at that time – Kim, Michelle and Melody. As we would visit each time, we became more emotionally involved. It was exciting to our family that year when we learned Dorothy could spend Christmas with us. I'll always remember driving on the back road behind the kitchen to the gym to pick her up. The road was wet with red Nash County clay. I almost got stuck but made it around to pick her up in the recreation area.

We then started taking another little girl, Robin Anderson ('74-'75), home with us each visiting weekend. We started out as a visiting family for Robin, but then we soon became her monthly sponsor.

Our love for the Children's Home was growing by leaps and bounds. We began praying about our feelings and asked the Lord to send us wherever; and, you guessed it, we were soon answering the call to become full-time house parents. Dave and Sandy Thick, house parents at Smith Cottage, played a big part in our becoming house parents at State Cottage. We met with Mr. Sam Weeks (Superintendent '73-'77) and his wife, Gladys, and they hired us. We were the second set of house parents to go into State Cottage.

Joyce and I moved our family to State Cottage on campus in June 1975. We had a co-ed cottage of boys and girls—brothers and sisters. This was definitely an adjustment, as we had never had boys. We had eight boys and four girls besides our three girls. The ages of the children in the cottage ranged from five to fifteen. Our own youngest daughter was two and a half. The boys and girls in our college were Roger Worley ('74-'79), Teresa Ann Worley ('74-'86), Betty Worley ('74-'84), Dorothy Johnson ('74-'81), Jeff Johnson ('74-'81'), Allen Johnson ('74-'80), Donnie Dement ('71-'81) and Jimmie Dement '68-'76), Tim Mills ('73-'82), James Speight, Jr. ('72-'78), David Jackie Speight ('72-'79) and Roy Speight ('72-'79).

I continued to work a full-time job at Swift & Company in Wilson, North Carolina and would come home in the afternoon and help Joyce all I could with the kids. Mr. Clarence Mitchell, house parent and maintenance supervisor had been diagnosed with cancer and was quite sick at this time. He knew his situation and worked with me to gradually relinquish his job responsibilities. It was not easy for him to give up a job he loved, but he wanted the Home to continue in good shape. I would sit with him in the evening as he told me his experiences and maintenance issues on campus. I did the best I could to stay on top of maintenance problems during the evening hours. I, too, was a house parent and barber to our eight boys. I'd cut their hair when needed. This was a skill I learned in earlier years.

Our girls were always on the same schedule as our cottage children. They all had the same bedtime, except on our day off, which was one day a week. We would take our girls to Raleigh sometimes and treat them to a night out. We would always take them out to eat on this night. This was the only time they had their parents to themselves.

My family continued this lifestyle for a year and a half. We had given our resignation to go home in December—Christmas—of 1976. We had a baby on the way, due in May of 1977. We moved back to our home in Black Creek, North Carolina. Our son Brian was born May 28, 1977. I continued working full time at Swift & Company. When Brian was three months old, the company closed and I had to look for another job. I went to work at Carolina Packers in Smithfield but was not happy. Joyce and I began praying about something different for me.

In November 1977, Stewart Humphrey (Superintendent '77-'81) called and wanted to meet with me. Clarence Mitchell had passed and the Children's Home needed someone to help with maintenance. I met Stewart on a Saturday morning, November 6, 1977. I still remember the meeting. I entered the office and he was sitting behind his desk. He had tears in his eyes. He ask me if I'd consider coming back to work at the Home. He told me, "I know we can't pay you the money I feel like you're making." I told him I was not really happy with my present employment with Carolina Packers Company, but I need to pray about it and would get back with him after discussing with Joyce. Within one week from the Saturday morning I'd made my decision and notified Stewart I'd like to work for the Home if we could agree on my needs to support my family. We sat down with my expenses and he come up with compensation for me to make the change and start working for the Children's Home with me staying at home (off campus), driving to the Home each day from Black Creek. I was hired as Director of Physical Affairs. I did this for the next 17 years. I had to furnish my own vehicle and gas to go back and forth to work.

In June 1993, we moved back to the Children's Home to live on campus. Our children were all out of the nest, except for Brian. He was a junior in High School. We moved into the Taylor House, in which we currently reside. Dr. Bobby Taylor was the President/CEO ('82-'07) at this time. Again, the Lord was definitely in this move, as we loved our home in Black Creek where all our children had grown up. The Lord gave us complete direction and we knew that this was the right move. We have been back on campus now 17 years this coming June 2010. Our experience here at the Home has been, and continues to be, a blessing. Everything is not always a bed of roses, but the good always outweighs the bad. We have met and continue to meet a lot of wonderful people.

One of my experiences was when one of the male residents asked to borrow the Home's maintenance pickup. He wanted to pull his John boat out of the pond to do some repairs on it. After he loaded the boat and starting driving back to the campus, he rounded the curve on the dirt road (at that time it had not been paved), and lost control of the truck, hit a tree and totaled the truck. A state trooper was called—no one was hurt—just the truck. The boy did have a North Carolina driver's license—yeah!

Another experience, on Thursday, September 16, 1999 Hurricane Floyd made landfall in North Carolina. We lost about 50 trees on and around the campus. The Home was without power for approximately 11 days. We had no generators and stores in Wilson were out of stock. We called around and found two generators in Marion, North Carolina. We worked around the clock to keep the generators running and rotated to keep refrigerators going and water in the water tower running. During the day, everyone pitched in, including neighbors, to clean up the campus. The American Red Cross furnished our most appreciated lunches.

A few years later we experienced a major ice storm and the campus was crippled without power for nine days. We were blessed to have generators this time (6) to keep the campus going.

Another experience was when our son, Brian, about four years old, got one of his fingers cut almost off. He had to have surgery, but that did not stop him from wanting to come to work with me. Brian is now almost 33 years old and still loves to help me on his days off. Brian is a North Carolina licensed auctioneer.

One of my fond memories while working at the Home is a gift from one of the residence. J. C. lived in Central Cottage and worked with me in the summer cutting grass and the afternoon after school during the school year. He was a very good worker and I enjoyed him. Sometimes I would give him change to purchase a soda. When he left the Home, he gave me a $2.00 bill which is now framed and hangs in my office. He came by to see me before he left and said he wanted me to have it for being so good to him and he wanted me to remember him. I still do!!

Another memory is the time I nearly caught two girls and two boys from Middlesex trying to climb the water tower about 9:30 p.m. one evening. When they saw me approaching, they scampered down the tower ladder and left on their car.

Thanksgiving on campus is always special to me. We gather in Heritage Hall for our campus Thanksgiving dinner. It is a special night with a little program, scripture reading and a few songs. It's usually held on Tuesday before Thanksgiving.

I dug the hole for a time capsule buried in the basement of the church. We looked for the first time capsule placed in the wall of Heritage Hall in the '40's, but could not find it. Before remodeling, we dug out places in the left corner and tried our best to find it, but did not have any luck. I crawled under the kitchen and looked several places. There is a lot of broken glass near the corner. I spent an hour under the building and a half day looking for it.

Joyce and I have enjoyed all the Free Will Baptist Churches and everyone who has had a part in visiting us during our time at the Home. It is always a blessing when visitors come on campus. I have thoroughly enjoyed and am very grateful to all the businesses that have supported and donated things to keep the maintenance department going through these years—Whitley Electric, Douglas Whitley, Durward Stancil Refrigeration, Water Guard (pool supplier), Jim Moyer, Irie Supply, Insco, Parker's Barbecue, Bill Ellis, Henry Manning, Stallings' Brothers, Wilson Glass and Mirror and lots of others, including Deans Oil Company.

In 2007, I was honored by the Home. A memorial bench was placed in front of the chapel. On the bench is inscribed: In Honor of Don Batchelor for 30 Years of Services 11-06-2007. I remember it was a real heart-touching service they did to honor me. I really don't feel like I deserved it. Some people say they sacrifice to work at the Home. I don't feel like I sacrifice to be here. I enjoy it. If you enjoy it, it is not a sacrifice. Dr. Bobby Taylor was President/CEO when I received the tribute.

Two weeks ago a boy came over to help me work after school. He told me he was depressed. I looked at him and said, "Look son, I'm not going to charge you one penny for what I'm about to tell you. This place is trying to provide for you. You need to take that at heart. Listen to me real good. Make the best of it until you can get back with your family. I don't know your situation, but I share this with you, hoping you'll have a brighten day.

You make the best of it until things get better." He looked at me and said, "Thank you, I needed to hear this from you."

We really can't help why a child is at the Home and the child cannot help for being here. But each child can make the best of it. And, it's our responsibility to make the best of it to provide a good home until children return to the people they call family.

Joyce and I wish our love to all the children, past and present.

See page 471. Location #3, bell mounted on two metal poles. Last location before current location above entrance to dining hall.

34

Omitted Stories, History and Tidbits

1920-2010

This book omits many stories and people of the family that were not woven into memoirs by writers. Even so, these bits of information are historically imperative in telling the story of the Children's Home. Some absent facts, experiences and people are integrated in this chapter. A number of significant specifics were omitted, not because lack of importance, but forgotten or not viewed by writers as something they felt others wanted to read. Some writers thought their story needed to be told for them to heal. Still, other writers decided not to include some experiences for personal reasons.

Too, within this chapter is information becoming available during researching and writing of the book. For the first time, some information is no longer oral history but now believed to be written Children's Home history.

Bonnie Farmer (1940-'75)

Back Row R-L: Bonnie Farmer standing with Concert Choir

Bonnie Farmer worked for the Children's Home at different intervals during the 1940's ('40's-'75). During that time, she became a full-time employee of the Home, but the exact date is not known. She remained an employee until she retired December 31, 1975.

Miss Bonnie was the Children's Home "public relations officer" before there was even a development office. Even though she worked in various positions, she was hired (1940's) to establish a Concert Choir. This Choir was made up of the children in care. For many years the Choir, under her direction, traveled the State visiting churches and presenting religious programs in song. There is an affectionate remembrance of Miss Bonnie in the communities and families in and with which she stayed as she traveled.

After her retirement, she moved into the Free Will Baptist Retirement Homes, which had duplex apartments on property adjacent to the Children's Home campus; she lived there until the late 1980's when she moved to a retirement home (Brook Field Retirement Home, Lillington, NC) to be near nieces and nephews.

On October 19, 1907 she was born to George Leonidas Farmer and Dora Grady Farmer of Wayne County. She has a sister Mary Emma Jones who resides in Southern Pines, North Carolina.

Miss Bonnie (92), died Thursday, November 4, 1999, and her funeral service, was held at Tyndall Funeral Home, Mount Olive, North Carolina. Dr. Bobby Taylor ('82-'07) participated in her funeral. She is buried in the Farmer Family Cemetery in Mount Olive.

Julia Rebecca Edwards Davenport (1969-'09)

Dr. Bobby Taylor and Julia Rebecca Edwards Davenport

Rebecca Davenport served five terms on the Board of Directors spanning from 1969-90. During her service, she served on numerous committees, as well as vice chairperson, and chair of the Board for seven years; she provided leadership, guidance, and concern. At the end of her last term, the Board of Directors elected her as an Emeritus member, an honor she held until her death. During her last term, she was honored by the North Carolina Child Care Association (1990), as Trustee of the Year.

Rebecca found herself involved in the Home's ministry through her parents who visited the Home on many occasions while she grew up. This was the beginning of what would be decades of her dedicated service to the Home. She had a concern and a passion for the children of the Home. She made it a point to visit often, and to visit early so she would have the opportunity to visit the children and staff. She was always concerned and wanted to ensure everyone was doing well and that the ministry of the Home was fulfilling its mission.

Rebecca was born March 26, 1916 and passed December 14, 2009. Dr. Bobby Taylor participated in her funeral and burial, December 17, 2009 at Reedy Branch Original Free Will Baptist Church, Winterville, North Carolina.

Blackie of the North Woods (1876-'63)

M.L. Cummings

The children called him Mr. Cummings. He never worked at the Orphanage, nor was he an alumnus of the Home. No one can tell you when he first came to the Home or when he left. He ate meals with the staff and children in the dining hall and he slept in the boys' building. If any of the boys wanted to chat, he'd take time to talk with them. He preached at the Home from time to time, but no one remembers him preaching in church. Always, Preacher Cummings' preached under a tree or out of the back of his jeep and usually the jeep was parked in the flower garden. Sometimes, he held up chains from his prison years. Occasionally, he would dress in his black and white prison garbs and talk about the penalty for sin. He was always "old" in our eyes.

No one knew then and no one knows now how Mr. Cummings got the name "Blackie of the North Woods". Everyone knew of Mr. Cummings; the boys probably knew him better, but no one really knew him. If you converse with anyone who was on campus during the years he appeared, you'd get snippets of him.

Jacob Lane ('46-'58), "I remember, when I was about age 10, seeing him preaching under a pecan tree. He wore a round, black-felt hat, black suit, white shirt, black shoes and a black bow tie."

Martin Morris ('52-'59), "Yes, I remember Mr. Cummings. When he was placed in the rest home, I was assigned to clean out his closet. He had black and white striped prison clothes. He was pretty intelligent."

Winfred Winstead ('44-'51), "When they called on him to bless our food at dinner, he always prayed a long prayer."

Sudie Mixon, dietician at the Home for many years, remembered Mr. Cummings this way, "Mr. Cummings walked with dignity. He did not have good hearing. When he died, a group of concerned citizens pooled their money to bury him."

The person who seemed to know him more was House Parent Mary Mitchell. She always was doing something for him when he was on campus, sometimes weeks at a time. In a conversation in 2000, she recalled, "He died in a rest home, but lived at the Orphanage a short time before his health deteriorated. He kept his clothes in his car and dirty clothes were cleaned at the dry cleaners. He told me once that he deserted his wife and two sons. He did not blame his sons for having nothing to do with him. Mr. Cummings made his living preaching. He would stand on street corners, wearing black and white striped prison clothes as he preached the gospel and sold his book for fifty cents."

The following background information is told by Moses LaFlaver Cummings (*Blackie*) in his 32-page paperback book, *Avenues Leading to Crime,* copyrighted in 1947:

"*Blackie's mother, a schoolteacher, moved from America to Canada in 1848. His father was a blacksmith. Their first child was a "brown-eyed, black-haired" girl named Unita. Four years after her birth, during a blizzard, her father, late for dinner for the first time, staggered into their once happy home all covered with snow and blood. The faithful husband and father, on his way home that night, had met up with the tempter in the form of a friend, who persuaded the curly-headed smithy to stop into a public house and have a social drink, which awoke within him a terrible appetite inherited from his ancestors.*

"*Unita's father continued his drinking binge for many months. "The faithful wife and mother never ceased to pray for her erring husband; and to her surprise, one night he returned home sober and knelt by the side of his wife and girl and gave God his heart. He commenced life over again by establishing the family altar in the home, and learned to love and serve God better as the days passed by.*

"*The family moved to rural Northern Canada, where they lived in a log cabin and Unita's father became a blacksmith for farmers and lumberjacks. God gave them the desire of their hearts, a beautiful baby boy, with jet-black hair and big brown eyes. The lumberjacks named him Blackie.*

"*During Christmas 1878, while gazing into their fireplace and talking of their children's future, the parents had a premonition. As they gazed into the fire, a vision seemed to rise out of the flames. The father sees his boy grown up to manhood with the terrible appetite for drink leading him captive, and he shudders as he thinks of how near that awful appetite came to wrecking his own life. The mother sees her Gypsy ancestors, with their wagons and tents and their roving, restless spirit, and she shudders at the thought of her boy inheriting the wanderlust. The desire of the parents' hearts is that he may grow up to be a preacher of righteousness.*

"*In 1881, Blackie's mother died from the "Great White Plague." Near death, with tears in her eyes, she asked for Blackie. She handed him her Bible saying, "Take it, my darling, and when you can read you will find a message in its back pages from a dying mother to her only boy. You will also find within its pages a chart from your mother's God that, if followed, will lead you to where she is going soon.*

"*After those few words, sister lifted little Blackie up so that he could kiss her thin pale cheeks. She smiled as he backed out of the room, holding the little Bible in one hand and waving the other at the 'bestest mother he had ever known'.*

"*Blackie's father remarried. In the winter of 1889, an epidemic called "la grippe", very similar to the flu, swept across Canada. His father dying, Blackie, age 13, hooked* up the faithful old horse to the sleigh and drove many miles to the city for the family doctor. It was a cold night and he stopped at a hotel to get warm. "He went to the sitting room, just off of the barroom. Lumberjacks spied Blackie all covered with snow and shivering, and ordered the bartender to fix him several hot toddies. Not realizing it might make him intoxicated, they wrapped blankets and furs around him, put him in the sleigh and the horse took him back home through a blinding blizzard.

"He returned home intoxicated. His father, tears trickling down his thin pale cheeks, thought of the vision he had seen leap out of the flames. The shock of seeing his only boy intoxicated proved fatal, and a few days later he died. A few days after his death, the stepmother auctioned off all the family's belongings, including the blacksmith shop and cabin. After the sale, the stepmother returned to her people, and Unita, age 17, went to work in the city. Blackie just drifted from one job to another.

"Blackie had not seen his sister for three years when he found out she was in the hospital. At the hospital, "She told him of the man who had wronged her and then left her when she was about to become a mother. He vowed he would kill the man who had dared to treat his orphan sister in such a way. He located his sister's betrayer working in a railroad yard.

"Shortly after midnight, Blackie managed to get within a few feet of the man without being seen. Unconscious of any danger, the man was waiting with a lantern in his hand for a fast-approaching train. The engineer saw the switchman's lantern go under the wheels and stopped the engine. A little later the crew found a hunting knife sticking in a pole with a note, 'Unita is avenged.'

"Afterwards, Blackie committed robberies in Canada, Ohio and Florida. In Florida, he was arrested, found guilty and sentenced to the convict mines of Florida. On his release, he turned to drinking and petty crimes. In 1901, Blackie "met a beautiful, brown-eyed, black-haired Canadian girl and married her. They were happy and prosperous, and God gave them two beautiful black-eyed boys.

"Blackie again turned to alcohol and left his family. In 1913, while lying near the San Francisco Bay, considering suicide, his soul took advantage of his drink-crazed mind. Blackie could see his faithful wife, with her eyes swollen from weeping over her erring husband. He could see his little boys as they cried themselves to sleep because daddy didn't come home." He thought, now it was time for him to end the miserable life that had caused so much sorrow and so many heartaches. No one loved him now.

"Blackie decided to end his life in the chilly waters of San Francisco Bay. On his way to the Bay, he spotted a Salvation Army Band and followed the band to church. As the band played, Blackie knelt at the altar and gave God his heart. That night, September 13, 1913, he preached his first sermon. He didn't know how to offer up a flowery prayer, he prayed the little prayer he had learned at his mother's knees, in the north *woods: Now I lay me down to sleep, I pray the Lord my soul to keep; and if I should die before I wake, I pray the lord my soul to take."*

Maybe through osmosis, maybe it was the will of God, our Children's Home family accepted Mr. Cummings. Regardless when he would show up, life continued as usual with no interruptions in our daily lives.

Blackie died December 26, 1963 and is buried in Marsh Swamp Original Free Will Baptist Cemetery, Sims, North Carolina. Reverend R. H. Jackson (Superintendent '55-'56) officiated his funeral. Blackie was 87.

Jimmy Cantrell (1953-'64)

Jimmy Cantrell

During the early 50's, I was in the concert class one summer. Our class toured eastern North Carolina singing and giving our program almost daily the entire summer at Free Will Baptist Churches. We'd usually arrive at the church of our scheduled performance in late morning or early afternoon. Church families would be waiting for us to provide our housing for the day and evening after church. Another boy and I always stayed together in homes, as we were the only boys in the class. On one occasion, we were assigned to stay with a Christian man who picked us up in the church parking lot. Everything went well until the evening hours. The other boy and I slept together in a bed. During the night, the man crawled into bed with us and started touching us. We ran into the bathroom and locked the door, sleeping the night in a bathtub. I never did report his advances. I thought that, if I did report it, I wouldn't be believed; or, if I was believed, I would be blamed for what happened. I also felt that, if I did report it, I would be a victim of disciplinary action as a result of coming forward. Knowing that the concert class brought in money in the form of donations, I did not think anyone would care as long as we continued to bring in money. I carried this incident for over 50 years before I finally told someone. To this day, it's still personally embarrassing but I feel this should be told. I hope it will provide information for administrators in the future and, by doing so, another child will not have to experience what I went through that night.

Foy Watson (1951-'63)

L-R *Eddie, Betty Jean, Foy Watson*

My brother Eddie ('47-'56) said when he lived in the old boys' building before I came there, Petey Mitchell would take him into the bathroom every morning and beat him with that board that he always used. I didn't stay in the old boys' building very long, but I do remember them putting me on the top bunk to sleep the first day I was at the Orphanage; after I wet the bed that night, they moved me to the bottom bunk.

"Eddie and I had to wear rubber pants and were made to walk up and down the bedroom isle, while the other boys were encouraged to laugh at us. Petey beat both Eddie and me and we were both thrown in the cold showers. Yes, Eddie did sleep on the floor to prevent being beaten or thrown in a cold shower by Petey, if he found the bed wet when he made his wake-up round early in the morning. I remember waking up during the night and my bed was wet so I tried to dry my sheets on the radiator before Petey found out the next morning.

"When I think back to those childhood days, I was well into my teens before I was able to stop wetting my bed. All the boys had to take a bath before they went to bed so very few or no one took a bath in the mornings before school. I know there were times when I would get up in the morning and put a dry pair of underwear on and cover up my wet bed with my spread because I didn't want anyone to know that I had wet the bed. Now when I think back, I know that I had to smell of urine when the weather was warm or when I got hot. When you are accustomed to these smells, you don't smell them but others do. How I wished that someone had told me that I needed to take a bath because they could smell the urine on me. I hope that future caretakers will realize the importance of this.

"One thing that was very embarrassing were the times that everyone had to remove the sheets from the beds to air out the mattress and the center of my mattress was rotted out from being wet on so much.

Alumni Association Presidents

In Chapter 1, the Reverend Dr. James A. Evans writes of an Alumni Association in 1943. The function of the Association, other than financial support, is not clear as there are no minutes or records from that period. The first Homecoming is believed to be in 1946 and it may be the Association ceased to function afterwards. We do known nearly 40 years after the first child was admitted to the Home, alumni wanting formal recognition, formed an association in 1962. The alumni wanted to be involved in the future of their "family" and Home. In 1962, the first meeting of the new assocation was held in the chapel and officers were elected. Horace Mixon, an employee and alumnus of the home, was elected the first president. A constitution was adopted by the Association July 11, 1982.

1962 – 1963	Horace Mixon ('23-'34)
1963 – 1965	Ralph Pate ('33-'41)
1965 – 1967	Steve Worthington ('54-'63)
1967 – 1969	Charles Harrell ('38-'51)
1969 – 1971	Andrew Hartsfield ('59-'69)

1971 – 1974	Nancy Smith Lane ('49-'60)
1974 – 1978	Jerry Smith ('49-'60)
1978 – 1982	Charles Warren ('67-'73)
1982 – 1984	Mickey Newton ('59-'71)
1984 – 1992	Doris Ann Lancaster Hudson ('55-'63)
1992 – 1996	Judy Warren Aycock ('67-'77)
1996 – 1998	Margie Herring Matthews ('52-'62)
1998 – 2000	Randy Faircloth ('67-'75)
2000 – 2003	Phil Mercer ('53-'68)
2003 – 2006	Margie Herring Sullivan ('52-'62)
2006 – 2007	Alice Little Rouse ('46-'55)
2007 – 2009	Alma Pope Woodard ('53-'66)
2009 –	Randy Faircloth ('67-'75)

Some of the Alumni Association interests through the years:

- Purchased stain glass mural behind baptistery in Memorial Chapel.
- Funded the outside church bulletin board as a memorial to alumnus Sandra Mercer ('53-'65) who passed June 15, 1965.
- Funded lights on the Children's Home sign at Middlesex.
- Sent children to Cragmont numerous years.
- Help fund construction for tennis court.
- Make donations to Alumni Endowment Fund in memory of deceased alumni.
- Association petitioned the Town of Middlesex to change the road named "Orphan Home Road" from Hwy 264 to the Children's Home. The name was changed to "Children's Home Road", later changed to Buck Deans Road at the request of Administration at the home.
- Continue to be a voice for Alumni in preservation of the Home and support of administration to keep the doors open for children.

Children's Home Board of Directors Alumni Representative

An alumnus did not attend Board of Directors meetings until the Alumni Association was formed. The Association elected representatives to attend meetings. Even then, the representative had no vote, only token representation for former children of the Home. It was not until 1978 an alumnus could cast a vote for board action.

Following is alumnus Jerry Smith's ('49-'60) remembrance of how the alumni were given representation by the State Convention of Original Free Will Baptist.

"In 1973, I visited Reverend C. F. Bowen and expressed desire of alumni to have an alumnus appointed to the Children's Home Board of Directors by the State Convention. Reverend Bowen pointed out that Alumni Presidents attend board meetings at the Children's Home. I acknowledged to him that Alumni Association Presidents did attend board meetings. I then made Reverend Bowen aware alumni representatives had no votes on board matters and alumni wanted a recorded vote on board issues. Reverend Bowen was President of the State Convention at that time. He seemed cool to changing the constitution to allow alumni a vote.

"Early 1974, I visited Pa Smith (Superintendent '51-'54 & '56-'58) and shared the same information I had shared with Reverend Bowen. Pa was interested in official alumni representation on the board and agreed to work with me in presenting the request to the State Convention that year, when it met in Kenan Memorial Auditorium, Kenansville, North Carolina. On September 11-12, the State Convention met. Convention rules required changes in the constitution be presented and the following year voted on. On the second day of the convention, Pa and I met with a committee and made the request. It was made in the form of a motion to the convention with Pa seconding the motion.

"The 1975 State Convention was held at the American Legion building, Wilson, North Carolina. When I arrived at the convention, Pa met me at the door. He said someone in the convention was trying to stop the appointment of an alumnus to the board by the convention. A motion had been made and seconded to study the amendment to the constitution more and wait another year before voting. Before the vote to delay the vote to another year, Pa went to the front of the auditorium and gave an emotional talk to vote down the motion to delay the constitutional change vote. The motion failed. The amendment was then passed. Afterwards Pa said to me. 'Duck, you'll never be voted on the Board of Directors at the Children's Home. There are some who are very dissatisfied with this constitutional change.' I told Pa I had no desire at the time to serve on the board. I thanked him for his support. For sure, without his support, the motion would not have been passed that year. The first State Convention approved alumnus to serve on the Board of Directors of the Children's Home was Mildred Johnson Penny ('38-'48). She was voted to the board for a three-year appointment 1975-78."

The following alumni have been representatives on the Children's Home Board of Directors:

Appointments by Alumni Association
1962 – 1963 Earl Tippett ('28-'40)
1963 – 1965 Ralph Pate ('33-'41)
1965 – 1967 Steve Worthington ('54-'63)
1967 – 1969 Charles Harrell ('38-'51)
1969 – 1971 Andrew Hartsfield ('59-'69)
1971 – 1974 Nancy Smith Lane ('49-'60)
1974 – 1975 Jerry Smith ('49-'60)

Appointments by Convention of Original Free Will Baptists
1975 – 1978 Mildred Johnson Penny ('38-'48)
1978 – 1982 Charles Warren ('67-'73)
1982 – 1990 Mickey Newton ('59-'71)
1990 – 1997 Jerry Smith ('49-'60)
1998 – 2010 Judy Warren Aycock ('67-'77)
2010 -   Billy Hines ('54-'62)

Children's Home History

The Free Will Baptist Historical Collection in the Moye Library, Mount Olive College, is an excellent resource for materials on the history and contributions of the Children's Home. Curator Gary Fenton Barefoot is open to receiving future materials that will add to the Children's Home historical collection. He is happy to assist you.

In addition to cataloged materials accessed through the on-line catalog are several collections of papers in the Manuscripts Collection with materials/references to the Children's Home. Included:
George Stevenson Papers – Alumnus ('42-'52)
M. E. Tyson Papers - Superintendent ('35-'40)

James A. Evans Papers – Superintendent ('40-'49)
J. C. Griffin Papers – Board of Directors – ('22-'26)
Stephen A. Smith Papers – Superintendent ('51-'55 & '56-'58)
Jerry Smith Writings – Alumnus ('49-'60)

Microfilmed minutes of the Children's Home Board from 1915 – 2008 Children's Home Newsletter/periodical *"Young People's Friend"* and *"Children's Home life."* The Children's Home may have things that are not available at the college library. The Original Free Will Baptist Headquarters in Ayden does not have Children's Home historical information.

L-R: George Stevenson & Curator Gary Barefoot

An alumnus from the Home, George Stevenson ('42-'52), was instrumental in founding of the Free Will Baptist Historical Collection. Curator Gary Fenton Barefoot writes about the early beginning of the Historical Collection at the college: "George and I were freshmen at Mount Olive College in the fall of 1957. George was a history "nut" and knew much about everything. I learned early on that he knew much about the history of the Free Will Baptist Church in North Carolina. I worked in the library and at that time there existed a file drawer and a glass display cabinet that contained some historical items of Free Will Baptists—mainly some printed minutes of varying years, some quite early. There were copies of disciplines (treatises), a copy of the original Harrison and Barfield History of the Free Will Baptists in North Carolina, an old hymnal or two, some pictures of various denominational enterprise buildings and people, some items from Ayden Seminary and Eureka College and a miscellany of other things. Mrs. Mildred Councill, the librarian at the time, had basically turned the materials over to Dan Fagg, then Dean and history professor, to sort and organize. As he was busy, he suggested that George and I might do that since we were both Free Will Baptists. That was the beginning of the Free Will Baptist Historical Collection and with Mr. Fagg's help, we made some organization out of the file and displayed some items. After we left two years later to attend the University of North Carolina at Chapel Hill, the Collection grew some as people learned that someone was collecting Free Will Baptist historical items at Mount Olive Junior College (Library). Both of us pursued our interest in the Collection as we worked in the North Carolina Collection at the University of North Carolina. George was good at seeking out items from bookstores, etc. We kept in contact with Mrs. Councill and occasionally returned to work some on the Collection at the College. After I returned as librarian in 1965, I inherited the job of trying to develop the Free Will Baptist Historical Collection. George was always interested and made many gifts to the collection, but his greatest gift was his expertise in organizing the Collection. After I did a list of Subject Headings for the subject classification of the Collection, he created a classification system based on an expansion of the Library of Congress Classification System. We still use that system as well as the subject heading list. George continued his interest in the work of the Collection and the endowment that he left in his will to the Collection is ample proof of his interest in and appreciation for the Free Will Baptist denomination."

Tidbits

Daniel Rouse ('55-'62) has filmed Free Will Baptist Children Home homecomings from 1989-present. He has the homecomings on CD and available for your purchase *($20.00 per year)*. These CD's provide an excellent history of activities of each homecoming held second Sunday in July each year. Daniel can be contacted at his home address to acquire a CD. His address: 614 N. 7th Street, Smithfield, North Carolina 27577. Phone: 919-934-4330.

All Alumni writers in *The Family* were recorded in the *REGISTER OF INMATES* bookwhen they were admitted to the Orphanage/Children's

Home and their discharged date was recorded in the Register when they left. The *REGISTER OF INMATES* book is still being used today.

Chester Eugene Page was admitted July 15, 1940 and discharged May 21, 1957. He is believed to have been a resident of the Children's Home longer than any child.

On Founder's Day, May 22, 2010, Heritage Hall was rededicated and the campus bell was relocated to its final location. Alumnae, alumnus, staff and a current resident participated in the Bell Ceremony. Ringing for each decade were 1920's Fannie Holland '25-'35; 1930's Sterling Skinner '37-'43; 1940's Nancy Smith '49-'60; 1950's Margie Herring '52-'62; 1960's John Elmore '58-'65; 1970's Judy Warren '67-'77; 1980's Mary Ann Hopkins '89-'96; 1990's Joyce Batchelor '97-'10; and 2000's Devonte' H '09-current.

W. Burkette Raper ('36-'44), became the President of Mount Olive college in 1954, at age 26; he was the youngest college president in the United States. When he retired as president in January 1956, he was the longest-tenured president in the nation. He died August 1, 2011. In attendance for his memoriam was Dr. J. Matthew Pinson, President of the Free Will Baptist Bible College, Nashville, Tennessee, Alumni President, Yvonne Rouse ('55-'69), and the longest serving governor in North Carolina, The Honorable James B. Hunt, Jr.

Footnote: The author has made reasonable efforts to insure the accuracy of this chapter. If there are omissions or mistakes, please inform him.

35

We Have Accepted the Challenge

The Reverend Ray Wells

The Reverend Ray Wells and Julie

This January 15th, an article in *"The Wall Street Journal"* caught my attention. Titled "The Best Thing About Orphanages," and written by Richard B. McKenzie who grew up in another orphanage in North Carolina, the article reported research recently released by Duke University researchers on a multi-year study of 3,000 orphaned children. The central premise was children reared in orphanages were no worse off than being raised by family and most often performed better than those reared in foster care.

McKenzie writes more in the column about his survey of 2,500 alumni from 15 orphanages in America. Of the many areas in which "orphans" do better than their counterparts is in education and life in general. He points out, "White orphanages had a 39% higher rate of college graduation in the same age general population, and less than 3% had hostile memories of their orphanage experience."

McKenzie's findings seem to reflect those reared in our Children's Home in Middlesex. Among the alumni writers in *The Family*, our denomination is to be proud of their careers that include a social worker for the blind, high school teacher, elementary school teacher, real estate appraiser, school bus driver, telecommunications expense management consultant, decorated Viet Nam marine captain, (ret.) air force major, business proprietor, writer, county tax administrator, county social service director, college president, decorated world war II B-17 bombardier tech. sgt., stay-at-home mom, archivist/historian, minister and administrative assistant.

The Original Free Will Baptists have taken very seriously the words of Matthew 19:14: "Let the little children come to me and do not forbid them; for of such is the Kingdom of Heaven". From 1913, when the proposal was made to consider establishing a home for orphans to the present, Original Free Will Baptists have fulfilled and will continue to fulfill those words. We have accepted the challenge in Matthews. The church has provided a place of physical growth, spiritual growth and unconditional love for children who otherwise would have never had the chance to experience any of those things. The Original Free Will Baptist Church has rallied time and time again to ensure that the doors of the Children's Home stayed open and the needs of every child were met.

Original Free Will Baptists have, in my opinion, always been a compassionate and caring people. There is no greater evidence of this than the relationship between the churches and the Free Will Baptist Children's Home. Since the first children were admitted to the Children's Home in May of 1920, the Original Free Will Baptist Church has constantly and consistently supported the ministry of the Home.

In order to illustrate this relationship, I feel it is necessary to share some of the things the church has done to insure the continuance of service to the children residing at the Home. I have gleaned much of this history from the book *A History of Original Free Will Baptists* by Dr. Michael R. Pelt.

During the 1930's, the era of the Great Depression, the one cause that aroused the sympathies of many Original Free Will Baptists was the Orphanage at Middlesex. The home at that time had taken in more children because of the impact of the depression. Every medium available to the superintendent and the board was used to keep before the Free Will Baptists the needs of the Orphanage. If anyone could not send money, he was encouraged to bring food and clothing. Such items were provided by many churches and taken to the home so that the physical needs of the children could be met.

The church once again showed its commitment to the home when, during World War II, the church and individuals were challenged to purchase government bonds in the name of the home and designated the proceeds for the building of the chapel. This again was an indication that Free Will Baptists not only cared for the physical well-being of the children in its care but also for their spiritual well-being also. The chapel was completed in 1952 and stands today as a constant reminder that with God, all things are possible.

From 1960 through 2009, the Children's Home has undergone many changes. The Home, formerly known as the Orphanage, provides for services for children of broken homes and abusive family relationships. The Home has been licensed by the North Carolina Department of Human Services and accredited by the Council on Accreditation of Services for Families and Children.

In my 40 years of ministry, I have never served a church that did not have a passion for the Children's Home. Those churches, like many more have at one time or another, opened their homes and hearts to the children and in doing so, they have been privileged to touch lives and make a difference in those lives.

Over the years, the operation of the Children's Home has changed and the church has changed also. Because of government guidelines, our churches are no longer able to bring children to the homes of church members for weekends, holidays or summer vacations. Many lasting and loving relationships developed between the church and the child they had "adopted". To compensate for that, the church has adopted new ways of maintaining a connection with the children. Now, instead of the one child coming to a particular church, many churches are inviting all of the children to visit. The churches plan meals, games, fellowship and worship opportunities for all the children. Many of churches plan outings that include the Children's Home. One Original Free Will Baptist church has an annual paper product drive and invites all other Original Free Will Baptist Churches to participate and the products are collected during a Carolina Mudcats' baseball game at the Five County Stadium near

Zebulon, North Carolina. The AA Mudcats are a Cincinnati Reds minor league team. The Children's Home also asked churches to send a gift of $100.00 at Christmas so every child will receive a gift or gifts and no one is left out. These changes have allowed the church to become involved with all the children and not just one or two. I believe this is more beneficial to the children and more of a blessing to the church.

Since the first children entered the Children's Home in 1920, a lot of things have changed. The majority of the children at the Home are from broken homes and abusive home environments. We are no longer an "orphanage"; we are truly a children's home.

I once heard this comment, "I don't know why we need a children's home, none of the children there are Free Will Baptists." If, indeed, there are no Free Will Baptist children there, we should be thankful. We should also be thankful that, if ever any Free Will Baptist child needed a place, we can provide a refuge for them.

As an Original Free Will Baptist minister for 42 years, I have had the privilege to know and to work with several of the superintendents of the Children's Home. My association with those men goes back to and includes, Reverends Dr. James Evans ('40-'49), S. A. (Pa) Smith ('51-'55 & '56-'58), R. H. Jackson ('55-'56), J. Wilbert Everton ('58-'62), M. L. Johnson ('62-'69), Edward Miles ('69-'71), Cedric Pierce ('71-'72), Graham Lane ('72), Sam Weeks ('73-'77), Howard Cayton ('81-'83), Bobby Taylor ('83-'07), and current President/CEO Gary Lee ('07-present).

Of those who have served as superintendent, four of them have pastored the Marsh Swamp Original Free Will Baptist Church, the church that I have pastored for the past 30 years. The Marsh Swamp cemetery is also the final resting place for Traveling Evangelist Elder M. L. Cummings referenced in several memoirs. Inscribed on Elder Cummings' tombstone are the words "Known as Blackie of the North Woods."

In my capacity as President of the Convention of Original Free Will Baptists from 1994-1998, I had the privilege to serve on the Board of Directors of the Children's Home and saw first-hand that the needs of the children always came first. Some of those former residents I have also known. I had the privilege to be the pastor of the author of this book, Jerry Smith ('49-60). No one has impacted the Original Free Will Baptist Church as Children's Home Alumnus Dr. Burkette Raper ('36-'45), President Emeritus of Mount Olive College.

Dr. Raper was the second president of Mount Olive College. Eighteen writers in *The Family* attended Mount Olive College.

I am proud to be a member of the Original Free Will Baptist Church. A church early in its existence chose, as one of its primary ministries, the care of children. Because of the efforts of Original Free Will Baptist Churches and individuals, the doors of the Children's Home have never closed, no child has ever been turned away and, as long as there are Original Free Will Baptist Churches, it will remain that way.

Footnote: Reverend Wells has been pastor of Marsh Swamp Original Free Will Baptist Church, Sims, North Carolina for over 30 years. He was President of the Convention of Original Free Will Baptists 1994-98. He writes this chapter at the request of the author of The Family. Pastor Wells was asked to write what the Children's Home means to Original Free Will Baptists.

Afterword

    I'm especially proud of J. Andrews Smith for caring enough about the Home to have the vision to see the need to collect the real stories of the experiences so many have shared with us. This book will serve as a reminder of the intimate relationships and forever memories which are etched into the hearts and minds of individuals touched by this Home.

    During the past fifteen years, I have been blessed to be part of the Free Will Baptist Children's Home family and ministry. I came to the Home as a young professional hoping to make a difference in the world. I have learned so much more than I could have imagined. After some time here, I discovered it was truly a place of caring. The environment at the Home is family oriented. Our relationship with one another and the children we care for is close. The staff care for one another, the children care for each other, and our community cares for this ministry. Words of appreciation will never accomplish the heartfelt thanks to all who have supported this ministry throughout our history. The history of the Free Will Baptists denomination's commitment to children and their families has remained strong. Our relationship with the churches and countless individuals who support this ministry have provided us with the necessary financial support needed to continue the mission of the Home. Of those children who have found their way to this Home through difficult circumstances, many survived uncertain futures. For the true orphan, the Home became the most important home they have ever known. We acknowledge children today do not see our Home as the only home they have. Yet, everyone who has been here has experienced something which is unique and important to them. All can enjoy the campus, receive necessary help and leave with confidence in themselves.

Many wonderful memories have been made on our campus. Just like many years ago, even today children have first-time experiences while living at the Home. Traditions at the Home have changed over time, but the core components of who we are and what we have been commissioned for remains unchanged. It is simply not enough to offer food, clothing, and shelter. We are committed to spiritual development, emotional support and educating young people.

During the past nine decades, the Home has experienced many changes. Organizations in society have sometimes been required to change to meet the needs of their community. The community of children needing a place to live has certainly changed, but our mission to provide a safe home has remained the same. As I travel throughout the state, I am constantly learning about the challenges faced by many child care institutions such as ours. Our industry has seen many changes as child welfare systems have been revamped in an effort to bring consistency and hopefully better services to children and families. Regardless of the implications, our commitment will remain the same. Children living at the Free Will Baptist Children's Home will continue to receive needed services.

By studying our history and listening to the many accounts of those who grew up or worked at the Home, it is clear there were times when things were done not as well as they could have been. Today, as we acknowledge the difficult times, we are also reminded of the good ones.

Recently, as I took time to walk the campus, I was reminded of the purpose of our ministry. We live in a world it seems where so many things go wrong. We can complain endlessly about something. Instead, let' take time to reflect on the good things we experience and enjoy. I would rather be right where I am than any other place. Personally, for me the Children's Home is a beautiful place - a place which GOD continues to bless each day. I pray daily for all of our staff, especially our children's service workers. Sacrifices are made by many who labor here daily by choice. For those of us who have seen, heard, or experienced the change in a life the Children's Home can bring, it truly is a blessing. I have peace in my heart each day to press forward for the work of children. We are sometimes the only ones to represent them.

As I represent the Children's Home ministry I do so with a humble heart and much appreciation to everyone who shares with this ministry

Gary Lee
President/CEO

Footnote: *Gary Lee was appointed President/CEO of the Original Free Will Baptist Children's Home on January 1, 2008. May, 2008, in above photo, he led children and staff in National Day of Prayer observance. Gary started working at the Home October 1, 1994 as Director of Church and Public Relations. On November 11, 1997, he was appointed Vice President of Operations and served in this capacity until becoming President/CEO.*

Acknowledgements

 I may be the only person to have talked with every writer contributing to *The Family*. Like writing a biography, the author takes a journey with that person into his life. So, it was with writers for this book. Although many of the writers and I listened to the same dinging of the bell for meals, attended church and events in our childhood, my journey with them was another passage inscribing this book. We conversed on an adult level looking back in time. There were times of tears, times of laughter, and times of healing. To each one, I will forever be grateful for their passion and for their strength of will to tell their stories.

 In addition to those submitting their memoir, other resources were invaluable. These people made available their time to assist me in bringing to life the stories you've read. I am forever grateful to these wonderful people:

Gary Fenton Barefoot – Curator of the Free Will Baptist Historical Collection, Gary gave his time to research for the book. His help with factual verification saved me time and miles of travel.

Cynthia Batten – While the Children's Home made available information for the book, Cynthia worked tirelessly with me and other alumni in gathering information as needed. She is the administrative assistant of the Children's Home. She lives in Kenly, North Carolina.

Carl Daughtry – His visit to a library and newspaper office numerous times to research newspapers saved me many miles of travel. He resides in Rocky Mount, North Carolina.

Margie "Herring" Sullivan ('52-'62) – While memoirs are verbatim, many writers asked for help in writing their story. Many alumni mailed memoirs in their handwriting. Margie gave countless hours editing before memoirs were returned for writers approval before publishing. Because of her support for the book, she did the editing during time of recovery from her liver transplant. She resides in Wilson, North Carolina .

Cathy "Hines" Campbell ('57-'66) – She spent endless time searching grave sites for Joseph L. Griffin and Willey R. Watson. Without her interviewing skills, one memoir would not be in the book. She, too, did research in the Free Will Baptist Historical Collection. She resides in Greenville, North Carolina.

Stewart Humphrey ('70-'72 & '77-'81) – I am grateful for his help with book layout. He resides in Weaverville, North Carolina

Donna Jacobs – She did restoration for pictures in the book. Without her skills, the book cover would have been different. She resides in Elizabeth City, North Carolina.

Gary Lee – President/CEO of the Children's Home was most supportive when asked for help. He not only encouraged writing the book, he made available historical information available at the Home.

Brenda "Mitchell" Overton ('46-'65) -- She took the time to read the final manuscript and proofed changes before publication. She supports publication of this book. She lives in Raleigh North Carolina.

Lynna Mitchell – Publisher and General Manager of Tazewell County Free Press, she has encouraged my writing as a columnist for her newspaper since 1996. Without her support and patience while my writing skills developed through the years, this book could not have been possible. The press is located in Richlands, Virginia.

Melissa Anne Poteat – Author and niece of George Stevenson, Jr.('43-'52), she worked with me formatting the book for LuLu Press publication. Her books can be viewed at her website. She lives in Marion, North Carolina.

Nancy "Smith" Lane ('49-'60) – My sister did research for the *Register of Inmates* and compiled the list for publication. She resides in Angier, North Carolina.

Susan Smith – I am very grateful to my wife for her support and patience during my early morning and late evening writings and times away from home. In addition, she endured my mood changes after a phone conversation with an alumnus or reading what an alumnus had written. She has been the steadiest force by my side during this journey. She deserves my utmost thanks.

George Stevenson ('42-'52) – He gave so much encouragement and advice for the writing of this book. Sadly, he passed before publication.

Joyce "Stevenson" Poteat (42'-52) – She took the time to read the final manuscript and proofed changes before publication. She supports publication of this book. She lives in Marion, North Carolina.

Elvin and Carol Stone – They were supportive and opened their home for my stays many nights after my visits in eastern North Carolina researching the book. In a way, they've become my adopted family and I know there's always love, friendship, a hot meal and bed for me in their home. I can never fully thank them for what they've been to me. They reside in Kenly, North Carolina.

Legal consultation was provided by attorneys Heather Newton, Allen Thomas, and Jerry Smith Jr. Their advice was most helpful.

APPENDIX I

REGISTER OF INMATES
1920-79

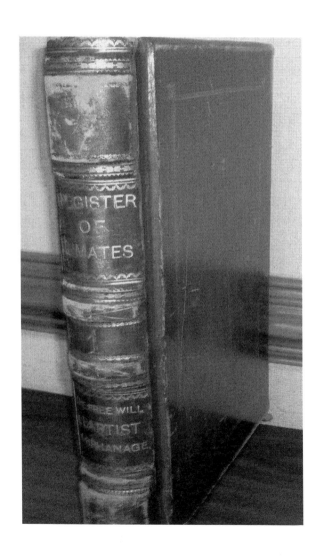

Order	Name	Admitted	Discharged
1	Whitley, Nellie	5/23/1920	6/5/1927
2	Whitley, Helen	5/23/1920	9/3/1930
3	Whitley, Dorothy	5/23/1920	5/7/1932
4	Whitley, Carl	5/23/1920	8/4/1931
5	Rawls, Cecil	5/28/1920	10/11/1920
6	Rawls, Vera	5/28/1920	10/11/1920
7	Rawls, Robert	5/28/1920	10/11/1920
8	Rawls, Vernon	5/28/1920	10/11/1920
9	Harrison, Inez	6/8/1920	10/30/1920
	Returned	8/29/1921	12/12/1927
10	Harrison, Elouise	6/8/1920	10/30/1920
11	Harrison, Lina C.	6/8/1920	10/30/1920
	Returned	8/29/1921	5/20/1933
12	Morten, Martin Asa	6/21/1920	6/8/1932
13	Martin, Lela	7/2/1920	5/17/1926
14	King, Robert Glenn	7/7/1920	5/13/1921
15	King, Isabel	7/7/1920	5/13/1921
16	King, Nettie Lee	7/7/1920	5/13/1921
17	West, Grace	8/2/1920	5/17/1927
18	West, Agnes	8/2/1920	06/26/1930
19	Martin, Charles	9/29/1920	5/28/1926
20	Martin, Larry	9/29/1920	5/22/1932
21	Martin, Alice Mae	9/29/1920	1/17/1934
22	Martin, David H.	10/17/1920	6/22/1928
23	Martin, Theodore B.	10/17/1920	12/12/1929
24	Taylor, Joseph L.	10/18/1920	*1921-1924
25	Taylor, Alsey	10/18/1920	*1921-1924
26	Winstead, Audry	10/2/1920	5/16/1929
27	Flemming, John R.	1/12/1921	3/24/1928
28	Flemming, Sarah M.	1/12/1921	9/27/1931
29	Flemming, Wilbert	1/12/1921	9/27/1931
30	Howell, Hazel	2/17/1921	8/19/1928
31	Howell, Ethel	2/17/1921	8/19/1928
32	Howell, Ester	2/17/1921	5/7/1932
33	Howell, Evelin	2/17/1921	8/28/1934

34	Whitley, Ebber	4/5/1921	10/4/1922
35	Whitley, Iddo	4/5/1921	4/6/1928
36	Williams, Troy	4/16/1921	1/7/1927
37	Williams, Salie	8/16/1921	8/30/1928
38	Nobles, William S.	8/22/1921	9/26/1927
39	Williams, Dillie	6/4/1921	12/5/1930
40	Williams, Cay Lee	6/4/1921	8/17/1932
41	Williams, Maggie	6/4/1921	12/16/1934
42	Hawkins, Myrtle Mae	8/24/1921	8/20/1928
43	Hantley, Oswald	8/28/1921	1/21/1923
44	Howell, Leslie	8/30/1921	7/26/1922
45	Howell, Marvin	8/30/1921	6/2/1927
46	Howell, Haywood	8/30/1921	10/9/1931
47	Flemming, Pearl	9/4/1921	7/25/1925
48	Barnes, Ruth	9/7/1921	9/27/1931
49	Williams, Nannie	11/22/1921	8/8/1929
50	Williams, Nellie M.	11/22/1921	5/8/1931
51	Kennedy, Luke Ray	11/29/1921	5/4/1923
52	Kennedy, Owen E.	11/29/1921	5/4/1923
53	Ledford, Frances	3/5/1922	7/11/1928
54	Ledford, Claude	3/5/1922	3/7/1929
55	Sills, Ruthey R.	6/8/1922	1/8/1925
56	Sills, William R.	6/8/1922	1/8/1925
57	Braswell, Charles	7/25/1922	12/24/1926
58	Braswell, Leland	7/25/1922	12/24/1926
59	Braswell, Herbert	7/25/1922	12/24/1926
60	Griffin, Joseph	9/11/1922	8/11/1929
61	Griffin, Elmer	9/11/1922	5/8/1931
62	Griffin, Russell	9/11/1922	5/8/1931
63	Liggins, Lula	2/5/1923	8/6/1930
64	Davis, Jan	5/23/1923	5/12/1927
64	Davis, Neta	5/23/1923	5/12/1927
66	Mixon, Alice	7/26/1923	11/11/1927
67	Mixon, Milan	7/26/1923	2/5/1928
68	Mixon, Beulah	7/26/1923	7/23/1931
69	Mixon, Horace	7/26/1923	1/20/1934
70	Mixon, Lula	7/26/1923	7/19/1937
71	Mitchell, Thelma	9/4/1923	12/5/1930

72	Mitchell, Clarence	9/4/1923	12/31/1932
73	Watson, Mallie C.	10/12/1923	7/10/1933
74	Watson, Leroy Pate	10/12/1923	1/9/1935
75	Watson, Wiley Robertson	10/12/1923	8/11/1929
76	Hales, Elizabeth	12/22/1923	5/12/1935
77	Grundstaff, Robert	12/12/1924	9/19/1927
78	Linston, Mary	12/16/1924	7/13/1927
79	Linston, Haleen	12/16/1924	12/22/1931
80	Linston, Albert B.	12/16/1924	12/16/1933
81	Linston, John	12/16/1924	5/24/1936
82	Linston, Ivy H.	12/16/1924	1/3/1938
83	Rouse, Rena	1/14/1925	3/10/1929
84	Rouse, Celester	1/14/1925	5/2/1932
85	Rouse, Virginia	1/14/1925	5/2/1932
86	Rouse, Isabell	1/14/1925	5/18/1932
87	Davis, Ester	6/7/1925	5/12/1927
88	Bissette, Rachel	6/18/1925	5/8/1931
89	Rich, Alfred A.	6/23/1925	8/2/1930
90	Rich, William H.	6/23/1925	8/2/1930
91	Holland, Fannie	7/12/1925	6/22/1935
92	Baker, Woodrow	7/24/1925	5/8/1931
93	Baker, Clayton	7/24/1925	5/8/1931
94	Bissette, Mavis	9/21/1925	5/8/1931
95	Wells, Randolph	9/27/1925	5/10/1931
96	Wells, George	9/27/1925	5/10/1931
97	Creekmore, Opie	10/17/1925	3/12/1933
98	Creekmore, Thesmon	10/17/1925	8/12/1934
99	Creekmore, Rufus	10/17/1925	6/5/1935
100	Pridgeon, J.B.	6/17/1926	9/4/1928
101	Parker, Fred	7/2/1926	12/2/1939
102	Parker, Hazel	7/2/1926	12/2/1939
103	Davenport, Cynda	1/5/1927	5/7/1932
104	Davenport, Phoebe	1/5/1927	5/20/1934
105	McCaskey, Joseph	1/17/1927	7/26/1931
106	McCaskey, Charles	1/17/1927	7/26/1931
107	Harris, Clara	7/17/1927	8/10/1940
108	Miller, Estella	7/17/1927	9/10/1939
109	Hedgepeth, James	7/22/1927	12/19/1927

110	Proctor, Troy	7/24/1927	8/22/1937
111	Proctor, Clay	7/24/1927	8/22/1937
112	Silverthorn, Della	7/24/1927	7/1/1938
113	Silverthorn, Dennis	7/24/1927	3/28/1936
114	Silverthorn, Lenwood	7/24/1927	2/28/1935
	Readmitted	9/21/1936	4/1/1939
115	Davis, James	9/18/1927	8/29/1937
116	Carter, Woodrow	10/9/1927	5/1/1938
117	Earwood, Kathleen	10/17/1927	5/21/1935
118	Proctor, Lucille	12/8/1927	7/1/1936
119	Proctor, Pauline	12/8/1927	5/17/1932
120	Brewer, Robert	1/3/1928	9/14/1936
121	Brewer, Zella Francis	1/3/1928	5/8/1941
122	Moore, Mary Russel	1/5/1928	5/8/1931
123	Moore, Paul E.	1/5/1928	5/8/1931
124	Sutton, Woodrow W.	1/3/1928	5/4/1930
125	Armstrong, Raymond	6/4/1928	6/18/1935
126	Armstrong, Annie May	6/4/1928	4/20/1936
127	Freeman, Jack	7/15/1928	1/3/1936
128	Freeman, Elmer	7/15/1928	4/30/1941
129	Freeman, Carl	7/15/1928	5/11/1942
130	Tippett, Earl	7/24/1928	5/1/1938
131	Tippett, Hazel	7/24/1928	9/8/1940
132	Langely, Nellie	8/19/1928	4/25/1941
133	Langely, Virginia	8/19/1928	8/27/1941
134	Rogers, James	8/31/1928	7/20/1936
135	Foreman, Henry	10/25/1928	12/5/1930
136	Foreman, Ametta	10/25/1928	12/5/1930
137	Foreman, Della	10/25/1928	7/25/1931
138	Ellis, Mary	11/7/1928	7/1/1939
139	Muse, Rachel Mae	8/20/1929	7/6/1930
140	Muse, Henry F.	8/20/1929	7/6/1930
141	Warwick, Norma G.	9/19/1929	9/7/1933
142	Warwick, James E,	9/19/1929	9/17/1933
143	Adams, Albert D.	10/7/1929	12/22/1938
144	Hill, Nina	11//20/1929	8/1/1936
145	Hill, Louise	11/20/1929	7/17/1938
146	Craft, Lexine	12/2/1929	12/28/1940

147	Craft, Beulah	12/2/1929	1/1/1931
148	Craft, Eppie J.	12/2/1929	7/19/1937
149	Craft, Ruth	12/2/1929	6/25/1940
150	Craft, Stephar H.	12/2/1929	1/1/1939
151	Lewis, Ruth G.	10/7/1930	2/1/1938
152	Lewis, George H.	10/7/1930	11/20/1930
153	Smith, Daisy	10/9/1930	1/1/1937
154	Smith, Joseph	10/9/1930	1/1/1937
155	Smith, Pearl	10/9/1930	1/1/1937
156	Smith, John	10/9/1930	1/1/1937
157	Smith, Elsie	10/9/1930	1/1/1937
158	Moore, Eloyse	10/22/1930	5/19/1939
159	Moore, Bertha	10/22/1930	5/31/1943
160	Croom, Walter	12/5/1930	5/8/1939
161	Swim, Florence	12/5/1930	9/2/1942
162	Hawkins, Frank	12/11/1930	3/4/1939
163	Hawkins, Bruce	12/11/1930	4/27/1942
164	Langley, Kathleen	10/19/1931	4/24/1942
165	Hodgers, Ralph	7/29/1932	8/1/1939
166	Hodgers, Willie E.	7/29/1932	8/1/1939
167	Hodgers, Margaret	7/29/1932	8/21/1942
168	Bissett, James R.	8/12/1932	11/5/1937
169	Bissett, Annie Lee	8/12/1932	5/7/1941
170	Bissett, Maggie Lee	8/12/1932	6/14/1943
171	Bissett, Vernon	8/12/1932	9/12/1946
172	Ange, Calvin	8/17/1932	5/15/1941
173	Ange, Golde Jr.	8/17/1932	2/9/1940
174	Ange, Vergia	8/17/1932	4/24/1942
175	Holoman, Lillian	11/13/1932	4/26/1941
176	Holloman, Cora Blanch	11/13/1932	4/21/1942
177	Warbritton, Louise	5/5/1933	8/29/1943
178	Warbritton, Gladys M.	5/5/1933	5/9/1940
179	Warbritton, Anne C.	5/5/1933	4/21/1942
180	Hatem, Thelma J.	6/1/1933	3/3/1943
181	Pate, Ralph	8/12/1933	4/27/1941
182	Pate, Annie Lee	8/12/1933	6/30/1942
183	Pate, Linwood	8/12/1933	4/27/1943
184	Pate, Mary Evelyn	8/12/1933	4/27/1943

185	Brickhouse, Victoria	8/16/1933	5/12/1940
186	Brickhouse, Ray	8/16/1933	5/10/1934
187	Jones, Odell	9/11/1933	4/25/1941
188	Jones, Estelle	9/11/1933	7/26/1942
189	Johnson, Virginia	11/30/1933	9/3/1934
190	Johnson, Hazel Grey	11/30/1933	9/3/1934
191	High, J.B.	12/19/1933	7/8/1942
192	High, Joseph H.	12/19/1933	10/20/1942
193	Watson, Felix	4/9/1934	9/16/1941
194	Watson, Irene	4/9/1934	6/28/1944
195	Watson, Josephine	4/9/1934	11/00/1944
196	Jarman, Bert Kenneth	10/4/1934	11/28/1935
197	West, Nancy C.	11/6/1934	10/1/1942
198	West, Iona	11/6/1934	7/26/1943
199	West, Robert D.	11/6/1934	9/10/1944
200	West, James G.	11/6/1934	2/17/1948
201	Tart, Mary Lois	11/6/1934	8/1/1939
202	Allen, Sarah Hope	3/7/1935	8/8/1942
203	Allen, Nancy Catherine	3/7/1935	8/8/1942
204	Allen, James Albert	3/7/1935	8/19/1936
	Readmitted	8/20/1937	5/22/1942
205	Allen, Benjamin H.	3/7/1935	8/8/1942
206	Rose, Willie Lee	4/4/1935	8/7/1935
207	Rose, James	4/19/1935	8/7/1935
208	Sexton, James	5/8/1935	12/14/1935
209	Sexton, Mary Agnes	5/8/1935	12/14/1935
210	Sexton, Dorothy	5/8/1935	12/14/1935
211	Tripp, Hicks	10/8/1935	5/14/1942
212	Tripp, Mary Agnes	10/8/1935	6/11/1945
213	Baker, Alton Lee	10/21/1935	8/29/1936
214	Thompson, Maurice	12/13/1935	4/28/1938
	Readmitted	9/3/1938	9/1/1941
215	Thompson, Thelma	12/13/1935	4/28/1938
	Readmitted	9/3/1938	12/21/1942
216	Thompson, Thelma	12/13/1935	4/28/1938
	Readmitted	9/3/1938	12/21/1942
217	Braswell, Linwood	4/28/1936	12/20/1938
218	Braswell, John Gilbert	4/28/1936	12/20/1938

219	Raper, Burkett	7/17/1936	7/1/1945
220	Raper, James Earl	7/17/1936	8/1/1945
221	Raper, Mary Lou	7/17/1936	4/29/1943
222	Snipes, Sidney	1/2/1937	7/24/1943
223	Snipes, P.G.	1/2/1937	5/1/1943
224	Skinner, Marvin E.	1/4/1937	9/1/1943
225	Skinner, Sterling	1/4/1937	2/28/1943
226	Skinner, Elva E.	1/4/1937	10/1/1942
227	Martin, Gerald	2/24/1937	1/24/1942
228	Thompson, Elizabeth	8/15/1937	3/5/1938
229	McGhee, Julian	9/5/1937	8/20/1943
230	McGhee, James	9/5/1937	8/20/1943
231	Stocks, Earl N.	9/17/1937	11/25/1937
232	Stocks, Earline	9/17/1937	12/21/1937
233	Stocks, Elsie	9/17/1937	12/21/1937
234	Allen, Bettie Jo	9/30/1937	8/1/1942
235	Allen, James F.	9/30/1937	8/1/1942
236	Allen, Annie	9/30/1937	8/1/1942
237	Butts, James	8/17/1937	5/30/1950
238	Butts, Alvin Earl	8/17/1937	1/20/1942
239	Butts, Joe	8/17/1937	2/14/1944
240	Brantley, Jonathan	11/27/1937	8/12/1944
241	Harrell, Hilda	1/21/1938	7/1/1953
242	Harrell, Charles	1/3/1938	5/22/1951
243	Harrell, Henry Ashley	1/21/1938	4/4/1946
244	Harrell, Lucy G.	1/21/1938	10/5/1944
245	Lucas, Billie Ray	4/7/1938	10/9/1943
246	Lucas, William Jack	4/7/1938	10/9/1943
247	Lucas, Woodard J.	4/7/1938	10/9/1943
248	Johnson, Mildred L.	9/28/1938	5/6/1948
249	Johnson, Rena	9/28/1938	9/30/1944
250	Thompson, Elizabeth	9/3/1938	12/21/1942
251	Powell, Billie Ray	10/1/1938	8/20/1949
252	Powell, James	10/1/1938	5/30/1950
253	Caulder, Manie	1/5/1939	6/1/1945
254	McLawhorn, Verna G.	6/6/1940	6/27/1944
255	Page, Charles	7/15/1940	5/23/1954
256	Page, Chester Eugene	7/15/1940	5/21/1957

257	Butts, Edna Lois	7/26/1940	5/1/1942
258	Sawyer, Lily Virginia	11/18/1940	7/31/1943
259	Watson, Robert F.	12/7/1940	7/22/1948
260	Merritt, Alene Grace	1/18/1941	8/18/1943
261	Merritt, Charles Ray	1/18/1941	8/18/1943
262	Merritt, Jesse James	1/18/1941	8/18/1943
263	Merritt, Gene	1/18/1941	8/18/1943
264	Shingleton, Bennie T.	5/12/1941	11/2/1943
265	Shingleton, Marvin E.	5/12/1941	11/2/1943
266	Taylor, Hugh B.	5/15/1941	11/30/1946
267	Taylor, Louise	5/15/1941	11/30/1946
268	Taylor, Joyce C.	5/15/1941	11/30/1946
269	Taylor, Margaret E.	5/15/1941	11/30/1946
270	Taylor, Garland	5/15/1941	11/30/1946
271	Bryant, Eloise	5/15/1941	11/14/1941
272	Bryant, Rabion	5/15/1941	6/11/1954
273	Rollins, Dorothy	9/14/1941	9/28/1941
274	Rollins, Annie Mae	9/14/1941	9/28/1941
275	Rollins, Doris Ruth	9/14/1941	9/28/1941
276	Lewis, Mary Francis	10/30/1941	12/22/1950
277	Kittrell, Mary Ann	12/30/1941	8/16/1946
278	Kittrell, Robert E.	12/30/1941	8/16/1946
279	Kittrell, Charlie	12/30/1941	4/16/1946
280	Stevenson, Helen E.	4/29/1942	11/27/1944
281	Stevenson, Joyce M.	4/29/1942	2/1/1952
282	Stevenson, George Jr.	4/29/1942	2/1/1952
283	Stevenson, Haywood	4/29/1942	2/1/1952
284	Tucker, Silvia J.	5/28/1942	12/20/1946
285	Tucker, Ernest Jr.	5/28/1942	12/20/1946
286	Bright, William Earl	1/1/1943	9/14/1946
287	Bright, Nathaniel E.	1/1/1943	9/14/1946
288	Lane, Mary L.	1/26/1943	5/25/1954
289	Lane, William R.	1/26/1943	2/28/1954
290	Lamn, Willard	1/15/1943	12/27/0944
291	Lamn, Ray Jr.	1/15/1943	12/27/1944
292	Hanney, Richard	2/6/1943	7/12/1943
293	Hanney, Jimmy	2/6/1943	7/12/1943
294	Huff, Mary Idella	2/20/1943	12/14/1947

295	Huff, James Lee	2/20/1943	12/14/1947
296	Moore, Wheatie	2/22/1943	12/20/1946
297	Williams, Bobbie	3/4/1943	6/12/1948
298	Williams, Preston	3/4/1943	6/12/1948
299	Williams, Ester M.	3/4/1943	6/12/1948
300	Wilson, Dorothy	5/14/1943	1/19/1946
301	Warren, Rosalyne	5/31/1943	5/21/1956
302	Warren, Willis Owens	5/31/1943	6/28/1953
303	Tyson, Christ Abelle	6/18/1943	6/18/1952
304	Tyson, Eugene	6/18/1943	5/30/1955
305	Tyson, Dorothene	6/18/1943	5/25/1954
306	Wood, Louella	8/19/1943	7/1/1945
307	Jones, Larry	8/20/1943	12/31/1945
308	Jones, Hazel Jean	8/20/1943	12/31/1945
309	Baldwin, Dannie Lee	8/22/1943	10/14/1943
310	Outlaw, Jule Benjamin	11/26/1943	5/5/1952
311	Outlaw, Rudolph	11/26/1943	5/19/1952
312	Jones, Helen M.	1/1/1944	12/31/1945
313	Wood, Carol G.	1/1/1944	7/1/1945
314	Winstead, Metta Lou	3/11/1944	5/30/1955
315	Winstead, Ernest G.	3/11/1944	5/22/1951
316	Winstead, Winfred M.	3/11/1944	5/27/1952
317	Winstead, Robert D.	3/11/1944	3/23/1953
318	Durham, Bettie L.	8/2/1944	6/15/1946
319	Willard, Jesse	8/2/1944	6/15/1946
320	Durham, Margaret	8/2/1944	6/15/1946
321	Bradshaw, Franklin D.	9/16/1944	9/4/1951
322	Bradshaw, Thelma E.	9/16/1944	5/25/1954
323	Hinson, Charles Ray	9/19/1944	1/23/1958
324	Mills, Kathleen	9/18/1944	9/17/1946
325	Mills, Robert R.	9/18/1944	9/17/1946
326	Gay, Jimmie E.	10/10/1944	8/6/1947
327	Gay, Fernie	10/10/1944	8/6/1947
328	Cockrell, Ann Shirley	2/24/1945	7/12/1946
329	Cockrell, Bettie J.	2/24/1945	7/12/1946
330	Cockrell, Mark T.	2/24/1945	7/12/1946
331	Powell, Larry D.	4/20/1945	1/29/1952
332	Gasperson, Roy Lee	4/20/1945	07/22/1957

333	Gasperson, Velma P.	4/20/1945	8/16/1958
334	Gasperson, Mildred. L.	4/20/1945	7/5/1952
335	Baker, Mary E.	5/1/1945	6/4/1948
336	Baker, Bennette	5/1/1945	6/4/1948
337	Baker, John D.	5/1/1945	3/15/1946
338	Reddick, Thomas	5/1/1945	7/25/1946
339	Jones, Ronnie L.	6/3/1945	12/31/1945
340	Darden, Christine	6/1/1945	5/28/1950
341	Darden, Evelyn J.	6/1/1945	5/30/1955
342	Tripp, Louis L.Jr.	7/14/1945	12/31/1947
343	Butts, Tiny	1/1/1946	8/12/1952
344	Butts, Teeny	1/1/1946	8/25/1952
345	Butts, Lydia L.	1/1/1946	1/3/1953
346	Duncan, Lois D.	1/26/1946	12/7/1952
347	Duncan, Edna	1/26/1946	11/8/1955
348	Duncan, Doris	1/26/1946	5/20/1958
349	Little, Irvin T.	3/1/1946	5/21/1956
350	Little, Doris L.	3/1/1946	5/30/1955
351	Little, Carrold	3/1/1946	5/25/1953
352	Little, Alice M.	3/1/1946	5/30/1955
353	Little, Joyce F.	3/1/1946	11/1/1956
354	Pope, Jimmie A.	8/10/1946	5/31/1947
355	Page, Donald Ray	8/10/1946	5/31/1947
356	Lane, David J.	8/27/1946	1/19/1952
357	Lane, Jacob J.	8/27/1946	5/27/1959
358	Lane, Patricia Ann	8/27/1946	5/20/1958
359	Lane, Robert L.	8/27/1946	5/27/1959
360	Lane, Durwood	8/27/1946	7/27/1952
361	Bryant, Alton	12/29/1946	6/15/1958
362	Rogers, Loyce Nicholas	12/30/1946	6/15/1958
363	Rogers, Lindsay Hal	12/30/1946	7/22/1957
364	Rogers, John Dirial	12/30/1946	9/14/1952
365	Mace, George William	12/30/1946	3/1/1953
366	Mace, Sam Ray	12/30/1946	4/6/1955
367	Mace, Wayne Arthur	12/30/1946	5/21/1957
368	Rowe, John Thomas	6/21/1947	5/15/1954
369	Watson, Lillie Fay	8/1/1947	2/25/1954
370	Watson, Betty Jean	8/1/1947	5/20/1958

371	Watson, Edward Wallace	8/1/1947	5/21/1956
372	Hill, Josie Pearl	12/29/1947	5/30/1955
373	Price, Glennie Mae	3/19/1948	11/24/1952
374	Price, Shelby Jean	3/19/1948	5/21/1957
375	Rogers, Gardiner Barry	7/14/1948	1/14/1961
376	Norris, Peggy Joyce	9/11/1948	5/30/1955
377	Thigpen, Clyde Earl JR.	5/23/1949	5/23/1952
378	Thigpen, Joyce	5/23/1949	5/23/1952
379	Thigpen, Justin	5/23/1949	5/23/1952
380	Thigpen, Nellie Jean	5/23/1949	5/23/1952
	Readmitted	2/2/1957	6/22/1960
381	Thigpen, Bobby Gene	5/23/1949	5/23/1952
	Readmitted	2/5/1957	6/7/1962
382	Jones, Arthur Vinton	7/22/1949	6/23/1955
383	Jones, Caroleen	7/22/1949	8/10/1957
384	Jones, Cora L.	7/22/1949	5/31/1961
385	Smith, Nancy Ann	8/27/1949	6/3/1960
386	Smith, Jerry A.	8/27/1949	6/3/1960
387	Jackson, Margaret J.	8/29/1949	12/21/1956
388	Jackson, Judy Katherine	8/29/1949	12/21/1956
389	Thigpen, Lois	8/27/1949	5/26/1953
390	Jones, Shelby Jean	6/24/1951	6/1/1955
391	Little, James Richard	7/21/1951	11/1/1956
392	Watson, Foy JR.	7/16/1951	6/10/1963
393	Pope, Mary Belle	1/7/1952	5/29/1961
394	Pope, Nancy Lou	1/7/1952	10/17/1961
395	Pope, Daisy L.	1/7/1952	6/10/1963
396	Herring, Bobbie	6/13/1952	10/31/1959
397	Herring, Evelyn Mae	6/13/1952	6/10/1963
398	Herring, Margie E.	6/13/1952	6/7/1962
399	Teasley, Ben W. Jr.	3/8/1952	11/1/1953
400	Nix, Dorothy Ann	7/11/1952	7/4/1953
401	Nix, Mannon A. III	7/11/1952	8/8/1953
402	Nix, Elmo Lee	7/11/1952	8/8/1953
403	Stallings, Jerry Lynn	7/19/1952	1/26/1962
404	Stallings, Joel C.	7/19/1952	1/26/1962
405	Miller, Lory B.	7/20/1952	6/23/1960
406	Lane, Sally Rae	7/19/1952	9/6/1952

407	Morris, Martin J.	8/23/1952	6/14/1959
408	Morris, Jack Leon	8/23/1952	12/20/1957
409	Morris, Bertha Louise	8/28/1952	6/14/1959
410	Dail, Harry Thomas	9/30/1952	10/22/1952
411	Dail, Kenneth Charles	9/30/1952	10/22/1952
412	Dail, Russell Lee	9/30/1952	10/22/1952
413	Hardee, Lula	9/24/1952	6/10/1963
414	Hardee, Lucy M.	10/24/1952	6/10/1963
415	Alexander, Daniel	11/28/1952	8/25/1960
416	Alexander, Deanna R.	11/28/1952	8/25/1960
417	Cantrell, James B.	2/23/1953	8/2/1964
418	Cantrell, David Ray	2/23/1953	6/30/1965
419	Cantrell, Diane Kay	2/23/1953	7/1/1966
420	Coward, Nuriel	8/18/1953	12/18/1953
421	Coward, Judy Ann	8/18/1953	12/18/1953
422	Heath, John William	8/24/1953	11/22/1962
423	Heath, Wilbert Earl	8/24/1953	8/28/1960
424	Heath, Michael Faye	8/24/1953	6/3/1964
425	Heath, Nancy Sue	8/24/1953	9/1/1967
426	Heath, Marshall	8/24/1953	12/13/1968
427	Pope, Alma Ruth	8/23/1953	7/31/1966
428	Waller, Harold Eugene	9/1/1953	6/3/1964
429	Mercer, Ona G.	9/19/1953	06/03/0964
430	Mercer, Sandra E.	9/19/1953	6/15/1965
431	Mercer, Philip Ray	9/19/1953	10/15/1968
432	Wiggs, Robert G.	11/15/1953	5/26/1954
433	Wiggs, Nestis	11/26/1953	4/16/1954
434	Hester, Patricia Deans	6/6/1954	6/10/1963
435	Worthington, Ernest Glenn	6/21/1954	8/24/1966
436	Worthington, JoEtta	6/21/1954	6/7/1962
437	Worthington, Raymond S.	6/21/1954	6/21/1959
438	Worthington, Ronald	6/21/1954	9/6/1963
439	Worthingtn, Stephen	6/21/1954	6/10/1963
440	Jones, Martha L.	7/15/1954	9/30/1965
441	Hines, William E.	8/24/1954	6/7/1962
442	Hines, Jesse J.	8/24/1954	6/7/1965
443	Lloyd, Ida F.	9/20/1954	11/5/1955
444	Langston, Bobbie J.	6/6/1955	6/5/1969

445	Langston, Gerald Lee	6/6/1955	9/11/1967
446	Rouse, Joan Yvonne	6/14/1955	6/5/1969
447	Rouse, Isaac Daniel Jr.	6/14/1955	2/29/1964
448	Rouse, Stephen	6/14/1955	9/15/1966
449	Lancaster, Doris Ann	8/30/1955	6/10/1963
450	Lancaster, Thomas E.	11/22/1955	6/30/1965
451	Lancaster, William Ray	11/22/1955	9/15/1966
452	Worthington, Brenda	12/31/1955	6/9/1965
453	Worthington, Ted W.	6/18/1956	6/1/1969
454	Worthington, Albert R.	6/18/1956	6/10/1963
455	Davis, Betsy Ann	8/29/1956	6/1/1969
456	Hines, Flora G.	1/9/1957	6/7/1962
457	Hines, Sylvia Catherine	1/9/1957	7/31/1966
458	Harris, John Allen	5/27/1957	7/31/1966
459	Harris, Ray Murphy	5/27/1957	6/5/1969
460	Joyner, William Marvin B.	6/17/1957	11/26/1959
461	Marvin (Ben)	NO DATES	
462	Joyner, Joyce R.	6/17/1957	11/26/1959
463	Joyner, Helen	6/17/1957	11/26/1959
464	Barbour, Stacy Otis	8/12/1957	6/30/1964
465	High, Shirley Ann	8/29/1957	12/13/1968
466	Driver, Patrticia Ann	8/29/1957	3/2/1970
467	High, James H.	8/29/1957	3/13/1969
468	Lloyd Jr., Alex	10/19/1957	8/16/1958
469	Sugg, Eula Mae	6/16/1958	6/1/1969
470	Sugg, Sidney Earl	6/16/1958	6/3/1970
471	Sugg, Linda Lou	6/16/1958	6/7/1965
472	Letchworth, Kathleen	7/2/1958	3/30/1960
473	Letchworth, Debra J.	7/2/1958	3/30/1960
474	Elmore, Ottis Ashford	9/5/1958	9/30/1965
475	Elmore, John Bailey	9/5/1958	9/15/1965
476	Elmore, Loucindy	9/5/1958	5/1/1969
477	Elmore, Dwight Patrick	8/23/1959	6/5/1972
478	Newton, Larry Mitchell	8/20/1959	6/4/1971
479	Newton, Deborah R.	8/20/1959	6/3/1970
480	Hartsfield, Joe Andrew	8/22/1959	6/5/1969
481	Williams, Margaret A.	10/13/1959	12/6/1961
482	Moore, Patricia Lee	6/28/1960	10/20/1969

483	Elmore, William C.	7/4/1960	5/31/1973
484	Batts, Georgia E.	7/1/1960	9/1/1972
485	Batts, Deborah Joan	7/1/1960	5/31/1972
486	Batts, Brenda F.	7/1/1960	12/1/1972
487	Batts, Elizabeth A.	7/1/1960	8/9/1968
488	Thomas, Jeff	10/18/1960	8/15/1970
489	Thomas, Terry	10/18/1960	10/31/1971
490	Thomas, Fred	10/18/1960	6/23/1971
491	Whitley, Johnny Ray	6/26/1961	6/5/1969
492	Whitley, James A.	6/26/1961	6/5/1969
493	Lamm, Margaret L.	8/21/1961	9/7/1967
494	Lamm, Willie Mann Jr.	8/21/1961	9/7/1967
495	Lamm Anna Marie	8/21/1961	9/7/1967
496	Brickhouse, Phillip W.	7/3/1962	1/30/1966
497	Pittman, Bobby Ray, Jr.	7/6/1962	6/13/1964
498	Pittman, James E.	7/6/1962	6/13/1964
499	Pittman, Pamela J.	7/6/1962	6/13/1964
500	Halloway, Stanley W.	7/9/1962	7/1/1967
501	Halloway, George L. Readmitted	7/9/1962 6/27/1968	7/1/1967 7/17/1970
502	Halloway, Theresa C. Readmitted	7/9/1962 6/27/1968	7/1/1967 7/17/1970
503	Elmore, Ronald S.	8/7/1962	3/8/1975
504	Elmore, Donald E.	8/7/1962	5/1/1974
505	Hill, Mary F.	11/30/1962	10/31/1971
506	Hill, Martha J.	11/30/1962	8/26/1973
507	Hill, Judy Lynn	11/30/1962	6/7/1974
508	Hill, Brenda Day	11/30/1962	6/30/1978
509	Hill, Odolph Jr.	11/30/1962	7/30/1976
510	Langston, Katherine M.	4/17/1963	6/3/1970
511	Hicks, Michael Wayne	6/25/1963	9/30/1965
512	Hicks, Talmadge L.	6/25/1963	9/30/1965
513	Connor, Nancy Carol	12/30/1963	4/15/1970
514	Connor, Edward E.	12/30/1963	10/31/1971
515	Connor, Patricia Lee	12/30/1963	11/19/1970
516	Connor, George Ray	12/30/1963	3/1/1973
517	Connor, Connie E.	12/30/1963	8/25/1973
518	Anderson, Doris Marie	12/31/1963	2/17/1970

519	Matthews, Johnny Lee	9/1/1964	8/24/1966
520	Matthews, James D.	9/1/1964	8/24/1966
521	Lee, Sharon E.	9/12/1964	3/9/1970
522	Lee, Rebecca	9/12/1964	7/14/1974
523	Pittman, Timothy R.	9/28/1964	12/18/1976
524	Lee, James K.	10/4/1964	9/25/1974
525	Lee, Donna June	10/4/1964	11/22/1978
526	Merritt, Jimmie Leon	3/17/1965	6/5/1972
527	Edwards, Nancy G.	7/7/1965	7/22/1967
528	Edwards, Eddie Terry	7/7/1965	7/26/1971
529	Edwards, Dolphus	7/7/1965	6/27/1973
530	McLawhorn, Betty J.	7/9/1965	7/16/1976
531	Anderson, Dennis O.	7/14/1965	3/18/1974
532	Anderson, Donnie	7/14/1965	9/25/1975
533	Anderson, Sandra Key	7/14/1965	7/6/1977
534	Anderson, Vivian J.	7/14/1965	9/1/1976
535	Lee, Vickie	7/25/1965	12/10/1977
536	Corbett, Dorothy Marie	9/3/1965	6/22/1970
537	Corbett, James Conna	9/3/1965	6/22/1970
538	Corbett, Berta Lee	9/3/1965	6/22/1970
539	Hill, Douglas Lee	12/2/1965	8/30/1970
540	Hill, Gary Thomas	12/2/1965	12/12/1975
541	Guthrie, Anthony L.	12/2/1965	7/18/1980
542	Tebo, Janice F.	7/20/1966	9/30/1975
543	Jones, Jimmie R.	7/22/1966	12/12/1973
544	Jones, Anthony R.	8/1/1966	3/2/1970
545	Jones, Evelyn Lynn	8/1/1966	10/30/1969
546	Jones, Valerie N.	8/1/1966	3/2/1970
547	Jones, John E.	8/1/1966	3/2/1970
548	Jones, Angela G.	8/1/1966	3/2/1970
549	Gay, Donald Ray, Jr.	8/10/1966	1/19/1976
550	Gay, Ronnie Ray	8/10/1966	1/19/1976
551	Gay, John Lee Allen	8/10/1966	8/9/1976
552	Gay, Delma Lee	8/10/1966	10/1/1977
553	Clifton, Leon Ralph Jr.	2/24/1967	1/1/1968
554	Clifton, Teresa Lois	2/24/1967	1/1/1968
555	Clifton, John Michael	2/24/1967	1/1/1968
556	Clifton, Gregory Phillip	2/24/1967	1/1/1968

557	Warren, Kenneth Ray	2/27/1967	6/5/1972
558	Warren, Charles G.	2/27/1967	8/18/1973
559	Warren, Thelma Lou	6/27/1967	9/11/1972
560	Warren, Judy Lynn	6/26/1967	4/30/1977
561	Warren, Mary Ann	6/26/1967	1/5/1970
562	Faircloth, Richard W.	6/27/1967	1/31/1978
563	Faircloth, Randy A.	6/27/1967	8/16/1975
564	Faircloth, Terry Lenn	6/27/1967	5/12/1979
565	Faircloth, Johnny Dale	6/27/1967	8/19/1976
566	Woodard, Ivey Joyce	8/28/1967	6/7/1973
567	Woodard, Julia Betsy	8/28/1967	2/28/1977
568	Cannon, Julia Mae	8/30/1967	7/1/1968
569	Cannon, Deborah D.	8/30/1967	7/1/1968
570	Cannon, Nancy L.	8/30/1967	7/1/1968
571	Bottoms, Bobby W.	1/24/1968	2/9/1978
572	Joyner, Michell Ray	2/6/1968	6/10/1977
573	Modlin, Ruth Ann	2/7/1968	2/24/1970
574	Benedict, Derek Alan	3/6/1968	10/20/1970
575	Benedict, Morris Dale	3/6/1968	10/20/1970
576	Renee, Gerri	6/25/1968	10/20/1970
577	Alford, Sally Lavon	6/25/1968	8/24/1977
578	Nichols, John Bennett	6/28/1968	1/23/1978
579	Nichols, Stephen Ray	6/28/1968	1/16/1979
580	Nichols, Angela Gail	8/7/1968	11/4/1981
581	Dement, Deborah Jean	8/13/1968	5/18/1972
582	Dement, Peggy Sue	8/13/1968	9/16/1974
583	Dement, Willard Ray	8/13/1968	6/23/1974
584	Dement, Jimmie Allen	8/13/1968	6/8/1976
585	Marlow, Deborah A. Readmitted	1/2/1969 10/5/1978	3/14/1978 9/1/1980
586	Marlow, Penny M. Readmitted	1/2/1969 9/6/1976	9/7/1970 3/11/1977
587	Elks, Dorothy L.	8/30/1970	8/17/1973
588	Elks, Timothy W.	10/31/1970	11/26/1975
589	Jones, Janise Faye	1/8/1971	3/4/1978
590	Garris, Brenda Faye	1/24/1971	8/1/1977
591	Schnell, Mollie Lynn	1/24/1971	12/21/1978
592	Garris, Cliffard B.	1/24/1971	6/8/1976

593	Dement, Margaret N.	6/21/1971	10/9/1981
594	Lanier, Donna Kay	8/16/1971	12/21/1972
595	Lanier, Pamela A.	8/16/1971	12/21/1972
596	Lanier, Wendy R.	8/16/1971	12/21/1972
597	Leggett, Everett S.	8/19/1971	11/28/1971
598	Leggett, Johnnie K.	8/19/1971	11/28/1971
599	Mansur, Samie	8/30/1971	6/27/1976
600	Dement, Bonnie	10/23/1971	8/15/1975
601	Dement, Donnie	10/23/1971	2/17/1981
602	Utley, Sharon A.	12/1/1971	4/30/1972
603	Utley, Tammy Kaye	12/1/1971	4/30/1972
604	Utley, Angela L.	12/1/1971	4/30/1972
605	Anderson, Andrew L.	4/8/1972	12/21/1978
606	Whitley, Patricia A.	8/7/1972	11/5/1973
607	Whitley, William H.	8/7/1972	11/5/1973
608	Speight, David J.	8/27/1972	8/22/1979
609	Speight Jr, James W.	8/27/1972	11/1/1978
610	Speight, Ray Bert	8/27/1972	8/22/1979
611	King, Julie Ann	1/11/1973	6/9/1977
612	Cone, Cathy Francine	3/3/1973	6/6/1975
613	Cone, Debra Lynn	3/3/1973	6/6/1975
614	Cone, Donna Gwen	3/3/1973	6/6/1975
615	Eason, Virgile Lee, Jr.	8/2/1973	11/8/1975
616	Eason, Jeffrey Michael	8/2/1973	11/8/1975
617	Eason, Richard Allen	8/2/1973	11/8/1975
618	Eason, Sandra Gail	8/2/1973	11/8/1975
619	Davidson, Ellen Lee	9/4/1973	8/16/1975
620	Davidson, Lounenia P.	9/4/1973	8/16/1975
621	Davidson, Mettie Lenn	9/4/1973	8/16/1975
622	Sasser, Donald Lee	9/4/1973	4/3/1974
623	Sassr, Albert M.	9/4/1973	4/3/1974
624	Mills, Linda D.	10/2/1973	12/31/1980
625	Mills, Timothy A.	10/2/1973	6/11/1982
626	Mills, Kimberly Ann	10/2/1973	6/11/1982
627	Brantley, Debbie J.	12/12/1973	2/22/1974
628	Christian, Rebecca M.	12/29/1973	11/27/1974
629	Jones, Brenda S.	1/5/1974	8/25/1978
630	Jones, Judy Carol	1/5/1974	8/25/1978

631	Jones, Kenneth Earl	1/5/1974	9/30/1985
632	Hopkins, Ramona Ann	5/14/1974	3/30/1984
633	Griffin, Johnny Wayne	5/14/1974	11/21/1986
634	Johnson, Dorothy F.	7/29/1974	1/16/1981
635	Johnson, Jeffrey Roger	7/29/1974	1/16/1981
636	Johnson, Allen Dean	7/29/1974	2/25/1980
637	Anderson, Donald Ray	9/16/1974	7/18/1975
638	Anderson, Robin E.	9/16/1974	7/18/1975
639	Worley, Audrey	9/29/2974	7/6/1977
640	Worley, Betty Yvonne	9/29/2974	8/31/1984
641	Worley, Roger Lee	9/29/2974	10/5/1979
642	Worley, Teresa Ann	9/29/2974	3/28/1986
643	Bass, Richard Charles	10/21/1974	4/5/1975
644	Bass, William Anthony	10/21/1974	4/5/1975
645	Summerlin, Rosa Lee	1/25/1975	6/12/1979
646	Summerlin, Sharon Y.	1/25/1975	6/12/1979
647	Lamm, Mary Ann	4/14/1975	6/27/1977
648	Lamm, Robert J.	4/14/1975	6/27/1977
649	Sasser, Debbie J.	6/25/1975	9/1/1980
650	Wilerson, Donna M.	8/16/1975	6/10/1978
651	Whitehurst, Louise M.	9/3/1975	6/10/1978
652	Joyner, James R. Jr.	9/3/1975	6/16/1978
653	Joyner, Jesse Leon	9/3/1975	6/16/1978
654	Crawford, Todd Scott	11/1/1975	8/6/1976
655	Crawford, Travis Sean	11/1/1975	8/6/1976
656	Rhodes, Randy Ray	11/13/1975	9/00/1982
657	Rhodes, Lucinda M.	11/13/1975	6/15/1985
658	Rhodes, Dorothy S.	11/13/1975	5/14/1984
659	Webb, Cynthia D.	2/29/1976	7/8/1983
660	Ellis, Pamela Jean	3/7/1976	1/24/1980
661	Anderson, Dale Allen	4/24/1976	12/26/1977
662	Thigpen, Billy F. Jr.	6/5/1976	10/11/1976
663	Thigpen, Jennifer M. J.	6/5/1976	10/11/1976
664	Smith, Michelle E.	7/19/1976	7/26/1977
665	Smith, Melissa Dawn	7/19/1976	7/26/1976
666	Norman, Michael F. II	7/19/1976	7/26/1976
667	Williams, Linwood J.	8/12/1976	12/3/1976
668	Hartley, Jimmy Allen	8/26/1976	6/5/1981

669	Hartley, Vickie Darlene	8/26/1976	6/5/1981
670	McCowan, Kelly Darlene	8/26/1976	6/5/1981
671	Corker, Trent Scott	10/9/1976	6/10/1977
672	Stephens, Jonathan P.	11/12/1976	8/30/1980
673	Stephens, Michael A.	11/12/1976	8/30/1980
674	Stephens, Melissa F.	11/12/1976	8/30/1976
675	Langsworthy, Steven	12/9/1976	7/17/1982
676	Langsworthy, Anthony	12/9/1976	7/17/1982
677	Lycykowskie, James Jr.	1/20/1977	2/25/1978
678	Barber, Melinda Gail	3/3/1977	6/9/1978
679	Lamm, Millard W.	3/3/1977	6/9/1978
680	Barbour, Susan Ann	4/6/1977	2/27/1978
681	Rhodes, Ronhie E.	5/6/1977	5/14/1978
682	Wall, Robert Lee	8/16/1977	3/24/1978
683	Wall, Clayon Mark	8/16/1977	3/24/1978
684	Joyner, Paul Woodard	8/23/1977	10/21/1977
685	Beamon, Joseph C.	8/23/1977	10/21/1977
686	Perkins, Heidi Lynn	8/23/1977	6/8/1984
687	Poole, Raymond Keith	1/30/1978	6/29/1978
688	Webb, Dallas Perry	1/30/1978	6/29/1978
689	Webb, Gregory Allen	1/30/1978	6/29/1978
690	Worley, Lois Mae	4/6/1978	6/11/1986
691	Jones, Lakey Lee Jr.	7/9/1978	10/24/1980
692	Arthur, Harold E. Jr.	7/16/1978	7/27/1981
693	Arthur, Rebecca L.	7/16/1978	7/27/1981
694	Hyman, Connie Faye	8/25/1978	10/24/1980
695	Arthur, Margaret A.	8/22/1978	7/27/1981
696	Guthrie, Donna F.	11/3/1978	6/8/1979
697	Gurthrie, Robert E.	11/3/1978	6/8/1979
698	Willis, Angela Sue	2/28/1979	7/6/1979
699	Willis, Ronald C. Jr.	2/28/1979	7/6/1979
700	Willis, Crystal G.	2/28/1979	7/6/1979
701	Willis, Sherry A.	4/5/1979	7/6/1979
702	Lycykowski, Tammy	7/5/1979	9/3/1979
703	Houston, Stephen C.	7/9/1979	11/1/1979
704	Houston, Brett A.	7/9/1979	11/1/1979
705	Houston, Theresa L.	7/9/1979	11/1/1979
706	Moore, Linwood Jr.	7/12/1979	8/28/1981

707	Moore, Kimberly Dawn	7/12/1979	8/31/1979
708	Wilson, Sherry L.	9/3/1979	10/27/1979
709	Wilson Jr., A.D.	9/3/1979	10/27/1979
710	Wilson, Anna Michelle	9/3/1979	10/27/1979

*Actual discharge date not recorded. It is assumed Joseph and Alsey Taylor left sometimes between 1921-24.

Footnote: The author has made reasonable efforts to insure the accuracy of the Register of Inmates for the years 1920-1979. If there are omissions or mistakes, please inform the author or the Free Will Baptist Children's Home. He has strived to create an historical record that includes all the children (1920-'79) who called FWB Children's Home their "home" at some point in their lives. Permission to publish was granted by Gary Lee, President/CEO.

APPENDIX II
Superintendents, Executive Directors and Presidents
1919-07

Superintendents, Executive Directors, and Presidents

Brother C. H. Dixon
1919-1926

Elder L. H. Williamson
1926-1927

Brother C. G. Pope
1927-1928

Elder J. R. Howard
1928-1934

Elder J. W. Alford
1934-1935 (acting)

Reverend M.E. Tyson
1935-1940

Rev. James Evans
1940-1949

Brother M. Cozart
1949-1952

Rev. S. A. Smith
1952-1953 & 1956-1959

Rev. R. H. Jackson
1953-1956

Rev. William Fuston
1959-1962

Rev. M. L. Johnson
1962-1969

Mrs. Pearl Johnson
1969- (acting)

Rev. Edward M. Miles
1969-1971

Rev. Calvin D. Pierce Jr.
1971-1972

Rev. A. Graham Lane
1972-1977

E. Howard Caylor
1981-1983

Rev. Sam Wright
1975-1977

Rev. J. Stewart Humphrey
1977-1993

Dr. Bobby Taylor
1993-

Footnote: Photos were first published by Free Will Baptist Children's Home, Inc. in 2005. Gary Lee, President/CEO granted permission to use in this book.

Index

A

Adams, Albert D.- p. 507
Albermarle Cottage- p. 160, 173-176, 182, 186, 191, 217, 240, 245-246, 250, 264, 356- 357, 414, 449, 467
Alexander, Daniel- p. 515
Alexander, Deanna R.- p. 515
Alford, J.W. Elder- p. 14,524
Alford, Sally Lavon-- p. 519
Allen, Annie- p. 510
Allen, Benjamin H. – p. 509
Allen, Hope p. 73
Allen, James Albert- p. 509
Allen, James F. – p. 510
Allen, Nancy Catherine- p. 509
Allen, Sarah Hope- p. 509
Alumni/Alumnus (Middlesex)-p. 10-11, 36, 42, 59, 62, 203, 219, 245, 274, 279, 284, 288-289, 370, 391, 408, 440, 463- 466, 470, 479, 485, 487, 490-491, 493, 495
Alumni Association- p. 17,357,447,466,485-487
Alumni Endowment Fund- p. 486
Anderson, Andrew L. - p. 408,520
Anderson, Dale Allen- p. 521
Anderson, Dennis O.- p. 518
Anderson, Donald Ray- p. 521
Anderson, Donnie- p. 518
Anderson, Doris Marie- p. 518
Anderson, Phillip- p. 274
Anderson, Robin E. – p. 472,521
Anderson, Sandra Key- p. 518
Anderson, Vivian J. - p. 518
Ange, Calvin- p. 508
Ange, Golde Jr. - p. 508
Ange, Verga- p. 508
Armstrong, Annie May-p. 507
Armstrong, Raymond- p. 507
Arthur, Harold E. Jr. - p. 522
Arthur, Margaret A. - p.522
Arthur, Rebecca L. – p. 522

B

Baker, Alton Lee- p. 509
Baker, Bennette- p. 513
Baker, Clayton- p 506
Baker, John D. - p. 513
Baker, Mary E. - p. 513
Baker, Woodrow- p. 506
Baldwin, Dannie Lee- p. 512
Ballard, Hobert- p. 34
Ballard, Jerry- p. 127
Ballard, Reverend & Mrs. p. 127, 128
Barbeque- (July 4th, Thanksgiving)-p. 27; (Parker Brothers)- p. 149, 217, 246, 346, 376, 381-382, 464, 475
Barber, Melinda Gail- p. 522
Barbour, Dovie- p. 277, 317, 361-362, 378, 405-406
Barbour, Stacy Otis- p. 277, 317, 378, 408, 516
Barbour, Susan Ann- p. 522
Barefoot, Gary Fenton- p. 488, 489, 500
Barn:
   (Dairy)- p.14, 16, 45, 51, 84, 86-88, 95, 100, 104, 107, 119, 160, 189, 191, 245, 434; (Horse)- p. 88, 95, 97, 191; (Stock)- p. 14, 82, 95, 233; (Storage)- p. 91, 95, 272, 299; (Tobacco)- ("Pack house")-p. 96, 102, 110, 114, 215, 275, 299
Barnes, Ruth- p. 505
Bass, Richard Charles- p. 521
Bass, William Anthony- p. 521
Batchelor, Brian- p. 473- 474
Batchelor, Donald-p.470
Batchelor, Joyce- p. 470, 472- 473, 475- 476, 491
Batchelor, Kim- p. 472
Batchelor, Melody- p. 472
Batchelor, Michelle- p. 472
Batten, Cynthia - p. 500
Batten, Gladys- p. 67, 70, 74
Batts, Brenda F. - p. 517
Batts, Deborah Joan- p. 517
Batts, Elizabeth A. - p. 517
Batts, Georgia E. - p. 517
Beamon, Joseph C. – p. 522
Benedict, Derek Allen-. P. 519
Benedict, Morris Dale- p. 519
Bennett, Elder J.R. (Randall)-p. 14, 26, 35, 213, 373, 434, 524
Between The Sheets-(Substituted Words on Hymns) -p. 129
Bible League Service (Sword Drills)-p. 57-58, 281, 293, 376, 391
Biddy House- p. 241
Big Blue – p. 274, 407
Bissett, Annie Lee- p. 508

Bissett, James R. – p. 508
Bissett, Maggie Lee- p. 508
Bissett, Vernon- p. 508
Bissette, Mavis- p. 506
Bissette, Rachel- p. 29, 506
Blood Brothers- p. 331, 335
Boone, Gwen- p. 501
Bottoms, Bobby W. – p. 519
Bowers, H.C. p. 57
Bowers, Rev. C. F. -p. 57,487
Bowers, Rose- p. 57
Boxes: Rabbit- p. 86, 92, 219, 242, 251, 334: Squirrel - p. 334
Boys: *Chicken* -p. 103,172,316; *Dairy*- p. 103, 172; Farm– p. 316,340, 386, 414; *Hog* - p. 104, 172, 318; *House*- p. 102, 107, 173, 316, 340, 346, 386, 414; *Kitchen*- p. 102, 105, 107, 114, 122, 172, 214-215, 276, 282, 299, 316; *Laundry*- p. 316, 341, 361, 374, 386; *Yard*- p. 340, 342, 386, 414
Boys Dormitory Building- p. 23, 25, 44, 70, 74-75, 78, 81-82, 92, 95, 97, 116, 119, 124-126, 147, 163, 166-168, 172, 191, 198, 203, 228, 240-242, 245, 254, 272, 278, 306, 308, 315, 324, 332, 339, 341-342, 347, 362. 374, 380, 383-384, 395, 408, 414, 417, 435-436, 479, 484
Bradshaw, Franklin D. – p. 155-156, 190, 193,512
Bradshaw, Thelma E. – p. 155-156,218,512
Brantley, Debbie J. – p. 520
Brantley, J0nathan- p. 510
Braswell, Charles- p. 505
Braswell, Herbert- p. 505
Braswell, John Gilbert- p. 510
Braswell, Leland- p. 505
Braswell, Linwood- p. 509
Braxton, Brother W. J. – p. 12
Brewer, Robert- p. 507
Brewer, Zella Francis -. 507
Brickhouse, Phillip W. – p. 517
Brickhouse, Ray- p. 509
Brickhouse, Victoria- p. 509
Bright, Nathaniel E. p. 511
Broughton, Alma (Concert Class)-p. 46, 54
Bright, William Earl- p.511
Bryant, Alton (nickname-"Sack")- p.230, 247,256,320,343,437,439,513
Bryant, Eloise- p. 44, 511
Bryant, Rabion (nickname-"Rabbit")- p. 126, 131, 148, 166, 171, 180, 230, 239, 511
Buddy System- p. 124
Bull ("Tojo") - p. 87,107
Burton, Mary- p. 166-170, 186, 235, 236
Butts, Alvin Earl- p. 510
Butts, Edna Lois- p. 511
Butts, James (JC) – p. 190, 436, 510
Butts, Joe – p. 510

Butts, Lydia – p. 513
Butts, Teeny – p. 216, 513
Butts, Tiny – p. 513

C

Campus- ("Orphanage")- p. 5, 10, 24, 28, 54, 58, 62, 93, 202, 216-217, 229, 233, 250, 263, 272, 274, 277- 278, 292, 316, 318, 322, 324-325, 332-333, 335, 337, 339-343, 346, 350, 356, 362-363, 366., 369-370, 374, 376, 399-400, 414-415, 432-433, 442, 445- 446, 454-456, 462, 467-469, 470, 473, 474-475, 480, 498
Cannon, Deborah D. p. 519
Cannon, Julia Mae- p. 519
Cannon, Nancy L. p. 519
Cantrell, David Ray- p. 437,515
Cantrell, Diane Kay- p. 515
Cantrell, James, B. (Jimmy) - p. 338, 403, 437, 440, 483, 515
Carolina General Hospital- (Dr. Kerr)- p. 14, 68, 73
Carroll, Ms. – p. 292
Carter, Woodrow- p. 507
Casey, Elder J.F. - p. 12
Caulder, Manie- p. 77, 510
Cayton, Howard- p. 454, 459
Cemetery:
    Baptist- p. 187; Cabin Free Will Baptist-p. 311:; Calvin Freewill Baptist Church – p. 4; East Duplin Memorial Gardens- p. 382; Evergreen- p. 221, 440; Farmer Family- p. 478; Garris- p. 38; J.H. Evans)-p. 4, 21 ; Lucas Family- p. 79; Marsh Swamp Original Free Will Baptist Church- p. 406, 408-409,483, 495; Moore's Church- p. 30; Oakwood- p. 440 Reedy Branch Original Free Will Baptist- p. 479
Central Cottage- p. 474
Chapel/Church Services- p. 16, 25, 44-45, 57- 58, 203, 229, 231, 234, 238- 239, 245, 250, 254, 257, 269, 273, 281, 293, 321, 347, 360, 365, 376-378, 382, 391, 396, 401, 406- 408, 433, 467, 469, 475, 485, 494, 500
Chicken Picker- p. 71, 276
Children's Home Road-(Buck Deans Road)- p. 28, 486
Chores- p. 100, 199-201, 210, 231, 257, 299, 308, 373-374, 386, 396, 414- 415, 423, 462- 463
Christian, Rebecca M.- p. 520
Churches:
    Black Jack Free Will Baptist-p.206, 291; Black Mountain Free Will Baptist-p.194; Cedar Hill Baptist- p.34; Creswell Free Will Baptist-p.205; Daniel's Chapel- p. 339, 382; Deep Run Free Will Baptist-p. 43; Edgemont Free Will Baptist-p.60, 77; Elm Grove Free Will Baptist-p.37-38; First Free Will Baptist (Kinston)-p.310; First Free Will Baptist (Wilson)-p.286; Free Union Free Will Baptist-p.298, 359; Friendship Free Will Baptist-p. 365; Greeneville First Free Will Baptist-p. 268; Holly Springs Original Free Will Baptist-p.405; Hopewell Original Free Will Baptist- p. 404; Johnston Union Free Will Baptist-p.339, 382; Kenly Free Will Baptist- p. 373; Lee's Chapel Original Free Will Baptist-p.224, 259, 385 Little Rock Free Will Baptist- p. 53; Marlboro Free Will Baptist- p. 264; Marsh Swamp Original Free Will Baptist-p.405-409,495-496; Memorial Chapel-p.85, 90, 97, 122, 126,

129, 135, 160, 191, 233, 297, 370, 407-408, 439, 467, 486; Middlesex Baptist-p. 123-124; Pleasant Grove Free Will Baptist-p. 454; Rooty Branch Baptist- p. 76; Shady Grove- p. 12; Snow Hill Original Free Will Baptist -p. 405; St. Mary's Free Will Baptist- p. 472; Stony Hill Free Will Baptist-p.122-124,128,135; Union Grove Free Will Baptist-p. 390

Clifton, Gregory Phillips- p. 519
Clifton, John Michael- p. 518
Clifton, Leon Ralph Jr. – 518
Clifton, Teresa Lois p. 518
Coach A. - p. 142
Coats, W.R. - p. 12
Cockrell, Ann Shirley- p. 512
Cockrell, Bettie J. p. 512
Cockrell, Mark T. – p. 512
Cone, Cathy Francine- p. 520
Cone, Debra Lynn- p. 520
Cone, Donna Gwen- p. 520
Connor, Connie E. p .517
Connor, Edward E. – p. 351, 517
Connor, George Ray- p. 517
Connor, Nancy Carol- p. 517
Connor, Patricia Lee- p. 517
Corbett, Berta Lee –p. 518
Corbett, Dorothy Marie- p. 518
Corbett, James Conna- p. 518
Corker, Trent Scott- p. 522
Corporal Punishment- p. 16, 156, 241, 273, 281- 282, 451
Coward, Judy Ann- p. 515
Coward, Nuriel- p. 515
Craft, Beulah- p. 508
Craft, Eppie J. - p. 508
Craft, Lexine- p. 508
Craft, Ruth p. 508
Craft, Stephar H. p. 508
Crawford, Todd Scott, p. 521
Crawford, Travis Sean – p. 521
Creekmore, Opie – p. 506
Creekmore, Rufus- p. 506
Creekmore, Thesmon- p. 506
Cows- (Guernseys/Holstein/Jerseys)- p. 100, 107, 160
Croom, Walter & Mrs. p. 159, 162, 226, 229, 436, 508, 524
Concert Choir (Class)- p. 14, 20, 37, 41, 46, 75, 98, 202- 203, 218, 238, 244, 264, 280-281, 321-323, 325, 327, 362, 372, 388, 415, 477- 478, 483- 484
Cottages- p. 8, 265, 299, 339, 350, 366, 407, 415, 433- 434, 442-444, 450,456, 460, 462-463
Cragmont- p. 486
Cronk, Trula- p. 70
Cummings, Reverend Moses ('' Blackie of the North Woods") - p. 131-134, 332, 479-483, 495

D

Dail, Harry Thomas- p. 515
Dail, Kenneth Charles- p. 515
Dail, Russell Lee- p. 515
D., Jesse- p. 157-158
Darden, Christine- p. 126, 513
Darden, Evelyn J. – p. 237, 271, 273, 513
Daughtry, Carol- p. 500
Daughtry, Velva- p. 51, 65, 66
Davenport, Cynda - p. 506
Davenport, Phoebe- p. 506
Davenport, Rebecca- p. 453, 478, 479
Davidson, Ellen Lee- p. 520
Davidson, Lounenia P. – p. 520
Davidson, Mettie Lenn- p. 520
Davis, Betsy Ann- p. 516
Davis, Ester – p. 506
Davis, James – p. 507
Davis, Jan- p. 505
Davis, Neta - p. 505
Davis, J.E. - p. 12
Day Room (Drawing Room)- p. 126, 193, 265, 274, 284, 311, 347, 376
Deans, Elder B.B. – p . 12, 85, 94
Deans, Gordon-p. 85
Dement, Bonnie – p. 520
Dement, Deborah Jean- p. 519
Dement, Donnie- p. 472, 520
Dement, Jimmie Allen- p. 472, 519
Dement, Margaret N. – p. 520
Dement, Peggy Sue – p. 519
Dement, Willard Ray- p. 519
Dildy, Bebe- p. 273, 277- 279, 290
Dildy, Ginny – p. 273, 277
Dildy, Leslie ("Papa") - p.273, 277, 290
Dining Hall –p. 13, 25, 33, 40, 44- 45, 51-52, 58-59, 65-66, 68-70, 72, 82, 89, 114, 120, 122, 126, 127, 147, 149, 152, 161, 169, 178, 191, 198-200, 203, 214, 217, 223, 229, 234-235.237, 239, 240, 250, 254, 265-266, 269-270, 278, 292, 308, 316, 319, 333, 341, 356, 360, 362, 363, 373, 386, 390, 400, 407, 415-416, 460, 462, 469, 471, 479
Dinner Bell- p. 25, 37, 40, 45, 62, 147, 203, 214-215, 229, 233-235, 265-266, 292- 293, 308, 356-358, 360, 366, 377, 386-387, 395, 414- 415, 433, 470- 471, 491, 500
Dormitory Style Building- p. 8, 302, 339, 350, 460
Driver, Patricia Ann – p. 516
Driveway- p. 84-86, 254, 266, 272, 282, 294, 307, 311
Duke Foundation- p. 98, 303
Duncan, Doris- p. 253, 266, 513
Duncan, Edna- p. 513

Duncan, Lois D. –p. 513
Dunn, L.B. - p. 14
Durham, Bettie L. p. 512
Durham, Margaret- p. 512

E

Eagles, Mr. (Farm Manager) - p.157
Earnings- p. 323
Earwood, Kathleen- p. 507
Eason, Jeffrey Michael- p. 520
Eason, Richard Allen- p. 520
Eason, Sandra Gail- p. 520
Eason, Virgile Lee, Jr. – p. 520
 Edgerton, Louise- p. 77
Education (School System) - p. 17
Edwards, Dolphus (Denny)- p. 424-425, 518.
Edwards, Dr. & Mrs. A.B. – p. 248
Edwards, Eddie Terry- p. 299-300, 315, 351, 518
Edwards, Nancy G.- p. 518
Electric Milkers -p. 107
Elks, Dorothy L. p. - 519
Elks, Timothy W. – p. 519
Ellis, Mary – p. 507
Ellis, Pamela Jean- p. 521
Elmore, Donald E. – p. 385, 387, 392, 517
Elmore, Dwight Patrick- p. 383, 385, 387, 392, 516
Elmore, John Bailey- p. 385-386, 437, 491, 516
Elmore, Loucindy- p. 385-386, 392, 516
Elmore, Ottis Ashford - p. 385-386, 389, 392, 427, 516
Elmore, Ronald S. - p. 385, 387, 392, 437, 517
Elmore, William C. (Claudius) - p. 385, 387, 392, 424-425, 437, 517
Evans, Anna- p. 64-65, 77-79, 159, 163
Evans, Faye- p. 44, 64, 79, 90, 105, 159, 160-164, 177
Evans, J. Arthur (Nickname- "Log Roller")-p. 64-66, 75, 77-79, 159, 162-163)
 Evans, Kay Nell-(p. 64- 65, 77, 79, 159, 163
Evans, Lorraine- p. 64- 65, 70, 159, 163
Evans, Nettie-("Granny")- p. 76, 78-79,107-109,111-114,159-160
Evans, Reverend Dr. James A.- p. 12, 14, 17, 43-45, 55-57, 59-61, 64-65, 69, 71, 73-77, 79, 81, 159-160, 173, 175, 177, 189, 224-225, 227-228, 234, 263, 440, 485, 488, 495, 524
Everton, Hattie Mae- p. 216-217, 270, 337-338, 367, 380, 384
Everton, James Wilbert ("Wilbur")- p. 495, 524
Everton, Jeff- p. 339, 380
Everton, Randy- p. 339, 380, 382
Everton, Rebecca- p. 339, 380-382

F

Faircloth, Johnny Dale -p. 519
Faircloth, Randy A.- p. 383, 420, 485, 519
Faircloth, Richard W. – p. 421, 519
Faircloth, Terry Lenn- p. 421, 519
Family- p. 10-11, 48, 63, 195-196, 198, 200, 208, 215-216, 246, 265, 279-281, 290, 297, 299, 309, 320, 357, 370, 384, 397, 408, 418, 422-423, 430, 438, 446- 447, 455-456, 458, 461-463, 477, 485, 497
Farm Building ("Home Farm")- p. 32, 86, 95, 103-105,342,404, 444
Farm Yard ("Other Farm")- p. 85-90, 92-95, 97, 102, 108-109, 121, 129, 154, 160, 233-234, 250, 327-328,346, 395, 405, 423, 432- 433, 436
Farmer, Bonnie- p. 194, 202-203, 244, 270, 276, 280-281, 283, 322, 362, 373, 377, 379, 388, 403, 477- 478
Feed Storehouse- p. 86- 87, 93, 95, 97, 201
Fields ("Meadow Strip")-p. 86, 105, 118, 201, 278, 327, 343, 363, 396, 423
Fitzgerald, Janie Bell- p. 77
Flemming, John R. (Johnny)- p. 421, 504
Flemming, Pearl- p. 505
Flemming, Sarah M.- p. 504
Flemming, Wilbert- p. 504
Food Pantry ("Store Room")- p. 25, 82, 215, 282, 340, 446
Foreman, Ametta- p. 507
Foreman, Della- p. 507
Foreman, Henry- p. 507
Freeman, Carl- p. 507
Freeman, Elmer- p. 507
Freeman, Jack- p. 507
Freewill Baptist Historical Collection- p. 488-490, 501
Fund (Anna Phillips Education Loan Fund)-p. 57, 60
Furnace (Steam Boiler)-p. 67, 85, 95, 147, 155, 189, 272, 341, 436, 469

G

Games: Board- p. 231; Checkers-p.231; Croquet- p. 271; Fox in the Hole- p. 116
Fruit Basket Turnover- p. 273; Hitting Rocks- p. 231; Hopscotch- p. 265
Horseshoes- p. 231; I'm going to Jerusalem-p. 106; Jump Board- p. 237, 261
Jump Rope- p. 261; Marbles- p. 230-231; Monopoly- p. 231; Mother May I -p. 271
Pile Up-p. 343; Ping-Pong- p. 231; Post Office- p. 273; Red Rover- p. 343; Simon Says- p. 170; Spin the Bottle- p. 273; Steal the Baker- p. 343; Watermelon- p. 247-248
Garden: Flower- p. 84-85,118,239,277,297,300,319,327,342,356,365-366,381,480
   Vegetable- p. 90-92,106-107,362,374,382
Garner, Archer-p. 319
Garner, Mr. & Mrs. Francis- p. 318
Garner, Pamela - p.319
Garner, "Twinkle Toes"- p.319
Garris, Brenda Faye - p. 519

Garris, Clifford B. - p. 520
Garris, Roger-p.38
Garris, Wilbur Asa- p.37
Gasperson, Mildred L. - p. 513
Gasperson, Roy Lee (nickname- "Gap") – p. 231, 248, 320, 513
Gasperson, Velma P. (Ruth) - p. 233, 320, 513
Gay, Delma Lee- p. 439, 518
Gay, Donald Ray- p. 518
Gay, Fernie- p. 512
Gay, Jimmie E. – p. 512
Gay, John Lee Allen- p. 439, 518
Gay, Ronnie Ray- p. 439, 518
Genesis House Emergency Shelter- p. 468
Girls: Dining Hall- p. 415; Kitchen- p. 86, 106-107, 120, 148, 215, 252, 416
  Laundry- p. 341; Tough- p. 276
Girl's Dormitory Building- p. 12, 23, 34, 40, 44, 47, 60, 67, 69, 77-78, 82-85, 90, 92, 93, 95,
  103-104, 115, 118, 125-129, 153, 155, 166, 171, 191, 193, 198,200-202, 215, 228, 250,
  252, 263-265, 269, 278, 290, 294, 306, 308-309, 319, 342, 347, 361, 363, 372-373, 375,
  378, 395, 408, 433-435, 471
Goat ("Billy")-p. 89, 253, 407
Griffin, Addie- p. 18, 20-21
Griffin, Alton- p. 20, 22
Griffin Brothers- p. 5, 18, 20
Griffin, Elmer- p. 18, 20-21, 505
Griffin, J.C.- p. 488
Griffin, Johnny Wayne- p. 521
Griffin, Joseph- p. 14, 18-22, 29, 31, 37, 44, 245, 500, 505
Griffin, Lela- p.19
Griffin, Lewis- p. 18
Griffin, Lillian - p. 19
Griffin, Robert- p. 19, 21
Griffin, Russell- p. 18, 20-21, 505
Griffin, Sallie V. - p. 19-21
Grinder (Sausage)- p. 103
Grown Folks Table- ("Head Table")-p. 52, 271, 400
Grundstaff, Robert – p. 506
Guthrie, Robert E. – p. 522
Guthrie, Anthony L. – p. 518
Guthrie, Donna F. – p. 522

H

Hales, Elizabeth- p. 506
Halloway, George L. – p. 517
Halloway, Stanley W. - 517
Halloway, Theresa C. – p. 517
Hamlen, Virginia- p. 262

Hander- (Tobacco Boy) - p. 110
Hanney, Jimmy- p. 511
Hanney, Richard- p. 511
Hantley, Oswald- p. 505
Hardee, Lucy M. – p. 155, 515
Hardee, Lula- p. 515
Harper, Annie Francis- p. 46
Harper, Blackledge- p. 46
Harrell, Charles- p. 73, 105, 118-119, 125, 162, 379, 485, 488, 510
Harrell, Henry Ashley- p. 510
Harrell, Hilda- p. 44, 70, 510
Harrell, Lucy G. – p. 510
Harris, Clara- p. 506
Harris, John Allen- p. 516
Harris, Ray Murphy- p. 351, 516
Harrison, Elouise- p. 504
Harrison, Inez- p. 504
Harrison, Lina C. 504
Hartley, Jimmy Allen- p. 157-158, 522
Hartley, Vickie Darlene- p. 522
Hartsfield, Joe Andrew- p. 351, 438, 485, 488, 516
Hatem, Thelma J. (nickname - "Possum") -p. 39, 44, 508
Hawkins, Bruce – p. 508
Hawkins, Frank- p. 508
Hawkins, Myrtle Mae- p. 505
Heath, John William--p. 305, 381, 438, 515
Heath, Marshall (Glenn)- p. 298, 305, 307, 351, 424, 440, 515
Heath, Michael Faye -p. 305-306, 515
Heath, Nancy Sue- p. 305, 322, 363, 515
Heath, Wilbert Earl (nickname- "Scram") -p. 305, 327, 331, 334-335, 345, 360, 438, 515
Hedgepeth, Charles- p. 241
Hedgepeth, James - p. 507
Hedgepeth, Mr. & Mrs. Clifton- p. 270
Heritage Hall- p. 58, 469, 470-471, 475, 491
Herring, Alice- p. 262,279-280,290
Herrin, Bobby- (nickname- "Archie")- 263-264, 279, 282, 290, 437, 514
Herring, Evelyn Mae- p. 261, 263-264, 266, 279, 282, 290, 514
Herring, James- p. 262-263,279,290
Herring, Janice – p. 262,279-280
Herring, Lillie- p. 68
Herring, Margie E. -p. 249, 260, 279, 322, 402, 485, 491, 500, 514
Herring, Norma- p. 261
Herring, Tommy-p.262,279-280,290
Herring, William- p. 261
Herring, Willie R. -p. 261,279, 290
Hester, Patricia Deans- p. 268, 369, 515

Hicks, Michael Wayne – p. 517
Hicks, Talmadge L. – p. 517
High, J. B. – p. 509
High, James H. (Johnny) – p. 322, 516
High, Joseph H. – p. 509
High, Shirley Ann- p. 516
Hill, Brenda Day- p. 517
Hill, Douglas Lee- p. 518
Hill, Gary Thomas – p. 518
Hill, Grover C. - p. 270, 316
Hill, Grover Jr. (Nickname-"Peanuts")-p. 316
Hill, Helen- p. 270, 316
Hill, Josie Pearl- p. 191, 214, 514
Hill, Judy Lynn- p. 517
Hill, Louise – p. 507
Hill, Martha J. – p. 517
Hill, Mary F. – p. 517
Hill, Nina – p. 507
Hill, Odolph Jr. – p. 517
Hines, Flora g. p. 266, 270, 371-372, 516
Hines, Jesse J, - p. 366, 372, 390, 437, 515
Hines, Sylvia Catherine (Cathy)- p. 38, 302, 371, 403, 500, 516
Hines, William E. (Billy) (nickname- "Turkey")- p. 153, 233, 239, 320, 512
Hinson, Charles Ray (nickname- "Wiley") - p. 153, 233, 239, 320, 512
Historical Summary- p. 467
Hodgers, Margaret- p. 508
Hodgers, Ralph – p. 508
Hodgers, Willie E. – p. 508
Hog Houses-p. 14, 45, 90, 95
Holland, Fannie- p. 36-38, 491, 506
Holloman, Cora Blanch- p. 508
Holloman, Lillian- p. 508
Homecoming- p. 44, 48, 63, 217, 245, 285-286, 358, 364, 370, 374, 408, 433, 463, 466, 470, 485
Hopkins, Ramona Ann- p. 521
Horses ("Mary, Silver")-p. 88
House Parents-(Father/Mother)-p. 8, 172, 265, 294, 302, 316-318, 350-351, 372, 378, 386, 389, 400, 405-406, 436, 442-443, 462-463, 472-473
Houston, Brett A.- p. 522
Houston, Stephen C. – p. 522
Houston, Theresa L. – p. 522
Howell, Ester- p. 504
Howell, Ethel – p. 504
Howell, Evelin - p. 504
Howell, Haywood - p. 25, 505
Howell, Hazel- p. 504

Howell, Leslie – p. 505
Howell, Marvin- p. 505
Huff, James Lee- p. 512
Huff, Mary Idella- p. 512
Humphrey, Linda- p. 441
Humphrey, Mark- p. 441
Humphrey, Stewart- p. 441, 445, 454, 471, 501, 524
Humphrey, Todd- p. 441
Hunt, James B. Sr. - p. 406
Huskins, Juanita- p. 400
Hyman, Connie Faye- p. 522

I

Inmates- p. 8, 31, 49, 283, 466
Institution- p. 6, 49, 81, 263, 337, 356
Institutional Children- p. 11, 49, 63, 184, 234, 446-447
Institutional Discipline-(Punishment)- p. 294
Institutional Upbringing- p. 11, 235
Ironing/Sewing Room- p. 44, 66, 83, 203-204

J

Jackson, Connie- p. 338
Jackson, Jo Ann – p. 233
Jackson, Judy Katherine- p. 233, 514
Jackson, Margaret J, (Jo Ann)- p. 233, 514
Jackson, R.H. - p. 270, 278, 338, 356, 409, 483, 495, 524
Jackson, Wilhelmina- p. 338
Jacobs, Donna- p. 501
Jarman, Bert Kenneth – p. 509
Johnson, Allen Dean – p. 472, 521
Johnson, Dorothy F. – p. 472, 521
Johnson, Hazel Grey- p. 509
Johnson, Glenda- p. 405
Johnson, Jeffrey Roger – p. 472, 521
Johnson, M. L. (Milton) – p. 285. 302-303, 337, 339-340, 349-350, 364, 377, 379, 404-407, 409, 415-417, 421-422, 495, 524
Johnson, Mildred L. – p. 46, 488, 510
Johnson, Pearl – p. 302, 337, 339, 404, 406, 409, 420-422, 524
Johnson, Rena – p. 510
Johnson, Virginia – p. 509
Johnson, Wanda- p. 406, 409
Jones, Angela G. – p. 518
Jones, Anthony R. – p. 518
Jones, Arthur Vinton (nickname- "Hog Eye") – p. 230, 232-233, 514
Jones, Brenda S. – p. 520

Jones, Caroleen (Carolyn) (nickname- "Gabby")- p. 233, 320, 514
Jones, Cora L. – p. 236, 274, 283, 514
Jones, Estelle- p. 66, 509
Jones, Evelyn Lynn- p. 518
Jones, Hazel Jean- p. 512
Jones, Helen M. p. 512
Jones, Janise Faye- p. 519
Jones, Jimmie R- p. 518
Jones, John E. – p. 518
Jones, Judy Carol – p. 521
Jones, Kenneth Earl – p. 521
Jones, Lakey Lee Jr. - p. 522
Jones, Larry – p. 512
Jones, Martha L. – p. 515
Jones, Mr. & Mrs. E. L. -p. 277, 279
Jones, Odell – p. 66, 74, 79, 509
Jones, Ronnie L. – p. 513
Jones, Shelby Jean – p. 514
Jones, Valerie N. – p. 518
Jordan, Charles Dr. – p. 59-60
Joyner, Helen – p. 516
Joyner, James R. Jr. – p. 521
Joyner, Jesse Leon – p. 521
Joyner, Joyce R. – p. 516
Joyner, Michell Ray- p. 519
Joyner, Paul Woodward – p. 522
Joyner, William Marvin B. – p. 516

K

Kennedy, Luke Ray- p. 505
Kennedy, Owen E. – p. 505
King, Isabel- p. 504
King, Julie Ann – p. 520
King, Nettie Lee- p. 504
King, Robert Glenn – p. 504
Kitchen- p. 25, 33, 40, 62, 65, 67, 69-70, 82, 85, 89, 91, 95, 102, 104-106, 112, -114, 121, 148-149, 160, 177-179, 181, 199, 200, 203-204, 215, 223, 229, 241, 248, 252, 265, 270, 272, 274-276, 308, 315-317, 340-342, 350, 361, 373, 395-396, 415-416, 438, 462, 472, 475
Kittrell, Charlie – p. 76, 511
Kittrell, Mary Ann – p. 511
Kittrell, Robert E. – p. 511

L

Ladies Aid Society- p. 98-99, 126
Lamm, Anna Marie- p. 517
Lamm, Margaret L. – p. 517
Lamm, Mary Ann- p. 521
Lamm, Millard W. – p. 522
Lamm, Robert J. – p. 521
Lamm, Willie Mann Jr. – p. 517
Lamn, Ray Jr. – p. 511
Lamn, Willard – p. 511
Lancaster, Doris Ann – p. 354-357, 485, 516
Lancaster, Thomas E. (Tommy) – p. 354, 390, 437, 516
Lancaster, William Ray (Willie) – p. 354-357, 437, 516
Lance, Mrs. - p. 237
Lane, Durwood – p. 188, 241, 513
Lane, Graham - p. 495
Lane, Jacob J. (nickname- "Slugger") – p. 188, 248, 256, 330- 331, 368, 437, 480, 513
Lane, Mary l. – p. 511
Lane, Patricia Ann – p. 188, 200, 253, 513
Lane, Robert L. (nickname- "Toe") – p. 188, 230, 233, 245, 345, 437, 513
Lane, Sally Rae - p. 515
Lane, William R. (Pat) – p. 103, 111*112, 114, 117, 151, 247, 511
Langely, Nellie – p. 507
Langely, Virginia– p. 507
Langely, Kathleen– p. 508
Langston, Bobbie J. – p. 360, 437, 516
Langston, Gerald Lee - p. 516
Langston, Katherine M. –p. 517
Langsworthy, Anthony – p. 522
Langsworthy, Steven – p. 522
Lanier, Donna Kay –p. 520
Lanier, Pamela A. – p. 520
Lanier, Wendy R. – p. 520
Laundry Room- p. 25, 40-41, 47, 55, 67, 70, 78, 83, 93, 95, 189, 199, 264, 317, 320, 341, 346, 361, 373-374, 434, 436, 460
Lawhorn, Velma- p. 37-38
Ledford, Claude –p. 505
Ledford, Frances – p. 25, 505
Lee, Donna June – p. 518
Lee, Gary (President/CEO)-495-496, 499, 501, 524
Lee, James K. – p. 518
Lee, Rebecca – p. 518
Lee, Sharon E. – p. 518
Lee, Vickie – p. 518
Leggett, Everett S. – p. 520
Leggett, Johnnie K. – p. 520

Letchworth, Debra J. – p. 516
Letchworth, Kathleen – p. 516
Lewis, George H. – p. 508
Lewis, Margaret- p. 77
Lewis, Mary Francis – p. 511
Lewis, Ruth G. – p. 508
Library- p. 16
Liggins, Lula – p. 505
Lightning- ("Electrical Storm")-p. 4, 29-21,30, 37, 212, 245, 287, 413, 434
Linston, Albert B. – p. 506
Linston, Haleen – p. 506
Linston, Ivy H. – p. 51, 506
Linston, John – p. 506
Linston, Mary – p. 506
Little, Alice M. – p. 197-198, 204-205, 214, 264, 485, 513
Little, Carrold – p. 189-190, 197-198, 205, 513
Little, Doris L. –p. 197-198, 205, 214, 513
Little Girl's Room- p. 44-45
Little, Irvin T. (Sam) – p. 214, 513
Little, James Richard –p. 197, 205, 266, 514
Little, Joyce F. – p. 197, 205, 513
Little, Lottie- p. 201
Little, Sam- p. 214
Lloyd, Jr. , Alex – p. 516
Lloyd, Ida F. –p. 515
Loopers (Tobacco Women)-p. 110-111, 275, 328
Lucas, Billie Ray- p. 510
Lucas, Carlton- p. 317
Lucas, Daisy- p. 270, 316-317
Lucas, James Cornell ("Luke")-p. 270, 316-317
Lucas, Patsy- p. 317
Lucas, William Jack- p. 510
Lucas, Woodard J. – p. 44, 510
Lucy- p. 32
Lycykowski, Tammy – p. 522
Lycykowski, James Jr. – p. 522

M

Mace, George William – p. 513
Mace, Sam Ray – p. 320, 513
Mace, Wayne Arthur – p. 320, 438, 513
Mad Itch- p. 77
Maiden, Emma- p. 270, 341
Mansur, Samie – p. 520
Marlow, Deborah A. – p. 519
Marlow, Penny M. – p. 519

Martin, Alice Mae- p. 504
Martin, Charles – p. 504
Martin, David H. – p. 504
Martin, Gerald – p. 510
Martin, Larry – p. 26, 504
Martin, Lela- p. 504
Martin, Theodore B. – p. 504
Marvin (Ben)- p. 516
Massey, Mr. - p. 88
Matthews, Christopher- p. 285-286, 288, 290
Matthews, Gerald-p. 285-286
Matthews, James D. – p. 518
Matthews, Johnny Lee – p. 518
Matthews, Lillian Elizabeth- p. 290
Matrons- p. 8, 29, 44, 46, 51-52, 57, 64, 67, 74, 147, 172, 199, 201, 228, 234-235, 237, 241, 244-245, 258, 265, 268, 270, 273-274, 277, 283, 286, 294, 306-309, 361, 364-366, 370, 414
McCaskey, Charles – p. 506
McCaskey, Joseph – p. 506
McCourtney, Charles (nicknames: "Ches, Goat Man") -p. 333
McCowan, Kelly Darlene – p. 522
McGhee, James – p. 510
McGhee, Julian – p. 73-74, 510
McLawhorn, Betty J. – p. 518
McLawhorn, Verna G. – p. 510
Mc Leod, Ravin- p. 225
Mc Swain, Clyde F. - p. 7
Memorial Chapel- p. 85, 90, 97, 122, 126, 129, 135, 160, 191, 233, 297, 370, 407-408, 439, 467, 486
Mercer, Leona- p. 40
Mercer, Ona G. – p. 296, 304, 322, 515
Mercer, Phillip Ray – p. 296, 351, 361, 397, 437, 439, 485, 515
Mercer, Sandra E. –p. 4, 215, 282, 296, 302, 304, 309-311, 369-370, 377, 402, 405, 427-428, 485, 515
Merritt, Alene Grace – p. 511
Merritt, Charles Ray- p. 511
Merritt, Gene– p. 511
Merritt, Jesse James – p. 44, 511
Merritt, Jimmie Leon – p. 351, 518
Miles, Reverend Edward W. - p. 408, 495, 524
Mill- p. 130
Miller, Estelle- p. 506
Miller, Leroy B. (nickname- "Lace")- p. 322, 367, 514
Mills, Kathleen – p. 512
Mills, Kimberly Ann – p. 520
Mills Linda D. - p. 520
Mills, Robert R. – p. 512

Mills, Timothy A. – p. 472, 520
Mitchell, Arleatha- p. 433
Mitchell, Brenda Lee- p. 317, 432-433, 438, 501
Mitchell, Clarence (nicknames- "Oscar, Petey") – p. 26-28, 71, 74-75, 171-172, 174, 176, 189, 194, 228-229, 234-235, 247, 249, 281, 300-302, 316-318, 324, 326-328, 342-344, 380, 386, 389, 400, 414-415, 420, 422-423, 425-426, 432-433, 440, 472-473, 484, 506
Mitchell, Eiffie- p. 433
Mitchell, Henry- p. 300, 414, 417
Mitchell, Lynne- p. 501
Mitchell, Mary Price- p. 171-173, 175-176, 189, 229, 234, 240, 242-243, 245, 273, 298, 316, 324, 327, 333, 365, 380-381,, 386, 389, 400-401, 414-415, 417, 432-433, 440, 480
Mitchell, Steve- p. 298, 317, 433, 440
Mitchell, Thelma (Rulli) (nickname- " Aunt Kay")- p. 270, 272, 283-284, 294, 316-317, 359-362, 370, 372, 378, 402, 405-406, 433-434, 440, 506
Minshew, Othal Rose- p. 277, 279
Mixon, Alice – p. 212, 505
Mixon, Beulah – p. 212, 505
Mixon, Charles – p. 213, 215, 247, 317, 363
Mixon, Horace – p. 26, 192, 194, 212, 214, 216-217, 221-222, 250, 270, 322, 328, 367, 423, 485, 505
Mixon, Lula – p. 215, 505
Mixon, Milan – p. 212, 505
Mixon, Peggy- p. 193, 212-213, 317, 322, 373
Mixon, Sudie Mrs.-p. 105, 160-161, 176-178, 180, 193-194, 212-213, 221, 240, 242, 246, 251-252, 270-271, 273, 275-277, 283, 317, 322, 329, 334, 340, 361, 366-368, 373, 377, 387, 480
Modlin, Ruth Ann – p. 519
Money Crops- p. 108, 192, 203, 374
Moore, Bertha – p. 508
Moore, Eloyse – p. 508
Moore, Kimberly Dawn – p. 523
Moore, Linwood Jr. – p. 523
Moore, Mary Russel – p. 507
Moore, Patricia Lee- p. 517
Moore, Paul E. – p. 507
Moore, Wheatie – p. 512
Morgan, Dorothy- p. 56, 163-164
Morris, Annie- p. 240, 251, 259
Morris, Bertha Louise – p. 266, 278, 283, 293, 515
Morris, Dalton- p. 240, 251, 259
Morris, Jack Leon (nicknames- "Abel, Benedict")- p. 320, 515
Morris, Martin J, (nickname-"Cain")- p. 320, 480, 515
Morten, Martin Asa – p. 504
Mules: (p. 192, 213, 215, 253)-Gladys- p. 31 ; Molly- p. 31; Lightning- p. 89; Rhoda- p. 31;Thunder- p. 89
Muse, Henry F. – p. 507
Muse, Rachel Mae – p. 507

N

New Building- p. 82, 92, 126, 131, 170, 173-174, 265
Newell, Josephine Dr.– p. 240, 249, 269, 399, 402-403, 405
Newton, Deborah R. – p. 393, 395, 516
Newton, Heather- p. 502
Newton, Larry Mitchell (Mickey) – p. 351, 383, 393, 422, 486, 488, 516
Nichols, Angela Gail – p. 519
Nichols, John Bennett – p. 519
Nichols, Stephen ray – p. 519
Nicknames:
  Abel- p. 345; *Bad Eye* -p. 345; *Bo-* p. 429; *Cain-* p. 345; *Chi-Chi-* p. 345; Dobie- p. 345 Doc- p. 360; Duck- p. 230, 241, 247, 251, 259, 313, 320, 344, 347, 358, 368, 383; Ears- p. 345, 360 Elvis- p. 345; Garcia- p. 345; Hanged- p. 345; Herb- p. 230, 247, 320; Higgy- p. 345, 360, 429; Hi-Tie- p. 345; Hog Eye- p. 230; Lace-p.345; Me-Too- p.345; Moose- p. 230, 361; Oscar- p. 300; Owl- p. 360; Petey-p.249, 300-301, 316, 324, 326-328, 342-344, 389, 396, 414-415, 420, 422-423, 425-426; Preacher- p. 345; Presley- p. 345; Rabbit- p. 126, 131, 148, 166, 171, 180, 230; Reno- p. 345; Rod- p. 230, 320, 343, 345, 437; Sack- p. 230, 247, 320, 343, 345; Sarge- p. 345; Scram- p. 327, 331, 334-335, 345, 360; Slugger- p.230; Soapy- p. 230, 345, 360, 361; Stony- p. 345; Tarzan the Turkey Slayer- p. 249; Tink- p. 381; Tip Toes- p. 345; Toe- p.230, 247, 345; Turkey- p. 230, 345, 360, 375, 429; Yogi- p. 360
Nix, Dorothy Ann – p. 514
Nix, Elmo Lee – p. 514
Nix, Mannon A. III –p. 514
Nobles, Betty & Herman- p. 151-152
Nobles, William S. - p. 505
Norman, Michael F. II – p. 521
Norris, Peggy Joyce –p. 214, 233, 514

O

O' Donell, Ray- p. 285
Orchard- (Apple)-p. 89- 90, 95, 97,337,346,432; (Pecan)- p. 118,277,363,480
Orphans- p. 8, 14, 30-31, 33, 45, 202-203, 208, 233, 261, 263-264, 266, 274, 278, 283-284, 289-290, 292, 298, 303, 320-322, 331, 333, 337, 339, 352-353, 358, 364, 370, 379, 383, 394, 418, 423, 427, 433, 467, 492-493, 498
Orphans ("Half Orphans")- p. 14,348
Orphan Shoes- p. 10
Orphan Siblings-("Brother/Sister")- p. 10, 202, 208, 259, 284, 290, 309, 311, 320, 357, 258, 440, 446, 455, 472
Orr, Dr. P. B. -p. 23
Outlaw, Jule Benjamin (JB) – p. 190, 512
Outlaw, Rudolph – p. 512
Owens, Daisy- p. 270

P

Page, Charles – p. 131, 190, 510
Page, Chester Eugene (nickname- "Rod") –p. 230, 247, 320, 343, 345, 386, 436-437, 491, 511
Page, Donald Ray – p. 513
Parker, Annie P. -p. 169-170, 173
Parker, Fred – p. 506
Parker, Hazel – p. 506
Pasture (Woods)- p. 86, 89, 92-95, 100-103, 109, 115, 120, 153-156, 163,, 239, 245-246, 331, 334-335, 343, 367, 420
Pate, Annie Lee – p. 43, 47, 54, 508
Pate, Benjamin Franklin- p. 43
Pate, Bessie Harper- p. 43
Pate, Linwood- p. 43, 47-48, 64, 508
Pate, Mary Evelyn–p. 43, 47-48, 64, 509
Pate, Ralph – p. 43, 47-48, 64, 245, 274, 485, 488, 508
Peele, Robert P. – p. 66
Pelt, Mildred- p. 59
Pelt, Reverend Chester H. – p. 59
Pen: Hog- p. 25, 92, 95, 103-104, 111, 117, 160, 318, 396; Turkey- p. 301, 374, 396, 438
Perkins, Heidi Lynn – p. 522
Phelps, Shireyan- p. 20-22
Physical Care: Diphtheria-p.14; Mental test- p. 14; Tuberculin Test- p. 14; Typhoid Vaccination- p. 14; Vision Test – p. 14; Wasserman Test- p. 14
Pierce, Cedric- p. 495
Pittman, Bobby Ray Jr. – p. 517
Pittman, James E. – p. 517
Pittman, Pamela J. – p. 517
Pittman, Timothy R. (nickname- "Birdman") – p. 429-430, 516
Pond ("Tippetts Millpond")-p. 129-131, 190-191, 205, 216, 233, 238, 272, 298, 343, 367, 432, 445, 467, 474
Poole, Raymond Keith – p. 522
Pope, Alma Ruth (Johnnie Faye)- p. 276, 291, 294, 309, 402, 515
Pope, Annie- p. 294
Pope, C.G. - p. 14, 25, 32-33, 484, 524
Pope, Daisy L. – p. 276, 291, 294, 514
Pope, Jimmie A. - p. 513
Pope, Mary Belle –p. 276, 291, 293, 514
Pope, Nancy Lou – p. 266, 276-277, 291, 294, 514
Poteat, Melissa Ann- p. 501
Poultry House ("Chicken House")-p. 14, 34, 45, 52, 89-90, 94-95, 102-103, 241, 250, 258, 338, 396
Powell, Billie Ray – p.
Powell, Carl - p. 270, 317
Powell, E.C. - p. 30-21, 99, 182-183, 399
Powell, Iris- p. 270, 317
Powell, James – p. 510

Powell, Lambert (Lanny)-p. 317
Powell, Larry D. – p. 512
Prayer Service (Worship) - p. 16, 57, 199, 360, 376, 391
Preparation for Independent Living- p. 468
Prescott, M.C. p.12
Price, Glennie Mae- p. 514
Price, Shelby Jean – p. 320, 514
Pridgeon, J.B. – p. 506
Proctor, Clay – p. 507
Proctor, Lucille – p. 507
Proctor, Pauline – p. 507
Proctor, Troy – p. 507
Pump House (Maintenance Building) - p, 25, 41, 45, 83, 85, 93, 95, 171, 271-272, 309, 319, 342, 344, 363, 438, 470

R

Raper, Barney- p. 53-54
Raper, Catherine- p. 53-54
Raper, James Earl – p. 50-51, 53-54, 510
Raper, Mary Lou – p. 50-51, 53-54, 510
Raper, Rose -p. 54, 63, 284
Raper, W. Burkette (President, Emeritus-Mount Olive College)- p. 44, 49-51, 53-54, 56, 63, 71, 79, 187, 191, 221, 233, 284, 286, 349, 382, 384, 406, 440, 495, 510
Rawls, Cecil – p. 504
Rawls, Robert – p. 504
Rawls, Vera – p. 504
Rawls, Vernon – p. 504
Ray, Charles- p. 153
Razor Strap- p. 158-159
Red, Big- p. 124
Red, Little- p. 124
Reddick, Thomas – p. 513
Refrigerator Room ("Cooler")-p. 84,162,362
Register of Inmates- p. 11, 490
Renee, Gerri – p. 519
Residents- p. 8, 297, 313, 468, 495
Rhodes, Dorothy S. – p. 521
Rhodes, Lucinda M. – p. 521
Rhodes, Randy Ray – p. 521
Rhodes, Ronhie E. – p. 522
Rice, Reverend Clifton- p. 43
Rich, Alfred A. – p. 24, 29-31, 33-35, 37, 506
Rich, Lee- p. 24
Rich, Ray- p. 24-25
Rich, William H. 23, 29, 31, 34, 37, 506
Roger's Cottage-p. 417

Rogers, Gardner Barry – p. 276, 360-361, 438, 614
Rogers, James - p. 507
Rogers, John Dirial – p. 190, 215, 513
Rogers, Lindsay Hal –p. 247, 320, 343, 513
Rogers, Loyce Nicholas – p. 190, 192-194, 513
Rollins, Annie Mae –p. 511
Rollins, Doris Ruth – p. 511
Rollins, Dorothy –p. 511
Rose, James – p. 509
Rose, Willie Lee – p. 509
Rouse, Celester – p. 506
Rouse, Isaac Daniel Jr. (nickname- "Moose")- p. 230, 359-361, 437, 439, 490, 516
Rouse, Isabell – p. 506
Rouse, Joan Yvonne – p. 359-360, 516
Rouse, Rena – p. 506
Rouse, Stephen (nickname- "Soapy")- p. 230, 345, 360-361, 437, 516
Rouse, Virginia- p. 506
Rowe, John Thomas – p. 231, 513

S

Salt Box- p. 113
Sanderson, Ms. (Granny)-p. 268,270,317,320
Sasser, Debbie J. – p. 521
Sasser, Donald Lee –p. 520
Sassr, Albert M. – p. 520
Sawyer, Lily Virginia – p. 44, 511
Schnell, Mollie Lynn – p. 519
Secret Meeting Places- p. 272
Service Road- p. 85, 90, 95, 102, 121, 127
Sexton, Dorothy – p. 509
Sexton, James – p. 509
Sexton, Mary Agnes – p. 509
Shearon, Faustima- p. 76-77
Shingleton, Bennie T. – p. 511
Shingleton, Marvin E. p. 511
Shit Slinger-(Manure Spreader)-p. 103
Shop- p. 14, 83, 87, 95, 121, 342
Sick Bay (Infirmary)-p. 78
Sills, Ruthey R. – p. 505
Sills, William R. – p. 505
Silverthorn, Della – p. 507
Silverthorn, Dennis – p. 507
Silverthorn, Lenwood – p. 507
Singing For Our Supper- p. 202-203, 388
Skinner, Elva E. - p. 465, 510
Skinner, Marvin E. – p. 115, 465, 510

Skinner, Sterling – p. 44, 115, 117, 465-466, 491, 510
Smith, Ada- p. 46
Smith, Andrew George- p. 225-226, 251, 253, 259
Smith, Bertha-("Ma")-p.243, 270, 316, 337-338, 372, 383, 400, 402-403,407
Smith, Daisy – p. 508
Smith, Elsie – p. 508
Smith, Frankie- p. 227
Smith, Jerry A. (nickname- "Duck") – p. 1, 4, 7-9, 11, 181-182, 185, 187, 221-222, 225-230, 232-235, 237, 240-242, 247, 251, 253-255, 259, 274-275, 284, 289-290, 313, 320, 344-345, 347, 358, 360, 364, 368, 383, 388, 401-402, 435-437, 439, 485, 487-489, 495, 497, 514, 525
Smith, Jerry Jr. - p. 502
Smith, John – p. 508
Smith, Joseph- p. 508
Smith, Martha- p. 222, 257-258
Smith, Mary Ann- p. 227
Smith, Melissa Dawn- p. 521
Smith, Michelle E. – p. 521
Smith, Mike- p. 227
Smith, Mildred- p. 259
Smith, Nancy Ann- p. 181-182,185, 222, 225-226, 228-234, 240, 244, 248-249, 251-252, 255, 257-259, 401, 437, 485, 488, 491, 501, 514
Smith, Pearl – p. 508
Smith, Rhonda- p. 227
Smith, Stephen- p. 226
Smith, Stephen- ("Pa") – p. 189, 195, 218-219, 240-241, 243-245, 270, 281-282, 292, 297, 299, 316, 337-338, 372, 383, 399-401, 407, 436, 487, 489, 495, 524
Smith, Susan- p. 501, 525
Smith, Vonnie- p. 227
Smith Cottages- p. 264, 275, 317, 462, 472
Smoke House- p. 27, 82, 95, 112-114
Snipes, P.G. – p. 510
Snipes, Sidney – p. 510
Speight, David J. – p. 472, 520
Speight, Jr., James W. – p. 472, 520
Speight, Ray Bert – p. 472, 520
Sports:
    Baseball-p.204, 215, 217, 231, 246-247, 249-251, 254, 272, 301, 319, 328, 335, 343-345, 348, 365, 368, 376, 381, 388-389, 394, 396, 402, 417, 422, 494; Basketball- p.141-142, 204, 249, 251, 254, 267, 319, 328, 335, 343, 345, 348, 363, 366, 368, 375-376, 388-389, 396; Football- p. 328, 343, 388, 396, 417
Stable- p. 86, 95
Stallings, Jerry Lynn – p. 438, 514
Stallings, Joel C. (nickname- "Higgins") - p. 438, 514
Stanley, Ray- p. 261
Stanley, Walter- p. 279
State Cottage- p. 472

State Dental Department- p. 14, 45, 182
Steam Press-(Ironer) - p. 67, 83
Stephens, Jonathan P. – p. 522
Stephens, Melissa F. – p. 522
Stephens, Michael A. – p. 522
Stevenson, George Jr. – p. 9, 79-80, 87, 95, 116, 187, 230, 488-490, 501, 511
Stevenson, Haywood – p. 76-77, 81-82, 166, 187, 233, 511
Stevenson, Helen E. – p. 81, 187, 511
Stevenson, Joyce M. – p. 77, 81, 187, 501, 511
Stocks, Earl N. – p. 510
Stocks, Earline- p. 510
Stocks, Elsie- p. 510
Stocks, Mr. & Mrs. Herman- p. 270, 318
Stone, Elvin & Carol – p. 502
Stove (Cook)-p. 102, 105, 172, 178
Study Hall- p. 25, 33, 146, 148, 171, 178, 216, 272, 324, 332, 346, 386, 414
Styman, Mrs. S.H. – p. 76
Sugg, Eula Mae- p. 516
Sugg, Linda Lou- p. 516
Suggs, Sidney Earl- p. 351, 383, 516
Sullivan, Michael- p. 286-290
Summerlin, Rosa Lee - p. 521
Summerlin, Sharon Y. – p. 521
Superintendent's Home- p. 13, 25, 74, 85, 90, 97, 109, 127, 129, 162, 191, 231, 342, 444
Sutton, Woodrow W. – p. 507
Swim, Florence – p. 508
Swimming Pool- p. 25-26, 33, 95, 213, 271-272, 363, 375, 382, 407-408, 436

T

Tart, Mary Louise – p. 509
Taylor, Alsey - p. 504
Taylor, Bobby Dr. (President/CEO)- p. 22, 453, 466, 474-475, 478-479, 495-496, 499, 501, 523-524
Taylor, Garland – p. 511
Taylor House- p. 474
Taylor, Hugh B. – p. 511
Taylor, Joseph l. – p. 504
Taylor, Joyce C. – p. 511
Taylor, Louise – p. 511
Taylor, Margaret E. – p. 70-71, 511
Taylor, Stephen- p. 453-455, 462
Taylor, Wesley- p. 453-454, 462
Teasley, Ben W. Jr. – p. 514
Tebo, Janice F. – p. 518
Tenant House- p. 96
The Young People's Friend- p. 232, 238, 489

Thick, Dave & Sandy- p. 472
Thigpen, Billy F. Jr. – p. 521
Thigpen, Bobby Gene –p. 232, 266, 282, 318, 439, 514
Thigpen, Clyde Earl Jr. – p. 514
Thigpen, Jennifer M. J. – p. 521
Thigpen, Joyce – p. 232-233, 514
Thigpen, Justin – p. 233, 514
Thigpen, Lois- p. 215, 268, 514
Thigpen, Nellie Jean – p. 268, 292, 514
Thomas, Allen- p. 502
Thomas, Fred – p. 517
Thomas, Jeff– p. 351, 517
Thomas, Terry – p. 351, 517
Thompson, Elizabeth – p. 510
Thompson, Maurice – p. 509
Thompson, Thelma- p. 509
Time Capsule- p. 45, 59, 469, 475
Tipett, Earl – p. 41-42, 75, 77, 488, 507
Tipett, Hazel – p. 507
Threshing Machine- p. 86
Tripp, Hicks – p. 67, 75, 509
Tripp, Louis L. Jr. –p. 152-153, 513
Tripp, Mary Agnes- p. 509
Tucker, Ernest Jr. – p. 511
Tucker, Silvia J. – p. 511
Tyson, Christabelle- p. 191, 512
Tyson, Dorothene (Doris) – p. 193, 218, 512
Tyson, Elder M. E. – p. 14, 488, 524
Tyson, Eugene (nickname - "Herb")- p. 155, 214, 230, 242, 247, 320, 512
Twins- p. 5, 222, 225, 227, 229, 232, 240

U
Utley, Angela L. – p. 520
Utley, Sharon A. – p. 520
Utley, Tammy Kaye – p. 520

V
Vacation Bible School- p. 57, 59, 233, 281, 376
Valedictorian- p. 5, 210, 237, 260, 267
Valentine, Elder- p. 127, 133
Vespers- p. 128-129

W
Wall, Clayton Mark – p. 522
Wall, Robert Lee – p. 522

Waller, Harold Eugene- p. 322-323, 438, 515
Warbritton, Anne C. – p. 508
Warbritton, Gladys M. – p. 508
Warbritton, Louise – p. 508
Warren, Charles G. – p. 383, 410, 485, 488, 519
Warren, Judy Lynn – p. 410, 413, 485, 491, 519
Warren, Kenneth Ray – p. 383, 410-413, 417, 519
Warren, Mary Ann- p. 410, 413, 519
Warren, Rosalyne – p. 155, 512
Warren, Thelma Lou- p. 410, 413, 519
Warren, Willis Owens – p. 512
Warwick, James E. – p. 507
Warwick, Norma G. – p. 507
Wash House- p. 14, 37, 64, 67, 95
Watering Cylinder- p. 108
Watson, Betty Jean - p. 320, 484, 514
Watson, Edward Wallace (Eddie) – p. 233, 245, 254, 320, 438, 484, 514
Watson, Felix = p. 509
Watson, Foy Jr. (nickname - "Tarzan the Turkey Slayer") –p. 216, 249, 320, 334-336, 338, 341, 367, 382, 438, 484, 514
Watson, Irene – p. 71, 76, 509
Watson, Josephine – p. 509
Watson, Leroy Pate – p. 506
Watson, Lillie Faye – p. 193, 209, 218, 320, 379, 513
Watson, Mallie C. – p. 506
Watson, Robert F. (Bobby) – p. 71, 511
Watson, Wiley Robertson – p. 4, 29-31, 35, 37, 44, 245, 500, 506
Webb, Cynthia D. – p. 521
Webb, Dallas Perry – p. 522
Webb, Gregory Allen – p. 522
Weeks, Gladys- p. 472
Weeks, Sam- p. 472, 495, 524
Well- p. 96
Wells, George –p. 506
Wells, Julie- p. 492
Wells, Randolph – p. 506
Wells, Roy- p. 492, 495
West, Agnes – p. 504
West, Catherine- p. 72
West, Grace – p. 504
West, Iona – p. 509
West, James G. – p. 509
West, Nancy C. – p. 509
West, Robert D.– p. 509
Wetherington, Elder L. H. – p. 14, 524
Whitehurst, Louise M. – p. 521

Whitley, Carl – p. 12, 217, 460, 466, 504
Whitley Center- p. 468
Whitley, Dorothy – p. 12, 217, 459, 466, 504
Whitley, Ebber – p. 505
Whitley, Helen – p. 12, 217, 459, 466, 504
Whitley, Iddo- p. 505
Whitley, James A. = p. 517
Whitley, Johnny Ray – p. 346, 517
Whitley, Nellie – p. 12, 217, 459, 466, 504
Whitley, Patricia A. – p. 520
Whitley, William H. – p. 520
Wiggs, Nestis – p. 515
Wiggs, Robert G. – p. 515
Wilerson, Donna M. – p. 521
Willard, Jesse - p. 512
Williams, Bobbie– p. 512
Williams, Bonnie- p. 45
Williams, Cay Lee – p. 505
Williams, Dillie – p. 505
Williams, Ester M. – p. 512
Williams, Linwood J. – p. 521
Williams, Maggie – p. 505
Williams, Margaret A. – p. 516
Williams, Nannie – p. 505
Williams, Nellie M. – p. 505
Williams, Preston – p. 512
Williams, Salie – p. 505
Williams, Troy – p. 505
Williford, Melia ("Mama")-p. 223-227, 234-235, 239-240, 245, 251, 253-255, 259
Willis, Angela Sue – p. 522
Willis, Crystal G. – p. 522
Willis, Ronald C. Jr. – p. 522
Willis, Sherry A. – p. 522
Wilson, Jr. A.D. – p. 523
Wilson, Anna Michelle – p. 523
Wilson, Dorothy – p. 512
Wilson, Sherry L. – p. 523
Winburne, Lena- p. 148, 171, 173, 180, 203, 214
Winstead, Audry- p. 504
Winstead, Ernest G. – p. 512
Winstead, Metta (Lou) – p. 214, 320, 512
Winstead, Robert D. – p. 512
Winstead, Winifred M. – p. 480, 512
Wolfe, Fred- p. 55-56, 249
Wood Box- p. 105-106, 110-111
Wood, Carol G. –p. 512

Wood, Louella – p. 512
Woodard, Ivey Joyce- p. 519
Woodard, Julia Betsy – p. 519
World's Troubles- p. 94, 138
Worley, Audrey – p. 521
Worley, Betty Yvonne – p. 472, 521
Worley, J.H. – p. 58, 66, 127, 133
Worley, Lois Mae – p. 522
Worley, Roger Lee – p. 472, 521
Worley, Teresa Ann – p. 472, 521
Worthington, Albert R. – p. 516
Worthington, Brenda (Ann) – p. 322, 365-366, 369-370, 390-391, 516
Worthington, Ernest (Glenn) – p. 314-315, 437, 515
Worthington, Joe Etta – p. 266, 273, 275-276, 283, 313-315, 322-323, 403, 515
Worthington, Raymond S. (Stuart)- p. – 216, 313-315, 358, 365, 383, 438, 515
Worthington, Ronald – p. 313-314, 437, 515
Worthington, Stephen (nickname-"Reno") – p. 313, 345, 403, 431, 485, 488, 515
Worthington, Ted W. – p. 351, 365-366, 383, 422, 516

Photo taken by Susan Smith

About the Author

J. Andrews Smith grew up in Middlesex, North Carolina. He is a graduate of Mount Olive Junior College, Barton College, and the University of North Carolina at Chapel Hill. Since 1996 he has been a columnist with *Tazewell County Free Press,* Richlands, Virginia. He has authored several books and been published in numerous newspapers. He now lives in the mountains of North Carolina.

Made in the USA
Charleston, SC
06 August 2015